Silenced

Silenced

How Apostasy and Blasphemy Codes Are Choking Freedom Worldwide

PAUL MARSHALL AND NINA SHEA

with a Foreword by
KYAI HAJI ABDURRAHMAN WAHID

OXFORD
UNIVERSITY PRESS

OXFORD

UNIVERSITY PRESS

Oxford University Press, Inc., publishes works that further
Oxford University's objective of excellence
in research, scholarship, and education.

Oxford   New York
Auckland   Cape Town   Dar es Salaam   Hong Kong   Karachi
Kuala Lumpur   Madrid   Melbourne   Mexico City   Nairobi
New Delhi   Shanghai   Taipei   Toronto

With offices in
Argentina   Austria   Brazil   Chile   Czech Republic   France   Greece
Guatemala   Hungary   Italy   Japan   Poland   Portugal   Singapore
South Korea   Switzerland   Thailand   Turkey   Ukraine   Vietnam

Copyright © 2011 by Paul Marshall and Nina Shea

Published by Oxford University Press, Inc.
198 Madison Avenue, New York, New York 10016

www.oup.com

Oxford is a registered trademark of Oxford University Press

Library of Congress Cataloging-in-Publication Data
Marshall, Paul.
Silenced : how apostasy and blasphemy codes are choking freedom
worldwide / Paul Marshall and Nina Shea.
p. cm.
Includes bibliographical references and index.
ISBN 978–0–19–981226–4; 978–0–19–981228–8 (pbk.)
1. Censorship—Religious aspects—Islam.   2. Blasphemy (Islam)
3. Apostasy—Islam.   I. Shea, Nina.
II. Title.
Z658.I77M37 2011
364.1'88—dc22   2011004600

1 3 5 7 9 8 6 4 2

Printed in the United States of America
on acid-free paper

To Shahbaz Bhatti, our friend and a lifelong champion of religious freedom,
and to Salman Taseer, Governor of Punjab, both murdered in 2011,
for opposing Pakistan's blasphemy laws; and to the late
Abdurrahman Wahid and Nasr Hamid Abu-Zayd, who devoted
their lives to an Islam of religious freedom.

CONTENTS

PART III   THE GLOBALIZATION OF BLASPHEMY

PART IV   MUSLIM CRITICISM OF APOSTASY AND
BLASPHEMY LAWS

PART V   CONCLUSIONS

ACKNOWLEDGMENTS

Silenced: How Apostasy and Blasphemy Codes Are Choking Freedom Worldwide is a project of the Hudson Institute's Center for Religious Freedom. The Center is deeply grateful for the generosity of the Fieldstead Foundation, the Lynde and Harry Bradley Foundation, and donors who wish to remain anonymous.

This large book would not have been possible without the assistance, criticism, and advice of a large number of people, including Omolade Adunubi, Reza Afshari, Mohsine el Ahmadi, Fouad Ajami, Mustafa Akyol, Ali Alyami, Barbara Baker, Rev. Justo Lacunza Balda, Maarten G. Barends, Hamouda Fathelrahman Bella, Cheryl Benard, Peter Berger, Peter Berkowitz, Ladan and Roya Boroumand, Jennifer Bryson, Ann Buwalda, Christopher Catherwood, Felix Corley, Paul Diamond, Saidu Dogo, Khalid Duran, Cole Durham, Imam Talal Eid, Aaron Emmel, Tom Farr, Willy Fautre, Steve Ferguson, Roger Finke, Arne Fjeldstad, Felice Gaer, Fatima Gailani, Most Rev. Macram Gassis, Robert George, Joseph Ghougassian, Brian Grim, Rev. Marcel Guarnizo, Wisnu Hanggoro, Kristanto Hartadi, Tom Holland, the late Samuel Huntington, Ed Husain, Mujeeb Ijaz, Emeka Izeze, Zuhdi Jasser, Philip Jenkins, Rebiya Kadeer, Mehrangiz Kar, Joseph Kassab, Firuz Kazemzadeh, Magdi Khalil, Amjad Khan, Leonard Leo, Natan Lerner, James D. Le Sueur, Bernard Lewis, David Little, Habib Malik, Ted Malloch, Salim Mansur, Walter Russell Mead, Mariam Memarsadeghi, Kevian Milani, Hedieh Mirahmadi, Douglas Murray, Azar Nafisi, Asra Nomani, Ugochukwu Okezie, Mary Okosun, Abdul Oroh, Lekan Otufodunrin, Nadia Oweidat, Marcello Pera, Ruud Peters, Dan Philpott, Anthony Picarello, Elizabeth H. Prodromou, Tina Ramirez, Peter Riddell, Michael Rubin, Vinay Samuel, Lamin Sanneh, Jonathan Schanzer, Stephen Schwartz, Roger Severino, Timothy Samuel Shah, the late M. L. Shahani, Peter Skerry, Zainab Al-Suwaij, Amir Taheri, Jenny Taylor, Frank Vogel, Kam Weng, Nicholas Wolterstorff, and Atilla Yayla.

We also received valuable assistance from the Abdorrahman Boroumand Foundation, the American Center for Law and Justice, the Becket Fund for Religious Liberty, Compass Direct, the Egyptian Initiative for Personal Rights, the Federalist Society, Forum 18, Human Rights Without Frontiers, Institute for Gulf

Affairs, the Nigerian Civil Liberties Organization, the Pew Forum on Religion and Public Life, and the Sudan Human Rights Organization.

The Center for Religious Freedom has profited from the able research of a number of very talented interns. We would like to thank Bonnie Alldredge, Harry Baumgarten, Alex Benard, Justine Desmond, Stephanie Ferguson, Jean Marie Hoffman, Katelyn Jones, Soumaya Lkoundi, Andy Marshall, Jeff Pan, Adam Parker, Karen Rupprecht, Amanda Smith, Samuel Trihus, and John Wasaff, for their diligent and excellent work as research interns.

Anisa Afshar, Maneeza Hossein, and Samuel Tadros provided invaluable research for several chapters, and Daniel Huff and Aaron Meyer of the Middle East Forum provided analyses of U.S. and international legal standards. Dwight Bashir, Kit Bigelow, Janet Epp Buckingham, Elizabeth Cassidy, Jamsheed K. Choksy, Mark Durie, David Forte, Darara Gubo, Matius Ho, Ziya Meral, Shastri Purushotma, Flemming Rose, Steven Snow, and Angela Wu read and commented on portions of the manuscript.

We also benefited from the assistance of several Hudson colleagues, including Alex Alexiev, Shmuel Bar, Zeyno Baran, Anne Bayefsky, Eric Brown, John Fonte, Hillel Fradkin, Herb London, Hassan Mneimneh, Katherine Smyth, Grace Terzian, and Richard Weitz.

Ulil Abshar-Abdallah, Governor Al Haji Sani Ahmed, Ali Al-Ahmed, Ayaan Hirsi Ali, Abdullahi Ahmed An-Na'im, Essam El Eryan, Saad Eddin Ibrahim, Carsten Juste, Amjad Mahmood Khan, Jytte Klausen, Ahmad Syafii Maarif, the late Nurcholish Madjid, Ahmed Subhy Mansour, the Rt. Rev. Michael Nazir-Ali, Festus Okoye, Din Syamsuddin, Prince El-Hassan bin Talaal, and the late Sheikh Al-Azhar Tantawi patiently answered our questions.

Our special thanks to Abdullah Saeed for kindly agreeing to provide an essay arguing on the basis of Islam that there should not be civil penalties for blasphemy and apostasy. Abdullah Saeed's essay is adapted from his *Freedom of Religion, Apostasy and Islam*, published by Ashgate Publishing.

We are grateful to Abdurrahman Wahid and Nasr Hamid Abu-Zayd for their contributions—the foreword and "Renewing Qur'anic Studies in the Contemporary World"—that we commissioned; and we are greatly saddened by their deaths during the book's production. C. Holland Taylor of LibForAll gave valuable advice and assistance and permission to publish these two pieces. Wahid, "Gus Dur," was cofounder and senior advisor of LibForAll, while Abu-Zayd was the Academic Director of its International Institute of Qur'anic Studies. LibforAll's Kyai Haji Hodri Ariev also gave editorial advice.

We are especially grateful to Lela Gilbert and Elizabeth Kerley, who provided major assistance in writing, editing, and in all phases of this book. Cameron Wybrow did excellent work on copyediting. Cynthia Read of Oxford University Press was, as always, careful, patient, and encouraging.

We thank Allen Tesler, Chairman of the Board of the Hudson Institute, and the directors, as well as Hudson President Ken Weinstein, and Center Advisory Board

Chairman Chair James R. Woolsey, for their belief in the work of the Center for Religious Freedom.

We would like to thank all the above for their work, assistance, and patience, and we emphasize that the above are not responsible for any errors in the book; nor should it be assumed that they agree with all of its contents.

This book is a project of the Center for Religious Freedom, a privately funded research center of the Hudson Institute. The Center promotes religious freedom as a component of U.S. foreign policy. For further information contact: Hudson Institute's Center for Religious Freedom, 1015 15th St NW, Washington DC 20005; http://crf.hudson.org/.

AUTHORS AND CONTRIBUTORS

Authors

Paul Marshall

Paul Marshall is a Senior Fellow at the Hudson Institute's Center for Religious Freedom and the author and editor of more than twenty books on religion and politics, especially religious freedom, including, more recently *Blind Spot: When Journalists Don't Get Religion* (2009), *Religious Freedom in the World* (2008), *Radical Islam's Rules: The Worldwide Spread of Extreme Sharia Law* (2005), *The Rise of Hindu Extremism* (2003), *Islam at the Crossroads* (2002), *God and the Constitution* (2002), *The Talibanization of Nigeria* (2002), *Massacre at the Millennium* (2001), *Religious Freedom in the World* (2000), *Egypt's Endangered Christians* (1999), *Just Politics* (1998), *Heaven Is Not My Home* (1998), *A Kind of Life Imposed on Man* (1996), and the best-selling, award-winning survey of religious persecution worldwide *Their Blood Cries Out* (1997). He is the author of several hundred articles, and his writings have been translated into Russian, German, French, Dutch, Spanish, Portuguese, Norwegian, Danish, Albanian, Japanese, Malay, Korean, Arabic, Farsi, and Chinese. He is in frequent demand for lectures and media appearances, including interviews on ABC Evening News; CNN; PBS; Fox; the British, Australian, Canadian, South African, and Japanese Broadcasting Corporations; and Al Jazeera. His work has been published in, or is the subject of, articles in the *New York Times, Wall Street Journal, Washington Post, Los Angeles Times, Washington Times, Boston Globe, Dallas Morning News, Christian Science Monitor, First Things, New Republic, Weekly Standard, Reader's Digest*, and many other newspapers and magazines.

Nina Shea

An international human-rights lawyer for thirty years, Nina Shea is Senior Fellow of the Hudson Institute, where she directs the Center for Religious Freedom, a foreign-policy center she helped found in 1986. For seven years ending in 2005, she helped organize and lead a coalition of churches and religious groups that worked to end a religious war in South Sudan against Christians and traditional African believers, which led to the 2005 Comprehensive Peace Agreement and culminated in a vote for South Sudan to secede and become an independent country in 2011; she is a long-time advocate for persecuted religious minorities around the world; and she has authored and edited three widely acclaimed reports on Saudi Arabia, which translate and provide original analysis on official Saudi textbooks and educational materials. She regularly presents testimony before Congress, delivers public lectures, organizes briefings and conferences, and writes frequently on issues pertaining to religious freedom in American foreign policy. Her best-selling 1997 book on anti-Christian persecution, *In the Lion's Den*, remains a standard in the field. Her writings and articles about her advocacy have been published in the *Wall Street Journal, Washington Post, Christian Science Monitor, Weekly Standard*, and *Huffington Post*, among others, and she is a frequent contributor to *National Review Online*. Since 1999, Shea has served as a congressionally appointed Commissioner on the U.S. Commission on International Religious Freedom, an independent federal agency. She previously served as a U.S. public delegate to the United Nation's main human rights body, appointed by both Republican and Democratic administrations, and currently serves as a commissioner on the U.S. National Commission to UNESCO.

Contributors

Abdurrahman Wahid

The late Abdurrahman Wahid was President of Indonesia, the world's largest Muslim country, and head of Nahdlatul Ulama, the world's largest Muslim organization. An outspoken critic of radical Islam, he has been recognized by members of all religions throughout the world for his defense of religious and ethnic minorities and promotion of religious liberty for all. Among the many positions he has held are cofounder and senior advisor of LibForAll, which generously arranged for his foreword to this book.

Nasr Hamid Abu-Zayd

The late Nasr Hamid Abu-Zayd was Academic Director of the International Institute of Qur'anic Studies (IIQS), a branch of LibForAll Foundation. He is the author of numerous scholarly works on Islam in both Arabic and English and is known for developing a humanistic interpretation of the Qur'an. Formerly Professor of Arabic Literature at Cairo University, he left when Egypt's highest court ruled that, because of his views, he was an apostate and must be forcibly divorced from his Muslim wife. He also received death threats from Ayman Al Zawahiri of Al-Qaeda. Abu-Zayd held the Ibn Rushd Chair of Humanism and Islam at the University for

Humanistics in the Netherlands and was awarded the Ibn Rushd Prize for Freedom of Thought in 2005. He died in Cairo on July 5, 2010.

Abdullah Saeed

Abdullah Saeed, originally from the Maldives, is Sultan of Oman Professor of Arab and Islamic Studies at the University of Melbourne. He obtained his B.A. in Arab/ Islamic Studies in Saudi Arabia in 1986 and his doctorate at the University of Melbourne in 1992. He has written on the interpretation of Islamic texts, Islam and human rights, and religious freedom, among other areas. Together with his brother Hassan Saeed, former Attorney General of the Maldives, he authored the book *Freedom of Religion, Apostasy and Islam* (2004), which is currently banned in the Maldives.

FOREWORD

God Needs No Defense

KYAI HAJI ABDURRAHMAN WAHID

Nothing could possibly threaten God who is Omnipotent and existing as absolute and eternal Truth. And as *ar-Rahman* (the Merciful) and *ar-Rahim* (the Compassionate), God has no enemies.

As revered Muslim intellectual K. H. Mustofa Bisri[1] wrote in his poem "Allahu Akbar": "If all of the 6 billion human inhabitants of this earth, which is no greater than a speck of dust, were blasphemous...or pious...it would not have the slightest effect upon His greatness."

Those who claim to defend God, Islam, or the Prophet are thus either deluding themselves or manipulating religion for their own mundane and political purposes. We witnessed this in the carefully manufactured outrage that swept the Muslim world several years ago, claiming hundreds of lives, in response to cartoons published in Denmark. Those who presume to fully grasp God's will, and dare to impose by force their own limited understanding of this upon others, are essentially equating themselves with God and are unwittingly engaged in blasphemy.

As Muslims, rather than harshly condemning others' speech or beliefs and employing threats or violence to constrain these, we should ask: Why is there so little freedom of expression and freedom of religion in the so-called Muslim world? Exactly whose interests are served by laws such as Section 295-C of the Pakistani legal code, "Defiling the Name of Muhammad," which mandates the death penalty for "blasphemy"? Pakistan's Federal Shari'a Court has effectively defined this law as:

> reviling or insulting the Prophet in writing or speech; speaking profanely or contemptuously about him or his family; attacking the Prophet's dignity and honor in an abusive manner; vilifying him or making an ugly face when his name is mentioned; showing enmity or hatred towards him, his family, his companions, and the Muslims; accusing, or slandering the Prophet and his family, including spreading evil reports about him or his family; defaming the Prophet; refusing the Prophet's jurisdiction or judgment in any manner; rejecting the Sunnah; showing disrespect, contempt for or rejection of the rights of Allah and His Prophet or rebelling against Allah and His Prophet.[2]

Rather than serve to protect God, Islam, or Muhammad, such deliberately vague and repressive laws merely empower those with a worldly (i.e., political) agenda and act as a "sword of Damocles" threatening not only religious minorities, but also the right of mainstream Muslims to speak freely about their own religion without being threatened by the wrath of fundamentalists—exercised through the power of government or mobs—whose claims of "defending religion" are little more than a pretext for self-aggrandizement.

No objective observer can deny that Pakistani society—like so many others in the Muslim world—has undergone a process of coarsening under the influence of such laws, in tandem with the rise of religious extremism and the loss of true spirituality, without which the profound meaning and purpose of Islam remain veiled from human understanding.

The renowned Qur'anic injunction, "Let there be no compulsion in religion" (2:256), anticipated Article 18 of the Universal Declaration of Human Rights[3] by over thirteen centuries and should serve as an inspiration to Muslim societies today, guiding them on the path to religious freedom and tolerance.

In its original Qur'anic sense, the word *sharia* refers to "the way," the path to God, and not to formally codified Islamic law, which only emerged in the centuries following Muhammad's death. In examining the issue of blasphemy and apostasy laws, it is thus vital that we differentiate between the Qur'an—from which much of the raw material for producing Islamic law is derived—and the law itself. For while its revelatory inspiration is divine, Islamic law is man-made and thus subject to human interpretation and revision.

Punishment for apostasy is merely the legacy of historical circumstances and political calculations stretching back to the early days of Islam, when apostasy generally coincided with desertion from the caliph's army and/or rejection of his authority and thus constituted treason or rebellion. The embedding (i.e., codification) of harsh punishments for apostasy into Islamic law must be recognized as a historical and political by-product of these circumstances, framed in accordance with human calculations and expediency, rather than as the eternal dictate of Islamic *sharia* on the issue of changing one's religion.

The historical development and use of the term *sharia* to refer to Islamic law often lead those unfamiliar with this history to conflate man-made law with its revelatory inspiration, and thereby to elevate to the status of Divine the products of human understanding, which are necessarily conditioned by space and time.

On the one hand, *sharia*, properly understood, expresses and embodies perennial values. Islamic law, on the other hand, is the product of *ijtihad* (interpretation), which depends on circumstances (*al-hukm yadur ma'a al-'illah wujudan wa 'adaman*) and needs to be continuously reviewed in accordance with ever-changing circumstances. This is necessary to prevent Islamic law from becoming out of date, rigid, and noncorrelative, not only with Muslims' contemporary lives and conditions, but also with the underlying perennial values of *sharia* itself.

Throughout Islamic history, many of the greatest *fiqh* (Islamic jurisprudence) scholars have also been deeply grounded in the traditions of *tassawuf*, or Islamic mysticism, and have recognized the need to balance the letter with the spirit of the law. The profoundly humanistic and spiritual nature of Sufi Islam facilitated the accommodation of different social and cultural practices as Islam spread from its birthplace in the Arabian Peninsula to the Levant, North Africa, the Sahel and Sub-Saharan Africa, Persia, Central and South Asia, and the East Indies archipelago. By many estimates, a majority of the Muslim population in most of these regions still practice a form of religious piety either directly or indirectly derived from Sufism. And the greatness of traditional Islamic art and architecture—from the wonders of Fes and Granada, to Istanbul, Isfahan, Samarkand, and Agra—bears testimony to the long line of Sufi masters, guilds, and individual artists who strove to ennoble matter, so as to transform our man-made environment into "the veritable counterpart of nature, a mosaic of 'Divine portents' revealing everywhere the handiwork of man as God's vice-regent."[4]

Indeed, the greatness of classical Islamic civilization—which incorporated a humane and cosmopolitan universalism—stemmed largely from the intellectual and spiritual maturity that grew from the amalgamation of Arab, Greek, Jewish, Christian, and Persian influences. That is why I wept upon seeing Ibn Rushd's commentary on the *Nicomachean Ethics*, lovingly preserved and displayed, during a visit some years ago to Fes, Morocco. For if not for Aristotle and his great treatise, I might have become a Muslim fundamentalist myself.

Among the various factors that have contributed to the long decline of Arab and Muslim civilizations in general, and have greatly hindered their participation in the development of the modern world, was the triumph of normative religious constraints, which ultimately defeated the classical tradition of Islamic humanism. Absorption of "alien" influences—particularly in the realm of speculative thought—and the creation of individual, rational, and independent sciences not constrained by religious scholasticism were defeated by internal control mechanisms exercised by religious and governmental authorities, thus paralyzing Muslim societies.

These same tendencies are still on display in our contemporary world, not least in the form of severe blasphemy and apostasy laws that narrow the bounds of acceptable discourse in the Islamic world and prevent most Muslims from thinking "outside the box" not only about religion but also about vast spheres of life, literature, science, and culture in general.

Religious Understanding Is a Process

Anyone who is sincere in understanding his or her faith necessarily undergoes a process of constant evolution in that understanding, as experience and insights give rise to new perceptions of the truth. For as God states in the Qur'an: "We will display Our Signs upon the horizon, and within themselves (humanity), until it is clear to them that God is the Truth (*al-Haqq*)" (41:53).

Nothing that exists is self-sufficient, other than God. All living things are inter-dependent and owe their very existence to God. Yet because God's creatures exist within time and space, their perceptions of truth and reality differ from one to the next, conditioned by their personal knowledge and experience.

As referenced above, Islam views the world and whatever information we may obtain from it as signs leading to knowledge of God. Muslim scholars traditionally classify three stages of knowledge: *First*, the science of certainty ('*ilm al-yaqin*), which is inferential and concerns knowledge commonly held to be true, whether by scientists, intellectuals, or *ulama* themselves. *Second*, the vision of certainty ('*ain al-yaqin*) represents a higher level of truth than the first. At this stage, one directly witnesses that information about an objective phenomenon is indeed true and accurate. *Third*, the truth or reality of certainty (*haqq al-yaqin*), that is, truth that reaches the level of perfection through direct personal experience, as exemplified by a saint's mystical communion with God.

The fact that the Qur'an refers to God as "the Truth" is highly significant. If human knowledge is to attain this level of Truth, religious freedom is vital. Indeed, the search for Truth (i.e., the search for God)—whether employing the intellect, emotions, or various forms of spiritual practice—should be allowed a free and broad range. For without freedom, the individual soul cannot attain absolute Truth, which is, by Its very nature, unconditional Freedom itself.

Intellectual and emotional efforts are mere preludes in the search for Truth. One's goal as a Muslim should be to completely surrender oneself (*islâm*) to the absolute Truth and Reality of God rather than to mere intellectual or emotional concepts regarding the ultimate Truth. Without freedom, humans can only attain a self-satisfied and illusory grasp of the truth, rather than genuine Truth Itself (*haqq al-haqiqi*).

The spiritual aptitude of any given individual necessarily plays a key role in his or her ability to attain the Truth, while the particular expression of Truth appre-hended by one person may differ from that of the next. Islam honors and values these differences, and religious freedom itself, recognizing that each human being comprehends God in accord with his or her own native abilities and propensities, as expressed in the *Hadith Qudsi*[5]: "*Ana 'inda zann 'abdi bi*," ("I am as my servant thinks I am"). Of course, one's efforts to know God (*mujahadah*, from the same root as *jihad*) should be genuine and sincere (*ikhlas*), leading to a state of self-tran-scendence. In such a state, humans experience God's ineffable Presence and their own annihilation. Muslim fundamentalists often reject this notion because of their shallow grasp of religion and lack of spiritual experience. For them, God must be understood as completely transcendent (*tanzih*) and far beyond the reach of humanity, with no hope for anyone to experience God's Presence. Such views are mistaken, for as the Qur'an itself states: "Whichever way you turn, there is the face of God" (2:115).

Nothing can restrict the Absolute Truth. Sufism—whose purpose is to bring Muslims to the third stage of knowledge, that is, the truth and reality of certainty (*haqq al-yaqin*)—emphasizes the value of freedom and diversity, both as reflections of God's will and purpose and to prevent the inadvertent or deliberate conflation of human understanding, which is inherently limited and subject to error, with the Divine. Faith (*îmân*) and surrender to God (*islâm*) on a purely intellectual level are not enough. Rather, a Muslim should continuously strive (*mujahadah*) to experience the actual Presence of God (*ihsan*). For without experiencing God's Presence, a Muslim's religious practice remains on a purely theoretical level; *islâm* has not yet become an experiential reality.

Sanctions against freedom of religious inquiry and expression act to stop the developmental process of religious understanding dead in its tracks. They conflate the sanctioning authority's current, limited grasp of the truth with ultimate Truth itself, and thereby transform religion from a path to the Divine into a "divinized" goal, whose features and confines are generally dictated by those with an all-too-human agenda of earthly power and control.

We can see this process at work in attempts by the Organization of the Islamic Conference (OIC), the United Nations General Assembly, and the UN Council on Human Rights to restrict freedom of expression and institute a legally binding global ban on any perceived criticism of Islam, to prevent so-called "defamation of religion." Whether motivated by sincere concern for humanity or political calculation, such efforts are woefully misguided and play directly into the hands of fundamentalists, who wish to avoid all criticism of their attempts to narrow the scope of discourse regarding Islam, and to inter 1.3 billion Muslims in a narrow, suffocating chamber of dogmatism.

While hostility toward Islam and Muslims is a legitimate and vital concern, we must recognize that a major cause of such hostility is the behavior of certain Muslims themselves, who propagate a harsh, repressive, supremacist, and often-violent understanding of Islam, which tends to aggravate and confirm non-Muslims' worst fears and prejudices about Islam and Muslims in general.

Rather than legally stifle criticism and debate—which will only encourage Muslim fundamentalists in their efforts to impose a spiritually void, harsh, and monolithic understanding of Islam upon all the world—Western authorities should instead firmly defend freedom of expression, not only in their own nations, but also globally, as enshrined in Article 19 of the Universal Declaration of Human Rights.[6]

Those who are humble and strive to live in genuine submission to God (i.e., *islâm*) do not claim to be perfect in their understanding of the Truth. Rather, they are content to live in peace with others, whose paths and views may differ.

Defending freedom of expression is by no means synonymous with *personally* countenancing or encouraging disrespect towards others' religious beliefs, but it does imply greater faith in the judgment of God, than that of man. Beyond the daily headlines of chaos and violence, the vast majority of the world's Muslims

PART I

INTRODUCTION

1

Introduction

The Threat of Blasphemy Restrictions

On February 14, 1989, an elderly Iranian ayatollah pronounced a religious decree on blasphemy that targeted a novelist half a world away. His proclamation created a tremor whose strength has intensified so that it now threatens to fracture the very foundations of Western free society.

In his landmark edict, Iran's Supreme Leader Grand Ayatollah Khomeini called for "all zealous Muslims to execute quickly wherever they find them," the British author Salman Rushdie and all others involved with his new book, *The Satanic Verses*. Khomeini was not deterred by the fact that Rushdie, born a Muslim in India and at that time living in London, had no connection to Iran. Khomeini had simply found the work offensive and wanted to ensure that "no one will dare to insult Islamic sanctity" ever again. As Iran's highest official, he also needed to shore up his political legitimacy following the end of an inconclusive and devastating war with Iraq.

International headlines reported the many ensuing bounties put on Rushdie's head, his hasty retreat to a safe house, and the murder of his Japanese translator and the assaults seriously injuring his Norwegian editor and his Italian translator. However, most Westerners gave the incident little thought. Those who did saw it as a quirk, a unique outburst by an insular and arcane ruler asserting a preposterous claim to direct the actions of Muslims worldwide. Rushdie himself, though perpetually under threat because the decree was never revoked, was feted by politicians and literary figures and remained a celebrity, and his books continued to sell well. At the time, the West was far from shaken.

Few foresaw that Khomeini was, in fact, spearheading a religious trend with political undertones, propelled by a zeal not seen in the West for several centuries. His edict signaled a new worldwide movement to curb freedoms of religion and speech through the export and enforcement of Muslim blasphemy rules that were already suppressing minorities and dissenters in Muslim-majority countries. All this took place in the context of a revival of reactionary forms of Islam, supported heavily by the political rulers and spiritual authorities of both Shia Iran and Sunni Saudi Arabia, who fiercely compete for power in the Muslim world.

Sunni authorities soon outdistanced Shia Iran's lead, generating a proliferation of fatwas and demands to stop purported Western blasphemy and related sins of apostasy, heresy, and "insulting Islam."[1] Over the ensuing years, Western film-makers, legislators, writers, journalists, political analysts, social activists, religious dissidents, and cartoonists have been targeted. As this book describes, this intimidation and violence has been not intended ostensibly only to protect Islam from criticism and rejection. It also serves the narrower political purpose of shielding from criticism those who claim the right to rule in the name of Islam.

This trend intensified after the attacks on the United States on September 11, 2001, as Islam and Muslim governments were publicly scrutinized, criticized, and sometimes ridiculed in the West to an extent never seen or permitted in Muslim lands. Whether Shia or Sunni, Muslim authorities feared that Western critiques could weaken their religious claims and their rule. The response of many Muslim-majority states, including those that describe themselves as "secular," has been to demand that Western governments punish all those within their borders who have purportedly insulted Islam. In so doing, they, like Khomeini, have departed from a long tradition, based on the opinion of Islamic legal scholars, that offenses committed by non-Muslims in non-Muslim countries are no concern of Islamic law.

These events played out against the backdrop of Islamist terror in the United States, Bali, Madrid, London, and elsewhere. That violence, while carried out for different reasons and involving other actors, amplified a sense of intimidation accompanying the Muslim antiblasphemy movement in the West. The movement itself, however, was never simply the demand of an apparent extremist fringe that could be marginalized; its strength was further demonstrated when the cause was taken up and mainstreamed by governments in the Muslim world—secular and religious—united within the Organization of the Islamic Conference (OIC).

The Saudi-based OIC and its fifty-seven members gave the antiblasphemy movement weight and traction. While the West largely understood religious freedom as a right of an individual, the OIC reinterpreted it to mean respect for religion itself, specifically Islam and everything Islamic. The OIC and its members were responsible for placing "defamation against religions"—in practice, a code term for Islamic blasphemy restrictions—onto the human rights agenda of the United Nations. This was done in an attempt to shape a new international human rights regime that would supplant existing laws that protect individual freedoms; the new laws would instead protect religions, particularly Islam. In the best-known international blasphemy episode, usually known as the Danish cartoons crisis, it was the OIC that amplified the event and gave global momentum to the backlash that made it so traumatic. There were certainly a multiplicity of actors, motives, and agendas in scores of countries. The overall trajectory, however, was to give heft to a decades-long, multiparty campaign, combining international lobbying, lawsuits, threats, and violence. The intention was to export restrictions on "insulting Islam" and blasphemy to the rest of the world.

Today, OIC countries are demanding that the West curb the intertwined individual freedoms of religion and expression—rights that have been enshrined in some constitutions for two hundred years, as well as recognized, since the founding of the United Nations, as universal fundamental human rights under international law. Nevertheless, the Western world has often been dilatory and confused in its response to the OIC's demands, not least because its lacks clarity about what dangers they entail and what lies behind them. Most of the discussion about "insulting Islam," doubtless shaped about memories of the Rushdie affair and Danish cartoons, has focused naively on questions of trying to curb "hate speech," and what are more generally thought to be insults, and of how to accommodate such demands within free societies.

Later in this book, we will examine how Western countries are faring in their undertaking to balance Muslim demands and fundamental rights and freedoms. But, before analyzing this, we must take a step back to examine whether such accommodation is desirable or even possible. We argue that the current imposition of curbs on perceived anti-Islamic speech—whether called blasphemy, defamation of Islam, insulting Islam, or anti-Islamic hate speech—is incompatible with the freedoms that define democracy and individual human rights.

The heart of the problem lies in determining precisely what specific forms of expression the OIC countries seek to limit in the West. There are no clear definitions of religious defamation or religious hate speech. Similarly, no common practice regarding blasphemy crimes exists within the OIC membership. Many Muslim expectations are based on amorphous rules expressed in practices that vary from country to country and evolve and expand over time. Within countries that have such restrictions, definitions are generally left to case law, commonly unwritten, and often determined by the subjective and sometimes self-serving opinions of local authorities. The nature of what is being asked of the non-Muslim world is, therefore, obscure.

Also, within most Western countries, discrimination and incitement to violence against Muslims and others are already understood to be crimes, which implies that speech crimes against Islam must include something far wider. As our survey reveals, the freedom to debate, to reject, to refuse to respect, to criticize religious ideas, and to worship according to one's conscience are essential to religious freedom. Blasphemy restrictions coerce religious conformity and forcibly silence criticism of dominant religious ideas, especially when those ideas support, and are supported by, political power. When politics and religion are intertwined, there can be no free political debate if there is no free religious debate.

In contrast to the West, many OIC countries have their own limits on speech regarding Islam, which control not only ridicule and mocking language, but also what can be expressed, analyzed, and argued in the political, cultural, social, economic, and religious realms; in fact, these limits are major means of social and political control. To give a clearer understanding of what leading OIC governments mean when they call for the internationalization of legal bans on blasphemy and insults to Islam, we first examine the contemporary situation within those countries.

Muslim-Majority Countries

To demonstrate the wide-ranging effects of restrictions on blasphemy, in part II, we survey restrictions on purported blasphemy, apostasy, insulting Islam, and similar offenses as they are applied in leading Muslim countries. We pay special attention to countries in the forefront of the international campaign to ban "defamation of religions" and "incitement to religious hatred," such as Saudi Arabia, Iran, Pakistan, Egypt, as well as over a dozen other members of the Islamic Conference. This is a long survey—there is much to survey—but we make no claim to completeness in the countries covered or in events within those countries. Indeed we have documentation on many more cases (in the West as well as in Muslim-majority countries) that, for reasons of space, we have not included, and the number of cases increases daily. Our goal is simply to illustrate the range of actions, words, and thoughts that are being repressed in these countries and to suggest the degree of religiously based repression that is currently taking place.

Our findings are deeply troubling. They reveal social and political patterns that have disturbing implications for human rights, political freedoms, development, and security. Three themes emerge from our study that should be of particular concern to the West.

First, coercive measures in OIC states that are ostensibly intended to ensure respect for Islam are used to curb the freedom not only of far-flung irreverent cartoonists but also of native scholars, writers, dissidents, religious reformers, human rights activists, converts from Islam, members of post-Islamic religions, and anyone else whose utterances depart from locally dominant variants of Islam. These laws establish a broad deterrent to critiques of Islam and all matters Islamic. Frequently, this includes protections for those who rule in the name of Islam, such as governments themselves. Freedoms of religion and expression are sharply curtailed. Related political and academic freedoms and the right to due process are also circumscribed.

Second, blasphemy laws and restrictions, by their nature, foster a closed religious orthodoxy and punish independent and innovative thinking. In the contemporary struggle of ideas within Islam, those who are empowered by such restrictions are the extremists, who use law and intimidation to determine which ideas are accessible and acceptable in their society. In contrast, Muslim religious and political reformers, who protest the extremists' agenda and work to lift their societies out of stunting, ideological conformity, are the first to be silenced. In other words, blasphemy laws suppress the very voices that seek to reconcile the Muslim world with modern pluralism.

Third, terms such as "blasphemy" and "insulting Islam" are invoked without precision. Protestors, complainants, and even courts frequently alternate between the terms, require no proof of intent, and offer novel understandings of what constitutes such transgressions, often without any historical foundation. For instance, Malaysia outlaws anything that might contain "twisted facts that can undermine the faith of Muslims." Under Pakistan's blasphemy laws, violations can be "by any imputation, innuendo or insinuation, directly or indirectly." Basic principles of fairness are undermined, and speech is broadly deterred by such murky standards.

Chapter 2 gives an overview of the Kingdom of Saudi Arabia, providing perhaps the broadest scope to blasphemy and apostasy prohibitions. The Saudi government uses its position as custodian of Islam's two holiest shrines, Mecca and Medina, to assert that its Wahhabi interpretation of the faith is the authoritative one. Effectively, this means that Muslims of different views, whether Shias, Sufis, reformers, or political dissidents, may find themselves condemned as apostates. For example, the opening fatwa of a Saudi government educational pamphlet rebukes a European imam for his "infidelity" because he "casts doubts about the infidelity of Jews and Christians." This is a serious charge since, according to the country's textbooks, which are available online, it is permissible to kill someone for such infidelity, though within the Kingdom itself, prison terms and flogging are more likely.

Saudi Arabia's Shia minority, including Ismailis, suffer disproportionately for blasphemy offenses. Among those of the majority Sunni population convicted in recent years were democracy activists, who were imprisoned for using "un-Islamic" terminology, such as *democracy* and *human rights*. Among those given prison terms and lashes for "mocking religion" were teachers who discussed the Bible in class and made favorable comments about Jews and who had written articles arguing that the dominance of radical Islamists over Saudi university culture had harmed the quality of cultural programs.

In chapter 3, we describe trends in Iran. Since its 1979 revolution, Iran has had few rivals in suppressing its population in the name of enforcing the state's religious orthodoxy. Private attacks on those deemed religiously deviant are relatively scarce, but the regime itself targets Baha'is, Jews, converts, Sufis and Sunnis, and increasingly, anyone seen as a political threat. Those deemed possibly dangerous to the powers-that-be include human rights and women's activists and, especially, Shia intellectuals and clergy who criticize the regime. Since the government claims that Shia Islam is its source of authority, it is particularly susceptible to critiques based on alternative interpretations of Islam. For example, Grand Ayatollah Hossein Ali Montazeri, one of the architects of *Velayat-e Faqih*, Iran's system of rule, was detained for six years for his religious criticism of the structure he had helped create. He mocked Ayatollah Khomeini's edict calling for the death of novelist Salman Rushdie and stated that Iran's "jailing the enlightened and the elite of society for false reasons" is "condemned and illegitimate."

In applying the regime's statutes on blasphemy and apostasy, Iran's judges frequently reference their own interpretations of sharia. With little consistency, they convict people on undefined charges such as "friendship with the enemies of God," "dissension from religious dogma," or "propagation of spiritual liberalism." Punishments for these charges include amputation, burning, starvation, and execution. Under Mahmoud Ahmadinejad's presidency, conditions have deteriorated even further, and the increased demonization of Baha'is, Jews, Sufis, and opposition figures may indicate darker days ahead.

In contrast to Saudi Arabia and Iran, Egypt has been regarded as a moderate or secular country. It is also one of the leading international proponents of a universal blasphemy law, and, in 2009, Egypt joined with the United States in sponsoring a UN resolution urging states to take "all necessary measures" against religious hate speech. As chapter 4 shows, Egypt's own laws against insulting a heavenly religion or "creating sectarian strife" have been used to repress criticism of the government and to prevent religious moderation and heterodoxy. Egypt's reformist Muslim intelligentsia, as well as the Christian community and other minorities, have borne the brunt of the repression. Quranists—a Muslim religious reform movement stressing political freedom—have been sentenced for "insulting religion due to unorthodox Islamic beliefs and practices." Quranist Sheikh Subhy Mansour sought political asylum in the United States after being persecuted for his reformist writings, including his book arguing against the death penalty for apostasy. The late Muslim reformer Abu-Zayd, whose essay appears later in this book, was declared an apostate by the court of Cassation, Egypt's highest court, and had to flee Egypt before his marriage was compulsorily dissolved by the courts. The state-funded Al-Azhar University, which the regime consults, has issued a fatwa against the Baha'is, calling on the state to "annihilate" them as a "lethal spiritual epidemic." It has also called for the punishment of Muslims who convert to Christianity, and it has taken the lead in banning books by reformers.

There are other dangers apart from the Egyptian government for those accused of blasphemy. Charges of insulting Islam inflame passions, and extremists have manipulated crowds to incite deadly riots. In 2005, for example, a newspaper reported that a play performed in St. George's Church in Alexandria had "insulted Islam," resulting in a 5,000-strong mob attack on eight churches, with four killed and ninety injured. In another incident, the late Naguib Mahfouz, the only Arab winner of the Nobel Prize in Literature, was stabbed and partially paralyzed by an extremist who thought that his novels insulted Islam.

Pakistan, which has also taken the lead in introducing the OIC's annual antidefamation resolutions at the UN, has codified some of the world's most draconian antiblasphemy laws, which can carry a life sentence or the death penalty. As chapter 5 details, in Pakistan, while there have been no official executions for blasphemy, extremists have frequently murdered the accused before, during, or after adjudication, even when there was an acquittal. Lynch mobs, whipped into hysteria by accusations of blasphemy broadcast from mosque loudspeakers, have assaulted, typically with impunity, thousands of coreligionists and families of the accused, attacking their houses of worship, homes, and businesses, and destroying entire villages.

Muslim reformers are silenced. Author Younus Shaikh was sentenced to life in prison for "deviating from the teachings of the Quran" by criticizing *rajam* (stoning for adultery). A vastly disproportionate number of cases involve the Ahmadi and Christian minorities, who are particularly vulnerable since, in blasphemy cases, their testimonies count for less than that of Muslims. In Punjab in 2009, after an unsubstantiated accusation that a Qur'an had been desecrated, at least seven Christians were burned alive and over fifty houses torched. Credible reports indicated that extremist groups linked to Al-Qaeda were involved. In 2011, extremists murdered Minorities Minister Shahbaz Bhatti and Governor Salman Taseer for calling for abolition of the blasphemy laws.

Chapter 6 describes how Afghanistan's 2004 constitution, drafted with the financial support and legal guidance of the United States and the United Nations, contains a clause asserting that no law can contradict Islam—a law that is often the basis for punishing apostasy and blasphemy. Abdul Rahman, a Christian convert who was imprisoned, was later freed, and subsequently fled the country after international pressure, is the most widely known instance, but there is an ever-lengthening list of such cases, especially involving Muslim journalists. The editor of the magazine *Haqooq-i-Zan* (Women's Rights) was imprisoned for blasphemy for arguing against the apostasy law. Sima Samar, the minister for Women's Affairs, was accused of blasphemy for her criticism of the adoption of Islamic law but was spared after international protest erupted. In 2008, a student journalist was condemned to death, a sentence later commuted, for downloading and circulating material on women's rights under Islam. Despite the presence of NATO forces and UN agencies, religious repression—even in government-controlled areas of Afghanistan—appears to be increasing.

Chapter 7, "The Greater Middle East," describes some events in Algeria, Jordan, Morocco, Turkey, Yemen, and elsewhere in the area. Despite their very great differences from one another, each also represses expression deemed insulting to Islam. Algeria has been cracking down on Christians because of fears of conversions, especially among the Kabyle people. There has been a similar pattern in Morocco. In both countries, this might also be tied to fears of conversions by Sunnis to Shiism, and the connection this might have to Iranian influence. Jordan is similar and has also pressured Muslim journalists and a poet. Libya, though varying with Qadafi's idiosyncrasies, has usually been far harsher in its treatment of converts. In Yemen, Jews, Baha'is, converts, and journalists have been persecuted, and several leading Muslim scholars have declared that those pushing for the reform of marriage laws were apostates. In Turkey, the minority Alevi Muslims suffer widespread discrimination, while writers and other reformers, as well as converts, can be accused of insulting the "Turkish nation," which can incorporate a religious dimension because Islam is regarded as an integral part of the Turkish nation.

Chapter 8, "Africa," covers three countries: Nigeria, the largest by population; Sudan, the largest by area; and Somalia, which is, in 2011, probably the most religiously repressive area in the Muslim world. In Nigeria, with the growth of more militant forms of Islam, accusations of apostasy and blasphemy have led to riots and murders, with certainly hundreds, and probably thousands, dead. There are also violent militias, such as Boko Haram, which appear to regard everyone else as a blasphemer or apostate who must be attacked. Somalia is torn between rival jurisdictions and rival militias, none of which is open to political or religious difference. Among them is the radical Islamist Al-Shabab—the Union of Islamic Courts—movement. It enforces its radically repressive version of sharia, which bans music and bells, destroys graves and anything else that it believes smacks of Sufism, and is embarked on a policy of exterminating every Christian in the country, including by beheading children. Apart from its genocide of minorities and political repression, Sudan executed its leading Muslim scholar for apostasy and implicitly charged a UN Special Rapporteur with blasphemy, and its agents declared hundreds of thousands of Nuba Muslims apostates who deserved death.

Chapter 9, "South and Southeast Asia," covers Bangladesh, Indonesia, Malaysia, and the Maldives. The Maldives bans all religion except Sunni Islam and has used religious restrictions to crack down on religious and political reformers. The other three countries have reputations for moderation, some of them deserved, but there seems to have been an intensification of religious repression in recent years. In Bangladesh and Indonesia, Ahmadis are repressed, as are heterodox groups and Muslims who express reformist and modernist views. While there is government repression, a larger problem is violence by mobs and militias that the government cannot or will not control. Malaysia has had ongoing legal struggles over the conversion of Muslims to other religions, is trying to restrict the religious words that non-Muslims may use, and, claiming that its population is easily confused and so should not be exposed to a range of views, is also repressing heterodox and reformist Muslims.

This survey of Muslim countries provides insights into the wide range, significance, effects, and baleful consequences of laws and vigilante actions against those accused of insulting Islam in the Muslim world. It is only against this background that the dangerous possibilities such restrictions pose to the rest of the world—either through the United Nations or by direct pressure on Western governments—can be seen.

Attempts to Internationalize Blasphemy Restrictions

In part III, "The Globalization of Blasphemy," we give an overview of attempts to transplant restrictions on "insulting Islam" to the West. These instances have occurred in particular Western countries and in the United Nations, taking place in commissions, conferences, courts of law, or in the streets through vigilante action. Some of the larger and more famous examples in the West have had such a complex and long-lasting international backlash and effect that they must be treated as special cases. These are detailed in chapter 10 and include the continuing affair of *The Satanic Verses*, renewed when author Salman Rushdie was given a knighthood by the British government. We also focus on the so-called Danish cartoons crisis of 2005–6, which continues to reverberate when the images are republished or forbidden to be printed, as in 2009 when Yale University Press censored them and other images from a book detailing the cartoons crisis itself. Other examples include the *Newsweek* account of a Qur'an flushed down a toilet at Guantanamo, a report which was later disproved; Pope Benedict XVI's controversial speech at Regensburg; and Dutch parliamentarian Geert Wilders's provocative film, *Fitna*. One feature of these upheavals was that they frequently involved political manipulation. For example, the Danish cartoons were first published in September 2005 and later republished, even in Egypt, Morocco, and Indonesia, without any outcry. It was only in January 2006, following a decision by the OIC in its Mecca meeting to make an issue of the caricatures, when riots, violence, and boycotts erupted and some 200 people were killed.

Chapter 11 moves from wide international upheaval over blasphemy accusations to more formal efforts to legislate antiblasphemy laws through international fora, particularly the United Nations. This chapter examines a twenty-year campaign driven by authoritarian governments to subject international human rights standards to an undefined version of Islam. The campaign includes the promotion of the 1990 "Cairo Declaration on Human Rights in Islam" and, in the 1990s, blasphemy-based threats against the UN Special Rapporteur on Sudan, Gaspar Biro, and the Special Rapporteur on Contemporary Forms of Racism, Racial Discrimination, Xenophobia, and Related Intolerance, Maurice Glele-Ahanhanzo. The main effort has been the OIC's push, begun in 1999, to use the United Nations to win official endorsement for a global ban on blasphemy against Islam. First called "defamation of Islam," then retitled "defamation of religions" at the insistence of other delegations, a resolution had been debated and adopted annually for more than a decade in the United Nations. This effort had been losing support and the resolution was not proposed in the Human Rights Council in March 2011. It is being replaced with an initiative, which also has some Western support, to establish an international religious hate-speech standard, relying on undefined terms such as "incitement to hostility" and "negative stereotyping."

Related questions are being debated in Western national law. Many Western countries already accept the principle that their governments should limit religious criticism. Chapter 12 investigates how these countries are creating, amending, and enforcing laws that limit what may and may not be said about religious beliefs. These laws range from literal blasphemy bans, originally intended to protect Christianity, to twentieth-century hate-speech prohibitions, devised primarily as antiracism measures, but which are now increasingly applied to religious categories as well. While largely anachronistic, some blasphemy laws have been used to prosecute offenses against Islam; for instance, in Finland in 2009, a city politician was convicted of "violating the sanctity of religion" for deriding the Muslim prophet and Muslim child marriages. Most European Union countries, as well as the EU itself, affirm that restrictions on speech should protect individuals rather than religions, but the conflation by Muslim complainants of insults to the religion with insults to the individual is widespread, as shown in our case examples. Proceedings brought against actress Brigitte Bardot in France, writer Mark Steyn in Canada, two Christian pastors in Australia, and others, involved complaints arising from speech critical of Islam and not personal insults. Most worrisome about the use of hate-speech laws against religious criticism—which is increasing, although not systematic—is its chilling effect. A growing number of publishers, journalists, filmmakers, and artists are acknowledging that they are shying away from Islamic subjects in their work. At both the national and international levels, it appears the West has begun to answer Muslim demands, not with a unified and principled defense of fundamental freedoms, but with religious hate-speech laws, which are just as arbitrary and vague as Muslim blasphemy regimes.

While legal strictures on religious speech are dangerous, a more pervasive, and in many ways deeper, problem is violence and threats of violence against those accused of insulting Islam. Chapter 13 sheds light on the effects of this violence not only on politicians and lawmakers but also on ordinary Muslims living in the West, converts from Islam, and others who are intentionally outspoken, defiant against Islamist strictures, attempting to reform ideas, or simply careless with words. A pattern of violent intimidation is becoming familiar in Western society. Such intimidation is especially evident in some Muslim communities, in which threats of violence follow in the wake of whatever words and actions are deemed "insulting to Islam."

The gruesome 2004 murder and near decapitation of director Theo van Gogh in Holland, and the related death threats against Somali-born ex-Muslim Ayaan Hirsi Ali, powerfully illustrate this growing trend. The murderer, Mohammed Bouyeri, made it clear that he was not enraged for any purely personal reasons. Instead, he declared, "From now on, this will be the punishment for anyone in this land who challenges and insults Allah and his messengers." The West still remains a relative haven for free debate, for voices of Islamic reform, and for those with unorthodox views of Islam. But Western states and international organizations stand at a crossroads between a robust defense of free speech and a flaccid response to the persistent encroachment of antiblasphemy restrictions, whether imposed through legislation, and court decisions, or enforced outside the reach of law by radical vigilantes.

Muslim Criticism of Apostasy and Blasphemy Laws

This book is not a work on Islamic law or history, nor does it analyze the development of apostasy and blasphemy concepts. Our concern is to survey the contemporary use and effects of such accusations and threats. Clearly, however, one of the most important means of combating these threats to individual freedoms of religion and expression is in the war of ideas itself. It is vitally important to show that temporal punishments for purported blasphemy and apostasy are not necessary within Islam and can, in fact, be understood as a departure from and a threat to Islam. There is no consensus on this. For example, Sheikh Qaradawi, perhaps the most widely consulted Islamic authority for the West, equivocates on the issue. Even a Muslim chaplain at Harvard wrote in 2009 that there was "great wisdom (*hikma*) associated with the established and preserved position (capital punishment) and so, even if it makes some uncomfortable in the face of the hegemonic modern human rights discourse, one should not dismiss it out of hand."[2]

In light of such statements, we asked three highly respected Islamic scholars to address this issue, which they did in three original essays included in this book. As committed Muslims, they are known for respect for Islam and they certainly deplore and oppose insults to God and to their religion. But, they argue carefully and strenuously that Islam does not require temporal punishments for blasphemy or apostasy.

The late Kyai Haji Abdurrahman Wahid's "God Needs No Defense" serves as the book's "foreword." Wahid was the president of Indonesia, the world's largest Muslim country, and the head of Nahdatul Ulama, the world's largest Muslim organization. His essay outlines the nature of religious belief itself and argues eloquently that God does not need to be defended from blasphemy. It maintains that blasphemy accusations stem from the politics of early Islam, when apostasy meant desertion from the caliph's army. In today's very different world, temporal punishments for blasphemy and apostasy threaten true faith itself, which always includes growing and seeking the truth.

In chapter 14, "Renewing Qur'anic Studies in the Contemporary World," the late Professor Abu-Zayd, who was forced to flee Egypt because of his work, emphasizes that blasphemy and apostasy accusations are used "strategically" to prevent the reform of Muslim societies. His essay stresses the diversity in contemporary and historical Islam and outlines the varied modes of interpretation used by Muslims. In particular, while carefully never reducing Islam to history, it emphasizes that we need to understand its historical context: "how it developed in Arabia and other parts of the world." Only in this way can we understand how Islam should be manifest in our own place and time.

In chapter 15, "Rethinking Classical Muslim Law of Apostasy and the Death Penalty," Abdullah Saeed—some of whose writings have been banned in his native

Maldives—argues that current human rights discourse is not Western but is shared by many Muslims. Like Abu-Zayd, he emphasizes the need to understand early Islam, especially the "post-prophetic period," during which apostasy laws were shaped. In a setting of armed conflict, apostasy meant joining a non-Muslim enemy and so threatening the community of believers. Later, the Abbasids curtailed religious dispute lest it undermine their claims to legitimacy, and so apostasy was akin to treason. Since most Muslims do not now live in closed tribes, apostasy is no longer related to desertion or treason and should not be treated as if it were.

Blasphemy Threats: Interconnecting the West and the Muslim World

In this survey, we seek to cover three things. First, we provide an overview of the actual practice and the consequent dire effects of current blasphemy and apostasy restrictions in some major contemporary Muslim countries. Second, we outline ongoing attempts over the last two decades within the UN system to conform international human rights standards to blasphemy and apostasy restrictions. Finally, we give an overview of the growth of increasing antiblasphemy demands in the West, by force of law and by extralegal threats and violence, imposed on those suspected of insulting Islam. We also examine the consequent chilling of debate and the self-imposed silence taking place within the broader community.

However, important as these three elements of the survey are, even when considered discretely, it is essential to note that these are not three separate trends. They are deeply interwoven, and their significance is best revealed when their interconnections are seen. For this reason, our survey seeks to elucidate six crucial themes and arguments, each of which stems from reciprocal interaction between the Muslim world and the West.

First, it will be shown that within the Muslim world itself, laws and violence against those accused of insulting Islam are not in the least limited to what are commonly regarded, at least in the West, as insults or mockery. These strictures include lethal persecution of those, such as Baha'is or Ahmadis, who are though to believe that there has been a prophet after Muhammad. They also justify the persecution and murder of those who convert from Islam to another religion or who simply no longer believe as Muslims. Targets inevitably include Muslim minorities, such as Shias in Saudi Arabia or Sufis in Iran, who are deemed deviant, if not outright heretical. Familiar targets of antiblasphemy laws are Muslim dissidents, liberals, and reformers, especially when they challenge the entrenched power of regimes and organizations that claim to represent Islam.

The span of specific victims is very broad. A Pakistani Muslim, who tripped onto a stove and accidentally singed himself and a Qur'an, was apprehended by vigilantes and burned to death for his transgression. Egyptian Nobel literature prizewinner Naguib Mahfouz's realistic portrayals of the complex lives of Cairene

Muslims were deemed threatening, and he was stabbed nearly to death. The current Somali campaign seeks to exterminate every Christian in the country. A former Afghan minister for Women's Affairs and Iranian and Saudi political reformers have faced threats and allegations. When we debate the meaning of "insulting Islam" or "defamation of religion," we should not do so in an abstract or antiseptic style, but bear in mind who the victims are.

Second, when countries in the OIC seek to introduce bans on defaming religion or insulting Islam into the international system through the United Nations, or through pressure for domestic legal change in the West, their agenda goes far beyond silencing Danish cartoonists or Dutch political provocateurs or providing so-called protection to individual Muslims in the West, who are already legally protected against violence, personal defamation, and discrimination. In most OIC states, the targets of such suppression are the disadvantaged, the religiously different or nonconforming, and the politically and religiously questioning. If these countries' pressure to ban religious defamation in the West succeeds, they will have taken a major step in exporting their own system of repression into the free world.

Third, if the limits on speech that have been debated at the United Nations become human rights law, virtually all critical analysis of anything claimed to be Islamic could be viewed as a human rights violation, one that UN member nations would be bound to silence and punish. The range of items that will be interpreted as "insulting" is likely to be extremely broad and unpredictable. For instance, in September 2005, complaints by some Muslim customers that the swirl on the lid of Burger King ice cream cones resembled the Arabic word for *Allah* led the fast-food chain to withdraw thousands of ice cream tubs. Nike had similar problems with one of its logos, and an Islamist website claimed that the glass cube built by Apple Corporation outside its midtown Manhattan store was an insult to Islam since it was shaped like the Kaaba, the Muslim shrine in Mecca.[3]

More disturbing are bans on longstanding and legitimate subjects of inquiry and debate, including Muslim practices regarding women, non-Muslims, violence, stoning and corporal punishments, and dress. This list must also include criticism of hate-speech laws themselves; such criticisms have already been challenged in Western courts as an example of Islamophobia. It is true that convictions in such cases have been infrequent, but that is not reassuring, because the trials themselves produce a broad chilling effect; there are uncertainties about what specific speech might be prohibited. For example, in 2009, criticism of Islamic veiling of women triggered prosecution in Great Britain but not in France, where the critique was made by President Sarkozy himself. Furthermore, even a successful defense can be disastrously expensive. An Australian lower court convicted two Christian preachers for "vilifying" Islam by, according to the court, selectively quoting from the Qur'an. Although the charges were eventually dropped, the case took three years and cost the defense over $100,000 in legal fees. Even with acquittal, in cases like these, the defendant's reputation and livelihood may be damaged.

The publicity stemming from being involved in a legal case of this sort also increases the threat of extralegal violence. This, as we will show, is already a far graver danger in the West than the legal process itself. Among the most prominent Western victims of these attacks and threats are novelist Salman Rushdie, cultural editor Flemming Rose, critical documentarist Theo van Gogh, feminist Ayaan Hirsi Ali, philosopher Robert Redeker, and Anglican bishop Michael Nazir-Ali. Among other victims of laws and threats in the West are Muslims who criticize reactionary interpretations of Islam. Muslim parliamentarians like Naser Khader in Denmark or German Green party politician Ekin Deligoz and prominent Muslim women's advocates such Mimount Bousakla receive serious threats, as do a myriad of writers and scholars, artists, and journalists.

The pages that follow reveal that self-censorship for fear of offending Muslims is now becoming common in Western discourse, extending far beyond rude or uncivil language. In 2008, BBC head Mark Thompson warned of "a growing nervousness about discussion about Islam and its relationship to the traditions and values of British and Western society as a whole." In 2008, publisher Random House canceled the publication of Sherry Jones's novel *The Jewel of Medina* because it feared violence by some Muslims. In this case the fears were well founded; in September 2008, the home and office of the British publisher that bought the rights to the novel were firebombed. In 2009, Yale University Press refused to include a photograph of the *Jyllands-Posten* "Danish cartoons" even though it was publishing a book, authored by Jytte Klausen, that was advertised by YUP itself as the "definitive" study of those cartoons.

Fourth, if international blasphemy restrictions are accepted, authoritarian regimes will have an additional weapon with which to protect themselves from any criticism from abroad, just as they have often used religious restrictions to ward off criticism domestically. These regimes are seeking a new world consensus on human rights, consistent with the 1990 Cairo Declaration, one that subordinates individual freedoms and rights to particular interpretations of Islamic law. Their simple syllogism is that if they claim to represent Islam, and one cannot criticize Islam, then one cannot criticize them. Already in the 1990s, when UN Special Rapporteurs criticized OIC countries for violations of international human rights standards—standards that those countries previously had accepted—the rapporteurs were threatened for purportedly insulting Islam.

Fifth, if we accept restrictions on "insulting Islam," we will betray those dissidents who fight for freedom under repressive regimes in the Muslim world, especially those Muslims for whom Islam holds the promise of political and religious freedom. We betray them by accepting the arguments and rationale, and thus becoming the de facto allies, of their persecutors. This is so whether their persecutors are Islamist governments such as those of Saudi Arabia or Iran, authoritarian regimes seeking Islamic legitimacy such as that of Egypt, or vigilantes and terrorists who seek to maim and destroy those with a different interpretation of Islam. In accepting these restrictions, we implicitly accept the rationale offered by their persecutors, which holds that the law should stop statements and activities deemed by some to be religiously insulting. In effect, this signals that repressive governments are right to silence dissenters, artists, minority faiths, and others who do not conform religiously. In acquiescing to proposals for legislation banning "insulting Islam", the West would implicitly embrace a view of Islam and its teachings against which reformers argue and have fought. Muslim reformers are often isolated enough in their own countries; for the West to further ideologically isolate them would amount to a grave betrayal.

Sixth, by surrendering to Islamic antiblasphemy restrictions, we will undercut our own security. The Muslim world is torn by strife over the meaning and future of Islam. Some of the most strident voices in that struggle press for reactionary forms of Islam, and out of their Islamist ideologies emanate terrorism and other forms of religious violence and repression. If we acquiesce in the legitimacy of repressing religious debate, then we boost those who are or would be our enemies, and we undercut those who are our natural allies. In abiding by such strictures ourselves, we politically disarm ourselves by making discussion, debate, and analysis of Islam and its various interpretations out of bounds.

PART II

MUSLIM-MAJORITY COUNTRIES

Introduction to Muslim-Majority Countries

The relation between Islam and the state varies widely across the world's forty-plus Muslim-majority countries. The constitutions of eleven of these countries describe their political orders as secular. An additional eleven have no mention of any Islamic or secular nature. Another twenty-two do give Islam some stated constitutional role. Ten of these declare themselves to be constitutionally Islamic states and also say that Islam is the official religion of the state. The other twelve declare Islam the official state religion but do not declare the country itself an Islamic state. Of these latter twenty-two, fifteen declare that Islamic law, principles, or jurisprudence is a source of, or limitation on, legislation.[1] There is also variation within these categories. Countries in which Islam has a legal status may also provide for freedom of religion, belief, expression, association, and assembly and also incorporate or reference international human rights standards in their legal systems. Furthermore, in many cases, Islam's role is limited to certain areas of law, often family and personal status law.

However, despite this continuing variety, the last three decades have seen an increasing radicalization across the Muslim world: in more long-standing regimes, as in Saudi Arabia; in regimes that came to power in a coup or revolution, as in Sudan, Somalia, and Iran; by creeping constitutional or legislative change, as in Pakistan; by provincial-level governments, as in Nigeria and Malaysia; and through local intimidation by Islamists, as in Bangladesh, Indonesia, or Yemen.

This radicalization has produced increasing pressure and attacks in Muslim-majority countries on those accused of having in some way insulted Islam, especially affecting four groups. One group is those, such as the Baha'is or Ahmadis, who believe, or are thought to believe, that there has been a prophet after Muhammad, and who are thus castigated as heretics. Another is those who leave Islam or convert to another religion, who may be attacked as apostates. The third is Muslim minorities, such as Shias in Saudi Arabia or Sufis in Iran, who are deemed deviant, if not outright heretical. The fourth is Muslim dissidents, liberals, or reformers, especially if they challenge the entrenched power of regimes that claim to be representative of Islam.[2]

In the following chapters we will survey the myriad threats to and attacks on these groups in Muslim-majority countries, both by the state and (often more commonly) by "society"—from calculated assaults by vigilantes and terrorists to sudden violence from enraged mobs. The dangers come not only in countries that are generally regarded as religiously repressive states, such as Iran, Saudi Arabia, Pakistan and Afghanistan, but also in many other countries often regarded as more moderate, such as Algeria, Jordan, or Morocco. To be sure, there remain Muslim-majority countries, such as Mali, in which freedoms of religion and speech are protected, but other traditionally moderate countries, even Indonesia, face increasing problems.

Another feature of current restrictions is that terms such as "apostasy," "blasphemy," and "insulting Islam" are invoked without any precision; militias, mobs, and even courts frequently alternate between the terms and come up with new terms of their own, often ones lacking any historical foundation. Whatever particular charge is used, the effect is the same: religious minorities are often threatened and persecuted, critics of the regime may be imprisoned or killed, and debate about the nature of Islam is stifled.

Saudi Arabia

Ali Al-Misaad, a twenty-five-year old Ismaili Shia native of Najran city, was stopped by members of the religious police on June 12, 2002, for listening to music while driving his car. The police told him to listen to the Qur'an instead; they claimed that he then insulted the Qur'an by calling it "boring." On August 17, he was convicted by Judge Hamed Abdullah Al-Dosary of insulting Islam and sentenced to eight years in prison and 2,000 lashes. He was only released after serving eight months, when well-connected relatives staged an intervention on his behalf.[1]

Hail Al-Masri, a Yemeni national, worked as a fruit seller in Jeddah. According to some of his roommates, his real crime was not getting up in time for dawn prayers. When a more hard-line roommate insisted that he do so, Al-Masri became irritated. He told his roommate to leave him alone. But he didn't stop there. He also criticized the mutawa'in—the religious police—and his roommate's newfound religious fervor. In so doing, he used a slang expression, roughly translated as "damn your religion," a relatively common phrase. But the roommate filed a complaint with the court, and Al-Masri, who surely never thought he could be executed for the heated words he had spoken to his roommate, readily confirmed that he had angrily told him to leave him alone. Originally, he was sentenced to 600 lashes and two years in prison. Then, on January 7, 2003, a higher court in Jeddah, under Judge Ali al Zahrani, sentenced him to be beheaded on the charge of insulting religion. Astonished at the verdict, Al-Masri tried to flee the courtroom by jumping from the third-floor window, sustaining serious neck injuries.[2]

In August 2008, Gulf News *reported that a Saudi man who worked for The Commission for Promotion of Virtue and Prevention of Vice had killed his daughter because she became a Christian. Using the nickname "Rania," she had stated in an online posting several days earlier that she was being pressured by her family; they had discovered a cross on her computer screen and Christian articles that she had written. The paper reports that she was burned to death and that her tongue had been cut out.[3]*

Country Overview

Since its unification in 1932, the Kingdom of Saudi Arabia has been controlled by the Al Saud family, which rules in partnership with the Wahhabi clergy according to an extreme interpretation of Sunni Islam, commonly known as Wahhabism. About 85 to 90 percent of the population is Sunni, about 10 to 15 percent Shia, of whom about one-fifth is Ismaili. Foreign workers, including Muslims, Christians, Hindus, and Buddhists, comprise six to ten million, about one-quarter of the in-country population.[4] The government is an absolute monarchy, and the *Majilis al-Shura* (Consultative Council), with members appointed by the monarch, has no significant power. Its legal system is based on sharia, with its jurisprudence ostensibly drawn from the strict Hanbali School of sharia. According to the 1992 Basic Law, the Qur'an and Sunna are the constitution.[5]

Islam is the official religion, and all nationals must be Muslim. The court system and much of the policing is controlled by the Wahhabi religious establishment. Saudis are denied freedom to choose or change their religion; noncitizens, including Muslims, are strictly controlled. Public practice of all non-Muslim religions is forbidden. Christians and Jews are officially viewed, as taught in government textbooks, as "enemies of the believers," unless they have a recognized "compact with the Muslims" by which their lives and property are respected, though they must abide by sharia.[6] Hindus, Buddhists, Sikhs, and also Shias and Sufis, as well as adherents of other religions, may be regarded as polytheists. The minority Shia community, living mainly in the eastern provinces, also suffers severe discrimination. Wahhabis frequently condemn as heretics, polytheists, and apostates those sects, groups, and movements within Islam that are not Salafi or other extreme Sunnis. The highest Saudi religious official, who was appointed by the government to his post, the late Grand Mufti Bin Baz, condemned Sufis in his government-published writings as "doomed to destruction." Saudi state religious tracts exported worldwide teach that freedom of thought must be rejected since "[f]reedom of thinking requires permitting the denial of faith."[7] All media are subject to religious censorship, though some officially allowed speech has had more latitude in recent years.

The U.S. State Department reported in 2009 that, often, "mosque speakers prayed for the death of Christians and Jews, including at the [state-sponsored] Grand Mosque in Mecca and the Prophet's Mosque in Medina." Such preachers, who receive government salaries, also often "end Friday sermons with a prayer for the well-being of Muslims and for the humiliation of polytheism and polytheists."[8]

Saudi officialdom promotes extreme religious intolerance. On March 17, 2008, a bill came before the Saudi Consultative Council calling for "an international pact for respecting religions . . . and [to] prohibit insulting them in any way" in order to combat a purported "onslaught on Islam" such as "the blasphemous cartoons and films being published in Denmark, the Netherlands, America, and the like." However, the council soundly rejected the measure, with at least one member arguing that approving the measure would "make it obligatory to recognize some religions and will facilitate establishing places of worship for them in Muslim countries."[9]

The same intolerance pervades the educational system. A study presented at the December 2003 Second Forum for National Dialogue found that boys' school texts on Islam "legitimiz[e] the violent repression of the 'other' and even his physical elimination because of his views on disputed issues. . . . These things may create a misapprehension that violent treatment of the 'other' is a task in which the pupil is obliged to take an interest." Among the purported signs of unbelief were referring to God by nonstandard names, such as "the Absolute Power," or saying that "religion is not in the hair," with reference to a bearded man. Statements that could credit a force other than Allah with producing results, such as "Development programs will eliminate poverty and ignorance," could indicate polytheism. Other Muslims, such as "Jahamiyya, Mu'tazila, Ashariyya, and Sufis, were deceived, and have deviated from the right path." Celebrations of the prophet's birthday are "imitating Christians" and redolent of "polytheism and deeds that are forbidden."[10] On June 11, 2008, the U.S. Commission on International Religious Freedom reported that a twelfth-grade *Tafsir* (Qur'anic interpretation) textbook (still online in 2011) teaches that it is permissible "to kill an apostate (a convert from Islam)" (*Tafsir*, Arabic/Sharia, 123). A twelfth-grade *Tawhid* (monotheism) text states, "Major polytheism makes blood and wealth permissible," meaning that polytheists can be killed or robbed with impunity (*Tawhid*, Arabic/Sharia, 15). In Saudi interpretation, "major polytheists" can include Shias and Sufis, as well as Christians, Jews, Hindus, and Buddhists.[11]

Despite Saudi assurances since the 2003 National Dialogue that it has changed its texts, studies by the Hudson Institute's Center for Religious Freedom in 2008 and 2011 found that the Ministry of Education's religious curriculum still taught hatred of Jews, Christians, Westerners, infidels, polytheists, and apostates, and it approved murder with impunity of members of many of these groups. For example, they assert that "building mosques on graves is an expression of poly-theism" and that "major polytheism makes blood and wealth permissible."[12] These texts are posted on the ministry's website, are required for all Saudi public schools, and are sent free to numerous mosques, Muslim schools, and libraries throughout the world.

The law combines royal decrees and sharia, in which, apart from commercial matters, there is no unified code. Rules are often vague and subject to judicial idi-osyncrasies; due process is severely deficient and, at times, wholly lacking, with religious police often summarily punishing their targets. Judicial proceedings, when they occur, are often closed to the public.[13] Apostasy is, in principle, subject to sharia *hudud* rules, which means that the punishment—death—is believed to be fixed by divine order and not subject to judicial discretion, though the king has commuted sentences and pardoned those convicted of such offenses. People may be accused of witchcraft, without any clear definition of the offense, and can be executed on the grounds of *ta'zir*, which focuses on the severity of the act and the turpitude of the offender.[14] The threshold for conviction in witchcraft cases is low and might even be a mere accusation. In May 2009, the religious police announced "a new national strategy for combating sorcery in the Kingdom," but its details are not public.[15]

Frequently, apostasy charges also lack evidence. In a 1970 memorandum on human rights sent to international organizations, the government asserted that the prohibition on Muslims changing their religion was because of "a Jewish conspiracy which was plotted in the early days of Islam" in which "[t]he Jews...craftily thought to let some of them join Islam then renounce it in order to make the Arabs suspect their religion and be misled." Hence, a law was created preventing a Muslim from changing his religion "so that nobody could join Islam excepting after making a rational and scientific study of its doctrines ending with his permanent acceptance of the Muslim creed." Its aim was to prevent "evil men...from joining Islam," hence "extirpating malicious elements who have been persisting in spreading evil on Earth."[16]

Christians

The Saudi government forbids the practice of any non-Muslim religion, as well as many forms of Islam, within the kingdom. Bringing in non-Muslim religious literature and symbols is generally banned, as well as Qur'ans and other Islamic items of non-Saudi origin, though the government now says they may be brought in for personal use only and kept out of the public eye. Until 2007, signs posted in Saudi airports warned openly of this practice.[17] In recent years, the government has said it will not stop nonapproved religious practices if they are private and discreet, and there appears to have been a reduction in such interference. However, the *mutawa'in* still attack non-Muslims, who are also subject to apostasy and blasphemy accusations and, like "Rania," described above, private attack.

In 2001, Saudi authorities arrested fourteen expatriate Christians in Jeddah. One of them, an Ethiopian named Worku Aweke, had a passport with the name Ismail Abubakr, a Muslim-sounding name he had officially taken, probably to help find work in the kingdom. Suspected of being an apostate, he was beaten savagely and when, in January 2002, his fellow prisoners were taken to the Breman deportation center as a prelude to deportation, he was transferred to the Matta Jail in Mecca. Since his case attracted international attention, he was not charged with apostasy but was deported in March 2002, along with Filipino Christian Dennis Moreno.[18]

On November 29, 2004, the religious police took Saudi citizen Emad Alaabadi to prison on charges of having converted to Christianity two years earlier. There are reports that other Saudi Christians were arrested at the same time, but their names remain unknown.[19] Reportedly, Alaabadi has since been released and lives in Saudi Arabia under heavy restrictions.[20] In May 2007, U.S. diplomats received information about another Saudi convert who was reportedly tortured and scheduled for trial. His fate, like his name, remains unknown.[21]

On January 13, 2009, Hamoud Bin Saleh was arrested for comments posted on his blog criticizing the Saudi judiciary and discussing his conversion to Christianity. Authorities blocked the blog, which Google subsequently locked for an alleged terms-of-service violation. The company reportedly reactivated his site on February 5 due to popular outcry. On March 28, 2009, Bin Saleh was released but forbidden to leave Saudi Arabia or appear in the media. However, he defiantly continued to blog. He attributed his freedom to do so to the pressure that the Arab Network for Human Rights Information had put on the Saudi authorities. His blog was shuttered once more, but, so far, Saudi authorities appear to have been relatively lenient, especially given Saleh's outspoken critiques and his clear "apostate" status.[22]

Ahmadis

Ahmadis also suffer in Saudi Arabia. On December 29, 2006, forty-nine Ahmadi expatriates were arrested in Jeddah, apparently on orders from Interior Minister Prince Nayef. They had just completed noon prayers at a rented guesthouse where they held monthly meetings. Their technical offense, mentioned by the police but never pressed as a formal charge, was meeting to pray without a permit. The next day, they were transferred to Buraiman Prison.[23] At least six other Ahmadis were arrested in early January 2007, and all were eventually deported. When some of the Ahmadis' employers attempted to obtain their release, they were turned away with the words, "There is an order from Nayef, so don't come to try to release them." One detainee said that interrogators pressured him to reveal the names of other Ahmadis in the country. Two additional expatriate Ahmadis were arrested in February 2007.[24]

Shias

Probably the brunt of Saudi Arabian religious repression falls on its Shia minority, who are excluded completely from the state's extensive religious media and broadcasting programming.[25] State online textbooks condemn Shias as "polytheists."[26] Common Shia practices, such as celebrating Muhammad's birthday or visiting the tombs of renowned Muslims, are in principle forbidden, though may be permitted in parts of the Eastern Province, a largely Shia area. In mixed Shia and Sunni areas, authorities limit public observances of Ashura, in which Shias mark the martyrdom of the Prophet's grandson, Ali. Shia books and tapes may be banned.

While Shia judges may use their own sharia school to rule on inheritance, family law, or endowments, there have been only seven such judges, all based in the Eastern Province, with three serving on an appeals court. In other cases, Shias must appear in Sunni sharia courts. Government departments may also refuse to implement rulings issued by Shia judges. Courts may also ignore Shia testimony or give it less weight than that of Sunnis.[27]

A 2001 fatwa by Sheikh Abd al-Rahman al-Barrak, who then held a royally approved position on a religious council, declared that Shias are *raafidah*, "rejecters of religion," who cannot be "a group of Muslims."[28] In December 2006, apparently for emphasis, he issued another fatwa proclaiming them heretics and apostates, "bearing all the characteristics of infidels." On January 21, 2007, Sheikh Abdullah bin Abdulrahman bin Jibrin declared that Shias are heretics and apostates who cooperate with Christians to kill Sunnis—especially in Iraq—and that they should be expelled from Sunni Muslim countries.[29] On June 1, 2008, twenty-two Saudi sheikhs, including al-Barrak and bin Jibrin, publicly denounced Hezbollah and also Shias in general as "a sect that the Jews inserted in the body of the Muslim Ummah a long, long time ago."[30] Shia Sheikh Tawfiq Al-Amer was imprisoned for a week because he condemned the statement and said that the authors spoke only for themselves and not for all Sunnis.[31]

Sadeq Abdul Karim Malallah, an advocate for the rights of Saudi Shias, was first imprisoned at the age of seventeen in 1988 for throwing stones at a police car.[32] During his imprisonment, he was reportedly physically abused and was transferred to a *Mabahith* prison after he resisted a judge's pressure to abandon his Shia faith in return for a lighter sentence. Malallah was then accused of making blasphemous statements while in jail, including the statement that Muhammad, not God, had authored the Qur'an. Although he recanted the alleged offending statements before the court, the judges stated that the statements' severity made it impossible to waive the penalty for blasphemy despite his repentance. His appeals to a higher court and to King Fahd were both denied, and he was publicly executed by beheading on September 3, 1992.[33] In 2002, as many as seventeen Saudi Shias were facing execution or life imprisonment for heresy.[34]

In February 2007, a Sunni human rights activist was placed under arrest for meeting with leading Shia cleric Sheikh Hasan al-Saffar.[35] Between fall 2008 and spring 2009 alone, Saudi security forces reportedly intervened to ban a Shia funeral procession, seized banners intended to mark the start of Ashura, broke up a Shia religious assembly and arrested its organizer, arrested four brothers who had arranged Shia activities, and arrested two Shia religious leaders. One of them—Sheikh Ali Hussein Al-Amar, arrested on May 17, 2009—was charged with financing Shia religious activities.[36]

In May 2008, Ali Sibat, a Shia Muslim from Lebanon who claimed to offer psychic predictions and advice on his popular show on Lebanese satellite television, was arrested by the *mutawa'in* while on pilgrimage to Mecca and Medina. After being held for over a year, he was sentenced to death on November 9, 2009, for practicing witchcraft. His lawyer states that he was deceived into believing that if he made a confession, he would be released. Instead, he was forced to appear on a Saudi religious TV program and repeat the confession, which was then used to help convict him.[37]

In February 2009, religious police filmed Shia women on pilgrimage at a cemetery in Medina believed to be the burial place of many of Muhammad's descendents. The women's male relatives, outraged by this invasion of privacy, insisted that the police turn over the footage, but they were arrested for their efforts on the women's behalf. This set off riots by thousands of Shia pilgrims, many of whom were arrested or injured. There are reports that government forces fired live ammunition, and one Shia scholar reportedly was stabbed at the entrance to the Prophet's Mosque by a man shouting, "Kill the rejectionist." However, the Interior Ministry denied that anyone had been injured. In early March, King Abdullah declared that those arrested would be released, but, in March, there was a second wave of arrests. Since this incident, Saudi authorities have increased efforts that interfere with Shias praying collectively.[38]

Ismailis

While Shia in general suffer discrimination, one particular group, Ismailis, suffers even worse treatment. The Organization of the Islamic Conference summit held in Mecca in December 2005 did not even acknowledge Ismailis as Muslims. Ismailis in the kingdom are forbidden to publish their own prayer books. In September 2006, at least sixty Ismailis were in prison over riots that occurred in 2000. In 2008, at least eighteen remained in jail.[39]

Hadi Al-Mutif is probably Saudi Arabia's longest-serving blasphemy prisoner. He enrolled in the Najran police training camp, where, in December 1993, during afternoon prayers, he allegedly made a joke about praying on "the penis of the prophet." Al-Mutif denies this.[40] Three people reported him, and he was arrested on January 20, 1994. Soon after, he was transferred to the custody of the secret police—the Mabahith—whom he states beat him and deprived him of sleep. In December 1994, he was tried in Najran General Court on charges of "insulting the Prophet." Al-Mutif says that the judge told him not to deny the charges unless he wanted to be returned to the Mabahith for additional "interrogation." After six short hearings, in which he was denied legal representation, he was sentenced to death for apostasy. His family asked the head of the Saudi Commission on Human Rights, Turki Al-Sudairy, to intervene, and he sent letters to the king asking that Al-Mutif be given a clean cell and his health be monitored.[41]

Al-Mutif went on a hunger strike on September 5, 2006, that ended on September 13, after he had collapsed on September 11. Prison officials responded by placing him in solitary confinement, without access to medical care, where he reportedly attempted suicide twice during the first month. After two messages that Al-Mutif taped about his case were played on Al-Hurra television, the government moved him from Najran General Prison to solitary confinement in the Mabahith's maximum-security prison in Najran, where he has remained. Many observers believe that his Ismaili faith was one reason that he was sentenced to death. His superiors had reportedly criticized his Ismaili faith prior to turning him over to the police, and the judges in the case displayed anti-Ismaili bias. The Chief Judge of the appeals court declared, "You are a corrupt minority. You don't belong to Islam in any form. You have no creed or religion." International organizations have pleaded for his release which is perhaps why the death sentence has not yet been carried out. However, he was denied the customary furlough to attend his father's funeral. In 2015 USCIRF was told by Saudi officials that his only recourse is a king's Pardon, (In 2006, an Ismaili high-school student was sentenced to fourteen years in prison and to 4,000 lashes for uttering the same phrase that Mutif had allegedly used.)[42]

On April 23, 2000, tensions erupted into violence between security forces and Ismailis in Najran, considered the spiritual seat of the Sulaimani Ismailis. Based on differences between the Sunni and Ismaili systems of calculating its exact date, police had closed all Ismaili mosques during Eid al Fitr, a provocative act somewhat comparable to closing all churches on Christmas. Security forces then raided an Ismaili mosque, arrested an imam, and charged the imam with "sorcery."[43] Over 100 Ismailis (some reports say 400 to 500), including prominent religious leader Hajj Mohamed Al-Saadi, were arrested, and two Ismaili teachers—Sheikh Ali bin Dhib al-Mahan and Mahdi bin Dhib al-Mahan—were charged with sorcery.[44] Many of those detained reported torture, including beatings, electric shock, stress positions, sleep deprivation, and forced confessions. Seventeen received death sentences, and sixty-five received life terms. Often, the trials were secret, and some were unaware that they had even been tried and sentenced.[45] In December 2002, Al-Saadi was released, the sentences of the seventeen men on death row were reduced to ten-year prison terms, and others' prison terms were shortened.[46]

On January 15, 2002, Ahmad Turki al Sa'ab, an Ismaili leader, was arrested after giving an interview to the *Wall Street Journal* in which he criticized Saudi policy toward Ismailis. On February 4, 2002, two others—Hamad 'Ali Daseeny al-Hutailah and Hamad Qulayan al-Zbeyd—believed to have been present during the interview, were also arrested. The government says they threatened national security through contact with foreign entities.[47] The only direct quotation from al Sa'ab in the final *Journal* article was, "We love our country, but we believe that the government is making a mistake against us." Al Sa'ab was not permitted counsel, was reportedly tortured, and, on April 23, 2002, was sentenced to seven years in prison and 1,200 lashes.[48] His sentence was later reduced to half a year in jail, probably in order to deflect international criticism in a high-profile case.[49] Al Sa'ab was rearrested on May 13, 2008, along with six other Ismailis, after he presented King Abdullah with a petition signed by seventy-seven Najran residents requesting the release of Al-Mutif and seventeen people in prison since the 2000 riots and listing grievances against the governor of Najran province.[50]

Sufis

Many Sufi rituals and literature are prohibited by Saudi authorities. The late Sufi leader Sheikh Mohammed Alawi al-Maliki was labeled an apostate by some Wahhabi clerics and barred from teaching in the Grand Mosque in Mecca, even though his father and grandfather had both taught there.[51] In 2003, sixteen men from the Al Jouf region were arrested for possessing Sufi literature, and Saudi authorities temporarily closed a weekly Sufi gathering in 2005.[52]

There have been some signs since 2003 that Sufis may be able to practice their faith more easily. In June 2004, Sheikh al-Maliki was invited as a Sufi representative to a royally authorized assembly on religious reform. In October, then–Crown Prince Abdullah attended the Sheikh's funeral, which drew more than 200,000 people.[53] The popular Wahhabi cleric Salman al-Odah also met with Sufi leader Abdallah Fadaaq in spring 2006.[54] However, the destruction of Sufi shrines and restrictions on Sufi literature continue. Followers of the Shafi'i and Maliki schools of sharia are prohibited from leading prayers at the Grand Mosque and are often castigated as Sufis by their critics.[55]

Sunnis

Like others, many Sunni victims have been accused of blasphemy, not necessarily because of theological arguments, but because of brief, often off-the-cuff comments, or because they are alleged to be sorcerers. In May 2005, the religious police arrested Fawza Falih for allegedly practicing witchcraft. She was sentenced to death in April 2006, reportedly because of several accusations, including one from a man who claimed her sorcery caused his impotence. In September 2006, an appeals court overturned this sentence and returned the case to the lower court, which nonetheless reinstated it, claiming that protecting "the creed, souls, and property of this country" demanded her execution. While imprisoned, Falih, who is illiterate, was reportedly coerced into fingerprinting a confession of whose content she was unaware.[56]

Egyptian pharmacist Mustafa Ibrahim, who lived in Arar, was accused of using black magic to separate a neighbor from his wife. As evidence, authorities cited books, candles, and herbs discovered in his residence. The Saudi Press Agency later reported that Ibrahim had "confessed to adultery with a woman and desecrating the Qur'an by placing it in the bathroom" at a local mosque.[57] As with many other cases, there are concerns that his confession was extracted under torture. In April 2007, Ibrahim was sentenced to death because, by "violating the boundaries set by God," he was no longer a Muslim but an apostate. He was executed in November 2007.[58]

In early 2007, Sabri Bogday, a Turkish barber in Jeddah, had a dispute with an Egyptian neighbor, who then reported him to the police. According to the Egyptian, during their altercation, Bogday had cursed God and Muhammad. The case was first heard on June 13, 2007, and, after eight hearing sessions, on March 31, 2008, the court declared that the alleged remarks proved him guilty of apostasy and then sentenced him to death. On May 1, 2008, the Mecca appeals court declined to overturn his sentence.[59] Turkey's prime minister, Recep Tayyip Erdogan, and the head of the Turkish parliament's Human Rights Commission, sought a reprieve for Bogday, and Turkish president Abdullah Gul wrote to King Abdullah on his behalf.[60] However, because the punishment was considered *hudud*, religiously required, Bogday was not eligible for a pardon. On further appeal, if his crime were judged to be disbelief, he could repent and avoid the death penalty, but if judged heresy, he could not.[61]

In what was turning out to be a very bad year for Turkish barbers in Saudi Arabia, in May 2008, authorities arrested Ersin Taze, who owned a barber shop in Riyadh, for "insulting the Prophet Muhammad." Several charges were dropped due to lack of evidence. According to one Turkish diplomat, "The [Turkish] embassy, after knowing that Taze is being implicated falsely, requested Prince Salman to intervene.... The prince ordered local officials to speed up the trial or release the accused if there is no evidence against him." Taze was released on May 30, 2008.[62]

Sunni Reformers

Other Sunnis are persecuted because they seek cultural, political, and religious reform. Like that of Iran, Saudi Arabia's government regards itself as the embodiment of Islam, so criticism of the ruling powers can be treated as criticism of Islam itself. One Jeddah businessman lamented of the clergy: "If you are against them, you are against Islam. If you criticize them, you criticize Islam."[63] This also raises the issue of *takfir*, accusing people, including Muslims, of apostasy, which can be interpreted by fanatics as a justification for murder. Though, since the beginning of Saudi Arabia's own terrorist scare in 2003, the Interior Ministry has launched a reeducation campaign that attempts to discredit *takfiri* thinking; officials continue to condemn Muslims with differing views as "unbelievers."[64]

Sheikh Saleh al-Lihedan, then head of the Supreme Judiciary Council, on September 9, 2008, issued a fatwa making it permissible to kill the owners of satellite TV stations that "broadcast immorality" (an authorization he later said applied only to proper authorities and following a trial). His fellow cleric, Abdallah Ben Jabreen, then on the Council of Senior Religious Scholars, defended him: "[T]hose (writers) and journalists and satellite TVs who attack scholars, and particularly well-known sheikhs, and publish bad bulletins about them—they must be punished…even by lengthy imprisonment…or by dismissing them from their jobs, and flogging and rebuking."[65] In February 2010, Sheikh Abd al-Rahman al-Barrak declared that whoever permitted the mixing of men and women in places of education and employment "is an infidel.…Either he retracts or he must be killed."[66] In the opening fatwa of a government booklet distributed in 2005 by the Saudi embassy in the United States, the late Grand Mufti Bin Baz responded to a question about a Muslim preacher in a European mosque who said "declaring Jews and Christians infidels is not allowed." Bin Baz accused the unnamed European cleric of apostasy: "He who casts doubts about their infidelity leaves no doubt about his own infidelity." This echoes long-standing and widely distributed official religious edicts that "innovative imams" are "heretics and their prayers are invalid."[67]

In 2001, during a class about ideas of love in poetry, teacher Mohammad Al-Suhaimi, who taught Arabic literature at middle- and high-school levels in Riyadh, said that love is a "noble thing."[68] When asked if love was not all about marriage, he replied that in a typical Saudi marriage, where the couple often do not know each other well before the wedding, "the emotions tend to be amiability and compassion." He also said that music, forbidden by Wahhabi hard-liners, is a gift from God, although adding that its permissibility is disputed. He explained, "I asked my students to love God instead of fearing Him.…I teach teenagers who need love and affection at a difficult period in their lives. I will not turn everything in their lives into fear and terror, especially their relationship with God."[69]

Based on remarks by some students, critics contended that Al-Suhaimi endorsed premarital sex and recommended that students reduce their fear of God. He was then suspended, and complaints were brought to Prince Abdul Rahman bin Abdul Aziz, Deputy Minister of Defense and Aviation, who had Al-Suhaimi arrested, without filing any formal charges.[70] After twenty-two days in prison, Al-Suhaimi staged a hunger strike and was released, but, in 2003, he was tried on allegations of encouraging adultery, sodomy, masturbation, music, and smoking tobacco. He was also accused of degrading the prophet Muhammad and his teachings. The five accusing students were fifteen years old at the time and were apparently under pressure from an Islamic Studies teacher to incriminate Al-Suhaimi. Al-Suhaimi responded that he had never made any such statements concerning sex but had rather been discussing love, and other students in the class were willing to corroborate his version, but they were not given the opportunity to testify.[71] While he was ultimately found innocent of apostasy, he was found guilty of "un-Islamic behavior" and, on March 9, 2004, sentenced to 700 lashes and three years' imprisonment. After he publicly recanted his supposedly blasphemous statements and declared his faith in Islam, his sentence was reduced to 300 lashes. He received a royal pardon in December 2005, was released from prison, was eventually reinstated as a teacher, and began to write a weekly column in *Al-Watan* newspaper.[72]

One of the more famous cases of blasphemy and related laws to repress political dissent concerns reformers Ali al-Domaini, Abdullah al-Hamid, and Matrouk al-Faleh. The three men were part of a group of thirteen first arrested in March

2004 in connection with a petition they had circulated advocating the creation of a constitutional monarchy.[73] Their ten colleagues were released in exchange for a promise to desist from pro-reform activities, but al-Domaini, al-Hamid, and al-Faleh rejected the deal. As a result they were accused of offenses including "incitement against the Wahhabi school of Islam" and, according to the Center for Democracy and Human Rights in Saudi Arabia, "introducing 'Western terminology'" in their calls for reform. On May 15, 2005, al-Faleh received six years in prison, al-Hamid, seven, and al-Domaini, nine for "stirring up sedition and disobeying the ruler."[74] In August 2005, King Abdullah pardoned all three. However, in February 2007, al-Faleh was rearrested, probably due to his criticism of the prison conditions for several other Saudi reformers—themselves jailed for organizing a women's protest over the lengthy detention without charge of alleged terror suspects.[75]

Mohammad Al-Harbi was a high-school chemistry teacher in Ein Al-Juwa, Al-Qassim. In mid-2004, he was accused by other teachers and some of his twelfth-grade students of "mocking religion," "praising unbelievers," preventing students from performing ablutions, and practicing witchcraft. They also claimed that Al-Harbi had ridiculed bearded men, an especially dubious charge in light of the fact that Al-Harbi himself had a beard. He responded that Islamic studies teachers were angered by his passionate lectures attacking terrorists and extremists after the 2003 Al-Hamra Compound explosions and were looking for a pretext to remove him. He had reportedly also drawn the ire of colleagues by talking positively about the Bible, speaking favorably of Jews, and supporting the use of critical thinking to reconcile apparent contradictions between the Qur'an and the Sunna. Following the complaints, the Ministry of Education transferred Al-Harbi to an administrative post and tried him for blasphemy. His attorney, Abdul Rahman Al-Lahem, said the trial violated many legal procedures, since no witnesses other than those responsible for the complaint testified. Nor was Al-Harbi allowed to question the complainants. Also, jurisdiction over a case involving "sacrilege" properly belonged to a special religious court. In November 2005, Al-Harbi received a sentence of 750 lashes, to be given at a rate of fifty each week over the course of fifteen weeks, and three years in jail. The case drew substantial domestic and international attention; in early December, then–Crown Prince Abdullah, and now king, overturned the sentence.[76]

Rabah Al-Quwayi was a journalist in the northern city of Hail and a frequent blogger on many liberal websites, most of which have since been shut down by the government. His posts concentrated on the dangers of Al-Qaeda attacks on the Arabian Peninsula and denounced illiberal Wahhabi practices, such as ritual book burnings.[77] He received many death threats, and, on November 15, 2005, the day after he questioned the authorities' case against Al-Harbi, his car was destroyed, and a note left stated, "This time it is your car but next time it is you. Return to your religion and forsake heresy..."[78] When Al-Quwayi filed a complaint with the police about the attack on his car, the Mabahith decided to investigate the soundness of his religious beliefs instead. He was arrested on April 3, 2006, and charged with "doubting the [Islamic] creed" and "harboring destructive thoughts." His accusers also claimed that he promoted homosexuality because he had written that it is a genetic predisposition. He was released in mid-April after being forced to sign a statement saying that he had denigrated Islam and not been a true Muslim but that he would defend Islamic values in his future work. The Committee to Protect Journalists reports that if he had refused to sign the statement, he would have been charged with the capital crime of *riddah*, apostasy.[79]

Hassan al-Maliki, a theologian, lost his job at the Ministry of Education and spent time under virtual house arrest after challenging Wahhabi teachings. He criticized early Muslims, the Salafis, for allowing the Umayyad caliphs to establish a dictatorship that demanded unquestioning obedience in the name of Islam, and he suggested that contemporary Wahhabis carried on this unfortunate tradition. In 2007, he lamented that the Saudi educational system taught that "whoever disagrees with Wahhabism is either an infidel or a deviant—and should repent or be killed." Sheikh Saleh Al-Fawzan, who authored the portions of the curriculum that al-Maliki criticized, responded to the criticism by threatening to behead him, proving al-Maliki's point as perhaps nothing else could have done. Al-Maliki was barred from leaving the country, and his books have been banned.[80]

On December 11, 2009, Saudi journalist Nadine Al-Bdair wrote in an Egyptian newspaper that Islamic leaders should issue an edict allowing women, as well as men, to marry up to four times. She claimed that the ancient reasoning, that the father of the child would be unknown if the woman got pregnant, is now obsolete because of technological advances. As a result, she faced charges of blasphemy, as did Magdy Al Galad, the editor in chief of the newspaper that published the article.[81] In March 2010, Al-Bdair was also indicted for insulting the prophet on her TV program on Al-Hurra channel.[82]

Closing

Under King Abdullah, there have been recent signs of slight moderation in the kingdom, but the monarch's reputation as a reformer so far seems overblown. Announced policies have not materialized into actual practices or changes on the ground. Because of sweeping attacks by state-approved and state-financed clerics on anyone who departs from Wahhabi orthodoxy as a blasphemer or apostate, Saudi Arabia remains perhaps the most repressively controlled Muslim country in the Sunni world. The kingdom is also aggressive in seeking to make its form of Islam the dominant one in the world, and it spends billions of dollars to do so. It has been the largest purveyor of Islamic educational materials worldwide, and, due to its role as custodian of the two holiest shrines in Islam, its religious authority is given special legitimacy. If it continues successfully to export its currently held Wahhabi views, the future will be bleak for minorities, thinkers, writers, and reformers throughout the Muslim world and beyond.

One indication of Wahhabi views of intellectual life beyond the kingdom's borders was given by then–doctoral candidate Sa'id ibn Nasser Al-Ghamdi. His dissertation at Imam Muhammad Ibn Saud Islamic University in 2000 accused more than 200 Arab intellectuals of heresy and apostasy and thus implicitly legitimized attempts to kill them. Those implicated included renowned Egyptian author and Nobel Prize winner Naguib Mahfouz, who had previously been stabbed by Islamic extremists, as well as Egyptian intellectual Nasr Abu-Zayd, who fled to the Netherlands when Islamists attempted to forcibly divorce him on account of his views, and who is a contributor to this book. Al-Ghamdi also attacked noted Syrian author Adonis, Egyptian intellectuals Taha Hussein and Hassan Hanafi, Egyptian author Jaber Asfour, Syrian poet Nizar Qabbani, Palestinian poet Mahmoud Darwish, Iraqi poet Badr Shakir Al-Sayyab, Egyptian poet Amal Dankal, Libyan poet Muhammad Al-Fayturi, Yemeni poet 'Abd Al-'Aziz Al-Maqalih, Saudi intellectual 'Abdallah Al-Ghadhami, Moroccan author Mohamed Choukri, Egyptian author Qassem Amin, Palestinian poet Mu'in Bsisu, Palestinian poet Tawfiq Ziad, Palestinian author Ghassan Kanafani, Palestinian author Emil Habibi, Egyptian intellectual Rifa'a Al-Tahtawi, Egyptian intellectual Sa'id 'Ashmawi, Egyptian author Yusuf Idris, and Sudanese author Al-Tayyib Salih. For this, Al-Ghamdi was awarded his doctorate summa cum laude.[83]

Al-Ghamdi's dissertation evolved into a book, *Deviation from the Faith as Reflected in [Arab] Thought and Literature on Modernity*, published in 2003. In a review, Egyptian poet and literary critic Abdallah Al-Samti writes: "Al-Ghamdi believes that modernism is a foreign plant intended to complete the West's colonialist domination over the Muslim countries . . . [He] does not leave a single detail of modern culture—large or small—uncriticized. His criticism . . . reaches various levels of revilement, racism and accusation of heresy." Al-Ghamdi's proposals for handling the accused writers' deviant behaviors are similar to, in Al-Samti's words, "the recommendations of the Inquisition." Furthermore, he did not stop with his cultural critique but addressed the political sphere, as well, berating "secular" Arab rulers and regimes, labeling them "apostate" and thus calling for their deaths.[84]

As one might expect, one of the dangers of throwing about charges of apostasy and blasphemy with promiscuous abandon is that the accusers themselves are subject to the same charges. Following NATO attacks in Afghanistan in 2001, a number of Saudi clerics, including the prominent legal scholar Hamoud bin Oqla al-Shuiabi, pronounced the entire Saudi royal family infidel on the grounds that "whoever backs the infidel against Muslims is considered an infidel."[85] After an April 2004 suicide attack on a Saudi government building, the radical Brigade of the Two Holy Mosques claimed responsibility for striking the "apostate" Saudi authorities.[86] In a video released in July 2010, Al-Qaeda then–second-in-command Ayman Al Zawahiri denounced the house of Saud as Arab Zionists for their support of a peace proposal concerning Israel.

3

Iran

Hojjatoleslam Hassan Yousefi Eshkevari was trained as a cleric in the religious center of Qom. He has been published widely in scientific and religious periodicals, served as Director of the Ali Shariati Research Center, and was contributing editor of now-banned newspaper Iran-e Farda, *a contributor to* the Great Encyclopedia of Islam, *and editor of the* Encyclopedia of Shi'a.[1] *Eshkevari participated in the 2000 Heinrich Böll Institute conference in Berlin, and, before attending, in an interview with Iran Press Service he criticized compulsory veiling for women and said that mixing religion and politics "spoils, corrupts and empties both of their substance" and that no leader should have powers above those of the constitution. At the conference itself, he spoke on the topic of dictatorship and its history, and his speech was criticized publicly by conservative clerics in Iran, including the Supreme Leader Khamenei. Critics compared his statements on separation of state from religion and unveiling of women to Salman Rushdie's "anti-Islamic" statements.[2]*

Eshkevari went from Berlin to Paris for medical treatment and was arrested on his return to Iran in August 2000. In October of that year, he was tried behind closed doors by the Iranian Special Court of the Clergy on charges of apostasy, corruption on earth, waging war against God, conduct unbecoming a clergyman, insulting Islamic sanctities, and spreading lies, and, on October 17, he was sentenced to death. He appealed, and in May 2001, the appeals court overturned the death sentence but upheld a seven-year sentence—four years for "insulting Islamic sanctities," in particular, for his comments about veils, one year for attending the conference, and two years for speaking against the Islamic Republic and "spreading lies." He was released on February 6, 2005, having served two-thirds of his sentence: he was prohibited from wearing cleric's robes, as one condition of his release.[3]

Zabihollah Mahrami was called before the Islamic Revolutionary Court in Yazd on September 6, 1995, and questioned about his Baha'i faith as part of an unsuccessful attempt to persuade him to renounce his beliefs. On January 2, 1996, he was put on trial for apostasy, and the prosecutor argued that, based on a 1983 newspaper announcement and another 1985 document, Mahrami had renounced the Baha'i faith and declared himself a Muslim. The court minutes read: "Mr. Mahrami . . . followed the wayward Baha'i sect until the year 1981 . . . when he recanted Bahá'ism in a widely distributed newspaper and announced his acceptance of the true religion of Islam. . . ." The court asked him again what his religion was, and Mahrami affirmed that he was a Baha'i. He was then sentenced to death—a verdict based not on any statute but on quotations from the writings of Ayatollah Khomeini. On appeal, the

Supreme Court confirmed the death sentence. In December 1999, due to a presidential amnesty on the eve of the birth of Prophet Muhammad, Mahrami's sentence was commuted to life imprisonment. On December 19, 2005, he was reported dead in prison, purportedly from a heart attack; however, before his death he was believed to have been in good health.

On June 3, 2008, twenty-eight-year-old Tina Rad, a Christian, was arrested for committing "activities against the holy religion of Islam," while her husband, thirty-one-year-old Makan Arya, also a Christian, was charged with "activities against national security." Rad was accused of attempting to convert Muslims by reading the Bible together with them in her residence. Security officials seized personal belongings, including all of the couple's videos, CDs, DVDs, and books, in addition to their computer and television set. They were jailed for four days, leaving their four-year-old daughter, Odzhan, alone. Tina Rad was tortured so severely that she was unable to walk when she was released. Security officials also told the couple that in the future they would be charged with apostasy and that Odzhan would be taken away from them and put in an institution. One officer told Rad that authorities could frame her and her husband as drug smugglers, a charge that can lead to the death penalty. The family's shop windows have been smashed, and they have received repeated threats from the surrounding community and anonymous phone calls. In June 2009, the family fled from Iran.[4]

Country Overview

Iran's population is around seventy million. Comprising 89 percent Shia Muslims, 9 percent Sunni Muslims, 0.5 percent Baha'is, and 0.5 percent Christians, as well as small and diminishing numbers of Jews, Zoroastrians, and Mandaeans, the Iranian state is intertwined with Shia religion. That relationship was intensified when, in 1979, the Pahlavi monarchy was toppled and Ayatollah Ruhollah Khomeini led a revolution producing a regime controlled by Shia Islamic jurists.[5]

According to Khomeini's revolutionary doctrine, state institutions that embody the establishment of Shia Islam include: (1) the *Vali Faqih*, or Supreme Leader (initially Khomeini, who declared himself to be the representative of Imam Mehdi, the "hidden Twelfth Imam" of traditional Shia belief); (2) the *Majles-e Khobregan*, Council of Experts, comprising eighty-three clerics who choose the successor to the Vali Faqih if he dies in office; (3) the *Shura-ye Negahban*, Council of Guardians, made up of six clerical jurists chosen by the Supreme Leader and six other Muslim jurists, which ensures that legislation is compatible with Islamic precepts and must approve all presidential and parliamentary candidates; and (4) the *Shura-ye Tashkhis-e Maslahat-e Nezam*, Committee to Determine the Expediency of the Islamic Order, or the Expediency Council, comprising senior state leaders, which arbitrates legal and theological disputes in the legislative process.

Iran combines republican and theocratic elements, but the latter far outweigh the former. The Guardian Council "screens" candidates who seek to run for Parliament, the Presidency, or the Council of Experts. By disqualifying all the candidates it deems insufficiently Islamic, which are most of them, the Guardian Council undercuts democratic choice. In addition, the elected bodies have limited power, and their decisions can be vetoed by the unelected ones. Ali Afshari aptly calls this a "vicious cycle": the Supreme Leader appoints all six clerical voting members of the Guardian Council (the six nonclerical members are advisors who cannot vote); the Guardian Council assesses the qualifications of all Assembly of Experts' candidates; and, to close the loop, the Assembly of Experts approves the Supreme Leader and is the only body that can impeach him.[6] Khomeini announced that government rule stemmed from the "absolute dominion of the Prophet of God" and stood above "all ordinances that were derived or directly commanded by Allah."[7]

Iran's June 2009 elections seemed to bring the Islamic state's authority into question. A popular uprising filled the streets of Tehran and other Iranian cities with tens of thousands of dissenters—in a movement popularly called the "Green Revolution"—who protested the purported landslide reelection of President Ahmadinejad over Mir Hussein Mousavi, election results that were eventually confirmed by Supreme Leader Ali Khamenei. Since then, despite brutal crackdowns within the country, outspoken dissatisfaction with the regime's hard-line rulers has continued. There are signs of divisions within the regime, but, at the time of this writing, it is not clear what effect the upheaval will have on Ayatollah Khomeini's 1979 Islamic Revolution.

Blasphemy and Apostasy

Questioning the theological doctrines that undergird the regime may be understood as blasphemy and apostasy. Iranian legislation does distinguish the terms; however, in practice, the authorities often use them interchangeably, and sometimes in an apparently ad hoc fashion, to punish those who challenge the regime or to repress those, such as Baha'is, whose very existence is held to be a violation.

The Iranian penal code defines blasphemy as a serious crime, and Article 513 states, "Anyone who insults the Islamic sanctities or any of the *imams* or her Excellency *Sadigheh Tahereh* [a respectful adjective to describe Prophet Muhammad's daughter Fatima] should be executed if his insult equals to speaking disparagingly of Prophet Muhammad. Otherwise, he should be imprisoned from one to five years."[8]

In all of the Penal Code's 729 articles, none specifically define, regulate, or criminalize apostasy. The word itself is mentioned only in Article 95 on adultery and Article 180 on the consumption of alcohol, and then indirectly: "[I]f a person is to be punished according to *Haad* [for adultery or intoxication] the punishment will not be revoked even if he is insane or apostate."

However, there is mention of apostasy in other legal provisions, which function as de facto apostasy laws. Article 167 of the constitution, Article 214 of the Criminal Procedure Act, Article 8 of the Modified Act on Establishment of General and Revolutionary Courts, and Article 42 of the Regulations Governing Special Court for the Clergy are used to convict and punish apostasy. In addition, Article 26 of the Press Law states, "[W]hoever insults Islam and its sanctities through the press and his/her guilt amounts to apostasy, shall be sentenced as an apostate and should his/her offense fall short of apostasy he/she shall be subject to the Islamic penal code." Article 29 of the Councils Law states, "[T]hose who are convicted of apostasy by competent courts are deprived of being candidates in elections."[9]

In practice, the principal article used to punish apostasy is Article 167 of the constitution, which states that if there is no codified law, the judge "has to deliver his judgment on the basis of authoritative Islamic sources and authentic *fatwa*."[10] It is important to understand that the "judges" and "courts" in such cases have sweeping powers. Many Iranians charged with undermining national security, apostasy, blasphemy, or other "crimes" described in this chapter were tried by Islamic revolutionary courts.

These courts, created immediately after the 1979 revolution, are notorious for lack of due process, use of torture either as punishment or to obtain confessions, and other gross violations of human rights. There are no juries, and the judges, who are religious figures, also function as prosecutors and sometimes as investigators. Defendants have no legal representation, "trials" may last only a few minutes, and verdicts cannot be overturned or appealed. The judges are believed to know the "right path" (*serate mostaqim*) and have accepted every means—including beating, lashing, solitary confinement, amputation, rape, sexual abuse, burning, starvation, and strangulation—to force defendants to follow it. The enforcement mechanism of these "divine" laws is the Ministry of Intelligence and National Security, also known as SAWAMA, the Revolutionary Guards, the *Basiji* paramilitary groups, and the pseudo-official Partisans of the Party of God (*Ansar-e Hezbollah*). This apparatus works under the command of the Supreme Leader.[11]

In this system, even if there is no codified offense, a judge can punish apostasy if there is a relevant *fatwa*. One source of such fatwas is Ayatollah Khomeini himself, an "authoritative Islamic source" whose writings are frequently used by Iranian judges to justify executions. Khomeini's *Tahrir-al-Vasileh* is probably the main source used to address apostasy, and in it he says, "A national apostate will be caused to repent and in case of refusing to repent will be executed. And it is preferable to give a three-day reprieve and to execute him on the fourth day if he refused."[12] This use of noncodified law has two consequences. First, when engaged in dialogue with the international community, the government can always claim that there is no such crime as apostasy and that no one in Iran has been ever prosecuted for this crime.[13] Second, judges have very large discretion in whether to describe something as apostasy and how it will be punished.

In only a few cases has the regime executed anyone on an explicit charge of apostasy. In most instances, the regime uses a selective interpretation of possible surrogates of apostasy and blasphemy to prosecute those who might challenge its "divine" authority. Dissidents may be charged with *inter alia,* "friendship with the enemies of God," "hostility towards friends of God," "corruption on earth," "fighting against God," "obstructing the way of God and the way towards happiness for all the disinherited people in the world," "spreading lies," "insulting the Prophet," "acting against the national security," "distributing propaganda against the government of Islamic Republic of Iran," "attracting individuals to the misguided sect of Baha'ism," "insulting Islam," "calling into question the Islamic foundations of the Republic," or even "creating anxiety in the minds of the public and those of Iranian officials." It often appears that, when there is nothing else handy with which to charge a person, the Islamic government brings charges of apostasy, which has the added convenience of carrying the death penalty.

There are also indications that the legal situation may worsen. In February 2008, a draft of a new proposed Islamic penal code was presented for discussion in the Iranian parliament (*Majlis*) that, for the first time, would make the death penalty for apostasy and heresy a legal stipulation in the criminal code.[14] Because the proposed law uses the word *Hadd,* it would make the death penalty for apostasy mandatory and bar any reduction or annulment of this sentence. This law would be a special danger to liberal thinkers, to those who leave Islam, and to Baha'is. Any adherent of a non-Muslim religion with one parent who was Muslim when he or she was conceived would also be declared apostate under the proposed law.

Following is a translation, made by the Baha'i community, of relevant sections of the proposed law:[15]

Section Five: Apostasy, Heresy, and Witchcraft

Article 225-1: Any Muslim who clearly announces that he/she has left Islam and declares blasphemy is an apostate.

Article 225-2: Serious and earnest intention is the condition for certainty in apostasy. Therefore, if the accused claims that his/her statement had been made with reluctance or ignorance, or in error, or while drunk, or through a slip of the tongue or without understanding the meaning of the words, or repeating words of others; or his/her real intentions had been something else, he/she is not considered an apostate....

Article 225–3: There are two kinds of apostates: innate (*Fetri*) and parental (*Melli*).[16]

Article 225–4: Innate Apostate is someone whose parent (at least one) was a Muslim at the time of conception, and who declares him/herself a Muslim after the age of maturity, and leaves Islam afterwards.

Article 225–5: Parental Apostate is one whose parents (both) had been non-Muslims at the time of conception, and who has become a Muslim after the age of maturity, and later leaves Islam and returns to blasphemy.

Article 225–6: If someone has at least one Muslim parent at the time of conception but after the age of maturity, without pretending to be a Muslim, chooses blasphemy is considered a Parental Apostate.

Article 225–7: Punishment[17] for an Innate Apostate is death.

Article 225–8: Punishment for a Parental Apostate is death, but after the final sentencing for three days he/she would be guided to the right path and encouraged to recant his/her belief and if he/she refused, the death penalty would be carried out.

Article 225–9: In the case of a Parental Apostate, whenever there appears to be a possibility of recanting, sufficient time would be provided.

Article 225–10: Punishment for women, whether Innate or Parental, is life imprisonment and during the sentence, under the guidance of the court, hardship will be exercised on her, and she will be guided to the right path and encouraged to recant, and if she recants she will be freed immediately.

Article 225–11: Whoever claims to be a Prophet is sentenced to death, and any Muslim who invents a heresy in the religion and creates a sect based on that which is contrary to the obligations and necessities of Islam, is considered an apostate. [This article seems to be particularly directed at Baha'is.]

Article 225–12: Any Muslim who deals with witchcraft and promotes it as a profession or sect in the community is sentenced to death.

Article 225–13: Assistance to the crimes in this chapter, in case there is no other punishment assigned to it by law, is punishable by up to 74 lashes in proportion with the crime and the criminal.

Article 112's extension of the punishment for "threatening Iranian national security" to those outside of Iran's border is especially dangerous in a government whose former "Supreme Leader" passed a death sentence on Salman Rushdie, has dispatched agents overseas to murder its opponents, and whose members have called for the death of Scandinavian editors and cartoonists, among others.[18] On September 9, 2008, the Iranian parliament passed the bill by 196 votes for, seven against, and two abstentions. It then went to committee for review.[19] In February 2010, Amnesty International reported that the provisions on apostasy had been removed from the bill in committee but that they could be reintroduced.[20]

Baha'is

The Baha'i religion began in Iran in the nineteenth century and originated from another religious movement, the Babis. The Babi movement began in 1844 with the Bab, Seyyed Ali Muhammad, a merchant from Shiraz, and gained many followers. However, it soon encountered hostility, especially from the Shia clergy. Officials ordered the imprisonment, torture, and death of thousands of adherents. After being imprisoned for a time, the Bab was executed in 1850. In 1863, Baha'u'llah, Hossein Ali Nouri, one of the followers of the Bab, announced that he was "Him Whom God Shall Make Manifest." He was immediately imprisoned and subsequently banished to Iraq, Turkey, and Israel, which were all part of the Ottoman Empire. He passed away in 1892 in exile in what is now Israel.[21]

Many Muslims consider Baha'is apostates because they are held to believe that Baha'u'llah is a true prophet and that the Bab is the return of the Twelfth Shia Imam, contradicting the Muslim belief that there is no valid religious revelation after Muhammad. Baha'is also believe that each of the world's major religions represents an evolution in God's message to mankind, hence that Islam is not the last and most complete religion. The Iranian Islamic regime also claims that, because the Baha'i World Center is located in Israel, Baha'is are Zionist spies and a threat to national security. In May 1996, the Head of the Judiciary called Baha'is "an organized espionage ring."[22]

Since the Islamic Revolution, the regime has killed more than 200 Baha'is merely because of their religious beliefs. Another fifteen have disappeared and are presumed dead, and more than 10,000 have been removed from posts in universities and government. Baha'i properties, including cemeteries, houses of worships, schools, libraries, private houses, real estate, businesses, and even furniture, have been confiscated by the regime. Members of Baha'i Local Spiritual Assemblies and the National Spiritual Assembly have been summoned to the notorious revolutionary courts and executed after summary closed-door "trials." Nine members of the National Spiritual Assembly were abducted and executed, and their families were refused access to their bodies.[23]

Article 297 of the penal code, which previously stipulated that a lesser amount of "blood money" (*diyeh*) be paid to families for the deaths of non-Muslims than for Muslims, was amended in 2004 to allow equal payment in each case. However, this change does not apply to Baha'is; their blood is held to be *Mobah*, which means that they may be killed with impunity.

Since Baha'is are banned from attending university, they opened their own underground university, the Baha'i Institute of Higher Education. Classes are conducted in private homes. In September 1998, the government began a nationwide attack against the university, and in at least fourteen different cities, thirty-six faculty members were arrested and had property destroyed or confiscated. In March 1999, four of the arrested professors, Sina Hakiman, Farzad Khajeh Sharifabadi, Habibullah Ferdosian Najafabadi, and Ziaullah Mirzapanah, were sentenced to between three and ten years under Article 498 of the penal code. The court verdict said they had established a "secret organization" engaged in "teaching against Islam, and teaching against the regime of the Islamic Republic."[24]

From 2006 on, the Iranian government has used new tactics to block Baha'is from university. In June 2006, 500 of the 900 Baha'i students who took the university entrance exam for the coming academic year received a passing score. Two hundred successfully enrolled, but most were expelled when university authorities became aware they were Baha'is. Officials also told almost 800 of the more than 1,000 Baha'is who completed the exam in June 2007 that their files were "incomplete," thus preventing their enrollment.[25] Many non-Baha'i students object to this discrimination. In December 2008, twenty-six students at Goldasht College in Kelardasht refused to take their first-term final examination to protest the dismissal of one of their classmates, Ameed Saadat.[26]

Baha'is are also forbidden to teach their faith to their children. Security forces have attacked houses where classes are held, arrested the adults, and confiscated books and anything related to Baha'i identity. Religious teachers have been imprisoned or executed by the regime. Mona Mahmudnizhad, a sixteen-year-old, and nine other women were hanged in 1983 for teaching Baha'i religious classes to Baha'i children. The government has forbidden Baha'is to have any official assembly or administrative institutions, and so they are forced to conduct their prayers and monthly ceremonies by rotating among private houses. Security forces routinely raid houses in which they believe there is a gathering, arrest family members, imprison them without charge for weeks or months, then release them with threats that if caught again they will face more serious consequences.[27]

Since Ahmadinejad's Election

The persecution of Baha'is has increased since Ahmadinejad's election in 2005. On October 29, 2005, a letter allegedly written on instructions from Ayatollah Khamenei by the Chairman of the Armed Forces Command, Major General Seyyed Hossein Firuzabadi, instructed officials including the Ministry of Information and the Commanders of the Army, Police and Revolutionary Guards, to provide the command with information for "a comprehensive and complete report of all the activities of [Baha'is and Babists] for the purpose of identifying all the individuals of these misguided sects."[28] The regime has also intensified its propaganda. There has been growing condemnation of Baha'is on radio and television programs, and even weekly anti-Baha'i broadcasts specifically aimed at evoking hatred of the community. This has led to increased social harassment, including threats and physical attacks.

On February 16 and 17, 2007, there were similar attacks by a masked intruder on the homes of two elderly Baha'is. Eighty-five-year-old Behnam Saltanat Akhzari was killed in the assault, while seventy-seven-year-old Baha'i Shah Beygom Dehghani died several weeks later.[29] In the eight months leading up to January 2007, sixty-three Baha'is were arrested. October and November 2008 saw an additional wave of arrests.[30] On January 26 and 27, 2009, eight Baha'is were arrested in Tehran and Mash-Had. Of the Tehran detainees, a judiciary spokesman said, "These people were not arrested for their faith. The six Baha'is are accused of insulting religious sanctities...."[31]

The government has also specifically targeted the Baha'i leadership and, in May 2008, arrested six members of the ad hoc national leadership group, Mrs. Fariba Kamalabadi, Mr. Jamaloddin Khanjani, Mr. Afif Naeimi, Mr. Saeid Rezaie, Mr. Behrouz Tavakkoli, and Mr. Vahid Tizfahm. Intelligence agents entered and searched their homes before taking the occupants away. The seventh member of the leadership group, Mrs. Mahvash Sabet, had been arrested in early March after receiving a summons from the Ministry of Intelligence in Mashhad on the pretext of questioning her about a burial in a Baha'i cemetery.[32] When Nobel Prize laureate Shirin Ebadi agreed to defend the seven leaders, she was immediately and vociferously attacked in the government-controlled news media as well as denied access to her clients' files.[33] Iranian-Japanese-American journalist Roxana Saberi, held in Evin prison for a month on espionage charges before her release under international pressure, reported that Mrs. Kamalabadi and Mrs. Sabet were being held there in a shared, four-by-five-meter cell, where they had to sleep on the floor, after both having previously been in solitary confinement. Ms. Saberi stated, "We have already seen infringements of their rights from the very beginning, including being held incommunicado, being interrogated while blindfolded, and having no access to a lawyer for months and months."[34] Charges against the seven include espionage for Israel, "insulting religious sanctities," "spreading corruption on earth," and "propaganda against the state."

After postponements in 2009, a trial took place on June 12–14, 2010, and the seven Baha'i leaders were then sentenced to twenty years imprisonment. On September 15, 2010, after an appeals court revoked three of the charges against them, the sentences were reduced to ten years.[35] However, in March 2011, the seven were informed by prison authorities without explanation that their term of incarceration had now reverted to the lower court's original ruling of twenty years.[36]

The U.S. Department of State, the U.S. Commission on International Religious Freedom, the European Union, and a concurrent House of Representatives and Senate resolution condemned the prisoners' plight.[37] In a rare open letter to Iran's Prosecutor General, the Baha'i International Community has said that "what is at stake is the very cause of freedom of conscience for all the peoples of your nation."[38]

However, the Prosecutor General, Ghorbanali Dari-Najafabadi, has said, "The corrupt cult of the Baha'i organization in all its rankings is illegal and is not recognized officially—their dependence on Israel, their anti-Islam posture and opposition to the regime of the Islamic Republic is corrosive and the danger it poses to national security is evident and documented."[39] In February 2009, more than 200 Iranian intellectuals signed an open letter of apology for their country's treatment of the Baha'i community.[40] The Baha'i community has historical reason to be concerned about their leaders' arrests and sentencing: Bani Dugal, principal UN representative of the Baha'i community, notes that "this latest sweep recalls the wholesale arrest or abduction of the members of two national Iranian Baha'i governing councils in the early 1980s—which led to the disappearance or execution of 17 individuals."[41]

Days before the trial was set to commence, Iranian authorities arrested another thirteen Baha'is, allegedly in connection with antiregime protests on the holy day of Ashura, and claimed to have discovered weapons and ammunition in their homes. They were taken to a detention center to sign a document prohibiting them from future demonstrating—though none had taken part in demonstrations. This group included relatives of some of the leaders previously arrested. As of January 2010, forty-eight Baha'is were imprisoned in Iran, with sixty arrested since March 2009.[42] A second group of thirteen Baha'is, again including a relative of the arrested leaders, was placed under arrest on February 10 and 11, while ten of those arrested in January remained in detention.[43] The regime is also trying to stigmatize protesters through association with Baha'is; *Kayhan*, a regime-linked paper, declared in a January 5, 2010, headline, "The So-Called God-Loving Mousavi's Men Turned Out to Be Baha'is and Terrorists." There have also been photographs of pro-government demonstrators carrying signs asserting that opposition leader Mir Hussein Moussavi is a Baha'i.[44] Examples of the many persecuted Baha'is include the following:

Musa Talibi

Four months after his arrest in Isfahan in June 1994, Musa Talibi was sentenced to a ten-year prison term on charges of "acting against the internal security of the Islamic Republic of Iran" and "attracting individuals to the misguided sect of Baha'ism." He appealed. After retrial in February 1995, his sentence was changed to eighteen months beginning on the date of his arrest. However, prosecutors objected to this reduction, saying the court had not considered the fact that Talibi, a practicing Baha'i, had claimed, while detained in 1981–1982, to have converted to Islam and was therefore an apostate. Based on this allegation, he was subjected to a further trial, and, on August 18, 1996, the Islamic Revolutionary Court, Branch Number 31, sentenced him to death. On January 28, 1997, on appeal, the Iranian Supreme Court of Iran upheld the death sentence. A February 1997 report by the Islamic Republic News Agency (IRNA), the Iranian news agency asserted that Talibi had been found guilty of espionage, but his death sentence was in fact based on an apostasy charge. As noted above, apostasy was not then listed as a crime under the Iranian Penal Code. On May 28, 2003, he was released, but without any documentation from the authorities as to his legal status.[45]

Ruhollah Rowhani

In 1985, Ruhollah Rowhani was sentenced to two years' imprisonment, with an additional year of internal exile in the village of Najafabad, because of his Baha'i faith. Rowhani, by this time a fifty-two-year-old father of four, was imprisoned in September 1997 and kept in solitary confinement for the rest of his shortened life. He was charged with apostasy for allegedly converting a Muslim to the Baha'i faith, a "crime" that even Khomeini had not called apostasy. In addition, the woman whom he was accused of converting asserted that she had not converted and that she had been raised a Baha'i. She was never arrested or charged. Rowhani was denied a lawyer and any legal proceeding at all. On July 20, 1998, his family was told that they could see him for one hour, the first time that he had breathed fresh air in three months. The next day, they were called to the prison to collect his body. Despite their appeal for more time to enable other relatives to attend the funeral, they were given only one hour to bury him. From the rope marks on his neck, it appeared that he had been hanged—the first Baha'i executed since March 1992.[46]

Baha'i Open Letter to President Khatami

In November 2004, for the first time, the Baha'i community wrote an open letter to then-President Khatami calling for an end to their persecution. It criticized government measures aimed at keeping Baha'is out of universities, including the false registration of Baha'i students as Muslims. It also highlighted passages in the Qur'an and Islamic law forbidding violence and supporting religious freedom and pointed out that Iran is bound to respect freedom of religion under the Universal Declaration on Human Rights and associated covenants, to which it is a signatory. It concluded with a call for "immediate action to ensure the emancipation of the Iranian Baha'i community."[47]

The Baha'i community in Yazd submitted a copy to government authorities. Shortly thereafter, the government attacked Baha'is throughout the country and launched a campaign of vilification in the media. On March 8, 2005, one Baha'i who had distributed the letter received a three-year prison sentence; another was tried in absentia and given a one-year sentence.[48] Authorities also arrested Baha'is who distributed copies in other cities. On May 16, 2005, nine Baha'is "were charged with 'creating anxiety in the minds of the public and those of the Iranian officials.'"[49]

Attacks on Baha'is have also spilled over onto those who defend them. In March 2006, Shirin Ebadi, an outspoken human rights lawyer, who was awarded the 2003 Nobel Peace Prize for her work promoting women's and children's rights in Iran, received death threats in a letter signed by an extremist group, the dysphemistic "Association Hostile to Apostate Baha'is." The association told her, "We are warning you for the last time, if you continue, you will pay for committing treason against your country and Islam."[50]

Christian Converts

Christianity has a long history in Iran: the Church of St. Mary in the northwest is considered by some historians to be the world's second oldest surviving church. Today, there are over 300,000 Christians, most ethnic Armenians: the Armenian Apostolic Church has 110,000 to 300,000 adherents, the Assyrian Church of the East about 11,000, the Chaldean Catholic Church about 7,000. Protestants include Presbyterians, Anglicans, the Assyrian Evangelical Church, and the Assemblies of God.[51] Despite this long history, and the Iranian constitution's recognition of Christian minority rights, the Islamic Republic often portrays Christianity as sympathetic to the West, and thus the regime interferes with and discourages Christian religious practices.

Since the beginning of 1979, the government has persecuted Protestants with close surveillance, forced exile, and even the prosecution, execution, or murder of converts and church leaders, especially if they are thought to be connected to conversion. Church leaders have been pressured to sign pledges to refrain from evangelizing Muslims and even to prevent Muslims from attending church. Reportedly, leaders of the Assyrian, Armenian Orthodox, and Presbyterian churches have signed the statement. The Assemblies of God and Brethren churches have refused.[52] Authorities keep copies of membership cards for evangelical congregations, which participants must carry, and conduct identity checks outside congregational centers. Church leaders must inform the Ministry of Culture and Islamic Guidance before admitting new church members, and worship services are permitted by the government only on Sundays.[53] In the mid-1990s, authorities, especially agents of SAWAMA, closed down the 160-year-old Iranian Bible Society and all Christian bookshops; prohibited the printing of Bibles or other Christian literature in the Farsi language; banned Christian conferences; shut down Protestant churches in Gorgan, Mashhad, Saari, and Ahvaz; and targeted converts.

In the 1990s, many evangelical, especially Pentecostal, church leaders were targeted in a campaign to destroy their leadership, and several of those more recently targeted by the regime have been their children. Pastor Hossein Soodmand was hanged on December 3, 1991, after two months of imprisonment and torture. He left behind his wife, Mahtab, who was blind and four children ages ten to fifteen. The authorities did not allow her a final visit with her husband, and she suffered a complete breakdown.[54] Presbyterian elder Robert Manaserian and Reverend Edmun Sergisian, of the Presbyterian Church in Tabriz, were tortured, as was Soodmand's successor in Mashad, Mohammad Sepehr.[55] On August 21, 2008, Soodmand's thirty-five -year-old son, Ramtin Soodmand, was arrested, as were four other Christians.[56] Reverend Mehdi Dibaj was arrested in 1979 and

1983 and, without trial or charges, spent ten years in prison, several of them in solitary confinement, and was tortured and faced mock executions.[57] His wife, who was threatened with death by stoning unless she denied her faith, divorced Dibaj and married a fundamentalist Muslim.[58] Dibaj was released on January 16, 1994, due to international pressure and internal lobbying. However, on July 5, 1994, his body was found in a forest west of Tehran, and his family's request for an independent autopsy was rejected. Twelve years after Dibaj's murder, on September 26, 2006, authorities arrested his daughter, Fereshteh Dibaj, and her husband, Reza Montazami, at their home in Mashhad, where they operated an independent church.[59]

Just three days after Dibaj's release, his friend Haik Hovsepian Mehr, secretary-general of the Assemblies of God and Chairman of the Council of Protestant Ministers of Iran, disappeared in Tehran. The police subsequently claimed that they discovered his body in the street and, being unable to identify it, buried him immediately in a Muslim cemetery.[60] In 2001, it was revealed that Saeed Emami, Vice Minister at the Ministry of Intelligence and National Security (SAWAMA), had ordered Mehr's murder along with other activists and authors.[61] Mehr's positions were taken over by Rev. Tateos Mikaelian, who disappeared on June 29, 1994. His body was found shot in the head execution-style.[62]

Recent Cases Involving Christian Converts

As with other religious minorities, persecution of converts has increased in recent years.[63] In May 2008, there were ten arrests in connection with converts, including Mohsen Namvar, who had been arrested in 2007 and tortured for baptizing Muslim converts. He was arrested again in May 2008 and so severely tortured that he continued to suffer fever, severe back pain, high blood pressure, uncontrollable shaking of his limbs, and short-term memory loss. He and his family have subsequently found refuge in Turkey. Eight other converts were also arrested that month in Shiraz and later released.[64]

On July 26, 2008, Ministry of Intelligence and National Security agents attacked a house-church in the town of Malak, in the suburbs of Isfahan, arresting eight men, six women, and two children. The detainees included a couple in their sixties, who were savagely beaten and had to be taken to intensive care in Shariati Hospital in Isfahan. They died shortly thereafter. On August 9, 2008, a Christian Kurd, Shahin Zanboori, was arrested in the southwestern city of Arak. To obtain information on other converts, Zanboori says police hung him from the ceiling and beat his feet. His arm and leg were broken during interrogations.[65] One young woman convert, who used the pseudonym Caty, was beaten so severely by her family that she is at risk of permanent disability from spinal injury.[66]

In recent years, arrests of Christian converts seem to have accelerated. In the wake of ten Christians' arrests in Tehran in January 2009, one source in that city said that "there are more arrests, of Christians as well as Baha'i, in the last several months among them than in maybe the whole 30 years before."[67] According to one Tehran pastor, arrests follow a predictable pattern of leaders being thrown in prison, beaten in order to obtain information on other converts, and then released after a few weeks.[68] The summer of 2009 saw a wave of arrests of Christians. Ten Christian converts were arrested in Shiraz in June 2009, eight were arrested in Rasht on July 29 and 30, and twenty-four were arrested in Amameh on July 31. Seven of the latter group were jailed in Evin prison until September 2, when they posted deeds to their houses as bail and were released.[69]

On March 5, two Christian converts, Maryam Rostampour, 27, and Marzieh Amirizadeh Esmaeilabad, 30, were jailed in Evin prison on charges of "acting against state security" and "taking part in illegal gatherings." On August 9, they appeared in court, where the judge asked them to return to Islam and, when they refused, ordered that they be returned to their prison cells "to think about it." Authorities failed to provide needed medical care for Esmaeilabad, who suffers from spinal pain, an infected tooth, and severe headaches. The two women were acquitted of "anti-state activities" on October 7, but charges of apostasy and propagating Christianity, to be handled by a different court, remained pending. They were released without bail, an unusual development in such a case, on November 18, 2009 and, in May 2010, were acquitted of all charges. However, they were told that if they continued with Christian activities, they would be punished, and, on May 22, they fled the country.[70]

The crackdown continued into 2010. Seven Christians were arrested in Shiraz on January 11, 2010, and, with the exception of one not born Muslim, told they had committed apostasy.[71] On February 2, 2010, Pastor Wilson Eisavi of the Assyrian Evangelical Church in Kermanshah, was arrested, tortured, and charged with baptizing Muslims. He was released temporarily, but his church has been compelled to close.[72] In mid 2011, evangelical pastor Yousef Nadarkhani was sentenced to death for apostasy.

The Jewish Community

Jewish history in Iran dates back to the Babylonian Exile, but after the establishment of Israel in 1948, many Iranian Jews immigrated to Israel. As of 1979, about 80,000 remained, but of those, around 20,000 emigrated within months of the Islamic Revolution. By the late 1980s, the population was estimated to be about 20,000 to 30,000. Although the Iranian constitution in principle recognizes Jews as a legitimate religious minority and grants them the right to practice their faith freely, since the revolution, they have been one of Iran's most persecuted minorities.

Since the Islamic Revolution, about thirteen Jews have been executed, most accused of spying for Israel or the United States. Another fourteen have disappeared, allegedly while in the custody of the Revolutionary Guards, and at least four have been murdered, probably by groups such as *Ansar*. The government has never seriously pursued the perpetrators of these murders. Hundreds of other Jews have been arrested on vague charges and live under constant surveillance. The regime has often killed or imprisoned Jews based on accusations that they have supported or engaged in espionage for Israel. Zionism is a crime, and Zionists are treated as traitors and criminals.[73] The regime has long promoted anti-Semitism and Holocaust denial.[74] Ahmadinejad has also, famously, called for Israel itself to be "wiped off the map."[75] The Islamic regime has created conditions in which the Jewish community and its representative in Parliament practice self-censorship and are extremely reluctant to speak about their situation.

While few Jews have been charged explicitly with blasphemy or apostasy, the regime's loose use of these and related terms indicates that Jews are persecuted, in part, as guilty or potentially guilty of religious crimes. In the case of Habib Elqanian, this was made explicit. Elqanian, a Jewish community leader, was executed on May 9, 1979. Apart from espionage and support for Israel, the charges against him included: "(1) Friendship with the enemies of God; hostility towards the friends of God.... (4) Spending funds and benefits which have been derived from the exploitation of Iranians to construct belligerent usurper Israel, which is against Islam and God. (5) Corruption on earth in the form of destroying society's human resources. (6) Fighting against God, the Prophet, the Representative of the Twelfth Imam, and against our disinherited people. (7) Obstructing the way of God and the way towards happiness for all the disinherited people in the world. Obstructing Islamic and human values. (8) Corruption on earth...." Amnesty International notes that the charges include the only instance known "of a non-Muslim being charged with a Qur'anic offence. Part Three of the indictment against him reads: 'Taking into consideration [the text of parts one and two of the indictment] and applying specified and unspecified verses of the Holy Qur'an ... and other words transmitted by the Tradition of the saints it is requested that the defendant be sentenced to death and that his property and that of his family be confiscated.'" The government Tribunal ordered the confiscation of the defendant's property and that of his immediate family, and he was executed within hours of being sentenced.[76]

Zoroastrians

Though Khamenei has referred to them as *kaffers* (infidels), Iran's Zoroastrians are recognized as a religious minority under Article 13 of the 1979 (amended 1989) constitution; and, as a "people of the book," a "heavenly religion," with secondary *dhimmi* status, they have some protection and receive somewhat better treatment than some other religious minorities. Also, since Zoroastrians usually do not seek converts, they generally do not suffer from the individual and communal repression that the regime visits on people suspected of "proselytising"

Muslims.[77] However, in 1978, Khomeini described the Shah's regime as an "anti-Islamic regime that wishes to revive Zoroastrianism."[78] They, too, are regarded as unclean; have fewer legal rights than Muslims; are barred from the higher ranks of the executive, legal, or judicial branches of government, as well as, of course, groups such as the Council of Guardians; and must take exams in Islamic theology in order to gain higher education. Government agents frequently plaster their temples and schools with portraits of Shia dignitaries in place of depictions of the Zoroastrian prophet, Zarathustra, even though Zoroastrian monuments are often protected because of their place in Iran's cultural heritage.[79]

In November 2005, when members of Iran's minority religious communities were pushing discreetly for less discrimination against their members, Khamenei's aide, Ayatollah Ahmed Jannati, Chairman of the Council of Guardians and an advisor to Ahmadinejad, denounced non-Muslims as "animals who roam the Earth and engage in corruption." In response, Kourosh Niknam, the Zoroastrian member of the legislature, rebuked him, saying, "Non-Muslims not only are not beasts, but if Iran has a glorious past and a civilization to be proud of then all Iranians owe those to the people whose ancestors lived here before the advent of Islam.... Those who sully the Earth are humans who do not show respect for the other creatures of God." Niknam was ordered to be tried by a tribunal of the Revolutionary Courts on charges of failing to show respect toward Iran's leaders and of disseminating false information. He escaped with a warning that this time Muslims were being tolerant but that they might not be so in the future.[80]

Sunni Muslims

Sunni Muslims, totaling approximately six million, compose the largest religious minority in Iran and pose a problem for the authorities, since the government maintains that Shia Islam is the basis of the regime and, indeed, of all human relationships. The regime generally does not use the same repressive tactics against Sunnis that it uses against other minorities, since this might harm Iran's relations with other Islamic countries. However, Shia zealots who practice widespread discrimination against Sunnis have not been restrained, nor has anti-Sunni violence been punished. On April 27, 2010, the government banned Sunnis from holding prayers at state universities and military camps and earlier forbade communal Friday prayers held in homes in Isfahan, Shiraz, Kerman, and Yazd.[81] The situation of Sunni minorities is further complicated by the fact that they tend to be ethnic minorities such as Turkmen, Arabs, Baluchs, and Kurds, living in the southwest, southeast, and northwest. The line between ethnic persecution and religious persecution can be blurred, and so-called ethnic attacks may include forms of religious repression and vice versa.[82]

After Ahmadinejad became president in 2005, a number of mass demonstrations and uprisings took place among Sunni minorities, and all were severely suppressed by security forces. Arab Iranians in Khuzestan demonstrated peacefully between September 2005 and January 2006 to protest economic deprivation and discrimination. Seven were killed when security forces repressed the demonstrations, and thirteen were executed after a one-day trial on charges of having taken part in bombings.[83] On July 6, 2005, Kurdish activist Shivan Qaderi was killed in Mahabad by security forces. He had been dragged behind a car, and, when photographs of his mutilated body were spread on the Internet in August 2005, there were massive demonstrations and rioting in Iranian Kurdistan. Protesters demanded that Qaderi's murderers be arrested and tried; at least seventeen people died when government forces responded by firing live ammunition. Authorities also detained other prominent Kurdish journalists and activists.[84]

In the predominantly Sunni province of Sistan-Baluchistan, the moderate and Sunni cleric Moulavi (a Sunni religious title) Ahmad Narouee was arrested in October 2008. An advocate of peaceful dialogue with Shia Iran, in spite of the killings of nearly 400 members of his clan since 1979, Narouee has been held incommunicado. Two other Sunni clerics, Moulavis Muhammad Yousof Sohrabi and Abdoulghodus Mallazahi, were executed in 2008 following a televised confession that they had been deliberately and actively causing Sunni–Shia divisions. More than 130 people in the Sistan-Baluchistan province, primarily Sunnis, have been executed or killed for similar charges since 2004.[85]

Sufis

Sufism has a long history in Iran and, depending on how restrictively it is defined, has up to five million practitioners, amongst both Shia and Sunni. Sufi meditative and mystical approaches arouse deep antagonism among the country's clerical rulers, who often regard them as heretics. After Ahmadinejad came to power, the demonization and persecution of Sufis increased significantly. One of the largest attacks took place in early 2006 in Qom, the center of Shia learning in Iran.[86]

In September 2005, Ayatollah Hossein Nouri-Hamedani, an Islamic scholar in Qom, labeled Sufis a "danger to Islam," and, in February 2006, security forces cracked down on them. Government-controlled newspapers ran articles attacking Sufis, the governor of Qom charged them with foreign ties, and leaflets describing them as enemies of Islam were spread by paramilitaries. Clashes broke out for two days after police attempted to shut down a *husseinieh*, or Sufi house of worship, on February 13. Human rights groups report that Sufis, including women and children, were protesting peacefully when the police, aided by members of the conservative Islamic organizations *Fatemiyon* and *Hojjatiyeh*, attacked those in the building. In addition to beating the protesters, police used tear gas and explosives, injuring hundreds.

On February 14, 2006, after the newspaper *Kayhan* quoted senior clerics in Qom saying that Sufism should be eradicated from the city, government forces razed the husseinieh and surrounding houses, and arrested more than 1,000 people. Over

170 were held in Fajr prison and reportedly tortured to obtain confessions to be read on national television. Authorities released some detainees only after they had signed agreements promising to report to intelligences offices and not attend Sufi meetings in Qom. On May 4, 2006, fifty-two Sufis were sentenced to a year's imprisonment and seventy-four lashes, as were their lawyers, Farshid Yadollahi and Omid Behrouzi, who additionally received a five-year prohibition on practicing law.[87]

On October 10, 2006, the residence of Sufi leader Nurali Tabandeh in Gonabad, in Khorasan province, was surrounded by approximately 300 security personnel.[88] Commentators suggest that the government wanted to avoid any large gathering of Sufis, since dervishes from throughout the country travel annually to Gonabad to celebrate Eid al-Fitr, the end of Ramadan, with Tabandeh.[89] He was arrested on May 21, 2007, apparently without formal charges.

In November 2007, many Shia clerics complained because Iranian state television had covered the Rumi International Congress, which celebrated the 800th anniversary of the birth of Rumi, a Persian poet and mystic. Deputy Culture Minister Mohsen Parviz then responded with a statement implying that Sufism should not be promoted in Iran. A week later, following a confrontation in the Western city of Borujerd between members of a Sufi lodge and Shias from a nearby mosque, police and Special Forces used tear gas to storm the lodge, injuring dozens, and made arrests. Government forces also partially demolished a Sufi monastery, called Hossaini-ye Nematollahi Gonabadi, in the same city.[90]

A dervish hosseinieh was demolished in Isfahan on February 18, 2009.[91] On the following day in the same city, forty dervishes were arrested by agents from the Ministry of Intelligence.[92] According to one report, more than 800 were arrested in Tehran on February 22, 2009, and charged with public order and security offenses after gathering to protest the demolition. Of these, 100 were sent to Evin prison for interrogation and fifteen kept in solitary confinement over the course of three months. As one dervish says, "Anyone who stands up to the current regime is charged with waging a war against God or trying to overthrow the Islamic establishment."[93]

Shia Reformers

The regime's suppression of religious views is not limited to religious minorities. Any Shia Muslim who questions doctrine, or the unrestricted power of the clergy and the supreme leader, or questions any part of the religious establishment, can be accused of some version of "insulting Islam." Many Shia religious leaders, including clergy, human rights activists, women's rights activists, journalists, writers, and lawyers have been charged with blasphemy or even apostasy because they have dared to question or criticize any of the regime's "divine" rules. Apart from Hojjatoleslam Hassan Yousefi Eshkevari, discussed above, the following are some of the more prominent cases.

Abdolkarim Soroush

Abdolkarim Soroush, or Souroush, born Husayn Haj Farajullah Dabbagh, is a world-famous Muslim intellectual who argues for the reconciliation of Islamic and democratic traditions, most especially in Iran, his birthplace. In 1980, he was invited by the regime to return from the United Kingdom, where he was teaching, to help incorporate Islamic studies into the nation's higher education. While eager to educate his fellow Iranians about Islam and its heritage, Soroush quickly became disillusioned by the regime's coercive nature. He began to argue for the need to interpret religious practices, though not "essences," according to the needs of each time in history. In 1983, he stopped working for the government and began teaching at the University of Tehran and publishing articles challenging the Mullahs' rule and their mixing political power with religion. The prominent Iranian journalist and political dissident Akbar Ganji was one of his students.[94]

Soroush's open criticism of the regime resulted in his arrest on May 10, 1996, and interrogation by the Ministry of Information. Ministry officials warned him not to lecture at the university or to travel abroad. At other public lectures, thugs have attacked him with clubs and knives—apparently with the approval of the regime. Both Tehran and Isfahan universities barred him from holding or attending public programs on their campus. He was then summarily dismissed from his job and prohibited from teaching and routinely threatened with death.[95] Due to these pressures, he left Iran in 2000 and has since been a visiting scholar at Harvard, Princeton, Yale, Columbia, the Free University of Amsterdam, Berlin's Wissenschaftskolleg, and Georgetown University. In 2004, he received the prestigious Erasmus Prize and, in 2005, was named by *Time* magazine as one of the world's leading 100 public intellectuals. In July 2004, despite threats against his life, he returned for a time to Iran.[96]

During a 2008 interview, Soroush stated directly that he believed the Qur'an represented a "prophetic experience." Thus, he has explained, Muhammad "was at the same time the receiver *and* the producer of the Koran," and the "words, images, rules and regulations" of the Muslim Holy Book came from a human mind "imbued with divinity and inspired by God" rather than represented a word-for-word transcription of God's revelation. While his statements drew accusations of heresy from some Iranian clerics, Supreme Leader Ayatollah Khamenei surprisingly interjected that such statements should be refuted using "religious truths" rather than "by declaring apostasy and anger."[97]

Ayatollah Sayed Hossein Kazemeyni Boroujerdi

Ayatollah Boroujerdi has emphasized that "there is no compulsion in religion" and advocates the separation of religion and state. Since 1996, he has been repeatedly summoned before the Special Court for the Clergy and imprisoned. However, he has continued to lead and teach his followers. On June 30, 2006, he led a large Islamic ceremony at Tehran's Shahid Keshvari Stadium. In subsequent months, security agents twice attempted to arrest him but were unable to do so. They did arrest members of his family, as well as some of his religious students. On September 7, 2006, he was summoned to appear before the prosecutor for the Special Court for the Clergy. Fearing what might happen, he wrote urgent appeals to Pope John Paul II, Javier Solana, who was head of the Council of Europe, and Kofi Annan, then UN Secretary General, telling them his life would be in danger if he appeared before the court. On September 28, security forces arrested about forty of Boroujerdi's followers and took them to the notorious Evin prison, run by the Ministry of Intelligence. One was held in solitary confinement for twenty-two days, and another was tortured and had to be transferred to the Taleqani hospital with a presumed heart attack.[98]

On October 8, security forces arrested Boroujerdi, as well as about 300 of his followers, at his residence in what became a violent confrontation. More of his family, reportedly including his eighty-six-year-old mother, were arrested and taken to prison with him. Some followers have been released, and others rearrested, while Boroujerdi continues to be held at Evin prison, suffering from Parkinson's disease, high blood pressure, diabetes, and kidney and heart problems, some of which are due to previous imprisonments and torture. His health has significantly worsened in prison, and he has been denied medical attention. Due in part to this refusal, on July 22, 2007, Boroujerdi started a hunger strike and was transferred to a hospital; he had reportedly lost sixty-six pounds since his arrest and had been tortured.[99] In December 2008, he was transferred to a prison in the city of Yazd, which seems to have exacerbated his health problems. His visitation rights have been gradually reduced to the point that daily contacts with the outside world have been denied and weekly visits reduced to one every forty-five days.[100] On August 19, 2009, perhaps due to health problems, Boroujerdi was transferred to Evin prison.[101] The thirty charges against him include "waging war against God," which carries the death penalty, "publicly calling political leadership by clergy unlawful," and publicly using the term "religious dictatorship" instead of "Islamic Republic."[102]

Mohsen Kadivar

Shia legal and religious scholar Mohsen Kadivar has been frequently disparaged by many other clerics for his criticism of the regime and his attempts to reconcile Islam and modern democracy. The fact that Kadivar, who was educated in a Shia seminary in Qom, argues carefully on the basis of Islam makes him one of the most formidable critics of the Islamic Republic. In 1999, his criticism resulted in his conviction and sentencing to eighteen months by the Special Court for the Clergy for "propagating against the sacred system of the Islamic Republic of Iran" and "publishing untruths and disturbing public minds."[103] He subsequently moved to the United States and has taught at Duke University.

The conservative clerical establishment's hostility to Kadivar is rooted in his analytical writings, going as far back as 1994, on Shia religious theories of government. Particularly incensing to many clerics was his critique of *Velayat-e Faqih*, the theory of political doctrine instituted by Khomeini in 1979 that places both temporal and spiritual power in the hands of a Shia cleric. Though critiques have been articulated by various scholars, Kadivar remains the most prominent and thorough in questioning the religious authenticity of this effective dictatorship. His three-volume *The Theories of the State in Shiite Jurisprudence* is a comprehensive attack on the principle of government by divine mandate. Kadivar examines the four sources that comprise the basis for the Velayat-e Faqih—the Qur'an, tradition (*Sonnat*), consensus of the Ulama, and reason (*Aghl*)—and he systematically undermines Khomeini's doctrine. Ultimately, he concludes: "The principle of Velayat e-Faqih is neither intuitively obvious nor rationally necessary. It is neither a requirement of religion nor a necessity for denomination. It is neither a part of Shiite general principles nor a component of detailed observances. It is, by near consensus of the Shiite Ulama, nothing more than a jurisprudential minor hypothesis." Kadivar goes on to say that, because the principle is expounded by clerics rather than by Allah, it is neither sacred nor infallible. He then insists that, as long as clerics possess no divine right to rule, Muslims are free to select their government in a democratic republic.[104] His writings attempt to resolve contradictions between traditional Islamic teachings and a modern understanding of human rights. While he advocates neither a "modern Islam" nor an "Islamic modernity," he has identified his writings as a search for "some interpretation of Islam [that is] compatible with a version of Modernity."[105]

Though not required to wear clerical robes, and despite numerous attempts by Iran's clerical courts to defrock him, he insists on wearing his clerical robes while teaching, speaking and writing about democracy. In this way, he aims to exemplify a dedication both to the spiritual message of Islam and to the possibility of an Islamic democracy.[106] In an interview with *Spiegel* during the summer of 2009, Kadivar called instead for "a truly Islamic and democratic state, a state that respects human dignity and does not refuse the rights of women, a state where people can freely elect their religious and secular leaders."[107]

Hashem Aghajari

Hashem Aghajari is a veteran of the Iran–Iraq war, a former political activist with the Warriors of the Islamic Revolution, and a former history professor at Tarbiat Modares University in Tehran. On June 19, 2002, on the twenty-fifth anniversary of the death of philosopher Ali Shariati, he delivered a speech entitled "Islamic Protestantism" to students in the western Iranian city of Hamedan. As one of Shariati's followers, he argued that the clergy should not be seen as mediators between God and mankind, and he questioned the Shia doctrine of emulation in his oft-quoted words, "Muslims are not monkeys to blindly follow the clerics." He went on to say: "Religion has performed badly when it has gone along with power.... Those who believe Islamic jurisprudence is a kind of divinity on earth, that it cannot be criticized, or judged by the law, must enter debates with Islamic thinkers and let voters choose.... Governments that suppress thinking under the name of religion are not only not religious governments but are not even humane governments.... It is time for the institution of religion to become separated from the institution of government."[108] Aghajari's speech threatened hard-line clerics; he was arrested on August 8 on charges of "insulting Islam" and, in November 2002, sentenced to death for blasphemy and apostasy.[109] This verdict led to widespread student protests and calls to reconsider the case and revoke the death sentence. Partly as a result, in January 2003, the Supreme Court annulled the verdict and sent it for retrial. However, the case was sent back to the same trial court, and, in May 2004, the court once again sentenced Aghajari to death. In June, the Supreme Court annulled this once more and assigned the case to branch 1083 of the Public Court of Tehran.

The third trial began on July 10, 2004, with a crowd of fanatics gathered at the court entrance chanting, "Aghajari deserves death penalty." The court charged him with four new offenses: "insulting religion and religious authorities" (articles 513, 514), "propaganda against the Islamic regime" (Article 500), and "publishing lies" for the purpose of inciting public opinion (Article 698). None carried the death penalty. In the course of the trial, Aghajari asserted that he was being tried for the "sin of thinking" and that "the Islam I believe in is an Islam which defends human rights, freedom, and democracy."

On July 20, the court found him not guilty of "propaganda against Islam" and "publishing lies," but guilty of "insulting religion." Under Article 513 he was sentenced to five years imprisonment, the maximum punishment for blasphemy, with two years off for time previously served. He was also suspended from all social services for an additional five years. On July 31, 2004, he was released on bail of one billion rials (more than $100,000), raised by friends. He returned to his teaching position but rarely speaks in public.

Abdollah Nouri

Abdollah Nouri was the Minister of the Interior for a total of four years in both President Rafsanjani's and President Khatami's first-term cabinets, serving until 1998. He was also one of the highest-ranking clergy to support the leading dissident cleric, Ayatollah Hussain Ali Montazeri, described below, and founded *Khordad*, a paper that allowed discussion of taboo subjects such as the limits on the Supreme Leader's powers, the rights of unorthodox clerics and groups to air their views, the right of women to divorce, and even whether laughing or clapping were un-Islamic. Soroush was one of its contributors.[110]

Nouri was arrested and put on trial on November 27, 1999, on charges including using his newspaper to insult the prophet Muhammad and his direct descendants, insulting Ayatollah Khomeini, backing political parties wanting a secular Iran, and seeking friendly ties with the United States and Israel. The prosecutor cited articles in *Khordad* that stated people should be allowed to clap, whistle, and cheer at concerts and political rallies, that criticized divorce laws and the Islamic legal precept of *qisas* (retaliation), and that said of the clergy that "absolute power corrupts absolutely." Nouri refused to back down, and he criticized regime clerics for reneging on promises of democracy and for defending a repressive system, which he believed violated Qur'anic precepts. He also declared, "I totally reject the court, its membership, and its competence to conduct this trial... what has happened to us, to our revolution, to our faith... that one group of clerics can make allegations against another like this?" Nouri's challenge of the court's legitimacy also questioned Khomeini's legacy. Khomeini had established the clergy court by personal decree to deal with rising resistance to Islamic rule, and Nouri, citing the 1980 constitution, said that not even "the leader"—a reference to Khomeini—could establish courts outside the framework of the constitution.[111]

The Special Court for the Clergy reached its verdict on the same day as Nouri's arrest and trial. It found him guilty on fifteen counts, including publishing sacrilegious articles, opposing the teachings of the founder of the Islamic Republic, antireligious propaganda, insults against Khomeini, destabilization of public opinion, and advocating relations with the United States. Under the vagaries of Iranian legal practice, these charges could amount to heresy, with an attendant death penalty, but he was instead sentenced to five years' imprisonment and fined fifteen million rials. However, in October 2002, he was released after his brother, Alireza Nouri, a member of Parliament, was killed in a car accident. Mehdi Karroubi, the Speaker of the Parliament, wrote to the Supreme Leader asking that Nouri be freed out of consideration for his grieving father.[112]

Ayatollah Hussein Ali Montazeri and Mojtaba Lotfi

After religious student and blogger Mojtaba Lotfi posted on the Internet a sermon from the oppositionist Ayatollah Hussein Ali Montazeri, he was arrested in the city of Qom on October 8, 2004, and charged with "spreading false information about the Supreme Guide." Montazeri's son-in-law, Mojtaba Feiz, also had his home searched but he was not detained.[113] Three days after the arrest, the pro-regime newspaper *Jomhouri Eslami* said that Lotfi was "one of the carriers of false information via the anti-revolutionary media."[114] This was not Lotfi's first arrest. In 2004, shortly after posting an article titled "Respect for Human Rights in Cases Involving the Clergy," he was arrested and sentenced to three years and ten months in prison, though he was released on bail, pending an appeal hearing that was never scheduled.[115]

Many commentators believe that the real target of the arrest was Montazeri, a prominent religious critic of the regime who also met with political reformers and encouraged them to unite to challenge Ahmadinejad in the then-upcoming elections. Montazeri had major religious stature, being a *grand marja*, a source of emulation, and, until 1989, was believed to be the designated successor to Supreme Leader Ayatollah Khomeini. However, a falling-out with Khomeini over Montazeri's criticism of the regime's restrictions on freedom and human rights ended that possibility. Montazeri strenuously objected to the mass executions that took place in the period leading up to Khomeini's death and stated after the 1989 fatwa against Salman Rushdie that "[p]eople in the world are getting the idea that our business in Iran is just murdering people." He also taught that apostates should not be subject to earthly punishments.[116] He was placed under house arrest in October 1997, and his religious school was forcibly closed. However, in part through use of the Internet, he continued to criticize the regime and issue dissenting religious fatwas, including one demanding equal rights for Baha'is.[117]

Due to Montazeri's religious stature, advanced age (born 1922), and large following, the regime remained cautious about targeting him directly and so tried to intimidate and silence him by attacking those, such as Lotfi, who posted his sermons. The sermon Lotfi posted called Ahmadinejad to task for calling Iran "the world's freest country." It challenged Ahmadinejad: "Why do your words not match your deeds inside the country? You call Iran the freest country in the world when you are outside, but inside Iran you deprive us of our basic and legal rights." He went on to say that even he, a key participant in the Islamic Revolution of 1979, had had his property confiscated and his speech censored and, if this could happen to him, how much worse it must be for the average people of Iran.

Lotfi was held for six months and unofficially released on August 28, 2005. Because of the nature of his release, the regime did not confirm the completion of his sentence, and so the original charges and sentence remained in force. Due to the poor conditions under which he was held, as well as prior medical problems, Lotfi's health deteriorated in prison, and he was seriously ill at the time of his release.[118] In late 2008, he was rearrested, spent fifty days in solitary confinement, and was eventually sentenced to four years in prison and five years of exile. Charges included spreading the views of Ayatollah Montazeri. He was ordered to cease any activities related to cultural issues and not to publish his works.[119]

On September 14, 2009, following the disputed Iranian elections, Montazeri wrote on his website that Iran had become a "military regime" rather than an Islamic government: "The regime has savagely suppressed million-strong protestors who were legally objecting to the election outcome. A large number were arrested, and an unknown number were martyred in notorious jails." He called upon senior clergy to stand in solidarity with the Iranian people and urged them to speak out: "The grand ayatollahs are well aware of their influence on the regime. . . . Their silence may give the wrong impression to people that the grand ayatollahs approve of whatever is underway."[120]

Montazeri's death from a heart condition on December 20, 2009, sparked student protests, while thousands flocked to Qom to pay their respects. Other grand ayatollahs visited his home. A number of travelers to Qom were arrested before reaching the city, and mourners there clashed with the *Basij* after what was perceived as insulting behavior by the latter.[121] In the wake of his death, fellow Grand Ayatollah Youssef Sanei, also a source of emulation, sent a condolence telegram interpreted by *Al-Ahram* as a sign that Sanei hoped to take Montazeri's place as a spiritual leader of the reformists. Shortly thereafter, the pro-government Qom Theological Lecturers Association ruled that Ayatollah Sanei's religious pronouncements should no longer carry weight, although other clerical bodies quickly opposed the move. Sanei's residence in Qom also came under attack by pro-government demonstrators.[122]

Post-Election Opposition Protesters

After the renewal of protests in Iran in December 2009, Ayatollah Khamenei and government loyalists called for protesters to be arrested and put to death for offending God and the prophet, as well as for insulting Ayatollah Khomeini.[123] As part of this effort, the government charged opposition members with religious crimes, especially *mohareb*, or "making war against God and His Prophet." As early as June, a regional prosecutor issued a warning to "the few elements controlled by foreigners who try to disrupt domestic security" that "the Islamic penal code for such individuals waging war against God is execution."[124] Hard-line General Muhammad-Ali Aziz Jaafari has been quoted as saying, "Those who demonstrate against the system are waging war on Allah," and cleric Abbas Vaez-Tabasi has asserted that "[t]hose who are behind the current sedition in the country . . . are mohareb [enemies of God] and the law is very clear about punishment of a mohareb."[125]

The charge of *mohareb* has also been raised in a number of cases involving protesters but in some cases has been thrown out by the courts. Several members of a group of sixteen protesters, arrested over their involvement with demonstrations on the holy day of Ashura in 2010, were charged with mohareb, a decision that drew protest in an open letter from sixty Iranian intellectuals, largely expatriates. Their letter asserted, "[I]f protesting is making war against God, then we are all warriors." Exiled Iranian former president Abolhassan Bani Sadr also criticized the regime for abusing the term "enemy of God."[126] Nonetheless, a twenty-year-old university student connected with the Ashura protests was charged with mohareb, among other offenses, on February 3. The prosecutor claimed that part of the student's crime consisted in his participating in a prayer service at which former President Rafsanjani gave a sermon.[127] At least two oppositionists had been executed for mohareb by this time, and at least ten death sentences for mohareb had been issued by February 10.[128] On March 4, 2010, mohareb was among the list of charges leveled against another group, this time of nine people, sentenced for their involvement with the Ashura demonstrations. Eight of those accused were sentenced to prison terms, and the ninth to death.[129]

Closing

The Iranian regime uses accusations such as apostasy, blasphemy, heresy, and even sorcery in a profligate and inconsistent manner to punish those individuals it sees as a threat to its rule, including religious reformists, intellectuals, student activists, religious minorities, and women's rights activists.[130] When expedient, it adds other charges not defined in statute such as "propagandists against the government of Islamic Republic of Iran," "friendship with the enemies of God," "hostility towards friends of God," "corruption on earth," "fighting against God," "obstructing the way of God and the way towards happiness for all the disinherited people in the world," "dissension from religious dogma," "spreading lies," "insulting the Prophet," "distributing propaganda against the government of Islamic Republic of Iran," "attracting individuals to the misguided sect of Baha'ism," "insulting Islam," "propagation of spiritual liberalism," "promoting pluralism," "calling into question the Islamic foundations of the Republic," and even, our personal favorite, "creating anxiety in the minds of the public and those of Iranian officials." Court reasoning in such cases may be taken from the writings of Khomeini or others considered authoritative, and the resulting punishments include beating, lashing, solitary confinement, amputation, life or lengthy imprisonment, execution, and extrajudicial punishments such as rape, sexual abuse, burning, starvation, and strangulation.

As noted above, this inconsistency suggests that, when there is nothing else with which to charge a person, the regime uses some variant of apostasy, which conveniently can carry the death penalty. The targeted undesirables can be Baha'is, whose very existence is treated as a crime, converts to Christianity, Jews, Sunnis, Sufis, or Shia religious or political reformists whom the state punishes for speaking their minds. Those charged with "apostasy" include Mahrami, who was never a Muslim; the Soodmans, father and son, who chose a religion other than Islam; Talibi, because he allegedly signed a document that stated his religion as Islam; and Rowhani, because he allegedly converted a Muslim woman to the Baha'i religion. Mekhoubad was executed because he spoke to relatives in Israel and America, and Hovsepian Mehr was murdered because he preached Christianity. Aghajari was charged because of speeches in which he challenged some Islamic practices. The only apparent consistency is the use of these laws to persecute and silence religious minorities and Muslim dissidents.

Under the presidency of Mahmoud Ahmadinejad, conditions have deteriorated, and the increased demonization of Baha'is, Jews, and Sufis indicates darker days ahead. This is especially so in light of proposed reforms to the penal code that would give the regime a sharper tool with which to eradicate its undesirables. Although Ahmadinejad's victory in the June 2009 elections remains disputed in the eyes of many reformers, and although the massive demonstrations in its wake may have revealed fractures in the regime's political support system, the Islamic Republic of Iran's iron grip is likely to remain firm against dissenters, and may even tighten, as long as clerical rule survives.

4

Egypt

On July 15, 2005, Sayed Al Qimni, one of Egypt's most accomplished writers on religion—and one who has been heavily censored—received a death threat from Al-Qaeda in Iraq. Though he asked the police for protection, none was forthcoming. Two days later he received another letter from Al-Qaeda, this time saying that a team of five assassins had been organized and planned to "cleanse their own sins through his blood" by "ripping his head off." The letter called Qimni "one of the walking dead" and threatened him with "the bullet of a passing car or a nearby rooftop." Qimni was given a week to repent. He decided to stop writing, giving interviews, and attending debates, explaining that, while he had resisted numerous threats to himself personally, recent letters had also threatened to kill his children and had described their whereabouts in detail. A year later, however, he announced his return to writing and fighting the Islamists.[1]

On July 16, 2007, Shaymaa al-Sayed, a twenty-six-year-old woman who had converted to Christianity several years before, was attacked in the street, along with her husband, by members of her family—they had been searching for her for four years. Police took al-Sayed into custody, ostensibly to protect her from the family, but then transferred her to the custody of State Security in Cairo. There she was tortured, including by electric shocks, and was photographed naked. On July 23, she was released to her family in Alexandria, who dragged her screaming from the police station and beat her severely before driving away with her.[2]

On March 29, 2009, during a discussion of the Baha'i religion on the Al-Haqiqa television program, Press Syndicate Board Member Gamal Abdel Rahem denounced one of the guests, Baha'i activist and dentistry professor Basma Gamal Musa. He declared that Musa was an "apostate" and ranted to his viewers, "This woman should be killed." A Baha'i caller to the program reported that his Egyptian village, al-Shuraniya, was "full of Baha'is." For five days after this announcement, Baha'i homes in the village, 200 miles south of Cairo, were attacked with firebombs, their water supplies were cut off, and local Baha'is received death threats. Although no one was reported injured, the police detained six people.[3]

Country Overview

Gamel Abdel Nasser, who led a coup in 1952 that overthrew Egypt's monarchy, established a repressive police state and restricted the role of Islamic sharia to family law. However, in 1971, his successor, Anwar Al-Sadat, revised Article 2 of the constitution to read, "Islamic jurisprudence [sharia] is *the* principal source of legislation" (emphasis added), a change whose influence is still percolating through the legal system. Though the main body of law remains civil, the influence of sharia has been increasing, especially with the pressure exerted by groups such as the Muslim Brotherhood, *Al-Ikhwan Al-Muslimeen*, which emerged in the 1920s with the goal of establishing a pan-Islamic state. Until the 2011 revolution, the Brotherhood was illegal in Egypt under a law prohibiting political parties based on religion, but it fielded "independent" candidates and remains strong despite years of persecution and official banning. The Muslim Brotherhood functions today as one of the most powerful Islamist movements in the world.

After Sadat's assassination in 1981, Hosni Mubarak became president and declared a state of emergency that was renewed every three years since. Numerous radical Islamist groups became particularly violent in the 1980s and '90s, attacking security forces, tourists, Christians, and moderate Muslims. These attempts at insurgency were met with heavy repression by the authorities, as well as restrictions on political and civil liberties, which have continued even after the armed infrastructure of radical Islamist groups was largely eradicated by 1998. To control extremism, the government has extended its legal control to all mosques, which, by law, require licenses. However, a large number of Egypt's mosques remain unlicensed and operate outside of state control.

While Iran and Saudi Arabia are well known for their repression of religious dissent, Egypt has also been cracking down on departures from official Islam. The result is that the country's intellectual and cultural life, which once set the pattern for much of the Arab world, has become increasingly stultified. Although Articles 40, 46, 47, and 48 of the constitution guaranteed equality before the law—freedom of belief, freedom of opinion, and freedom of the press—the political reality has been very different. The religious establishment has defended the government against political Islamist groups and in return is given authority over religious matters, including banning books, issuing fatwas on apostasy, and filing court suits.[4] The doctrine of *hisba*, which entitles any Muslim to take legal action against anyone he considers harmful to Islam, provides Islamists extensive opportunities to harass intellectuals and others who arouse their displeasure. While no law specifically forbids blasphemy or apostasy, Article 98(f) of the penal code, which prohibits "ridiculing or insulting heavenly religions," functions as a de facto blasphemy or apostasy law. The law, in principle, also forbids insulting Judaism and Christianity, but in practice only alleged insults to Islam are prosecuted, including by Muslims who object to the official version of Islam.[5] This situation fans religious violence and bigotry.

In the early months of 2011, Egypt entered a period of turmoil. Beginning on January 25, 2011, hundreds of thousands of demonstrators, inspired by the overthrow of the regime in Tunisia, began to gather in Cairo's Tahrir Square, calling for a democratic and free Egypt. When the military refused to repress the demonstrators by lethal force, on February 11, 2011, longtime President Mubarak resigned. The military announced that elections were slated for approximately fall 2011, a deadline that many opposition parties said was too soon to allow them to organize. Meanwhile, Egypt's repression of religious minorities has continued and intensified with violent attacks on Copts in particular.

The majority of Egypt's eighty-three million people are Sunni Muslims. There is a small number of Shias and Baha'is, and fewer than 100 Jews. Egypt's Christians, predominantly Coptic Orthodox, comprise some 10 to 15 percent of the population and thus constitute by far the largest non-Muslim minority in the Middle East. The Coptic Orthodox Church is an ancient community, dating from the first century of the church.

Religious Minorities

Baha'is

Due to widespread accusations that they are heretics, blasphemers, or apostates, Baha'is are probably the most repressed religious group in Egypt. The community originally consisted of people from Iran, but Egyptians have also converted, and Egypt's Baha'i population now numbers several thousand. In the 1920s, Egypt's highest ecclesiastical court declared the religion's independence, saying, "The Baha'i Faith is a new religion, entirely independent, with beliefs, principles and laws of its own, which differ from, and are utterly in conflict with, the beliefs, principles, and laws of Islam. No Baha'i, therefore, can be regarded a Muslim or vice-versa...."[6] Law 263, passed in 1960, deprives Baha'is of legal recognition and also prohibits Baha'i institutions and community activities, while all Baha'i community properties, including cemeteries, were seized by the government under Nasser. On December 15, 2003, the state-funded Islamic Research Center (IRC) of Al-Azhar University issued a fatwa declaring Baha'is apostates and urging the state to "annihilate" the community. Most Baha'is are known to the security services, and many are harassed and subjected to surveillance. State security cracked down on them in 1965, 1967, 1970, 1972, 1985, and 2001, arresting several hundred people. In early 2001, the government arrested eighteen people in Sohag on suspicion of insulting a heavenly religion and violating the law abolishing Baha'i institutions. They were released in October of that year.[7]

In earlier years, Baha'is were allowed to list their religion on identity papers, but the Ministry of the Interior declared that only the three "heavenly" religions—Islam, Christianity, and Judaism—could be recorded on the new identity cards.[8] Since Baha'is would not lie about their religion, they were forced to go without such cards. One Baha'i, Diya Nur al-Din, had a handwritten birth certificate from 1982 stating his Baha'i faith. In 2001, his new (and compulsory) computerized birth certificate replaced this with the word "other." Human Rights Watch reports:

> In his case, because he has a Muslim name, CSD officers told him he had no practical choice but to identify as Muslim. Diya's 23-year-old sister, Sama, has a dash in the religion entry on her birth certificate. Her 2001 comput-erized ID card, however, identifies her as Muslim. Their father, Nur al-Din Mustafa, has a birth certificate that says he is Baha'i and a paper ID card with a dash in the religion line. Their mother, Tahra, has a paper ID card that identifies her as Christian, in accordance with her family name, despite the fact that her birth certificate leaves her religion blank, indicating that she comes from a Baha'i family.[9]

Without identity cards, one cannot register children in school, open bank accounts, or establish a business. Law 143/1994 requires all citizens by age sixteen to obtain an identification card featuring a new national identification number. Those dis-covered without identity cards during random police inspections are detained until the card can be provided. This has forced many Baha'is to stay at home in fear of being arrested.

Baha'is proposed that the Interior Ministry write "other" in the religion box on the cards, but the Ministry refused and instead offered passports, which contain no religious identification. This led to speculation that the government wanted to make Baha'is emigrate to avoid ongoing insecurity. Baha'is then filed a lawsuit to revoke the Ministry's decision and, on April 4, 2006, won its case. The following month, in preparation for an appeal, the Ministry consulted the IRC of Al-Azhar University, which issued a fatwa declaring the Baha'i faith a "heresy," and referenced its 1985 opinion labeling them as "apostates" who supported Zionism and imperialism. On October 16, 2006, the pro-government newspaper *Roz Al-Youssef*, in addition to declaring Baha'is apostates, claimed that they threat-ened public order and advised that they be "watched carefully, isolated and moni-tored."[10] On December 16, 2006, the Supreme Administrative Court overturned the lower court ruling, arguing that the government could place restrictions "respecting public order and morals" and that listing the Baha'i faith in identity documents constituted a religious rite that violated public order, which in Egypt is based on sharia. It then attacked what it said were the heretical characteristics of the Baha'i faith.[11]

The Baha'is brought a new lawsuit represented by the Egyptian Initiative for Personal Rights (EIPR), asking the Court of Administrative Justice to recognize that Baha'is have a right to obtain documents without any religious affiliation and without being forced to falsely identify as Muslim or Christian. On January 29, 2008, the court ruled that the plaintiffs Hussein Hosny Bekeit and Raouf Hendy

Halim could have a dash placed in the religion entry of their IDs.[12] However, Baha'is still reported barriers in enrolling their children in school, and, by July 2008, none had received the documents that the court ordered to be issued. In summer 2008, the Ministry of Religious Endowments distributed a book to all mosques in Egypt attacking the Baha'is. On August 1, 2008, *Al-Akhbar* newspaper reported that the then sheikh of Al-Azhar, Muhammad Sayyed El-Tantawi, had repeated his previous assertion that recognizing the Baha'i community would be "a departure from Islam and the teachings of divine religions . . . and that no one can be allowed to recognize it as a religion. . . ."[13]

Despite this resistance, on March 16, 2009, a Supreme Administrative Court decision, not subject to appeal, upheld a right to legal identification without stipulating a religion. Hossam Bahgat, executive director of the EIPR, said it was "a major victory for all Egyptians fighting for a state where all citizens must enjoy equal rights regardless of their religion or belief."[14] The Interior Ministry ordered that civil status regulations be revised accordingly.[15] On August 8, 2009, Imad and Nancy Rauf Hindi each received an identity card that had a dash in the religion section, so that in Egypt, Baha'is are now sometimes jokingly referred to as the "-" religion.[16] By the end of 2009, some seventeen identification cards and seventy birth certificates had been issued to Baha'is.[17]

This new identity card represents an important step; however, the government, while granting Baha'is exemption from having their religion on their documents, still has not included the word "Baha'i" and so still refuses to officially recognize the Baha'i community.[18] Furthermore, the new national IDs can only be used by unmarried Baha'is: since the authorities still resist recognizing Baha'i marital status, even divorced or widowed Baha'is have still not been permitted to have new ID cards with the religion status line remaining blank.[19]

Other forms of persecution continue, including the attack on the village of al-Shuraniya, described above. In April 2009, Ahmed Omar Hashim of the parliamentary Joint Commission on Defense, National Security, Arab Affairs, and Religious Endowments, and the previous president of Al-Azhar University and ruling party Religious Committee head, claimed that Baha'is "pose a greater threat to national security than extremists and terrorists because they are a product of Zionism," and the Joint Commission demanded that a law be passed declaring Baha'ism illegal. Extraordinarily, Hashim cited the burning of Baha'i homes as evidence of the dangers created by Baha'ism.[20]

Copts

Coptic Christians are often attacked after facing accusations of "insulting Islam." On January 1, 2000, after a dispute in a store involving two Muslims and a Copt named Surial Gayed Isshak, the Christian community in the village of El-Khosheh was attacked by an outraged mob. Twenty-one Christians were murdered, one Muslim was accidentally killed, and scores of homes and businesses were destroyed. On February 27, 2003, two men were sentenced in connection with the death of the Muslim man, but all ninety-three other defendants were acquitted. The longest sentence given was to Isshak, who received three years of hard labor for "insulting a heavenly religion"; Amnesty International categorized Isshak as a "prisoner of conscience." The Egyptian government also leveled charges against people who tried to investigate and publicize the attacks, including the area's Coptic bishop, Bishop Wissa, who was charged with, among other things, "insulting a heavenly religion."[21]

In October 2005, a mob of at least 5,000 people surrounded St. George's Church in Alexandria after the newspaper *Al-Midan* reported on October 13 that a play had "insulted Islam" by featuring a Copt who resisted becoming a Muslim. The play had been performed at St. George's two years earlier but had allegedly appeared on a newly discovered CD. In the riots, four people died and ninety were injured. There were attacks on seven other churches in Alexandria, as well as on cars and Coptic businesses, and a mob surrounded another church as far away as Cairo. In the days following, anonymous taggers marked Coptic houses in Alexandria with crosses, in what was generally assumed to be a sign to aid future attackers. Many Christians remained home in fear. Death threats against Alexandria priests and against Coptic Pope Shenouda III also appeared on extremist websites.[22]

On August 8, 2007, Egyptian security forces arrested Adel Fawzi Faltas, head of the Canada-based Middle East Christian Association (MECA), and his associates, photographer Peter Ezzat Mounir and Adeeb Ramses Kosman. Authorities took the three men to Lazoghly prison, State Security headquarters. They were accused of distributing religiously defamatory books and of "insulting Islam" on the United Copts website, which is based in the United Kingdom. MECA had been advocating that Egyptian converts from Islam to Christianity should be able to change their religious identity legally. A few days before his arrest, Faltas had interviewed a convert from Islam to Christianity on the Internet. On November 5, 2007, they were released. However, on November 10, police in Cairo arrested two other members of the group, Wagih Yaob and Victor George. On November 10, 2007, MECA's lawyer, Mamdouh Azmy, was also arrested.[23]

Converts from Islam

The late Sheik Muhammad Tantawi of Al-Azhar University said, "It is forbidden for any Muslim to change his religion in Egypt," and, on May 1, 2007, the *Sout el Oma* newspaper reported that Interior Minister Habib el-Adly had sent a memo to the Administrative Court arguing that Islam, as the state religion, demands the death of any Muslim man who leaves the faith, while a female apostate "should be imprisoned and beaten every three days until she returns to Islam."[24] In early July 2010, Sheikh Youssef Al-Badri, a member of the Supreme Council for Islamic Affairs, an affiliate of the Egyptian Ministry of Al-Awqaf (Islamic Endowments) stated on state television that converts from Islam "should be killed."[25] Even if such prescriptions are not carried out, converts may face forced annulments and the loss of child custody rights; with regard to female converts, Egypt's highest court has ruled that "a woman apostate does not originally have the right to marry either a Muslim or a non-Muslim; she is considered dead, and the dead is [sic] not subject to marriage."[26]

Faced with such official statements and the risk of attack, converts may avoid going to church altogether or surreptitiously leave their houses to attend services, and some Christian women don veils to go home when services are over. In addition to threats and violence from extremists and family members, converts face official legal hardship. Rather than protecting them, security officials often join in the mistreatment. Converts can be charged under Article 98(f) of the penal code, which prohibits using religion to "promote or advocate extremist ideologies, ignite strife, degrade any of the heavenly religions, or harm national unity or social peace."[27] Also, because their very existence may cause unrest among some Muslims, the police may accuse them of causing religious division. Even without formal charges, under Egypt's emergency law, police can hold converts indefinitely. Convert Osama Gomaa Maatouq was first detained by State Security on April 11, 2008, and, as of July 17, 2010, had been held without charge or official registration despite several court orders that he be released. In 2010, Egyptian embassies who had been contacted by European members of Parliament, claimed that Maatouq had been released, but it appears that he was moved to a new prison, Minya Al-Amoma, under the name Abdel-Latif Gomaa Maatouq. Human rights advocates believe that State Security may have altered his name so he would not show up in inquiries into their records.[28]

Between October 18 and 24, 2003, security forces detained twenty-two people for allegedly creating false Christian identity papers for other former Muslims and for themselves. Those arrested were mostly women. During interrogation, the police pressured them to return to Islam and sought to find the names of other converts and people who had helped them. The detainees were all beaten, several were tortured, and at least one of the women, Mariam Girgis Makar, 30, suffered sexual abuse. Another detainee, Isam Abdul Fathr, died while in custody. Makar, a mother of two young daughters, who had moved from Cairo to Alexandria after converting to Christianity with her husband, was the last to be released, on bail, on December 3, 2003.[29]

Following the crackdown, on October 26, 2003, an association, the Christian Converts of Egypt, issued a declaration on their plight, calling for international attention and stating, "For many years, we have been struggling for the simplest of our human rights, the freedom of belief and the freedom of worship. We have been imprisoned, tortured, followed by the security police, and subjected to all forms of abuse for our faith...." Such a declaration is a most unusual step, since converts usually hide and avoid drawing attention to themselves.

As with the Baha'is, one of the major problems for Christian converts is the government's refusal to change their religion on their identity cards. Hence, many Christians are treated as if they are Muslims. This is especially a problem because Egyptian family law is based on religion, and sharia applies to any family in which at least one parent is Muslim.[30] Since sharia law forbids Muslim women to marry outside their religion, Christian women identified as Muslim cannot marry Christian men.[31] Desperate to marry, they may acquire forged Christian IDs. When the police discover this, they have the authority to forcibly divorce such women from their husbands. At other times, the women may be arrested and tortured. Recently, the government has been cracking down on marriages with forged documents. On October 12, 2008, Coptic priest Metaos Wahba, of Saint Mary Church in Giza, was sentenced to five years imprisonment for alleged "forgery," since he had performed the wedding of a Christian man and a woman who had converted to Christianity from Islam. He was convicted despite having been unaware that the woman's papers were forged. Two witnesses at the wedding were also sentenced to five years imprisonment for "forgery." The newlyweds have gone into hiding.[32]

Among the many converts persecuted in Egypt is Gasir Mohammed Mahmoud, who converted to Christianity in 2003. When his family learned of this, his adoptive father sought the help of local Muslim sheikhs, who issued death threats against Gasir for apostasy. His mother then asked police to protect him from being killed, but her pleas fell on deaf ears. Instead, Gasir was detained by security officials and tortured, including reportedly having his toenails ripped out. On January 10, 2005, he was forcibly confined to Cairo's El-Khanka mental hospital and kept in solitary confinement. Mahmoud recalled, "They filled the room with water, to prevent me from sleeping." After international publicity, he was released June 9, 2005, but he remained in hiding.[33]

On April 6, 2005, Baha al-Aqqad, then fifty-six, and a recent convert to Christianity, was arrested and held in Doqqi prison. He was never informed exactly what he had been accused of, although the repeated interrogations centered on "insulting Islam." He was also beaten severely by another prisoner over rumors that he was converting others to Christianity and baptizing them. His lawyer was told that he was being held under emergency laws on suspicion of "committing blasphemy against Islam" or "insulting a heavenly religion." Though he was not formally charged, his detention was renewed every forty-five days until he was released without explanation on April 28, 2007.[34]

In 2002, when her family discovered that Siham al-Sharqawi had fallen in love with a Copt at tourism school in 2000, they beat her and continued to do so whenever they suspected she had managed to see him. On October 28, 2003, she was tied to a dining room chair and beaten but managed to escape from the home. On August 26, 2004, she was baptized, and three months later, on November 22, al-Sharqawi married her Christian boyfriend using a false Christian name to procure a marriage certificate. Subsequently, she was forced to stay inside her home in

Alexandria to avoid being seen. She later moved to Luxor and then to Qena, where, on November 22, 2007, police arrested her. Witnesses said that police treated the woman like a prostitute although it was her third wedding anniversary. She was interrogated for four days, insulted, and threatened with beatings.[35]

Some Christians may not realize that the government considers them Muslim until years after their conversion. In the case of sisters Shadia and Bahia El-Sisi, for example, a conviction came forty-five years after the alleged offense. The background was that, in 1962, their father had left home and converted to Islam. Three years later, he moved back home, reconverted to Christianity, and obtained forged documents stating that he was Christian. In 1996, this was discovered by police, who detained him and told him that he was a Muslim and that therefore his daughters were also Muslim. Neither sister knew of their father's doings decades before, and their identity documents had always listed them as Christians. Shadia, who had been married to a Christian for twenty-five years, was threatened with forced divorce. In November 2007, she was sentenced to three years in jail, purportedly for committing fraud on her identity documents since, in 1982, she had listed "Christian" on her marriage certificate. In early 2008, she was released when the attorney general said that the judgment was based on false information. Bahia, who went into hiding when Shadia was detained, came out when her sister was released and was then tried and convicted for identifying herself as Christian on her marriage certificate. She was freed pending an appeal. If she continues to be regarded as Muslim, then her husband will be forced to convert, or their marriage will be annulled by the court. In that case, her children will be reregistered as Muslim, with her daughters also facing possible involuntary marriage annulment.[36] In principle, this procedure of retroactive forcible conversion could carry on through many generations.

On December 17, 2008, twenty-two-year old Martha Samuel Makkar was arrested at Cairo's airport on charges of forging official documents as she attempted to leave for Russia with her husband and two sons, aged four and two. Five years earlier, she had converted to Christianity, changed her name from Zeinab Said Abdel-Aziz, and married a Christian, Fadel Thabet. Subsequently, not only was she persecuted by the police, but also her family attempted to kill her. There are reports that Makkar was sexually assaulted by Egyptian police at El-Nozha police station; at the National Security office in Heliopolis, she was assaulted by other prisoners while in detention; and she was also tortured to force her to return to Islam.[37] On January 24, 2009, she was granted bail but not before the judge said she should be killed for leaving Islam.[38]

There are no reliable figures on the number of converts from Islam in Egypt, since the government refuses to recognize them, and they often live in hiding, but the number is likely to be several thousand. Many converts are afraid to speak of their new views, while others move in the hope of beginning a new life where they are not known. Unfortunately, Egypt's identity cards make religious anonymity nearly impossible, and government officials are able to abuse converts wherever they go.[39]

Challenging Apostasy Restrictions in the Courts

Despite exposing themselves to attack, in recent years, several people who have converted from Islam have challenged the Egyptian government's refusal to recognize their conversion. Most of these are people who were born Christian, converted to Islam, often for reasons of marriage, and then decided to convert back. On April 24, 2007, the Court of Administrative Justice ruled that recognizing reconversion to Christianity by individuals who had been born Christian and previously converted to Islam would violate sharia apostasy prohibitions and that the government was not required to grant such recognition.[40] The case was appealed, and on February 9, 2008, the Supreme Administrative Court ruled that twelve Christian-born Muslims could convert back and have their identity documents changed to reflect this. However, the ruling was narrow and worded only to apply to those twelve. Moreover, the court also said that the reconverts should have the words "formerly declared Muslim" on their IDs. This would essentially mark them as apostates and expose them to persecution and attacks by extremists and security officials.[41]

While the appeal to the Supreme Administrative Court was being heard, the government consulted Al-Azhar about reconversions. Al-Azhar's fatwa committee described them as "grave crime[s] that cannot be met with leniency." In line with these statements, Judge Muhammad Husseini appealed to Egypt's Supreme Constitutional Court to review the constitutionality of Article 47 of Egypt's civil law—cited by the Supreme Administrative Court to justify accepting the reconversions—on the grounds that it violated Article 2 of the constitution.[42]

Meanwhile, there were signs that the administrative court's decision was not being enforced. On March 9, 2008, the newsweekly *Watani* reported that a request for new documents from one of the twelve reconverts, Bishay Farag Bishay, was rejected by Egypt's Civil Status Department on the grounds that their computerized system allowed them to enter only one word in the religion section. With the constitutional court case delayed indefinitely, and the Ministry of the Interior refusing to follow administrative court decisions, reconverts had little hope in the near term of having their religion recognized.[43]

As distinct from "reconverts," no Muslim-born convert to Christianity has won the right to have his new religion recognized. One who has been trying to do so is Mohammed Ahmed Hegazy, who converted to Christianity in 1998. Shortly after, he was tortured by the police for three days and was held again for ten weeks in 2002 in conditions he describes as being like a "concentration camp." On August 2, 2007, when his wife was expecting a baby, who would have to be raised as a Muslim, Hegazy filed a court case challenging the government's refusal to recognize his conversion. After receiving death threats, he went into hiding. The Minister of Religious Endowments, Mahmoud Hamdi Zakzouk, publicly stressed the legality of capital punishment for converts, and Hegazy's lawyer, Mamdouh

Nakhla, withdrew from the case after receiving death threats and being told by Egyptian State Security that he might be killed.[44]

At a January 15, 2008, hearing, Islamist lawyers demanded that apostasy be outlawed, and a dozen Islamist lawyers tried to attack Hegazy's attorneys. On January 25, 2008, when asked what he would do if his son did not return to Islam, Hegazy's father said, "I will kill him with my own hands. I will shed his blood publicly."[45] On January 29, 2008, the Supreme Administrative Court ruled that Hegazy could not have his conversion recognized since "monotheistic religions were sent by God in chronological order" and, therefore, one cannot convert to "an older religion." Hegazy tried to flee the country but was unable to get a passport, and he went into hiding.[46]

Another Muslim-born convert who has challenged the law is Maher El-Gohary, now named Peter Ethnasios. On August 4, 2008, he filed to change his official religion from Islam to Christianity. He had converted some thirty years previously, and his main motive for going to court was that his fourteen-year-old daughter, who had been forced to attend Muslim classes at school, was, at age sixteen, scheduled to be issued an identity card designating her faith as Muslim, which would make it illegal for her to marry a Christian.[47] On February 22, 2009, about twenty Islamist attorneys demanded that he be convicted of apostasy and sentenced to death. Given the risk to his safety, El-Gohary could not attend the hearing; when he had sought to obtain the documents for his lawyer, Nabil Ghobreyal, to act on his behalf, registry office employees beat him.[48]

In order to proceed legally with the conversion, the court asked him to provide a conversion certificate from Egypt's Coptic Orthodox Church, something that had previously proved almost impossible. Realizing it would be difficult to obtain the certificate in Egypt, El-Gohary traveled abroad, returning with a conversion certificate from a church in Cyprus that the Coptic Orthodox Church officially accepted in April 2009.[49] Despite the certificate, the judge rejected his appeal. In spite of this setback, El-Gohary vows to continue his quest for official recognition as a Christian Egyptian.[50] Near the end of March 2010, fifteen-year-old Dina El-Gohary, his daughter, ventured out of hiding in Alexandria to get some water and had acid thrown on her; it damaged only her jacket.[51]

Muslims

Religious Censorship

One method that the state, in cooperation with Al-Azhar and other establishment Sunni bodies, uses to control Muslims' thoughts is the censorship of religious works. Egypt also censors works that have little to do with religion, as well as works by non-Muslims. However, the major goal of censorship is to ensure that nonapproved views of Islam are not circulated.[52] The earlier part of the twentieth century was comparatively free: in 1937, Ismail Adham was even able to publish his *Why Am I an Atheist*. But the situation worsened dramatically after 1952, when Egypt's ostensibly secular military rulers established close links with the Al-Azhar religious establishment in order to combat Islamic political groups. Under Anwar Sadat and Hosni Mubarak, this relationship has strengthened. Al-Azhar itself, as well as the Council of Ministers, the Ministry of the Interior, and the Ministry of Education, has censorship powers. In 1985, Al-Azhar's IRC was authorized to advise on censoring books it deemed heretical. In 2003, it received power to recommend confiscation of "publications, tapes, speeches, and artistic materials deemed inconsistent with Islamic law," though a court order was necessary for the actual confiscation. In June 2004, Al-Azhar's inspectors were given authority to confiscate any publications dealing with Islam.[53]

In 1981, the Ethical Court in Cairo ordered the destruction of 3,000 copies of *One Thousand and One Nights* and jailed the publisher for "corrupting the morals of the young." In 1997, the IRC listed 196 books that should be banned, and a High State Security Court ordered Sayed Al Qimni's *God of Time* to be banned based on the IRC's recommendation. In 1998, two books by Khalil Abdel Karim were seized because the IRC disapproved of their content, and the March 19 issue of the *Cairo Times* was banned for including an interview with Abdel Karim on the grounds that it "harmed the image of Al-Azhar," and the magazine was subsequently banned from being printed in Egypt.[54] Haydar Haydar's novel, *Banquet for Seaweed*, was originally published in Syria and available in Egypt since 1983. In 2000, the book was reprinted in the Ministry of Culture's Arab Classics series, but Haydar was accused of apostasy because of it. The pro-Islamist newspaper *El Shaab* called the novel an attack on Islam, which led to riots by Al-Azhar students, and Al-Azhar called for it to be burned.[55] Bannings and confiscations have continued and even increased in the twenty-first century, including bannings of books by noted authors and reformers such as Salah El Din Mohsen, Khalil Abdel Karim, Gamal Al-Banna, Nawal Al-Sadawi, Naguib Mahfouz, and Mohammed Futuh.[56]

Al-Azhar's censorship of views at variance from its official version of Islam also directly restricts academic freedom. Probably the institution most affected has been the American University in Cairo (AUC), since other universities usually already follow Al-Azhar's rules. On May 13, 1998, the Minister of Higher Education ordered the removal of Maxime Rodinson's book *Muhammad* from the curriculum, claiming that it contained fabrications harmful to respect for the prophet and Islam. The government censor then banned seventy other titles that the university had tried to import. Between May 1998 and April 1999, out of a total of 450 books reviewed, the censor's office reportedly declared eighty-nine books impermissible for sale in the AUC bookstore.[57]

Shias

Egypt's government also represses Shias, who comprise perhaps one percent of the population. Egypt's Shias are commonly divided into two groups: those whose families immigrated more than a century ago from Syria, Lebanon, and Iran, and those, often known as Neo-Shias, who are more recent converts from Sunnism.[58] Both groups have suffered numerous crackdowns, especially since the 1979 Iranian Revolution, including in 1988, 1989, 1996, and 2002. More than 100 have been arrested.

On March 22, 2004, Shia leader Mohamed Ramadan Hussein El-Derini was arrested by the State Security Intelligence service (SSI) and detained without charges for fifteen months. On four occasions, the Supreme State Security Emergency Court ordered his release, but, each time, the Minister of the Interior countered by issuing a new administrative detention decree, saying that he was "under the influence of Shia ideas."[59] The government released him after a 2005 report by the UN Working Group on Arbitrary Detention declared that he was "detained solely on the basis of his religious beliefs." There are credible reports that El-Derini was repeatedly tortured. He was again arrested on October 1, 2007, for making claims about torture in Egypt in his book *The Capital of Hell*, as well as for preaching Shia doctrine.[60]

In June 2009, a wave of arrests of Shias began with the detention of cleric Hassan Shehata, along with some of his followers. By the end of the year, there were reports of as many as 300 arrests. Among the charges that have been leveled against those detained are holding extremist views that go against true Islam as well as organizing, and possibly being linked to, members of a Hezbollah cell.[61]

Religious Reformers

Book banning is not the most serious barrier that Sunni intellectuals face in Egypt. The authors are also accused of being anti-Islamic and blasphemers or heretics and perhaps apostates. Most attacks have a similar pattern: a reactionary Islamic writer attacks the author's work, and then media assaults quickly follow. This is often followed by members of the Muslim Brotherhood in Parliament attacking the government for allowing such offensive materials to be published and then threatening, and actually attacking, those accused. Some prominent cases follow.[62]

Farag Foda

Farag Foda, one of Egypt's best-known liberal thinkers, was a role model for many others, since he was one of the first to attack the Islamization of society that began in the 1970s and 1980s. He was born in 1945 and became a professor of agriculture. Foda resigned from the liberal El Wafd Party in 1984 after it formed an electoral alliance with the Muslim Brotherhood, and then he tried unsuccessfully to establish a new party, Al Mustaqbal.[63]

His book *Terrorism* attacked violent Islamic groups, not only for their actions, but also for their religious rationale. His book *The Trick* criticized the infiltration of financial markets by Islamic banks and "money investing companies" and the role these companies played in fundamentalist political campaigns; he correctly prophesied their eventual collapse, in which many Egyptian families lost their money. His *A Discussion About Secularism* defended the separation of religion and the state and mocked Islamist interpretations of the Qur'an and hadith, which had led them to issue fatwas banning people from eating cucumbers and bananas because they had sexual meaning. Perhaps his best-known work is *Absent Truth*, which argues that a pious Islamic state has never existed, and he discusses atrocities and killings from the first caliph Abu Bakr to the end of the Arab Caliphate of the Abbasids.[64] His 1990 *To Be or Not to Be* was banned, and he was brought into state security for questioning.[65]

In January 1992, the Cairo Book Fair held a debate between him and three Islamist thinkers, attended by hundreds of Islamic activists, and his rebuttal of Islamist arguments and championship of a free society were probably the primary reason for his subsequent murder. Though he received numerous death threats, he continued speaking undeterred, until, on June 8, 1992, he was shot dead by two men riding a motorcycle outside his office in Nasr City. The killers also injured his son Ahmed and a friend.[66] The group Gamaat Islamia claimed responsibility for the murder, accusing Foda "of being an apostate, of advocating the separation of religion from the state, and favoring the existing legal system in Egypt rather than the application of Sharia." Scholars at Al-Azhar denounced the way he was killed but still held that he was an apostate who deserved to die. During the murder trial, Sheikh Mohamed El Ghazali declared that it was the right of any Muslim to kill an apostate and that, although this usurped the role of the state, he should not be executed.[67]

Ahmed Subhy Mansour commented on the trial:

> They have succeeded in converting the trial of Farag Foda's killers to a trial for Farag Foda himself. They made out of that trial an occasion to terrorize their opponents. The defense in the case demanded that the testimony of some advocates of political Islam should be heard. Their leader gave his verdict that whoever opposes the application of Islamic sharia is an apostate who deserves to be executed, and that any person from the public who kills him should not be punished by the authorities, even though such a person has taken away the right of the state by taking the law into his own hands.... The newspapers of political Islam very happily welcomed it. No less enthusiasm was shown by their supporters working in the government official newspapers.[68]

Gamal Al-Banna

The name Al-Banna is usually associated with Hassan Al-Banna, founder of the Muslim Brotherhood. However, Gamal Al-Banna, born in 1920, rejected his famous brother's ideology and has, himself, aroused controversy through more than forty books. In 1946, he published *A New Democracy*, with a chapter titled "A New Understanding of Religion," highly critical of the Brotherhood. After his book *Rationalization of Renaissance* was banned because of its criticism of the 1952 military takeover, Al-Banna stopped writing on Islamic matters and instead wrote extensively on workers' issues. He also founded the Egyptian Association for the Care of Prisoners and Their Families, which brought him more problems with the government. In the 1980s, with the reemergence of political Islam, he returned to Islamic issues and published *Islam and Rationalism, No and No Again*, and *Islamic Movements: Pros and Cons*. One of his most famous books was *Towards a New Islamic Jurisprudence*, in which he called for a new Islamic theology. In 2005, his book *The Responsibility for the Failure of the Islamic State* was banned after an IRC ruling that it deviated from Islamic orthodoxy.[69]

Al-Banna's major theme is that "no Islamic revival can be achieved without a direct return to the Holy Qur'an and a reexamination of the Sunna," free from interpretations by ancestors influenced by the spirit of their age. He maintains that "a narrow isolationist position, taking the example of a long-gone society as the best example ... contradicts the essence of Islam ..." Al-Banna has maintained that the Sunna "should never have the same weight as the Qur'an" and "must be judged by the Qur'an, not the other way around."[70] Along with fellow reformers Saad Eddin Ibrahim and Sayed Al Qimni, he held a conference in Cairo on October 5–6, 2004, called "Islam and Reform." It asked for reliance on the Qu'ran as the sole authentic source for reviewing the Islamic heritage and a radical revision of "Islamic scholarship relating to Islamic Jurisprudence and the Sunna, the Traditions of the Prophet."[71] Not least because of its call for institutional reform, the conference was heavily criticized by Tantawi, the late head of Al-Azhar, who said that research centers that participated in the seminar have a "destructive influence" and "must be stopped and brought to trial." Tantawi, who participated in interreligious dialogues himself, also claimed that the "participation of Western research centers" in the discussion "is a mark of shame." He called participants "a group of religious deviants, one of whom has already been indicted on charges of treason; thus it is forbidden to deal with them...."[72]

Speaking on the topic of freedom and Islam at the Alexandria Library on May 26, 2007, Al-Banna emphasized that "the prophet stressed freedom in all his acts and dealings," but the current religious establishment "decides the death penalty for an apostate." He added that the Prophet did not punish apostasy and that [t]here is no contradiction between complete freedom of thought and religion because religion is built on belief.... This can only exist in an environment which allows liberal examination and pious scrutiny." He added, "There is no freedom without the freedom to print and publish, to form political parties, organizations, trade unions and the rest of civil society's organizations ..." He has also advocated granting women equality with men. In *The Veil*, he challenges the dogma requiring women to wear headscarves and argues that it does not derive from Islam but from earlier cultures.[73]

Concerning the Baha'i cases described above, Al-Banna argued, "I believe that it is in their right that they are documented as Baha'is in the ID Card and official documents."[74] He also defended the right of Mohamed Hegazy to convert from Islam to Christianity: "There is not one word in the Quran dictating the death penalty on those who depart from the Muslim faith. The Quran never mentions a worldly punishment..."; such punishment, for Al-Banna, was invented as a political tool to protect rulers.[75] He also continues to criticize Al-Azhar: "The problem is that the Islam propagated now by religious institutions... is the Islam of the Jurists... these Islamic thinkers were geniuses," but they "cannot be liberated from their time."[76] Al-Banna remains highly critical of the Muslim Brotherhood, saying: "There is no such thing as an Islamic state. It is impossible to create...."[77]

Nasr Hamid Abu-Zayd

In 1955, Nasr Hamid Abu-Zayd, though only twelve years old, was imprisoned on suspicion of sympathy with the Muslim Brotherhood. By 1981, with support from the Ford Foundation and after studies at the University of Pennsylvania, he received a doctorate from Cairo University for research on Qur'anic interpretation and began teaching there in the Department of Arabic Language and Literature.[78] In May 1992, seeking promotion to full professor, he presented the tenure committee with two of his academic books, *Imam Shafai and the Founding of Medieval Ideology* and *The Critique of Religious Discourse*, in addition to eleven journal articles. Two referees' reports recommended promotion. However, the third, by the influential Abdel Sabour Shahin, an advisor to President Mubarak, said his research was an affront to Islam. There is some speculation that Shahin's hostility was partly due to the fact that *The Critique of Religious Discourse* criticized Islamic investment companies for which Shahin worked as a consultant.[79] Based on Shahin's negative report, the committee ruled seven to six that Abu-Zayd did not deserve promotion. The Arabic department and the Faculty of Arts both objected to this ruling, but the Council of Cairo University adopted it. Abu-Zayd appealed to the administrative court to overturn this decision but lost his appeal in 1993.[80]

Abu-Zayd's major troubles began when, in a front-page story, a pro-Islamist newspaper accused him of abandoning his faith in Islam.[81] At the end of 1993, Islamist lawyers, led by Youssef El Badry, former member of Parliament and imam of a Paterson, New Jersey, mosque from 1992 to 1993, filed a lawsuit demanding the breakup of Abu-Zayd's marriage to Ibtihal Younes. The case was based on the claim that Abu-Zayd was an apostate and a Muslim woman cannot be married to a non-Muslim.[82] On January 27, 1994, the Giza Personal Status Court rejected the suit because the plaintiffs lacked a direct interest in the case, but, on June 14, 1995, the Cairo Appeals Court ruled that Abu-Zayd was an apostate and that, therefore, his marriage was null and void. Six days later, a group of Al-Azhar scholars urged the government to compel Abu-Zayd to repent by applying the "legal punishment for apostasy."[83]

On June 21, 1995, Islamic Jihad declared that, under Islamic law, the professor should be killed.[84] He was condemned during mosque prayers, and many sheikhs, particularly in Cairo, called for his death. Facing these threats, on July 23, 1995, he and Ibtihal went to Leiden, Netherlands, where he had a standing offer to teach at the university. He later stated, "I'm not afraid of death. What I'm afraid of is a disability that may result from an assassination attempt, like what happened to Naguib Mahfouz."[85]

The court battles continued even after he left the country. On August 5, 1996, the Court of Cassation, the highest court, sustained the Court of Appeals verdict and announced "the separation of the first defendant Dr. Abu Zayd from his wife, the second defendant, because of the former's apostasy and because she is a Muslim." It also called on him to repent and return to Islam, which was "a light to the people." The verdict further stated that apostasy was a crime that could be punished in accord with "Quranic punishments," that this might be grounds for a further judicial case, and that the "exiting from Islam is a revolt against it and this is reflected upon the person's loyalty to Shari'a and state"[86] The ruling also condemned Abu-Zayd's positions on Christians paying additional taxes (*jizya*) and slavery. It stated, "The defendant's proposition, that the requirement of Christians and Jews to pay *jizya* constitutes a reversal of humanity's efforts to establish a better world, is contrary to the divine verses on the question of *jizya*," which are "not subject to discussion." It also said that his denunciation of the ownership of slave girls was "contrary to all the divine texts which permit such."[87] The divorce ruling was suspended in September 1996 by the Giza Court of Emergency Matters, but the declaration of apostasy remained in place.[88] This led to a flood of cases in subsequent years wherein Islamist lawyers "filed some eighty lawsuits against the Egyptian government, against artists and intellectuals, academics and journalists, all in an attempt to make Sharia law the law of the land," and often won.[89]

When asked about the death threats against Abu-Zayd, Abdel Sabour Shahin, who helped initiate the witch hunt against reformers, said, "The prescribed penalty for apostasy is execution, but an apostate has to be given a chance to repent.... Let him renounce his ideas. Let him publicly burn his books."[90] In some kind of rough justice, Shahin himself soon faced apostasy charges. His book *Adam, My Father* concluded that Adam was not the first human form, but the first human being. El Badry, his former ally against Abu-Zayd, then proclaimed that Shahin is "more dangerous than Al Qimni or Abu Zayd, because everyone knows that they are non-believers, whereas Shahin has the status of a preacher."[91]

Ibtihal returned to Egypt several times to review theses at the University of Cairo, but Abu-Zayd himself stayed away until the last years of his life, when he visited quietly, since he remained a target for Islamists. He died in a Cairo hospital on July 5, 2010. His books remain unavailable in Egyptian university libraries and even in the Alexandria Library, and he maintained, "I criticized the religious discourse and its social, political, and economic manifestations, and this threatened the interests of some institutions."[92]

Sayed Al Qimni

Sayed Al Qimni, born in 1947, has published thirteen books on themes including mythology, such as *Moses and the Last Days of Tal El Amarna, Prophet Abraham, The Story of Creation, The Legends and the Heritage, Ozories*, and *God of Time*; Islamic history, such as *Islamic Issues, The Hashemite Party and the Establishment of the Islamic State*, and *The Wars of the Prophet's State*; and attacking Islamic political movements and the religious establishment, such as *Thank You Bin Laden, The People of Religion and Democracy*, and *The Ghosts of Heritage and the Heritage of Ghosts*.[93]

He analyzes early Islam from the perspective of myth and avoids being labeled an apostate by using only sources approved by Al-Azhar. However, as one commentator has said, "Many of his conclusions would make Nasr Hamed Abu-Zayd blanch." Despite being banned by Al-Azhar and, until recently, virtually unobtainable in Egypt except as photocopies, his books have provoked widespread debate, and outraged Islamists label him an apostate and call for his death. He has been shot at but says, "I had kids with me. It was a warning. If they wanted to kill me, they could have."[94] On August 17, 1997, the High State Security Court, on the IRC's recommendation, ordered the confiscation of his *God of Time*. On July 7, 2004, the IRC recommended the confiscation of his *Thank You Bin Laden*, accusing its author of apostasy and insulting the Companions of the Prophet.[95] In 2005, on Al Jazeera's highly-rated show *The Other Direction*, Al Qimni was widely regarded as having defeated an Islamist in a debate subsequently posted on YouTube, leading to renewed death threats.

In July 2009, in what appeared to be a brief liberalizing literary trend, the Ministry of Culture bestowed the State Award of Merit in Social Science on Al Qimni. As in the case of Hassan Hanafi, who was honored in the same month, conservative Islamists protested vigorously. Islamist Sheikh Youssef al Badri stated on televison that Al Qimni was more of a "disaster" than Salman Rushdie: "Salman Rushdie, everyone attacked him because he destroyed Islam overtly. But Sayyid al-Qimni is attacking Islam and destroying it tactfully, tastefully and politely." Nabih al-Wahsh filed a suit demanding the award be cancelled as Al Qimni is "derisive of Islam." The government-backed religious institution Dar-al-Ifta promulgated a fatwa that, while not identifying Qimni by name, has been interpreted by the Cairo Institute for Human Rights Studies as "effectively declar(ing) him an infidel."[96]

Ahmed Subhy Mansour and Quranism

Ahmed Subhy Mansour taught at Al-Azhar from 1973 to 1987, and in 1980, he received his doctorate there in Muslim history. His troubles, both with fundamentalists and with the Egyptian regime, began in 1985. His work stressed the centrality of the Qur'an combined with skepticism about the hadith, or sayings of the prophet, and he was consequently accused of being against Islam. In November 1987, the government imprisoned him and twenty-four associates for two months, asserting that he was calling on Muslims to abandon Islam. On November 30, 1987, an article in *Al Ahram*, Egypt's most prestigious paper, claimed he rejected the Sunna and insulted the Companions of the Prophet. On December 5, 1987, *Akhbar Alyoum* described him as an "Enemy of the Sunna."[97]

Farag Foda defended Subhy Mansour, and the two together sought to establish a new political party, the Future Party. After Foda was assassinated, Mansour helped establish the Egyptian Association for Enlightenment, one of whose goals was tolerance between Muslims and Christians. Between 1993 and 2000, he worked with several organizations, including the Egyptian Organization for Human Rights, and with a prominent democracy advocate, Saad Eddin Ibrahim, at the Ibn Khaldoun Center, chairing the center's weekly debate forum and working on curriculum revision. On May 4, 1999, the Muslim Brotherhood's *Alsha'ab* paper, described his educational materials as a Zionist project attacking Islam. On May 16, 1999, *Alsayasy Al Masry* described them as a "Conspiracy to teach Zionist ideology."

After Saad Eddin Ibrahim's arrest and the government's closure of the Ibn Khaldoun Center in June 2000, Mansour and twenty of his associates, now labeled "Quranists," were arrested in October 2001, and he escaped to the United States on October 15, 2001. On March 5, 2002, eight of his associates were convicted in a state security Emergency Court of violating Article 98(F) of the penal code, which forbids insulting a "heavenly religion." Two received three-year prison sentences, and the others received one-year suspended sentences since they were not convicted of actually propagating Quranism.[98]

His books cover a wide range. His 1985 *The Prophets in the Holy Qur'an*, which was banned, argued that the Qur'an shows that Mohammed was not infallible and that he would not intercede on the Day of Judgment. His 1990 *The Qur'an: The Only Source of Islam and Islamic Jurisprudence*, also banned, argues that the Qur'an is properly the only source of Islam.[99] In 1994, the Egyptian Organization for Human Rights published his *Freedom of Speech: Islam and Muslims*, which argued that freedom of speech in Islam should be unlimited and that, historically, Muslims, beginning with the Umayyads and Abbasids, have restricted it for political reasons. Of his twenty-four books, he was unable to publish six, and seven were banned.[100]

Mansour has also argued that a penalty of apostasy "is a fabricated tradition created and applied two centuries after the Prophet Muhammad's death . . . to provide the totalitarian rulers with a religious justification to eliminate their opponents. . . ." In particular, he argued against the common Muslim belief that freedom of religion applies only to not being a Muslim or to joining Islam, but not to leaving Islam. Had God intended to confine compulsion to only joining religion, He would have said, "There should be no forcing INTO joining religion," but He wanted to exclude all types of compulsion in all matters that are related to religion. So He said, "There is no compulsion IN religion."[101]

Like many religious reformers, Mansour also advocates political and social reform. Consequently, he defends Middle Eastern minorities, including the Kurds and the Copts. Similarly, accusations of apostasy are often tied to political repression. In Mansour's words, people suggesting "progressive opinions" will be accused of "opposing the application of Shariah. Such opposition will be interpreted as committing apostasy."[102]

Attacks did not stop after his escape to the United States. On March 29, 2005, Islamist writer Fahmy Howeid wrote in *Al Ahram* that reformers, including Mansour, worked with Jews and were backed by neoconservatives and the CIA. Among those allegedly supporting the project, Howeid singled out Paul Wolfowitz, then assistant secretary of defense, and James Woolsey, past director of Central Intelligence Agency.[103] In October 2009, Mansour was threatened on an Al-Qaeda-linked website that described him as "an infidel whose blood is *halal* to be shed" and an apostate.[104]

In Egypt itself, attacks on Quranists intensified. In May and June, 2007, five were arrested and charged with "insulting religion." They were beaten and also held in the same cells as Islamists, which placed their lives in danger. One was Amr Tharwat, who had worked for the Ibn Khaldoun Center in monitoring elections. Later, two additional defendants were added—Mansour himself, resident in Virginia, and his cousin, Osman Mohamed Ali. Investigators examined Mansour's books, including the ones rejecting the killing of apostates.[105] In October 2008, Quranist blogger Reda Abdelarahman Ali, a relative of Mansour, was arrested and faced charges of defaming Islam. He was released three months later, after the High National Security Court ruled that "arresting people solely on the basis of their religious beliefs is not acceptable." Mansour reports that in detention prisoners have been "severely beaten and humiliated" and "electrified" to make false confessions.[106]

Other Reformers

Given the range of Egyptian cultural life, many other examples can be given. Salah El Din Mohsen, whose *Lecture of the Heaven* and *Memoirs of a Muslim* and *Shivers of Enlightenment* were banned, was sentenced on January 27, 2001 to three years in prison with hard labor for insulting a heavenly religion. Also in 2001, Manal Manea, an outspoken atheist, received three years in prison for blasphemy against Islam.[107] Metwalli Ibrahim Metwalli Saleh, whose unpublished research rejected the idea that apostates should be killed and that a Muslim woman could not marry a non-Muslim man, was arrested in May 2003 and, although the Supreme State Security Emergency Court ruled eight times that he should be released, was held until April 23, 2006.[108]

Dissident intellectuals are also harassed through religious litigation. Islamist lawyer Nabih el Wahsh has filed over a thousand *hisba* cases, though the majority of these were dismissed by Egypt's prosecutor general. He initiated a suit seeking to revoke the State Award of Merit given to Sayed Al Qimni on the ground that

Qimni's writings "deride Islam" and urged that Minister of Culture Farouk Hosni be removed for permitting the award. In 2001, El Wahsh sought, but failed, to have feminist writer Nawal El Saadawi forcibly divorced from her husband, arguing that her opinions proved that she was "an infidel," and, in 2007, he sought the revocation of her Egyptian citizenship. In 2008, El Saadawi won this case and returned to Egypt from the United States, to which she had fled. In October 2009, Naguib Gobraiel—a defense lawyer allegedly assaulted by El Wahsh during the Hegazy case—turned the tables and took El Wahsh to court for abuse of *hisba* charges. Gamal Eid of the Arabic Network for Human Rights Information described *hisba* cases as "a threat hovering over the heads of all intellectuals in Egypt."[109]

Egyptian novelists have also suffered. The most notable was Naguib Mahfouz, the Arab world's only winner of the Nobel Prize in literature. In 1989, he called Iran's Ayatollah Khomeini a terrorist over his death fatwa against Salman Rushdie and asserted, in a joint declaration with eighty other intellectuals, "No blasphemy harms Islam and Muslims so much as the call for murdering a writer."[110] On October 14, 1994, he was stabbed by a member of Gamaat Islamia after Omar Abdel Rahman, the "spiritual leader" of the first attack on the World Trade Center in New York, issued a fatwa against him because of his 1959 novel *Children of the Alley*. The novel had been banned in Egypt, and Rahman claimed that if Mahfouz had also been punished "in the proper Islamic manner," that is, killed, then Salman Rushdie would not have dared to publish his *Satanic Verses*. Mahfouz survived the attack but was permanently disabled.[111]

Closing

Egypt's Muslim Brotherhood has shown some weakness in recent years but remains the most powerful opposition force in the country. One reason for the Brotherhood's strength is that the regime has choked off civil society for decades, thus preventing any challenges and ensuring that the short-term choice is either the Brotherhood or the government. Egypt's reformers are often connected through formal and informal networks. Those described in this chapter, Foda, Al Banna, Al Qimni, Abu-Zayd, and Mansour, as well as others, such as blogger Abdel Kareem Nabil Suleiman, have major differences from one another, but most have sought to be faithful Muslims; they have suffered similar fates, and they have usually supported one another despite their differences.[112] They have also been democracy advocates—several have cooperated with Saad Eddin Ibrahim and his work for human rights, democracy, and an open society. They have advocated freedom of religion and speech and been defenders of the Baha'is and the Copts. In particular, they have criticized civil penalties for apostasy, which, in the vicious circularity of radical Islam, is one reason that they have been labeled apostates. Hence the regime's policies have also choked of the possibilities of religious freedom and religious renewal.

Egypt faces an uncertain future. If it is to have political renewal, one necessary avenue is through religious freedom and thus open religious debate.

As Magdi Khalil has written:

> The advocates of terrorism live comfortably—most of them are rich. Advocates of enlightenment live in hardship, and fund their writings from their own pockets. Some of them are not able to pay their own health bills... advocates of hatred and terrorism distribute their books in abundance, sometimes for free; the advocates of enlightenment oftentimes have a hard time finding a publisher. If they do find a publisher or pay the costs of publication themselves, their books get banned... the advocates of terrorism are stars in Arab societies, and are sometimes given forums in mosques, schools, colleges, newspapers and satellite stations.... Violence may recede as a result of security measures, but terrorism first and foremost is ideas, and it cannot be defeated except through opening windows of light to scatter this obscurantist thought.[113]

5

Pakistan

On February 5, 1997, a torn Qur'an was found in a mosque about a mile from the predominantly Christian village of Shanti Nagar. Some locals maintained that the book was torn by Raji Baba, a Christian resident of Shanti Nagar, since his name and address were written on some loose pages, even though Baba himself was illiterate. Speeches on mosque loudspeakers in nearby Khanewal city and other villages accused the Christians of Shanti Nagar of having burned a copy of the Qur'an. They demanded that faithful Muslims unite to take revenge on the Christians for this alleged act of blasphemy. Shanti Nagar was attacked by a mob of tens of thousands of enraged Muslims. Despite the presence of 300 to 400 police, the rioters burned 326 houses and fourteen churches.[1] There is evidence that at least seventy people were abducted, most of them young girls and women. These hostages were forced to spend one or two nights in the custody of Muslim culprits; several were raped, and some were forcibly married.[2]

In January 2008, in Punjab province, four Ahmadi boys and one man were arrested without any evidence. The accused—three fourteen-year-olds, one sixteen-year-old, and a forty-five-year-old man—had received permission to pray at the local mosque. However, when offensive graffiti was subsequently found on the walls of the mosque's bathroom, the Ahmadis were arrested and charged with blasphemy. The accuser, Liaquat Ali, was among those who saw the graffiti and decided that the act must have been committed by an Ahmadi. A local teacher and leader of an anti-Ahmadi movement, Shahbaz Qasim, agreed and accused the four boys of drawing the graffiti on the instructions of the forty-five-year-old man, Mubashar Ahmed. According to the official complaint, "only they could be responsible for the offense" as they were the only "non-Muslims" in the mosque. The inspector in the case, Khalid Rauf, confirmed that the police did not have any substantial evidence linking the boys with the crime, but, nevertheless, they raided the boys' and Ahmed's homes on January 28 and arrested them all. Within four hours of the arrests, all five had been charged under Article 295-C.[3]

On May 29, 2001, Mohasib, a daily newspaper in Abbottabad, published an article, "Darhi aur Islam" (Beard and Islam), written by Jamil Yousfi, a well-known poet and author of twelve books. In it, he argued against some religious leaders' claims that without a beard one could not be a true Muslim. He explained that in the prophet's lifetime even non-Muslims wore beards. He also criticized self-proclaimed teachers of Islam for exploiting Islam for their personal gain. That same day, in response to Yousfi's article, Mohasib's premises were sealed off, and the paper itself was banned until June 5. Four journalists were arrested:

> *Mohammed Zaman, the editor, Shahid Chaudhry, the managing editor, Shakil Tahirkhelvi, the news editor, and Raja Haroon, a subeditor. The police registered a case under sections 295-A and -C, based on a complaint lodged by the religious group Waqar Jadoon of Khatme Nabuwat Youth Force. Other religious groups, including Jamiat Ulama-e-Isloam and Sipah-e-Sahaba, held a protest at Abbottabad on June 8, in which they denounced the article and demanded death sentences for the writer and journalists.*[4]

Country Overview

Pakistan was created as a home for the Muslims of British India, based on the belief that Hindus and Muslims constituted two nations. Although its population of 176 million is over 90 percent Muslim, it was not intended by its founders to be an Islamic state. In 1947, independence leader Muhammad Ali Jinnah pledged that Hindus, Christians, Parsis, and other religious minorities would enjoy equality with the Muslim majority. Three days before the country's official founding, he stated: "You are free; you are free to go to your temples, you are free to go to your mosques or to any other places of worship in this State of Pakistan. You may belong to any religion or caste or creed—that has nothing to do with the business of the State."[5] In March 1949, the "Objectives Resolution," which was to help guide the constitutional drafting process, stressed "pluralism both within Islam and among non-Islamic religions."[6]

Yet, despite being 18 percent Shia, 3 percent Ahmadi, 2 percent Christian, 2 percent Hindu, and 2 percent "other," including Baha'i, animist, Buddhist, and Parsi, Pakistan has not embraced pluralism and has moved away from many of its founders' principles. Successive governments have subjected much of Pakistan's public life to so-called Islamic principles and have introduced purported sharia into civil and criminal law. While political and religious reformers have sought respect for the rights of all citizens, they have had to struggle continuously with reactionary elements, especially among the *ulema*. Religious reformers, such as the esteemed scholar Fazlur Rahman, who sought to look to the Qur'an and Sunna as a "source of generic values, not specific rules," have faced threats, including accusations of blasphemy. Rahman himself was forced to flee the country and became a professor at the University of Chicago, where he shaped a generation of students. This was America's great gain but Pakistan's great loss.[7]

These internal tensions led to an unstable legal system. The 1956 constitution was abrogated in 1958; the 1962 constitution was abrogated in 1969. The 1973 constitution, though not abrogated by the later martial law regime, was subject to so many amendments that by the 1980s, it was effectively a new constitution.[8]

These changes each gave an increasing role to Islam. The 1956 constitution's references to Islamic sources were tailored to avoid making sharia itself a source of law. However, the 1973 constitution, introduced under Yahya Khan, contained Islamist-leaning provisions. Section 1(1) named the country the "Islamic Republic of Pakistan, hereinafter referred to as Pakistan." Section 2 stated: "Islam shall be the State religion of Pakistan." Section 41(2) required the president to be a Muslim, and Section 227(1) required that all laws "be brought in conformity with the injunctions of Islam as laid down in the Holy Quran and Sunnah...and no law shall be enacted which is repugnant to such Injunctions."[9] It also established the Council of Islamic Ideology to advise Parliament on the compatibility of laws with Islamic law.[10]

After the separation of Bangladesh in the 1970s, the prime minister, Zulfiqar Ali Bhutto, strengthened ties with the Gulf States, looking to Saudi Arabia, the United Arab Emirates, and Kuwait as sources of aid and trade. In 1977, he outlawed alcohol, gambling, and nightclubs and declared that sharia law would be established and enforced. Since Bhutto was deposed in 1977 by a military coup led by General Zia ul-Haq and was hanged on murder charges in 1979, he never implemented these changes. However, as part of a pattern whereby the ulema's influence tends to strengthen under military rule, Zia accelerated legal Islamization. Having a power base only in the armed forces, and lacking democratic legitimacy, he claimed that God spoke to him in a dream and charged him with creating an Islamic state in Pakistan.[11] Zia subsequently introduced compulsory prayers in government offices during working hours, enforced fasting during Ramadan, and encouraged "Islamic standards" in newspapers, TV, radio, the arts, and magazines.[12]

On February 10, 1979, the anniversary of the prophet's birth, *hudad* ordinances were introduced, prescribing amputation, stoning, and whipping for theft, robbery, unlawful sexual intercourse, false accusation of unlawful sexual intercourse, and the consumption of alcohol. Zia also established Shariat Benches at the High Courts, the Federal Shariat Court, and the Shariat Appellate Bench at the Supreme Court to oversee the implementation of sharia criminal law and to evaluate the laws' consistency with sharia.[13]

Blasphemy Laws

It was under Zia that Pakistan's notorious blasphemy laws were introduced. Until then the penal code had criminalized only the "injuring or defiling (of) a place of worship, with intent to insult the religion of any class."[14] In the 1980s, sections 298-A, -B, and -C and 295-B and -C were added, creating what are now generally known as the blasphemy laws.

Section 298-A, added in 1980, stipulates: "Whoever by words, either spoken or written, or by visible representation, or by any imputation, innuendo or insinuation, directly or indirectly, defiles the sacred name of any wife, or members of the family of the Holy Prophet (peace be upon him) or any of the righteous Caliphs or companions of the Holy Prophet (peace be upon him) shall be punished with imprisonment of either description for a term which may extend to three years, or with fine or both." (Sections 298-B and -C, added in 1984, are specifically directed against Ahmadis and are discussed below).

Section 295-B, added in 1982 (incorporated through the implementation of Ordinance I) requires: "Whoever wilfully defiles, damages or desecrates a copy of the Holy Quran or of an extract therefrom, or uses it in any derogatory manner or for any unlawful purpose, shall be punishable with imprisonment for life."

Section 295-C, added in 1986, requires: "Whoever by words, either spoken or written, or by visible representation, or by any imputation, innuendo, or insinuation, directly or indirectly, defiles the sacred name of the Holy Prophet Muhammad (peace be upon him) shall be punished with death, or imprisonment for life, and shall also be liable to fine."[15] The stakes were raised even higher when, in 1990, the Federal Shariat Court ruled, "The penalty for contempt of the Holy Prophet...is death and nothing else." While this is in principle binding, the government has not yet amended the law, which means that the provision for a life sentence still formally exists, and the government uses it as a concession to critics of the death penalty.[16]

With these sections, Pakistan now enforces some of the world's strictest anti-blasphemy laws. They apply only to purported blasphemies against Islam, not against any other religion. While the legal system does not yet include apostasy as such, the Islamization of the law means that any Muslim who decides to leave Islam might well be killed.[17] According to the Pew Research Center, 78 percent of Pakistanis support the death penalty for apostates from Islam.[18] Some lawmakers have also proposed an act imposing the death penalty for male apostates and imprisonment until "penitence" for females. Under this bill, the Apostasy Act of 2006, the property of an apostate would be transferred to his Muslim heirs, and the children would be appointed a legal guardian.[19]

Despite their severity, these vaguely worded statutes do not define blasphemy clearly and contain few safeguards against false accusations. Any person can bring blasphemy charges against another, relying only on circumstantial evidence that may amount merely to a bare accusation, with no requirement to prove intent. This invites serious abuses, particularly against non-Muslims, since their testimony in such cases can be given less weight in court, if not ignored entirely. The testimony of a male non-Muslim in an Islamic court can carry half the value of a male Muslim's testimony, and that of a non-Muslim woman carries one fourth. A non-Muslim may be required by the courts to pay a double penalty to a Muslim he has wronged, while a non-Muslim receives only half of the penalty owed him by a Muslim. In some situations neither a woman nor a non-Muslim is allowed to testify at all. The government has considered amending the blasphemy laws to provide heavy penalties for false accusations, but currently the testimony of a single Muslim is still sufficient to convict a non-Muslim.[20] Under international pressure, and in the light of numerous false blasphemy accusations, in 2005, the Pakistani government established the legal requirement for senior police officials to probe all blasphemy charges before filing formal complaints, but this measure appears to be grossly inadequate.

Blasphemy accusations and laws continue to be used against political adversaries, personal enemies, and unpopular minorities, especially religious minorities. Amnesty International reports that most cases are motivated not by blasphemous actions but by "hostility toward members of minority communities, compounded by personal enmity, professional jealousy or economic rivalry." About half of those accused under the blasphemy laws are Muslims, but a disproportionate number belong to religious minorities. Ahmadis and Christians—3 percent and 2 percent of the population respectively—have taken much of the brunt of intimidation and punishment; Hindus, at 2 percent, also suffer disproportionately.[21] Amnesty International noted in 2007 that the laws are so vague that "they encourage, and in fact invite, the persecution of religious minorities or non-conforming members of [the] Muslim majority."[22] The U.S. Commission on International Religious Freedom reports that the laws "are often used to intimidate reform-minded Muslims, sectarian opponents, and religious minorities, or to settle personal scores." Sometimes cases are brought against those who may be mentally ill.[23]

One of the strangest incidents occurred in Okara on July 28, 2001, when a Muslim and five Christian boys were arrested on blasphemy charges. The boys, ten to fifteen years old, were treating a wounded donkey, and the medicine they used on its wounds streamed in different shapes. A small group of Muslims declared that the boys had written holy names on the donkey, and some extremists demanded that they be arrested for insulting Islam. The boys were arrested, and even the donkey was briefly taken into custody. After an investigation, the police released the children, since many locals submitted affidavits testifying to their innocence.[24]

Pakistan's government says it does not have exact numbers of people charged under blasphemy laws, and other sources offer differing estimates. However, these sources provide some clues to the scale of accusations and arrests. The U.S. State Department says that in the four years up to 2002, some fifty-five to sixty Christians a year were charged with blasphemy. Pakistan's National Commission for Justice and Peace reports that from 1986 to August 2009, at least 964 people were accused. Of these, 479 were Muslims, not including 340 Ahmadis, 119 Christians, 14 Hindus, and 10 of unknown religion. The commission also reported that in the first six months of 2005, sixty people in Punjab alone were the targets of blasphemy complaints; of these, fifty-three were charged. In 2005, eighty Christians accused of blasphemy were in prison. In 2005, thirty-nine Ahmadis were in detention awaiting trial on blasphemy charges, and eleven were serving time.[25] As noted below, data kept by the Ahmadi community itself suggest far higher numbers for Ahmadis charged with blasphemy under various laws.

A greater threat than legal punishment is extralegal attacks, sometimes by vigilantes or mobs and sometimes by the police themselves. While nobody has yet been officially executed under the blasphemy laws, since the 1980s, over thirty accused have been killed, some only minutes after being acquitted. Many others informally accused of blasphemy have also been killed or assaulted, and there have been numerous mob attacks on houses of worship, homes, and businesses.[26] Often the police and security forces fail to take effective action to protect those under attack. The BBC has suggested that, because of blasphemy accusations, "[h]undreds of people have been lynched since the mid-1980s."[27]

For example, Amnesty International reports, "Niamat Ahmer, a teacher, poet and writer, was murdered by extremists in 1992. Bantu Masih, aged 80, was stabbed and killed in the presence of the police in 1992, and Mukhtar Masih, aged 50, was tortured to death in police custody. In 1994, Salamat Masih, aged 12, and Rehmat Masih, aged 42, and Manzoor Masih, aged 37, were fired on in front of the Lahore High Court by extremists, after the former two had been acquitted of blasphemy. Manzoor Masih died on the spot, while Salamat and Rehmat sustained serious injuries. One of the judges in that trial, Arif Iqbal Bhatti, was later murdered."[28] In July 2010, two Christian brothers in Faisalabad were accused of writing a pamphlet critical of Muhammad and, while being escorted by police from a district court, were shot dead. A police officer was critically wounded when unidentified gunmen opened fire.[29]

In 2000, Lahore High Court Judge Nazir Akhtar said publicly that Muslims have a religious obligation to kill anyone accused of blasphemy on the spot, with no need for legal proceedings. Despite a later retraction, this statement shows the degree of prejudice and violence surrounding the issue of blasphemy.[30]

Blasphemy laws also target freedom of the press. On January 9, 2001, a mob burned the printing press of *The Frontier Post* at Peshawar for publishing what it believed to be a blasphemous letter. The protestors, mainly college and *madrassa* students, demanded the publishers be severely punished and promised two million rupees to anyone who would murder Ben Dzac, the author of the letter, who was Jewish. Though the police were present at the newspaper's office, they made no effort to stop the violence. The paper's premises were sealed off by the district administration, and news editor Aftab Ahmed, chief reporter Imtiaz Hussain, feature writer Qazi Ghulam Sarwar, subeditor Muawar Mohsin, and computer technician Wajih-ul-Hassan were charged with blasphemy.[31] In the wake of a series of cartoons of Muhammad being posted online, mainly from America, in May 2010, the government blocked access to YouTube and Facebook websites, which together account for about 25 percent of Internet traffic in the country, to stop Pakistanis from being able to view blasphemous material. The government later said that it would also monitor Google, Yahoo, Amazon, MSN, Hotmail, and Bing for offensive content, while seventeen less well-known sites would be blocked.[32]

Ahmadis

The Ahmadi community, also called *Ahmadiyya*, was founded by Hadhrat Mirza Ghulam Ahmad (1835–1908) in the Punjabi village of Qadian, now in India, in 1889. It has followers in some 166 countries, who usually identify themselves as a movement for spiritual renewal within Islam that emphasizes the wisdom and philosophy that underlie its teachings.[33] Ahmadis typically support tolerance and universal human rights and consistently denounce militant Islam.[34] One of the best-known Pakistani Ahmadis, Abdus Salam (1926–96), received the Nobel Prize in Physics in 1979.

However, most Muslims do not accept Ghulam Ahmad's teachings and maintain that he claimed to be a prophet even though Islam teaches that there can be no prophet after Muhammad. Hence, although Ahmadis consider themselves Muslims, their differences have been deemed by many Muslims sufficient to place them outside Islam. Ahmadis in Pakistan and elsewhere face religious and political attacks and are often declared apostate.[35] They are targeted by government policies, which reinforce discrimination and attacks against them, and by blasphemy laws, the Hudad Ordinances, and even specific anti-Ahmadi laws and constitutional provisions.

In 1974, Section 260(3) of the 1973 constitution was amended to declare that a Muslim believes "in the absolute and unqualified finality of the Prophethood of Muhammad (peace be upon him), the last of the prophets, and does not believe in, or recognize as a prophet or religious reformer, any person who claims to be a prophet, in any sense of the word or of any description whatsoever, after Muhammad (peace be upon him)." This is understood to declare that Ahmadis are not Muslims.[36]

Some blasphemy laws specifically target Ahmadis, described as Quadianis.[37] According to Section 298-B:

(1) Any person of the Quadiani group or the Lahori group (who call themselves Ahmadis or by any other name) who by words, either spoken or written, or by visible representation:
  (a) refers to, or addresses, any person, other than a Caliph or companion of the Holy Prophet Muhammad (Peace be upon him), as *Ameer-ul-Mummineen*, *Khalif-tul-Mumineen*, *Khalifa-tul-Muslimeen*, *Sahaabi* or *Razi Allah Anho*;
  (b) refers to, or addresses, any person, other than a wife of the Holy Prophet Muhammad (Peace be upon him), as *Ummul-Mumineen*;
  (c) refers to, or addresses, any person, other than a member of the family (*Ahle-bait*) of the Holy Prophet Muhammad (Peace be upon him), as *Ahle-bait*; or
  (d) refers to, or names, or calls, his place of worship as *Masjid*; shall be punished with imprisonment of either description for a term which may extend to three years, and shall also be liable to fine.

(2) Any person of the Quadiani group or Lahori group (who call themselves Ahmadis or by any other name) who by words, either spoken and written, or by visible representation, refers to the mode or form of call to prayers followed by his faith as *Azan*, as used by the Muslims, shall be punished with imprisonment of either description for a term which may extend to three years, and shall also be liable to fine.

Section 298-C states:

> Any person of the Quadiani group or Lahori group (who call themselves Ahmadis or by any other name), who, directly or indirectly, poses himself as a Muslim, or calls or refers to, his faith as Islam, or preaches or propagates his faith, or invites others to accept his faith, by words, either spoken or written, or by visible representations in any manner whatsoever outrages the religious feelings of Muslims, shall be punished with imprisonment of either description for a term which may extend to three years and shall also be liable to fine.

Together, these laws prohibit Ahmadis from calling themselves Muslims, from naming their children Muhammad, from nearly any public expression of their faith, and from anything else that could be construed as insulting the "religious feelings" of Muslims.[38] A constitutional challenge to these laws was dismissed by the Pakistani Supreme Court in 1993 on the grounds that the Pakistani state was entitled to "protect" Islamic terms from use by non-Muslims and was necessary for law and order, given that "Ahmadi religious practice, however peaceful, angered and offended the Sunni majority in Pakistan."[39]

As American-Ahmadi leader Mujeeb Ijaz reported, an Ahmadi in Pakistan can even fear being arrested for "saying *assalam-o-lekum* to another Muslim."[40] There is even a requirement for Pakistani Muslims seeking passports to denounce Ahmadi beliefs by declaring in writing:

> I do not recognize any person who claims to be prophet in any sense of the word or of any description whatsoever after Mohammad (peace be upon him) or recognize such a claimant as prophet or a religious reformer as a Muslim.

And, more directly:

> I consider Mirza Ghulam Ahmad Quadiani to be an imposter nabi and also consider his followers whether belonging to the Lahori or Quadiani group, to be NON-MUSLIM.[41]

Ahmadis have faced decades of severe persecution in Pakistan, with their mosques burned and cemeteries desecrated. They are also prohibited from making the pilgrimage to Mecca or burying their dead in Muslim graveyards. Their literature is often confiscated, their attackers are rarely prosecuted or punished, and police complicity in attacks is ignored.[42]

Ahmadis are also disproportionately subject to blasphemy and related charges, such as "hurting the religious feelings" of Muslims. The U.S. State Department reported in 2002 that, since 1999, 316 religiously motivated criminal cases, including blasphemy, had been brought against Ahmadis, some for "crimes" such as wearing an Islamic slogan on a shirt.[43] For example, in July 2002, Zulfiqar Goraya was arrested and charged for "posing as a Muslim," based on greeting cards he had sent out that included a Qur'anic verse and Islamic salutations.[44] In October 2006, police charged Mohammed Tariq with blasphemy because he had allegedly removed anti-Ahmadi stickers placed inside a bus.[45] An Ahmadi-related website estimates that, between April 1984 and December 2008, 756 Ahmadis were charged with illegally displaying the *kalima*, a traditional Islamic testament of faith, 37 with offering a call to prayer, 44 with posing as Muslims, 161 with using Islamic words and epithets, and 679 for preaching. The same estimate reports over 900 other charges of violating section 298-B and -C, 258 cases under 295-C, and more than 24 for distributing pamphlets criticizing the laws against them.[46] The following are five out of hundreds of such incidents.

Attar Ullah Warraich, from the Bahawalnagar district, in Punjab province, was charged with violating section 298-B on September 8, 1999. The accusation, by members of the radical Khatam-e Nabuwwat organization, alleged that he had built a minaret and a niche in a mosque adjacent to his house, possessed a copy of the Qur'an, and taught Ahmadiyyat. He responded that he had not had the mosque built, that it had been there decades, that he did not own the land on which it stood, and that he was not its caretaker. The judge concluded that a Qur'an had been found in the mosque, as had Ahmadi literature, and that Warraich had built the mosque in its current form. The judge then inexplicably added that the mosque may have been built before the passing of section 298-C made it a criminal offense, but that Warraich "should have changed the shape of the mosque after the said amendment." Since he was a first-time offender and an illiterate farmer, the judge claimed to exercise leniency and on January 31, 2000, sentenced Warraich to rigorous imprisonment for two years with a fine of Rs. 2,000.[47]

On July 31, 2000, Ghulam Mustafa, Hamid, Maqsud Ahmad, and Mian Fazil were charged under sections 298-C and 295-A for "injuring the feelings of Muslims" in Bharokay Kalan, Sialkot district. They had allegedly dared to watch an Ahmadiyya television program in a garage that had its door open because of the mid-summer heat. However, Ghulam Mustafa, who was head of the Daryapur Ahmadiyya community, had never even been to Bharokay. Subsequently fifty local men gave written testimony that the allegations against the trio were false. Still, two of the men were kept in detention for at least a year.[48]

On September 7, 2008, the anchorman for the religious television program *Alam Online*, Dr. Amir Liaquat Hussain, urged Muslims not to be afraid to kill Ahmadis, and two other Islamic scholars on the program supported him. Within twenty-four hours, six vigilantes found their way into the Fazle Umer Clinic in Mirpur Khas city and killed forty-five-year-old Dr. Abdul Manan Siddiqui, who was shot eleven times. The killers waited at the hospital until the doctor was pronounced dead and then fearlessly walked out the front door. Meanwhile the police registered the killers as unknown. A second killing occurred forty-eight hours after Hussain's statement was broadcast. Yousaf, a seventy-five-year-old rice trader and local Ahmadi leader, was shot as he went to pray in Nawab Shah. He was hit three times and died on his way to the hospital. No arrests were made.[49]

In March 2009, in Sillanwali Tehsil, Punjab province, fifteen Ahmadi men were arrested when a local radical religious leader complained that the building they were using for worship resembled a mosque, in violation of Section 298-C, which forbids Ahmadis to pose as, or call themselves, Muslims "or in any manner whatsoever to outrage the religious feelings of Muslims." Although Ahmadis had been using the facility for decades without a word of official complaint, the police complied with the radical leader's demands. Three of the fifteen were detained and denied bail.[50]

In one of the most horrific attacks in recent years, on May 28, 2010, gunmen attacked two Ahmadi mosques or worship centers (in Pakistan it is illegal to call them *masjid*, mosques) during Friday prayers in Lahore, firing shots and setting off grenades. The attacks took place within minutes of each other at locations several miles apart, and ninety-three people were killed. It took the police several hours to regain control, and, when they entered the mosque, several of the attackers blew themselves up with suicide vests packed with explosives. It was reported that the Pakistan Taliban claimed responsibility for the attack. While Ahmadis suffer frequent violent attacks, this is the first coordinated one bearing the mark of careful planning by militants.[51] A week later, the former prime minister, Nawaz Sharif, shocked much of the country by referring to Ahmadis as his "brothers and sisters."[52]

Christians

Christians, some 2 percent of the population, are mainly descendants of converts from Hinduism and suffer widespread abuse and harassment because of their religious beliefs and usually very low socioeconomic status. This leaves them particularly vulnerable to blasphemy accusations.[53] Following are a few examples out of many hundreds.[54]

After a disagreement with a Muslim neighbor in 1996, Ayub Masih, a Christian, was accused of speaking favorably of Salman Rushdie, author of *The Satanic Verses*. On November 6, 1997, one of Ayub's accusers, Mohammad Akram, shot the defendant outside the court, wounding him. Although there were firsthand accounts of the crime, the police refused to investigate Akram. Many of the Muslim defense lawyers and judges in the case also received death threats. On April 27, 1998, a court in the Punjab town of Sahiwal sentenced Ayub to death for alleged blasphemy, relying only on the complainants' statement. A lower appeals courts upheld the sentence, as did the High Court. During his six years in prison, there were at least two attempts on his life.[55] Eventually, his lawyer was able to prove that Akram had used the conviction to force Ayub's family off their land and to acquire control of it himself.[56] On August 16, 2002, Ayub was acquitted by the Supreme Court, who ordered his immediate release from the high-security cell in the Multan New Central Jail. Faced with ongoing death threats, Ayub quietly left Pakistan in early September 2002. Not only had he lost nearly six years in prison, but also he had forfeited his home simply because a contentious neighbor wanted his land.

Ayub's death sentence may also have provoked the death, perhaps by suicide, of prominent Catholic bishop John Joseph of Faisalabad. On May 6, 1998, Bishop Joseph was shot in the same courtroom and at the same spot where Ayub had been shot; he died on the steps of the courthouse. Many Pakistani Christians interpreted his death as a protest against the blasphemy law, and thousands marched at his funeral to protest his death and to oppose the laws. Hundreds were arrested, and two Christians were jailed on blasphemy charges because of remarks they allegedly made. One, Ranjha Masih, was sentenced on April 26, 2003, to life imprisonment and a 50,000-rupee fine on the charge of desecrating a sign on which was printed a declaration of Islamic faith: Ranjha had allegedly thrown a stone that hit the sign. Ranjha worked for the Pakistan People's Party (PPP), and the accusation against him came from a political opponent.[57]

In an especially peculiar accusation, Aslam Masih (Masih is a common Christian surname in Pakistan referring, in Arabic, to the Messiah) of Faisalabad, an illiterate Christian man in his mid-fifties, was arrested in November 1998 on charges that he had hung verses from the Qur'an in a charm around a dog's neck.[58] Court testimony indicates that some local Muslims resented seeing a Christian as a successful farmer and so refused to pay him for animals he had sold them. Subsequently, they stole all of his animals and filed a blasphemy case. Some locals then beat him up and handed him over to the police, where he faced further abuse. When his case was finally heard three and a half years later, a mob often gathered outside the courtroom while the prosecution produced only hearsay evidence against him. Nevertheless, he was found guilty in May 2002 and given two life sentences.[59] He was often placed in solitary confinement and regularly beaten by other prisoners so that he became traumatized and suffered memory loss. After four and a half years, during which his family was allowed to visit him only three times, the Lahore High Court finally acquitted him on June 4, 2003. The appeals hearing took only five minutes, and, in overturning the conviction, Justice Najam ur-Zaman criticized the prosecution, noting that their chief witness had retracted his statement. However, Aslam has had to remain in hiding, with continuing threats on his life and against those who have sheltered him. On one occasion, arsonists set ablaze the house in which he was hiding.[60]

Yet another Christian named Masih—Younis Masih, age twenty-nine—was arrested and charged with blasphemy in September 2005 near Lahore, after locals told police he made derogatory remarks against Islam and Muhammad. He told Shahbaz Bhatti, who was then head of the All Pakistan Minorities Alliance, that dozens of Muslims attacked him on September 10, 2005, when he asked them not to sing loudly, because his nephew had died, and his body was still lying at home. On May 30, 2007, Younis Masih was sentenced to death. His appeals continue.[61]

In early July 2009, Imran Masih, a Christian living in Faisalabad, was accused of having desecrated the Qur'an. Following a common practice, Imran had cleaned out waste paper from his shop and burned it in the street. A nearby shop owner, possibly motivated by a business rivalry, accused him of burning pages of the Qur'an and blaspheming against Islam and its Prophet. He repeated the accusation to other Muslims, by some reports through a mosque loudspeaker. Imran was subsequently attacked, beaten, and tortured by an angry mob, which also looted his shop. Police intervened to stop the beating, but then they themselves detained Imran. On January 11, he was convicted of violating Sections 295-A and -B of the penal code and received a life sentence, as well as a fine of over $1,000 for intentionally burning the Qur'an so as to "foment interfaith hatred and hurt the feelings of Muslims."[62]

Several of the most brutal attacks against Pakistani Christians in recent years began on July 30, 2009, in the village of Korian, home to around 100 Christian families. Several days after a Korian family was accused of throwing torn pieces of a Qur'an in the air at a wedding ceremony, where guests threw money in the air according to custom, mosque loudspeakers began calling for attacks against Christians. A mob of angry Muslims, armed with guns and explosives, used trucks to break through walls and gasoline to start fires. Approximately sixty houses were destroyed, two churches were ransacked, and livestock was stolen. Many families were able to escape and hide in the fields, where they watched their homes burn to the ground.[63]

The blasphemy charges and attendant violence soon reached the town of Gojra, where, on August 1, a crowd of around 1,000 Muslims, believed to be connected to the Taliban-linked Sipah-e-Sahaba militant group, attacked local Christians. Over forty homes were razed, and at least seven Christians were killed, six of whom (including two children) were burned alive. The independent Human Rights Commission of Pakistan (HRCP) found, in a report released on August 4, 2009, that the police had been aware of plans for the attack in Gojra, which appears to have been premeditated, but had not acted to stop it. "The police remained silent spectators," said Zahid Iqbal, a local councillor. According to the HRCP, calls for Muslims to "make a mincemeat of Christians" in retaliation for the alleged blasphemy had come from Gojra mosques the previous night.[64]

Following the Gojra riots, Shahbaz Bhatti, then Minister of Minority Affairs, declared that "[t]he blasphemy law is being used to terrorize minorities in Pakistan."[65] Asma Jahangir, chair of HRCP, stated that Pakistan was witnessing a "pattern" of rising violence against religious minorities, while local politicians protect the violators "and keep their names out of police reports."[66] On October 1, Pope Benedict XVI met with President Asif Ali Zardari of Pakistan and discussed the growing trend of anti-Christian violence in Pakistan, and there was talk of amending the laws.[67]

Despite these discussions, blasphemy convictions against Christians continued in 2010. On February 25, Qamar David received a twenty-five-year prison sentence for allegedly outraging Muslim religious feelings by disseminating blasphemous text messages concerning Muhammad and the Qur'an.[68] In early March, a Christian couple were found guilty of desecrating the Qur'an after allegedly touching it without first washing their hands. Witnesses at the trial asserted that the couple had used the Qur'an in a black magic ritual and that they had written the Muslim profession of faith on the walls of their home. The couple, Munir Masih and Ruqqiya Bibi, were sentenced to twenty-five-year jail terms.[69] On June 19, 2010, Rehmat Masih, believed to be eighty-five years old, was arrested by police in Jhumray and sent to Faisalabad District Jail. He had been accused of blasphemy by a Muslim neighbor, Muhammad Sajjid Hameed, with whom he had a land dispute.[70] In November 2010, Asia Bibi, a mother of five, was sentenced to death for blasphemy in the town of Sheikhupura, near Lahore.[71]

Hindus

According to the 1998 census, Hindus, including scheduled castes, comprise almost 2 percent of Pakistan's population and are concentrated in the province of Sindh. They suffer from discrimination, economic hardships, and religious persecution and are often randomly attacked in general retaliation for attacks, or perceived attacks, on Muslims in India. They are also targeted by blasphemy accusations, although perhaps not as frequently as Ahmadis or Christians are targeted.

One example took place in July 2001. A Hindu, Ram Chand, who lived in Chack, Bahawalpur district, was constructing a bathroom floor for Mohammed Safdar. Safdar accused the laborer of defiling the name of the Prophet by carving it on a brick and took the brick to the village head. Deeply offended by this so-called act of blasphemy, local Muslims attacked homes and other property belonging to Hindus and also beat up Hindu women and children. Meanwhile, the police arrested Chand and his son, Ram-Yazman, charging them with blasphemy. Local Muslims reacted to these charges even more ferociously, blocking the road for hours and demanding that all Hindus be expelled from the area. Police arrested twenty Muslims for attacking Hindus.[72]

On April 9, 2008, a Hindu factory worker in Karachi, Jagdesh Kumar, was beaten to death by coworkers after allegedly making remarks that blasphemed against Islam. Factory guards made a failed attempt to take Kumar into protective custody, while police officers who responded to the incident were later suspended for their failure to take proper action to prevent Kumar's death.[73]

Muslims

While charged proportionally less than religious minorities, Muslims, including Shias, Sufis, and Muslim reformers, but excluding Ahmadis, account for about half of those targeted by blasphemy accusations. In fact, adherents of the Deobandi school of Islam, from which the Taliban sprang, and which has been increasing its strength throughout much of Pakistan, have been carrying out a largely underreported violent campaign against Pakistani Shias and Sufis on the grounds that they are apostates.[74]

Mohammed Yousuf Ali, of Lahore, a Sufi mystic, was charged with blasphemy based on accusations that he claimed that he was a prophet. He denied the charge, and several of the prosecution witnesses admitted that they did not fully understand what he was actually teaching. However, the local media vilified him, and his trial was held in camera. On August 5, 2000, he was convicted of blasphemy under section 295-C and sentenced to death, thirty-five years of hard labor, and a fine. Ali was kept in Kotlakpat Jail in Lahore under poor conditions; he became ill, developing difficulty in speaking and in using his fingers, but was denied adequate medical treatment.[75]

Zahid Shah was charged with blasphemy and was jailed in September 1994. His detention was based on a complaint by an imam, Maulvi Faqir Mohammed, who said that Zahid had desecrated the Qur'an and made derogatory remarks about Muhammad.[76] In 1997, he was released on bail by a local court and went to live with his brother at Faisalabad while the case was pending. In 2002, he returned home and unwisely became involved in an argument with some locals. Upon hearing that he had returned, Faqir Mohammed convened a *Panchayat*—council of elders—on July 5, 2002. After evening prayers, the imam broadcasted a fatwa over mosque loudspeakers, urging people to kill Zahid. Assailants broke into his house, hauled him outside, and beat him with iron rods and sticks in front of his wife and brother. His brother begged for mercy and promised that the accused would leave the village forever, but neither the mob nor the imam accepted these pleas. After Zahid lost consciousness, the mob dragged him to the village's main intersection, where people from nearby villages quickly gathered; and when he regained consciousness, the mob stoned him to death. Police arrived hours later, did not arrest anyone, and did not send the body for an autopsy. No case was registered against the culprits because Zahid's relatives were afraid to press charges. Several days later, the police did arrest thirty people, including the imam, for their role in the stoning.[77]

Some cases developed over allegations of what appears to be accidents. In 1996, one man slipped and fell onto a stove while holding a Qur'an. A page was burned, and the unfortunate individual was imprisoned. After a cleric incited them against the alleged blasphemer, a mob accosted and burned him alive in his jail cell while he was awaiting trial.[78]

A blasphemy accusation similarly provoked the murder of Najeeb Zafar, owner of a leather factory in Muridke in Punjab and a member of one of Pakistan's leading industrialist families, by other factory workers on August 5, 2009. A factory supervisor, Qasim, objected when he saw Zafar taking down an old wall calendar and remove tape from it since the calendar had "holy verses" on it. After quarreling with the owner, Qasim incited factory workers and local residents with a charge of Qur'an desecration, and they stormed the factory, seized weapons from security guards, and murdered Zafar and an employee.[79]

The Pakistan government's ongoing war against the Taliban overlaps with repression of purported blasphemy. In February 2009, the government and the Taliban signed a short-lived agreement pledging to enforce sharia law in the Swat Valley region, partially in recognition that the Taliban were already in effective control. A spate of violence followed in the frontier provinces and tribal areas. In March 2009, three days after a threatening letter arrived at a Peshawar mausoleum commemorating the seventeenth-century Sufi poet Baba, a bomb exploded and damaged a portion of the shrine. The letter had warned against further promotion of "shrine culture" and spoke disparagingly of the fact that women were coming to pray at the shrine as well as men.[80] On July 1, 2010, there was a suicide bomb attack by three people on the Data Darbar shrine in Lahore, which commemorates an eleventh-century Sufi saint, Ali bin Usman, and is probably Pakistan's most popular Sufi shrine. The attacks took place on a Thursday evening, the most popular evening for crowds to gather; fifty-two people were killed and nearly 200 wounded. Although there was no claim of responsibility, Islamist extremists often accuse Sufis of being heretical, and officials maintain that it was the work of Punjabi Taliban.[81]

Muslim Reformers
Mohammad Younas Shaikh

According to scholar Akbar Ahmed, "perhaps dozens" of Pakistani educators that have spoken out in favor of reforms have faced blasphemy accusations from their students. Among them is Dr. Mohammad Younas Shaikh, a professor who taught at the medical college in Islamabad. He did post-graduate studies in Dublin and London, and he was a participant in the Pakistan-India Forum for Peace and Democracy, a member of the South Asian Fraternity, the South Asian Union, and the Human Rights Commission of Pakistan. In 1990, he started an organization called "The Enlightenment," dedicated to discussing Islam in a contemporary context. As its name indicates, it draws inspiration from the European Enlightenment and Renaissance. However, Shaikh still considers himself a devout Muslim and draws inspiration from the Qur'an.[82]

On October 1, 2000, Shaikh had suggested at a meeting of the South Asian Union that the line of control in Kashmir between India and Pakistan should become the international border. In response, a Pakistani officer threatened him, saying, "I will crush the heads of those that talk like this." The following day, Shaikh reportedly stated in response to a student's query that Muhammad was neither a prophet nor a Muslim before he was forty, since there was at that point no Islam (according to Islamic teaching, Muhammad received Qur'anic revelation when he was forty). Shaikh was also reported to have said that Muhammad had not observed Muslim practices regarding circumcision or the removal of underarm hair before that age.[83]

Some students thought he contradicted the Muslim belief that Muhammad was predestined to become a prophet and hence was blasphemous. That evening, one of them, who was also employed at the Pakistani Foreign Ministry, complained to a cleric that the doctor had blasphemed.[84] An organization that frequently targets alleged blasphemers (usually Ahmadis), called the Movement for the Finality of the Prophet, lodged a complaint against him and also incited a mob that threatened to burn the college and the local police station.[85] On October 4, Shaikh was arrested on blasphemy charges.

His trial took place in closed session in the Central Jail. Even his lawyers received a fatwa calling them apostates, and their childrens' lives were threatened.[86] On August 18, 2001, he was found guilty and sentenced to death.[87] He spent two years in solitary confinement in the Central Gaol in Rawalpindi. The two judges on the Lahore High Court could not reach an agreement on his appeal, and a senior judge to whom the case was referred on July 15, 2002, did not make a decision for over a year. On October 9, 2003, this judge found the original judgment unsound. However, he opted to remand the case back to a lower court for retrial rather than acquit Shaikh. At the retrial, Shaikh conducted his own defense and was acquitted on November 21, 2003. He says he was inspired by Sir Thomas More's speech in *A Man for All Seasons*. To avoid further attacks, he was released secretly. He remained in Pakistan for a time but, when his accusers sought to appeal his acquittal, fled to Europe.[88]

Faraz Jawad

On July 7, 2002, during mosque prayers, Faraz Jawad, an American Navy engineer who was visiting his family in Jaranwala, objected to the imam's political speech that cursed the Pakistan government and the Americans. He said to the imam, "Instead of cursing America, you should teach us Islam." The imam, Hafiz Abdul Latif, demanded that those in the mosque kill Jawad on the spot since he was an American and, as such, an enemy of Muslims. Jawad managed to escape with his relative Mohammed Naeem. In response, dozens of people attacked Naeem's house, armed with iron rods, sticks, and other weapons. Naeem called the police, who dispersed the mob, but only after promising the rioters that Jawad would be charged with blasphemy. Jawad contacted the U.S. embassy, which intervened and asked the government to save his life. Police subsequently charged the imam and twelve villagers with disturbing the peace, inciting the people's religious feelings, and attacking Faraz Jawad's relatives.[89]

Najam Sethi

Najam Sethi, the chief editor of one of Pakistan's most respected English newspapers, *Daily Times*, is Cambridge-educated and a recipient of the Committee to Protect Journalists' International Press Freedom award. He is well known for his paper's stance against Islamic extremism. In July 2008, he received death threats, including a picture of a man whose throat had been slit, for publishing a cartoon of Umme Hassan, the director of a radical women's madrassa, who was teaching her students to wage jihad. Hassan, as well as local clerics from the Red Mosque, condemned the cartoon as blasphemous and in so doing, according to Mr. Sethi, "have provoked people to kill me and my staff."[90]

Closing

In Pakistan, as in other countries with blasphemy laws, people can, in practice, be charged with any of a range of vague offenses, such as damaging "religious feelings." Rules of evidence are commonly violated, and the laws are very frequently used to settle private disputes, grudges, and vendettas. During blasphemy hearings, religious extremists often pack courthouses and threaten the accused, especially if there is the possibility of an acquittal. To make matters worse, in a vicious ratchet effect, those who question the blasphemy laws can then themselves be accused of questioning Islam, thus becoming suspects under the very law that they have challenged.

   This ratcheting effect came into stark and violent relief in early 2011, when two brave politicians were brutally murdered specifically because of their calls to repeal the laws. Salman Taseer, a Muslim, was the governor of Punjab, Pakistan's wealthiest and most populous state, and a friend of President Zardari. He was also a voice of moderation, one of the most prominent in the country, who worked for a free society and fought for the rights of all Pakistanis, Muslim and non-Muslim. He publicly called for a pardon for Asia Bibi and persistently criticized the blasphemy laws, calling them a "black law," and arguing that they were pivotal to the future of the country. On January 4, 2011, he was killed by one of his own security guards, Mumtaz Qadri, who has since been feted as a hero in much of Pakistan. Taseer's daughter, Sara, observed, "This is a message to every liberal to shut up or be shot."[91]

   Then, on March 2, 2011, Shahbaz Bhatti, federal Minster of Minority Affairs and the highest-ranking Christian politician in the country, was shot dead as he was visiting his mother. In leaflets left at the scene, Al-Qaeda and the Pakistani

Taliban Movement in Punjab claimed responsibility for killing the "infidel Christian." Bhatti, who has been compared to Martin Luther King, devoted his life to religious freedom and other human rights, was well aware that he was targeted for death, and, in a video he left to be played in the event that he was killed, said he would not change his principles and was ready to die for his work.[92]

As we have seen, so far, none of the convicted in Pakistan has in fact been judicially executed, in part because the trials can take many years, and scheduling an execution can take even longer. However, mobs and vigilantes have killed hundreds of the accused.[93] This intimidation means that while, in elections, the vast majority of Pakistanis reject radical parties, a free press and free debate on religion and politics is quashed. A *New York Times* report summarizes the country's predicament: "[A]n intolerant, aggressive minority terrorizes a more open-minded, peaceful majority, while an opportunistic political class dithers, benefiting from alliances with the aggressors."[94] However, when former President Musharraf sought to change the laws, militants warned, "If the government tries to finish it, the government itself will be finished," a threat personified in the killings of Taseer and Bhatti.

A more hopeful note was struck when, on March 9, 2011, Pakistan's embassy to the United States held a memorial service for Bhatti, and Ambassador Husain Haqqani's moving eulogy went far beyond formal diplomatic niceties and cut to the heart of the matter:

> "[M]y colleagues in the embassy from all wings of the embassy, from our accounts department to our military leaders who serve here, to the diplomats, and to the non-diplomatic staff in this embassy—we all discussed this and it was our collective decision that we will not only pay tribute to Shahbaz Bhatti today but also to use this as an occasion to reiterate our commitment to a pluralist Pakistan, a tolerant Pakistan, a moderate Pakistan—a Pakistan in harmony with the rest of the world.... For the sake of Pakistan, for the sake of Islam, for the sake of humanity, and for the sake of Shaheed Benazir Bhutto, Shaheed Salman Taseer, and now sadly our brother Shahbaz Bhatti, it is time for us to stand up, courageously against intolerance, against discrimination and against extremism. My friends, "If not now, when?"

Haqqani concluded: "Those who would murder a Salman Taseer or a Shahbaz Bhatti deface my religion, my prophet, my Koran and my Allah. Yet there is an overpowering, uncomfortable and unconscionable silence from the great majority of Pakistanis who respect the law, respect the Holy Book, and respect other religions.... This silence endangers the future of my nation, and to the extent the silence empowers extremists, it endangers the future of peace and the future of the civilized world.... When a Shahbaz Bhatti is murdered, and we remain silent, we have died with him."[95]

Afghanistan

In a 2002 interview with the Washington Post, Sayed Abdullah described being brutally tortured for months by Taliban agents. Abdullah, a Red Cross employee with some knowledge of English and an interest in the world outside Afghanistan, had a 500-book library that included two Bibles, one in English and one in Dari. In late 1999, the Taliban's Intelligence Division took him into custody and searched his house. When they found the two Bibles, they immediately assumed they'd found evidence that Abdullah was an apostate. Abdullah maintained throughout every interrogation that he was still a Muslim and tried to explain, "I have those books for information, for learning, not for changing religions. Everyone should know about other religions and other parts of the world." His Taliban adversaries were unimpressed with this explanation and instead tortured him repeatedly. Meanwhile, they demanded that he inform them about whom he was working for and provide them with names of others he had converted. A prison record found after the fall of the Taliban listed Abdullah as jailed for "belonging to the Christian religion." He stated that his torturers chanted, "God is blessing us. God will reward us," as they beat him and repeatedly accused him of being a Christian convert. Eventually, Abdullah made a false confession in order to end the torture. A Taliban official then threatened him with death: "We will take you to the roof of the Ministry of Communications.... First we will burn you. Then we will throw you over the edge so that everyone can see you and know the punishment for converting from Islam." Eventually, Abdullah's mother was informed about his situation and was able to bribe officials to obtain his release. Because of what he endured in the Taliban's prisons, Abdullah now requires a brace to stand and suffers from chronic pain as well as problems with his kidneys, short-term memory, hearing, and sight.[1]

In August 2007, approximately 100 Afghans demonstrated in the southeastern region of Khost after American soldiers presented local children with soccer balls decorated with the flags of various countries. One of the flags was that of Saudi Arabia, which carries the Islamic declaration of faith, the shehada. Afghan parliamentarian Mirwais Yasini explained the problem: "[T]o have a verse of the Koran on something you kick with your foot would be an insult in any Muslim country around the world." A U.S. spokesperson expressed regret for the unintentional offense caused by the gifts.[2] The following month, the Afghan parliament announced, "The people's representatives want them (U.S.-led forces) to formally apologize out of respect for public opinion and sentiment...we, representing the people of Afghanistan, want our friendly forces to respect the culture and tradition of people in their activities."[3]

Country Overview

After the withdrawal of Soviet forces in 1989 and the toppling of the communist government in 1992, the Taliban ("students") militia seized control of much of the country and installed a highly repressive version of Islam. In response to the terrorist attacks of September 11, 2001, the United States launched a military campaign aimed at toppling the Taliban and eliminating the Al-Qaeda terrorist network's safe haven there. Afghanistan ultimately adopted a new constitution and a new government, which has since been led by Hamid Karzai. The population of the country is about thirty million; of that, approximately 80 percent is Sunni, 19 percent is Shia, including a small Ismaili community, and 1 percent is "other," including Sikhs, Hindus, Christians, and, in 2008, one remaining Jew. There is a correlation between religious and ethnic identities: the Sunni population comprises mainly Pashtuns, Turkmen, Uzbeks, and Tajiks, while the Shia Muslims are mainly Hazaras, with some Qizilbash from the mountainous central highlands. Though many Sikhs and Hindus fled the country during the Taliban's rule, approximately 1,500 Sikh and 100 Hindu families remain, along with a Christian community consisting of 500 to 8,000 people. A handful of Sikh and Hindu temples are left in the country, along with one official Christian church and one Jewish synagogue.

The Taliban's Continuing Depredations

The Taliban has persecuted, and, where it can, continues to persecute, anyone who does not adhere to its reactionary brand of Islam, and the vast majority of its victims have been Muslims. When in power, they also specifically targeted anybody thought to be connected to criticism or conversion of Muslims. On January 8, 2001, reputed leader Mullah Mohammed Omar made a radio announcement warning that his government would execute both apostates from Islam and any non-Muslim who attempted to convert Muslims. Omar also decreed that any owners of bookshops offering texts that criticized Islam, or that even discussed other religions, would receive a five-year jail sentence.[4]

In August of that year, Taliban officials arrested eight foreign Christians working for the Shelter Now International (SNI) aid organization, claiming that they had been "trying to convert Afghan Muslims to Christianity." Two women from the group had been arrested on August 3 while presenting a Christian film to an Afghan family, and the six others were arrested on August 5. Taliban agents cited Dari-language Christian materials as evidence of the employees' involvement in "proselytism."[5] Sixteen of the organization's Afghan employees were also arrested, although their friends and coworkers maintained that they were all firmly Muslim. Unlike the foreigners, the incarcerated Afghans were not allowed visitors, and Taliban representatives said they might face death or life imprison-ment. The Taliban even detained sixty-four children who had been in contact with the aid workers, holding them until any possible "Christian influences" on them could be eradicated.[6] In keeping with their assertions that there was a "larger conspiracy" behind SNI's alleged proselytism, the Taliban closed the offices of two more Christian relief agencies, SERVE and the International Assistance Mission (IAM) and expelled their foreign workers at the end of August. After the expul-sion, officials exhibited Bibles and Christian videos they claimed to have seized from the foreigners to prove their point. Thirty-five Afghan employees of IAM were later arrested when Taliban officials ordered them to pick up their salaries at the planning ministry.[7] Following the September 11, 2001, attacks on the United States, President Bush listed the release of the foreign workers among the demands made on the Taliban. On September 27, the Taliban said it would resume their trial. When the Taliban evacuated Kabul on November 13, they confined their prisoners in a steel container and drove them south: they were freed on November 15 when Northern Alliance troops liberated the prison in which they were held.[8]

Even after its collapse as a government, the Taliban continued its practices wherever it could. On July 1, July 15, July 23, July 28, and August 7, 2004, Taliban supporters murdered five Afghan converts to Christianity by stabbing or beating them to death. In the first case, a Taliban representative, Abdul Latif Hakimi, phoned Reuters and announced that "Taliban dragged out Assad Ullah and slit his throat with a knife because he was propagating Christianity." Hakimi warned foreign aid workers, whom he accused of proselytizing, that "they face the same destiny as Assad Ullah if they continue to seduce people." Local sources said Ullah was killed in broad daylight at a local market and his body dragged around the marketplace as an example to those who might have been swayed by his teachings.[9]

Between May and July 2005, at least six Afghan Muslim clerics who criticized the Taliban were murdered. The first, Maulvi Abdullah Fayyaz, had declared that Taliban leader Omar could no longer claim the title "leader of the faithful," which he had assumed in 1995. Twelve other clerics were killed in 2006, and eleven were killed in 2007, either for supporting the government or for declaring that terror-ism is against Islam.[10]

On July 19, 2007, Taliban forces kidnapped twenty-three South Korean Christians from Saemmul Presbyterian Church who were visiting Afghanistan as short-term volunteers. They killed two and freed two others after the South Korean government agreed to negotiate directly with them. On August 28, the South Korean government agreed to pull its 200 military support personnel out of Afghanistan by the end of 2007 and to block missionary activities by South Korean evangelical groups as a condition of the remaining hostages' release. The government said that they had merely confirmed the existing timetable to with-draw troops and that an agreement to withdraw South Korean volunteers and missionaries had already been made.[11]

The New Constitution

The vicious persecution by the Taliban regime of anyone whose practice differed from its version of Islam is well known, and persecution has lessened since they were deposed. However, with respect to blasphemy and apostasy provisions, particularly in the media, Afghanistan remains highly repressive. The Afghan constitution, adopted under American auspices in January 2004, borrows heavily from what it describes as Islamic principles.[12] Article 1 identifies the state as an "Islamic Republic," and Article 2 declares Islam the state religion. More worrisome, Article 3 sets forth the vague mandate that "no law can be contrary to the beliefs and provisions of the sacred religion of Islam." Article 35 declares that Afghans can only form political parties if "the program and charter of the party are not contrary to the principles of the sacred religion of Islam." Article 54 declares that the state should ensure "the elimination of traditions contrary to the principles of the sacred religion of Islam." Article 130 states that where statutory law does not directly cover a case, courts are to make decisions according to the Hanafi school of jurisprudence. Article 131 permits the use of Shia jurisprudence if only Shias are party to the dispute. The president is constitutionally required to be a Muslim and, with all Ministers, to swear to obey and support "the provisions of the sacred religion of Islam." Supreme Court justices must take similar oaths.

The constitution does not state what the principles of Islam are. But, whatever they are, they are the law, and "ignorance about the provisions of laws" (Article 56) will be no defense against them. Article 149 protects all such articles and declares, "The provisions of adherence to the fundamentals of the sacred religion of Islam and the regime of the Islamic Republic cannot be amended." Hence, undefined principles that cannot be amended are Afghanistan's ultimate legal authority.

Chief Justice Shinwari

The 2004 constitution's initial major interpreter was Afghanistan's first post-Taliban Supreme Court Chief Justice, Fazil Hadi Shinwari, who added his own unique perspectives to the justice system. At the time of his appointment, he was leader of the Council of Islamic Scholars.[13] In January 2002, he announced that he would enforce strict sharia penalties, including amputations for theft, lashing or stoning for adultery, and possible executions for non-Muslim proselytizers. He explained, "We can punish them for propagating other religions—such as threaten them, expel them and, as a last resort, execute them, but only with evidence."[14]

In February 2002, National Public Radio reported, that Afghanistan's chief justice found a sword in his office when he moved in and thereafter kept it above his desk to enforce what he considers Islam's three essential rules: first, that a man should politely be invited to accept Islam; second, that if he does not convert, he should obey Islam. "And if he does not do that, then the third option is to use that sword and to behead him."[15]

In 2006, the Afghan parliament rejected President Karzai's renomination of Shinwari to head the Supreme Court, and Abdul Salam Azimi, who boasted sounder legal credentials and has kept a somewhat lower profile than his predecessor, replaced Shinwari.[16] However, this does not appear to have made much difference in legal interpretations of blasphemy and apostasy provisions. Local municipal and provincial judges often ignore statute laws and base their judgments on their personal understanding of sharia, tribal codes of honor, or local customs. *Shuras*—Islamic legal consultations that handle, by some estimates, 80 percent of cases—do not recognize any constitutional rights, and women and minorities frequently suffer rights violations at their hands.[17] In fact, many areas are not under the effective control of the Kabul-based government and are subject to the dictates of the Taliban or other violent groups.

Restrictions on Blasphemy and Apostasy

Statutes are interpreted through, and may be supplemented or replaced by, the judge's view of what Islam demands. This has led to calls to execute those thought guilty of apostasy or blasphemy if the individual is a male over age eighteen or a female over age sixteen and of sound mind. The sentence may be dropped if those accused recant their actions within three days.

In March 2003, police confiscated hundreds of images of Muhammad from Kabul shops, and there are reports that images of the Caliph Ali, as well as of Jesus and Mary, were also taken. The Supreme Court promptly prohibited the sale of posters depicting the prophet or other religious figures.[18] Chief Justice Shinwari claimed, without evidence, that the images "were printed in Iran by Jews because they have old enmity with Islam and want to insult the prophet."[19]

The Ulema Council, a council of senior Muslim scholars whose pronouncements carry enormous weight in Afghanistan, sought to close the major private television station, Tolo TV, which opened in October 2004, on the grounds that it is "immoral and anti-religious." One Tolo employee, charged by Shinwari with "corrupting society," was murdered in May 2005. A presenter for the station's music shows fled Afghanistan after receiving death threats. In March 2008, the lower chamber of Parliament passed a resolution to stop the broadcasting of "un-Islamic" activities, such as dancing, on television. In April 2008, the Ministry of Information and Culture ordered private broadcasters to cease carrying Indian soap operas, which conservatives had declared "contrary to the principles of Islam."[20]

In May 2008, a cleric and some members of Parliament complained that the magazine *Sobh-e-Omid* had published a blasphemous article concerning an October–November 2007 Iranian-sponsored book exhibition held in Herat, which included books criticizing the caliphs, the prophet's companions, and Bibi Ayesha, one of Muhammad's wives. The cleric, Mawlawi Faruq Hosayni, charged Iran with disseminating blasphemous materials in order to create religious discord and faulted the Ministry of Information and Culture for failing to stem the import of offending Iranian books. Mobarez Rashedi, Deputy Minister of Information and Culture, promised to look into the case if given copies of the blasphemous texts.[21]

Baha'is

As in many other Islamist jurisdictions, Baha'is in Afghanistan are singled out for oppression. On May 20, 2007, the General Directorate of Fatwas and Accounts, a body under the Supreme Court that advises on religious questions not dealt with by the law, declared that all converts from Islam to Baha'ism are apostates and that all Baha'is are infidels. The ruling may render invalid the marriages of Baha'is who are married to Muslims. The status of second-generation Baha'is, who may be accused of blasphemy although they were born into Baha'i families rather than converting from Islam, is uncertain.[22]

On April 9, 2007, one Baha'i, born into that faith, was arrested after his Muslim wife revealed his religious beliefs to authorities. The wife also applied for divorce, claiming she could not legally be married to a non-Muslim. Following international inquiries into the case, authorities released him on May 11, 2007. At that point, he had been in jail for thirty-one days without being charged, although, under the penal code, authorities can jail suspects for no longer than fifteen days without charges unless the courts grant an extension, which had not been given in this case. He fled Afghanistan with several family members.[23]

Converts

In a case widely reported in the international media, Abdul Rahman was arrested for apostasy in February 2006 after police learned that he had converted to Christianity sixteen years earlier. At that time, he had been living in Peshawar, Pakistan, and was employed by a Christian relief agency working with Afghan refugees. His wife obtained a divorce shortly after his conversion, and his parents in Afghanistan took custody of the couple's two infant daughters. Rahman had traveled through Europe seeking asylum for nine years before being deported back to Afghanistan in 2002.

In the months before his arrest, he had been seeking to regain custody of his children, and when he went to the local police for questioning, he was carrying a Bible and freely admitted to being a Christian.[24] The prosecutor, Abdul Wasi, said that he would drop the case if Rahman agreed to convert back, "but he said he was a Christian and would always remain one." After Rahman's refusal, Wasi told the court, "He is known as a microbe in society, and he should be cut off and removed from the rest of Muslim society and should be killed."[25] One prison employee told reporters, "We will cut him into little pieces.... There's no need to see him." Other inmates in the Kabul jail also threatened him, so he was transferred to the high-security Policharki prison.[26] In Friday sermons, clerics demanded his execution.[27]

At his hearing, when Rahman was asked to confess that he had apostatized from Islam, he responded, "No, I am not an apostate. I believe in God." On March 26, in an interview with the Italian daily *La Repubblica*, Rahman stated, "I am serene. I have full awareness of what I have chosen. If I must die, I will die." After intense international pressure, Afghan officials, citing "problems with the prosecutors' evidence," said they needed time to decide if Rahman was mentally fit to stand trial. They acknowledged that a psychiatric evaluation would be difficult since, if Rahman were taken to an Afghan hospital, "he would be killed immediately."[28]

In reaction to the case's dismissal, 700 protestors, including many clerics, gathered in Mazar-e-Sharif and chanted slogans including "Death to Christians," "Death to America," and "Abdul Rahman must be executed!" Without a formal vote, the lower chamber of Parliament demanded that Rahman not be allowed to leave the country.[29] He was released on March 27 and two days later fled to Italy, whose government had offered him asylum. Meanwhile, there were repeated calls in Afghanistan for him to be brought back and killed.[30] Abdul Rauf, despite his previous opposition to the brutal tactics of the Taliban, declared that he would kill Rahman if he could: "If other people want to join Islam, we encourage and appreciate them. But ours is the complete and final religion. If you leave it, that is like throwing God away." On October 12, 2006, Italian photojournalist Gabriele Torsello was kidnapped and offered in exchange for Rahman, though later released without concessions to his captors.[31]

The Rahman case drew wide attention, but similar cases attracted little notice, sometimes because they occurred in remote areas and were dealt with locally. Also, at times, those targeted asked that their cases not be publicized for their own protection. *Compass Direct News*, one of the best sources on such matters, reports that while the Rahman case proceeded, police raided other Afghan Christians. Two were arrested, and one convert was attacked by six men who beat him unconscious. Others received threats.[32] In March 2006, three other Afghan converts, as well as some of their family members, were "harassed." In another case, a Christian convert was jailed on charges of homicide, and while he was in jail, another inmate, who came to know of his religious beliefs, killed him. In 2006, another convert was killed by his father-in-law, although no arrests were made.[33]

Spiegel Online interviewed another Afghan convert, who used the pseudonym Hashim Kabar, who reported that at the time of his conversion, "[T]here were a lot of churches," and Afghans could practice Christianity above ground. However, this ceased when the Taliban took power. Kabar survived only by pretending to be a Muslim when questioned by the police or visited by Muslims associates. In 2010, even in areas controlled by the Karzai government, converts must now hold services in private and on days other than Sunday to throw off suspicion, must shift locations, and often do not possess Bibles for fear that their homes will be searched. On May 30, 2010, the Afghan National Assembly (which includes the parliament, Wolesi Jirga, and senate, Meshrano Jirga) stated that the government should search, find, arrest, and execute all Afghans who have converted from Islam to Christianity, and dozens of Afghan Christians have fled their homes and even the country.[34]

Coalition Forces

There have been controversies concerning allegations of blasphemy against coalition troops. In March 2009, students from Nangarhar University demonstrated against "an alleged desecration of the holy Qur'an" and blocked the Kabul-Jalalabad highway. The demonstrators believed that Polish soldiers had insulted the Qur'an while searching mosques in Ghazni province. They dispersed peacefully after a parliamentary resolution asking the international community to "leave Afghanistan and stop insulting Islam" was passed.[35] On October 25, 2009, violent protests rocked Kabul as students from Kabul University burned an effigy of President Obama after allegations that U.S. troops had desecrated a Qur'an. United States officials denied the accusation and accused the Taliban of spreading false rumors.[36] In January 2010, further protests took place in the Garmsir district, when International Security Assistance Forces, including Muslim soldiers, were accused of desecrating a Qur'an. Afghan police claim that a demonstrator killed a guard, which prompted the police to open fire on the crowd of 1,000, killing at least six people. NATO maintains that no Qur'ans were desecrated.[37]

In May 2009, a controversy arose when a year-old video surfaced showing U.S. troops serving in Afghanistan distributing Bibles in Pashto and Dari. There was an immediate outcry that the troops were "proselytizing," a violation of the U.S. military code of conduct. The soldiers denied it and claimed that the Bibles had been sent, unsolicited, by a church in the United States. The incident led to a major uproar among many Afghans and has raised awareness of the dangers to possible "apostates" in the country. However, the possession of local-language Bibles does not demonstrate that troops were attempting to convert Afghans. Indeed, the implication that it is an offense for an Afghan to be given, or to have, a Bible is a rather draconian view. Still, U.S. Colonel Greg Julian insists that the video footage was taken out of context and that the Bibles were never distributed. The U.S. military was quick to confiscate and destroy the Bibles: "The decision was made that it was a 'force protection' measure to throw them away."[38]

At least one Afghan, "Ahmed," a recent convert to Christianity, has met secretly with U.S. troops at the Kabul Afghanistan International Airport in order to join Christians with whom he can pray. Ahmed first learned of Christian teachings when his English instructor offered him an English-Dari Bible. Ahmed hid the Bible under his mattress, where his mother later found it. Thrown out of his parents' home and forced to marry a relative in hopes that the marriage might renew his Muslim faith, he prays during his weekly services "for a day to come in which there is freedom of religion in Afghanistan and each and every person can practice what they believe."[39]

Shias

Shias in Afghanistan may also suffer discrimination and persecution from the majority Sunnis. Above we described how the magazine *Sobh-e-Omid* in 2007 ran into trouble because of its coverage of an Iranian-sponsored, and Shia, book exhibition. In May 2009, following complaints from a local governor that certain Shia texts insulted Sunnis, the Afghan government dumped over 1,000 of the texts into a river. The government's action appeared to be an attempt to smooth over tensions between Sunnis and Shias but had the opposite effect. Many Shia leaders called the act a "humiliation for all Shiites" and insisted that a joint commission of Sunnis and Shias should have first reviewed the complaints. Deputy Culture Minister Aleem Tanwir claimed that the books' incorrect statements about Muhammad were offensive to Sunnis and therefore "dangerous to the unity of Afghanistan." However, merchants who ordered the books insist that there was nothing offensive about them and that the destruction was rooted in anti-Shia prejudice.[40]

Reformers

Blasphemy and apostasy allegations, by the government or violent groups, are also used to silence those who hold to reforming versions of Islam. Many of the accused are journalists, but one of the earliest targets was Sima Samar, a cabinet member in Afghanistan's 2002 interim government.

Sima Samar

On June 10, 2002, a letter to the *Mujahed* newspaper—the party organ of Burhanuddin Rabbani's Jamiat e-Islami party—accused Sima Samar, minister for Women's Affairs in the Afghan interim government, of telling a Canadian journalist, "I don't believe in sharia." The letter, labeling her "Afghanistan's Salman Rushdie," pronounced, "Our people know what punishment awaits anyone who insults Islam and the Prophet," and called on the authorities to investigate "and prepare the appropriate punishment." *Mujahed* also printed a front-page article condemning Samar.[41] She denied the charge and said, as a Muslim, "I have built hospitals and schools with 25,000 students. This is my jihad and it is what I supported and have done since the Russians were here. I believe in human rights and in women's rights and in peaceful speaking."

Samar was also deputy chairwoman of a *loya jirga*, a grand council of Afghan leaders, held at the same time as the controversy and was denounced there for her advocacy of the rights of women and rejection of the *burka* and other supposedly Islamic restrictions. She was also stigmatized as a member of the minority, mainly Shia, Hazara ethnic group.[42] She also received threats of violence, including some from men dressed as police officers. Chief Justice Shinwari declared that "the Supreme Court of Afghanistan thinks she cannot hold official jobs any more," and the court allegedly summoned her to face blasphemy charges, but, according to one court source, the case was dropped after "she denied the accusations and said she was a Muslim woman."

However, the attacks led to Samar's resigning her ministerial positions and taking a lower- profile job as leader of the Afghan Independent Human Rights Commission.[43] Despite his earlier statements, Shinwari insisted that the court was reassured of Samar's Islamic faith and had not barred her from the Women's Affairs post, while President Karzai maintained that he had permitted Samar to choose freely between either of the positions.[44]

Sayeed Mir Hussein Mahdavi and Ali Reza Payam Sistany

On June 17, 2003, Shinwari ordered the arrest of newspaper editors Sayeed Mir Hussein Mahdavi and Ali Reza Payam Sistany, an Iranian national, for allegedly insulting Islam. Mahdavi was chief editor, and Sistany was deputy editor of the newspaper *Aftab*, which had published two articles questioning interpretations of religious texts and the role of Islam in Afghan politics. Afghan intelligence agents also confiscated copies of *Aftab* from shops, temporarily closed the paper's office, and forbade its staff from publishing in the future.[45] One article, "Holy Fascism," published on June 11, criticized warlords for committing crimes in the name of Islam and raised questions about conservative religious leaders. It also asked, "If Islam is the last and most complete of the revealed religions, why do the Muslim countries lag behind the modern world?" and argued that the new Afghan constitution should accept an interpretation of Islam suitable for modernity.[46]

Mahdavi described his work as "a sort of Luther-like challenge to Islamic fundamentalism," suggesting that "the general history of Islam in Afghanistan had been almost entirely accompanied by violence and repression," and he asked "why ordinary Muslims were bound by clerics' interpretations of Islamic law." The other article carried the title "Religion + Government = Tyranny."[47]

On June 25, Mahdavi and Sistany were released pending legal proceedings, and the paper was granted permission to resume operations. However, protests in Kabul, claiming that they had "humiliated Islam" and demanding their execution, drove them into hiding. In early August, word leaked to the press that, on July 17, the Supreme Court agency responsible for issuing fatwas had called for a death sentence against the two journalists. Mahdavi then fled with his family to Islamabad, where he remained in hiding until October, when he received asylum in Canada. Sistany also received asylum outside of the country.[48]

Ali Mohaqeq Nasab

In October 2005, Ali Mohaqeq Nasab was arrested for publishing "un-Islamic" articles. A liberal Shia cleric, he had spent many years in exile, including in Iran, where he ran into trouble by challenging the government's religious legitimacy. He returned to Afghanistan in 2004, hoping to take advantage of greater political openness, and became the editor of the magazine *Women's Rights* (*Haqooq-i-Zan*), described by Kim Barker of the *Chicago Tribune* as "a curious mix of Western pop and women's issues." It questioned strict sharia practices, including temporal punishments for apostasy, amputations for thieves, lashing or stoning for adultery, and giving a man's court testimony twice the value of a woman's testimony. Nasab contended, as a general principle, that the precepts of sharia must be open to human questioning and interpretation.[49]

In September, part of the Afghan Supreme Court apparatus concluded that Nasab's writings contradicted the Qur'an and cited a hadith, stating, "Whoever changes or denies any verses of the Holy Qur'an will legitimize their own execution."[50] President Karzai's religious advisor, Mohaiuddin Baluch, also thought the articles contradicted the Qur'an and referred the matter to the Attorney General. On October 1, when Nasab went to the authorities seeking protection from followers of a cleric who had branded him an infidel, he was instead himself arrested. Nasab was put on trial before a public security court, where, according to the head of the Afghanistan Independent Human Rights Commission, it was "very obvious" that "without respect to rules and procedures, they were going to punish him."[51] On October 22, he was sentenced to two years' imprisonment for blasphemy. The presiding judge, Ansarullah Malawizada, admitted: "[T]he Ulama Council sent us a letter saying that he should be punished so I sentenced him to two years' jail." The Ministry of Information and Culture's media commission, which President Karzai's office believed had jurisdiction over the case, maintained that Nasab was innocent but was unable to void the court's decision.

In Nasab's view, the sentence illustrated the failure of Afghan democracy: "I made one mistake. When I heard there was democracy in my country, I came back... I didn't know that still there was no democracy... and still there is the culture of the Taliban regime." He also contends that there were political and discriminatory motives behind his conviction, since he is a Hazara and therefore part of a group that has historically been marginalized. He has continued to promote his ideas and even gave a televised statement from prison seeking a debate with his clerical opponents. Chief Prosecutor Zmarai Amiri warned that "there are some people who speak irresponsibly through television and newspapers, without knowing anything about Islamic law, the Afghan constitution or Afghan law. We have decided to arrest and interrogate these people." One person who had publicly advocated for Nasab's release was held briefly for questioning in November 2005.[52]

Both prosecution and defense challenged the sentence. The former pressed for the death penalty, and the latter sought an acquittal. The Attorney General's office proclaimed, "According to sharia law, if he does not repent and if he does not return to his religion, he should be executed." The head of the public security court, Alhaj Ansarullah Maulavi Zada, maintained that the trial had been a lost opportunity for Nasab to repent: "We listened to him a lot. We gave him a three-day trial. But he couldn't answer the court. He was not showing any kind of remorse. He still said changing your religion is forbidden but is not a crime." Nasab responded, "I haven't committed any sin to repent for. If I'm not a sinner, then why should I repent? . . . I'm a Muslim, and what I mentioned in my magazine doesn't have a single conflict with my religion. I'm more of a religious person than they are."[53]

On December 21, 2005, Judge Muzafarudeen Tajali of the Kabul High Court reduced Nasab's sentence to six months and suspended parts of the new, shortened sentence; his having been in prison since October 1 allowed for his release the following day.[54] The court only agreed to shorten the sentence after Nasab apologized for the articles. However, in a subsequent interview with Radio Free Europe, he affirmed that, "in my view, apostasy is not a crime." Due to continuing threats, he fled to Iran.[55]

Sayed Pervez Kambakhsh

On October 27, 2007, Sayed Pervez Kambakhsh, a twenty-three-year-old journalism student, was arrested over an article that criticized the position of women in Muslim society. He had distributed the article, written by an Iranian then living in Germany, to his classmates at Balkh University after discovering it online. The article, "The Koranic Verses That Discriminate Against Women," questioned the right of men in Muslim societies to have several wives while women are permitted only one husband. Kambakhsh said that he hoped to start a discussion on women's rights in Afghanistan.

Some students who saw the article complained to the authorities, and Kambakhsh was accused of being its author, which he denies. He was brought to face charges of blasphemy in the highly conservative city of Mazar-e-

Sharif.[56] Prosecutors argued that the piece mocked Islam and the Qu'ran by suggesting that Muhammad ignored women's rights. In December 2007, the case was referred to the Ulema Council, which called for him to be executed, rather than to the media commission, the appropriate body authorized under Afghan law.[57]

Kambakhsh's older brother, Sayed Yaqup Ibrahimi, says that the trial, which took place in a closed session with three judges, lasted for five minutes. Some reporters' groups contend that the trial was really a ploy intended to intimidate Ibrahimi, who had recently accused an Afghan politician of ties to violent crime. Kambakhsh says he was not permitted to have an attorney or to speak in his own defense. The regional Attorney General responded that the defendant chose to forgo an attorney.

Kambakhsh's accusers claim that he confessed to writing parts of the article—including the part that said, "The prophet Mohammad wrote verses of the Holy Qur'an just for his own benefit." Kambakhsh maintains that he made this admission only under torture. On January 22, 2008, he was convicted of blasphemy and sentenced to death under Article 130 of the constitution, which states that when there is no national law, the court should decide in accordance with the Hanafi school of Islamic jurisprudence.[58] After the sentencing, some Afghan journalists were warned by a deputy Attorney General of Balkh province that if they took up Kambakhsh's case, they also would face arrest.[59] The Afghan Senate initially expressed its support for the death sentence but, in the face of international protest, said that this approval had been a "technical mistake." It affirmed that the defendant should have the right to counsel but also that "[t]he nature of the sentence, considering the judiciary's independence, would be up to the court itself."[60]

Kambakhsh sought to appeal the verdict but, due to fear of retribution by opponents, initially had difficulty finding a lawyer. His case then went before the Kabul appeals court. In a June 15, 2008, preliminary hearing, the presiding judge, Abdul Salam Qazizada, spoke as if already convinced of Kambakhsh's guilt, demanding of the defendant, "Just tell me why you did these things...It is clear that this text belongs to you." He went on to imply that some of the classmates should also have been arrested.[61]

On October 21, 2008, the appeals court heard the charges, and the prosecution's case nearly fell apart. A fellow student, Hamed, who had earlier testified that Kambakhsh had given him the offending article, replied no when asked if he stood by his statement, and he added that he had been forced to make the statement after a literature professor escorted him to the university director's office, and two strangers, whom he believed were from the National Security Directorate, ordered him to write a statement against Kambakhsh. Hamed testified, "I wrote what they told me. I was scared. They threatened my mother, my father..." When prosecutor Akhmad Khan Ayar hinted that he could be tried for perjury, Hamed replied, "I accept responsibility." During the trial, several professors from Balkh

University testified that they had complained because Kambakhsh asked provocative questions in class. Shahabuddin Saqeb, a teacher in the sharia faculty, said, "He asked questions that made it seem that he was not sure of his beliefs." Despite these flaws in the prosecution's case, the appeals court, while overturning the death penalty, sentenced Kambakhsh to twenty years in prison.[62] On September 7, 2009, he was released after serving twenty months when President Karzai granted him amnesty.[63]

Ghaus Zalmai

In November 2007, Ghaus Zalmai, formerly an outspoken journalist, who was then a spokesman for the Attorney General, was arrested for publishing a Dari translation of the Qur'an. The translation had been made by U.S. resident Qudratullah Bakhtiarinejad and edited by Mullah Qari Mushtqaq; 6,000 copies were printed and ready for distribution. The text, titled "A Fluent Translation of the Holy Koran," differed from earlier translations in that it was entirely in Dari, that each verse was not accompanied by its Arabic equivalent, and that it was a literal line-by-line translation.

This publication led to protests and an emergency debate in Parliament that denounced the book and called for its confiscation. Niamatullah Shahrani, Minister for the Hajj and Religious Affairs, warned, "This book...is a conspiracy by international Zionism and other groups which is designed to eliminate Islam." Chief Justice Abdul Salam Azimi said, "This is a plot against the religion of Islam." Zalmai's employer, the Attorney General, issued a warrant for Zalmai's arrest, and police captured him at the Pakistani border as he attempted to flee. The translation's editor, Mullah Mushtaq Ahmad, went into hiding. A Supreme Court representative said that Zalmai's punishment would depend on exactly how problematic an investigatory commission found the translation to be."[64]

Dr. Sher Ali Zarifi, chair of the investigating commission, stated that "the contents of this book show that its writers and editors are members of a religious pluralism movement in the West." He cited what he regarded as significant deviations in the translation, including the omission of any direct statement on the punishment for certain sins (e.g., stoning for adultery). Zarifi also criticized one chapter that seemingly called on Muslims to examine the holy texts of other faiths as well as the Qur'an and another that permitted them to question some verses of their own sacred book.

Zarifi made these remarks at the November 25 Afghan Academy of Sciences conference, "Scientific Investigation into the Causes and Facets of the Conspiracy to Alter the Koran." While participants overwhelmingly saw the translation as the product of an assault on Islam, some at least disagreed with Zarifi's harsh condemnation of Zalmai. The academy's Mohammad Hassan Tawhidi, for instance, noted, "It is not a great sin if you make some mistakes in a literal translation of the Koran. It is impossible, I think, to translate the Holy Book the way it is supposed to be." He also argued that the supposedly omitted directive to stone adulterers was not part of the Qur'an but was developed on the basis of hadiths.[65]

On September 12, 2008, Zalmai and Mushtqaq were each sentenced to twenty years in prison. Two of Zalmai's brothers, who had been arrested on charges of trying to help him flee, were freed after spending seven and a half months in jail.[66] In March of 2009, an appeals court upheld the convictions. Chief Judge Abdul Salam Qazizada believed that the two were in fact guilty of modifying the Qur'an—a crime that can be punishable by death. Abdul Qawi Afzeli, Zalami's lawyer, plans to appeal and take the case to the Supreme Court.[67]

Nazari Paryani and the *Payman Daily*

On January 10, 2009, *Payman Daily*, a small paper in Kabul, printed an article that apparently questioned the validity of religions associated with divine revelation. This was considered blasphemous by the Ulema Council and the Government Media Discipline Commission, and, despite a formal apology, the editor, Nazari Paryani, was arrested along with members of his staff. The paper was subsequently closed. A former editor, Razaq Mamoon, insisted that the offending article had previously been published on an Afghan website and had been mistakenly reprinted instead of another article with a similar name.[68]

Paryani was held for nine days and received death threats after his release. There has been controversy as to the legality of his detention. Din Mohammad Mobarez Rashidi, a representative of the Minister for Information and Culture, criticized the collective arrest of the *Payman* reporters and said the matter should have been referred to his ministry's Media Violations and Complaints Assessment Commission. Afghan National Journalists Union (ANJU) spokesman Fahim Dashti acknowledged that the article was illegal but said that, since an immediate apology was offered, Paryani's detention was unwarranted. While it is encouraging that the Afghan government has been openly criticized in this case, the criticism has largely centered not on freedom of press but rather on the premise that the article was published "mistakenly."[69]

Closing

In the time since the fall of the Taliban government and following the adoption of the 2004 constitution, Afghanistan has quickly established, or reestablished, itself as one of the world's worst places to discuss competing views of Islam.[70] Students, human rights activists, journalists, editors, poets, and translators have been arrested, charged, tried, and imprisoned on vague charges of blasphemy, apostasy, and insulting Islam that have no foundation in statute. Their offenses are simply declared by religious scholars, and the accused can be subject to short "trials" with no counsel, before judges who may have already decided their guilt. Afghanistan has said that its regime and law are Islamic. But if Islam cannot be discussed, much of the country's law and politics have been placed beyond discussion and, therefore, beyond reform.

The Greater Middle East

On January 15, 2007, the Moroccan magazine Nichane *published the article "Jokes: How Moroccans Make Fun of Religion, Sex and Politics," which poked fun at Islam, Muhammad, and the late king of Morocco, Hassan II. Driss Ksikes, the magazine's editor, and Sanaa al-Aji, the author, were put on trial for "damaging the Islamic religion, lacking proper respect for the king, and publishing writings contrary to public morals." The prosecutor asked for five-year prison sentences, closure of the magazine, and a permanent ban on their work as journalists. They were given three-year suspended sentences, banned from working for two months, and each fined $8,000 for blasphemy. The magazine itself was banned for two months.[1]*

In April 2007, three Turkish Christians at the Zirve publishing house in Malatya were murdered. Among the victims were two converts from Islam, Necati Aydi, who had converted after a chance meeting with a Christian Turkish woman whom he eventually married, and Ugur Yuksin. The third victim, Tilmann Geske, was a German living in Malatya with his wife and three children. The victims were tortured before their throats were slit. Five suspects reportedly claimed to have been acting to foil a plot to undermine Islam and divide Turkey. Identical notes found inside each of the victims' pockets read, "We did this for our country. They are attacking our religion." Defense attorneys claimed that the victims had engaged in inappropriate evangelistic activity and that the suspects were therefore acting in defense of the nation, as such activity would allegedly undermine Turkey's secular state.[2] As the trial progressed, there were ongoing plausible allegations that the murders, as well as the 2006 assassination of Catholic priest Andrea Santoro and the 2007 slaying of Hrant Dink, are tied to the activities of the shadowy ultranationalist group Ergenekon, which has also been alleged to be involved in plotting a coup.[3]

Introductory Remarks

In preceding chapters, we have surveyed apostasy and blasphemy restrictions in some of the greater Middle East's most religiously repressive states. We have also focused on Egypt, a country often regarded as moderate or secular, but in which religious controls and religiously motivated abuses are pervasive. Similar circumstances can be found in various forms elsewhere in the region, occurring in such countries as Algeria, Jordan, Libya, Morocco, Turkey, and Yemen, although in these countries there are usually fewer examples of religious repression. As in other settings, the major problems faced by apostates are in personal status law, wherein they can, in some cases, become legally nonexistent.

These countries have their own particularities. The Jordanian and Moroccan monarchies are comparatively less religiously repressive than many of their neighbors. Algeria is a relatively secular country whose government wants to maintain order after suffering a brutal civil war with an Islamist insurgency, and it so seeks to repress anything that might lead to social and religious tension. In Yemen, the competing power centers, tribal structures, religious divisions, and insurgencies combine to make life very difficult for those who do not conform to the religious majority's traditions; at times, even those who do conform to the country's religious norms suffer abuse.

Turkey is perhaps the most idiosyncratic country in its treatment of blasphemy-related matters. Apart from recently increased vigilante attacks on Christians, it also has some religiously based repression of non-Muslims, different Muslims, novelists, journalists, and reformers, not only by Islamist elements, but also by nationalists. These abusers are often secular but regard Sunni Islam as an integral part of "Turkishness" and practice repression in the name of nationalism.

Algeria

After a bloody war, Algeria declared its independence from France in 1962. The 1963 constitution has been revised numerous times and is based on an amalgam of French and Islamic legal precepts. A military coup overthrew the country's first president in 1965, and the military has continued to dominate politics. Of Algeria's current total population of about thirty-three million, 99 percent are Sunni Muslim, and Islam is the state religion. In 1992, Algeria entered a state of emergency when the military intervened to prevent the likely electoral victory of the Islamic Salvation Front (FIS). Radical Islamic terror groups responded violently, carrying out massive, often random, and brutal killings of civilians. Many victims were non-Muslims or those opposed to Islamism.

Today, radical Islamic groups have less support among the general public, and they face close scrutiny by the government for possible security-related offenses. Nevertheless, while the government claims to protect the fundamental liberties of its citizens, many Muslim reformers and writers and non-Muslims continue to face persecution for their beliefs. Under the 2001 revised penal code, Algerians can be imprisoned for up to twelve months for offending the president and up to five years for offending Islam. The new code also makes the act of offending other religions punishable for up to three years.[4]

On February 28, 2006, the government passed Ordinance 06–03, regulating worship by non-Muslims. Article 2 of the ordinance guarantees religious freedom and respect for different religions. However, its implementation has made it more difficult for non-Muslims to practice their religious beliefs. For example, Article 5 declares, "Structures intended for the exercise of religious worship are subject to being registered by the State, who assures their protection." In practice, many places of religious worship have never been approved and thus are operating illegally in the eyes of the state. Meanwhile, Article 11 states that anyone who "incites, constrains or utilizes means of seduction tending to convert a Muslim to another religion" can be imprisoned for up to five years and fined up to 1 million dinars (about \$16,000 US).[5]

Initially, the regulation was not strictly enforced. Then, in December 2007, political leaders from the al-Nadha Islamic party demanded that the government "slow the activity of Christian missionaries in the country." This may have reflected concern in government circles that Christianity was growing among the non-Arab Kabyle people (the growth of Christianity in Algeria is largely in the Berber, not Arab, regions).[6] In response, officials tried, incongruously, to equate Christian evangelism with terrorism, asserting that Christians threatened Algeria's Islamic identity. By February 5, 2008, authorities had initiated a program of restricting missionaries, and, by April 11, the government had ordered half of all Algerian Protestant churches to close. Government officials claim that Muslims are under the same restrictions, but this does not appear to be true. Some observers believe that President Abdelaziz Bouteflika is reaching out to Islamists for support and trying to distract the public from complaining about domestic concerns.

Fears of Apostasy

Whatever the motivations for increased enforcement of 06–03, religious freedom in Algeria has deteriorated precipitously since its passage. As one Catholic leader put it, "This is very new, to be considered as an enemy of the country."[7] These new pressures may have been mitigated somewhat by pressure from the international community. For example, on June 6, 2008, more than thirty U.S. congressional representatives sent a letter to President Bouteflika protesting the 2006 law, as well as expressing concern about the general persecution of Christians in Algeria.[8] Meanwhile, participants in the UN Human Rights Council have questioned the compatibility of 06–03 with both Article 18 of the Universal Declaration of Human Rights and Article 36 of Algeria's own constitution. In response, however, much of the Algerian press has alleged that the country is under attack from "outsiders," and there is speculation that the government may respond by increasing its control over religious rights.[9]

For example, on June 7, 2008, in response to criticism of the government's recent stance toward Christians, the Minister of Religious Affairs, Ghoulamullah Bouabdellah, accused churches of collaborating with outsiders to destabilize the country; he even repeated his February 2008 equating of Christians and terror-ists.[10] While Islamists support these recent developments, many Algerians are growing weary of their government's intolerance of religious minorities, and this made religious freedom an issue in the April 2009 Algerian presidential elections.

At the same time, Christians faced legal battles. On June 20, 2007, five Algerian Christians were brought before a court for possessing religious literature and preaching Christian doctrine. The five were fined and sentenced to one year in prison, though whether the sentence was fully carried out is not clear. A week later, another Christian was brought before a court after giving a Bible to under-cover police officers who were posing as interested, potential converts. The offi-cers arrested him and confiscated all the Bibles in his possession. On February 5, 2008, three Christians were told that they would be sentenced to three years in prison and charged 500,000 dinars ($8,000 US) for attacking religion.[11]

Those who convert from Islam to another religion face both official and unoffi-cial pressure. On March 29, 2008, Habiba Kouider, a thirty-five-year-old Algerian convert to Christianity, was riding a public bus from Oran to her home in Tiaret, where she attended a Bible school. Police confronted her on the bus and detained her after finding Bibles and other Christian literature in her handbag. After twenty-four hours of interrogation, she was brought before a state prosecutor, who allegedly offered to close the case if she would return to Islam. Otherwise, in his words, "If you persist in sin you will undergo the lightning of justice."[12]

After she refused to renounce her faith, Kouider was officially accused of "practicing non-Muslim religious rites without a license." When her defense attorney argued that there was no such charge under Algerian law, the prosecutor responded that Kouider's possession of several copies of the Bible suggested that she was planning to distribute them in violation of Ordinance 06–03 (which gives rules for religious worship by non-Muslims). The defense countered that her pos-session of Bibles did not prove anything and that the charges were baseless. Meanwhile, the judge reportedly confiscated the notebooks of journalists attending the trial, despite the defense's objection that, since the trial was public, the press had a right to be present.[13]

The prosecutor demanded that she be sentenced to three years in prison, and a Tiaret court was scheduled to rule in May 2008. The verdict was postponed and postponed again on December 31, 2008, probably because of the international attention Kouider's trial had received.[14] The police, however, weren't finished with her. On June 1, 2008, five plainclothes officers detained her and, after a humili-ating body search, interrogated her for two hours, asking, "Why did you convert to Christianity?" Although Kouider was eventually released, the episode demon-strates the Algerian authorities' animus toward conversion.

In early June 2008, police found Bibles in a car belonging to Rachid Muhammad Essaghir and an associate, and, on June 18, they were put on trial in Tissemsilt for "distributing documents to shake the faith of Muslims." Together with church leader Youssef Ourahmane, they were also charged with "blaspheming the name of the Prophet and Islam," as well as threatening a Christian convert who had reconverted to Islam. The man who claimed to have been threatened, Shamouma Al-Aid, had first encountered the Christian group in July 2004 and had claimed that his family was persecuting him for converting to Christianity. Ourahmane maintained that the church took care of him and only later discovered that he was in touch with Islamic fundamentalists while professing Christianity. Ourahmane says he believes Al-Aid used Christians to get money and information and subsequently funneled it to the radicals. Ultimately, the church excommunicated Al-Aid, at which point he made his accusations of blasphemy and threats.[15] Essaghir, Ourahmane, and another Christian, Djallal, were convicted of insulting Islam and the prophet but won their case on appeal.[16]

Further problems erupted around Tafat Church in Tizi-Ouzou, about sixty-two miles east of Algiers. The church—part of the Protestant Church of Algeria—opened in 2004. Until 2009, it met in a small rented building. In November 2009, it opened its doors in a new location to its nearly 350 congregants, many of whom were converts from Islam. On December 26, 2009, around fifty Muslims blocked the way of people trying to attend a Christmas service. The protestors were reportedly irritated that a new church building had opened near their homes and that it was being frequented by many visitors from outside the area. These Muslims feared that their own young people could be lured to the church with promises of money or cell phones. On December 28, a mob broke into the new church structure, stealing the sound equipment; two days later, the building's electricity service was cut off. Youssef Ourahmane said, "[I]t was the first time to my knowledge that this happened... Having hundreds of Christians coming to meet and different activities in the week, this is very difficult for Muslims to see happening there next door, and especially having all these Muslim converts. This is the problem." In early 2010 there were six blasphemy- and apostasy-related court cases pending against Algerian churches and Christians.[17]

Muslims

There is increasing concern over conversions to Shia Islam, because of possible ties to Iran. Also, as in much of the Arab world, critical Muslim writers can be targeted as "dangerous to Islam."[18] One example is novelist Anouar Ben Malek, who has been criticized for offending Islam and for expressing hatred against Muslims and their prophet in his most recent work, *Oh Maria*. His historical novel recounts a brutal period in the history of Christian-Muslim relations, and the dialog contains the sort of inflammatory language that Muslims and Christians might have employed in attacking one another in those days. Ben Malek insists that the language is appropriate in its historical context and that the views espoused by the novel's fictional protagonists cannot be equated with his own views. So far, Ben Malek has not faced anything more serious than threats and condemnation in the Algerian media. But the maintenance of freedom of speech that touches on religions remains an uphill battle in Algeria.[19]

Ali Ahmad Said Asbar is often regarded as the greatest contemporary Arab poet and is more commonly known by his pen name, Adonis or Adunis. He is Syrian by birth and has established most of his reputation while living in Lebanon and, for the later part of his life, Paris. On October 13, 2008, he gave a lecture at Algeria's National Library arguing that Islamist attempts to impose their religion on society and the state are wrong. Islamists responded by accusing him of being an "apostate," something that, of course, could lead to his death. In the meantime, Algeria's Minister of Culture denounced his "ideological deterioration" and fired the library's director for inviting him.[20]

Jordan

In the Hashemite Kingdom of Jordan, King Abdullah holds broad executive powers and may dissolve Parliament and dismiss his cabinet, which he selects, at his discretion. The lower house of the National Assembly, elected through universal adult suffrage, is limited in its ability to initiate legislation and cannot enact laws without the assent of the upper house, which is appointed by the king. Of Jordan's 5.8-million population, 95 percent is Sunni Muslim, with 1 percent Shia and Druze, and 4 percent Christian, predominantly Greek Orthodox. The country is also 98 percent ethnic Arab, with a large Palestinian component, and 1 percent each Circassian and Armenian. The legal system is based on a combination of sharia and French codes, with sharia courts handling personal matters for Muslims—including marriage, divorce, child custody, and inheritance—while special tribunals of respective religious communities exercise jurisdiction over non-Muslims.

Converts can suffer from family violence. In 2003, Zena, an Iraqi widow who had converted from Islam to Christianity in Jordan, was kidnapped by her brother, who took her back to Iraq where he beat her daily in order to force her to return to Islam. She managed to escape, returned to Jordan, and was given protection by her church, but she has been on the run from her brothers who have come to Jordan to find her. She had been unable to gain asylum in a Western country.[21]

There are also some cases in which people accused of apostasy have had their rights removed by sharia courts, and they can become legally almost nonexistent. An important precedent was set in September 2004, when a convert to Christianity, Samer Muhammad Khair Talib al-Aidy, was arrested on charges of apostasy—the first case of its kind in modern Jordan. Samer refused to renounce his Christian faith and was found guilty and stripped of his civil rights. This judgment included the annulment of his marriage, his inheritance, and all documents that he had ever signed. The court ruling stated that he no longer had a legal religious identity and therefore possessed no property rights and could not be legally employed; it also declared his marriage annulled, and he could only remarry his wife if he converted back to Islam; potentially he could lose custody of his children. Having received death threats from his brothers, he fled the country and found asylum in the United States.[22]

In March 2008, Muhammad Abbad al-Qader Abbad, who had converted to Christianity fifteen years before, together with his Christian wife, Muna al-Habash, and Salam, one of his children, was beaten for his apostasy by the relatives of a convert living with the family. Abbad's father also reported him to the police and demanded custody of Abbad's two children. When Abbad went to the police to report the beating, he was charged with apostasy and brought before a sharia court. Abbad claimed that, due to his lack of real faith, he had never been a Muslim. As a result, the court sentenced him to a week's imprisonment for contempt of court. He was released on bail after he was hospitalized due to his injuries. At a second hearing, Abbad refused to deny his Christian faith and fled the country before the trial had ended, fearing that he would lose his rights and custody of his children. In June 2008, the court annulled his marriage *in absentia*.[23]

Article 5 of Jordan's 1998 Press and Publication Law forbids publication of "anything that conflicts with the principles of freedom, national responsibility, human rights, and values of the Arab and Islamic nation."[24] Two journalists, Jihad Al-Momani and Hussein Al-Khalidi, were arrested in January 2006 and charged with "denigrating the Prophets in public" and "insulting God," after they published three cartoons of Muhammad in the newspaper *al-Shihan*. Al-Momani, the chief editor, was immediately fired. In February 2006, each received a two-month prison sentence, although they were immediately released on bail.[25] Al-Momani says that he has received death threats.[26]

Jordan's grand mufti, Noah Alqdah Samas, accused Islam Samham, a Jordanian poet and journalist, of apostasy in 2008. There was terminology from the Qur'an in Samas's Arabic verses, along with lines that compared the poet's loneliness with the loneliness of Yusuf, a prophet from the Qur'an. Samham was accused by the Printing and Publication Department of "harming the Islamic faith and violating the press and publication law for combining the sacred words of the Qur'an with sexual themes."[27] He received death threats while waiting for the court's decision and on June 22, 2009, was sentenced to one year in prison and a $14,000 fine.[28]

Jordanian officials have also attempted to use the country's laws to prosecute foreign acts of blasphemy. Court orders have summoned Dutch MP Geert Wilders to appear before the Jordanian public prosecutor under charges of blasphemy and "contempt of Muslims" because of his anti-Islam film, *Fitna*.[29] Similarly, a Danish cartoonist and ten newspaper editors are being prosecuted *in absentia* for blasphemy and "threatening the national peace." The punishment for blasphemy in Jordan is up to three years of imprisonment, though it is unlikely that Jordan will be successful in forcing any extradition. However, Wilders has expressed concern that an arrest warrant issued through Interpol could lead to extradition from other countries that he may visit.[30]

Morocco

Since Morocco gained its independence from France in 1956, its royal family has ruled the country. The two legislative chambers serve as "debating" forums rather than as autonomous bodies, and the several opposition parties are weak. No political party is allowed to challenge the monarch's ultimate authority. About 99 percent of Morocco's thirty-one-million-person population is Sunni Muslim, and the remainder is Christian, Jewish, Hindu, and Shia. The constitution establishes Islam as the official religion and the king, now Mohammed VI, as "Commander of the Faithful and the Supreme Representative of the Muslim Community." As such, he is charged with ensuring "respect for Islam." Article 106 of the constitution says that the constitutional provisions related to the place of Islam cannot be changed.

The 1958 Press Code, amended in 2002, provides severe penalties for speaking ill of Islam. Article 29 of the code forbids the import of writings that "infringe the Islamic religion." Articles 38 and 41 establish a penalty of three to five years in addition to a 10,000- to 100,000-dirham fine for the publication of such writing. No similar law exists for infringing or offending other religions.[31] Christians who are foreign visitors or converts from Islam have been monitored, arrested without charge, and deported or imprisoned for missionary activity, an offense punishable by law. There are well-publicized cases of authorities punishing blasphemy.

The Moroccan government has also taken steps to outlaw literature comparing Islam and Christianity. In November 2008, it banned an issue of the French magazine *L'Express International* because it contained material deemed "offensive to Islam." The issue, dubbed "The Jesus-Mohammad Shock," contained a number of articles that drew similarities between the two religions—including comparing Jesus and Mohammad. The magazine's editors were surprised at Morocco's response since they had taken extra care to publish an issue that considered Muslim sensitivities and they released it during a period when the government was promoting interfaith dialogue with the West.[32]

Although voluntary conversion from Islam is in principle legally acceptable, the authorities have harassed "apostates" and others. Article 220 of the penal code prescribes a prison term of six months to three years for "anyone who employs incitements to shake the faith of a Muslim or to convert him to another religion." This has been used against Christians thought to be involved, directly or indirectly, in "proselytism." In 2010, International Christian Concern reported that Jamaa Ait Bakrim was serving a fifteen-year prison term for "proselytizing" and "destruction of goods of others." In 1993, Jamaa had returned to Morocco from Europe, where he converted to Christianity. In 1994, he was placed in a mental hospital in Inezgane for proselytizing. In 1996, he was sentenced to a year in prison for putting up a Christian cross in public. In 2001, he was prosecuted again, and, in 2005, he was sentenced to fifteen years and was being held in Prison Centrale, in Kenitra.[33]

The authorities have also, on occasion, interpreted Article 220 broadly, harassing those converts who have merely associated with other Christians and Muslims. Similarly, while the government permits the display and sale of Bibles in English, French, and Spanish, it limits access to those published in Arabic by blocking their import and sale, even though there is no law strictly prohibiting them.[34]

In July 2004, authorities initially confiscated and refused to renew the passports of five converts. Later, they all received their passports, but it has been reported that two of them were harassed and interrogated at length by the police.[35] In January 2005, a Christian convert named Hamid al-Madany was arrested without charge after a photocopy of his passport was found in the possession of a Western missionary who had been arrested for distributing Bibles. Hamid was released on bail, and in October 2005, all legal proceedings against him were dropped.[36] In 2010, extremists began posting images of dozens of Christian converts and their families on Facebook, calling them "hyena evangelists" who are trying to "shake the faith of Muslims," and giving their addresses.[37]

Foreigners

In one curious incident, Gilberto Orellana, the conductor of the San Salvador symphony orchestra, was living in Morocco, having been invited by Moroccan officials to teach at the prestigious National Conservatory. In December 1994, he was arrested, along with five Moroccan associates, and sentenced to a year in prison for the crime of proselytizing. Orellana admitted that at a dinner party, when asked, he had spoken to friends about his Christian faith. This was apparently what led to the police raid, nine days of interrogation, and a prison sentence. A few days later, he was released, taken to the Spanish border, and banished from Morocco for five years. Three of Orellana's five friends were released immediately. The other two, who were imprisoned with him, suffered physical abuse at the hands of the authorities. One was reportedly tortured with electric shocks; the other suffered a broken arm. The men were only released after they had made a declaration of Muslim faith.[38]

In November 2006, Sadek Noshi Yada, a German tourist, was sentenced to six months in jail and fined 500 dirhams for "shaking the faith" of Muslims by distributing books and CDs on Christianity to young Muslim Moroccans. Prior to this, the local media had declared that a secret Christian proselytizing campaign was being launched in the area.[39] In March 2009, five European women—four Spaniards and one German—were purportedly caught "red-handed" attempting to convert local Muslims to Christianity. The women were later expelled from the country, although subsequent reports indicate that they were not "proselytizing" at all, but simply holding a Bible study with twenty fellow Christians; all of them were arrested in Casablanca and held overnight for interrogation. Though Morocco prides itself on its religious tolerance (and it is much more tolerant than some other countries in its neighborhood), the number of Christians arrested in recent years for holding illegal religious gatherings does not speak well for its respect for freedom.[40]

On February 9, 2010, over sixty officers arrested eighteen Moroccan Christians and their American pastor in a private home. Of the Christians arrested, five were small children ranging in age from infant to four years old; the group was held and interrogated for fourteen hours. Eventually, they were released, and the American was deported. The group had been charged with "shak[ing] Muslims' faith and undermining the Kingdom's religious values" by trying to recruit Muslims for Christianity.[41] Following these arrests and vague accusations of "proselytism," the Moroccan government began to expel dozens of expatriate Christian workers. Further expulsions began in May 2010 until the total exceeded 100. The expulsions covered Christians of all denominations and included people who had been in the country many years, and several were married to Moroccans. Some were staff of an orphanage, the Village of Hope, which raised more than thirty Moroccan children in a family setting and had a policy of not proselytizing. Because of the expulsions, many of the children were separated from their adoptive parents. Several of the expulsions appeared to violate a Moroccan law stating that expatriates resident in the country for more than ten years cannot be deported unless they have committed a crime. The expatriates consistently maintained that they had not violated the law on proselytizing, but the country appeared to be sliding into intolerance of Christians.[42]

Muslims

In the Sunni-dominated country of Morocco, Shia Muslims also have a difficult time, and some of this is connected to political associations with Iran. In March 2009, Morocco cut off diplomatic relations with Iran, in part due to accusations that Iranians were attempting to spread Shia in Morocco. These allegations were based on Moroccan intelligence reports indicating that Iranian diplomats were working to spread Shiism throughout North Africa. The Moroccan government viewed this as extremely hostile and threatening, believing that it aimed "to alter the religious foundations of the Kingdom, [to] attack the foundations of the Moroccan people's ancestral identity, and to attempt to undermine the unity of the Muslim religion and the Sunni Maliki rite in Morocco."[43] On April 2, 2009, a spokesman stated: "[T]he Kingdom, whose foundations are grounded in Islam and the Sunni Maliki rite, can never tolerate serving as a hotbed for spreading Shiism and Christian proselytizing.... The freedom of belief does not mean conversion to another religion."[44]

Reformers can also face problems. In September 2009, six members of Morocco's Alternative Movement for Individual Freedom (MALI) were arrested near Mohammedia for eating publicly during Ramadan. The group is the first in Morocco to publicly demonstrate for the right not to observe Ramadan, and its members have been labeled "agitators" by the Islamic scholars of the local province. MALI's spokesmen denied being anti-Islam and argued that their stance was merely "in favor of individual freedom." The group members face up to six months' imprisonment.[45]

Turkey

Mustapha Kemal Ataturk's secular, nationalistic legacy still influences Turkish politics and culture, and Article 24 of the constitution forbids the state to be established on religious principles. Nevertheless, the country's population of seventy-three million is predominantly Muslim, mostly Sunni, though with ten to twelve million Alevis (see section following). Only 0.2 percent are Christian, Jewish, Baha'i, and Ezidi. This predominance of Islam creates tension between Turkey's secular constitution and its Islamic identity. Since November 2002, the Justice and Development (AK) Party, whose roots lie in the Islamic Welfare Party that was banned in 1998 for "conspiring against the secular order," has won sweeping majorities in three general elections by promising to end governmental corruption and put the country on a path toward European Union (EU) membership.

While the Turkish constitution provides for religious freedom, the state maintains tight control over religion, dictating the content of Friday mosque sermons and monitoring radio and television stations for "misuse of religion."[46] In Turkey, with its almost-century-old secular traditions, it is certainly possible to criticize religion and religious beliefs, including Islam. Turkish intellectuals can write critiques and analyses that would be banned, or worse, in much of the Muslim world. In this sense, there are not restrictions on blasphemy as such. However, one of the country's idiosyncrasies is that the state's defense of nationalism can almost include a ban on criticism of Islam. Article 301 of the penal code, passed in 2005, made it a crime to, inter alia, publicly denigrate "Turkishness," a provision amended in 2008 to refer instead to the "Turkish nation." At least fifty journalists have been charged under the article, including Nobel Prize–winning novelist Orhan Pamuk; the charges against Pamuk were later dropped.[47] This law can incorporate a religious dimension because Islam is regarded as an integral part of the Turkish nation. So, in a peculiar twist for a secular constitution, insulting Islam can be viewed as tantamount to insulting the Turkish nation and is therefore forbidden.[48] Also, Article 216 provides sentences of one to three years for openly inciting enmity or hatred toward another person based on religion and six months to a year for openly denigrating religious values.

A further complication for religious freedom is Turkey's so-called deep state, a term describing secular-nationalist circles in the army, police, and other elements of state administration.[49] Along similar lines, there have been allegations that an ultranationalist group, Ergenekon, has been involved in several cases of religious persecution, and prosecutors have been investigating the organization and making arrests, claiming that members have sought to mount a coup.

Turkey's unique blend of Islam and secular nationalism became evident in the murder of Hrant Dink, a man who defies easy categorization. Though in Turkey, he was often called the "voice of Armenians." Dink did not stress Armenian nationalism and was opposed to French and American bills on Armenian geno- cide.[50] Yet, when, as editor-in-chief of the weekly *Agos*, he was convicted in 2005 under Article 301 for "insulting Turkish identity" by referring to the 1915 mass slaughter of Armenians as "genocide," he became a target for nationalists.[51] On January 19, 2007, he was shot and killed outside of his Istanbul office. When questioned, the suspect in the murder, Ogun Samast, age seventeen, proclaimed, "I shot him after saying the Friday prayers. I'm not sorry...He [Dink] said 'I'm from Turkey but Turkish blood is dirty' and that's why I decided to kill him."[52]

While this case appears to stem from nationalistic rather than religious motives, in Turkey, the two can overlap, and Dink's alleged insult to Turkey appears also to have been construed by his killer as an insult to Islam. His Christianity, which had both Armenian Orthodox and Armenian evangelical influ- ences, may also have been a factor. Immediately after shooting Dink, Samast shouted, "I shot the non-Muslim."[53] Additionally, Yasin Hayal, who was arrested for inciting Samast to kill Dink, had an alleged history of militant Islamic activity.[54]

Erhan Tuncel, an informant and suspect in the case, had provided Trabzon police with information on the plot to kill Dink, but the police never followed up on it. Both Istanbul and Trabzon police have been accused of failing to use that information to prevent the murder, though they were acquitted of any legal wrongdoing. At Samast's initial arrest, police detained him in a tearoom rather than a prison cell. Stranger still, they lined up to have their photos taken with him, holding a calendar that read, "The soil of the motherland is holy, and it will not be abandoned."[55] As the trial progressed, possible links to the infamous Ergenekon have been alleged.

Along with Hrant Dink and Orhan Pamuk, other Turkish intellectuals, and especially authors, have come under fire for writings that supposedly insult Islam. In May 2009, novelist Nedim Gursel was charged under Article 216 with "humili- ating religious values and inciting religious hatred" in his novel *Allah'in Kizlari* (Daughters of Allah). In an unusual twist, Turkey's Directorate of Religious Affairs presented testimony against the defendant, stating that his work "insults not only Islam but also all celestial religions and caused disintegration in society." Gursel repeatedly emphasized that his book was fictitious, that it was not intended to offend, and that he himself was respectful of religious values. In fact, the case lacked almost any foundation, since the prosecution itself said that there was no evidence suggesting that Gursel's book had actually incited hatred. On June 25, 2009, Gursel was acquitted. He commented, "For an author to be prosecuted for a novel does not suit the Turkish Republic." He went on to say that his case showed a bizarre disconnect between the values espoused in Turkey's constitution and the realistic experience of its citizens.[56]

In October 2006, Hakan Tastan and Turan Topal, two Christian converts from Islam, were also charged under Article 301 for "insulting Turkishness," for inciting religious hatred under Article 216, and for compiling data on private citizens under Article 135. The charges were based on trips the two men had taken to Silivri to meet a teacher and a group of high-school students who had asked for a visit in connection with an Istanbul-based Bible correspondence course. The accusations against them included forming illegal cell groups, possessing weapons, promising money and jobs and education for conversion, and procuring sexual relationships with teenage girls to induce young men to convert. Tastan and Topal denied all of these charges.[57] Even the state prosecutor assisting the judge stated that there was "not a single concrete, credible piece of evidence" for the allegations. Moreover, all of the three accusing parties contradicted themselves in testimony. In July 2007, the two were additionally charged with "illegal collection of funds," but, once again, no substantive evidence was produced. In February 2009, the Ministry of Justice issued a decision saying the trial would continue under the revised version of Article 301.[58] There was a hearing on January 28, 2010, but it lasted only a few minutes since the prosecution failed to produce key witnesses.[59]

Evangelistic activity is actually legal under Turkish law. Indeed, the constitution protects the right to choose or change one's religion, as well the right to share it with others. However, a senior official in the justice ministry has referred to "missionary activity" as "more dangerous than terrorism," and the General Staff of the Directorate of Religious Affairs publicly labeled religious minorities "an internal threat, a danger and an enemy."[60] In one of the sermons that it issued to local mosques, the Directorate of Religious Affairs claimed in March 2005 that modern-day crusaders were attempting "[to exploit] ethnic differences and economic and political hardship to entice our children" and "[to] sever our people's links to Islam."[61]

Protestant churches, which are relatively new to Turkish society, and several of which are led by pastors who were formerly Muslims, have seen an increase in violence in recent years. Pastor Mehmet Sahin Coban, of a Protestant church in Odemis, was assaulted in May 2007; his church had previously been firebombed. In these and other cases, there has been little or no police response, and the Protestant community in Turkey has complained to Parliament about the neglect.[62] In August 2009, police rescued Ismail Aydin, whose organization seeks to spread knowledge of Christianity, after he was kidnapped at knifepoint by a man who declared, "[T]his missionary dog is trying to divide the country."[63]

Alevis

Of those whose beliefs deviate from the state's version of Islam, the ones who have experienced the most widespread problems (albeit less violence in recent years) are the Alevis. This Muslim group combines elements of both Sunni and

Shia Islam, while having its own distinctive features in oratory, poetry, and dance. It also allows men and women to worship together. Even though Alevis form approximately a quarter of Turkey's population, they are not formally recognized, their houses of worship are not recognized as such, and their beliefs are treated as a cultural rather than as a religious matter by the Ministry of Education. Alevis have brought more than 4,000 court cases alleging discrimination for the state's failure to incorporate their beliefs into the compulsory religious education.[64] In addition, the Diyanet, or Directorate of Religious Affairs, funds the salaries of Sunni imams, as well as other costs associated with Sunni practice, but excludes Alevi practitioners.[65]

The deadliest attack against Alevis in past decades took place in 1978, when violent mobs laid siege to the southeastern town of Karamanmaras, where, after a week of killing, raping, and looting, 111 Alevis were killed, thousands were injured, and much of the town was destroyed.[66] But Alevis have also suffered violence more recently. In 1993, thirty-seven people died when non-Alevi protesters coming from Friday prayers set fire to a hotel hosting an Alevi cultural festival. Police reportedly stood by and watched. In 1995, police were suspected of collusion with gunmen who targeted five teahouses in a poor Alevi neighborhood, an incident that sparked demonstrations that turned into riots, during which police shot and killed sixteen people.[67]

In February 2009, an Alevi family sued the Muratpasa district governorship to obtain an exemption for their daughter from attending religious classes. Although a 1990 court decision had restricted exemption to Christian and Jewish students, the Turkish court ruled in favor of the Alevis based on Article 24 of the Turkish constitution, which provides freedom of religion, and also on Article 9 of Europe's Convention for the Protection of Human Rights and Fundamental Freedoms. It is hoped that this case may open the way for other changes; embodying this hope on November 8, 2009, tens of thousands of Alevis demonstrated for equal rights.

On February 2, 2010, in another closely watched case, the European Court of Human Rights ruled, again on the basis of Article 9, that Sinan Işık, who in 2004 had asked that his identity card list his religion as Alevi rather than as Islam, had his religious freedom violated when this was not allowed. The court went further and held that "the violation in question does not lie in the rejection of the plaintiff's demand to specify his Alevi faith on his identity card, but in the mentioning, obligatory or optional, of religion on the cards." Even though since 2006, Turks have been allowed to leave the religion section of the identity card blank, the court ordered the removal of the section itself.[68]

Yemen

Yemen is beset by unrest from a dozen rival political parties, conservative tribal groups, secessionist activists, Iranian-backed Shias, and Al-Qaeda in the Arabian

Peninsula—all operating inside the borders. The population of twenty-one million is about 70 percent Sunni Muslim, 30 percent Shia Muslim (Zaydi), 0.1 percent Shia Muslim (Ismaili), and 0.1 percent Christian/Jewish/Hindu. Although it affirms adherence to the United Nations' Universal Declaration of Human Rights, Yemen's constitution stipulates that sharia law is the basis of all legislation.[69]

Article 103 of Yemen's 1990 Press and Publications Law prescribes fines and up to a year in prison for publication of anything that "prejudices the Islamic faith."[70] Baha'is and Jews have been under increased threat.[71] In June 2008, three Iranian, one Iraqi, and two Yemeni Baha'is were arrested and detained for suspected proselytism in a manner "incompatible with Yemeni law." It is also inhospitable to converts. In July 2000, a Yemeni court gave Mohammad Omer Haji, a Somali refugee and Christian convert, seven days to either return to Islam or be executed. Thanks to international pressure, he, together with his wife and infant child, found asylum in New Zealand. There were further arrests of converts in 2005, 2008, and 2009. On June 14, 2009, armed men kidnapped nine foreigners working at a hospital in Saada, reportedly because of rumors that they were Christian missionaries engaged in proselytizing.[72]

As elsewhere, not only non-Muslims or converts suffer under blasphemy and apostasy laws. In 2002, Samir al-Yusufi, editor of the newspaper *Al-Thaqafiya*, was charged with apostasy because his paper had serialized a book deemed blasphemous. The Ministry of Culture said the book, *Open City*, by Mohammed Abdelwali, used religious terms to describe sexual scenes and ordered it confiscated for insulting religion. The judge, for reasons that are not entirely clear, also banned reporting on the trial. The case was later dismissed at the intervention of "high-ranking officials."[73] Three other newspapers, the *Yemen Observer, Al-Hurriya*, and *Al Rai Al Aam*, were closed down for six months in February 2006 for republishing the Danish *Jylland-Posten* cartoons. The journalists and editors were imprisoned for a year and banned from writing for six months after their release. The prosecution had originally requested the death penalty. The prime minister ordered the newspapers to reopen in May 2006.[74] On March 21, 2010, in response to proposed legislation that would make marriage illegal for those under the age of seventeen, several leading Muslim scholars said that those people who were pushing for a ban on child brides were apostates.[75]

Closing

Middle East countries are diverse in their practices and their reasons for religious repression. Some, such as Morocco, are comparatively free; some, such as Algeria and Turkey, are relatively secular. Yet despite their greater freedom or secularity, these three countries, like others in the area, continue to punish blasphemy and apostasy offenses.[76] There also appears to be an increase in repression in the area.

8

Africa

On February 20, 2006, Florence Chuckwu, a Christian high school teacher in the capital of Nigeria's Bauchi state, was nearly killed after a student accused her of blasphemy. The area was already tense because of riots over the publication of the Danish cartoons. When Chuckwu noticed that one of her students was reading during her lecture and refused to stop, Chuckwu confiscated the book until after class, unaware that it was the Qur'an. The Muslim students in the class began to throw books at her and one shouted, "Kill her!" By the time her colleagues came to her rescue, she had already sustained serious head injuries. The students rioted and, in the ensuing frenzy, more than twenty Christians were killed and two churches burned down. Soldiers from the 33rd Artillery Field Brigade, in whose barracks the school is located, eventually dispersed the rioters. Chuckwu's present whereabouts are unknown.[1]

Musa Mohammed Yusuf, a fifty-five-year-old Somali, was the leader of an underground church in Yonday village, twenty miles from Kismayo. On February 20, 2009, members of Somalia's radical Islamist group al-Shebab arrived at his house to question him about Salat Mberwa, the head of another Christian fellowship. After being questioned, Yusuf fled to Kismayo. The next day the interrogators returned and, when told by his wife, Batula Ali Arbow, that Yusuf had fled, seized the couple's three sons—eleven-year-old Abdi Rahaman Musa Yusuf, twelve-year-old Hussein Musa Yusuf, and seven-year-old Abdulahi Musa Yusuf. The terrified mother later said, "I knew they were going to be slaughtered. Just after some few minutes I heard a wailing cry from Abdulahi (who was) running toward the house..." Batula fainted, and when she regained consciousness, she learned that two of her sons, Abdi and Hussein, had been beheaded.[2]

In 1992, the Kordofan state government in Sudan declared jihad on the Muslim and Christian people of the Nuba Mountains in central Sudan. In 1993, six government-sponsored Muslim clerics in Kordofan issued a fatwa in support of the jihad and declared: "An insurgent who was previously a Muslim is now an apostate; and a non-Muslim is a non-believer standing as a bulwark against the spread of Islam, and Islam has granted the freedom of killing both of them."[3] *This fatwa declared that the Nuba non-Muslims could be wiped out, as they were barriers to Islam, and that Nuba Muslims were now apostates who not only could be, but also should be, killed. Hence, half a million people were sentenced to death. Between May 1992 and February 1993, over 60,000 Nuba had already reportedly been killed and many of their villages burned to the ground. Death*

*squads targeted community leaders and intellectuals in particular, so
that the Nuba would remain without a voice. The army and Popular
Defense Force also disrupted trade and marketplaces to produce a
famine that would wipe out tens of thousands more Nuba. These conditions continued through the 1990s and, by 1998, prompted human
rights and refugee aid groups to identify the Nuba mountain region
as a target of genocide.*

Introductory Remarks

In much of Africa, Islam draws on Sufi traditions, and in the past, levels of religious violence have been relatively low. However, as elsewhere in the world, there
has been an increased radicalization that has led to more frequent accusations of
blasphemy and apostasy, and to ensuing violence.[4] To illustrate this, we will outline three countries—Nigeria, Somalia, and Sudan.

Nigeria, by population the largest country in Africa, has, in recent decades,
been ripped apart by violence between Muslims and Christians—sometimes triggered by blasphemy and apostasy allegations—that have cost thousands of lives.
More than anywhere else in the world, many people are killed because of rumors
of blasphemy taking place far beyond its borders, even in Denmark or Bangladesh.
There has been comparatively little state religious repression, though there has
been discrimination. The major threat is from mob violence, and the victims
include not only those accused but often also their coreligionists.

Somalia has no functioning central government, and religious violence is per-
petrated by quasi-state militias and mobs. One goal has been the extermination of
Somalia's Christians, who have been targeted by the Al-Qaeda-linked Al-Shabab
movement. While Al-Shabab is the worst, the country's other radical movements
also attack anyone that differs from their version of Islam, including some Sufis.
Due to this violence and the ceaseless warring between armed factions, Somalia
may be the most religiously repressive country in the world.

Sudan is the largest African country in area. Its predominantly Muslim North
has laws governing apostasy and blasphemy, and it has been the site of some of
the world's most significant blasphemy incidents. These have occurred against the
backdrop of a twenty-year civil war triggered in the mid-1980s in part because the
Islamist government sought to impose an extreme form of sharia on the South,
which is largely populated by Christians and followers of traditional African religions, thus sparking a rebellion. Over two million were killed in that conflict
before a fragile peace was established by the comprehensive peace agreement of
2005. Conflict reaching genocidal proportions also began in 2003 in Darfur, in
the West, though that does not appear to be tied to government interference in

religious matters. One of the most notorious blasphemy incidents was Sudan's execution of Mohamed Mahmoud Taha, a prominent Muslim intellectual and political leader. There have also been blasphemy-related death threats against UN Special Rapporteurs and government-backed pronouncements declaring that half a million people, the Nuba, should be killed as apostates. South Sudan gained independence in July 2011, amidst great insecurity.

Nigeria

With an oil-rich delta, a relatively recent transition from military rule, and by far the largest population (over 130 million) in Africa comprising over 250 ethnic groups, Nigeria would face an uphill battle for stability, peace, and religious freedom even without its religious differences. But those differences can be deadly. The country is almost equally divided between Muslims and Christians, with about 10 percent of the population retaining traditional beliefs. Muslims are the majority in the North, Christians are the majority in the South, and the two are mixed in the middle belt, which is often the scene of violent conflict. Such outbreaks have tribal and regional dimensions and involve issues of political power, land, and resources, but there is also persistent religious tension. Since 1999, sharia law has been imposed in many northern states, which has increased tensions and led to thousands of deaths.[5]

Religious freedom is protected in numerous clauses in the 1999 constitution. Article 1 forbids the federal or state governments to "adopt any religion as State Religion." Article 38 guarantees "freedom of thought, conscience and religion," while articles 15 and 42 forbid religious discrimination. Despite these provisions, however, by 2002, twelve northern states had extended sharia law beyond matters of personal status, and some had imposed Islam as a de facto official state religion in contravention of the constitution. Some proponents of sharia say their aim is to have a majority of states adopt sharia and then proclaim Nigeria an Islamic state.[6]

The constitution allows personal sharia law but guarantees the right of non-Muslims not to be subject to sharia courts. Yet, several northern states use sharia in disputes between Muslims and non-Muslims.[7] As noted, this expansion of sharia has led to conflicts in which thousands have died. The authorities have been largely ineffectual in preventing attacks, which, though stemming mainly from Muslim elements, are sometimes initiated by Christians. While neither blasphemy nor apostasy is explicitly punishable de jure, even in the sharia states, those accused face extrajudicial violence and persecution. Although the constitution guarantees the freedom to change religions, Muslims who become Christians are also frequently targeted as apostates. Strife has also broken out between Sunni and Shia Muslims, while animists continue to suffer in political, ethnic, and religious conflicts.

Converts

In October 1999, Ibrahim Shetima, a spiritual advisor to the late military Head of State, Ibrahim Abacha, was thrown out of his residence for becoming a Christian. According to Shetima: "I had to leave and they've been on my trail since. I have been hunted and harassed along with attempts to take my life."[8] In late May 2000, in renewed religious violence in Kaduna city, Father Clement Ozi Bello, a convert who became a Catholic priest in 1999, was brutally mutilated and killed. While thousands, both Christian and Muslim, were killed in mob violence in Kaduna in 2000, Bello appears to have been singled out for special treatment: fellow priest, Reverend Yakubu, reported, "They tied a rope round his mouth and dragged him into a culvert and left him there.... They plucked off his eyes."[9]

In 2002, converts Lawani Yakubu and Mohammed Ali Ja'afaru were arrested by an Islamic monitoring group created by the government of Zamfara to enforce sharia. The group had no legal power, since criminal law is a federal matter, but demanded that Yakubu and Ja'afaru be executed for apostasy. The presiding sharia judge, Awal Jabaka, correctly responded that he did not have jurisdiction, but the group said they would try to kill the two converts anyway. Yakubu and Ja'afaru fled, and their current whereabouts are unknown.[10]

In 2003, fifteen-year-old Salamatu Hassan was ambushed, gagged, and threatened with death by her uncle Malam Kasimu and some Islamic clerics for converting to Christianity. Before sending her back to her parents, Kasimu said, "If you were my daughter, I would have slaughtered you, killed you here, you bastard infidel, for turning away from Islam." Hassan's parents did not attack her but did reject her, leaving her homeless.[11] Sardauna Anaruwa Sashi, a thirty-year-old convert in Paiko, was seized by police on September 21, 2005. The officers asked him why he had converted but did not give him a chance to respond before they beat him. He was detained for four days and tortured.[12]

Blasphemy Accusations

In Gombe city, in March 2006, a Christian teacher was beaten to death at the hands of her students after being accused of desecrating the Qur'an.[13] On September 18, 2006, a Christian tailor named Jummai was talking with Muslim customers at her store in Dutse. When a Muslim woman named Binta called Jesus a drunkard for turning water into wine, Jummai retorted that if that were the case, Muhammad's many wives would make him a womanizer. Her comments were called blasphemous by some bystanders, and she was dragged before an adviser to the emir of Dutse, who ordered her to leave the area within two days or be killed. Her current whereabouts are unknown.[14] On June 12, 2006, Joshua Lai, a Christian high-school teacher in Keffi, in Nasarawa, was teaching an English class when a Muslim student, Abdullahi Yusuf, arrived late, with the excuse that he just was coming from prayers at the mosque. As a former Muslim, Lai knew that morning prayers could not have delayed Yusuf until 9 a.m., and Lai caned him—a typical punishment for students in Nigeria. Yusuf later accused Lai of blaspheming by saying, "I will flog the prophet Muhammad." That night, students burned down Lai's school residence as well as his home. The next day, he was evacuated to Abuja for his protection and, on October 16, 2006, was put on trial in Lafia for, among other things, blasphemy.[15]

Charges of blasphemy also lead to generalized violence, especially in the northern state of Kano. On September 29, 2007, a Christian teacher allegedly posted an insulting caricature of Muhammad in his classroom, and nine people were killed in the ensuing clash between Christian and Muslim youth. On October 5, 2007, another nine people, all Christians, were killed, and churches, shops, and houses were torched in reaction to a Bangladeshi cartoon purportedly defaming the Prophet. Two months later, hundreds rioted and attacked Christians over claims that a Christian had written an inscription on a wall disparaging Muhammad. On February 2, 2008, in Bauchi state, five churches were burned in retaliation for alleged defamation of the Qur'an by a female Christian student.[16] Muslims have also been victims of mob violence following blasphemy accusations. In August 2008, a Muslim man in Kano was beaten to death by angry youths because statements he had made the previous night were interpreted as blasphemous.[17]

One of the stranger incidents, which, unusual for Nigerian violence, received international publicity, concerned the Miss World competition, scheduled for Nigeria in 2002. Several Muslim clerics pronounced the pageant immoral. In response, Isioma Daniel, a journalist with *ThisDay* newspaper, wrote, "What would Mohammed think? In all honesty, he would probably have chosen a wife from one of them."[18] Daniel's comments sparked riots in Kaduna, where she lived, that lasted for four days, resulting in over 200 deaths and leaving thousands homeless. *ThisDay* printed an apology, but, in November 2002, Islamic authorities in Zamfara state issued a fatwa urging Muslims to kill Daniel. Federal Information Minister Jerry Gana pronounced the fatwa null and void, proclaiming, "The federal government . . . will not allow such an order in any part of the federal republic."[19] However, it was not clear how the government could prevent someone from acting on the fatwa. Daniel fled the country.

Boko Haram

In late July 2009, a militant Islamist group calling itself "Boko Haram," which roughly translates as "Western civilization is forbidden," began violent attacks around the town of Maiduguri. The group, which is also dubbed "the Taliban" by locals because of its censorious tactics, attacked police stations, prisons, schools, churches, and homes, burning almost everything in its path. The violence spread to Borno, Kano, and Yobe states where Boko Haram treated as infidel anyone— Christian or Muslim—who did not conform to its views. Although the vast majority of Nigeria's Muslims rejects the sect's doctrines, Christians were a particular focus of the violence. Many were abducted and forced, under threat of death, to renounce their faith. The riots continued for five days before police were able to stop them, and 700 people were killed in Maiduguri city alone. One arrested Boko Haram member, twenty-three-year-old Abdulrasheed Abubakar, confessed to receiving $5,000 and military training in Afghanistan, with the promise of $35,000 on his return there.[20]

Nigerian president Umaru Yar-Adua stated that intelligence agencies had been tracking Boko Haram and had regained control of the regions at risk. However, on August 9, 2009, the group released a statement aligning itself with Al-Qaeda and calling for jihad in response to the killing of its leader, Mallam Mohammed Yusuf. It further said it would "hunt and gun down those who oppose the rule of sharia in Nigeria and ensure that the infidel does not go unpunished."[21] In March 2010, it promised to continue its "holy struggle to oust the secular regime and entrench a just Islamic government."[22]

Somalia

With its clan and regional fragmentation, extremist religious groups, coups d'état, and war with neighboring Ethiopia, Somalia is one of the most dangerous and unstable countries in the world. Since independence in 1960, its history has been marred by relentless conflict, bloodshed, and poverty. In recent years, the Transitional Federal Government (TFG), enjoying UN recognition and Ethiopian interventionist military support, has fought with the more radical Al-Shabab— the Union of Islamic Courts, a group aligned with Al-Qaeda. While less extreme than Al-Shabab, which is not difficult, the transitional government also holds to a version of sharia requiring death for anyone who leaves Islam. Religious repression is endemic.[23]

Sufi Muslims have been branded as heretics and have experienced increasing persecution. Their clerics have been assassinated, their shrines labeled as idolatrous and burned down, and their cemeteries desecrated. Sufi graves have been opened and the bodies pulled out. Sufi leader Mohamed Sheikh has declared, "The living person can at least defend himself, but the dead cannot . . . destroying graves is despicable."[24] In March 2010, many Muslims marched to protest the destruction of clerics' tombs, some over 100 years old. In April 2008, a Muslim was stabbed after a clash between two groups over different interpretations of Islam.[25] Beginning in 2009, a Sufi group known as Ahlu Sunna Wal Jamaa has also formed militias to fight Al-Shabab.[26]

Some of the most intense repression is directed against Somalia's small Christian population; Islamist insurgents are conducting pogroms to exterminate Somali Christians.[27] The principal reason for this campaign of genocide is the Islamists' view that Islam is the only true Somali religion; hence, all Somali Christians must be considered apostates. Al-Shabab has destroyed Christian cemeteries and killed hundreds of Christians since 2005, a dire situation even further exacerbated by the perception that invading Ethiopian forces were Christian. In October 2006, Sheikh Nur Barud, vice chairman of the influential Somali Islamist group Kulanka Culimada, flatly declared, "[A]ll Somali Christians must be killed according to the Islamic law."[28] Foreign aid organizations are also attacked if they are alleged to be promoting Christianity. British Christian aid workers Richard and Enid Eyeington were murdered in October 2003 by militia fighters with possible links to Al-Qaeda.[29] Italian nun Sister Leonella Sgorbita, a sixty-five-year resident of Somalia, was fatally shot, together with her bodyguard, in September 2006. It is thought that her murder was related to Pope Benedict XVI's remarks at the University of Regensburg.[30]

But most attacks are against native Somali Christians and are not even confined within Somali borders; Somali refugees in Kenya face the same persecution. One of the most gruesome cases concerned Mansuur Mohammed, a twenty-five-year-old World Food Program worker. In September 2008, Al-Shabab members promised a feast to villagers in Manyafulka, who gathered in expectation of the customary slaughter of a goat, sheep, or camel. Instead, armed men brought out Mansuur, proclaimed him an apostate, and publicly beheaded him. One Al-Shabab member used a mobile phone to make a video of the slaughter, which was then sold in Somalia and neighboring countries to instill fear among those contemplating conversion.[31]

While Mansuur's case received some international press attention, scores of others have generally been ignored in the pandemic violence that prevails. On July 8, 2008, two Muslim men approached Sayid Ali Sheik Luqman Hussein, a twenty-eight-year-old convert to Christianity, and asked if he faced Mecca when he prayed. He answered that because he prayed to an omnipresent God, facing Mecca was unnecessary. Two days later, the men returned and shot him to death.[32] Ahmadey Osman Nur, a twenty-two-year-old convert, attended a September 2008 wedding conducted in Arabic, which few of the attendees understood. Nur asked for a Somali translation for himself and other guests, but the sheikh, who knew of Nur's conversion, was offended. He called Nur an apostate and ordered a guard to "silence" him. Nur was encouraged to leave the wedding and, when he did so, was shot dead.[33]

In November 2008, Salat Sekondo, a convert who lived in a refugee camp in Dadaab in northeastern Kenya, was attacked by a mob threatening to "teach him a lesson" for converting from Islam. He tried to escape by crawling out of a window, but the mob shot him in the shoulder and left him for dead. He later recovered, but others in his family were not as fortunate. The previous July, his relative Nur Osman Muhiji was stabbed to death by Islamic extremists while ten Christians he was attempting to smuggle from Kismayo, Somalia, remained hidden.[34]

Binti Ali Bilal was living in the village of Lower Juba with her ten children when, on April 15, 2008, she and her twenty-three-year-old daughter, Asha Ibrahim Abdalla—who was six months pregnant at the time—were asked by members of Al-Shabab if they were Christians, which they admitted. Binti and Asha were then beaten severely, raped repeatedly, held captive for five days, and left for dead.[35] There are other forms of brutality—the beheading of Christians has become common. On July 10, 2009, seven Somalis were beheaded for being "Christians" and "spies," and, on July 27, 2009, four Christians were kidnapped and beheaded after having refused to renounce their faith.[36]

There are also many examples of more recent cases. On September 15, 2009, when sixty-nine-year-old Christian Omar Khalafe was discovered in the port city of Merca carrying twenty-five Somali Bibles, Al-Shabab shot him dead. The Bibles were placed on his body as a warning to others. Khalafe had been a Christian for forty-five years.[37] In September 2009, Sheikh Arbow, a member of Al-Shabab, sent his wife to visit the home of forty-six-year-old Mariam Muhina Hussein with instructions to pose as a potential convert and ask to see a Bible. After Mariam Hussein was found in possession of Bibles, Arbow murdered her.[38] At about the same time, radicals noted that forty-five-year-old Amina Muse Ali, a Christian convert, refused to wear the veil. On October 19, 2009, members of the Islamic group Suna Waljameca killed her in her home in Galkayo.[39] On October 28, 2009, in Mogadishu, members of Al-Shabab detained twenty-three-year-old Mumin Abdikarim Yusuf after he was accused of trying to convert a young Muslim. On November 14, his body was found in the street: he had been shot, his front teeth were missing, and several of his fingers had been broken. There are many other such cases of abuse, torture, rape, and brutal murder of "apostates" and their families.[40] On January 1, 2010, another convert, Mohammed Ahmed Ali, was shot and killed by Al-Shabab.[41] On May 4, 2010, fifty-seven-year-old church leader Yusuf Ali Nur was killed when he was sprayed with bullets at close range by Al-Shabab in Xarardheere.[42]

The slaughter of the Christian population is not confined to converts. On March 15, 2010, Al-Shabab militants shot Madobe Abdi to death in Mahaday village; earlier in the month he had escaped a kidnapping attempt. He was an orphan who had been raised a Christian. The rebels forbade anyone to bury his body and ordered that it be left to the dogs as an example to other Christians.[43]

Sudan

Sudan has had a succession of military coups and brutal wars, interspersed with intermittent legal and constitutional changes, often promulgated in response to increasing Islamist pressure. Jafaar Numeiri seized power on May 25, 1969, in a coup led by leftist army officers, but, when in 1971 he faced a coup attempt by communist officers, he sought Islamist support by performing the Hajj and meeting with Muslim Brotherhood leaders. Also, hoping for economic support from the Saudis and political support from the Brotherhood, he agreed to implement sharia law. However, the Addis Ababa peace agreement with southern rebels, who were fighting against the North's programs of Islamization and Arabization, produced a compromised 1973 constitution, which tempered the call for an Islamic state.

This constitution was undercut in 1975 by amendments that curtailed basic human rights; and in September 1983, sharia law was imposed. In a land with a population of some forty million, about two-thirds Sunni Muslim, mainly living in the northern part of the country, about a quarter Christian, and about 10 percent traditional, mainly in the southern third of the country, this had major effects on religious freedom. Numeiri's first step was televised and theatrical, pouring thousands of bottles of whiskey into the Nile and bulldozing hundreds of thousands of beer cans. Numeiri sacked most of the prominent judges and created courts of "Prompt Justice" to implement sharia. The new judges lacked judicial experience and simply applied their own, often idiosyncratic, interpretation of sharia. Verdicts were carried out immediately, with no chance of appeal, and no lawyers could appear.[44]

Judicial amputations were conducted in public by prison guards, and there are reports that the first five victims died from blood loss. Between September 1983 and August 1984, in Khartoum province alone, there were fifty-eight public amputations, including twelve "cross limb" amputations (in which a hand and a foot on opposite sides of the body were removed). Most victims were poor Christian southerners. There were also public hangings followed by crucifixion. One of the first victims, described below, was seventy-six-year-old Mohamed Mahmoud Taha, a leading Muslim scholar and opponent of the regime.[45]

In 1985, a further coup, led by the National Islamic Front (NIF), an offshoot of Egypt's Muslim Brotherhood, suspended the constitution. Thousands were detained and tortured in secret "Ghost Houses." Regular police were augmented by Public Order police, who monitored "improper dress," indecency, prostitution, alcohol violations, and "public nuisances."[46] For the next nearly twenty years, the South waged a rebellion against Islamic rule. The government of Omar al-Bashir's, who came to power in 1989, was ruthless in prosecuting the North's side, and millions of civilians from the South were killed or displaced. Currently, hope for religious freedom and human rights in general, especially in the South, is linked to the implementation of a peace agreement between the North and the South, and the ending of the regime's genocidal attacks in Darfur, in the West.

The framework for North-South peace was the Comprehensive Peace Agreement (CPA) signed between the National Congress Party (NCP) and the Sudan People's Liberation Movement/Army (SPLM/A) on January 9, 2005. Under the CPA, the Interim Constitution gave some provision for human rights and religious freedom and stipulated that sharia law would not apply to the ten southern states; for non-Muslims in Khartoum, sharia was not automatically to apply. Article 1 recognizes Sudan as a "multi-religious" state and included rights to worship and assemble as a religious group, to communicate religious beliefs to the public, and to teach one's religion. The CPA culminated in a 2011 referendum in which the South voted to secede, and became independent on July 9 2011.

For those in the North, under section 126 of the criminal code, the legal penalty for apostasy remains death, though, as in many other settings, there is more
danger to accused apostates from vigilantes and mobs than from the legal process.[47] There are comparatively few recorded cases of formal charges against people for blasphemy and apostasy, but the country has been at the forefront of
several major blasphemy and apostasy cases. Recently, it attracted international
notoriety in the ludicrous "teddy bear incident," which we will outline below. But,
in 1985, Sudan conducted one of the most infamous apostasy trials in modern
history when it executed a man who was among the country's leading reformers
and scholars, Mohamed Mahmoud Taha.

Mohamed Mahmoud Taha

On January 18, 1985, Mohamed Mahmoud Taha was hanged for apostasy.
A leading figure of the religious and political opposition, Taha was charged for
disseminating deviant views of Islam that could create religious turmoil. He
was one of Sudan's leading Islamic scholars, a cofounder of the Sudanese
Republican Party, and an advocate for reform.[48] He was born in 1909 and in
1936 graduated from the University of Khartoum with an engineering degree
and went to work with Sudan railways. He also became involved in politics,
especially the independence movement that had begun in the late 1930s. In
October 1945, to avoid the widespread political patronage of the colonial
authorities, he cofounded the antimonarchical Republican Party. Shortly after,
the British imprisoned him for writing pro-independence pamphlets. He was
pardoned after fifty days but later that year was rearrested for leading a revolt
against the British in Rufa'ah. During his two years in prison, he began seriously to engage in his Muslim faith and, after his release, spent three more
years in self-imposed religious seclusion.

During this time, Taha concluded that the universal form of Islam was revealed
to Muhammad in Mecca, where the Prophet taught and lived a message of equality
and freedom despite being part of a persecuted minority. The Qur'an's later texts
were much more a response to particular historical conflicts around Medina. This
runs contrary to the many interpretations of the Qur'an that hold that Meccan
verses have been superseded by the later Medina teachings. In his *The Second
Message of Islam*, Taha argued: "Many aspects of the present Islamic sharia are not
the original principles or objectives of Islam. They merely reflect...time and the
limitations of human ability."[49] Taha believed that Medinan teachings were never
intended to be permanent, and he argued that humanity had developed to the
point at which it was ready to revive the Meccan verses and an Islam based on
equality and freedom. This would provide an alternative for Muslims who wanted
to embrace their faith but had doubts about the historical practice of sharia. In
October 1951, Taha emerged from seclusion and the Republican Party adopted his
understanding of the Qur'an, gradually becoming less of a political party and more

of a spiritual group. The party attracted many women because its emphasis on equality meant they could hold leadership positions.

After Sudanese independence in 1956, Taha was involved in drafting a new constitution but resigned due to government interference in the committee's work. In November 1958, before the constitution could be adopted, General El-Ferik Ibrahim Abboud seized power and dissolved all political parties. Taha clashed with Abboud's attempts at Islamization of the South and was later banned from speaking in public. In October 1964, when popular resentment against army rule forced Abboud to relinquish power, Taha revived the Republican Party and championed religious and political reform. He also spoke out internationally against Arab nationalism and the repressive forms of Islam practiced in Saudi Arabia and other Arab countries. In response, in November 1968, conservative Muslim groups pressured the authorities to try him for apostasy. Taha boycotted the trial, which issued a nominal verdict of guilty, but without any sentence.

On May 25, 1969, Colonel Jafaar Numeiri seized power. At first, Taha and the Republican Party supported the new regime, but in 1973, Numeiri banned him from lecturing in public and in 1983 introduced Islamic law in order to head off the growing Islamist following of his advisor, Hassan al-Turabi. Before implementing the laws, Numeiri imprisoned Taha and others of his group to prevent them from leading protests. After being released in December 1984, Taha published a pamphlet, "Either This, or the Flood," criticizing the laws and calling for freedom to debate Numeiri's Islamization. He asserted: "It is futile for anyone to claim that a Christian person is not adversely affected by the implementation of Shari'a.... It is not enough for a citizen today merely to enjoy freedom of worship. He is entitled to the full rights of a citizen in total equality with other citizens. The rights of southern citizens in their country are not provided for in Shari'a but rather in Islam at the level of fundamental Qur'anic revelation...."[50]

In response, public prosecutors pressed charges against Taha and four others for sedition, undermining the constitution, inciting unlawful opposition to the government, and disturbing public tranquility. At the January 8, 1985, trial, the accused refused to participate because they objected to the laws constituting the court and the very low caliber of the judges. The court's head, Al-Mukashfi Taha Al-Kabashi, also added a charge of apostasy, although there was no such provision in the penal code. Taha's supposed apostasy was based on his suggestion that women were entitled to equal shares with men in the Islamic law of inheritance and allegations that he renounced duties of jihad and daily prayer.

The court found all five guilty on all counts but added the proviso that they could be reprieved if they repented and recanted their views. On January 15, a special court of appeals upheld the lower court's finding but ruled that, because Taha was persistent in his apostasy, he did not have the option of repentance and reprieve. The decision received praise from Saudi sheikh Bin Baz, the head of the Muslim World League, based in Mecca. Other political leaders, such as Egyptian president Hosni Mubarak, asked for clemency, but Numeiri rejected their requests.

Taha's execution took place on the morning of January 18, 1985, in the court-yard of Kober prison in Khartoum North. Witnesses say that as he approached the red steel gallows, he looked defiant, smiling at the crowd before the hood was placed over his head. Many in the crowd jeered at him, chanting, "Allahu Akbar! Islam huw al-hall!" (God is great! Islam is the solution!) as his body fell through the trapdoor. After the execution, security forces flew his body by helicopter to an unknown destination in the desert west of Omdurman. The four men convicted with Taha recanted and were pardoned.

On April 6, 1985, Numeiri was overthrown by a popular uprising. Later that year, under a new transitional government, Taha's daughter, Asma, together with one of the four men convicted alongside him, initiated a constitutional suit to nul-lify the trial and execution. On November 18, 1986, the Supreme Court sided with Asma and ruled that Taha's trial and execution were null and void; Taha himself was, of course, unable to appreciate this legal victory.

Converts

In northern Sudan, under section 126 of the Sudanese penal code, any Muslim who converts to another faith is in principle subject to the death penalty. In prac-tice, suspected converts are subjected to harsh treatment. The U.S. Commission on International Religious Freedom reports that such converts "face societal pres-sures and harassment from the security services to the point that they typically cannot remain in Sudan... In contrast, government policies and societal pressure promote conversion to Islam."[51]

In 1991, Aladin Omer Agabni Mohammed converted from Islam to Christianity and was subsequently expelled from Gezira University and denounced by his family. Though no formal charges appear to have been filed against him, security police jailed him several times, tortured him, injected him with drugs, and threat-ened to kill him. On January 30, 2002, he tried to fly out of the country, but police stopped him at the airport, confiscated his passport, and beat him severely. Shortly thereafter, he went into hiding. Security officials searched his house and interrogated family members on his whereabouts but could not locate him.[52]

In June 1998, Mekki Kuku, a primary school teacher from the Nuba mountain region and the father of ten children, was arrested in Khartoum for converting from Islam to Christianity. He was imprisoned, tortured, and offered bribes to get him to recant. Eventually Abel Alier, former vice president of Sudan, intervened to end the torture and allowed Kuku a trial. However, while in prison awaiting his trial, Kuku suffered a stroke. He was subsequently released, and shortly afterward he fled the country.[53]

Mohammed Saeed Mohammed Omer became a Christian in December of 2000 while at university in New Delhi, India. When his parents learned of this, they ordered him to return home and said they would publicly disown him. When he returned on July 17, 2001, his family threatened to report him to security police if he did not recant, but he continued attending Christian meetings. On September 22, the family did report him, and he was arrested, tortured by the pulling off of three of his fingernails with pliers, and then returned to his family, who kept him under a form of house arrest. In 2003, Omer was able to flee to another country.[54]

Halima Bubkier of Sinar town, Khartoum, converted to Christianity in 2008. At first, her husband accepted her decision positively since, in the past, she had struggled with alcoholism. However, after news of her conversion spread, Islamists blocked her husband from breaking his fast at local communal meals because of his wife's conversion. He was so angry that he hurled a heavy chair at her, injuring her back. Then after removing all his belongings, he set the house on fire, destroying all of her possessions. She tried to find refuge with her older brother, but he also beat her and tried to knife her. She was then arrested for "disrespecting Islam." After three days, she was released; her present whereabouts are unknown.[55]

The "Teddy Bear" Blasphemy

Internationally, perhaps the most widely reported, and the most atypical, recent case of blasphemy in Sudan was the "teddy bear incident." In September 2007, as part of a lesson to primary school students on animals and their habitats, Gillian Gibbons, a fifty-four-year-old schoolteacher from Liverpool, England, used a teddy bear as a teaching tool. She asked the class to suggest their favorite name for the stuffed animal. Out of twenty-three students, twenty wanted to name the bear Muhammad, not directly after the prophet, but after one of the class's most popular boys.

On November 25, 2007, once news of the incident spread, Gibbons was arrested for insulting Islam's prophet, and, on November 28, she was formally charged under section 125 of the criminal law for insulting religion and inciting hatred. On November 29, she was found guilty of insulting religion and sentenced to fifteen days in prison followed by deportation. The following day, tens of thousands of protesters flooded the streets of Khartoum demanding her death for blasphemy. During the march, the protesters chanted, "Shame, shame on the U.K.," "No tolerance—execution," and "Kill her, kill her by firing squad!" Many protesters wielded machetes and swords, and government employees were involved in inciting the protests. On December 3, after two British Muslim peers, Lord Ahmed and Baroness Warsi, met with the Sudanese president, he pardoned her, and she returned to the United Kingdom.[56]

The United Nations and Gaspar Biro

Not content with its depredations within its own borders, in order to protect itself from criticism, Sudan has also pioneered attempts to use the United Nations to internationalize its blasphemy and apostasy restrictions. As described

more fully in chapter 11, one way Sudan sought to accomplish this was by charging a UN Special Rapporteur with blasphemy and indirectly threatening his life.
In 1994, the courageous UN Special Rapporteur on Sudan, Gaspar Biro, criticized
numerous Sudanese rights violations in his report to the UN Commission on
Human Rights. The greatest controversy emerged from his charge that Sudan
was in violation of international human rights agreements due to its sharia-
based penal code, under which crimes including adultery, theft, and apostasy
could lead to harsh corporal penalties or execution for anyone over the age of
seven.[57] Since Biro had said that the claimed Islamic sources of Sudan's penal
code were irrelevant to whether it was in conformity with its treaty-based human
rights obligations or not, Sudanese officials tried to silence him by calling his
report "flagrant blasphemy and a deliberate insult to the Islamic religion." The
government-controlled Sudanese press then compared him to Salman Rushdie
and demanded that he "bear the responsibility" for his statements.[58]

At the fiftieth session of the UN General Assembly in 1995–96, in response to
an inquiry as to why Biro had not been permitted back into Sudan to compile
information for a subsequent report, Sudan's Permanent Representative to the
UN warned: "[W]e don't want to speculate about his fate if he is to continue
offending the feelings of Muslims worldwide...as he did in his current interim
report"; and he implicitly threatened Biro's life, calling for the General Assembly
to "take the necessary remedial measures...otherwise no one would be in a position to guarantee that he would not face the fate of Mr. Salman Rushdie."[59]

Declaring the Nuba People Apostate

As described in the beginning of this chapter, one much less well-known use of blasphemy and apostasy by Sudan was far more momentous and involved some half a
million death sentences. Khartoum declared the population of the Nuba Mountains
apostate.[60] When civil war broke out again in 1983, many Nuba sided with the Sudan
People's Liberation Army (SPLA), based largely in the south with a majority non-
Muslim population. In response, the government organized the local Baggara Arab
tribes into a militia to fight the SPLA. This militia later became formalized as the
Popular Defense Force (PDF) and joined forces with the army in attempts to wipe out
the SPLA and the Nuba.[61] When the NIF came to power in 1989, the level of violence
against the Nuba escalated. In 1992, the Kordofan government declared jihad on the
Nuba, and, in 1993, six government-sponsored Muslim clerics in Kordofan declared
the Muslim insurgents apostates, who should be killed along with the nonbelievers
who stood in the way of Islam.[62] Hence, half a million people were sentenced to death.
The January 2005 peace agreement ended the conflict in the central Nuba region.
However, the fate of the Nuba Mountains is subject to future political negotiations
since it was not included in the referendum for the south and the area faces the
prospect of government-sanctioned sharia. It remains deeply scarred by the death,
slavery, or relocation of hundreds of thousands of its people.

Muslim Reformers

Mohammed Taha

Following the example of Mohamed Mahmoud Taha, Sudan has a tradition of innovative Muslim scholarship and reform.[63] One Muslim reformer who fell afoul of Sudan's blasphemy restrictions was Taha's namesake, Mohammed Taha. In May 2005, he was put on trial for blasphemy when the newspaper he edited, *al-Wifaq*, reprinted an article questioning the parentage of the prophet Muhammad. Eventually, the charges were dropped and he was released. However, during the trial, thousands of demonstrators gathered outside the courtroom calling for him to be put to death. On September 6, 2006, a group of armed men came to his house, forced him into a car, and drove him away. The next day, Taha was found beheaded on the main road of Khartoum. While no group has taken credit for the murder, most observers believe that Islamist vigilantes murdered a man they regarded as a blasphemer.[64]

Yasser Arman

Another notable Muslim reformer is Yasser Arman, the joint Secretary General of the Sudan People's Liberation Movement (SPLM), the primary political organization in the country's south, and a group that includes Muslims, Christians, and animists. In April 2009, in Parliament, Arman challenged a draft law on adultery. Adultery legislation in Sudan is a version of Islamic sharia law and, as it currently stands, permits death by stoning for married individuals and 100 lashes for the unmarried. In stating the SPLM's position, Arman objected to these provisions on the grounds that sharia law should not apply to non-Muslims. Simply put, he emphasized, "Some different societies... may not see adultery as a crime."

Afterward, several Sudanese media outlets suggested that, because of his stress on the limits of sharia, Arman, a devout Muslim, was no longer really a Muslim and was therefore guilty of apostasy. Though there have not appeared to be any murder attempts on him, he has received death threats from members of the ruling party, the National Congress Party (NCP). There are also concerns that imams in Khartoum will issue a fatwa against him.[65] Arman's ordeal paints a particularly dire picture for any attempts at criticism or reform of Sudan's status quo. If even the head of the largest opposition party cannot, in Parliament, safely voice disagreement on proposed laws without charges of impugning Islam and blasphemy, with the concomitant threat of death, the potential for change remains bleak.

Hassan Al-Turabi

Most surprisingly, similar allegations have dogged one of the progenitors of Sudan's Islamist regime—a man who has been involved in most of the political machinations in that country for decades and who, therefore, cannot be described as a reformer. Hassan al-Turabi had served as a high-placed religious advisor to the Numeiri and al-Bashir governments, sheltered Osama bin Laden in Sudan during the 1990s, and supported the 1985 execution of Mohamed Taha. Yet, he himself has been accused of apostasy for voicing liberal opinions concerning the status of women under Islam.

Al-Turabi has asserted that the testimony of men and women should carry equal worth in court and that mixed-gender prayers and even female prayer leaders should be allowed. He has also said that Muslim women need not cover their faces and that marriages between Muslim women and Jewish or Christian men are permissible. In response, Sudan's powerful Muslim Scholars Committee declared that he "should declare repentance or face the Sharia Hadd for heresy." Critics filed a legal complaint for apostasy against him, though so far without result.[66] Al-Turabi, who has roots in the Muslim Brotherhood and has alternated between political power and jail since the 1969 Numeiri coup, broke with his ally, Omar al-Bashir, in 1999–2000. He has since been arrested several times, most recently for his criticism of al-Bashir's actions in Darfur.[67] Whether the accusations of apostasy against him will ever be prosecuted remains to be seen.

Closing

While much of Africa remains religiously free, and a country such as Mali practices a very open form of Islam, the continent is also home to some of the most repressive Muslim regimes in the world and has the dubious distinction of being the site of much of radical Islam's most widespread nonstate violence. Current repression, due to restrictions on apostasy, blasphemy, and insulting Islam, is clearly not confined to the Middle East. Besides being present in Africa, it is, indeed, worldwide, as we will see in the next chapter, which provides some examples from South and Southeast Asia.

South and Southeast Asia

On October 31, 2003, Bangladeshi imam Aminur Rahman preached a sermon declaring that there would be no punishment if Muslims physically attacked Ahmadis. After making this proclamation, Rahman personally led an armed mob to attack the Ahmadi mosque in the Jhikargachha district of Jessore. Mohammed Shah Alam, the local Ahmadi imam, died from injuries received outside his mosque. One Ahmadi described the brutal attack and Shah Alam's murder:

> They started hitting us with bamboo sticks. They beat us and beat us. We tried to escape but it was not possible. Shah Alam was being beaten particularly harshly by Aminur Rahman and Shahid. They continued hitting us with the bamboo sticks, particularly on the head. I could see that Shah Alam was getting badly injured. They beat his brain out of his head. I could see it. We asked them to stop as we could see Shah Alam was dying and had to be taken to hospital. But they did not.

In 2009, Welhelmina Holle, a Christian teacher in Seram, part of Indonesia's Maluku Islands, was accused of blasphemy for allegedly insulting Islam in a comment she made while tutoring a sixth-grade student. The student reported the offense to his parents, and rumors quickly spread through the local Muslim community.

The local chapter of the Indonesian Ulema Council lodged a complaint with police, and the story spread even more rapidly. Soon 500 Muslims rampaged through Seram, clashing with police and local Christians and setting fire to sixty-seven homes as well as churches and a health clinic; many Christians took refuge in a nearby army barracks. Eventually, the police shut down all the stores and offices in that area. They took Holle into custody and subsequently named her, along with Muslim leader Asmara Wasahua, as a suspect in sparking the riots. She was charged with blasphemy under Article 156 of Indonesia's criminal code, which carries a maximum sentence of five years in prison.[1]

In recent years, political dissidents in Malaysia have been accused of "insulting Islam." In mid-2008, the Malaysian Islamic Development Department, the Federal Territory Islamic Religious Council, and the Federal Territory Religious Department lodged complaints against Raja Petra Kamaruddin, a member of the Selangor royal family. Raja Petra was editor of the website "Malaysia Today" and perhaps Malaysia's most prominent political blogger. Among other purported offenses, these governmental bodies alleged that his article entitled

"I Promise to Be a Good, Non-hypocritical Muslim" insulted Islam. On
September 12, 2008, he was arrested under the Internal Security Act,
and police confiscated his books and CDs. Also arrested were Teresa
Kok, an opposition parliamentarian, and journalist Tan Hoon Cheng.
Raja Petra was subsequently held without charge in a prison camp for
two months. This continued until Malaysia's high court finally ruled
that the government had overstepped its bounds.[2]

Introductory Remarks

Several countries covered in this survey—such as Saudi Arabia, Iran, Pakistan, and Afghanistan—are noted for having strong, extremist, Islamist movements. However, repression on the basis of "insults to religion" is not confined to these more radical countries. It is also present, and growing, in areas usually perceived as epitomizing open interpretations of Islam. This chapter will outline the situation in South and Southeast Asia, covering four countries: Bangladesh, Indonesia, Malaysia, and, very briefly, the Maldives. At least three of these are usually regarded as sites of moderate Islam, and two of them contain some of the Muslim world's largest populations. It should be emphasized that, in general, their brands of Islam are largely tolerant; they are not Iran or Saudi Arabia.

These countries have marked differences. Like Pakistan, Bangladesh represses Ahmadis, converts, and reformers, both by state action and by private violence, although at a much lower rate than in Pakistan. In Indonesia, the world's largest Muslim country by population, there has been increasing radicalization in recent years, with physical attacks on Ahmadis and converts from Islam. Most attacks are by mobs and vigilantes, although many local governments have also fallen under radical control. At the central government level, there has been increasing use of Article 156(a) of the criminal code, which bans defamation of religion. In Malaysia, there is increasing censorship of anything deemed by the government as likely to upset, insult, or confuse Muslims, categories that the government interprets expansively. There has also been a series of court cases undercutting the rights of Muslims to change their religion. While these cases are deeply troubling, Malaysia has so far generally dealt with them through the courts rather than through extrajudicial violence. The Maldives, an archipelago in the Indian Ocean, with very few non-Muslims, is becoming one of the world's most religiously controlled countries and is strengthening laws to further restrict its non-Muslim and dissident Muslim populations.[3]

As in other chapters, we do not try to list all recent incidents and attacks or to say all that might be said about the cases that we do cover. Even in the more moderate countries, doing so would amount to a very extensive account. But it is clear that apostasy- and blasphemy-based repression in these countries has been increasing. Violence in Indonesia and Bangladesh has grown rapidly over the last fifteen years, as has the number of Malaysian court cases on changing one's religion. In 2010, Malaysia even began to experience some religious violence.

Bangladesh

After its successful struggle for independence from Pakistan in 1971, Bangladesh was formally established as a secular state. However, in 1975, the government replaced Article 12 of the constitution, which stipulated a pluralistic and secular society, with a declaration that Islam would be among the nation's guiding principles. A 1988 constitutional amendment made Islam the state religion, although the constitution still formally grants religious freedom. According to the 2001 census, minority religions comprise some 10 percent of the population, and, of these, an estimated 90 percent are Hindu, with the rest divided mainly between Christians, primarily Roman Catholic, and Buddhists, though there continues to be a small Ahmadi presence. The rest of the population is officially categorized as Sunni Muslim.[4]

In 2001, in an effort to unify the legal system, the High Court ruled all fatwas illegal, a decision met with violent public protests. On the local level, village religious leaders have nonetheless continued to issue fatwas regarding specific cases, often involving "perceived moral transgressions" by women.[5] Meanwhile, radical Islamists complain about what they regard as the country's "pseudo-Islamization" and call for Bangladesh to be renamed the "Islamic Republic of Bangladesh" with a constitution based on sharia. While most Bangladeshi Muslims appear to want a state distinct from religious authority, radical Islamists campaign, including through widespread bombing, to transform the country into an Islamist state. The December 2008 national elections pitted the relatively secular Awami League against the Islamist Bangladesh Nationalist Party, which had pledged to enact blasphemy laws. The Awami League won in a landslide, gaining more than 250 of Parliament's 300 seats.[6] The league then committed itself to improving the plight of religious minorities, and, in April 2009, the prime minister, Sheikh Hasina, promised to repeal all laws and rules held to be discriminatory toward them.[7]

Despite this recent electoral rejection of Islamism, Bangladesh still sees widespread and virulent persecution of minority religious groups, especially of the Ahmadi community. This includes destruction of property, kidnapping, the killing of leaders, rape—often of young girls—and discrimination in education, employment, and property rights. Most Hindus have lost lands under old Pakistani laws against "enemies," which, in practice, has meant Hindus.[8] Jamaat-e-Islami, the country's largest Islamist party, pledged in the 2008 election campaign to enact a blasphemy law.[9] Although it did poorly in the election, persecutions and arrests on the basis of blasphemy charges have continued, despite the fact that the country has no blasphemy law.[10] While rejecting such practices, the more secular, democratic parties have been complacent, unwilling to address this persecution and, for electoral gain, sometimes even adopting Islamist rhetoric. The constitutional guarantees of religious freedom have been functionally deficient, as illustrated by the treatment of Ahmadis and dissidents such as Taslima Nasreen, Salahuddin Shoaib Choudhury, and Arifur Rahman, who will be discussed in the following pages.

Ahmadis

Perhaps the chief victims of quasi-legal blasphemy restrictions are the Ahmadis, about 100,000 of whom live in Bangladesh. As in Pakistan, Ahmadis have been declared non-Muslims and apostates by most religious and political leaders and have suffered relentless religious and political attacks.[11] Foreign Muslims have encouraged this rejection; in Bangladesh on February 28, 1997, the chief imam of the Prophet's Mosque in Medina, Saudi Arabia, Allama Dr. Shaikh Ali Bin Abdur Rahman Al Huzaifi, condemned Ahmadis as "traitors . . . misleading others by their self-made and false Quranic commentary." By January 9, 2004, the government had banned all Ahmadi publications, with the Home Ministry stating that the ban was intended to block any "publications which hurt or may hurt the sentiments of the majority Muslim population of Bangladesh." (On December 21, 2004, Justice A.T.M. Kharul Islam of the High Court ordered a stay on the ban.)

Attacks against Ahmadis have increased since the early 1990s. On October 30, 1992, the Bahshkibazar Ahmadiyya complex in Dhaka was attacked by over a thousand rioters, who burned books, including Qur'ans, set off some thirty-five crude bombs, and set the buildings on fire. At least twenty Ahmadis were injured. On October 8, 1999, a bomb killed six Ahmadis and severely injured several others at their mosque in Khulna. In November 1999, an Ahmadi mosque near Natore was ransacked, leaving thirty-five people injured. On October 15, 2002, after a brawl broke out outside the Upazila Parishod courthouse in Gajipur—where a case was being filed against Ahmadis—twelve Ahmadis were arrested for allegedly distorting verses of the Qur'an and hadith.

Often the police not only fail to provide adequate protection to Ahmadis but also directly participate in their persecution. Mohammad Mominul Islam describes how the police attacked him on July 19, 2004:

> Early in the morning, after the Fajr (dawn) prayers, a mob from the village surrounded my house, dragged me out, and tied me to a tree. Then they started beating me with sticks and rods. Then they carried me to the local market and beat me more, this time even more badly. Just when I thought I was going to die, local policemen came to the spot and took

me to another house and then the policemen asked me to leave the Ahmadiyya faith. When I refused, the policemen started beating me. Then they took me to the police station and put me in the lock-up where they handcuffed me and beat me again. The next morning, at about 11 o'clock, the policemen took me to the district headquarters of the police and beat me again.

Converts

Converts from Islam have also suffered persecution. On April 12, 2008, thirty-two-year-old businessman Rashidul Amin Khandaker converted to Catholicism while in Australia. When he telephoned friends back in Dhaka to tell them, several looted his house, threatening to harm his family if he told police about it. Since they could not reach Rashidul, Muslim leaders in Dhaka ordered his father, sixty-five-year-old Rahul Amin Khandaker, to disown his son and to remain confined to his house until his son could be punished: "If he comes to Bangladesh, you must hand him over to us and we will punish him."[12] Then, when Rahul had a stroke, no local doctor would treat him. One neighbor asked. "Why did you not sacrifice your son like cattle before telling the news to us?" In May 2008, Rashidul's brother wrote him, asking him to break off all contact since Muslim authorities had warned they would ostracize the family. While deeply grieved by his son's conversion, Rahul does not want to disown his son: "If all of my property and wealth is destroyed, I can tolerate that, but one thing I cannot tolerate is to carry the coffin of my son on my shoulders.... My son changed his faith according to his will, and our constitution supports this kind of activity."[13]

In Chakaria, in southeastern Bangladesh, a family of Christian converts was attacked in November 2008. Laila Begum, forty-five, was assisting a local NGO micro-credit agency when a group of Muslims demanded that a Muslim woman repay a loan even though Begum had already repaid it on her behalf. Upon her refusal, the group attacked her with sticks, iron rods, knives, and machetes. Her husband and son came to her rescue when they heard her screaming, at which point Begum reports, "They thrust at my son with machetes and a sharp knife and stabbed him in his thigh... They also beat the kneecap of my husband and other parts of his body." Her eighteen-year-old daughter was assaulted and partially stripped in front of the crowd. One attacker allegedly said, "Nobody will come to save you if we beat you, because you are converted to Christianity from Islam."[14] On September 25, 2009, William Gomes, a Catholic convert from Islam, fled his burning home after a group of Islamic militants stormed his house and accused him of apostasy. The riot was started after inflammatory sermons in a local mosque, from which the rioters went to Gomes's house and set it on fire.[15]

Reformers

Taslima Nasreen in Bangladesh and India

Taslima Nasreen has suffered ongoing persecution in her native Bangladesh, which continued even after she tried to settle in neighboring India. Born in 1962, the daughter of a village physician and a devoutly religious mother, she was trained as a medical doctor. Nasreen gradually became a critic of religion, a feminist, and a self-described atheist.[16] In the 1980s, she criticized Islam as a cause of the oppression of women, and her poem "Happy Marriage" depicted physical and emotional abuse within a marriage, matters rarely discussed openly in Bangladeshi society. In her novel *Lajja* (Shame), she explored the problems faced by Bangladesh's Hindu minority. She has won many awards, including the 1994 Sakharov Prize for Freedom of Thought from the European parliament and the 2000 Global Leader for Tomorrow award from the World Economic Forum.

The Bangladesh government banned *Lajja*, as well as other books written by Nasreen, while radical Islamist groups called for her to be killed. In 1993, following complaints about her newspaper columns, she was charged with "deliberately and maliciously hurting Muslim religious sentiments." After massive and sometimes violent Islamist demonstrations against her, she went into hiding. In 1994, the government ordered her detention, and, after two months, she surrendered to the High Court. Faced with the banning of her books, legal threats, and radical imams issuing fatwas demanding her death, she fled to Sweden after being released on bail and was granted asylum. However, after a decade in exile in Europe, mostly in Stockholm and Paris, she sought to settle in Kolkata (Calcutta), West Bengal, where much of India's Bengali population lives.

However, many in India's Muslim community also turned on her. In January 2004, upon her arrival in Kolkata, Syed Noor-ur-Rehman, a powerful Muslim cleric, promised "20,000 rupees ($440 US) to anyone who can tar her face or put around her a garland of shoes."[17] Hindu radicals passed out copies of *Lajja*, and Muslim radicals responded by burning the book and calling for her death. Despite this, successive Indian governments denied her requests for asylum. Some Indian Muslim groups asked for a ban on her 2002 autobiographical book, *Dwikhondito*, (Divided) and demanded that she be deported. In response, and while maintaining that *Dwikhondito*'s religious references were based on "universally accepted" works on Islamic history, she said that, to avoid hurting people's feelings, she would be willing to remove "controversial lines." On November 16, 2004, the Kolkata High Court banned the book, though the ban was lifted in September 2005 after an appeals court rejected it as "unjustified and untenable."[18]

In March 2007, the All India Ittehad Millat Council promised 500,000 rupees to anyone who beheaded Nasreen, an offer that would be rescinded only if she "apologizes, burns her books and leaves." On August 9, 2007, she was physically attacked by members, including some elected members, of the political party Ittahidul Muslimin at the launch of her book's Telugu translation, *Shodh*, in

Hyderabad, South India. One elected member threatened Nasreen with beheading were she ever to return to Hyderabad. The Hyderabad City Police also filed a case against her for "hurting the religious sentiments of Muslims."[19] In November 2007, the government of West Bengal told Nasreen that it could not ensure her security and deported her from the state. She moved to an undisclosed location— some reports say in a safe house run by India's intelligence bureau near Delhi.

On January 9, 2008, it was announced in Paris that Nasreen had been awarded the Simone de Beauvoir Prize for her writing on women's rights. On February 15, with great hesitation, the Indian government cautiously extended her visa for six months, but, the next day, West Bengal's Muslim clergy and political leaders warned that they would take to the streets if she were offered ongoing shelter. In March 2008, she short-circuited the debate by leaving India "voluntarily" and went to Norway. However, she returned to India on August 8, 2008, and is again at an undisclosed location. As she has noted, "If India gives in to the fundamentalists' demand to deport me, the list of demands will become an endless one. A deportation today, a ban tomorrow, an execution the day after. Where will it cease?"[20] Indian Muslim Ali Asghar Engineer defended the author's right to free expression. While agreeing "Taslima has written provocative articles on Islam," he argued, "We must counter it by arguing on the basis of Qur'an rather than attacking her physically. No one can cite a single verse of the Qur'an or any hadith to support violence against others, even enemies, as long as they are peaceful. On the other hand we can cite several verses from the Qur'an, to support dignified behavior."[21]

Salahuddin Shoaib Choudhury

Salahuddin Shoaib Choudhury, a man of moderate Islamic religious views, was the editor of *The Weekly Blitz* and has written about Al-Qaeda's activities in Bangladesh. He has also criticized anti-Israeli and anti-Semitic attitudes in Muslim-majority countries. His major difficulties began in 2003 when he developed an interest in Israel and started corresponding with an editor of *The Jerusalem Post*. This led to his article in the *Post* advocating peaceful relations between Bangladesh and Israel. He was then invited to the International Forum for the Literature and Culture of Peace conference in Tel Aviv to lecture on "[h]ow the media can foster world peace."[22]

On November 29, 2003, as he was about to board a plane on his way to Israel, he was arrested, and his passport was confiscated. He was blindfolded, beaten, and questioned by security officials for ten days to get him to confess to espionage for Israel.[23] He was initially charged with, inter alia, criminal conspiracy, sedition, and "deliberate and malicious acts intended to outrage religious feelings." He was held for seventeen months in hellish conditions and suffered isolation, torture, and denial of medical attention. He was released in April 2005 but faced more harassment, threats on his life, attacks on his newspaper's offices, and a pending trial. PEN Center USA awarded him its Freedom to Write Award in 2005, and the

Bangladesh Minority Lawyers Association gave him its Courageous Journalism Award in 2006. When the American Jewish Committee sought to present him with its Moral Courage Award in May 2006, Bangladeshi authorities again kept him from leaving the country, and he addressed the meeting via video.

While Choudhury was awaiting trial, about forty people, including senior members of the governing political party, looted his offices. He was beaten—his ankle was broken—and robbed. Police did not permit him to lodge charges against his assailants and also denied him any protection, so that he had to go into hiding. At his trial, in Dhaka on November 13, 2006, the presiding judge described his crimes: "By praising the Jews and Christians, by attempting to travel to Israel, and by predicting the so-called rise of Islamist militancy in the country and expressing such through writings inside the country and abroad, you have tried to damage the image and relations of Bangladesh with the outside world."[24] The charges could carry a sentence of up to thirty years' imprisonment or death. The case dragged on, and February 12, 2008, marked his forty-first court appearance in thirty-four months.[25] The only offense that the authorities have been able to pin on him is that he violated the Passport Act by seeking to travel to Israel, a country with which Bangladesh does not have diplomatic relations, which is an offense usually punishable by a small fine. In February 2009, a gang broke into his newspaper's headquarters, attacking the staff until they found him, brought him out to the street, and beat him in broad daylight, claiming the Mossad, the Israeli intelligence service, employed him. There is no indication that authorities intervened at all in the situation.[26]

Arifur Rahman

Arifur Rahman was the sole breadwinner of his family and supported his elderly mother, no mean feat for a twenty-three-year-old self-taught cartoonist in Bangladesh. As a young artist with a promising future, he drew comics for *Aalpin*, the weekly satirical supplement of *Prothom Alo*, the country's largest Bengali-language daily newspaper. In 2007, he won first prize in the national Anti-Corruption Cartoon Competition sponsored by *The Daily Star*. However, on December 18, 2007, he was taken into custody and interrogated about a cartoon titled "Naam" (Name) that he had published the previous day. The text of the cartoon shows a man addressing a boy:

> Q. Boy, what is your name?
>   - My name is Babu.
>
> Q. It is customary to mention Muhammad before the name. What is your
>   father's name?
>   - Muhammad Abu
>
> Q. What's this in your lap?
>   - Muhammad cat.[27]

Arif was certainly not the first to joke about the common practice in Islamic societies to name everything and everyone Muhammad, and similar items had circulated widely in previous years. Arif told police that he had not meant to hurt
anyone's religious feelings and that this was a common joke in his home village.
Aalpin's deputy editor was dismissed, and *Prothom Alo* not only apologized for
publishing an "impertinent" and "unacceptable" cartoon but also promised never
to publish Arif's work again. Despite these abject apologies, Arif was taken to
Tejgaon police station and held overnight. He was not told why he was being held,
given any opportunity to tell anybody his whereabouts, nor allowed access to a
lawyer.[28]

Arif was initially detained under Section 54 of the criminal procedure code,
which permits police to arrest suspects with neither a warrant nor orders from a
magistrate. Under the Bangladesh State of Emergency, he was not guaranteed any
legal representation. He was originally held for thirty days on the orders of a
deputy secretary of the Ministry of Home Affairs, with three-month extensions
ordered October 11 and again in January 2008. For over a month after his arrest,
he did not know of the detention order against him. While he was supposedly
being held in "preventive detention," the actual allegation against him was that he
had violated Section 295A of the penal code by "hurting religious sentiments"
with his cartoon.

Opportunistic Islamist politicians immediately jumped on the issue in an
attempt to silence a newspaper that had often been critical of the military regime.
There were street demonstrations and vandalism throughout Dhaka, with protests led by radical Islamist groups, including Hizbut-Tahrir Bangladesh (HT) and
Islami Shasantantra Andolon (ISA), under the auspices of the All Party Resistance
Committee. Demonstrators burned effigies of Arif and called for his death, as well
as for the deaths of his editor and publisher.[29] Islamists found a ready partner in
the military government, and a delegation led by Obaidul Haque—the *khatib*
(preacher) of the Baitul Mukarram, the national mosque—called on law and
information advisor Mainul Hosein and demanded cancellation of *Prothom Alo*'s
license and the arrest of its editor, along with others concerned, "for showing disrespect to the Prophet." After the meeting, Hosein told reporters: "It is a conspiracy
to destabilize the country. We are very concerned over the issue."[30]

Hizbut-Tahrir is active in many countries, and a spokesman of its U.K. wing
said that the cartoon and article were "deliberate attempts to ridicule Islam's
Prophet."[31] They launched protests in London, calling for the suspension of the
publications' licenses, the arrest of everyone involved with the cartoon, and the
reinstatement of sharia and Khilafah laws to "protect Islamic faith and values."
They also charged that Arif's cartoon was, together with the caricatures of
Muhammad published in Danish and Swedish papers in September 2005 and
August 2007, part of an international crusade against Islam.

The Paris-based Reporters Without Borders defended the cartoon as nothing
more than "a joke about cultural custom" and said that the "play on words had no

intention of attacking the Prophet" and called for Arif's immediate release.[32] On September 25, 2007, the Vienna-based International Press Institute also urged his release in the name of press freedom.[33] Nonetheless, the military regime continued to resist international pressure for press freedom.[34] After being held for six months in Dhaka's central jail, Arif was released in March 2008, but, in November 2009, he was found guilty of "hurting the religious sentiments of the Muslim community" and sentenced to six months' hard labor. Arif says he was not aware that a trial was even taking place and has asked his lawyers to inquire further.[35]

Accusations of blasphemy have also infected the political arena and have been used even against Islamist parties. On March 17, 2010, one of the leaders of the fundamentalist Jamaat-e-Islami party (JeI), Matiur Rahman Nizami, complained of the party's persecution by the government coalition and compared his own sufferings to those of Muhammad. He was then accused of blasphemy by Mohammed Syed Rezaul Haque Chandpur, Secretary General of the Tariqat Federation, which is part of the government alliance. After Nizami and two other JeI leaders, Ali Ahsan Mohammad Mojaheed and Nayebe Ameer Delwa Sayeed Hossain, repeatedly refused to appear in court to answer to the charge, they were arrested on June 29 and held for investigation.[36]

Indonesia

Indonesia's population of some 240 million is about 83 percent Muslim, 9 percent Protestant, 4 percent Catholic, 2 percent Hindu, and 1 percent Buddhist. Most Muslims are Sunni, though there may be up to three million Shiites in the country. Following independence, under President Sukarno, the country accepted the broad state ideology of *Pancasila*, now enshrined in the constitution's preamble.[37] It proclaims five principles: "One Lordship, just and civilized humanity, the unity of Indonesia, democracy guided by the wisdom of deliberations of representatives, and social justice for all the Indonesian people."[38] Article 29 of the constitution combines this commitment to monotheism with a commitment to religious freedom. It proclaims, "1. The State shall be based upon the belief in the One and Only God. 2. The State guarantees all persons the freedom of worship, each according to his or her own religion or belief."

It is the world's most populous Muslim country, and its religious communities have traditionally coexisted peacefully. However, Indonesian law only recognizes six faiths: Islam, Buddhism, Hinduism, Catholicism, Protestantism, and, as of January 2006, Confucianism. Consequently, other religious minorities can only register as social groups and thus are prohibited from performing certain types of religious activity. The Baha'ís have been banned, and Jehovah's Witnesses were banned from 1976 to 2001, while restrictions have been placed on others, especially Islamic groups regarded as heterodox. Atheism is also in principle banned on the grounds that it violates *Pancasila*, though the government does not seek out atheists. Conversions between faiths are legal and do occur, although, according to a 1979 decree by the Ministries of Religion and Home Affairs, proselytizing is illegal.

While religious groups have a wide range of freedoms, Article 156(a) of the criminal code states, "Those, who purposely express their views or commit an act that principally disseminates hatred, misuses or defames a religion recognized in Indonesia, face at maximum five years imprisonment." This provision has been enforced almost exclusively in cases of alleged heresy or blasphemy against Islam. In 1990, journalist Arswendo Atmowiloto published in the newspaper *Monitor* the results of a survey asking readers to name their heroes: then-president Suharto came in first, Atmowiloto came in tenth, and Muhammad came in eleventh. For this, the journalist was convicted of blasphemy and served five years.[39] On February 9, 2010, after challenges by the former president of Indonesia, Abdurrahman Wahid, and several human rights organizations, the Constitutional Court for the first time began to review the constitutionality of the 1965 law. Hendardi, the chairman of the Setara Institute for Democracy and Peace, argued that the law was used to intimidate Muslim and non-Muslim minorities, especially the Ahmadiyya. The government, as well as Islamist groups, has defended it.[40] On April 19, 2010, the Supreme Court, in an 8–1 decision, held that the law was constitutional. Before the ruling, Suryadharma Ali, Minister of Religious Affairs, said, "The law should be upheld because if it is annulled...Islam and the Quran could be interpreted at will and people and figures could declare new prophets and establish new religions."[41]

The largest challenges to religious freedom tend to come from social pressures, vigilantes, and militias rather than from the government. Since the late 1990s, there has been an escalation in radical Islamist activities, and, in addition, many provinces have instituted elements of Islamic law locally. Aceh is the only province with officially recognized Islamic law, but other local governments have also passed laws discriminating against religious minorities, and mobs and other forms of violence sometimes implement these.[42] To date, the government has not used its constitutional authority to overturn these laws.

Ahmadis

Ahmadis are one of the most heavily persecuted religious groups, as they are in many other Muslim-majority countries. In Indonesia, they have been deemed a heretical sect and, in 1980, the Indonesia Council of Ulemas (MUI)—a government advisory body—issued a fatwa declaring that the Ahmadis are not a legitimate part of Islam. Following this lead, in 1984, the Ministry of Religious Affairs banned Ahmadis from disseminating their teachings in Indonesia.[43]

Ahmadis are also subject to increasing violence. On July 15, 2005, some 10,000 people from the Indonesian Muslim Solidarity group attacked the Indonesia

Ahmadiyya Congregation (JAI) in Parung, Bogor, West Java. Though armed only with stones and batons, the attackers damaged and set fire to buildings while demanding that the 500 followers living there leave Parung within two hours. The mob leaders specifically cited the 1980 fatwa and a recent ruling issued by the Bogor branch of the MUI, calling for the Ahmadis to leave Bogor. The police detained none of the attackers. The coordinator of the Solidarity group, Habib Abdurrahman Ismail Assegaf, justified his actions by opining, "Ahmadiyah is not a Muslim group... It says that Prophet Muhammad was not the last (prophet) and that its followers can be a haji by carrying out a ritual right here in its compound, so they don't have to go to Mecca." The 500 Ahmadis left their compound, and, on July 18, 2005, JAI chairman Abdul Basit went to the Indonesian Legal Aid Foundation (YLBHI) for help in preparing legal measures against the MUI and the attackers.[44] Specifically, Basit wanted the MUI to annul the 1980 fatwa in order to prevent more violence against the Ahmadiyyah.[45] However, the MUI did the exact opposite. On July 26, 2005, its four-day national congress called for an end to "deviant secular and liberal Islamic thoughts" and renewed the fatwa.[46]

The renewal of the fatwa prompted yet more attacks, including the destruction of Ahmadi mosques as well as their headquarters near the city of Bogor.[47] On September 20, 2005, police detained thirty-five people for attacks against Ahmadis in Cianjur. According to one report, four mosques, three religious schools, and thirty-three houses were damaged. In response, the Cianjur regency banned all Ahmadi activities. In October 2005, the regional office of the Ministry of Religious Affairs in West Nusa Tenggara also banned the Ahmadis. While these regional bans were purportedly aimed at protecting the Ahmadis and keeping the peace, Ahmadis and their supporters justifiably believed that the government was punishing them and not their attackers.[48] Indonesian authorities often did little to prevent the attacks or prosecute those responsible, instead blaming the Ahmadis for "provoking" the violence.[49] In February and March 2006, 187 members of the JAI in Mataram, Lombok, had to flee to a refugee camp after local Muslims attacked their houses and mosques. The victims considered seeking asylum in another country.

On June 9, 2008, the Indonesian government, after persistent pressure from extremist groups, issued a joint ministerial decree ordering the Ahmadiyya community to stop all religious activity as long as they continued to describe themselves as followers of Islam. The decree states, "The followers... of the Indonesian Ahmadiyya Jama'at (JAI) are warned... to discontinue the promulgation of interpretations and activities that are deviant from the principal teachings of Islam."[50] The punishment for disobedience is up to five years in jail. The decree also states that those who attack Ahmadis would be punished, but this has not been systematically enforced. This decree echoed the Ulema Council view that the issue would be resolved if Ahmadis simply formed their own religion. However, apart from the Ahmadis' own views, Indonesia requires all its citizens to adhere either to Islam, Hinduism, Buddhism, Protestantism, Catholicism, or Confucianism. Unless this legal framework is altered, Ahmadis will have to find a way to align with the state-sanctioned religion closest to their own beliefs.[51]

The government decree did not formally disband the Ahmadiyya community, and in practice, they can maintain their faith but cannot propagate it. However, it represented a serious setback for Ahmadis in Indonesia and set the stage for more violence.[52] During 2008, twenty-one Ahmadi mosques were closed because of violence or intimidation in addition to those remaining closed from previous years.[53] Many have spoken out on their behalf, including the former president, Abdurrahman Wahid, who believed that banning the Ahmadis was a first step for many Islamic radicals toward creating an Islamic state. Still, Indonesia's Ahmadis remain under siege.[54]

Converts

While Christians in Indonesia have a great deal of freedom, converts from Islam to Christianity—and anybody thought to be involved in such conversions—have faced increasing threats. On September 1, 2005, three Indonesian Christian women were each sentenced to three years in prison for allowing Muslim children to attend their Christian Sunday school classes. The women, Rebekka Zakaria, Eti Pangesti, and Ratna Banjun, were charged under the 2002 Child Protection Act, which forbids "deception, lies or enticement" to lure a child from a state-recognized religion and provides a maximum penalty of up to five years in prison and a fine of 100 million rupiah. (Enticing a person to a recognized religion from an unrecognized religion would not violate this law, so the children of Ahmadis, Baha'is, and Jehovah's Witnesses are not protected.)

The court recognized that the three women had not converted any children and that, in fact, had told children who did not have parental permission to attend the class to go home. The women also showed photographs of Muslim children together with their parents at the Sunday school, proving that they had attended the class with parental consent. However, hundreds of Islamic extremists gathered outside the court and threatened to kill the judge if he did not find the defendants guilty. Rioters also brought a coffin to intimidate the defendants, purportedly threatening to bury them in the event that they were found innocent. This violent environment made it difficult for the judges to acquit the defendants. When the court announced that the three women were guilty of using "deceitful conduct, a series of lies and enticements to seduce children to change their religion against their wills," the large crowd in the courtroom screamed, "Allahu akbar!" The women were sentenced to three years in prison. Feelings about the case were so intense that even two years later, the defendants were released at 6 a.m. to avoid violence.[55]

On October 17, 2006, Muslim extremists in West Java kidnapped, brutally beat, and attempted to strangle a Muslim convert to Christianity. A Muslim extremist pretending to be interested in learning about Christianity first approached the man, a lecturer at several local religious institutions, whose name has been withheld for security reasons. This man studied with the lecturer and then asked him to accompany others on a trip to Lembang, a town near Bandung, and to bring along Christian books and cassettes. After getting into a van, he was strangled and hit in the head with a hammer before rolling out of the car and escaping to the nearest police station. The police later apprehended one of the extremists who had been delayed in a traffic accident.[56]

Heterodox Muslim Groups

Apart from Ahmadis, there has been repression of others from either heterodox Muslim groups or non-Muslim groups. The Al-Qiyadah Islamiyah sect, with approximately 4,000 members, holds that prayer only once daily, rather than five times daily, is sufficient and that Muhammad was not the last prophet. In October 2007, the Ulema Council (MUI) declared Al-Qiyadah Islamiyah "deviant," and, later that month, hundreds of people raided the homes of three of its members. Members were detained by police and soon were prosecuted. Twenty-one of the group's members applied to the East Java police for protection but were refused; instead, they were instructed to write a letter promising not to engage in proselytism.[57] On May 2, 2008, two members, Dedi Priadi, forty-four, and Gerry Lufthi Yudistira, twenty, were sentenced to three years in prison on the basis of Article 156. The previous month, the leader of Al-Qiyadah, Abdul Salam, was sentenced to four years for blasphemy.[58]

There has also been imprisonment of people with very idiosyncratic views or habits. On June 28, 2006, Sumardi Tappaya, a Muslim teacher from Sulawesi, was arrested after a relative reported that he whistled when he prayed. After the local MUI declared that the whistling was deviant, Sumardi was sentenced to six months for heresy.[59] On June 29, 2006, the Central Jakarta District Court sentenced Lia Eden, leader of Salamullah (God's Kingdom of Eden), to two years in prison for blasphemy. She was convicted for claiming that her son Abdul Rachman was the reincarnation of Muhammad, that she was the angel Gabriel, that she prayed in languages other than Arabic, and that she was the Virgin Mary.[60] On October 30, 2007, she was released but said that she would continue her teaching. On November 9, 2007, Rachman was sentenced to three years in prison for blasphemy.[61] In July 2009, Agus Imam Solichin, a leader of the Atrio Piningit Weteng Buwono sect, which does not consistently pray five times a day or fast, was sentenced to two and a half years in prison for violating article 156A.[62]

Muslim Reformers

Liberal Islam Network

On July 26, 2005, at the same congress that renewed its 1980 fatwa against the Ahmadis, the MUI issued ten other edicts, one of which banned the Liberal Islamic Network (JIL). This network began in meetings among Muslim intellectuals at the

Institute for the Studies on Free Flow of Information (ISAI) in Jakarta but soon attracted more people, formed a website, and began publishing online.

The radical Islam Defenders Front had already targeted one of JIL's founders, Ulil Abshar Abdalla. In 2002, a group of religious scholars, the Bandung Indonesian Ulemas Forum (FUUI), issued a fatwa saying he should be killed after he published an article in *Kompas* newspaper entitled "Freshening Up Islamic Understanding," in which he defended the freedom of people to choose their own beliefs and emphasized that Islam must be understood in its historical and cultural context. He insisted that aspects of sharia law, including amputations, were no longer applicable. Abdalla also called for an understanding of Islam that distinguished between what is "the creation of a local culture, and what are fundamental values...aspects of Islam that reflect the mirror of Arab culture, for example, do not need to be followed." A fatwa issued by Islamic clerics associated with Unity of Islam, the Prosperous Justice Party, and even the mainstream Muhammadiyah movement, accused Abdalla of blasphemy for saying that Muhammad was primarily a historical figure and for questioning the basis of Islamic law. One cleric who helped draft the fatwa, Athian Ali, stated, "[A]ccording to Islamic law, anyone who slanders Islam can be punished with death." The fatwa also pushed for Abdalla's arrest, but he remained free; however, for a time, he did have security guards.[63]

Muhammad Yusman Roy

In August 2005, East Java's Malang district court sentenced Muhammad Yusman Roy to two years in prison for inciting hatred after he challenged local clerics on the issue of bilingual prayers. Born to a Dutch Catholic mother and an Indonesian father, Roy embraced Catholicism as a teenager but converted to Islam in his early thirties. Like most Indonesian Muslims, Roy never learned Arabic. This can become a problem when performing *salat*, prayers recited by Muslims five times a day while facing Mecca; conservative Muslims interpret the Qur'an to require that *salat* be performed in Arabic. In 2002, Roy began translating *salat* prayers into Indonesian for himself and a few others at his boarding school in Malang. These unorthodox prayers went unnoticed at first, but that changed when he distributed tapes of himself to local mosques, performing the prayers in Indonesian. The Islamic Defenders Front confronted Roy during a debate at his school, and local and provincial ulema councils issued fatwas against him. At one point, police even posted guards at his house and school to protect him from angry mobs. In August 2005, he was put on trial and found guilty of inciting hatred through his challenge to local clerics. Curiously, he was acquitted of the further charge that his teachings deviated from Islam. He was released from prison on November 9, 2006, after serving eighteen months. He plans to continue to push for the adoption of bilingual prayers.[64]

Teguh Santosa

On February 2, 2006, the online edition of *Rakyat Merdeka* briefly republished one of the "Danish cartoons" from *Jyllands-Posten*, illustrating an article critical of the cartoons. After Muslim groups protested in front of *Rakyat Merdeka*'s offices, the cartoon was quickly taken down, having been posted for less than a day. However, the radical Islamic Defenders Front filed a complaint with the police. On July 19, Teguh Santosa, the chief online editor, was arrested and held briefly in Cipinang prison. He was charged with offending Islam, in violation of Article 156(a) of the criminal code. His trial began on August 31, 2006, and, on September 20, 2006, a Jakarta court dismissed the charges on the grounds of insufficient evidence.[65]

Malaysia

While there are exceptions, in Malaysia, religious identity is highly correlated with ethnicity. The majority of ethnic Malays are Muslim, and ethnic Indians and Chinese usually practice Buddhism, Christianity, or Hinduism. In the population of some twenty-six million, about 60 percent are Muslim, though this may be skewed by the fact that the constitution defines all ethnic Malays as Muslim. About 19 percent are Buddhist, 10 percent Christian, 6 percent Hindu, and 5 percent "other," including Confucian, Taoist, and traditional Chinese religions. Article 3 of the federal constitution provides that Islam is "the religion of the Federation," but "other religions may be practiced in peace and harmony." Article 11 provides, "Every person has the right to profess and practice his religion and...to propagate it." The civil justice system is applicable to all citizens, and there is a state sharia court system that has jurisdiction over Muslims in family law. When sharia court decisions affect non-Muslims, the defendants may, in theory, seek recourse in the civil courts.

In practice, the government significantly restricts non-Sunni Muslim beliefs and systematically discriminates against non-Muslims. Using guidelines issued by the Islamic Development Department, and with the consent of sharia courts, the federal government represses what it considers "deviant" interpretations of Islam and has prohibited over fifty deviant teachings, including Shia. So-called deviants may be arrested and detained in order to be "rehabilitated." The federal government also requires that all Muslim civil servants attend government-approved religion classes, and Islamic religious instruction is mandatory for Muslim children in public schools. The government has also rebuffed efforts at building interfaith coalitions to discuss religious freedom, maintaining that "matters concerning Islam could only be discussed by Muslims."

Censorship

As part of its efforts to prevent its Muslim population from being exposed to any nonapproved religious belief, under Section 7(1) of the Printing Presses and Publications Act of 1984, the Malaysian government restricts and bans books and other publications if it believes that they are contrary to the official version of

Islam. According to the government's Bernama news agency, between 2000 and July 2009, 397 books were banned.[66]

The censorship includes non-Muslim books. In 1986, the Interior Security Ministry banned the word "Allah" from publications of the non-Islamic community, on the grounds that this could confuse Muslims, though the ordinance was not always applied. This restriction is unusual since Arabic-speaking Christians have used the word for centuries, as have Christians in neighboring Indonesia. Apparently, the Malaysian government thinks its population is easily confused. In April 2005, the prime minister even declared that Malay-language Bibles should have the words "Not for Muslims" printed on the front, could only be distributed in churches or Christian bookshops, and could not be used in Malay homes. In 2003, the government stopped publication of a Bible in Iban, the language of an indigenous Malaysian tribe, ostensibly to prevent Christians from proselytizing.[67]

The ban on the use of "Allah" was invoked in December 2007 in a lawsuit, by the Islamic religious councils of seven Malaysian states and the Malaysian Chinese Muslim Association, against the Malay-language *Catholic Herald* magazine, published by the Catholic diocese of Kuala Lumpur. Christians responded that the use of "Allah" as a general term for God predates Islam, that the word is a variation of the Hebrew "Elohim," that it has been used for centuries, including in Malaysia, as a "common reference to God" by Christians and Muslims, and that only recently had Malay diction started to treat "Allah" as "the God of Islam." Christians also maintained that, in any case, Malaysia's constitutional guarantees of religious freedom allowed them to use the word.[68]

The Interior Security Minister sided with the Islamic councils and banned the magazine on the grounds that using the term "could increase tension and create confusion among Muslims."[69] While the *Herald* is generally distributed only in Catholic churches, some Muslims complained that the offending word could be found on the newspaper's website. In January 2009, the *Herald* was allowed to publish but was still prohibited from using "Allah." Malaysian authorities also asked the *Herald*'s publisher to mark the front of the paper with the words *terhad*, or "restricted" in Malay, as solely for distribution to Christians or churches.[70] On December 31, 2009, Judge Lau Bee Lan of the High Court ruled that Christians have "a constitutional right to use [the word] Allah," though only because the *Herald* was focused on reaching Christians. The government appealed for calm but quickly said that it would appeal, and, on January 6, Judge Lan suspended her judgment pending an appeals court decision. Subsequently, eleven churches were vandalized, some were firebombed, a Sikh temple was vandalized, pigs' heads were found in two mosques, two young Muslims desecrated a communion wafer, and the *Herald*'s lawyers' office was ransacked.[71]

Subsequently, Selangor state, using the relevant Selangor sharia Criminal Offences Enactment, 1995, which can carry sentences of up to two years in prison, said that non-Muslims should not use thirty-five "Islamic" terms including "Allah," *Firman Allah* (Allah's decree), *solat* (daily prayers), *Rasul* (prophet), *mubaligh* (missionary), *mufti, iman* (faith), *Kaabah* (the Holy cubicle), *Qiblat* (the direction in which the Muslims pray), and *haji* (Muslims who have done the pilgrimage). Mohammed Khusrin Munawi, director of the Selangor Islamic Religious Department (Jais), said: "These are listed under the Control and Restriction of the Propagation of Non-Islamic Religious Enactment. They cannot be used to promote religions other than Islam."[72]

Beginning in March 2009, government officials seized Christian books and other materials containing "Allah." By the end of the year, Malaysian port and customs authorities had impounded some 15,000 Bibles. The Christian Federation of Malaysia (CFM) said that this violated a 2005 agreement that it had with the government. It also created the problem that, since Indonesia, whose language is similar to Malay, has Bibles with "Allah" in them, Indonesian Bibles and other Christian literature could not be imported to Malaysia.[73]

Despite these increasing restrictions on non-Muslim literature, the government's major efforts are directed toward books that do not conform to its version of Islam or, as the official bulletins say, that contain "twisted facts on Islam that can undermine the faith of Muslims." Some of these are materials of more radical Muslims, including Wahhabis, while others are more liberal interpretations of Islam. In some cases, there is no obvious rationale, as when it banned Paul Marshall and others, *Islam at the Crossroads: Understanding Its Beliefs, History and Conflicts.* In June 2007, the Interior Security Ministry banned thirty-seven publications "containing twisted facts" on Islam. A spokesman for the interestingly named "Secretary of the Publications and Quranic Texts Control Division," Che Din Yusoh, said twenty-one of the publications were in English and published in the United States, the United Kingdom, and Jordan, while sixteen were in Malaysian and published in Malaysia and Indonesia.[74]

In July 2008, the control division banned more books and specified, with reference to the Printing Presses and Publications Act, that anyone reprinting or possessing the publications could be jailed for not more than three years or fined not more than RM 20,000 (about $6,000 US) or both. One of the banned books was *Muslim Women and the Challenge of Islamic Extremism* by Norani Othman, published in 2005, which the government thought might confuse Muslim women. Published by the Malaysian Muslim women's organization Sisters in Islam (SIS), the book summarized discussions among Muslim women's groups from Southeast Asia and the Middle East.[75] SIS describes itself as "Muslim women committed to promoting the rights of women within the framework of Islam. Our efforts to promote the rights of Muslim women are based on the principles of equality, justice and freedom enjoined by the Qur'an as made evident during our study of the holy text."[76] Sisters in Islam received no formal communication from the Ministry of Home Affairs or the Publications and Quranic Texts Control Division about the ban.[77] In December 2008, they appealed the banning in the Kuala Lumpur High Court, and, on January 25, 2010, Justice Mohamed Ariff Yusof said that the facts of the case did not justify the banning, especially since the book had previously been in circulation for two years without incident. He ordered the government to pay SIS's court costs.[78]

Converts

In recent years, Malaysia has faced increased controversy over a series of conversions from Islam to Hinduism, Buddhism, Sikhism, and Christianity. While there have been some threats and detentions, these cases, unlike in some other countries, especially in the Middle East, are usually addressed nonviolently and through a legal process. In practice, Muslims are restricted from converting to another religion. Ten states—Terengganu, Kelantan, Selangor, Perak, Kedah, Malacca, Pahang, Negeri Sembilan, Johor, and Perlis—have laws limiting the spread of other religions to Muslims.[79] The process for conversion in Negeri Sembilan is for the applicant to be counseled for a year by a mufti. If, after a year, the person still wants to convert, a sharia judge may permit the application. No other states have procedures for an applicant to leave Islam; in some, attempted conversion is punishable by a fine or jail term. Sharia courts have also traditionally denied requests for conversion out of Islam and have sentenced applicants to confined "rehabilitation."

A key case concerning conversion was that of Soon Singh. On May 14, 1988, Soon Singh, then seventeen, converted to Islam from Sikhism without the knowledge of his parents. Four years later, on July 16, 1992, he wanted to return to Sikhism and went through a Sikh baptism ceremony at a temple in Alor Star. He subsequently tried and failed to change his legal status as a Muslim and declare himself a Sikh. Although the sharia courts' jurisdiction was limited to specific itemized matters, not including apostasy, in 1999, the Federal Court, Malaysia's highest court, ruled that where there are provisions granting sharia courts authority to adjudicate on conversion to Islam, then jurisdiction to deal with apostasy could be read as "necessarily implied." The court also stated that Singh's initial conversion was voluntary and genuine and that he had to abide by his decision.[80]

In one of the most famous of Malaysia's conversion cases, in September 2005, the court of appeals, the federal middle-level appeals court, denied Lina Joy's request to change the religion on her national identity card from Islam to Catholic. She had been born into a Muslim family and given the name Azlina binti Jailani, but in 1990, she began attending Catholic mass and, on May 11, 1998, was baptized into the Catholic Church. Soon after, she tried to marry a Catholic, but Malaysia's Civil Registry of Marriages denied her request because the 1976 Law Reform Act stated that a registered Muslim could not marry a non-Muslim.[81]

She then applied to change the name and religion on her identity card, but, although her name change to Lina Joy was granted, she could not change her official religion without an order from the sharia court.[82] Knowing that the sharia courts had never granted such a request, and protesting that, as a Catholic, she was not under sharia court jurisdiction, she appealed to the civil courts. On April 18, 2001, the High Court ruled against her, saying that Malaysian Muslims were forbidden to renounce Islam. Although recognizing that Article 11 of the Federal Constitution guaranteed freedom of religion, the court ruled that this freedom had to be construed harmoniously with other provisions, including the Islamic ban on apostasy.[83] On September 15, 2005, the court of appeals also denied her request. Finally, on May 30, 2007, the Malaysian Federal Court upheld the two lower courts' verdicts, with Chief Justice Ahmad Fairuz Sheikh Abdul Halim reiterating that her request fell under the jurisdiction of the sharia court. Lina Joy was disowned by her family and fired from her sales job. She and her boyfriend, whom she is not allowed to marry, went into hiding out of fear of Muslim extremists who have threatened her.[84]

Some of the precedents established in Lina Joy's case continue to create problems. Revathi Massosai, though born to Muslim convert parents and given the Muslim name Siti Fatimah Abdul Karim, was raised as a Hindu by her grandmother, who called her Revathi Massosai. Massosai considered herself a Hindu and in 2001 officially changed her name to Revathi Massosai. In 2004, she married Suresh Veerappan, a Hindu man, but, when the couple tried to get a birth certificate for their daughter, the authorities learned that her birth certificate identified her as Muslim. Since in Malaysia it is against sharia for her to marry a non-Muslim, the authorities refused to give their daughter a birth certificate or recognize the marriage.

In January 2007, Massosai went to the Malacca Syariah High Court to request a change in her religion, but she was seized by the Islamic Religious Department in Malacca state and sent to the Ulu Yam religious rehabilitation camp in Selangor state for six months. There she was forced to pray like a Muslim, wear a headscarf, and eat beef, in direct opposition to the Hindu belief that cows should not be slaughtered.[85] The Islamic Religious Department also seized her fifteen-month old daughter from her husband and gave the child to Massosai's Muslim mother. As might be expected, Massosai's stint in religious rehabilitation had the opposite effect to that desired by the authorities. After her release, she told reporters, "Because of their behavior, I loathe Islam even more now. They say it's a school, but it's actually a prison."[86] She has been reunited with her daughter and husband, but the court required that she be placed in the custody of her Muslim parents and that she undergo weekly religious counseling.

Despite these doleful precedents, however, the later Siti Fatimah Tan Abdullah case provides some hope for Malaysians attempting to change their religion from Islam. Siti Fatimah, originally Tan Ean Huang, converted to Islam in July 1998 in order to marry an Iranian Muslim, Ferdoun Ashanian. She testifies that she never practiced Islam and, in practice, continued to follow Buddhist teachings.[87] Ferdoun later left her, and she petitioned to return officially to Buddhism. On May 8, 2008, the Islamic court of Penang, stressing her lack of genuine commitment to Islam, ruled that she was no longer a Muslim and allowed her to legally change her religious status. This decision marked the first time in Malaysia's recent history that an Islamic court has allowed a convert to leave Islam. In his ruling, Islamic high court judge Othman Ibrahim blamed the Penang Islamic Religious Council for not fulfilling its obligation to "ensure new converts understand and follow Islamic teachings . . . however, in this case nothing was done until the last moment when it was already too late."[88] Hizbut Tahrir Malaysia, an Islamic hard-line group, protested the ruling outside the court and declared, "In Islam, a person who insists on leaving the religion must be punished with death."[89] However, the sharia appeals court upheld the lower court's ruling.[90]

Heterodox Muslim Groups

Apart from banning Muslim literature deemed heterodox, the Malaysian government has also repressed some fifty people and groups that it deems deviant—including Shias and Ahmadis. In May 2009, the Selangor Council of Islamic Religion, the highest Islamic authority in Selangor state apart from the Sultan, banned the Ahmadiyya community from praying at the Bait-us-Salem mosque since "Ahmadiyya is not an Islamic Religion." Failure to comply could bring a fine and/or imprisonment up to one year.[91]

While sharia courts usually deal only with personal status law, they can also authorize government officials to arrest members of deviant sects. One notable and colorful example was the sect "The Sky Kingdom," alternatively called the "Teapot Group." Founded in the mid-1970s by the illiterate Ariffin Mohammed, known to his followers as Ayah Pin, "Father Pin," the group's 150 to 200 followers lived in a compound near Kampung Batu 13 village in the northeast of the country. The Sky Kingdom acquired its nickname because of their two-story-high teapot installed in 1998, which devotees said symbolized God's pouring of blessings on humanity. Critics said Sky Kingdom members believed that Ayah Pin was divine, a reincarnation of Buddha, Jesus, Shiva, and Muhammad.

In the mid-1980s, the office of Islamic affairs declared that the Sky Kingdom was a deviant group, and, in 1992, an Islamic court convicted four members for participating in "deviant practices" and ordered them to attend a rehabilitation program. When they refused, the court ordered them jailed; they continued to plead their case.[92] In 2001, Ayah Pin renounced Islam, and an Islamic court ordered him arrested and jailed for nine months, asserting that his views were corrupt, belittled Islam, and threatened public peace. When the authorities realized that the Sky Kingdom was attracting the attention of international media and converts from Islam, they went a step further. In May 2005, local authorities ordered the members to demolish the giant teapot and other structures, arguing that they were not allowed on agricultural land. The group refused, and, on July 20, 2005, the police raided the commune and arrested fifty-nine members.[93] Six were subsequently released: five were underage, and one ethnic New Zealander was born a Christian. However, the others were charged with disobeying the fatwa declaring

Ayah Pin's teachings deviant. In August 2005, by court order, state officials bull-dozed all nonresidential buildings on the group's main compound, including the teapot.[94]

One member, Kamariah, fifty-seven, was put on trial on March 2, 2008. She had originally claimed to be an apostate from the Sky Kingdom, in order to avoid charges for not obeying the fatwa against Ayah Pin. However, an Islamic high court ruled both that her apostasy was not sincere and that she had not truly abandoned all teachings contrary to Islam, so she was sentenced to two years in prison.[95] Ayah Pin himself fled the country in 2005 before the commune was raided and remained in exile close to the border in Thailand.[96]

Reformers and Political Dissidents

In recent years, political dissidents have also been accused of "insulting Islam." At the start of this chapter, we described one of these, Raja Petra Kamaruddin. On March 22, 2010, following a spate of accusations by radical Muslim activists that Sisters in Islam was misinterpreting religious principles, a group called the Malaysian Assembly of Mosque Youths filed suit against SIS, trying to force it to drop "Islam" from its name. Sisters in Islam's official name is SIS Forum (Malaysia), however it does use the phrase "Sisters in Islam" in its publications. Using its common and insulting assertion that Malaysian Muslims are very easily confused about their religion, the assembly's leader, Mohammad Nawar Ariffin, said that SIS "issues statements that contradict what other Muslims believe. It causes confusion among Muslims who might think that the group represents Islam."[97]

Maldives

The Maldives archipelago in the Indian Ocean is perhaps best known as a tourist destination, thanks to its brilliant waters and atolls, and as the country most at risk from rising sea levels. But it is also one of the most religiously repressive countries in the world. Like only a few other states, it bans all religions other than Sunni Islam. With sharia as the basis of law, it has restrictions on blasphemy and heresy, and, according to the 2008 constitutional revision, non-Muslims may not even be granted citizenship.[98] Article 36 of the constitution requires every citizen "to preserve and protect the State religion of Islam, culture, language and heritage of the country." In addition, the 1994 Protection of Religious Unity Act has been used to quash dissent and shun those suspected of converting. In 2004, Maldivian legislators began revising their fifty-year-old penal code, and several proposed revisions seek to implement punishments based on the sharia, perhaps including killing apostates.[99]

Its apparent uniformity notwithstanding, the country is caught between Islamist hard-liners and reformists, with a 2009 transfer of presidential power—the first in thirty years—marking what many hoped would be a more moderate, democratic era. Mohammad Nasheed, the new president, was formerly a political activist as well as a political prisoner who campaigned for democratic principles, including freedom of expression and protection of human rights.[100] However, his choice for Minister of Islamic Affairs, Abdul Majeed Abdul Bari, is a member of the Islamic fundamentalist Adaalath Party who has called music *haram*, or "forbidden." Control over Friday prayers and sermons has increased since Nasheed's election. In early 2010, Parliament was discussing a bill that would make it illegal to build non-Muslim places of worship or publicly practice non-Muslim faiths, with penalties of up to five years in prison. Foreigners would be allowed to worship in their homes.[101]

In 2007, Aishath Aniya, formerly the Maldivian Democratic Party's deputy secretary-general, was forced to resign and go into hiding after writing an article criticizing the notion that women must wear a veil lest men be tempted.[102] In 1998, the government detained a number of men and women, perhaps up to fifty, for allegedly converting to Christianity, and questioned another twelve. Some reports say that that they were forced to pray Islamic prayers and read the Qur'an during their detention.[103] On May 28, 2010, in a public meeting, thirty-seven-year-old Mohamed Nazim said he was no longer a Muslim. After some in the audience tried to attack him, police escorted him from the meeting and detained him. The Ministry of Islamic Affairs sent two scholars to counsel him while he was in custody, and, on June 1, Nazim offered a public apology on Television Maldives.[104]

Another example of the reformist-Islamist tension was the case of Hassan Saeed. Educated in Pakistan and Malaysia, in 2003, he became the attorney general at the age of thirty-three and embarked on a reformist agenda until his resignation in August 2007 because of differences with President Gayoom. In 2004, his book *Freedom of Religion, Apostasy and Islam*, which he coauthored with his brother Abdullah Saeed (a contributor to this volume), was published.[105] The book's stated aim is "to show that the punishment of apostasy by death cannot be justified by an appeal to the Qur'an or the practice of the Prophet." At first, the book was available in the Maldives, as elsewhere; but in 2008, it was banned by the Supreme Council on the grounds that it "contradicts principles of Islam that could mislead [the] common man." This took place during the 2008 presidential campaign, in which Hassan Saeed himself was an early contender.[106]

Religious censorship has continued, and in November 2008, the Ministry of Islamic Affairs blocked a website—www.sidahitun.com—on the grounds that it promoted Christianity. In defense of the ministry's action, prominent sheikh Ibrahim Fareed Ahmed stated of Maldivians, "If they have access to these websites, because their belief in Islam is weak, there might be a negative impact."[107]

While Maldivian citizens are stripped of religious freedom, so, too, are the approximately 80,000 migrant workers of many faiths who labor in the country. If not Sunni Muslims, they are restricted not only from practicing their religion but also from importing books and other religious materials. Moreover, the cramped quarters that the majority of these low-level workers live in make even illegal worship almost impossible.[108]

Closing

These four countries are diverse, but each demonstrates the dangers of blasphemy restrictions. In Bangladesh, Indonesia, and Malaysia, one destructive dynamic has been the willingness of larger, often nationalist, political parties to form coalitions, acceding to the demands of smaller Islamist parties in return for their support. A related trend is for those same parties to push for more Islamist policies in order to head off support for more radical elements. Each tactic gives greater political space for more radical currents. In Bangladesh and Indonesia, the central governments have usually been moderating influences, but in both countries they are weak. This has made possible Islamist repression by scattered regional and local governments. In the Maldives, successive governments have used state power to impose a suffocating and restrictive uniformity on a country that is already strikingly closed.

In particular, while Malaysian law creates major problems for those who want to change their religion, the country is also notable for its programs to suppress "deviant" groups, ideas, and even individual words that it thinks its Muslim population might possibly find "confusing." This claim, echoed in the Maldives, is at odds with the government's claims that it represents an open, modern Islam. Moreover, it is insulting to its energetic and increasingly educated population, implying that its citizens are not capable of dealing with different thoughts and ideas.

As Sisters in Islam says: "Ignorance is never bliss. By narrowing the space for open dialogue among citizens and squashing their quest for information and to read, the government's act can be deemed as 'promoting Jahiliah' as it will push us into a more suppressed world where we will blindly follow with no questions asked, lest it disrupts our small worldview...."[109]

PART III

THE GLOBALIZATION OF BLASPHEMY

Introduction to Western Countries and International Blasphemy

Bans on blasphemy, heresy, "insulting Islam," and similar purported offenses in the Islamic world aim, in part, to enforce religious conformity and temporal compliance by limiting the range of possible debate and discussion within Muslim societies. However, such restrictions can be fully effective only if the society is kept closed, something that is increasingly difficult for governments to achieve given the spread and accessibility of global media. Moreover, Muslims are currently settling in large numbers in the West, where they are an immigrant minority—an unusual situation in the history of Islam—and hence are often exposed to a much larger range of argument and criticism than previously. These changes, especially when compounded by political manipulation, have produced a series of legal, diplomatic, and violent clashes over claims of "insults to Islam" by Muslims and non-Muslims alike.

Though often driven by mob or vigilante violence encouraged by religious extremists, these clashes are also the product of organized efforts by Muslim-majority states, and sometimes by Muslim organizations in the West, to shape and use Western laws and institutions to suppress what they consider "insults" to their religion. The conflict now takes place in the United Nations, through direct diplomatic channels, and, increasingly, within Western countries. Legal efforts and violent intimidation directly undermine free speech for a broad and widening range of people, including reform-minded Muslims, those who have left Islam, and non-Muslims who have made controversial remarks ranging from intellectual commentary, critique, and questioning, to slight mockery, to strong condemnation. Death threats and violent attacks against alleged offenders, as well as against their unlucky conationals or coreligionists, also augment the legal offensive by producing naïve calls for new restrictions on discussing Islam simply for the sake of peace and social harmony. Such a move is not only likely to prove futile but also would enshrine in law the dangerous principle that people have the right to be "protected" from ideas that might offend them. Taken together, these growing pressures for the global enforcement of Islamic blasphemy norms threaten to fundamentally erode individual rights to freedom of religion and freedom of expression.

Islamic blasphemy rules first captured global attention with Ayatollah Khomeini's 1989 fatwa against Salman Rushdie, and, especially since 2005, they have made a conspicuous return to the world stage. Chapter 10 describes five cases, international in both origin and consequence, in which blasphemy strictures maintained in Muslim countries have come into direct and explosive conflict with a statement or work produced elsewhere in the world that has been called "insulting to Islam." Of these cases, the unlikely sounding Danish cartoons controversy of 2005–6 has produced singularly sweeping reverberations. In addition to placing those involved in the cartoons' publication in permanent danger and taking a toll on Denmark's economy, mob attacks and assassinations have claimed the lives of over 200 people utterly uninvolved with the "blasphemous" drawings. The experience also left its mark in the minds of Western political leaders and has heavily influenced subsequent discussions, which now often seem to center on how, not whether, to balance freedom and Muslim blasphemy demands. As with other cases, from the Rushdie fatwa onward, the cartoon crisis involved what seems a baffling plurality of motives at the local, national, and international levels—from three Danish imams' resentment over unflattering coverage in the newspaper *Jyllands-Posten*, to the Egyptian government's desire to parry a U.S.-led push for democratization in the Middle East. Despite the frequent mischaracterization of the crisis as a spontaneous eruption of rage from the "Muslim street," members of the Organization of the Islamic Conference (OIC) played a vital role in drawing and sustaining attention to the cartoons, as well as lending the reaction against them legitimacy and heft. Afterward, when the former Danish prime minister was tapped to lead NATO, Turkey used the cartoons episode to leverage two high-level appointments for its nationals within the West's most important military alliance. At all levels of this and other blasphemy protests, the political manipulation of religious motives has been prominent.

Incidents like the Danish cartoons crisis are also the result of sustained pressure by a range of actors on three main fronts for the global export of Islamic blasphemy norms. This pressure helps keep the issue alive in the West long after the protest of the month has faded from the headlines.

In the most formal of these efforts, detailed in chapter 11, the OIC has sought through the UN and other international fora to win official endorsement for a global ban on blasphemy against Islam. This effort in its current form began with a little-noticed 1999 resolution of the UN Commission on Human Rights that was initially called "defamation of Islam," then retitled "defamation of religions" at the insistence of other delegations; the resolution represented OIC countries' growing concern with and reaction to both human rights criticism of their practices and increasing attention to Islamist terrorism. Earlier, these governments had already sought to exempt themselves from established international human rights standards, leveling at least two allegations of "blasphemy" against UN Special Rapporteurs who raised sensitive human rights issues. Though these resolutions predated the Danish cartoons affair and even the terror attacks of September 11, 2001, they gained force in the wake of each incident. From 2006 onward, OIC resolutions have sought to assert that freedom of expression must be limited in the interest of other goals, purportedly including religious freedom.[1]

"Defamation of religions" resolutions eventually came under heavy fire, not only from Western countries, which usually opposed them, but also from many nongovernmental organizations (NGOs) and human rights experts. However, so far this criticism has not led to any substantive rethinking but only to a change in terms—the use of "advocacy of religious hatred" as a substitute for defamation. Alarmingly, in October 2009, the United States appeared to lend support to this effort by cosponsoring, with leading defamation-of-religions proponent Egypt, a resolution on freedom of expression that expressed concern about "negative racial and religious stereotyping" and, while not binding, urged states to combat "any advocacy of national, racial or religious hatred that constitutes incitement to discrimination, hostility or violence."[2] Free speech advocates won a small but essential victory when this resolution was dropped from the agenda of the commission's successor body, the Human Rights Council, in 2011.

The same questions are being debated in Western national law. Indeed, the disputes over wording at UN conferences in New York and Geneva reflect the fact that many Western countries already accept the principle that governments should determine what constitutes acceptable religious criticism. As outlined in chapter 12, these countries themselves enforce laws that limit what may be said about religious beliefs. Such laws include literal blasphemy bans, originally conceived to protect Christianity, and hate-speech prohibitions, devised mainly in the last half-century as antiracism measures that are now increasingly used to cover religious categories as well. In keeping with the EU's stated view that restrictions on speech should aim to protect individuals rather than religions, those blasphemy laws that remain on the books are usually weakly enforced and, in some cases, are effectively defunct. However, a few have nonetheless been used to prosecute offenses against Islam.

In contrast to blasphemy laws, the use of hate-speech laws is increasing. In practice, the dividing line between the two types of statutes, as well as the corresponding distinction between criticism of a religion and of its adherents, has proved fuzzy and has been rejected outright by some Muslim complainants who claim that any defamation of Islam also necessarily constitutes defamation of Muslims.

Finally, beyond the danger presented by Western legal restrictions, every debate on "insults to Islam" takes place in the shadow of a further problem, one deeply affecting not only politicians and polemicists but also ordinary Muslims living in the West, converts, and others who might make the wrong remark in the wrong place at the wrong time. While officials argue over the permissibility of a legal blasphemy ban, a pattern of violent intimidation, discussed in chapter 13, has already in practice established such a ban for large swaths of Western society, as it has done previously in Muslim-majority countries. This intimidation is particularly powerful within some Muslim communities, in which individuals may be targeted for any comment that deviates from extremist orthodoxy.

Together with the shock of international incidents such as the Danish cartoons crisis and the vague threat of legal charges, this intimidation has created a massive disincentive toward talking publicly about Islam, one that also affects Western Muslims' ability to debate the interpretation of their religion. The wide range of words and people targeted by threats demonstrates that limited legal measures to restrict certain kinds of speech are, to put it mildly, very unlikely to produce social harmony. Rather, as can be seen in Muslim-majority countries that already have such laws, state-sponsored speech bans typically lead to increasing sensitivity and ever-increasing demands to silence ideas that do not conform.[3]

Despite these pressures, the West still remains a relative haven for those wishing to voice reformist or critical views about Islam, yet it stands at a critical juncture between a renewed defense of free speech and an acceptance of ever-increasing limits on expressing controversial ideas. In light of most governments' at best ambiguous reaction to the controversies over *Jyllands-Posten*'s cartoons and Geert Wilders's *Fitna*, ongoing legal proceedings against certain critics of Islam, and a continuing climate of threat, particularly in Europe, facing those of whatever background who discuss matters that Islamist extremists have deemed off limits, it is unclear which way the Western world will turn.

Islam and Blasphemy on the International Stage, 1989–2011

The Satanic Verses, the famous novel penned by Salman Rushdie, was published in 1988. At the time of its release, a few British Muslims protested, mostly peacefully, against a work of fiction they perceived as insulting to Islam. Scattered demonstrations followed, some of them more violent than others. Then, in February 1989, Ayatollah Khomeini, Iran's Supreme Leader, expanded his claimed jurisdiction well beyond Iran's borders. He issued a fatwa—an Islamic legal pronouncement— saying that it is a duty of Muslims to track down and execute Rushdie, who is a British citizen from South Asia, for his purported blasphemy against Islam.

Khomeini's international death warrant drove Rushdie underground. It forced him to maintain constant security protection for nearly a decade. In the meantime, the novel's Japanese translator was murdered, other translators and publishers were assaulted, and U.S. bookstores and a hotel in Turkey were firebombed. In 1998, the beleaguered author emerged from hiding following a supposed deal between the British and Iranian governments. Rushdie is alive today, but hard-line elements of the Iranian regime continue to proclaim that the fatwa against him is still very much in effect.

In February 2006, twelve cartoons depicting Islam's prophet Muhammad unexpectedly triggered angry protests around the world. Although the cartoons had first been published five months earlier, in September 2005, in the Danish newspaper Jyllands-Posten, international violence and bloodshed, supposedly representing the spontaneous outrage of the "Muslim Street," did not occur until the following year.

On February 10, 2006, thousands of Muslims across Africa, Asia, and the Middle East set out from Friday prayers to demonstrate against the cartoons. Some of their protests ended in violence, despite calls by many religious leaders for them to remain peaceful. Egyptian demonstrators invoked the name of Osama bin Laden and burned a Danish flag.[1] Thousands in Kuala Lumpur, Malaysia, called for the destruction of Denmark, Israel, George Bush, and America.[2] In Karbala, Iraq, around 10,000 demonstrators burned Danish flags and called for breaking off Iraq's relations with Denmark.[3] Hamas organized a protest in which about 500 children trampled a Danish flag, carried a coffin bearing the word "Denmark," and demanded a boycott of Danish goods.[4] Police quelled riots in Hyderabad, India, with batons and tear gas.[5] Kenyan security forces used tear gas to keep hundreds of protesters away from the Danish embassy in Nairobi.[6] Pakistan and Afghanistan saw many of the worst riots. The cartoons continue to be *both vilified by Muslims and, from time to time, defiantly republished by advocates of free expression. All told, the Danish cartoons crisis has so far cost at least 241 lives internationally.[7]*

Dutch parliamentarian Geert Wilders was no stranger to controversy when, in November 2007, he announced that he had begun work on a film to illustrate "the intolerant and fascist nature of the Koran."[8] In January 2008, he announced a March release date for his film titled Fitna, an Arabic word meaning strife or discord. He stated that Fitna would link the Qur'an directly to violence and depict it as "the latest test to Western democracies since Nazism and communism."

In the aftermath of Fitna's appearance online, angry protests, threats, acts of vandalism, and accusations of blasphemy reverberated around the globe. Egyptian, Moroccan, and Bangladeshi cabinet ministers denounced the movie, with the latter calling it "mentally retarded." Sudan, Iran, Malaysia, and Indonesia spoke out against it, calling for boycotts and threatening various consequences. Pakistan's Foreign Ministry said that "insults to other religions could never be justified on the basis of freedom of expression" and demanded that the Dutch government bring charges against Wilders. On April 6, more than 20,000 people attended a Jamaat-e-Islami rally in Karachi to protest both Wilders's film and the Danish cartoons reprint.[9]

In Afghanistan on April 18, 2008, a roadside bomb killed Lieutenant Dennis van Uhm, son of newly appointed Dutch chief of staff Peter van Uhm. A Taliban spokesman claimed to have known van Uhm was in the vehicle and that the attack was part of an "operation against the Dutch"; "first it was because they have occupied our country and secondly it was in retaliation to the Dutch insult to our great prophet Muhammad."[10]

Introductory Remarks

In the following chapters, we describe blasphemy and hate-speech restrictions in the West, enforced either by the state or by vigilante action and mobs. We also describe the efforts by governments in the Organization of the Islamic Conference (OIC) and others, either through the United Nations or by direct pressure, to persuade or force Western governments to apply the same denial of freedom of speech and of religion as do OIC members. Some of these events and pressures are described in chapter 11 on the United Nations, in chapter 12 on legal developments in the West, and in chapter 13 on private violence. However, some of the major crises and developments concerning blasphemy and apostasy—reactions to the novel *The Satanic Verses*, the Danish and Swedish cartoons, the pope's lecture at Regensburg, and the doings of Geert Wilders—spill over these boundaries. They play out in the Muslim world and the West, the United Nations, and other international bodies, and they involve not only law but also mob violence, vigilantism, and terrorism. Hence, they need to be described here as a whole.

The *Satanic Verses*

Khomeini issued his fatwa against Salman Rushdie and the publishers of his novel on February 14, 1989, while also declaring February 15 a day of mourning over *Satanic Verses'* "poisonous and insulting subject-matter concerning Islam, the Koran and the blessed prophet." The ayatollah called for "all zealous Moslems to execute [Rushdie and others involved with the novel] quickly, wherever they find them, so that no one will dare to insult Islamic sanctity." He promised that anyone who was killed while complying with his edict would go directly to paradise. For the more earthly-minded, the 15th Khordad Relief Agency also offered a bounty for anyone who killed Rushdie: $2.6 million for an Iranian; $1 million for a foreigner.[11]

A densely written work of magical realism, Rushdie's novel had drawn attention of a decidedly nonliterary nature by touching on Islamic theology in several areas. The phrase "Satanic Verses" was derived from the story itself, which speaks of the tenth-century historian and Qur'anic commentator Abu Ja'far Muhammad ibn Jarir Al-Tabari. Al-Tabari's view, considered heretical by most Muslims, was that some of the verses Muhammad included in the Qu'ran, and then retracted, had come from Satan rather than the Angel Gabriel.[12]

The most controversial material in Rushdie's book involved a short section concerning a man called Mahound, a derogatory term for Muhammad that originated from medieval polemics against Islam. In his account of Mahound's story, Rushdie presents the origin of the verses in question as a case of opportunistic deception rather than diabolical intervention; he suggests that Mahound's revelation was the product of artifice. He also observes that Mahound seemed habitually to receive revelations suspiciously convenient for his own purposes at the moment. This substory has been interpreted as an attack on Islam, although Rushdie himself has called that an oversimplification. In fact, many who have protested the novel have not read it or even been familiar with its content.

The Mahound sequence also depicts a brothel in Mecca called The Curtain—which translates to *Al-Hijab*—with twelve prostitutes who assume the names and some of the features of Muhammad's wives. In other sections, the book contains an unflattering portrayal of Ayatollah Khomeini and a story that has been taken as a metaphor for the Iranian Islamic revolution. For the most part, Rushdie's attitude toward his subject matter is not entirely clear, particularly because the

Mahound and Iranian sequences appear only as the dreams of one of the central characters. But the work does appear consciously intended to challenge Islamic doctrine. Indeed, *Verses* includes one passage in which Mahound accuses a character named Salman of "blasphemy."[13]

Once the novel was proclaimed sacrilegious by many Muslim leaders, demonstrations ensued. There were violent protests in India (where the controversy over the novel and its prohibition began) and in Pakistan shortly before Khomeini's fatwa. The book was banned in Bangladesh, Egypt, India, Pakistan, and South Africa, among others. Already in November 1988, the grand sheikh of Egypt's Al-Azhar University, one of the most respected scholarly figures in the Muslim world, had called on British Muslim groups to seek legal means of suppressing the novel. He also asked that the OIC take action.[14] In late December, three Muslim ambassadors met with Britain's Home Minister.

Initially, Saudi Arabia took the lead in sponsoring denunciations of the novel.[15] Saudis and Saudi-backed organizations played a prominent role in anti-Rushdie efforts in Britain, which were considerable. Following publicity (though likely without authorization) from these organizations, Rushdie began receiving death threats in October 1988. A public burning of the novel, organized by the Bradford Council of Mosques, led local booksellers to withdraw *Verses* and 8,000 Muslims to demonstrate in London in late January 1989. Threats also targeted Rushdie's U.S. publisher, Viking Penguin.[16]

Then, on February 14, 1989, came the Iranian fatwa, which has received a mixed response from Muslims. Sayed Abdul Quddas, who had orchestrated the Bradford book-burning, said he was ready to act on the ayatollah's decree and declared, "every good Muslim is after [Rushdie's] life. He has tortured Islam and has to pay the penalty." On February 15, Rushdie's French publisher, Christian Bourgois, suspended publication of the book due to security concerns. In the United States, B. Dalton and Barnes and Noble initially refused to sell the book at all, although they later reversed their decisions. Waldenbooks agreed to sell it only from storerooms. On February 28, two California bookstores, and the offices of a newspaper that had published an article defending the book, were firebombed.[17]

At first, Rushdie asserted that he only wished his book had been more critical. "It seems to me," he said, "that Islamic fundamentalists could do with a little bit of criticism right now." On February 18, however, after a possible suggestion by Iran's president, Sayyid Ali Khamenei, that the fatwa might be reversed if he apologized, Rushdie stated: "I profoundly regret the distress the publication has occasioned to sincere followers of Islam. Living as we do in a world of many faiths, this experience has served to remind us that we must all be conscious of the sensibilities of others." Yet Ayatollah Khomeini promptly proclaimed, "Even if Salman Rushdie repents and becomes the most pious man of [all] time, it is incumbent on every Muslim to employ everything he's got, his life and wealth, to send him to hell."[18]

While Khomeini's death edict against a British citizen led the United Kingdom to freeze relations with Iran, it was Tehran that officially severed relations on March 7, after Britain refused to condemn Rushdie's book. In a statement carried by the Islamic Republic News Agency, Iran's government cited an alleged "anti-Islamic campaign" by "the world oppressors and the West, which find genuine Islam against their objectives and plots." Other Muslim countries, some of which had led their own efforts against *The Satanic Verses* prior to February 14, did not risk fully associating themselves with the Iranian fatwa. On March 16, the OIC declined to back the fatwa directly but condemned Rushdie's "blasphemous" novel and called on countries "to ban the book and take all necessary steps to protect sacred religious beliefs."[19]

Tensions in Britain soon escalated. On May 27, participants in an approximately 20,000-strong London demonstration shouted, "Rushdie must die," hung him in effigy, and delivered a petition to 10 Downing Street calling for the widening of Britain's blasphemy laws. Clashes with police led to eighty-four arrests. The violence inspired two Labour MPs, Keith Vaz, and Max Madden, to suggest banning the book; Vaz actually led 3,000 protesters "intent on burning an effigy of Rushdie." Other establishment figures were also less than sympathetic to the author. Historian Lord Dacre declared he "would not shed a tear if some British Muslims, deploring Mr. Rushdie's manners, were to waylay him in a dark street and seek to improve them."[20]

Following Khomeini's death in June 1989, the Iranian government attempted subtly to distance itself from his fatwa. It suggested that, while the decree could only have been altered by Khomeini himself, Iran's political leaders did not wish it to be treated as their handiwork, nor did they want it to become a complicating factor in their relations with Western governments. This, however, did little to ease the pressure on Rushdie and others affected by the fatwa. There were major demonstrations outside the headquarters of publisher Viking Penguin in January 1990, and a Viking spokesman said his organization had been the target of "a stream of threats and violence."[21]

Following his unsuccessful apology of February 18, Rushdie, still in hiding, insisted that the reaction was his attackers' problem, not his. Then, once again, he altered his position under pressure. In May 1990, some Britons suggested he should apologize and withhold a paperback version of *Verses*. This was to be done, at least in part, in order to improve relations with Iran, which was believed to have control over terror groups holding British hostages in Lebanon. In September 1990, Rushdie stated that "if people have been upset, I'm sorry," that he had not meant for his work to be interpreted as an insult and that his life in hiding was "hell." If Muslims wished to punish him, he noted, they already had. Only hours later, Britain announced it was resuming diplomatic relations with Iran, and British officials suggested Rushdie would no longer have to live in hiding.[22]

Nevertheless, Iranian Foreign Minister Ali Akbar Velayati told an interviewer that there was "no change . . . When somebody insults the main Islamic values and

Islamic principles, you cannot ignore it."[23] This was the first of many similar misunderstandings between Iran and the United Kingdom. Rushdie emerged from hiding for the first time in early December of 1990. At the same time, Iran's culture minister, Mohammad Khatami, reaffirmed the death sentence against him.[24]

In November, Rushdie stated on television that he agreed with Muslims that Britain's blasphemy laws were unfair, that they protected only Christianity and should be replaced with a law against incitement to religious hatred, a charge for which he was sure his own novel would not qualify. Meanwhile, when rumors surfaced that Rushdie was in talks with Muslim leaders, several British Muslims, including Dr. Kalim Saddiqui of the Muslim Institute and Abdal Chowdury of the British Muslim Action Front, took exception to the idea of any such discussion, asserting that the fatwa should not be lifted.[25] Nonetheless, Rushdie's talks with less militant British Muslims bore some fruit.

In late December 1990, after an extended discussion on the meaning of Rushdie's prose, Dr. Hesham El-Essawy of the Islamic Society for the Promotion of Religious Tolerance suggested that the novelist did not mean for the anti-Islamic remarks contained therein to be taken seriously. He also said that Rushdie had not been a Muslim believer when he wrote the novel but had since become one and was therefore not an apostate but a convert. El-Essawy proposed that Rushdie engage in a similar conversation with scholars at Al-Azhar.[26]

On December 24, 1990, in a statement witnessed by an Egyptian secretary of state and a number of Islamic scholars, Rushdie affirmed that he was a Muslim believer and declared that he did not personally "agree with any statement in my novel *The Satanic Verses* uttered by any of the characters who insults the prophet Mohammed, or casts aspersions upon Islam, or upon the authenticity of the holy Koran, or who rejects the divinity of Allah." He promised not to allow his novel to be published in paperback or retranslated "while any risk of further offense exists" and stated he would "continue to work for a better understanding of Islam in the world, as I have always attempted to do in the past." British Muslim leaders such as Iqbal Sacranie welcomed the statement but continued to call for the book's withdrawal from circulation.[27]

Assaults and Threats through the 1990s

Whatever respite these events provided for Rushdie personally, his statement did not end the danger to others associated with his work.[28] Professor Mushirul Hassan, an Islamic historian, was threatened with death by Indian Muslims in New Delhi after he called on the Indian government to lift a ban on the book. In Milan on July 4, 1991, a man claiming to be Iranian brutally assaulted Ettore Capriolo, the novel's Italian translator, who survived, despite being attacked with a knife as well as kicked and beaten on the head.[29]

A Pakistani Muslim attacked publisher Gianni Palma at the February 1990 press conference where he announced that he planned to issue a Japanese version. Raees Siddiqui, later to become president of Japan's Pakistan Association, told Palma that "we won't let you live." The Islamic Center of Japan pressed for bookstores not to stock the novel. On July 12, 1991, the Japanese translator of *Satanic Verses*, literature professor Hitoshi Igarashi, was stabbed to death in his university office. Siddiqui commented that it was "natural that Igarashi should be killed."[30]

In 1993, 100 Arab and Muslim writers submitted essays defending Rushdie and free speech, published as *Pour Rushdie: Cent intellectuels arabes et musulmans pour la liberté d'expression*.[31] Despite a ban on *The Satanic Verses* in Turkey, in February 1993, secular editorial writer Aziz Nesin, of the left-leaning Turkish paper *Aydinlik*, declared (apparently without the author's permission) that he would publish a Turkish translation. This decision produced calls in Iranian papers for the fatwa against Rushdie to be applied to Nesin as well. It also earned Nesin trouble with the Iranian public and authorities. When *Aydinlik* began carrying excerpts of the book in May, Turkish prosecutors initiated legal proceedings against the paper, and authorities seized copies of the paper. On July 2, a crowd of 10,000 protesters gathered outside a hotel in Sivas where Nesin and a number of other leftist intellectuals, primarily members of the Alevi Muslim minority, were meeting. The mob then attacked a cultural center, bookshops, cafes, and some cars outside the hotel. They finally set fire to the hotel itself and, for a time, blocked firefighters from reaching it. Thirty-five people died in the blaze; sixty were injured.[32]

On October 11, 1993, William Nygaard, owner and CEO of Aschehoug Forlag, the Norwegian publisher of *The Satanic Verses*, was shot three times while getting into a car outside his Oslo home. Although seriously wounded, he survived the attack. Nygaard had previously contacted the police about threats following *Verses'* initial Norwegian publication in April 1989.[33] The would-be assassin was never apprehended, and, in late 2010, police reopened the investigation after the publisher and the Norwegian Publishers' Association offered a reward for information "primarily to defend Norwegian values of freedom of expression."[34]

Throughout the decade, Iran's stance on Rushdie remained convoluted, and the novelist and his collaborators on *Verses* remained, and probably still remain, at risk.[35]

Salman Rushdie's alleged blasphemy in *The Satanic Verses* gained unusual prominence because of Ayatollah Khomeini, who was capable of inspiring considerable fear given his prestige among many Islamist radicals and his proclivity for orchestrating assassinations beyond national borders.[36] Yet, as is revealed by the threats and protests against *The Satanic Verses* predating Khomeini's edict, the effort to suppress Rushdie's work enjoyed a significant base of support beyond Iran. It is thus, perhaps, unsurprising that well after the ayatollah's death and the Iranian-British meeting that allegedly "meant everything" for Rushdie, outbursts of global anger over Rushdie's novel were easily reignited. More important, the implied principle introduced through international threats, protests, and violence in response to

Rushdie's novel lived on: the principle that blasphemy committed in the Western world should carry a penalty as if it were committed in a Muslim country.

Twelve Danish Cartoons

Some years later, in 2005, enormous turmoil resulted from allegations that, as reported in *Newsweek* magazine, a Qur'an had been flushed down a toilet at the U.S. Guantanamo Bay detention camp. The story was later refuted, but not before global rioting against America and its treatment of suspected terrorists. It was not, however, the actions of the U.S. government, but the editorial decisions of a private Danish newspaper, that came to occupy the center of the next international blasphemy controversy. Unlike the *Newsweek* imbroglio of the previous year, the Danish cartoons affair of 2006 concerned no allegations of specific government abuse. But, thanks to a group of dissatisfied Danish Muslims, popular Mideast-based Islamic leaders, and governments purporting to speak in the name of religion, twelve allegedly blasphemous drawings in a private paper—one with few readers in Islamabad or Cairo—became the seed of the widest-reaching international crisis regarding blasphemy in recent history.

Denmark's prime minister Anders Fogh Rasmussen steadfastly insisted that the illustrations in a private newspaper were not the concern of his government or any other. But his declarations fell on deaf ears as a wide range of Muslim leaders seized on the incident as a pretext to call for a blasphemy ban with global reach. In countries where such a ban had already taken hold, editors uniformly suffered state retribution for daring to display the cartoons, regardless of their reasons for doing so. Other more permissive countries were subject to boycotts, diplomatic pressure, and threats of violence as a result of their unwillingness to censor. The Western response in the face of these demands was mixed, with some officials touting freedom of expression, and others suggesting this freedom could not entail the right to insult religion. Some attempted to have it both ways.

Like *The Satanic Verses*, the Danish cartoons, having once been invoked across national borders as a quintessential Western offense against Islamic values, have remained controversial ever since. The running debate over the twelve drawings—initially published in support of the notion that the right to free expression necessarily includes "scorn, mockery and ridicule"—has drawn reactions across the board, from those who adamantly support that right, from those who oppose it on principle, and from those who believe it is an acceptable casualty of intercultural harmony.

The Cartoons and Their Origin

The twelve cartoons were originally published in Denmark's largest-circulation newspaper, *Jyllands-Posten. Jyllands-Posten* leans right of center but is far from being an organ of the xenophobic far right. As recently as May 2005, a *Jyllands-Posten* article on integration had won second place in a European Union contest on the theme "For Diversity. Against Discrimination."[37] Nonetheless, the paper also engaged in hard-hitting coverage of Islamic radicalism, and its staff had become concerned about the widespread fear in Europe of displeasing its Muslim population.

After Kare Bluitgen, the author of a Danish children's biography of Muhammad, was unable to find an artist willing to provide illustrations under his own name, Flemming Rose, *Jyllands-Posten*'s culture editor, asked all forty-two members of the Danish newspaper illustrators' union to draw images of Muhammad, as they envisioned him. The paper published the work of the dozen who participated.[38] According to editor-in-chief Carsten Juste, the cartoon project was intended to explore "whether self-censorship exists in Denmark to a greater degree than generally acknowledged."[39]

The September 30, 2005, issue carried an article by Rose warning that fear, whether warranted or not, was creating a climate of self-censorship in Denmark with regard to important issues surrounding "the most important cultural meeting of our times, the one between Islam and the secular, western society with its roots in Christianity." In addition to the children's book illustrations, he cited an art gallery that had taken down works deemed offensive by Muslims. He also described the desire for anonymity by the translators of a volume of essays criticizing Islam and discussed calls by a Muslim religious leader for Denmark's government to pressure the media into depicting Islam in a more positive light.

Rose argued that in a "temporal democracy...you must be ready to tolerate scorn, mockery and ridicule." Having served as a correspondent in the former Soviet Union, he added, "It is not by coincidence that people in totalitarian societies end up in prison for telling jokes or depicting dictators in a critical way." In his judgment, Denmark was "approaching a slippery ground, where no one can predict where self-censorship will end."[40] Rose's article was accompanied by the twelve images of Muhammad. These ranged widely, from a simple portrait of Islam's prophet walking in a desert, to the controversial image of Muhammad with a bomb in his turban, to a depiction of a frightened-looking cartoonist huddled over a portrait titled "Muhammad" as he drew.[41]

These cartoons could be considered offensive to Islam in two main regards. One is the unflattering manner in which several of the drawings depicted Islam's prophet, particularly in the case of the bomb-turban. Critics have interpreted this drawing as an accusation that Muhammad himself was a terrorist. But the cartoon's creator, Kurt Westergaard, has explained that he intended to satirize the hijacking of Islam by violent extremists.[42] Many also stressed that such images, by their very existence, contravene prohibitions by Muslims of any visual images of Muhammad whatsoever. However, there are numerous representations of Muhammad in historic Muslim art. Such works are housed in the Smithsonian, the Metropolitan Museum of Art, and Istanbul's Topkapi Palace. Images of

Muhammad appeared in illuminated manuscripts dating from as early as the thirteenth century and as late as the eighteenth century.[43]

Sunni Islam, in modern times, has prohibitions against depicting the Prophet or his companions. Sunni theologians at Al-Azhar University continue to prohibit his portrayal, as does the Muslim Brotherhood, and iconoclastic theology has been promoted with particular vigor by the conservative Wahhabi sect, supported by the Kingdom of Saudi Arabia.[44] Shia tradition is less stringently opposed to such depictions. Ayatollah Ali al-Sistani of Iraq, a prominent Shia cleric, suggests on his website that portraying the Prophet is not problematic as long as the depiction is respectful.[45] A primary reason for barring images of Muhammad is the prevention of idolatry, a concern that clearly did not apply to the cartoons.[46]

Although the cartoons were published in September 2005, international violence and bloodshed, supposedly representing spontaneous outrage in the "Muslim Street," did not occur until several months later. The change in atmosphere was due in no small part to the work of three controversial Danish imams, Raed Hlayhel, Ahmed Akkari, and Ahmed Abdel Rahman Abu Laban. They organized the Committee for the Defense of the Honor of the Prophet, which involved twenty-seven leaders of mosques or other Muslim groups, some extremely small but with a known radical bent, and sought to quickly make their displeasure known.[47]

Hlayhel, perhaps the most aggressive participant, while insisting that he made no threats, also warned, "When you see what happened in Holland and then still print the cartoons, that's quite stupid" (presumably referring to the murder of Theo van Gogh). A petition to the prime minister, Anders Fogh Rasmussen, circulated by the imams, received 17,000 signatures, even though other Danish Muslims voiced disapproval of the committee's activities.[48] A crowd of 3,000 showed up for a rally in Copenhagen on October 14.[49] By October, *Jyllands-Posten* had been forced to hire a security guard in response to numerous phone and e-mail threats against cartoonists, journalists, and editors. Nonetheless, while maintaining a respectful tone, *Jyllands-Posten* editor-in-chief Carsten Juste refused to apologize.[50]

Having failed to get the desired response through local channels, the self-appointed defenders of the Prophet decided to go global. Abu Laban contacted Muslim diplomats in Copenhagen, eleven of whom sent a letter to Denmark's prime minister requesting a meeting.[51] They raised the issue of the cartoons alongside three other examples of a claimed "on-going smearing campaign in Danish public circles and media against Islam and Muslims." Signatories of the letter declared that "Danish press and public representatives should not be allowed to abuse Islam in the name of democracy, freedom of expression and human rights" and called for the Danish government "to take all those responsible to task under the law of the land in the interest of inter-faith harmony, better integration and Denmark's overall relations with the Muslim world." The OIC also sent a letter along similar lines.[52]

Rasmussen, the prime minister, responded with a letter in which he reaffirmed his support for cross-cultural dialogue. But he also stated, "The freedom of expression is the very foundation of the Danish democracy," and that while concerned parties could bring cases of blasphemy or hate speech to court under existing laws, "it is for the courts to decide in individual cases."[53] Rasmussen refused to meet with the ambassadors.

Thus thwarted, the Danish imams organized delegations to spread cartoon rage across the Middle East. There, they displayed not only the *Jyllands-Posten* cartoons but also images from other Danish publications as well as three significantly more offensive, entirely unrelated drawings, whose origin is murky. The threesome made wildly exaggerated claims about repression against Muslims in Denmark; for example, asserting that they are not legally permitted to build mosques.[54] Representatives of the imams' group traveled to Cairo, Damascus, and Beirut. They received a particularly warm reception in Egypt and enjoyed the assistance of the Egyptian ambassador to Denmark in organizing high-level meetings. Meanwhile, word of the drawings spread.

By early December 2005, there were reports that the Pakistani Islamist party Jamaat-e-Islami had offered a large reward for anyone who killed one of the cartoonists.[55] By December 18, *Jyllands-Posten* faced "an avalanche of death threats against its staff," and the Danish Security and Intelligence Service (PET) had become involved. As the crisis continued to escalate, Danish Muslims unsuccessfully attempted to bring criminal charges against *Jyllands-Posten* on the basis of laws banning blasphemy and hate speech.[56]

At the same time, the cartoons were condemned as blasphemy by the OIC, the Muslim World League, and the Arab League, while the World Assembly of Muslim Youth charged Denmark with "Islamophobia."[57] In late December, the Islamic Educational, Scientific and Cultural Organization (ISESCO) threatened a political and economic boycott if no official apology was forthcoming from Denmark, and later it followed through on this threat. ISESCO's president, Abdulaziz Othman Altwajiri, described the cartoons as "a form of racism."[58] The December 2005 OIC summit in Mecca initially convened to discuss sectarian violence and terrorism but took up the cartoons issue, and the Danish imams' dossier was passed around on the sidelines.[59]

In the last days of January 2006, fifteen gunmen occupied an EU office in the Gaza Strip. They claimed that Norwegians (a Norwegian paper had republished some cartoons) and Danes would be barred from the area, and they demanded an apology from the two governments. A German NGO volunteer was briefly kidnapped from a hotel in Nablus, in the West Bank; and the Danish Red Cross and the Norwegian People's Aid Group withdrew employees from Gaza, the former citing "concrete threats." The Red Cross also pulled an employee from Yemen. Danish troops in Iraq began operating under an elevated alert level.[60]

Rasmussen repeatedly stressed that the government could not apologize for *Jyllands-Posten*, since "the Danish government and the Danish nation as such cannot be held responsible for what is published in independent media."[61] Contrary to OIC and UN pronouncements on the subject, he affirmed that "freedom of speech is absolute ... it is not negotiable."[62] In a January 31 statement, Rasmussen explained that "as my personal opinion I deeply respect the religious feelings of other people," and added, "I would never myself have chosen to depict religious symbols in this way." Nonetheless, he continued to maintain his position, stating, "freedom of expression ... is a vital and indispensable part of a democratic society."[63]

The Pen versus the Sword

Against this backdrop of mounting pressure and intimidation, a number of European newspapers decided to demonstrate their support for freedom of speech. On February 1, Germany's *Die Welt* reprinted the cartoons. Papers in France, Spain, Switzerland, the Netherlands, and Italy published the images on the same day.[64] *France Soir* and the Netherlands' *De Volkskrant* quickly became part of the story itself when they received bomb threats.[65]

On February 3, 2006, Rasmussen met with Muslim ambassadors and reiterated that, while he was "distressed" over the way the cartoons had offended some Muslims, "a Danish government can never apologise on behalf of a free and independent newspaper."[66] That same day, Sheikh Yusuf al-Qaradawi, a "special advisor" to the Muslim Brotherhood and widely followed figure in the Arab media, issued a fatwa that called for a "day of anger."[67] In a sermon broadcast on Qatar TV, he told his audience, "We are lions that zealously protect their dens, and avenge affronts to their sanctities. . . . We are a nation that should rage for the sake of Allah, His Prophet, and His book." He also called for a UN resolution against "affronts to prophets" and reiterated the boycott threat.[68]

As Rasmussen was meeting with Muslim leaders on Friday, February 3, protests surged across the Muslim world. Rioters railed against the cartoons, with crowds reaching tens of thousands in some places. Threats and bombings rocked the Palestinian territories. Demonstrations erupted in Somalia, with protesters in the country's northeastern region of Puntland marching on the buildings housing UN and NGO personnel. Protestors gathered outside the Danish embassy in Bangkok and trampled the country's flag; Indian police scattered protesters in Delhi with water cannons and tear gas.[69] Two protesters were killed and six police officers injured when demonstrators attempted to force their way into an American airbase in Bagram, Afghanistan, and hundreds of demonstrators in Laghman province called for "death to Denmark" and "death to France." One protester told the BBC that those behind the cartoons' publication "want to know whether Muslims are extremists or not"; as far as he was concerned, he went on to say, "Death to them and to their newspapers."[70]

On February 10, thousands of Muslims across Africa, Asia, and the Mideast set out from their mosques after Friday prayers to demonstrations against the cartoons, some ending in violence despite calls by many religious leaders for the protests to remain peaceful. On February 9, top Taliban commander Mullah Dadullah claimed that his organization had recruited 100 suicide bombers since the start of the controversy over Denmark's "blasphemous" cartoons. He offered a reward of 100 kilograms of gold to anyone who murdered the cartoonists.[71] In Afghanistan, by February 11, eleven people had died in riots.[72]

Next door in Pakistan, on February 14, bank guards in Lahore shot and killed two demonstrators in a crowd that was attacking buildings. In Islamabad, protesters had to be dispersed with tear gas.[73] Three people died in protests the following day. A 70,000-strong protest in Peshawar escalated into attacks on foreign businesses by youths wielding rocks and guns. Demonstrations across the country on February 16 drew tens of thousands of participants; there were 40,000 in Karachi alone, where rioters burned effigies of the Danish prime minister and called for breaking off relations with Denmark. A Kentucky Fried Chicken franchise in Peshawar—its connection to *Jyllands-Posten* unknown—was set ablaze. Attackers also targeted the offices of a Norwegian cell phone company. Turabal Haq of Jamat Ahl-e-Sunnat, the group responsible for the Karachi demonstration, declared, "The movement to protect the prophet's sanctity will continue until the pens of the blasphemous people are broken and their tongues get quiet."[74] Several protests ended in violence against diplomatic targets in Indonesia, Libya, Syria, Lebanon, and Iran. Denmark and Norway advised their citizens to leave Syria, and Denmark withdrew its ambassadors from Tehran, Jakarta, and Damascus, variously citing threats and a lack of host government protection.[75]

Attacks on Christians

In some cases, what began as anger at a group of largely secularist Danish cartoonists and editors also led to attacks against Christian targets. In Turkey, on February 5, a gunman murdered Italian priest Andrea Santoro, who had founded the magazine *Window to the Middle East* to encourage interfaith dialogue.[76] A Maronite church in Beirut, Lebanon, was stoned despite attempts by mainstream Sunni clerics to prevent such acts since, as one cleric in *Dar Al Fatwa* asked, "What do the people who live in Ashrafiyeh have to do with the people who published those blasphemous cartoons about our Prophet?"[77]

Pakistani protesters also targeted Christians. Rioters in Sukkur burned a Christian church after tensions over *Jyllands-Posten* were exacerbated by allegations that a Christian man had burned pages from a Qur'an.[78] On February 17, a crowd in the city of Kasur assaulted a United Presbyterian girls' school, breaking the windows and forcing the occupants to flee; the rioters also attempted to attack a Catholic church. In Peshawar, students and members of Islamist groups attacked a missionary school. At the behest of local Christian leaders, Muslim official Pir Ibrahim Sialvi reminded listeners on February 12 that Christians were "local people" and not involved with the cartoons.[79]

In Nigeria, cartoon demonstrations quickly gave way to attacks on Christians that set off widespread interreligious violence. On February 18, cartoon rioters in the northern states of Borno and Katsin set eleven churches alight and attempted to burn one man alive; sixteen people were killed.[80] Muslim rioters in the northern city of Maiduguri, carrying machetes and iron rods, burned thirty churches. In the melee, at least eighteen people, mostly Christians, died, including three children and one priest, Fr. Michael Gajere.[81] In Bauchi, also in the north, twenty-five people died in attacks against Christians, which may also have been linked to unfounded rumors of Qur'an desecration by a Christian schoolteacher.

Muslim Government Responses

Muslim government officials joined the protesters in wholeheartedly condemning the cartoons, but they took mixed stances on the demonstrations themselves. In some cases, they appear to have been directly involved, while in others the reaction to an issue initially publicized by governments now appeared to be growing beyond their control.[82] Given the difficulty of holding a truly spontaneous demonstration under Iran's and Syria's regimes, it was widely held that the regimes themselves were directly responsible for the protests that occurred on their territory.

Iran's Ayatollah Khamenei called violent protests in Tehran "justified and even holy," while the Iranian government cut trade ties with Denmark and President Mahmoud Ahmadinejad threatened a boycott of all countries in which the cartoons had appeared.[83] In India, an Islamic court issued a death fatwa against the cartoonists, and a minister in the state of Uttar Pradesh offered a reward of $11 million and the recipient's weight in gold for any successful cartoonist-killer.[84] Turkish prime minister Recep Tayyip Erdogan proclaimed that press freedom should have its limits; Pakistan president Pervez Musharraf claimed the cartoons were indefensible on grounds of free expression.[85] Afghan president Hamid Karzai called for "a strong measure" from western nations to prevent the appearance of offensive cartoons. Iraq's transportation ministry declared a freeze on its contracts with Denmark and Norway, and the Basra city council urged for Danish troops to be pulled from the country if Denmark's government would not apologize.[86] Indonesia's president, Susilo Bambang Yudhoyono, urged Muslims to accept apologies for the cartoons but also declared that their republication "sends a conflicting message to the Muslim community: that in a democracy it is permissible to offend Islam."[87]

Some leaders, while denouncing the caricatures, also condemned the cartoon violence. Malaysia's prime minister, Abdullah Ahmad Badawi, urged cartoon protesters to keep their response within reasonable bounds.[88] While charging the West with widespread "demonization of Islam and the vilification of Muslims," he also called for Muslims to refrain from "sweeping denunciations of Christians, Jews and the West."[89] Kuwait's Parliament called for legislation banning insults against religions and lauded Muslims' desire to defend Muhammad but also declared that "irresponsible acts...disfigure that emotion and makes it look like aggressiveness and destructiveness."[90] Iraq's Ayatollah Sistani, while condemning the "horrific action" of the cartoons' publication, also faulted "misguided and oppressive" parts of the Muslim community whose deeds "projected a distorted and dark image of the faith of justice, love and brotherhood." Elsewhere, newspapers were shut down and editors were arrested.[91]

On February 20, a number of leading Islamic scholars and professors, including the grand mufti of Egypt, issued a fatwa that denounced the cartoons' publication as "an entirely unacceptable crime of aggression." It also called on Muslims "to exercise self-restraint" and avoid "acts not sanctioned in Islam, such as breaking treaties and breaching time honored agreements by attacking foreign embassies or innocent people and other targets." However, the fatwa also urged the OIC and Muslim governments "to press the United Nations to issue a declaration criminalizing any insult to Muhammad, Jesus or Moses or to any other revered prophetic figure." Indeed, this officially endorsed prong of the antiblasphemy effort would remain an issue long after the violent protests died down.[92]

The Cartoons in the West: Press and Government Responses

Western countries saw a wide range of reactions to the cartoon controversy on the part of both government officials and private editors. While a number of papers published the cartoons to make a point, and a few others did so in the interest of reporting the news, many refrained from doing so out of fear of causing offense, suffering violence, or both. In the United States and the United Kingdom, the drawings went largely unpublished even as they came to dominate the news cycles. Meanwhile, statements from government officials ranged from one minister actually urging papers to reprint the cartoons, to a head of state urging the prosecution of a paper that had done so. In general, the notion that freedom of expression was somehow distinct from the freedom to insult or offend appeared to gain considerable traction.

Beyond immediate responses to the twelve caricatures, the cartoon controversy has become part of a far-reaching international debate on the parameters of freedom of expression. International and private Islamic organizations have echoed the position of Muslim governments, contending that freedom of speech (for those who accept the concept at all) does not cover religious insults. As a spokesman for Egypt's Muslim Brotherhood asserted, "We believe in free speech and a free press, but this does not give you the right to hurt me by hurting the prophet."[93] In Saudi Arabia, Sheik Abdul Rahman al-Seedes, of Mecca's Grand Mosque, not only declared that the Muslim world would "demand a trial" over the cartoons but also called for an international ban on insults to Islam.[94] This widely shared demand became a subject of contention between European institutions and Islamic organizations as they sought a resolution to the cartoon crisis.[95]

The Aftermath

Although the most concentrated furor of riots, threats, and diplomacy in connection with the *Jyllands-Posten* cartoons occurred during February 2006, the aftermath of the crisis has continued. In the UN, the incident has had a lasting effect on the tone of ongoing debates over "Islamophobia" and freedom of speech. Related legal cases brought in by France, Canada, and Denmark took years to resolve; and threats and violence from Islamist terror groups against those involved in the cartoons' production, and in some cases their conationals, have periodically resurfaced. Death threats against opposing voices continue to be heard.

In March 2006, Osama bin Laden declared that the cartoons were part of a "new Crusade" and warned of a response that would "make victorious our messenger of God." He stated that the loss of life in European bombings "paled (in comparison) when you went overboard in your unbelief and freed yourselves of the etiquettes of dispute and fighting and went to the extent of publishing these insulting drawings." Bin Laden also called for a boycott on goods from the United States and from European countries that had backed Denmark, and punishment of "those responsible for this terrible crime, committed by a handful of crusader journalists and others who have fallen from the faith." Al-Qaeda's second-in-command, Ayman al-Zawahiri, declared that "the hatred of Western crusaders, directed at the honorable prophet Muhammad…forces us to make a risky decision: Are we prepared to sacrifice ourselves and everything we own in the way of God or not?" In May, Al-Qaeda operative Mohammed Hussain posted on the Web a video calling for Muslims to "avenge your prophet." He announced, "We deeply desire that the small state of Denmark, Norway and France…are struck hard and destroyed…destroy their buildings, make their ground shake and transform them into a sea of blood."[96]

That same month, Pakistani journalist Hamid Mir reported that twelve terrorists were traveling to Denmark to kill the cartoonists.[97] Cartoon rage also apparently motivated one of three suspects arrested in August 2006 in connection with a plot to detonate bombs on German passenger trains, which failed only due to a problem with the detonators.[98] In May 2007, prosecutors listed the caricatures, together with the presence of Danish troops in Iraq, among the motives behind a thwarted plot to detonate a bomb somewhere in Copenhagen, for which four men were subsequently convicted and sentenced to jail terms.[99] In October 2007, a Danish convert to Islam, arrested with three others on terror charges, stated in court that his group had considered attacking Flemming Rose's house with a remote-controlled car bomb.[100] In September 2008, the U.S.-based security think tank Jamestown Foundation discovered plans to poison Denmark's water supply in retaliation for the cartoons on an Al-Qaeda-linked website.[101] In July 2008, an Islamist rebel leader was apprehended by government forces in Chad after a month of calling, according to Ahmat Mahamat Bachir, the country's Security

Minister, for a "holy war against Christians and atheists" that "would be launched from Chad to as far as Denmark."[102]

On February 12, 2008, Danish police arrested two Tunisians and a Danish man of Moroccan background in connection with a plot to assassinate Kurt Westergaard for drawing the turban-bomb cartoon.[103] Danish intelligence later revealed that the two Tunisians had cased Westergaard's home and learned his schedule. The younger of the pair, a martial arts expert, had planned to strangle the cartoonist.[104] While the younger Tunisian left Denmark voluntarily in August 2008, the elder remained under a "tolerated stay" policy, according to which even foreign nationals who have committed a crime may remain in Denmark if they will likely face ill treatment upon return to their country of origin. The Danish Supreme Court ruled in November 2008 that the evidence against him was inadequate to keep him in custody.[105]

Westergaard, whose drawing was most often singled out by critics as an example of Danish infamy, had, at the time of the arrests, been in hiding since early 2006. In November 2007, when word of a plot to murder him first surfaced, he had to relocate to a well-protected hotel room. February 15, three days after the revelation of the plot's details, he was evicted from the hotel for being "too much of a security risk."[106] Meanwhile, *Jyllands-Posten* editor Carsten Juste stated that his staff had "become more or less used to death threats and bomb threats since the cartoons, but it's the first time that we've heard about actual murder plans."[107]

On February 13, newspapers in Denmark, Spain, Sweden, and the Netherlands reprinted the offending cartoon in connection with their coverage of the arrests. *Berlingske Tidende* explained, "We are doing this to document what is at stake in this case, and to unambiguously back and support the freedom of speech."[108] In total, seventeen Danish papers that had originally declined to publish the cartoons now did so as a show of support for Westergaard; *Jyllands-Posten*, despite its previous apology, also reprinted them.[109] Flemming Rose linked the cartoon controversy to the cases of those accused of blasphemy in the Muslim world and argued: "In the West, there is a lack of clarity on these issues. People suggest that Salman Rushdie, Theo van Gogh, Ayaan Hirsi Ali, Taslima Nasreen and Kurt Westergaard bear a certain amount of responsibility for their fate. They don't understand that by doing so they tacitly endorse attacks on dissenting voices in parts of the world where no one can protect them."[110]

Terrorists cited the republication of the cartoons as the motivation for a new spate of threats. In April 2008, Denmark evacuated the staff of its embassies in Algeria and Afghanistan as a result of threats linked to the February cartoon republication.[111] On June 2, at least six Pakistanis died in an Al-Qaeda bombing of the Danish embassy in Islamabad, whose perpetrator said the act was retribution against Denmark's "infidel government" for the cartoon republication, and warned of further attacks unless the Danish government apologized.[112] In September 2008, Al-Qaeda released a video profiling the perpetrator of the attack and reiterating its threat to strike against "the Crusader states which insult, mock and defame our prophet and the Koran in their media and occupy our lands, steal our treasure and kill our brothers."[113]

In October 2009, two men living in Chicago were arrested for planning an attack on *Jyllands-Posten*'s offices in Denmark. (One of the conspirators told authorities he had suggested amending this plan and instead attempting to murder Flemming Rose and Kurt Westergaard.) The plot, code named the "Mickey Mouse Project," was discovered by the FBI and the PET. David Headley, born as Daood Sayed Gilani, and Tahawwur Hussain Rana, American and Canadian citizens respectively, admitted to receiving training in Pakistan from Lakshar-e-Taiba, a terrorist group. While in Pakistan, Headley met with Al-Qaeda operative Ilyas Kashmiri to set his plan in motion. He also traveled to Denmark to scout for targets; officials discovered short videos of the *Jyllands-Posten* office and other potential targets in his checked luggage after arresting him at the Chicago airport.[114]

On January 1, 2010, a man linked to the Somali terrorist group Al-Shabab broke into Kurt Westergaard's home with an axe and a knife. Westergaard, whose five-year-old granddaughter was also in the house, saved himself only by fleeing to a specially installed panic room in his house's bathroom. While his attacker attempted to break down the door and shouted, according to Westergaard, about "blood" and "revenge," the seventy-four-year-old cartoonist pressed a button to call police. Danish Intelligence later described the attack on Westergaard as likely "terror related." Facing two counts of attempted homicide in a Danish court, the suspect denied the charges against him in court. An Al-Shabab spokesperson, however, praised the assault and urged "Muslims around the world to target the people" like Westergaard.[115]

The global campaign of outrage over *Jyllands-Posten*'s alleged blasphemy took a heavy toll. In addition to extensive destruction of property, scholar Jytte Klausen estimates that, by 2006, at least 241 people had died in related violence. Many deaths occurred in Nigeria, followed distantly by Afghanistan and Libya.[116] It seems likely that much of the force of the crisis came from the intersection of institutionally amplified anticartoon rhetoric with existing conflicts and tensions.

Klausen, whose account of the crisis is often less than sympathetic to *Jyllands-Posten* and its project, concludes that, since the cartoon imbroglio, "New rules—formal and informal—apply that undoubtedly shrink the space for speech and artistic expression."[117] Her assessment proved uncannily accurate, as we discuss in chapter 13, when, in August 2009, Yale University Press, which had previously published at least four books containing images of Muhammad, refused to reproduce an image of the *Jyllands-Posten* issue containing the cartoons, along with other historic depictions of Muhammad, in a book chronicling the Danish cartoon affair—Klausen's own book, *The Cartoons That Shook the World*.[118]

Pope Benedict's Lecture at Regensburg

The Danish cartoons controversy might have appeared to some as a collision between religious and secular values, particularly given the Vatican's support for Muslim protests against insulting their religion. However, the next major global crisis involving a purported Western insult to Islam proved that religious leaders themselves are far from immune to such charges. This furor originated in an academic lecture by Pope Benedict XVI, given at Regensburg, Germany, on September 12, 2006, on the relationship between faith and reason. While discussing the place of reason in the Christian tradition, the pope quoted from a dialogue between the fourteenth-century Byzantine emperor Manuel Paleologus II and a Muslim Persian, which at one point turned to the question of holy war:

> The emperor...addresses his interlocutor with a startling brusqueness on the central question about the relationship between religion and violence in general, saying: "Show me just what Mohammed brought that was new, and there you will find things only evil and inhuman, such as his command to spread by the sword the faith he preached." The emperor, after having expressed himself so forcefully, goes on to explain in detail the reasons why spreading the faith through violence is something unreasonable. Violence is incompatible with the nature of God and the nature of the soul. "God," he says, "is not pleased by blood—and not acting reasonably is contrary to God's nature."[119]

The pope's primary purpose for the quotation was to elaborate on the emperor's key claim that "not to act in accordance with reason is contrary to God's nature," the theme to which he devoted the remainder of the lecture. He described a Muslim teaching that "God is absolutely transcendent"—not bound to rationality or even, in the view of one Islamic theologian, to His own word. The pope then contrasted that view with what he described as the Catholic position, based on the synthesis of biblical faith and Greek philosophy, "that between God and us, between his eternal Creator Spirit and our created reason there exists a real analogy." The bulk of the lecture focused on this heritage and the modern, mainly Western, challenges it faces. The pontiff called for faith joined with reason in the broad sense and contrasted this with either a positivist truncation of reason to exclude faith or a divorce between religion and rational inquiry.

However, many critics in the Muslim world quickly seized exclusively on Paleologus's assertion that Muhammad had brought "evil and inhuman things." In response, Vatican spokesmen emphasized that the pope had no wish to offend Muslims and hoped for respect and dialogue between faiths.[120] This explanation failed to quell the outcry. Notably, a Muslim Brotherhood official, who warned that the pope's remarks were likely to provoke "an extreme reaction," went on to explain that they "harm Islam more than the cartoons because they come from a leader who represents millions of people and not just from a journalist."[121]

Once again, Muslim government entities spoke alongside clerics in condemning a perceived insult to their faith. While some merely called the remarks ignorant or offensive, others characterized the speech as an effort to foster conflict among civilizations or even as a flashback to the Crusades. On September 14, 2006, the OIC stated that it "regrets the quotations cited by the pope on the Life of the Honorable Prophet Mohammed, and what he referred to as 'spreading' Islam by the sword," which show "deep ignorance of Islam and Islamic history."[122] The Gulf Cooperation Council demanded an apology and expressed its displeasure that the pope could make such remarks "at a time of multiple campaigns hostile towards Muslims."

Yemen's president denounced the pope. Malaysia's prime minister said the pope should apologize, withdraw his remarks, and "not take slightly the spread of outrage that has been created."[123] Hamas leader Minister Ismail Haniyah demanded that the pope "revise his comments and stop attacking Islam." Libya's General Instance of Religious Affairs stated that the alleged slander on Islam "pushes us back to the era of crusades against Muslims led by Western political and religious leaders." Jordan's Minister of Religious Affairs called for an immediate explanation, as did Egypt's Foreign Minister, and an Egyptian foreign ministry spokesperson said the comments worked to "reinforce calls for a war of the civilizations."[124] Iran's Ayatollah Khamenei described the pope's comments as "the latest chain of the crusade against Islam started by America's Bush."[125] Pakistan's government complained to the Vatican's diplomatic representative, and its Parliament said that Benedict "should retract his remarks" since they "have injured sentiments across the Muslim world and pose the danger of spreading acrimony between religions."[126]

In Turkey, the prime minister, Tayyip Erdogan, said that the pope's "ugly and unfortunate" remarks should be taken back.[127] Senior religious official Ali Bardakoglu claimed that Benedict's comment represented an "abhorrent, hostile and prejudiced point of view" that reflected the mind-set "of the Crusades" and called for the pope to apologize.[128] Bardakoglu asserted, "We also criticize the Christian world for its wrongs, but we never defame either Christ or the Bible or the holiness of Christianity."[129] Salih Kapusuz, deputy leader of the governing Justice and Development Party, said the pope had "a dark mentality that comes from the darkness of the Middle Ages," was attempting to "revive the mentality of the Crusades," and, as "the author of such unfortunate and insolent remarks," would be "going down in history in the same category as leaders such as Hitler and Mussolini." Opposition leaders, although secularist, also said the pope should apologize before visiting Turkey in November.[130]

In response to allegations of a "war on Islam," violence against indigenous Christians—whether Roman Catholic or not—promptly erupted. In Gaza on September 15, 2006, a Hamas official proclaimed to 2,000 protesters, "This is another Crusader war against the Arab and Muslim world." That same day, four improvised bombs exploded outside a Greek Orthodox compound in Gaza City, fortunately causing no injuries.[131] On September 16, gunmen targeted an Orthodox church; a caller from the Islamic Organization of the Swords of Righteousness claimed to have "carried out this shooting because of the pope's statement" and demanded a papal apology. Others armed with guns and Molotov cocktails assaulted four churches of various denominations in the West Bank city of Nablus; one gunman fired inside a fifth Nablus church, which was, in fact, Catholic. A group calling itself the Lions of Monotheism, which linked its action to the pope's lecture, firebombed Anglican and Greek Orthodox churches. Police were dispatched to the besieged churches, a Hamas parliamentarian denounced the attacks, and a leading Palestinian Muslim cleric called for Palestinian Christians to be protected. But at the same time, he called for "our Muslim and Arab countries not to receive the Pope so that he does not make any comments that may ignite fire and in order to avoid any assault on him that may ignite a religious war."[132]

In Iraq, a bomb went off at an Assyrian Catholic church in Basra on September 15, and an unknown militant group posted statements in mosques threatening to attack Iraqi Christians if the pope did not apologize. Islamic militants murdered two Assyrian Christians in the days following the speech, and Christian leaders warned Iraqi Christians to remain at home.[133]

In Egypt, Coptic leader Pope Shenouda III, very attuned to the precarious position of the Mideast's Christian minorities, said that he had not heard the pope's actual words but that "any remarks which offend Islam and Muslims are against the teachings of Christ," which "instruct us not to hurt others, either in their convictions or their ideas, or any of their symbols—religious symbols." He later stated that he "wish(ed) the Catholic pope had considered the reaction to his remarks" and that "criticizing others' faith breeds enmity and divisions."[134]

On September 16, newly appointed Vatican Secretary of State, Cardinal Tarcisio Bertone, stated that the pope "did not mean, nor does he mean, to make [the Byzantine emperor's] opinion his own in any way" but, "as is evident from a complete and attentive reading of the text," simply meant to issue "a clear and radical rejection of the religious motivation for violence, from whatever side it may come." He continued: "The Holy Father thus sincerely regrets that certain passages of his address could have sounded offensive to the sensitivities of the Muslim faithful, and should have been interpreted in a manner that in no way corresponds to his intentions. Indeed it was he who, before the religious fervor of Muslim believers, warned secularized Western culture to guard against 'the contempt for God and the cynicism that considers mockery of the sacred to be an exercise of freedom.'"[135] This statement failed to satisfy many critics. Morocco withdrew its ambassador from the Vatican, effective September 17, due to the pope's "offensive remarks."[136] A threat from the Mujahedeen Army of Iraq, perpetrators of numerous terror attacks, "to send you people who adore death as much as you adore life" led the Vatican to increase the pope's security.[137] Another Iraqi insurgent group, Ansar al-Sunnah, declared that it would attack Christians. Security for churches in several countries was tightened for the Sunday services to be held on September 17.[138] Their fears were realized when gunmen murdered a sixty-five-year-old Italian nun working in an Austrian-funded hospital in Mogadishu, Somalia; Sister Leonella Sgorbita was shot seven times, and her bodyguard was also killed. As she lay dying, the nun said she forgave her killers. The pope wrote that Sister Leonella's forgiveness of her attackers represented "the most authentic Christian witness, a peaceful sign of contradiction which shows the victory of love over hate and evil."[139]

On the day of these attacks, Benedict personally stated that he was "deeply sorry for the reactions in some countries to a few passages of my address" and noted that they "do not in any way express my personal thought." Such a statement of personal regret from the pope is a highly unusual event. The pontiff's comments were printed in Arabic in the Vatican newspaper *L'Osservatore Romano*.[140] The response was mixed.[141]

On September 20, the pope again expressed his "profound respect" for Muslims and said that "the negative words pronounced by the medieval emperor" do not "reflect my personal conviction." Again, the Muslim Brotherhood expressed dissatisfaction, although Iranian president Mahmoud Ahmadinejad stated that there was "no problem" now that Benedict had made it clear he did not endorse Manuel's remark. Meanwhile Mehmet Ali Agca, the Turkish man who had attempted to assassinate Pope John Paul II in 1981, warned Benedict from jail that his life would be in danger if he visited Turkey.[142]

Amidst this barrage of threats and denunciations, a number of voices in the West supported the pope's comments and the right to speak freely about Islam generally. German chancellor Angela Merkel, Italian prime minister Silvio Berlusconi, and Australian prime minister John Howard came to his defense.[143] On October 3, a plenary assembly of German bishops declared that "the Catholic Church and all people who, in Germany and throughout the world, respect and defend freedom of speech, will never allow themselves to be intimidated."[144] They also expressed concern over attacks against Christian minorities and particularly the murder of Sister Leonella, stressing the urgency for dialogue between Christianity and Islam and calling for Muslim governments to show reciprocity with regard to the religious freedom enjoyed by Muslims living in Germany.[145]

In a further effort to calm the controversy, on September 25, the pope met with ambassadors from twenty-one Muslim-majority countries—all those, except Sudan, that had diplomatic ties to the Vatican—as well as an Arab League representative. Once again, Benedict reaffirmed his respect for Muslims and the need for Christian-Muslim dialogue.[146] The pope's speech was broadcast live on Al Jazeera, and a representative of the Muslim World League, Mario Scialoja, expressed his approval.[147] However, the following day, an OIC summit declared that the pope should still "retract or redress" his Regensburg statement to prevent "tension between the Muslim world and the Vatican, to the detriment of the real interests of the two parties."[148]

Despite the pope's repeated attempted clarifications of his statements, there was continuing violence against Christians in Iraq. On October 4 and 5, gunmen opened fire on a Chaldean Catholic church in Mosul and injured one guard in an attack believed to be linked to outrage over the pope's speech. On October 9, a Syrian Orthodox priest, Father Amer Iskender of the St. Ephrem Church in Mosul, was kidnapped by militants who gave the priest's church two options: either to pay a $350,000 ransom or to provide $40,000 plus a statement denouncing Benedict's comments. The church, which had already clarified that it did not support the pope's comment, posted thirty billboards throughout the city criticizing the statement; and family members sought to raise the ransom money. In spite of these efforts, the body of Fr. Iskender, who appeared to have been tortured, was found beheaded and dismembered on October 11.[149]

The papal comments remained in the minds of Islamic militants as late as March 2008, when Osama bin Laden released an audio tape. Besides calling for Palestinians to take up holy war, bin Laden charged Pope Benedict XVI with facilitating a "new Crusade" against Islam. He also warned of repercussions for the republication of the Danish cartoons.[150]

In a more reasonable effort, on October 15, 2006, a group of thirty-eight Muslim scholars published an open letter to Pope Benedict in the U.S.-based *Islamica* magazine, which suggested an actual discussion of Benedict's views. This letter criticized a number of Pope Benedict's implications about Islam but also commended the pope's criticism of materialism, as well as his statements of regret and respect for Muslims following the controversy. The signatories told the pope, "We share your desire for frank and sincere dialogue and recognize its importance in an increasingly interconnected world." They also declared the murder of Sister Leonella and "any other similar acts of wanton individual violence" to be "completely un-Islamic." Several grand muftis, including that of Egypt, were among the signatories.[151]

Lars Vilks and "The Right to Blaspheme Religions"

In August 2007, Scandinavian cartoons once again made it back into the headlines. This time, the artist-provocateur was Lars Vilks from Sweden, whose caricature depicted Muhammad's head on a dog's body. Along with two similar drawings, it had been removed from a dog-themed art exhibition and rejected by several other art institutions on security grounds. However, public protests and international criticism began when regional newspaper *Nerikes Allehanda* published one of the dog drawings alongside an August 18 editorial on "the right to ridicule a religion." The op-ed stated: "A liberal society must be able to do two things at the same time. On the one hand, it must be able to defend Muslims' right to freedom of religion and their right to build mosques. However, on the other hand, it is also permissible to ridicule Islam's most foremost symbols—just like all other religions' symbols.... The right to freedom of religion and the right to blaspheme religions go together." The editorial also linked the galleries' wariness to host Vilks's drawings with the 2006 Danish cartoon crisis.[152] *Nerikes Allehanda*'s publication provoked a small, peaceful protest by about sixty Swedish Muslims. It also inspired a broader international controversy that took the editors by surprise, given that a number of other Swedish papers had previously published the cartoon.[153]

On August 27, the Iranian foreign ministry summoned Sweden's *charge d'affaires* in Tehran to complain about the cartoon.[154] Iran's president also chimed in to blame the cartoons on "Zionists" who "do not want the Swedish government to be a friend of other nations" since "they thrive on conflict and war."[155] On August 30, Pakistan's Foreign Ministry condemned *Nerikes Allehanda*'s "offensive and blasphemous sketch of the Holy Prophet (PBUH)" and warned, "Regrettably, the tendency among some Europeans to mix the freedom of expression with an outright and deliberate insult to 1.3 billion Muslims in the world is on the rise."[156]

While there were some threats in connection with Vilks's caricature, it did not produce anything like the violence of the Danish cartoons affair. However, as with other controversies, it created a lasting danger for its central figure. After Danish cartoonist Kurt Westergaard was attacked in January 2010, Vilks received telephone calls reportedly telling him, "Now it's your turn." In early March 2010, seven people were arrested in Ireland in connection with an international plot to kill the Swedish cartoonist. One plotter, American Colleen LaRose (who went by the Internet name of "Jihad Jane"), had been arrested in Philadelphia in late October 2009. LaRose and another American woman among those arrested in March, Jamie Paulin-Ramirez, are converts to Islam; the other suspects are reportedly Libyan, Algerian, Palestinian, and Croatian nationals. Five of those arrested in Ireland were quickly released, while the other two were held on unrelated charges. On March 4, LaRose was indicted on conspiracy charges; according to the indictment, she had agreed to murder a Swedish citizen (identified by a U.S. official as Vilks) after receiving orders to kill him and, in so doing, to frighten "the whole Kufar [non-believer] world." In 2011, both LaRose and Paulin-Ramirez pleaded guilty to the terrorism charges in U.S. federal court.[157] The conspirators reportedly felt that LaRose, a blond woman in her forties and a U.S. citizen, would be able to avoid unwanted attention during this assignment.[158]

Nonetheless, in relative terms, the Swedish cartoons' affair was a startling contrast with the previous year's events. Despite the similarities—a derogatory cartoon of Muhammad appearing in a Scandinavian paper alongside an editorial in support of the right to mock religion—and despite international attention, there was no mass response along the lines of that allegedly provoked by *Jyllands-Posten*. This suggests that, while mocking Islam is dangerous, global protests and violence on the level of the 2006 cartoon controversy do not materialize directly as a result of every insult that crosses a certain threshold of offensiveness—at least, not without assistance.

Geert Wilders's *Fitna*

Unlike most of the figures discussed thus far, the man at the center of the next major "insulting Islam" international crisis is self-avowedly anti-Islam. Dutch parliamentarian Geert Wilders was no stranger to controversy when, in November 2007, he announced that he had begun work on a film dedicated to illustrating "the intolerant and fascist nature of the Koran." A politician who had issued repeated denunciations, not only of Islamic extremism, but also of the Muslim religion itself, Wilders had been under around-the-clock police protection and living in a secret location since the 2004 murder of Dutch filmmaker Theo van Gogh.

He had previously attracted negative attention from abroad after, in a February 2007 interview, he stated that Muslims who wanted to stay in the Netherlands "must tear out half of the Koran and throw it away. I've read the Koran... and I know that there are enough awful things in it." He also said that Islam was "a violent religion" and that "if Mohammed lived here today I could imagine chasing him out of the country tarred and feathered as an extremist." While the Dutch Contact Organization for Muslims and Government "[didn't] want to react to the content [of Wilders's comment] because we cannot take it seriously," the Saudi government apparently took Wilders's words seriously enough to demand an apology from the Dutch government through its embassy in The Hague.[159] A Dutch foreign ministry representative explained that although Wilders's opinions were "not the point of view of the Dutch government," the MP enjoyed the "right to express himself." Wilders, who "would not dream of taking any of it back," found it "scandalous that a country which does not have freedom of speech teaches me a lesson."[160]

In January 2008, Wilders announced a March release date for his film, which he titled *Fitna*, the Arabic word for strife or discord. He promised that the film would link the Qur'an directly to violence, depicting it as "the latest test to Western democracies since Nazism and communism." Long before the planned release, and as Wilders seems to have expected, his claims caused an outcry both in the Netherlands and internationally.[161] Syria's grand mufti, Ahmad Badr al-Din Hassoun, told the European parliament that, if rumors that Wilders would destroy a Qur'an in the film were correct, "this will simply mean he is inciting wars and bloodshed... It is the responsibility of the Dutch people to stop him." In late February, a Dutch paper reported that Al-Qaeda had issued a death threat against Wilders.[162] Threats, recriminations, and saber-rattling echoed around the globe.[163]

The Dutch Islamic Federation sought legal action against Wilders, while the Netherlands' National Moroccan Council promised it would attempt to "neutralize the threat" of violence were the film to be released but noted that they could not guarantee the success of such efforts. Wilders refused to budge. He argued that the threats proved his point: "We can never allow people who use nondemocratic means, people who use violence instead of arguments, people who use knives instead of debates, we can never allow them to set the agenda."[164]

When television stations refused to show an unedited version of his film, Wilders opted to release *Fitna* online. Plans for a press showing were cancelled when security costs proved to be prohibitive.[165] Wilders's original website for the movie was shut down by U.S.-based host Network Solutions on the grounds that it potentially violated the company's policy on hate speech.[166] After being turned down by other prospective hosts, on March 27, *Fitna* was posted on the U.K.-based website LiveLeak. However, just two days later, LiveLeak was forced to take down the film "following threats to our staff of a very serious nature."[167] By this time, however, the film was readily accessible on numerous websites, including YouTube, which placed a disclaimer on the film: "The diversity of the world . . . means that some of the beliefs and views of some individuals may offend others."[168]

In its final version, *Fitna* contained footage of Islamist terrorist attacks interspersed with quotations from the Qur'an and hateful sermons by imams; it featured headlines from Dutch newspapers about immigration problems juxtaposed with images of Muslim protesters. The film implied an impending Islamic takeover of the Netherlands and included bar graphs showing the number of Muslims in the country. These graphs appeared alongside images of radical Islamist atrocities such as female genital mutilation, executions of gays, and a beheading under the heading "The Netherlands in the future?!" The film opened and closed with Danish cartoonist Kurt Westergaard's drawing of Muhammad with a bomb in his turban. (Westergaard has threatened to sue Wilders for copyright infringement.[169])

The rumored destruction of a Qur'an did not take place. The film opened with the sound of pages being torn, and then text states, "The sound you heard was a page being removed from the phonebook . . . For it is not up to me, but to Muslims themselves to tear out the hateful verses from the Qur'an." Additional text toward the end of the film charged that "Islam . . . seeks to destroy our western civilization" and called for "Islamic ideology" to be defeated as were Nazism and communism. In an unusually open show of agreement with those who believe Islam to be linked with brutality and violence, radical Islamist Omar Bakri stated, "If we leave out the first images and the sound of the page being torn, [*Fitna*] could be a film by the (Islamist) Mujahedeen."[170]

European officials widely denounced the film, and the Secretary-General of the OIC, Ekmeleddin Ihsanoglu, issued a statement on March 28 that called *Fitna* "a deliberate act of discrimination against Muslims, incitement for hatred and an act of defamation of religions."[171] Secretary-General Saleh S. Al-Wohaibi of the Saudi-backed World Assembly of Muslim Youth warned that "attacks" like Wilders's film would "lead to very serious repercussions, pushing mankind to a situation of chaos and conflict." He contended, "If we do something against Christianity or target Christian interests in retaliation, the Netherlands, Europe and the whole world would object."[172] This statement is remarkable, given that the Saudis already ban the practice of Christianity in their country, and its state-funded imams make regular vitriolic attacks on other religions.

The Egyptian, Moroccan, and Bangladeshi governments denounced the movie, while the Iranian government deemed it blasphemous and sought to compel the EU, the Netherlands, and even the United Kingdom (home of LiveLeak) to remove it from the Internet. In a note of protest to the Dutch embassy, a Malaysian Islamic opposition party claimed that the film, if not withdrawn, would "invite vengeance" from Muslims.[173] Indonesia and Pakistan added their voices to the complaints and demands for bans.[174]

There was also a push for legal action against Wilders. In Jordan, the same country in which prosecutors targeted Danish cartoonist Kurt Westergaard, a media group announced plans to press charges against Wilders. A campaign called "The Messenger of Allah Unite Us" sought a boycott of Dutch and Danish products. On July 1, Prosecutor General Hassan Abdalat charged Wilders with five offenses under Jordanian law, vowing that the Dutch MP would receive a subpoena "through diplomatic channels." He also suggested that if the Netherlands did not extradite Wilders, Jordan could seek to have him arrested elsewhere by Interpol. A representative of the Messenger of Allah campaign said Wilders could face up to three years in a Jordanian jail.[175]

At the April 2008 session of the UN Human Rights Council, which included the Universal Periodic Review of the Netherlands, numerous delegates called for the Dutch government to take action against Wilders. Several of them sought to redefine freedom of expression so that *Fitna* would not be protected. Egypt and Turkey urged Dutch leaders to take legal measures, while Pakistan claimed that *Fitna* violated articles of the International Covenant on Civil and Political Rights (ICCPR) and the International Convention on the Elimination on All Forms of Racial Discrimination (ICERD).[176] Citing Ministry of the Interior sources, an article in the Pakistan *Daily Times* stated that "the delegation would also tell the EU that if such acts against Islam are not controlled, more attacks on the EU diplomatic missions abroad could not be ruled out."[177] The report came in the wake of the car-bomb attack outside the Danish embassy in Islamabad that killed at least six people.[178] As described in chapter 12, Wilders also faced prosecution in his own country on charges of group insult of Muslims and inciting hate and discrimination against Muslims because of their religion and against non-Western foreigners because of their race, in 2011, he was acquitted.

Closing

These international incidents reflect the alignment of a widespread popular belief that insults to religion should be prevented with a growing campaign to crush by force any criticism of Islam. This is true not only in cases of terrorist violence but also in the more subtle pattern of holding governments responsible for "allowing" blasphemous works or statements in a free press. In the aftermath of the Danish cartoons crisis, the Parliamentary Assembly of the Council of Europe rightly declared that ideas "that may shock, offend or disturb the state or any sector of the population" are nonetheless protected by the freedom of expression.[179] Yet, as we shall see in the next chapter, the extent of many governments' commitment to this principle remains unclear. At the same time, attempts to undermine freedom of expression, whether genuinely spontaneous or carefully planned, continue in full force.

More positively, some reform-minded Muslims have taken issue with some of their coreligionists' reaction to *Fitna* as well as to the cartoons. Egyptian Ahmad Al-Aswani wrote:

> I do not think that cartoons, books, or films can harm a religion or affect the faith of those who adhere to it out of conviction...
>
> The ones who harm the Prophet are those who butcher and bomb innocents all over the world...
>
> The ones who harm the Prophet are those who call on the world to pass a resolution against disparaging religion, while they themselves denigrate other religions in each prayer in the mosques, as well as in their schools and on their satellite channels—and especially [the religion] of Christians and Jews, whom they curse in every prayer....
>
> The ones who harm the Prophet do not live in the West—they are among us, the Muslims.[180]

Legitimizing Repression

Blasphemy Restrictions in the United Nations

In 1994, Gaspar Biro, a young Hungarian lawyer and the UN Special Rapporteur on Sudan, concluded that Sudan was violating international human rights agreements due to what it claimed was its "sharia-based" penal code. Under this code, convictions for adultery, theft, and apostasy meant harsh penalties, including amputation or execution for anyone over the age of seven.[1] Biro said: "It does not matter in this context who the drafter is nor what the sources of inspiration of these norms are. In terms of human rights, the only question is whether or not the national legislation is compatible with the existing international instruments to which Sudan is a party."[2]

Sudan's UN delegation responded by calling Biro's report "flagrant blasphemy and a deliberate insult to the Islamic religion, for which the author of the report must be interrogated and condemned by all States and Organizations that respect human and peoples [sic] rights," and "brought to justice."[3]

When asked why Biro had not been permitted back into Sudan to collect information for a subsequent report, the delegation representative replied with a thinly veiled threat: "[W]e don't want to speculate about his fate if he is to continue offending the feelings of Muslims worldwide..." He then demanded that the UN General Assembly "take the necessary remedial measures to comfort the feelings of Muslims worldwide for the unwarranted challenge to Islam posed by those references, otherwise no one would be in a position to guarantee that he would not face the fate of Mr. Salman Rushdie."[4]

In 1998, Biro was replaced as Special Rapporteur to Sudan. Sudan continued many of its atrocities, now widely recognized as genocide, in the south for several years and commenced new ones in Darfur.

United Nations and Blasphemy: An Overview

In recent years, in what they say is an effort to quash culturally insensitive "insults to Islam," members of the Organization of the Islamic Conference (OIC) have sought to silence UN criticism of Islamic practices and values in their own countries and have used the UN human rights mechanisms as instruments for suppressing anti-Islamic speech generally. This effort began well before the Danish cartoon controversy and is a long-standing concerted campaign to shift international norms in the OIC's favor. The attempts to stop "insults" to Islam were at first primarily defensive and aimed at shutting down UN criticism of human rights abuses. This included promulgating a separate and distinct version of "human rights in Islam," whose entire content was declared subject to an undefined Islamic "sharia" law. The OIC members then sought, with some success, to give UN legitimacy to this parallel human rights regime—the only religion-based system to win such recognition. OIC members have also threatened several UN Special Rapporteurs for criticizing Islamic regimes. OIC governments did this on the grounds that, since the regimes claim to represent Islam, any criticism of them is necessarily an "insult" to Islam itself.

In 1999, some Muslim-majority states began to argue that the UN must condemn and prohibit what the OIC labels "defamation of religions," particularly of Islam. They have acknowledged that these "defamation of religions" resolutions are meant primarily to shield Islam and Muslims from criticism. The "defamation" push effectively seeks to redefine human rights in five ways, by:

1. treating religious matters under hate speech bans as if they were akin to racial matters;
2. granting rights to religions themselves rather than to individuals;
3. creating a new right not to be offended in matters of religion;
4. claiming that freedom of religion stands in opposition to freedom of expression;
5. giving an expansive interpretation to the exceptions to the right of freedom of expression.

Underlying this strategy is a rejection of the closely linked freedoms of expression and belief as universal, individual, and fundamental human rights.

The OIC succeeded in altering the mandate of the Special Rapporteur on Contemporary Forms of Racism, Racial Discrimination, Xenophobia, and Related Intolerance and eliminating the mandate of the Special Rapporteur on Sudan. Pressure was also brought against the Special Rapporteur on Freedom of Opinion and Expression. At the OIC's urging, the UN adopted nonbinding resolutions denouncing "defamation of religions" every year between 1999 and 2010, first by the UN Commission on Human Rights and then, when the commission was formally disbanded, by its successor, the UN Human Rights Council. Since 2005, the UN General Assembly also has adopted resolutions on "defamation of religions." After the 9/11 terrorist attacks, these resolutions emphasized the negative repercussions of such "tragic events" for Muslims, including the verbal linkage of Islam with terrorism. Since the 2006 Danish cartoon controversy, resolutions have also stressed the importance of placing limits on freedom of expression.

Initially, such "defamation" resolutions were adopted by consensus, but, in 2001, Western countries began voting against them, pointing to the resolutions' undue emphases on a single religion; to their protection of religion as such rather than of individuals; and to their potential for abuse in silencing debate within religions. The European Union (EU) and the United States have rejected the entire concept of "defamation of religions" as invalid in human rights discourse, which, they argue, should center on individual rights. The UN Special Rapporteur on Freedom of Religion or Belief has also criticized this concept, pointing out that religious freedom "does not include the right to have a religion or belief that is free from criticism or ridicule" and that restrictions on this basis threaten both free expression and religious freedom itself.[5] The West increasingly weakened support for these resolutions, and, at the sixteenth session of the Human Rights Council in 2011, the OIC refrained from introducing the resolution, sensing it would fail to pass.

Amidst these pressures, proponents began to adopt other tactics, including recasting their case as opposition to "hate speech." This push for expanded curbs on free speech based on existing prohibitions against incitement to racial and religious hatred is one which Western states seem ill-poised to resist; it remains a major reason for concern, since it is used to silence criticism of and debate within Islam, as well as criticism of those who violate human rights in Islam's name.

The Organization of the Islamic Conference

The OIC, a fifty-seven-member body, headquartered in Jeddah, Saudi Arabia, was founded in 1969 to respond to the Israeli-Palestinian conflict.[6] Particularly since the OIC's "Extraordinary Summit" in 2005 in Saudi Arabia, when discussion of the Danish cartoons helped ignite a global uproar, the OIC's leadership has grown vociferous in denouncing "Islamophobia." At its 2008 summit on Islamophobia in Dakar, Senegal, the OIC called for a "legal instrument" to ban defamation of Islam. The meeting resulted in the creation of its Observatory on Islamophobia, to protest crimes already banned by Western law, particularly vandalism against mosques, and offenses prohibited only by Islamic blasphemy rules, such as the sale of autographed copies of Danish cartoonist Kurt Westergaard's cartoon depicting Muhammad in a turban-bomb. This latter category also included calls to ban simple expressions of opinion, notably the "One Law for All" campaign against the establishment of sharia law in the United Kingdom. Also deemed "Islamophobic" was the association of internationally famous critics of Islam established by Danish parliamentarian Naser Khader. Khader is a self-described "cultural Muslim" who has sought to promote moderate Muslim voices and to emphasize the compatibility of Islam and democracy in Denmark.[7]

The latest 2008 OIC charter pledges the organization "to protect and defend the true image of Islam, to combat defamation of Islam, and encourage dialogue among civilizations and religions."[8] It has adopted a "Ten-Year Program of Action" that includes the resolution "Endeavor to have the United Nations adopt an international resolution to counter Islamophobia, and call upon all States to enact laws to counter it, including deterrent punishments." The article on Islamophobia on the OIC's website declares "offensive" the terms "Islamic fascists," "Muslim terrorists," and "Islamist fundamentalist extremists," and the group has made inroads in having the United States, the United Kingdom, and other governments adopt such lexicons.[9]

The Cairo Declaration on Human Rights in Islam

Beginning with the adoption of the "Cairo Declaration on Human Rights in Islam" in 1990, OIC governments have attempted to win acceptance of a human rights framework that they claim is based on Islamic tradition. In its introductory sections, the declaration lauds, "[T]he civilizing and historical role of the Islamic *Ummah* which God made the best nation," and expresses the hope to define " . . . the role that this *Ummah* should play to guide a humanity confused by competing trends and ideologies." In structure, the declaration mimics the Universal Declaration of Human Rights (UDHR), but in substance, it subordinates each of the UDHR's guarantees to an undefined Islamic law. The guarantee of free expression reads: "Everyone shall have the right to express his opinion freely in such manner as would not be contrary to the principles of the Sharia." Similarly, information "may not be exploited or misused in such a way as may violate sanctities and the dignity of Prophets, undermine moral and ethical values or disintegrate, corrupt or harm society or weaken its faith."

The declaration effectively bars debating Muslims about their religion, stating that "Islam is the religion of unspoiled nature. It is prohibited to exercise any form of compulsion on man or to exploit his poverty or ignorance in order to convert him to another religion or to atheism." Article 25 stipulates, "The Islamic Sharia is the only source of reference for the explanation or clarification of any of the articles of this Declaration."[10]

Thus, an undefined sharia is the governing rule, and other human rights principles must yield to it. The declaration is also premised on the fiction that there is a consensus in the Islamic world on sharia. Hence, if a state declares that its structure, policies, or acts are manifestations of sharia, and finds a compliant jurist to say that this is so, then it could claim a warrant to override any conflicting human right.

OIC efforts to win acceptance of the Cairo Declaration at the UN have met with some success. The declaration has been invoked in a number of official UN reports and in a resolution and is repeatedly cited in communications from OIC-member governments to the UN.[11] The UN has in effect, and without precedent, given stature to an instrument of an institution of one particular religion that undercuts the civil and political human rights enshrined by the world body and is controversial even among Muslims themselves.[12]

The UN has implicitly endorsed the notion of a unique Islamic version of human rights by staging several events on the subject. In 1998, at the suggestion of Iran, the UN hosted an OIC-sponsored seminar, "Islamic Perspectives on the Universal Declaration of Human Rights," which provided a platform for government-approved "experts" to promote sharia, while shutting out UN-registered nongovernmental organizations.[13] In 2002, the UN held a second seminar on human rights in Islam at whose conclusion, Mary Robinson, then UN High Commissioner for Human Rights, declared that "[n]o one can deny that at its core Islam is entirely consonant with the principle of fundamental human rights, including human dignity, tolerance, solidarity and equality" and that it "bestowed rights upon women and children long before similar recognition was afforded in other civilizations."[14] Even though demands for a separate, culturally specific rights regime would seem to suggest the contrary, Robinson declared, "No one can deny the acceptance of the universality of human rights by Islamic states."[15]

Attacks on UN Rapporteurs and NGOs

The first Muslim government attempt to exempt their states from human rights critiques occurred in 1994, when—as noted—the Sudanese government accused UN Special Rapporteur on Sudan Gaspar Biro of committing "blasphemy" with his human rights report. Sudan had support for its stance. In 1999, the Arab League submitted to the UN a pointed resolution defending Sudan from "foreign intervention" in its internal affairs. This resolution declared that all allegations of slavery in Sudan constitute "part of the campaign to mar the image of the Arabs and the Muslims and offend their community and civilization."[16] Sudan's massive human rights violations and war crimes against humanity continued and escalated to become what is now widely recognized as genocide.

In 1997, Indonesia's delegate for the OIC accused the UN Special Rapporteur on Racism of blasphemy for a passage in his report dealing with anti-Semitism. The rapporteur had included the statement, "Muslim extremists are turning increasingly to their own religious sources, first and foremost the Qur'an, as a primary anti-Jewish source." After Pakistan called it "an insult to Islam" and other states complained, the Commission on Human Rights adopted—without a vote— a resolution in which it protested the reference to the Qur'an and requested that it be deleted.[17] Thereafter, the section on anti-Semitism mentioned only Eastern Europe and the former Soviet Union as specific problem areas.[18] Thus, in the name of sensitivity to religion, an entire region of the world was exempted from UN scrutiny on anti-Semitism. Also under OIC pressure, the commission suspended its monitoring of Iran in 2002. As in the Sudanese case, Iranian human rights abuses continued apace. It was not until March 2011 that the UN's premier human rights body, which was by then the Human Rights Council, again decided to resume special reporting on human rights violations in Iran.

Following a protracted struggle with a group of NGO speakers, OIC states also demanded and obtained a de facto ban on mentioning Islamic institutions in the Human Rights Council. Despite the fact that these same governments have sought to promulgate a specifically faith-based declaration of human rights within the UN—in many cases citing Islam as a source in national laws and constitutions, and even organizing themselves into a self-proclaimed Islamic voting bloc—their sudden contradictory contention that Islam is not a proper topic for discussion within the council won over the council's leadership.

OIC-member states then used this implied ban as a means directly to silence their NGO critics within UN human rights fora.[19] Sudan charged in August 1997 that Christian Solidarity International (CSI)—an NGO that had spoken and worked against slavery in that country—had "offended Islam . . . by implying that [Islam] condoned an ideology of genocide, and by alleging that what CSI termed an 'Arab-Islamic State' could order the collective punishment of communities that resisted its programs by consigning them to slavery." Sudan also worked to get CSI's status as an official NGO with the UN revoked.

In March 2008, several NGOs questioned the Cairo Declaration's compatibility with the UDHR in a joint written statement to the council. The joint statement particularly noted references to sharia law and their implications for gender equality, religious freedom—specifically the right to change one's religion—and freedom of expression, and it criticized the "defamation of religions" resolution.[20] At the reference to sharia, both Egypt and Pakistan interrupted, the latter declaring that "[i]t is insulting for our faith to discuss sharia here in this forum." The council's president, Romanian Doru-Romulus Costea, accepted this point and asked the NGO to move on.[21] In June 2008, David Littman, speaking for several NGOs, attempted to read a statement on the situation of women in Muslim countries and was stopped by the Pakistani delegate, who voiced "strong objections on [sic] any discussion, any direct or indirect discussion, any out-of-context, selective discussion on the sharia law in this Council." Egypt rejoined, claiming that the council's discussion of sharia law was inadmissible.

Council president Costea affirmed that "this Council is not prepared to discuss religious matters in depth. Consequently we should not do it." His promise was put to the test when Littman, in the context of discussing female genital mutilation, stated, "We believe that only a fatwa from Al-Azhar Grand Sheikh Sayyad Tantawi . . . will change this barbaric, criminal practice." Egypt immediately responded, protesting, "This is an attempt to link bad traditional practices to Islam," and "Islam will not be crucified in this Council." The president once again ruled in Egypt's favor, seemingly placing out of bounds any discussion, not only of the contents of a fatwa or other religious edict, but also quite possibly of any legal system with a purported sharia basis.[22] Costea explained to reporters that, since discussions about religion would be "very complex, very sensitive, and very intense," only religious scholars should enter into such questions and that mention of religious causes for rights abuses would be "unhelpful, to say the least, for both the human rights in question and for a true, genuine dialogue among followers of various religions."

As an Amnesty International spokesman put it, "If Pakistan can come and say that that murder of women for some perverse sense of honor has nothing to do with universally recognized human rights, we're in trouble." Even outgoing UN High Commissioner for Human Rights, Louise Arbour, who had previously expressed some support for the OIC's campaign, said she feared that a council "which should be...the guardian of freedom of expression" was promulgating "constraints or taboos, or subjects that become taboo for discussion."[23]

While the Human Rights Council's president had cast his decision as an even-handed effort to avoid amateur theologizing, the selectivity of the OIC states' concern was clear. Despite their distress at the invocation of the name of Sheikh Tantawi, they had been remarkably unperturbed when Doudou Diène chastised evangelical leaders Jerry Falwell, Pat Robertson, and Franklin Graham for their "Islamophobic rhetoric." Meanwhile, Pakistan, for the OIC, had used the council itself to declare in September 2006 that "[t]he recent reference by Pope Benedict XVI to the Prophet Muhammad had hurt the sensibilities of Muslims."[24] Discussions of "hurtful" pronouncements by Islamic leaders, on the other hand, were to remain off-limits.[25]

The UN as Blasphemy Monitor: Resolutions 1999–2002

Beginning in 1999 in the UN Human Rights Commission, OIC members began a more coordinated campaign of blanket condemnation of any commentary they could construe as a "defamation" of Islam. Resolutions to this effect were then adopted regularly until 2011, when the OIC, sensing defeat, did not introduce the resolution in the council. (At this writing, it can not be foreseen whether the def-amation resolutions will be reintroduced in subsequent years and what their pros-pects for adoption would be.) Meanwhile, the West moved from unsuccessfully seeking compromise resolutions in 1999 and 2000 to opposing such resolutions altogether. The origin of these resolutions was a 1999 statement before the General Assembly made by Jordan's foreign minister, which protested purported efforts to "establish a linkage between Islam and those extremist and terrorist movements that hurt Islam and Muslims by using religion as a tool."[26] This opened the possibility that, since terrorists and rights violators themselves invoked Islam, criticism of them could be construed as an act of "defamation."

On the OIC's behalf, in 1999, Pakistan introduced an antidefamation resolu-tion for the first time, with Islam the only religion mentioned in the text.[27] Its delegate emphasized that "[t]here was a tendency . . . in the international media to portray Islam as a religion hostile to human rights, threatening to the Western world and associated with terrorism and violence, whereas, with the Quran, Islam had given the world its first human rights charter. . . . That defamation campaign was reflected in growing intolerance towards Muslims."[28] In 2000, the commission adopted a new compromise, "Combating defamation of religions," which focused on discrimination based on religion rather than issues of religious freedom per se.[29] India and the EU regretted the resolution's focus on a single religion and complained that its inclusion on the agenda distracted the commission from "promoting freedom of all religions and beliefs." Nonetheless, based on an informal "understanding" that the matter would not be raised again in the commission, they allowed its adoption without a vote.[30]

That understanding was proved false the following year, which motivated the West, for the first time, to actively oppose a "defamation" resolution. In introducing this resolution for the OIC, Pakistan asserted that Islamophobia was an emerging "form of contemporary racism," while the text itself singled out "defamation," rather than intolerance or discrimination, and asserted that "defamation of religions is among the causes of social disharmony and leads to violations of the human rights of their adherents." Though not binding, the resolution called for states "to provide adequate protection against all human rights violations resulting from defamation of religions."[31]

In a response that presciently diagnosed problems to come, the Belgian delegate explained that the EU had concerns about the text's emphasis on "the protection of *religions* rather than the human rights of *individuals*" and its tendency to "stress one religion above all others [emphasis added]." Belgium added that the sponsors had "invoked the General Assembly initiative on the elimination of crimes against women committed in the name of honor" as an instance of a recent increase of defamation of religions and that the "EU does not accept such a connection." The EU also protested that the draft resolution "seems to indicate that individual dissent from majority opinions and practices should not be tolerated in the interest of social harmony. The concept of defamation can easily be abused by extremists to censor all legitimate, critical debate within religions. . . . Freedom of expression and freedom of religion are fundamental components in promoting tolerance in societies."[32]

Nonetheless, the resolution passed on April 18, 2001, by a vote of twenty-eight to fifteen, with nine abstentions. The commission's Western members voted in opposition.[33] Thus, in the 2001 resolution, the principle of banning "defamation of religions" was established in the UN. In the aftermath of the attacks on the United States on September 11 of that year, the campaign on behalf of these resolutions acquired an additional focus. Already, by November 2001, Abdullah Al-Turki, Secretary-General of the Saudi-based Muslim World League, accused Western media of conducting a campaign of defamation against Islam and demanded that the UN prohibit defamation of religions, especially of Islam. The resolution the following year passed with virtually the same support as the 2001 resolution.[34]

Doudou Diène: UN Special Rapporteur on Contemporary Forms of Racism, Racial Discrimination, Xenophobia, and Related Intolerance

The 1999–2002 debates and resolutions show a consistent pattern. OIC-member states introduced draft resolutions citing concerns about what they termed defamation of religion, particularly of Islam. Other states, usually EU members, countered that the resolutions sought to give rights to religions as such, threatened freedoms of speech and of religion, and gave preeminence to one religion. In the first two years, the resolutions, though watered down by compromises, nonetheless passed by consensus, giving OIC states what they wanted. This also consumed valuable commission time and took attention away from the body's traditional concerns. Meanwhile, the commission's special reporting on Islamist states, such as Iran and Sudan, was dropped.

The OIC then expanded its strategy by involving the Special Rapporteur on Racism, Racial Discrimination, Xenophobia, and Related Intolerance. Seizing the new mandate that the OIC had advanced that allowed him to investigate alleged attacks on Islam, Special Rapporteur Doudou Diène, a jurist from Senegal, began issuing reports striking for their absence of evidence and their tendency to conflate all expressions of concern over Islamic extremism with "racist" assaults against Muslims. He published reports covering Islamophobia over the five years following his appointment until he left the post in 2008. Diène warned of "the equation of Islam with violence, terrorism and cultural and social backwardness by intellectual, political and media figures"; of "intellectual legitimization of overt hostility towards Islam and its followers by influential figures in the world of arts, literature and the media; of tolerance of such hostility in many countries"; and of a growing "logic of suspicion with regard to Islam."[35]

In general, he asserted that Islamophobia "has become the substitute ideology for a number of Cold War theoreticians."[36] He repeatedly inveighed against Harvard political scientist Samuel Huntington for his book *The Clash of Civilizations and the Remaking of the World Order*, a book that in fact shared Diène's concerns but which he mischaracterized, first as depicting "a confrontation between two culturally antagonistic blocks, the West and the Arab-Muslim world," and later as "an attempt to construct a theoretical and ideological justification for Islamophobia."[37] Despite his alleged disdain for Huntington's views, Diène himself put forward his own sweeping vision of a brewing "conflict between civilizations," featuring generalizations that far transcended any of the late Samuel

Huntington's more cautious formulations.[38] Notwithstanding his professed concern over negative stereotypes of Islam, Diène threw about stereotypes and one-sided accounts of European culture, citing the Crusades and the "re-conquest of [Al-Andalus]" in the fifteenth century.[39]

The Danish cartoon controversy allowed Diène to expand his thesis of an Islamophobia-driven clash of civilizations, with the defense of free expression being characterized as a weapon in the West's Islamophobic arsenal. He redefined "freedom of religion" to mean the right of a religion to freedom from criticism, astonishingly contending that the defense of free expression is itself an aggressive act.[40] He accused "governments, political leaders, intellectual personalities and the media" of having "radically set freedom of expression and freedom of religion against each other." Diène was apparently blithely unaware that that was exactly what *he* was doing. He did so when he cast religious freedom as a matter of protecting religions from hostile words rather than safeguarding the individual's freedom of conscience.[41]

Meanwhile, in those reports with a broader focus, Diène's treatment of "defamation" against other religions differed starkly from his statements on Islamophobia.[42] He depicted anti-Semitism and "Christianophobia" primarily in terms of reactions to Israel and the policies of Western states.[43] He was perfunctory in reporting on persecution of Christian minorities in Saudi Arabia and Pakistan.[44]

Asma Jahangir, Special Rapporteur on Freedom of Religion or Belief

One report, commissioned by the newly constituted Human Rights Council in the wake of the Danish cartoons affair, was exceptional. In 2006, the council sought a joint report from Doudou Diène and Asma Jahangir, who had been, since 2004, the UN Special Rapporteur on Freedom of Religion or Belief. Since Jahangir, a woman advocating human rights from Pakistan, had fought courageously for human rights, including religious freedom, the report they produced was, predictably, schizophrenic.

In the first section, Diène once again suggested that inflammatory Western rhetoric was the main obstacle to cultural harmony and that international legal limitations on criticizing Islam were the answer. In the second section, however, Jahangir offered a trenchant analysis of the deleterious effects of attempts to suppress criticism of religious views. Her section of the report provides one of the best contemporary analyses of the dangers involved in the concept of "defamation of religion." Accepting the legitimacy of bans on speech only in order to prevent direct incitement to violence or discrimination, she rejected the notion of a conflict between freedom of expression and freedom of religion or a new right to be protected from offense. She noted the oppressive potential inherent in blasphemy laws and emphasized the protection of individual rights.

Jahangir rejected the view that religions, as such, should be protected, since there are divisions both within and among religions. As a Pakistani Muslim human rights activist herself, and one who had suffered from religiously based attacks, she honed in on this essential point: "[I]ndividuals who belong to a majority religion are not always free from being pressured to adhere to a certain interpretation of that religion [and] should therefore not be viewed as parts of homogenous entities. For that reason, inter alia, international human rights law protects primarily individuals in the exercise of their freedom of religion and not religions per se."[45] In this context, she considered provisions from Article 18 of the International Covenant on Civil and Political Rights (ICCPR), which reads: "Everyone has the right to freedom of thought, conscience and religion; this right includes freedom to change his religion or belief, and freedom, either alone or in community with others and in public or private, to manifest his religion or belief in teaching, practice, worship and observance." Critically, Jahangir concluded that the right to freedom of religion "does not include the right to have a religion or belief that is free from criticism or ridicule" and that religious rules are not always generally applicable. She agreed that freedom of expression can be legitimately curtailed to suppress "advocacy that incites to acts of violence or discrimination against individuals on the basis of their religion," but she argued that defamation of religions per se "does not necessarily or at least directly result in a violation of their rights."[46]

While Article 20 of the ICCPR prohibits advocacy of national, racial, or religious hatred, Jahangir argued that this provision should only be applied to quash "incitement to imminent acts of violence or discrimination against a specific individual or group." And, while Article 4 of the Convention on the Elimination of All Forms of Racial Discrimination (CERD) prohibits "dissemination of ideas based on racial superiority or hatred" and "incitement to racial discrimination," Jahangir contended that "the elements that constitute a racist statement are not the same as those that constitute a statement defaming a religion," so similar legal measures would not necessarily be appropriate. She concluded with the warning that "[a]t the global level, any attempt to lower the threshold of Article 20 of the Covenant would not only shrink the frontiers of free expression, but also limit freedom of religion or belief itself." Most surprisingly, given Diène's involvement, the report concluded that "[t]he situation will not be remedied by preventing ideas about religions from being expressed."[47]

The UN, Post-2003

Neither Diène nor the OIC, however, was prepared to accept this conclusion. From 2003 onward, now often citing Diène's reports, OIC countries made more pointed attacks on freedom of expression in the Commission on Human Rights. Then, in 2004, the UN General Assembly (GA) took up the question of Islamophobia and, in the following year, for the first time in the GA, Yemen for the OIC introduced a text almost identical to those in the commission.[48] Despite opposition from the United States, the EU, and India, the resolution was adopted 101–53–20 (i.e., twenty abstentions).[49]

The 2005 resolution began to link "defamation of religions" to antiterror efforts, maintaining that, "in the context of the fight against terrorism and the reaction to counter-terrorism measures," defamation of religions is "an aggravating factor that contributes to the denial of fundamental rights and freedoms of target groups."[50] After the Danish cartoons controversy amplified the OIC's and others' allegations of defaming Islam, the campaign gained momentum. In December 2005, the UN High Commissioner for Human Rights, Louise Arbour, wrote to the UN deploring "any statement or act showing a lack of respect towards other people's religions."[51] The grand sheikh of Egypt's Al-Azhar University, and the OIC, at its 2005 "Extraordinary Summit" in Mecca, both decided "to have the United Nations counter Islamophobia."[52] In 2006, they were joined in this effort by Arab League leaders, and the Muslim Brotherhood's Yusuf al-Qaradawi urged "a binding resolution banning contempt of religious beliefs."[53]

By 2006, the United States began offering a more comprehensive critique, saying that the resolution "did not take into consideration basic rights which were held dear by many, including the freedom to express negative opinions about a specific religion or all religions in general." The EU rejected the validity of "defamation of religions," emphasizing the need to protect individuals rather than religions themselves: "Members of religions or communities of belief should not be viewed as mere particles of homogeneous and monolithic entities."[54] Meanwhile, the EU worked for a compromise text aimed at "incitement to religious hatred" rather than defamation.[55]

The Human Rights Council that replaced the discredited Commission on Human Rights in 2006 continued its predecessor's practices. Western opposition drew off support for the resolution year by year so that, by 2010, one passed with only a three-vote margin; and, in 2011, with memories still fresh of the assassinations of Pakistan minister Shahbaz Bhatti and governor Salman Taseer, the OIC, fearing defeat, did not introduce a defamation of religions resolution. It had been Pakistan, representing the OIC, that had introduced the antidefamation resolution adopted by the Human Rights Council at its very first session in June 2006.

In 2006, the council resolution had expressed "deep concern over the increasing trend of defamation of religions, incitement to religious hatred and its recent manifestations" and mandated the High Commissioner for Human Rights to investigate these issues, in addition to commissioning a report.[56]

By 2007, the council was back to adopting a resolution expressly entitled "Combating Defamation of Religions," cosponsored by Pakistan for the OIC and by Venezuela.[57] As usual, it mentioned specifically only the situation of Islam and

Muslims and once again took note of the 2005 Mecca summit.[58] The resolution drew strong protests from Western NGOs, including the Jubilee Campaign, the Becket Fund, Amnesty International, Human Rights Watch, and Freedom House.[59] That year, UN Secretary-General Ban Ki-Moon himself appeared to endorse criminalizing "defamation of religions" by declaring in one UN report, "A trend is emerging towards amending criminal codes to reflect the existence of the different phenomena constituting defamation of religions. The persistence of these phenomena, however, proves that further efforts need to be made."[60] Meanwhile, OIC delegates were increasingly vocal in deploring the menace of unrestricted free speech. During a 2007 Council on Human Rights discussion, the Egyptian representative, Ihab Gamaleldin, asserted that "the offensive publication of portraits of Prophet Muhammad...has highlighted the damage that freedom of speech if left unchecked may lead to. Not only by hurting the religious feelings of more than a billion people, but also to their freedom of religion and their right of respect for their religion."[61] Delegate Marghoob Saleem Butt of Pakistan remarked, "Unrestricted and disrespectful freedom of opinion creates hatred and is contrary to the spirit of peaceful dialogue and promotion of multiculturalism."[62]

The OIC members abstained from a council resolution on religious freedom, particularly distressed that it guaranteed the right to convert and that it made no mention of protecting religions from "defamation." The Saudi delegation said it could not "accept texts which go against the Islamic sharia."[63] The OIC, however, has not succeeded in gaining EU or U.S. approval of the "defamation of religions" concept. Without such Western support, passing a binding UN resolution remains elusive. However, OIC states have managed to obtain GA resolutions against "defamation of religions" in every session since the 2005 Mecca summit, and even nonbinding UN resolutions have the potential to be cited by international and national courts and over time enter into international law as "customary" laws.[64] The OIC's decision not to introduce a resolution against defamation of religions in the council's sixteenth session in 2011 was seen by the UN's Western bloc as an essential battle won in the struggle to preserve the principle of fundamental freedoms of the individual.

2008 and Beyond

Though defamation of religions resolutions would continue to be adopted in the UN's foremost human rights body until 2011, albeit with decreasing support, by 2008, the center of gravity in the UN had shifted to favor a religious hate-speech focus. Europe saw resolutions against hate speech as putting the emphasis properly on individuals rather than on religions. The OIC, however, viewed them as a convenient pretext to declare allegedly Islamic institutions off-limits for criticism and thus as a proxy for resolutions against religious defamation.

A new paragraph in the Human Rights Council's 2008 resolution contained the Orwellian assertion that protecting religions from "contempt" was "an essential element conducive for the exercise by all of the right to freedom of thought, conscience and religion." The 2008 text also relied on the conflation of racial and religious issues. It argued that a ruling by the Committee on the Elimination of Racial Discrimination permitting bans against "the dissemination of all ideas based upon racial superiority or hatred" should be equally applicable to speech inciting religious hatred. It gave a new mandate to the High Commissioner for Human Rights to seek out best practices among blasphemy laws, which resulted in a finding that, in fact, there is no common practice.[65] This was the first such resolution to pass by a plurality rather than a majority.[66]

In March 2008, the council further circumscribed protection for freedom of expression by adopting, with overwhelming support, an amendment introduced by Egypt (for the Group of African States), Pakistan (for the Organization of the Islamic Conference), and Palestine (for the Group of Arab States).[67] This amendment changed the mandate of the Special Rapporteur on Freedom of Opinion and Expression to report on the "abuse" of the right of freedom of expression by an act of racial or religious discrimination.[68] The U.S. ambassador stated that the revision "attempts to legitimize the criminalization of expression" and aims to place "restrictions on individuals rather than to emphasize the duty and responsibility of governments to guarantee, uphold, promote and protect human rights."[69] The Canadian delegate likewise argued that the resolution "turns the Special Rapporteur's mandate on its head."[70] A few months later, Secretary of State Condoleezza Rice stated that the United States was "concerned by efforts to promote a so-called defamation of religions concept...this concept seeks to limit freedom of speech, and that could undermine the standards of international religious freedom." Following Rice, the U.S. ambassador on international religious freedom, John Hanford, rejected the OIC approach to protecting religions for creating a "chilling effect upon the freedom of people to discuss their beliefs openly, to be critical openly." Hanford also warned of "cases in certain countries where people have been sentenced for apostasy or blasphemy that drew upon this precedent from a resolution that passed at the UN."[71] The resolution also alarmed the World Association of Newspapers and World Editors Forum, which warned that the council's "proper role is to defend freedom of expression and not to support the censorship of opinion at the request of autocracies."[72]

In 2008, following further controversies over alleged insults to Islam, the office of the UN High Commissioner for Human Rights held an "Expert Seminar" on the links between articles 19 and 20 of the ICCPR.[73] The result was an agreement that there were certain acceptable limitations on speech, but there was also disagreement on how extensive these limitations should be. Participants agreed that prohibitions were acceptable in genuine cases of "incitement to discrimination, hostility, or violence," as provided for in Article 20 of the ICCPR. (This article had been formulated in the 1960s by the Soviet bloc and had been adopted without any Western support.) The president of the council suggested that common ground could be reached by shifting from "defamation of religions" to "incitement to religious hatred."[74] Even within the West, which opposed the "defamation of religions" concept, there was growing support for shifting the debate over banning religious insults to the framework of hate speech or "incitement."[75] Doudou Diène's final report thus pronounced that "political and ideological polarization on the question of the defamation of religions is artificial. Indeed, analysis of international, regional, and national human rights instruments shows that provisions against inducement to national, racial or religious hatred are almost universal."[76] The OIC's head sought to make "it clear that the OIC was not looking for limitation or restrictions of freedom of expression beyond those set by Articles 19 and 20 of the ICCPR." To further emphasize that the "defamation resolutions" were not of an exceptional nature, the report stressed that "the EU has imposed stringent restrictions on hate speeches."[77]

However, on December 10, 2008, four freedom of expression monitors—from the UN, Organization for Security and Co-operation in Europe (OSCE), Organization of American States (OAS), and African Commission on Human and Peoples' Rights (ACHPR)—adopted an extraordinary joint declaration that emphasized the importance of "open debate about all ideas and social phenomenon in society and the right of all to be able to manifest their culture, religion and beliefs in practice" and lauded the abolition in many countries of laws "used to prevent legitimate criticism of powerful religious leaders and to suppress the views of religious minorities, dissenting believers and non-believers...." They argued that, although prohibitions on "incitement to hatred, discrimination or violence" were acceptable, "open dialogue that exposes the harm prejudice causes" should be the primary means of combating bigotry. Their declaration pointed out that the "defamation of religions" framework was unacceptable because it "does not accord with international standards regarding defamation, which refer to the protection of reputation of individuals."[78]

Nevertheless, in December 2008, the GA passed another resolution against "combating defamation of religions," albeit with reduced support. In fact, 2008 marked the first year, in both the GA and the council, in which "no" votes and abstentions together outweighed the votes in favor.[79] In the debate, speaking for the EU, France endorsed the approach of banning hate speech rather than defamation of religions, since "religious pluralism demanded the right of every individual to criticize, discuss and contest the values and convictions of others," and the "defamation of religions" concept "was not compatible with a discussion on human rights" due to its focus on religions rather than on individuals. The U.S. representative took a stronger stand for free speech, stating that while he agreed with certain concerns voiced in the resolution, "freedom of expression meant freedom also to challenge the ideologies of hate through more speech, more information and more dialogue, not less." He demanded an accounting from "those who misused United Nations resolutions to harass, torture or jail individuals for nothing

more than the expression of their opinions or beliefs." He also criticized the conflation of religion with race, which, by implying that "like an individual's race, one's
religion was a characteristic that could not be changed," contradicted the protections for freedom of religion in the UDHR: "Governments must respect the right
of individuals to choose any particular religion or none at all, as well as to change
religions and to manifest their religion in teaching, practice or observance."

Even the observer of the Vatican, which had supported the OIC position during
the Danish cartoons imbroglio, argued that while "in multicultural societies,
appropriate measures must be taken to guarantee respect for different faiths," the
"defamation of religions" approach "risked moving the focus from the basic right
of individuals and groups to the protection of institutions, symbols and ideas.
Furthermore, it could lend itself locally to support for laws that penalized religious minorities and stifled legitimate dialogue among persons of different faiths
and cultures." In his view, the best means for preventing hate speech and "acts
against (believers') convictions" remained "insuring the right of individuals and
communities to religious freedom," as established in the UDHR and other international rights declarations.[80]

Unfazed by these critiques, Pakistan and the OIC made certain that "defamation of religions" was again adopted as a resolution of the Human Rights Council
in 2009 and 2010, though losing votes each year.[81] The OIC delegate widened his
concern from allegedly Islamophobic politicians to "blasphemous" Islam-related
art collections, several of which, including those by artists of Muslim background,
had been exhibited in Europe and had provoked violent threats.[82] In 2011, however, taking note of rapidly dwindling support for the resolution, Pakistan and the
OIC lacked the confidence to introduce it at the sixteenth session of the council,
whose session took place around the time that two prominent Pakistani political
figures were assassinated for opposing Pakistan's national blasphemy laws. This
was a small but essential victory in the defense of individual rights to freedom of
expression and of religion.

International Treaties:
The Exception Becomes the Rule

International human rights treaties, which have been the foundation for global
human rights for nearly half a century, are turning out to be weak bulwarks against
a concerted OIC push for restrictions on negative commentary on Islam.
Proclaimed for their universality, these treaties have served as the legal basis for
individual freedoms since they originated but are now being twisted into a justification for suppression of such freedoms as the consensus behind them changes.
The UN's International Covenant on Civil and Political Rights (ICCPR, effective
1976) is the main treaty protecting an individual's rights to freedoms of religion
and of expression. It also sets forth vaguely worded exceptions to free expression

that are now being interpreted expansively, even by much of the West, to erode the ICCPR's core freedoms of both religion and expression.

The ICCPR's Article 18 establishes one's "freedom to have or to adopt a religion or belief of his choice, and freedom, either individually or in community with others and in public or private, to manifest his religion or belief in worship, observance, practice and teaching." This right was intended to protect individuals in the exercise of a religion of their choosing, not to protect religions or individuals from religious insult or criticism. However, new interpretations threaten to limit a person's right to dissent from specific religious teachings and practices. As discussed in chapter 12, European states, as well as OIC-member states, now argue that religious freedom includes the right of religious groups and individuals not to have their feelings injured and that this new right can conflict with, and take precedent over, the right to free expression.

The ICCPR's Article 19 protects the right to freedom of expression, which includes "freedom to seek, receive and impart information and ideas of all kinds, regardless of frontiers, either orally, in writing or in print, in the form of art, or through any other media of his choice." It also sets forth certain "necessary" restrictions—to protect "the rights or reputations of others," "national security" or public order, and health or morals (Paragraph 3). British courts have begun to prosecute religious hate-speech cases under "public order" laws. Article 20 (included by the then-Soviet bloc states over strong Western opposition) explicitly obliges states to prohibit "[a]ny advocacy of national, racial or religious hatred that constitutes incitement to discrimination, hostility or violence."[83] This provision is the one used in the West to apply religious hate-speech laws and limit the rights found in articles 18 and 19. Article 4 of the CERD (effective 1969) makes a more sweeping demand that states institute legal penalties for "all dissemination of ideas based on racial superiority or hatred," in addition to various forms of racial or ethnic incitement.[84] The OIC and some Western courts have declared anti-Islamic expression a form of racism.

The United States and some other states believe these restrictions are threatening free speech, prompting them, in ratifying the two instruments, to make reservations or interpretative declarations on behalf of free speech.[85] Nevertheless, several of these same countries are yielding under OIC pressure to silence criticism of Islam.

The United States Joins Consensus on a UN Hate-Speech Resolution

In May 2009, the United States campaigned for, and was elected to, a seat on the UN's Human Rights Council.[86] Whereas the Bush administration had declined to participate in the council because, like its predecessor, the Commission on Human

Rights, its lack of membership criteria opened membership to some of the world's worst human rights violators, allowing them to distort its work, the Obama administration argued that reform could be better achieved from within the body. The United States was soon put to the test on the issue of religious hate speech.

In its first council session, on October 2, 2009, in what American diplomats said was an effort to "reach out to Muslim countries," the United States, with Egypt, introduced a hate-speech resolution under the freedom of expression agenda item. Adopted by consensus, the resolution expresses concern about "negative racial and religious stereotyping" and, while not binding, "urges States to take effective measures to combat . . . any advocacy of national, racial or religious hatred that constitutes incitement to discrimination, hostility or violence." The incitement standard articulated here by America is very different from the narrow one allowed under the U.S. Constitution.[87] It was said to be an attempt to steer the OIC away from efforts to make religious speech bans binding by means of bans on "defamation of religions," or through amendments to the racial discrimination treaty, but no mention was made in the resolution of the European distinction between protecting individuals and protecting religions per se. Moreover, it appeared to suggest that the U.S. administration saw a need to roll back First Amendment freedoms.

In the speeches surrounding the joint resolution's adoption, Pakistan seized on the term "negative stereotyping" and equated it with "defamation of religion": "The OIC strongly believes that negative stereotyping or defamation of religions is a contemporary manifestation of religious hatred, discrimination, and xenophobia. . . . We further hope that today's consensus outcome will lead to better understanding of our concerns regarding defamation of religion, as well as to adopt the corresponding resolution by consensus in the future." Though the U.S. Supreme Court has decided that the U.S. Constitution allows only the criminalization of speech that incites to violence and lawless action that is imminent and likely, through this resolution, the United States gave encouragement to the worldwide criminalization of hate speech far more broadly, including when that speech incited to violence that was not "imminent" or "likely and to "hostility," a term that lacks a recognized legal definition.[88] The resolution proved controversial among human rights advocates, so much so that Secretary of State Hillary Clinton felt compelled to use the release of the State Department's annual religious freedom report later that month to reassert America's commitment to free speech. Her statement seemed to be a strong defense of free speech and outlined steps that could serve as a useful blueprint:

> Now, some claim that the best way to protect the freedom of religion is to implement so-called anti-defamation policies that would restrict freedom of expression and the freedom of religion. I strongly disagree. The United States will always seek to counter negative stereotypes of individuals based on their religion and will stand against discrimination and persecution. But an individual's ability to practice his or her religion has no bearing on others' freedom of speech. The protection of speech about

religion is particularly important since persons of different faiths will inevitably hold divergent views on religious questions. These differences should be met with tolerance, not with the suppression of discourse. Based on our own experience, we are convinced that the best antidote to intolerance is not the defamation of religion's [sic] approach of banning and punishing offensive speech, but rather, a combination of robust legal protections against discrimination and hate crimes, proactive government outreach to minority religious groups, and the vigorous defense of both freedom of religion and expression.[89]

However, her reference to "hate crimes," which omitted any explanation that in the United States these are traditional crimes with enhanced penalties and not stand-alone religious hate-*speech* crimes, was unfortunate. It lent itself to likely misinterpretation and confusion, particularly on the part of international audiences. The confusion was deepened by the remarks of the U.S. Assistant Secretary for Democracy, Labor and Human Rights, Michael Posner, who immediately followed her to the podium. His statement was ambiguous and could be understood as further asserting a new U.S. hate-speech policy based on the European dichotomy of embracing religious hate-speech bans to protect people's religious feelings, while rejecting blasphemy bans that protect religious doctrines.[90]

The U.S. State Department Legal Adviser, Harold Koh—who had written approvingly of "transnational jurisprudence," that is, integrating the United States into the international legal system and having American courts use international rules and decisions in their own decision-making—explicitly praised the U.S.-Egypt hate-speech resolution as among the administration's "important successes."[91]

"Durban II"

The conceptual shift from defamation to incitement was also manifested in the April 2009 Durban Review Conference against racism, popularly known as "Durban II." From the preparatory stages, OIC-member states had worked diligently to make "Islamophobia" and "defamation of religions" major topics, with Iran serving as a vice-chairperson and an informal "Friend of the Chair" of the Preparatory Committee.[92] A submission by the Asian group of states asked that governments "prohibit the transmission of racist and xenophobic messages" on the Internet and elsewhere. It called for a media code of conduct and instructed states "to take firm action against negative stereotyping of religions and defamation of religious personalities, holy books, scriptures and symbols." It also suggested that the review conference take note of Special Rapporteur Diène's recommendations on "defamation of religions" when issuing guidelines for states.[93] The OIC produced similar recommendations, and these themes were prominent in subsequent meetings and documents.[94] There was also at least one Durban-related attempt to make the "defamation" prohibition binding through the further conflation of racial and religious matters. In December 2008, an Algerian-led preparatory subcommittee proposed a revision of the CERD to include a "defamation of religions" ban. This, however, failed to pass.[95]

The United States, which had walked out of the first Durban conference along with Israel, sent a delegation to preliminary talks in February 2009 in hopes of arriving at a more acceptable program. However, by February 27, the United States announced that it would not participate in the conference unless there were major changes to the text, including dropping "the troubling concept of 'defamation of religion.'" The United States, Canada, Israel, and other Western countries withdrew, several withdrawing after an incendiary anti-Israel, anti-Semitic, and anti-Western diatribe on April 20 by Iran's President Ahmadinejad.[96]

Ultimately, the final Durban II document made no specific reference to "defamation of religions" but called for restrictions on speech more along the lines of existing national and international bans on incitement to religious hatred. It "deplore[d] the global rise and number of incidents of racial or religious intolerance and violence, including Islamophobia, anti-Semitism, Christianophobia and anti-Arabism, manifested particularly by the derogatory stereotyping and stigmatization of persons based on their religion or belief" (the mention of "persons" seems a clear concession to the EU's insistence that any restrictions on speech protect people rather than beliefs). It called for the legal prohibition of "any advocacy of national, racial or religious hatred that constitutes incitement to discrimination, hostility or violence."[97]

As a side event at the Durban conference, the Special Rapporteurs on Freedom of Religion (Asma Jahangir), Freedom of Expression (Frank LaRue), and Racism (Githu Muigai, who had replaced Diène) issued a joint statement that reiterated many of the most important criticisms of the "defamation of religions concept." Notably, the rapporteurs rejected the false opposition between freedom of expression and freedom of religion to assert that freedom of expression was instead "an essential aspect of the right to freedom of religion or belief" and thus merited legal protection. They continued: "While the exercise of freedom of expression could, in some extreme cases, affect the right to manifest the religion or belief of certain identified individuals, it is conceptually inaccurate to present 'defamation of religions' in abstracto as a conflict between the right to freedom of religion or belief and the right to freedom of opinion or expression." In addition, the rapporteurs pointed out that any analogy between racism and "defamation of religions" was flawed, since, while racial superiority claims were both reprehensible and wrong, "several religions are characterized by truth claims—or even by superiority claims—which have been traditionally accepted as part of their theological grounds."

Given these issues, the three experts lauded "the fact that the debate seems to be shifting to the concept of 'incitement to racial or religious hatred,' sometimes also referred to as 'hate speech,'" and issued a call to "anchor the debate on these issues in the relevant existing international legal framework, provided for by the ICCPR." Within this framework, the threshold of Article 20, which prohibits the advocacy of national, racial, or religious hatred that constitutes incitement to discrimination, hostility, or violence, "remained to be determined."[98] The experts concluded, "The strategic response to hate speech is more speech: more speech that educates about cultural differences; more speech that promotes diversity; more speech to empower and give voice to minorities, for example through the support of community media and their representation in mainstream media. More speech can be the best strategy to reach out to individuals' hearts and minds, changing what they think and not merely what they do."[99]

Nevertheless, the OIC, with support from the African states, continued, in the March 2010 Human Rights Council, to aim for a binding agreement to ban anti-Islamic speech through amending the CERD and through the resolution on the "defamation against religions," as well as through religious hate-speech restrictions already provided for in the ICCPR.[100] As previously noted, it dropped its push for a council resolution against "defamation of religions" in the sixteenth session of the council in 2011; it remains to be seen whether it will attempt to advance the resolution at a subsequent meeting.

Closing

Prohibitions on "defamation of religions" reflect the view that, in the realm of belief, government should serve as the arbiter and regulator of ideological orthodoxy rather than as the defender of individual freedom; this is the same principle operative behind many OIC states' own domestic laws against blasphemy and apostasy. The UN's "defamation of religions" resolutions seek to legitimize this idea by suggesting that speech criticizing religious beliefs is a human rights violation rather than the exercise of a protected human right. In reality, banning "defamation of religion"—effectively meaning Islam—contradicts existing precepts of human rights law.

Such a ban would serve to punish individuals who voice controversial opinions rather than those who employ violence to silence them. It would empower "the dubious claim that speech has violated religious freedom, not because it has incited violence *towards* a targeted group, but because violence has resulted *from* the targeted group."[101] These resolutions would also change the meaning of "defamation"—which, historically, has meant injuring a person's reputation through false statements—to any putatively negative portrayal of a religion or something or someone claiming to represent that religion.[102]

Resolutions banning "defamation of religions" stand little chance of being directly incorporated into international law, particularly so since the OIC dropped its campaign for them in the council in 2011. The effort to advance the concept, however, is far from dead. Blasphemy prohibitions are now being universalized at the UN through a back door. Traditionally narrow limits on free expression are being interpreted expansively to accommodate prohibitions against "religious hate speech," which, in turn, is explicitly interpreted by the OIC as a ban on "defamation of religions." This new twist on the meaning of fundamental rights would erode not only freedom of expression, but also that other "first freedom" with which it is inextricably linked: freedom of religion. Government efforts to side with religious authorities to coerce religious dissenters and minorities have long been understood not as a component but as a negation of the right to religious freedom. Religious freedom is guaranteed precisely to ensure that individuals can have religious disagreements without fear of temporal punishment. Outlawing speech that rejects or criticizes religion undercuts religious freedom itself.

The rapporteurs' May 2009 statement noted that, while cases of incitement to violence or genocide could often be relatively easy to identify—they offered the horrific example of the Hutu radio station that called for its listeners to kill Tutsis during the Rwandan genocide—they acknowledged that "incitement to *hostility*" (which is explicitly included as religious hate speech in a UN treaty) carries an inherent "risk of subjectivity."[103] The lines between legally protected criticism of ideas and unprotected incitement against a group are frequently muddled.[104] Furthermore, conflicting theologies render it impossible for governments to protect equally all religions or religious people from being offended by blasphemy. Prohibitions on blasphemy would tend to benefit the majority or the powerful.

Moreover, as our country chapters show, where religion and power are intertwined, states invariably draw on laws restricting speech critical of religion for other than purely religious purposes. Many OIC members silence their domestic opponents and critics through a wide variety of repressive measures, but one prominent tactic is to accuse such critics of "insulting Islam" or insulting the "Islamic regime." These accusations enable both the crushing of political dissent and the silencing of Muslims who question the official and dominant versions of Islam, including those who advocate versions of Islam that promote human freedom.

Operating within the UN is a concerted, twenty-year campaign to suppress human rights critique of authoritarian regimes that claim to represent and embody Islam and, under their logic, are thereby shielded from any critique under rules forbidding insult to Islam. International laws against apostasy and blasphemy, whether called defamation or hate speech, would legitimate this campaign, thus placing up to one-quarter of UN-member states beyond criticism. Furthermore, such laws could be interpreted not only as an endorsement of authoritarian regimes but also as a requirement of all UN-member states to repress anyone, anywhere in the world, whom those regimes accuse of blasphemy against Islam. International rights to freedoms of expression and religion for the individual would be undermined.

Religiously Incorrect

Islam, Blasphemy, and Hate Speech in Western Domestic Law

In 2007, popular Canadian writer Mark Steyn and Maclean's, English Canada's leading newsmagazine, were brought before three of Canada's human rights commissions by the same complainant, over the same article, one that excerpted from Steyn's best-selling book America Alone. They were accused of publishing material "likely to expose a person or persons to hatred or contempt."

In November 2007, the Canadian Islamic Congress (CIC) filed the three human rights complaints against Maclean's and Steyn for Steyn's piece "The Future Belongs to Islam."[1] According to the CIC, the article was harmful to Muslims' "sense of dignity and self-worth."[2] A CIC report on Maclean's, which contended the magazine was habitually "Islamophobic," also denounced Maclean's for "attacking multiculturalism and religious freedoms" and "attacking laws that provide protection to identifiable communities from the type of discriminatory journalism that Maclean's is engaging in." Steyn also came under attack for "the misrepresentation of legal action taken by Muslims against the authors of discriminatory publications as ganging up by Muslims in order to persecute writers and launch lawsuits on frivolous grounds"—in other words, he was attacked for criticizing the very statutes under which he and others might be penalized and for criticizing those who sought to penalize him.

The CIC filed complaints with the federal commission and with two provincial human rights tribunals—in Ontario and British Columbia. In the name of CIC leader Mohamed Elmasry, the complaints linked Steyn's purported offenses against Muslims to his denunciations of Canada's culture of political correctness. Elmasry alleged, among other things, that Steyn's article asserted that a "substantial number" of Western Muslims desire the imposition of "an oppressive branch of Shariah law" and would be willing to engage in terrorism; that Muslim immigrants to Europe bring with them radical ideas from places such as Nigeria and South Asia; that "a policy of multiculturalism is incapable of making Muslims in the West loyal to their countries of citizenship;" that "social democratic states are susceptible to being taken over by Muslims as a result of their social democratic policies;" and that, "in a few years, European (sic) will be 'semi-Islamified,' meaning that parts of it will be living under Shariah law or will have been taken over by Muslims."

None of the complaints succeeded. One of the judges, however, while saying that the tribunal did not have jurisdiction in the case, gratu- itously pronounced the defendants "Islamophobic" anyhow, but adding, "fear is not synonymous with hatred and contempt."³ The complaints against Steyn were also financially costly. Under Canadian law, com- plainants' legal fees are provided by the state while defendants' are not, even if the complaint fails.

A case in Finland raises the specter of anti-Islamic blasphemy charges being used by a Western government for political purposes against its opposition, without the involvement of any Muslim com- plainants or even commentators. In September 2009, a popular Helsinki City Council member was convicted of the offense of "defaming religions" for negative statements on his blog about Islam's prophet. The offender, twenty-eight-year-old Jussi Halla- aho, wrote a blog on anti-immigration and pro-free speech themes in which the state prosecutor, Mika Illman—a prominent supporter of hate-speech laws—was frequently criticized. Soon after Halla- aho's election to the city council, the government launched an inves- tigation into one of his blog postings from two years earlier, in which he had expressed views about the deportation of immigrants convicted of rape.

Finding no evidence of a hate-speech crime, the police dropped the case. The government then ordered the police to review every- thing Halla-aho had written.⁴ After trawling through his extensive blog site, the government charged the councilman for an entry concerning the free speech debate about what can be said about Islam. Halla-aho argued that it should not be illegal to call the prophet Muhammad a pedophile or Islam a religion that sanctifies pedophilia, since both claims could be shown to be true. This particular posting had appeared under the heading "Bait" for Mika Illman on the blogsite.

The court declared Halla-aho's reasoning inadmissible because "[l]ogic and so-called arguments of reason have no true significance in debating religious questions." Halla-aho was found guilty of defaming Islam and fined after the court ruled that he had not intended to engage in a sincere discussion of Islamic beliefs and that his statements would foster religious intolerance.⁵ Members of the Green Party, which had previously advocated for the repeal of Finland's blasphemy law, applauded the conviction.

In December 2004, pastor Daniel Scot and pastor Daniel Nalliah of the Australian Pentecostal group Catch the Fire Ministries (CTFM), ran afoul of Victoria state's Racial and Religious Tolerance Act of 2001, which outlaws "conduct that incites hatred against, serious contempt for, or revulsion or severe ridicule of, that other person or class of per- sons" based on religious belief or activity.⁶ The pastors were charged with criticizing Islam in connection with a public seminar on ministry to Muslims at which Scot spoke and for material on the Web and in a CTFM newsletter. Three converts to Islam had infiltrated the seminar for the Islamic Council of Victoria and had taken offense at what they heard. The council filed charges, accusing CTFM of inciting hatred against Muslims.[7]

The pastor's alleged offenses ranged from direct criticism of Qur'anic teachings to warnings about Muslim immigrants. Among them were criticisms "that the Qur'an promotes violence, killing and looting"; that it promotes abuse of women and domestic violence; "that Allah is not merciful and a thief's hand is cut off for stealing"; that terrorists are true Muslims based on the Qur'an; that Muslims are religiously obligated to fight Christians and Jews; and "that Muslims have a plan to overrun western democracy by the use of violence and terror, and to replace those democracies with oppressive regimes."

Judge Michael Higgins of the Victorian Civil and Administrative Tribunal held Scot liable because his remarks were "essentially hostile, demeaning and derogatory of all Muslim people, their God, Allah, the prophet Mohammed and, in general, Muslim religious beliefs and practices." The court reasoned that Scot's lecture gave an "unbalanced" view of Islamic theology; in fact, the judge, who showed no sign of expertise in the subject, ventured deep into theological territory.[8] Scot was found at fault for interpreting the Qur'an in accordance with "Wahhabists," which the judge opined "bear no relationship to mainstream Muslim beliefs and, in particular, Australian Muslims." He also stated that Scot's "credibility" was in doubt, in part because, during his defense, he had cited two Qur'anic verses that produced an unfavorable impression of Islam without citing a third that the Judge strangely described as "a pro-Islamic verse."[9]

Nalliah was found to have incited hatred of Muslims through a mix of political and theological assertions. In a newsletter article entitled "2002—Will Australia Be a Christian Country?" he had questioned why, in his view, Muslim immigrants receive visas to Australia more readily than Christian refugees. He also said that Christians are frequently killed in Muslim-majority countries, suggesting that Australian Christians could be killed and that other dangers could ensue from alleged Islamic infiltration of the West. In addition, Nalliah had posted on CTFM's Web site a third party's article that called Islam inherently violent, claimed that the Qur'an teaches hate, and "suggests that the prophet is a pedophile." This article was judged to have made "no attempt . . . to distinguish between moderate and extremist Muslims."[10]

The pastors were found in violation of the law and ordered by the tribunal to publish, under their names, a prepared statement that would have barred them for life from repeating their statements about Islam—and, in effect, from teaching what they believed as Christians. The pastors appealed and also lodged a complaint against Judge Higgins on the grounds that during the case he had himself "ridiculed" Scot's own religious beliefs. The Supreme Court of Victoria ordered a retrial on the basis that the lower court had paid insufficient attention to "the distinction between hatred of the religious beliefs of Muslims and hatred of Muslims because of their religious beliefs."

In June 2007, the Islamic Council dropped its suit.[11] Despite this favorable outcome, Pastor Scot noted that his defense had cost him "hundreds of thousands of dollars in legal fees." Not only had the ordeal lasted nearly three years, but it damaged his reputation, costing him speaking engagements. Anti-vilification laws, he argued, amounted to "blasphemy laws in disguise."[12]

Introductory Remarks

Despite clear Western opposition to the efforts of the Organization of the Islamic Conference (OIC) to legislate an international prohibition on "defamation of religions," the Western world equivocates between upholding the right to freedom of expression and calling for its curtailment in the name of religious sensitivity. Many Western countries, though not the United States, have laws prohibiting speech that insults religious groups or "incites to hatred and discrimination" and, to a lesser extent, laws on public order that are used to curb controversial statements on religion and bans on blasphemy.

Bans on hate speech had their origin in concerns about Nazism and have been justified as a necessary protection for minorities. More recently, the bans have come to prominence because of fear of religiously motivated violence against, and from, Muslim minorities. Demands to respect Islam are being answered, in part, by support for laws against hate speech. While in recent decades, Western blasphemy laws have been dying out, religious hate-speech laws, which focus on perceived injury to religious feelings, are serving as proxies for them.

There is no clear definition of "religious hate speech" in either national or international law, leaving individual countries and courts to develop their own interpretations and regulations. To some extent, these interpretations depend on whether the laws are based on international treaties prohibiting speech targeting people on the basis of religion, race, and other groupings, or whether they ban speech that specifically offends religious beliefs. Over the last century, bans on religious hate speech have increased while enforcement of blasphemy laws has declined. In both politics and law, the distinction between blasphemy bans and hate-speech laws has become increasingly blurred. The result is a direct denial of individual freedoms, an indirect chilling of speech, legal confusion, rising sectarian expectations of further restrictions, the exacerbation of tensions among religious groups, and secular courts being put in the untenable position of pronouncing judgment on the doctrines of a multitude of religions.[13]

Sacred Crimes and Human Feelings: The Evolution of Blasphemy in the West

Europe's history of blasphemy laws is a reminder that bans on religious criticism, dissent, and insult have not been the exclusive preserve of Islam. In Europe, blasphemy against Christianity has incurred penalties ranging from short prison terms, to physical mutilation for repeat offenders, to capital punishment. Through British colonial influence, blasphemy prohibitions spread to Australia and North America. In 1660, a Quaker woman was hanged on the Boston Commons for blasphemy, one of the last examples of execution for such crimes in what is now the United States.

By the close of the nineteenth century, most such Western laws were reformed to show leniency, fell into disuse, or were abolished. In the United States, there has never been a federal blasphemy law, and the six remaining state-level blasphemy laws are generally considered unconstitutional and are not enforced.[14] France abolished its blasphemy law in 1791.[15] England and Wales abolished theirs in 2008. A notable exception is Ireland, which, in early 2010, pleading constitutional necessity, introduced a blasphemy law that punishes speech "grossly abusive or insulting in relation to matters held sacred by any religion, thereby causing outrage among a substantial number of the adherents of that religion"; following protest, a referendum to stop the law is to take place.[16]

Most Western governments began to emphasize the need to protect believers, rather than religions, from offensive speech.[17] England's common law on blasphemy, originally justified on the grounds that speech contesting Christian doctrine was a danger to the nation, was redefined in the late 1800s to cover only material unduly harmful to human feelings. "Mere denial of the truth of Christianity" would no longer be an offense if couched in decent language, but attention would be paid to whether expressions were "calculated and intended to insult the feelings and deepest religious convictions of the great majority of the persons amongst whom we live."[18] There has been a gradual progression from protection of "God Himself," to "faith in God," to "securing religious peace."[19] Western blasphemy laws have been increasingly understood to serve the earthly goals of preventing hurt feelings and social disorder rather than the theological goals of protecting the sacred.[20]

Today, most Western blasphemy laws carry fines or prison terms measured in months and are now invoked only in rare cases involving an insulting treatment of religious figures or symbols.[21] The trickle of recent prosecutions of blasphemy against Christianity has generally resulted in dismissal, acquittal, or, more rarely,

the suppression of "offensive material" without additional penalties for its creators. With rare humor, a Munich court even held that the show *Popetown* was "too
dumb to be insulting."[22] More recently, Italian authorities have shut down websites
featuring offensive depictions of the Virgin Mary and the pope. In 2005, they also
brought charges against a comedian who joked crudely about the pope.[23] Greece
responded to a recent Council of Europe (CoE) survey by describing blasphemy
trials there as "rather frequent," though most end in acquittal.[24] In 2005, a prosecution in Greece against the Austrian author of a religious satire entitled *The Life of
Jesus* resulted in a lower court's decision to order the first Greek book ban in twenty
years, along with a six-month suspended sentence for the defendant. However,
after international pressure, the conviction was overturned on appeal.[25]

Nevertheless, blasphemy bans in Europe have not been ruled out in principle.
In the 1990s, the European Court of Human Rights—the court of last resort in
such cases for the member states of the CoE—upheld national authorities in
two major cases that restricted expression on grounds of blasphemy against
Christianity.[26] As recently as 2005, it upheld the conviction of a publisher based
in France for violating an Islamic blasphemy law in Turkey. Although the court
ruled against another Turkish blasphemy conviction the following year, it did so
on factual grounds; the expression at issue was not "an abusive attack on Muslims
or on sacred symbols of Muslim religion."[27] As the cases below show, there is a
growing interest in Europe in applying blasphemy or quasi-blasphemy bans to
protect Islam.

The European Court of Human Rights on Blasphemy

The European Convention for the Protection of Human Rights and Fundamental
Freedoms (1950), binding on all CoE states, guarantees freedom of expression.[28]
It does not explicitly provide for a right of religions to be protected from blasphemy or persons to be protected from religious offense, but it does permit
restrictions on expression in order to protect public safety, order, health, or
morals, as well as the reputation or rights of others. It is these restrictions that
the European Court relies on to uphold both blasphemy and hate-speech bans.
European regional judges have cited the rationale of protecting the "religious feelings" of groups and individuals and a "right not to be offended," rather than protecting the sanctity of religious teachings per se.

Using the same controversial tactic as the OIC at the UN, the European
Court has attempted to carve out a new right not to have religious feelings
offended from what was originally intended to be a narrow exception to a general right of free expression. European judiciaries now struggle to reconcile
freedom of expression with this "right" of protected feelings, with cases often
turning on whether the speech was a "gratuitous insult." The European Court

uses the criterion of "gratuitous" insult to allow a right not to be offended to trump freedom of expression, thus making an exception to free speech into the new rule.

For twenty years, the European Commission of Human Rights and European Court, in cases involving pornographic or mocking representations of sacred Christian figures, repeatedly held that authorities may legitimately ban publications, seize films, and punish their authors in order to protect the "rights of others"—namely, "the right of citizens not to be offended in their religious feelings."[29] While, with a restructuring, the commission became largely obsolete in 1998, the European Court has continued to maintain that freedom of expression includes "a duty to avoid as far as possible an expression that is, in regard to objects of veneration, gratuitously offensive to others and profanatory."[30] For much of Europe, religious freedom is coming to mean that people have a right to be protected from offense to their religious feelings that can override freedom of expression.

These rulings focus on whether the expression is "extreme," "provocative," or an "insult." While maintaining that religious persons "must tolerate and accept the denial by others of their religious beliefs and even the propagation by others of doctrines hostile to their faith," the European Court nonetheless asserts a state interest in regulating "the manner in which religious beliefs and doctrines are opposed or denied."[31] It has also asserted that there can be more state regulation of expression regarding religion than of politics, even though the two are often intertwined. It has also defended the ambiguity and unpredictability of blasphemy and religious hate-speech prohibitions by declaring that blasphemy "cannot by its very nature lend itself to precise legal definition" and that what might produce offense would "vary significantly from time to time and from place to place, especially in an era characterized by an ever growing array of faiths and denominations." These relativizing complications were simply deemed reasons to allow national authorities greater "flexibility" in adjudicating blasphemy cases.[32]

In 2005, for the first time, the European Court followed these precedents in upholding an Islamic blasphemy ruling. It supported Turkey, a member of the CoE, in *I.A. v. Turkey*, in which a publisher in France claimed that his freedom of expression had been violated by a Turkish court ruling that he had insulted "God, the Religion, the Prophet and the Holy Book." The director of the France-based Berfin publishing house, which had published a novel depicting fictional sexual excesses by the Islamic Prophet, had been sentenced to two years' imprisonment, later commuted to a fine. The European Court found it decisive that there had been "'provocative' opinions and abusive attacks on one's religion" and ruled valid the Turkish law's aim of "provid(ing) protection against offensive attacks on matters regarded as sacred by Muslims."[33]

Notwithstanding such cases, by the end of the twentieth century, the application of blasphemy laws in most Western countries was so sporadic that few authors of religiously provocative material faced a risk of prosecution. The censorship that does occur is selective and uneven. For instance, in the case of *Wingrove v. the United Kingdom*, a film was banned for blasphemy. Shortly before that, Martin Scorsese's *Last Temptation of Christ* received a classification certificate, permitting it to be shown, while Monty Python's *Life of Brian* was banned in some jurisdictions and permitted in others. In Italy, complaints over *Last Temptation* were dismissed for reasons of intent, though allegedly blasphemous websites have been closed.[34] Despite weak enforcement in recent decades, the criminalization of blasphemy survives as a valid legal principle at the European regional level, leaving open the possibility of a revival of national blasphemy bans.[35] Some Muslim groups now argue that fairness demands the application of these statutes to punish insults against Islam. The controversy over Salman Rushdie's *Satanic Verses* stimulated this debate.

Blasphemy Laws and *The Satanic Verses*

In the United Kingdom, Abdul Hussain Choudhury of the British Muslim Action Front, a group formed in response to Khomeini's fatwa against Salman Rushdie, sought to have the writer charged with blasphemous libel.[36] Choudhury also accused Rushdie of seditious libel, claiming that his novel caused "discontent" and mutual hostility among British subjects and harmed Britain's diplomatic relations with Iran and other Muslim governments, while instilling anger toward the United Kingdom among foreign Muslim populations. Both efforts failed.

The magistrate declined to prosecute Rushdie on the grounds that British blasphemy laws protected only religious beliefs that were part of Anglican doctrine, a decision later upheld despite the complaint of discrimination.[37] Among other issues, the court reasoned that expanding the scope of blasphemy restrictions would foster not social peace but "intolerance, divisiveness and unreasonable interference with freedom of expression." The panel added, "there are fundamental differences which would be capable of setting one religion against another under an extended law of blasphemy."[38] In July 1989, a minister at the Home Department wrote to British Muslim leaders, explaining that "an alteration in the law could lead to a rush of litigation which would damage relations between faiths."[39] Until its final abolition in 2008, Britain's blasphemy law remained applicable only to Anglican doctrine.

Despite this ruling, the Rushdie decision did not end debate over prosecuting offenses against Islam. Throughout most of the West, newer laws, expressly designed to protect religious minorities, are increasingly being adopted and applied to restrict speech thought to be religiously offensive. These laws have led to lawsuits aimed at settling sectarian differences of opinion, which was the very outcome against which the British panel had warned. Together with remaining blasphemy, public order, and related laws, they have created a complicated legal patchwork that threatens the right to speak freely about and within Islam.

Religious Hate Speech and a Right Not to Be Offended

While blasphemy laws are in decline, newer laws that perform many of the same social, if not theological, functions are becoming entrenched in many Western legal systems. In comparison to blasphemy laws, prohibitions against hate speech are of relatively recent vintage. While some countries, including Germany, passed such laws in the 1930s as a (futile) measure against Nazism, their major growth came after the Second World War.[40] Together with more narrowly targeted measures, including laws against Holocaust denial and prohibitions on the organization of fascist parties and use of their symbols, they reflect the traumatic memory of Hitler's genocide.[41]

As discussed in chapter 11, two principal international human right treaties—the ICCPR, protecting individual civil and political rights, and the CERD, protecting against racism—contain provisions banning hate speech, with the former containing a provision specifically compelling states to prohibit incitement to religious hatred, a provision that had been proposed by the Soviet bloc without Western group support. Several regional agreements also call for restrictions on hate speech. A 1997 recommendation by the CoE Committee of Ministers urged its member states to adopt "civil, criminal and administrative law provisions on hate speech."[42] A 2003 additional protocol to the CoE's convention on cybercrime calls for the criminalization of "distributing, or otherwise making available, racist and xenophobic material to the public through a computer system," as well as "publicly insulting via computer" groups "distinguished by race, colour, descent or national or ethnic origin, as well as religion, if used as a pretext for any of these factors," or persons because of their membership in such a group.[43] (The American Convention on Human Rights also bans advocacy of national, racial, or religious hatred but, at U.S. insistence, only when this constitutes "incitement to lawless violence or to any other similar action," rather than the broader formulation, when there is incitement to "hostility and discrimination."[44])

To ensure a common criminal law approach to the issue, in 2008, the European Union adopted a binding "Framework Decision" to criminalize certain expressions of racism and xenophobia. In so doing, all twenty-seven EU countries agreed to punish with at least one to three years' imprisonment, inter alia, intentional acts of incitement to religious "hatred": the new crimes could include the "distribution of tracts, pictures or other material." Formulated with neo-Nazi extremism as its target, the agreement also mandates the criminalization of genocide denial.[45] As a result of an intervention by the United Kingdom—which regulates religious hate speech less strictly than its racial equivalent—the EU formally compels prosecution only when religious hate speech functions as a cover for racism or xenophobia.[46] While reaffirming freedom of expression, it provides little clear guidance on how to reconcile tensions between this right and the obligation to prohibit hate speech.[47] National compliance by member states was required by November 28, 2010.

Many states have copied the ICCPR's "incitement to hatred" formula, though some have foregone adopting its particularly vague "incitement to hostility" language and only ban incitement when it is likely to result in violence or discrimination.[48] Other countries also, or instead, ban related offenses, such as defamation or insult of a protected group or its members. In England, hate-speech crimes are prosecuted as racially or religiously aggravated public order offenses.[49] Many such laws do not require proof of intent for conviction, while even fewer require that the speech in question lead to imminent lawlessness. As a result, as one legal scholar remarked concerning an Australian religious vilification statute, "one can 'incite' hatred without either the intention to do so or the effect of so doing."[50]

A 2008 study by the CoE's independent consultative body, the Commission for Democracy through Law (the "Venice Commission"), clearly shows the trend: of the forty-seven council-member states, all but Andorra and San Marino have adopted some type of hate-speech bans, with most covering religious hate speech, while blasphemy laws remain on the books in only eight states.[51]

The United States is exceptional in the strong protections it gives to freedom of expression under the First Amendment of the Constitution.[52] As the Supreme Court held in the 1969 case *Brandenburg v. Ohio*, under this amendment, freedoms of speech and press bar the government from forbidding "mere advocacy" of violence or of other criminal behavior save where such advocacy is directed to inciting or producing imminent and likely lawless action.[53] Generally, hate speech or speech that gives offense is, like blasphemy, constitutionally protected speech in the United States.[54] Offenses that are called "hate crimes," which some American states do have, simply amplify the penalty for traditional crimes in which the perpetrator was motivated by biases considered particularly detrimental to society but are not intended to penalize speech per se.[55] By contrast, European-style hate-speech codes punish hateful expression standing alone.[56]

American free-speech principles were questioned by at least some leading figures in September 2010, when a tiny Florida church threatened to burn a Qur'an, and again in April 2011 when the same church went through with the deed. These events in Gainesville received ample publicity and were exploited in Afghanistan by Taliban militants and other extremists to stage riots that resulted in the murder of a dozen people, including UN humanitarian workers and American military trainers. The American president, senior members of his administration, and American military commanders spoke out in a coordinated effort first to try to prevent, and then to condemn the Qur'an burning. More troubling, powerful American voices expressed doubts about American freedoms of speech and religion. Senate Majority Leader Harry Reid debated holding hearings on Qur'an desecration. Senator Lindsey Graham, a chief sponsor of a bill against flag burning, expressed his wish to "hold people accountable" for Qur'an burnings, since, while "free speech is a great idea," America is "in a war." Supreme Court Justice Stephen Breyer told an interviewer of his desire for a First Amendment exception that would allow punishing those who immolate the Qur'an. (He later retracted this.) These senior American leaders were, in effect, contemplating a law to protect Islam from negative expression—the first such U.S. federal law for any religion. In *Snyder v. Phelps* (2011), the Supreme Court reaffirmed the principle that speech cannot be banned because it is hurtful. Nevertheless, America's resolve to uphold its First Amendment rights will continue to be tested.[57]

In Europe, hate-speech prohibitions have often been wielded against neo-Nazis and are still used to prosecute anti-Semitic expressions. The prosecuted have included the authors of a vitriolic anti-Israeli article in *Le Monde*, a French comic who mocked Jews and accused them of "taking control of the media," a U.K. Foreign Office aide charged with lapsing into an anti-Semitic rant in connection with the February 2009 Israeli military action in Gaza, and a Christian Dior fashion designer charged with religious-based public insult after an anti-Semitic tirade in a Paris bar.[58] Over the years, these laws have been broadened to be used on behalf of a range of diverse causes and against a panoply of targets.[59] In Sweden, Australia, and Canada, they have been employed against Christian clergy, including those who made unpopular moral or theological pronouncements concerning homosexuality.[60] Although France has had no blasphemy law for centuries, there have been at least five group insult cases since the 1990s concerning material offensive to Christians and at least two convictions for making harsh remarks concerning Jehovah's Witnesses.[61] There are also examples in Europe of hate-speech laws being invoked to quell inflammatory and extreme speech uttered by Muslim hard-liners, but the major growth has been against critics or perceived critics of Islam.[62]

Legal Cases against Commentators on Islam

Since the 1990s, a growing number of people who have made negative remarks about Islamic matters, often in the context of opposing Muslim immigration to the West, have been prosecuted and even convicted under Western blasphemy and hate-speech laws, and the distinctions between the two prohibitions have proven far from clear. Even in those cases ending in acquittal, defendants have suffered major costs in time, money, and reputation in mounting their defense. Also, regardless of the outcome, the possibility of prosecution hangs over society, chilling public discussion of Muslim and Islamic beliefs and practices.[63]

Commentators on Islam and Immigration

Several hate-speech cases have centered on writings opposed to Muslim immigration to the West. In an early case, the application to Islam of what were originally intended as antiracism laws produced bizarre results. "Zola F," a cabaret artist of Pakistani Muslim background, pseudonymously published a book entitled *The Impending Ruin of the Netherlands, Country of Gullible Fools* and was sentenced in 1992 to a hefty fine under Dutch hate-speech laws. His book criticized Dutch tolerance of Islamic institutions and immigration, which its author warned would end in civil war and partition. As observers noted, the trial produced "the remarkable spectacle of a dark-skinned immigrant shouted down by the press and sentenced to a heavy fine for racism by white judges, while his white collaborators— the publisher and translator...were acquitted."[64]

Brigitte Bardot

In France, former screen star Brigitte Bardot was fined five times between 1997 and 2008 for inciting racial hatred. These charges centered on her condemnation of the ritual slaughter of animals during the Muslim holiday of Eid el-Kabir. Bardot, an animal-rights advocate, has urged that Eid killings be carried out in licensed slaughterhouses, where the animals would be stunned before being killed.[65] Her published statements also made repeated allegations of a Muslim immigrant "invasion" that would harm France.

First charged in 1996, after complaints from "antiracist" groups concerning an article in *Le Figaro*, Bardot was initially acquitted on the grounds that her editorial "condemned those who practice the slaughter of sheep and not the entire Muslim community," while her comments on immigration were statements of political opinion and thus enjoyed strong free-speech protections.[66] An appeals court disagreed, however, and handed her a 10,000-franc fine in October 1997.[67]

In 1998, she was fined for an article in a *National Front* paper, in which she charged that the slaughter of sheep by Muslims "covered France with blood every year" and connected this to attacks on civilians in Algeria: "They cut the throats of women and children, our monks, our officials, they will cut our throats one day and it will serve us right." She contended that this was a reference to Islamists, not all Muslims. The court ruled that while her criticism of slaughter practices was permissible, she was at fault for laying blame for killings in Algeria on "the Moslem community in general" and predicting that France would soon experience such crimes.[68]

Bardot was again fined in June 2000 for a passage, "Open Letter to my Lost France," in her book *Le Carre de Pluton*, and again four years later over another book, *A Scream in the Silence*, a best seller that condemned "the Islamization of France."[69] She was also convicted in 2008 and fined 15,000 Euros for a published letter to President Sarkozy, which mainly criticized ritual slaughter but included a statement that she was "tired of being led by the nose by this population that is destroying us, destroying our country by imposing its acts."[70] She declared to the court, "I will not shut up until stunning is carried out" before ritual slaughter.[71]

Oriana Fallaci

The late Italian journalist Oriana Fallaci faced a series of legal cases in multiple countries over her hostility toward Muslim immigration. In France in June 2002, the Movement Against Racism and for Friendship Between People (MRAP) sought a judicial order to quash French distribution of her book *The Rage and the Pride*, which the group's leader claimed "incites racial violence." Fallaci, who noted that she had received death threats because of her writings, responded that she "reserve[d] the right to sue MRAP for the insult 'racist.'" *The Rage and the Pride*, written as a reaction to the 9/11 terror attacks, was vitriolic in tone, criticizing the large size of Muslim families with the words "they multiply like rats" and Muslim prayer practices, claiming they "spend their time with their bottoms in the air, praying five times a day."[72] The case was dismissed on a legal technicality on November 20, 2002.[73]

In Switzerland, Geneva's Islamic Centre also sought to have the book banned and initiated proceedings to charge Fallaci under antiracism laws. The center's leader, Hani Ramadan, brother of Tariq Ramadan, complained that Fallaci was insulting the Muslim community as a whole with her words. (Hani Ramadan himself soon became a target of human rights proponents for writing an article in *Le Monde* expressing approval of stoning as a punishment for adultery).[74] Swiss authorities requested her extradition but were turned down by Italy's Minister of Justice.[75]

In Italy itself, Fallaci became embroiled in a running verbal and legal contest with Italian Muslim activist Adel Smith, who had responded to *The Rage and the Pride* with his own book, *Islam Punishes Oriana Fallaci*. Fallaci claimed that one passage in this book constituted incitement to murder her. She unsuccessfully attempted to bring charges against Smith, who then threatened Fallaci with a libel suit for claiming that he had made a death threat. Smith had already distinguished himself by campaigning to have a crucifix removed from his son's classroom, endorsing 9/11 conspiracy theories, and sending the mayor of Naples a bottle of cleaning liquid and an invitation to "stay at home" after she criticized his run for provincial office.[76]

Smith had discovered the potential of religious hate-speech laws in 2004. At that time, he had tried, unsuccessfully, to sue Pope John Paul II, then-Cardinal Joseph Ratzinger, and Cardinal Giacomo Biffi, for having stated, respectively, that in Islam "the richness of God's self-revelation" in the Christian Bible was set aside; that followers of religions other than Catholicism were in a "gravely deficient situation" with regard to salvation; and that Italy should resist "Islam's ideological attack" by seeking Catholic immigrants rather than Muslims. Smith said that these remarks violated Italy's constitution, which made all religions equal under the law, and that they amounted to "offense, injury and insult" of Muslims as well as "defamation and incitation to racial and religious hatred." The Union of Islamic Communities in Italy distanced itself from Smith.[77]

In 2005, he brought a complaint against Fallaci over her new book, *The Strength of Reason*, charging that it contained eighteen blasphemous statements. Among other provocative elements, the book warned of a Muslim plot to turn Europe into "Eurabia" through immigration, with the collaboration of certain elements of European society. At one point Fallaci called Islam a "pond" with water that "never moves, never runs, never purifies itself…It poisons, it kills."[78] A judge in northern Italy insisted on bringing Fallaci to trial for her "hostile expressions against every manifestation of the Islamic religion and world." He took particular issue with her contention that the distinction between "a good Islam and a bad Islam" was fallacious.[79] Trial proceedings were halted by Fallaci's death on September 15, 2006.[80]

With Fallaci's case in mind, the Italian Senate amended a Mussolini-era statute that prohibits "offend[ing] the state's religion, by defaming those who profess it" by expanding it to cover any "religion acknowledged by the state" and reducing the maximum punishment from two years' jail time to a 5,000-Euro fine. Smith himself was put on trial in 2005 for "offending the Catholic religion, through the use of scorn" in a television appearance at which he had called the Catholic Church a "criminal association" and Pope John Paul a "double-crosser." He was convicted and originally sentenced to six months in jail, which was later reduced to a fine of more than 6,000 Euros. Appearing suddenly solicitous of freedom of expression, he vowed to appeal.[81]

Seppo Lehto

In addition to the Halla-aho case, described above, Finland successfully convicted blogger Seppo Lehto, who received a prison term of two years and four months for defamation and incitement to ethnic and religious hatred for racially, religiously, and/or personally insulting statements on the Internet. Lehto had drawn heavy scrutiny after making public a video in which he drew Muhammad as a pig.[82]

Cartoons
Denmark

While verbal criticism or vitriol has regularly drawn the attention of Muslim activists and Western legal authorities, it is cartoons that have been at the center of most attention. The 2005–6 global crisis over *Jyllands-Posten*'s cartoons of Muhammad drew widespread Western legal attention, although cases against publishers in the West have generally failed. In Denmark itself, a complaint by Muslims against the paper was rejected by the Director of Public Prosecutions on March 15, 2006.

Officials considered charges concerning the cartoons under two statutes, one governing blasphemy and one on hate speech. Section 140 of the Danish criminal code states that "any person who, in public, mocks or scorns the religious doc-trines or acts of worship of any lawfully existing religious community in this country" may face up to four months in prison. Section 266b provides for a fine or up to two years in jail for "any person who, publicly or with the intention of wider dissemination, makes a statement or imparts other information by which a group of people are threatened, scorned or degraded on account of their race, colour, national or ethnic origin, religion, or sexual inclination."[83]

In the interest of protecting freedom of expression, the prosecutor held that both laws should be interpreted narrowly. He concluded that the cartoons were not merely "gratuitous" but had broader social significance that accorded them free speech protection. He also determined, "The drawings that must be assumed to be pictures of Muhammed depict a religious figure, and none of them can be considered to be meant to refer to Muslims in general." The prosecutor argued that those that did depict Muslims did not do so in a "scornful or degrading" fashion and that a "depiction of a religious figure" was not sufficient to meet Danish standards for a blasphemy ban.

With regard to Section 140, the prosecutor ruled on each drawing individually, noting that all but four were neutral. Of those, he found that the drawing that chastised Islam's Prophet for "keeping women under yoke" and the image of a sword-wielding Muhammad before two frightened figures in burkas were pro-tected commentary and not an attack against "religious doctrines and acts of worship." The drawing in which Muhammad tells two angry followers to "relax, it's just a sketch made by an infidel Dane from South Denmark," showed the Prophet rejecting violence and so was not scorn or mockery.

In their considerations, the prosecutors necessarily had to address what con-stitutes a correct portrayal of Islam and, in particular, to weigh evidence on the contentious issue of whether Islam is linked to violence. They noted, "The histor-ical descriptions of the Prophet's life show that while propagating their religion, he and his followers were involved in violent conflicts and armed clashes with per-sons and population groups that did not join Islam." With relevance to the fourth caricature, the now well-known image of Muhammad wearing a turban bomb, they clarified that "a depiction of the Prophet Muhammed as a violent person must be considered an incorrect depiction if it is with a bomb as a weapon, which in the context of today may be understood to imply terrorism." However, such depictions, while "incorrect" portrayals, did not qualify as "mockery," "ridicule," or "scorn." Thus, the prosecutor indicated that the two statutes did limit the range of permissible statements on religious subjects and that the paper had been wrong to imply that religious groups could not demand "special consideration."[84] However, the prosecutor further held that such "consideration" did not apply in this particular instance. Despite this carefully articulated decision, the Danish cartoons still became emblematic of blasphemy against Islam in the West.

Seven Muslim groups then brought a civil suit, which, in 2006, an Aarhus court ruled invalid after finding no intent to insult Muslims.[85] In 2008, an appeals court upheld that decision and further noted that, since there have been terrorist attacks committed in the name of Islam, Danish law permitted satire on the subject.[86] In October 2008, the Justice Ministry turned down an appeal to bring the case before Denmark's Supreme Court.[87]

France

Complainants in France and Canada initiated legal proceedings against those who republished the cartoons but were ultimately unsuccessful. In France, the Grand Mosque of Paris, joined by other Muslim organizations, launched criminal proceedings against the journal *Charlie-Hebdo*, which had reprinted two Danish cartoons and its own original Muhammad cartoon, and its director, Philippe Val, for "publicly abusing a group of people because of their religion."[88] According to Val's account, French authorities encouraged Islamic groups to push for legal action to block distribution of the relevant issue, but these attempts failed. Unfazed, President Jacques Chirac recommended the services of his personal lawyer to the groups, who subsequently filed racism charges and, together with the Union of Islamic Organizations of France, reportedly pressured a reluctant Paris Grand Mosque rector, Dalil Boubakeur, to commence a suit.[89]

Val declared that he published the cartoons to protest the sacking of another paper's director who had done the same.[90] One notable theme of his defense was that the cartoons he published did not constitute a hate-speech crime, because they had targeted "ideas, not men" or, as he explained in the *Wall Street Journal*, "not believers but religion when it is used as an alibi to perpetrate terrorist acts. When religion leaves the private sphere, it becomes an ideology like any other, and must accept to be criticized with the same virulence as any other ideology. That is the very essence of democracy."[91]

He received support from then–presidential candidate Nicolas Sarkozy, who had often been lampooned by the magazine, and who declared he preferred "too many caricatures to an absence of caricature."[92] On March 22, 2007, Val was acquitted. The court found no sign of a "deliberate intention of directly and gratuitously offending the Muslim community." The judgment emphasized such specific factors as the "context" of the drawings, that *Charlie-Hebdo* "is a satirical paper...that no one is obliged to buy or read," and that caricatures are by definition intended to go "beyond good taste."[93] The courts also relied on the arguments that some or all of the drawings targeted only fundamentalists, not all Muslims, and that they contributed to an ongoing public debate.[94]

Canada

One widely publicized case took place in Canada, where, on February 15, 2006, the Canadian Islamic Congress (CIC) lodged human rights complaints against the *Western Standard* and the *Jewish Free Press* for republishing the cartoons. The CIC claimed that the drawings incited hatred that had led to e-mail threats against it. Furthermore, it claimed that the *Western Standard* publisher, Ezra Levant, had defamed the group's representative personally since he was a follower and descendant of the Prophet Muhammad, as well as harmed the reputation of all Canadian Muslims.[95] Levant and *Jewish Free Press* publisher Richard Bronstein were also criticized by the general in charge of Canadian forces in Afghanistan and by the Canadian prime minister, Stephen Harper.[96]

The *Jewish Free Press* case was settled in March 2007. However, Levant remained a defiant champion of free speech and refused to repent. He noted that the initial complaint took issue with his defense of his editorial decision in other media, just as Mark Steyn's critics had denounced him for criticizing lawsuits of the very type they brought against him.[97] Formal proceedings before the Alberta Human Rights and Citizenship Commission began in January 2008, and Levant, who was asked questions about his motives for publishing the cartoons, complained that such an inquiry made citizens' private thoughts the business of the government, called the meeting an "interrogation," videotaped his own hearing, and even republished the Muhammad cartoons on his website during the inquiry.[98] He argued that it was a violation of basic Canadian law "for a government bureaucrat to call any publisher or anyone else to an interrogation to be quizzed about his political or religious expression." Levant noted that the complainants would be funded by taxpayers while the *Western Standard* had to fund its own legal defense, a situation he suggested would deter other journalists from writing about controversial topics.[99]

In February 2008, the CIC dropped its complaint, having come to "understand that most Canadians see this as an issue of freedom of speech, that that principle is sacred and holy in our society."[100] Levant still had to defend himself against a complaint by the Edmonton Muslim Council until August 2008, when the Alberta Commission decided that, while the cartoons were "stereotypical, negative and offensive," they were "not gratuitously included" but rather "related to relevant and timely news." Levant disputed the commission's implication that it could have penalized him had they not considered the cartoons properly contextualized: he maintained that the officials had "assume[d] the role of editor-in-chief for the entire province of Alberta."[101]

The Netherlands

The cartoon affair seems to have created a lingering suspicion of provocative caricaturists in the minds of at least one country's law enforcement officials. In mid-May 2008, a Dutch cartoonist, using the pseudonym Gregorius Nekschot, whose work had been published, among other places, on the late Theo van Gogh's website, was arrested, had his computer and other materials seized, and was briefly held by police after an Internet monitoring group told authorities his work was racist and insulting to Muslims. The group had received numerous complaints, many apparently coming from followers of Imam Abdul-Jabbar van de Ven, who has also publicly wished for Geert Wilders's death. Nekschot's cartoons linked immigrants, particularly Muslims, to crime, bestiality, and welfare dependence. Released after one day, he remained under suspicion of "insulting people on the basis of their race or belief, and possibly also of inciting hate." If prosecuted, he could face two years in prison or a fine equivalent to about $25,000.

The initial complaints about Nekschot's cartoons had been lodged in 2005, leading some to speculate that his arrest in 2008 was an effort to placate Muslim opinion after Geert Wilders's *Fitna* controversy. Officials claimed they had previously been unable to discover Nekschot's true identity, which he kept secret to forestall violent retribution from those offended by his work; both he and his publisher had received death threats. The arrest also led to protests from a number of Dutch politicians. Even some Muslim leaders suggested that the charges were excessive, with one remarking that Dutch officials appeared "more afraid" of alleged insults to Islam than were Muslims. A controversial figure whose work had been considered too vulgar for publication in mainstream outlets, Nekschot had been relatively unknown until the authorities took an interest in him, after which daily views of his website multiplied from a few thousand to over 100,000, and his cartoons began appearing in papers that had previously shunned them. Meanwhile, the media discovered during the course of the controversy that the government had established an "Interdepartmental Working Group on Cartoons" after the Danish cartoon affair, apparently to keep officials apprised of any drawings that might lead to future controversy.[102]

Politicians

Ayaan Hirsi Ali

As discussed previously, in 2003, Amsterdam prosecutors opened an investigation into, but did not prosecate, complaints that Ayaan Hirsi Ali—a vocal ex-Muslim, champion of Enlightenment values, and then a member of the Dutch parliament for the People's Party for Freedom and Democracy (VVD)—had incited hatred of Muslims. Since she was a Somali immigrant, this undermined the oft-cited "fighting racism" justification for the prosecution of critics of Islam.

She had called Islam's prophet a "perverse tyrant," comparing him to "all those megalomaniac leaders in the Middle East: Bin Laden, Khomeini and Saddam." Her anger was linked to present-day abuses against Muslim women: "Mohammed says that women must stay at home, wear a veil, cannot take part in certain activities, do not have the same inheritance rights as their husbands and can be stoned to death if they commit adultery." After she announced plans for a sequel to *Submission* (the film on abuses against Muslim women that led to the murder of its director, Theo van Gogh) that would deal with the treatment of homosexuals in Islam, a group of Dutch Muslims filed a civil lawsuit to prevent her making unnecessarily hurtful or offensive remarks, or blasphemous statements, against Islam.[103] In 2005, a judge found that although she had "sought the borders of the acceptable," her speech did not warrant prohibition. Though she prevailed, the defense cost her 8,000 Euros.[104]

Geert Wilders

The historically tolerant Dutch also prosecuted other politicians for speech critical of Islam, including MP and Party for Freedom (PVV) leader, Geert Wilders, who has built his political identity on challenging Islam. In March 2008, the Dutch Islamic Federation filed a case to bar the release of Wilders's film *Fitna* and to charge him for his anti-Islamic statements.[105] The suit focused on his calling the Qur'an a "fascist book" and Muhammad "a barbarian." Initially the case was dismissed.

In January 2009, following persistent legal efforts by complainants demanding Wilders's prosecution, the Amsterdam Appeals Court ruled that he should be charged with incitement to hatred and discrimination. It suggested that his "method of presentation" produced hatred; his offending technique apparently involved using "biased, strongly generalizing phrasings with a radical meaning, ongoing reiteration and an increasing intensity." His statements also "substantially harm the religious esteem of the Islamic worshippers." Wilders's criticism of Islamic beliefs was treated as a crime against Muslim people: "Wilders has indeed insulted the Islamic worshippers themselves by affecting the symbols of the Islamic belief as well." Thus, although "Islamic immigrants may be expected to have consideration for the existing sentiments in the Netherlands as regards their belief, which is partly at odds with Dutch and European values and norms," criticism of this belief must be limited, and the court sought to "draw a clear boundary in the public debate" on the matter.[106]

Attempts by Wilders to halt the case were turned down by the Dutch Supreme Court in May 2009 and by a lower court in January 2010. He was formally charged with violating the Dutch penal code, Article 137c (concerning group insult) and Article 137d (concerning incitement to hatred, violence, or discrimination).[107] According to a copy of the summons made public on Wilders's website, his offending expressions include, among many others: the claim that "a moderate Islam does not exist"; comparisons of the Qur'an to *Mein Kampf*; calls for the Qur'an to be prohibited; and calls to end "non-Western" immigration and to deport those who do not assimilate. Also cited were statements that "Islam is a violent religion," offered as an explanation for high crime rates among Moroccan youth, and that Muhammad would be expelled from the Netherlands were he alive today. The list includes denunciations of Dutch officials as "cowardly folks" who are "cooperat[ing] in the transformation of the Netherlands into Netherabia as a province of the Islamic super state Eurabia," along with the full content of his movie *Fitna*.[108]

In a move that led to predictions that the trial could become a referendum on Islam, Wilders's defense team planned to summon eighteen witnesses, including legal experts, experts on Islam, former Muslims, Islamic extremists—among the latter Muhammed Bouyeri, the murderer of Theo van Gogh—and popular Islamist leader and media figure Sheikh Yusuf al-Qaradawi. However, in early February 2010, the court approved only three witnesses. Those permitted, including outspoken American ex-Muslim Wafa Sultan, could testify only in closed session.[109] In October 2010, a Dutch judicial oversight body ordered that he be tried anew after finding that judges in the initial court proceedings appeared to be biased. Wilders was finally acquitted in June 2011.

Wilders's rhetoric also seemed to run afoul of British law, or at least policy, since, on February 10, 2009, after warnings of demonstrations by opponents, Home Secretary Jacqui Smith banned the Dutch MP on public order grounds from entering the United Kingdom. He had planned to speak at the invitation of members of the House of Lords and to show his film *Fitna*. The British ban drew protests from the Dutch foreign minister and a warning by Lord Pearson, who had invited Wilders, and by Baroness Cox, that "[o]ur western society, and indeed the majority of peaceful Muslims, are being intimidated far too much by violent Islamists."[110] When Wilders landed at Heathrow, he was sent back to the Netherlands.[111] (The United Kingdom has also barred entry to other controversial figures through similar "exclusion orders," including Sheikh Yusuf al-Qaradawi, and, in May 2009, it issued a list of sixteen banned individuals— mainly Islamist hate preachers but including American "shock jock" Michael Savage.)[112]

The Wilders travel ban was overturned eight months later by an immigration tribunal, whose chair declared that the government had shown no "[s]ubstantial evidence of actual harm" adequate to justify suppressing discussion on "matters that might form the opinions of legislators, policy makers and voters."[113] Wilders entered the United Kingdom in March 2010 and spoke at the House of Lords without incident about his controversial ideas.

The British National Party

In other cases, hate-speech laws have been invoked against extreme right-wing politicians, with equally questionable results. In December 2004, Nick Griffin, chairman of the anti-immigrant British National Party (BNP), was arrested, along with a number of colleagues, on suspicion of inciting racial hatred. Although other BNP members admitted to committing racially motivated crimes, Griffin's prime offense appears to have been calling Islam a "vicious, wicked faith." Another of the charges concerned his prediction, made in 2004, before the London Tube bombings of July 7, 2005, that local Muslims would one day stage a terror attack in Britain. In an Orwellian turn, a court official instructed jurors to exclude from consideration whether Griffin's statements were factually correct.[114] After the prosecution failed, the case was retried in November 2006, and Griffin was acquitted on all counts, while garnering valuable publicity.[115]

Other Politicians

In January 2009, far-right Austrian politician Susanne Winter was sentenced to a fine of approximately $30,000 and a suspended three-month prison term after being convicted of incitement and "humiliating a religion." A Muslim organization and private individuals had filed charges against her for calling Muhammad a "child molester," stating he had written the Qur'an in "epileptic fits," and accusing Muslim men in general of sexual misconduct. Winter had also received Islamist death threats for these statements.[116]

Other complaints concerned criticism of Muslim practices or representations of Muslims as a danger to society, with most eventually dismissed. In 2007, three members of the Danish People's Party (DF) were reported to police by an "antiracism" NGO for criticizing Muslim veils as a symbol of totalitarian repression comparable to Nazi swastikas. Prosecutors decided against pressing charges, citing "a particularly wide freedom of expression for politicians on controversial social issues."[117] In Switzerland, the Federal Court dismissed a local prosecutor's complaint over a poster issued by the Swiss People's Party (UDC)—an anti-immigration group also responsible for the 2009 referendum banning minarets in that country—that showed Muslims praying outside the Swiss parliament and urged voters to "Use your heads" and support UDC in the 2007 elections. Another UDC poster, featuring a woman in a burka and an image of minarets that resembled missiles atop the Swiss flag, was denounced by a federal antiracism body for "inciting hatred" and was banned from publicly owned spaces in some cities, but permitted in others.[118] In Sweden, Jimmie Akesson, of the small Sweden Democrats party, was reported to authorities by an "antiracism" group over an op-ed arguing in dramatic terms that Sweden was threatened by Islam's spread, which the group contended was hate speech. No prosecution ensued.[119]

Media

A U.K. media exposé of radical Muslim preachers triggered an investigation because it appeared to cast Islam in a negative light. In January 2007, Channel 4, a public-service television broadcaster, aired a documentary titled *Undercover Mosque* that showed preachers at some British mosques "condemning the idea of integration into British society, condemning British democracy as un-Islamic and praising the Taliban for killing British soldiers." In response, West Midlands Police, who some thought should have investigated the documentary's subjects, instead inquired whether Channel 4 could be prosecuted for inciting racial hatred. A Crown Prosecution Service lawyer argued that the way the statements were spliced "appears to have completely distorted what the speakers were saying."[120] In November 2007, Ofcom, Britain's media regulator, found that Channel 4 "had accurately represented the material it had gathered and dealt with the subject matter responsibly and in context."[121] West Midlands Police and the Crown Prosecution Service apologized and gave restitution of £100,000.[122]

Theology and Philosophy

As we already seen in Australia's *Catch the Fire Ministries* case, blasphemy and religious hate-speech laws also punish and chill those expressing certain theological beliefs. Another notable example occurred in France, where writer Michel Houellebecq was tried in September 2002 on charges of inciting religious hatred in an interview with a literary journal. Regarding his feelings about Islam, he stated, "You could call it hate." While rejecting all forms of monotheism, he claimed that "the stupidest religion of all is Islam." The Paris mosque rector demanded that Houellebecq be punished because "Islam has been reviled." Houellebecq responded that, in his own mind, his comments had been directed at beliefs, not people: "I have never shown any contempt for Muslims, but I still have as much contempt as ever for Islam." Asked if he still believed Muslims to be stupid, he replied, "I didn't say that. I said they practice a stupid religion." Stressing that Islam was not a race but a religion, he also argued, "You can't be racist against Islam." The court terminated the case, finding Houellebecq's remarks displayed "ignorance" about Islam, but not an intention to affront Muslims.[123]

Citizens

Charges have also been leveled at ordinary citizens for peaceful—albeit sometimes distasteful—expression about Islam. In 2006, a sixty-one-year-old German man, who sent toilet paper printed with the words "Koran, the holy Qur-an" to the media and mosques, was convicted under German law of disturbing public order and slandering religious beliefs. He had also sent a letter describing the Qur'an as a "cookbook for terrorists." His notes led to death threats against him, and, in July 2005, Iran's government sent a démarche to Germany's Foreign Ministry.[124] Prosecutors argued that his writings "posed a risk, under the cover of free speech, to peaceful coexistence" between cultures, and he was sentenced to a year's imprisonment—which was suspended for five years—and 300 hours of community service.

Angered by van Gogh's murder, a Dutch man hung in his window a poster advertising a far-right movement and stating, "Stop the tumour that is Islam. Theo has died for us. Who will be next?" After being convicted by two lower courts, he won on appeal, arguing that he was criticizing radical forms of Islam hostile to Western society.[125]

In Austria, Elisabeth Sabaditsch-Wolff was put on trial for a briefing on Islam that she gave to a gathering of an anti-immigration party in Vienna. A diplomat's daughter who had lived in Iran and Libya, she depicted Islam as a danger to Western values and spoke critically of the treatment of women. The court found that Austria's free-speech guarantees protected her from hate-speech charges. However, the case turned on the judge's reasoning that her statement that Islam's prophet Mohammed was a "pedophile" was false since his child bride Aisha (usually reported as age six at the time of marriage and nine at the time it was consummated) remained his wife when she turned 18. On February 15, 2011, the trial court found her guilty of defaming Islam's prophet and thus of vilifying Islam and fined her 480 Euros.[126]

Religious speech regulations were also invoked to police in a Muslim-Christian dispute in the United Kingdom, resulting in further rupture of social harmony. After a religious dispute with a guest in March 2009, Ben Vogelenzang and his wife, who owned a bed-and-breakfast hotel in Liverpool, were charged with the "religiously aggravated" use of "threatening, abusive or insulting words," an offense under the Public Order Act 1986 and subject to increased penalties in cases involving religious hostility, under the Crime and Security Act 2001.[127] The Vogelenzang's guest, sixty-year-old British Muslim convert Ericka Tazi, contacted the police following a heated religious debate with the Christian owners, which she claimed began when the hotelier saw her wearing an Islamic headscarf, or *hijab*. Tazi reportedly complained that Vogelenzang called her "a terrorist or a murderer" and labeled Muhammad a warlord, comparing him to Saddam Hussein and Hitler. Vogelenzang's wife, Sharon, was said to have described the headscarf as a form of "bondage." Vogelenzang, in turn, said Tazi called the Bible false and Jesus a minor prophet. The couple, who, according to various reports, had once either fostered or adopted a Muslim child, strenuously denied being Islamophobic. The charges were dismissed, but the case led to an 80 percent drop in business for the Vogelenzangs over a nine-month period.[128]

Reaction against "Hate-Speech" Laws

In both Australia and Canada, high-profile hate-speech cases have produced a political and, in the latter case, judicial backlash. The *Catch the Fire Ministries* case spurred calls to weaken Australia's religious vilification laws. The backlash was further exacerbated by frivolous complaints, including one by a convicted child sex offender, calling himself a witch, who claimed he had been vilified by a Salvation Army Bible class taught to prisoners.[129] Some Anglican, Catholic, Jewish, and Quaker representatives, as well as Muslim ones, lauded Victoria's Racial and Religious Tolerance Act for "exposing" the work of "religious extremist and race hate groups."[130] But the Anglican bishop of South Sydney, Robert Forsyth, argued that such laws could criminalize merely the "strong" expression of genuine convictions. Cardinal George Pell, Catholic archbishop of Sydney, warned that they would "end up curtailing free speech as well as deepening the rifts between different religious groups." He added, "Being part of Australian life means you can criticize and will be criticized, sometimes unfairly. That is one reason why we manage to live together in peace."[131]

The *Catch the Fire Ministries* case disillusioned one of the Religious Tolerance Act's main Muslim supporters about the wisdom of such laws. Amir Butler of the Australian Muslim Public Affairs Committee reported: "At every major Islamic lecture I have attended since litigation began against Catch the Fire Ministries, there have been small groups of evangelical Christians—armed with notepads and pens—jotting down any comment that might later be used as evidence in the present case or presumably future cases." As he wrote in *The Age* newspaper: "If we believe our religion is true, then it requires us to believe others are false." Vilification laws thus became "a legalistic weapon by which religious groups can silence their ideological opponents, rather than engaging in debate and discussion."[132]

In Canada, too, some Muslims have concluded that hate speech and blasphemy prosecutions are bad for Islam. The moderate Muslim Canadian Congress (MCC), which had warned that the CIC's allegations against Steyn and *Maclean's* would "serve no purpose other than to reinforce the stereotype that Muslims have little empathy for vigorous debate and democracy," lauded the case's dismissal. It also argued that the CIC's "editorializing," by gratuitously declaring the defendants' writings "Islamophobic," sent "a very dangerous message to moderate Muslims who reject Sharia and do not take inspiration from overseas Islamic countries or groups."[133] In effect, according to the MCC, Canada's human rights commission had "taken sides in the bitter struggle within Canada's Muslim community where sharia-supporting Islamists are pitted against liberal and secular Muslims."[134]

Alan Borovoy, one of the architects of Canada's human rights legislation and the general counsel of the Canadian Civil Liberties Association, has had second thoughts about the usefulness of hate-speech hearings. He lamented that Section 13.1 of the Canadian Human Rights Act, banning "hate messages," has been used or threatened to be used against a film sympathetic to South Africa's Nelson Mandela, a pro-Zionist book, a Jewish community leader, and Salman Rushdie's *Satanic Verses*—none of which bore the slightest resemblance to the kind of hate material or hate mongers that he thought were the law's original targets.[135]

Critics of the legislation argue that, as Ezra Levant has stated, "the process is the punishment," since those charged with human rights offenses must foot their own legal costs while the plaintiff pays nothing.[136] Borovoy added that "during the years when my colleagues and I were laboring to create such commissions, we never imagined that they might ultimately be used against freedom of speech...No ideology—political, religious or philosophical—can be immune...A free culture cannot protect people against material that hurts."[137] Concerns about the Canadian human rights process increased when, in mid-2008, reports became public that, in what appeared to be entrapment undertaken to elicit an incriminating response, serial complainant and former commission investigator, Richard Warman, had posted offensive messages on extremist websites under pseudonyms and using an unsuspecting neighbor's Internet connection.[138]

Amid growing controversy, in September 2009, Athanasios Hadjis of the Canadian Human Rights Tribunal found that Section 13 violated the Canadian Charter of Rights' guarantee of free expression, since its use was not "remedial"— an important criterion for the lawfulness of human rights commissions set forth in a previous Supreme Court decision—and instead had become punitive.[139] Hadjis chose not to enforce the statute in the case at hand, brought by Richard Warman— the man behind the majority of Canadian hate-speech cases—against far rightist Marc Lemire. As Hadjis lacks authority to officially invalidate the law, his pronouncements are not decisive and, in any event, leave intact a Canadian criminal provision against hate speech, which is prosecuted in Canada's regular judiciary. However, there is increasing doubt in Canada about the justice and efficacy of such laws.[140]

Hate-Speech Bill Draws Fire in Britain

When the U.K. parliament sought to transform its blasphemy laws into hate-speech bans, it led to one of the most thorough critiques of such laws within any Western nation.[141] However, the result was still confused: the bill was eventually adopted, but in a drastically neutered form. Meanwhile, the United Kingdom continues to prosecute hate speech under public order laws.

In 2001, British prime minister Tony Blair's government began efforts to ban "incitement to religious hatred" with a draconian penalty of up to seven years' imprisonment. Home Secretary David Blunkett contended it was necessary to "close a loophole" insofar as British law banned incitement on racial but not religious grounds. The Home Office emphasized the theoretical distinction between blasphemy and hate speech, and that the measure was for "protecting the believer, not the belief," or "people not ideologies."[142]

The bill was explicitly designed to replace the ancient blasphemy ban protecting Anglican Christianity and was widely regarded as a measure designed to protect Muslims. The Muslim Council of Britain (MCB) had long called for such legislation, and, in November 2004, a Guardian/ICM poll found that 81 percent of British Muslims wanted new legislation against incitement to religious hatred, while 58 percent agreed that "despite the right to free speech, in Britain people who insult or criticize Islam should face criminal prosecution."[143] Left-wing London mayor Ken Livingstone claimed that the legislation was needed to end affronts to multicultural decency, such as the insulting reception given his recent guest, Sheikh Yusuf al-Qaradawi, who drew angry criticism after reports that he supported suicide bombing, wife-beating, and the murdering of Jews.[144]

During the British parliamentary debates and in the ensuing media coverage between 2004 and 2006, skeptics, including academics, writers, comedians, and artists, led by comedian Rowan Atkinson, as well as MPs, members of the National Secular Society, and Christian groups, pilloried the proposed law.[145] Atkinson warned that it could ban Monty Python's *Life of Brian* and maintained "there should be no subject about which you cannot make jokes," stating, "In my view, the right to offend is far more important than any right not to be offended."[146]

Conservative David Davis, who also argued that "religion, unlike race, is a matter of personal choice and therefore appropriate for open debate," noted that the ban would "technically prevent what many people may regard as reasonable criticism of devil worshippers and religious cults."[147] Indeed, the self-proclaimed "high priest of British white witches" said that witches and satanists were likely to invoke the new laws against their critics.[148] Over 1,000 churches contended in a petition that it would not dampen religious hatred but might well have "the opposite effect" and would even criminalize "the mere quoting of texts from both the Koran and the Bible."[149] The bishop of Liverpool noted that even if the charges never made it to trial, "just the headline 'Bishop's sermon on ritual slaughter is referred to the Attorney General' would create an atmosphere of fear."[150] The Christian-identified Barnabas Fund feared the law could "silence organizations like ourselves from highlighting the persecution of Christians and other human rights abuses which occur within some religious communities."[151] Secularist ex-Muslim Maryam Namazie warned of dire repercussions for those who, like her, already faced violent threats and social ostracism for criticizing Islamic extremism: "Even in the heart of secular Europe and the West, women who have resisted political Islam no longer feel fully safe.... We are already called racists and Islamophobes whenever we speak for women and against Islam and its movement."[152] Salman Rushdie urged that the proposal be dropped and noted that enduring offense was "part of everyday life" in countries such as Britain and the United States.[153] He warned of attempts by right-wingers or racists to claim Muslims were engaging in hate speech, and by Muslims to prosecute writers like him.[154]

Conservative MP Boris Johnson, soon to replace Livingstone as Lord Mayor of London, after reading several Qur'anic passages on Jews, Christians, and unbelievers, called for the prime minister to clarify "why and how he thinks the repetition of those words in a public or private place does not amount to incitement to religious hatred of exactly the kind that the Bill is supposed to ban...If it does not...[the bill] is nonsensical and should be scrapped."[155] When the prime minister's spokesman declined to answer, this raised sufficient concern for a Muslim delegation to visit Home Office Minister Paul Goggins, who reassured them that the bill would not affect their right to preach or recite from Islam's sacred books.[156]

In early February 2005, the MCB sent letters to politicians, warning that their stance against the bill could cost them Muslim votes.[157] The Director of Public Prosecutions found it necessary to advise some Muslim groups, whose members were under the impression that the law "will protect them from people being rude or offensive about Islam," that it would not prevent rudeness about Islam, but only "the grossest form of conduct."[158]

The bill received a strikingly hostile reception in the House of Lords, where Lord Peston called it "the most illiberal measure" he had seen during eighteen years in Parliament. Speakers warned of complaints that could arise: Lord Mackay cited criticism of radical imams, of the sort in which government officials themselves had engaged; Baroness Turner cited condemnations of religious teachings on the position of women; and Lord Chan expressed concern that even a moderate Muslim's criticism of capital punishment for apostasy could trigger a complaint.

Lord Carey, former archbishop of Canterbury, suggested that the bill could be invoked against a speech he himself had made criticizing repressive Muslim governments, which had drawn complaints from Muslim leaders. And Lord Lester noted that the likely refusal of the attorney general to take up frivolous cases would "be used by extremists as evidence of the discriminatory operation of the law and will leave embittered those whose expectations were not fulfilled." Numerous speakers noted the law's potential chilling effect, which Baroness Miller suggested would create an incentive for booksellers to simply avoid shelving controversial works rather than risk prosecution.[159] Lord Carey later explained that when Muslim groups asked him to support their campaign against *The Satanic Verses*, he told them they were "living in a country and civilization where we are quite used to this."[160]

Ultimately, a group of Conservative and Liberal Democratic lords proposed an amendment that would confirm the right to ridicule, criticize, and insult religion, as well as the right to proselytize, while clarifying that only those intentionally inciting religious hate (rather than those whose speech or behavior was merely *likely* to do so) would be violating the law. The amendment also declared that behavior or speech must be threatening, rather than merely abusive or insulting, to pass the threshold for prosecution. This weakened version of the bill became law as the Racial and Religious Hatred Act of 2006.[161] Its passage still did not end the British prosecution of religious hate speech, since such cases continue to be brought under public order laws, as was seen in the 2009 *Vogelenzang* case. In 2008, England and Wales abolished the common law ban on blasphemy, spurred by outrage over Sudan's "teddy bear" blasphemy charges against a British teacher (see chapter 8).[162] The country's last successful blasphemy libel prosecution—and its first in over half a century—had been in the 1977 *Gay News* case, concerning a lewd poem involving Christian symbols.[163]

The Council of Europe Defends Hate-Speech Bans but Reveals Their Problems

There is widespread debate on whether to prosecute specific accusations of blasphemy and religious hate speech, and, as our brief review of some cases reveals, there is a bewildering array of laws applied and interpreted inconsistently and selectively across, and even within, countries.[164] Against this background, the Danish cartoon fracas prompted the CoE to develop a rationale and set of criteria for such laws in an attempt to promote greater consistency across the continent. However, the CoE's effort fails to square the circle. It attempts to embrace both free expression and also its curtailment through vague and arbitrary definitions and standards. In this process, the thinking developed to support the West's religious hate-speech bans is indecisive, self-contradictory, and sometimes intellectually dishonest. The CoE's best defense of such bans inadvertently supports the argument for their unworkability and undesirability.

The CoE Parliamentary Assembly (PACE) commissioned a report from its consultative commission specifically on "legislation relating to blasphemy, religious insults and hate speech against persons on grounds of their religion."[165] The consequent report, adopted in final form by the prestigious Venice Commission in October 2008, affirmed criminal penalties for "incitement to hatred, including religious hatred." It rejected penalties for blasphemy or religious insult that did not incite others to hate but, for such cases, noted appropriate legal alternatives to criminal sanctions, such as "restraints" or censorship and fines.

It stressed the need to negotiate "the right balance between freedom of religion and freedom of expression." By rejecting the traditional view, asserted by the UN Special Rapporteur on religion, that these two rights are parallel and complementary, it adopted the novel view advocated by the OIC that the right to religious freedom includes the right of religions not to be defamed and the right of religious believers not to feel insulted for their religious beliefs. (Some argue that four recent European Court hate-speech cases marked a turning point in its jurisprudence, establishing that "[a]n unconditional right not to be offended in one's religious feelings does not exist."[166] However, these cases turn on a judicial test entailing the very subjective distinction between acceptable and unacceptable forms of religious criticism rather than a rejection of the test itself or any clear guarantees of free expression.)

The Venice Commission explicitly acknowledged the significance of Europe's changing demographics in requiring attention to these issues, yet its response was markedly conflicted. In an oblique reference to the Danish cartoons and the van Gogh case, it endorsed the use of coercive governmental action to *placate* the "increasing sensitivities" of "certain individuals" who "have reacted violently to criticism of their religion." It directly allowed that such "sensitivities" could be considered by governments "in the short term... when, in order to protect the right of others and to preserve social peace and public order," they must limit freedom of expression. After thereby granting the right of a "heckler's veto," the Commission quickly followed with the hopeful thought that "democratic societies must not become hostage to these sensitivities and freedom of expression must not indiscriminately retreat when facing violent reactions."[167] On the societal level, it offered a prescription of self-censorship or "self-restraint," provided that "it is not prompted by fear of violent reactions, but only by ethical behaviour."

A follow-up resolution by PACE, which promulgated the Venice Commission's views, offered a series of justifications for limiting freedom of expression in religious matters.[168] It insisted that religious groups must tolerate critical public statements and debate about their activities, teachings, and beliefs but added the critical qualification, only insofar as such criticism does not amount to "intentional and gratuitous insults." It stressed that a distinction should be made between "matters which belong to the public domain, and those which belong to the private sphere." It cited approvingly the European Court of Human Rights' distinction between offensive "political speech," which is given legal protection, and offensive speech regarding "intimate personal convictions within the sphere of morals, or, especially religion," which is not. PACE rightly admonished that care should be taken in making such distinctions because prosecutions in this respect are "legion in other countries of the world." Nonetheless, it gave no useful guidance about which matters are which and how its member countries could avoid the legion of dire results.

This distinction between the political and the personal or moral or religious is untenable since virtually every religion has teachings about politics or a substantial bearing on politics. The distinction also depends on specific judgments regarding the statement's worthiness, its audience and range of distribution, and whether the speaker was fulfilling a public role; hence PACE gives an extremely wide opening to prosecutorial and judicial arbitrariness. As the Venice Commission itself was forced to acknowledge, "the boundaries . . . are easily blurred." Far from clarifying matters, these criteria establish contradictory legal rules for different people and even for the same person in different times and places.[169] This both directly and indirectly, through a chilling effect, undermines, among other rights, guarantees to individual freedom of expression, though, to be sure, PACE also acknowledges that freedom of expression is of "vital importance for any democratic society."

The CoE—Europe's most authoritative proponent of religious hate-speech laws—has set aside some basic principles of Western jurisprudence and set forth in their place vague and subjective criteria to guide the adjudication of this new offense. The CoE's inability to adopt a coherent definition of a crime of religious hate speech is the best testament to its inherent subversiveness, not only to individual freedoms, but also to fundamental principles of judicial fairness, due process, and rule of law. The selective and uneven enforcement of these crimes, and the attendant problems of rising sectarian resentments and frustrations that we have seen over the past twenty years, can only be expected to continue.

Closing

The view that ideologically troubling speech should be repressed to prevent social disorder or to protect members of certain groups from "hurt feelings" has converged with pressure to enforce Muslim blasphemy strictures. Viewed by the West as the institutionalization of altruistic ideals, or perhaps of political correctness, hate-speech and related laws are seen differently by the OIC. In the UN, the OIC has interpreted hate-speech and public-order restrictions on expression as bans against religious defamation; and in the West, such laws are increasingly used to enforce restrictions akin to OIC-style blasphemy rules.

Religious hate-speech bans, public-order laws, and the like are well suited as proxies for anti-Islamic blasphemy bans since, like blasphemy rules themselves, they defy definition and can be adapted to suppress negative commentary about virtually anything claiming Islamic legitimacy. According to the CoE and its experts, the crime of religious hate speech can only be identified on a case-by-case basis by the content, manner, and context of the expression at issue. However, unlike pornography, which, with its know-it-when-I see-it standard, also defies legal definition, religious views are far-reaching and include descriptive claims about the nature of the universe, human beings, and society, as well as normative claims about how we should live, what goals we ought to serve, and how we should organize families, communities, and states. The West has traditionally accepted open debate on religious teachings pertaining to philosophical matters such as the nature of right and wrong, social matters such as the place of women, political matters such as the definition of just war and the death penalty, and even the place of religion in society. Any or all of these issues could be placed beyond debate or critique by religious hate-speech laws.

Western hate-speech laws have already been applied in a variety of Islam-related cases. Defendants in trials have been Christian clergy, for theological arguments made in religious seminars; a mainstream conservative commentator, for an article published in a prominent Canadian news magazine; and a French novelist who expressed critical opinions about all monotheistic religions. Others have been targeted by accusations of Islamophobia or "inciting hostility" against Islam and have been put through the ordeal of a formal legal investigation, including a liberal Somali-born Dutch legislator, Danish editors who hoped to open a discussion on the state of freedom of expression in their society, and even British public television broadcasters reporting on radical Muslim preachers. So far, most of these cases have ended in dismissal or acquittal or have been followed by successful appeals. However, even when prosecutions fail, the tremendous costs to defendants of time, money, and reputation, together with rare successful convictions, mean that others have cause to think twice before voicing anything that could be accused of being a criticism of Islam or any other religion.

Feelings of offense—which often is the central standard of this class of speech bans—can be expected to rise and spread to wider areas of speech as political forces strive to create, manipulate, and inflame feelings of outrage. As scholars have documented, Muslim outrage has already been manufactured over irreverent cartoons depicting Islam's Prophet; tomorrow, it could be over women's rights, criminalizing homosexuality, the age of consent for marriage, the comingling in society of men and women, Western toleration of Ahmadis, Baha'is, Jews, converts, and Muslim reformers, or any of the issues discussed in the preceding Muslim countries chapters.

Beyond their chilling effect, these laws result in selective and arbitrary enforcement, turning as they do on subjective judgments by police, prosecutors, juries, and courts about whether the speech at issue concerns politics and "questions of public interest" or is a religious comment, whether it is "social commentary" or "gratuitous insult," whether it is aimed at a religious doctrine or against "intimate personal convictions within the sphere of morals or, especially, religion." We are urged to agree, as the European Court and CoE have repeatedly insisted, that freedom of expression includes the right to make statements that "offend, shock, or disturb" but also that, as the CoE's Secretary General, Terry Davis, explained in 2007, it "should not be regarded as license to offend."[170]

The question of whether someone is liable is now contingent on exceedingly fine and unworkable distinctions of legal and philosophical principle. Religious views are not merely arcane sets of terms, signs, and symbols of no legitimate interest to the nonbeliever. Contrary to the views of the European Court, socially relevant dimensions of religious discourse cannot simply be cordoned off from other elements that merely engage "intimate personal convictions," when believers themselves often view the one as the necessary extension of the other. It is no coincidence that, when Ayaan Hirsi Ali, Lars Hedegaard, and others criticize the oppression of women by Muslim fundamentalists, they also criticize Qur'anic verses pertaining to women that have been cited by these same fundamentalists. If religions include integrated beliefs with potential ramifications in personal, social, and political life, then debating matters of social interest requires the freedom to criticize every aspect of religion. Far from being a fringe issue, the right to express oneself freely and critically on religious questions cuts to the heart of freedom of religion, freedom of speech, and many other freedoms in liberal democracies.

If the wide-reaching and interconnected nature of religious belief makes it difficult to debate the moral teachings of a religion in isolation from its sacred narrative, it also complicates efforts to discuss any religious doctrines without affecting one's impression of that religion's believers. For Mark Steyn, Oriana Fallaci, Brigitte Bardot, and Geert Wilders, their unease about Muslim immigration reflected their negative views of Islam itself. However, in contrast to racism, even a hyperbolic treatment of religion and society is often linked to real debate over beliefs and values. Because religions include practices and doctrines as well as adherents, any effort to restrict negative speech about religious groups involves a perilous effort to disentangle advocacy of hatred from philosophical debate and social commentary.

There is also the problem of raising and then dashing Muslim expectations, which British policy makers recognized and the Venice Commission warned against.[171] Although Western diplomats and lawmakers have rejected bans on "defamation of religions" while still accepting the principle of suppressing hate speech against persons, in many domestic and international disputes, it is perceived defamation of Islam itself that has aroused most ire within Muslim communities. It is vital to note that the major global conflagrations over "insults to Islam," including the *Satanic Verses* affair, the response to *Newsweek*'s Qur'an desecration story, Pope Benedict XVI's Regensburg speech, the Danish cartoon controversy, and Wilders's *Fitna*, were centered on perceived blasphemy against Islam as a religion, rather than on any strictly personal insult. Many committed Muslims, as well as members of other religions, are far more concerned about criticism of their religion and its sacred symbols than they are of any criticism of themselves personally. If we accept the distinction between allegations against religions and allegations against persons, it is the former that has led to most controversy and outcry.

Amid inflamed passions surrounding a prominent case such as the *Jyllands-Posten* cartoons, those offended are unlikely to be mollified by even the most sober and well-reasoned arguments stressing the cartoons' function as social commentary or by the intention of the paper's editors in publishing them or (least of all) by the fact that the publication targeted a "religious figure" rather than Muslims as a group.

The selective policing and prosecuting of such crimes, caused in part by their vagueness, also leads to the criticism that officials, and the laws themselves, are biased when they deal with particularly "sensitive" groups or questions. When the Arab European League published a Holocaust cartoon in response to the Danish cartoons, it was prosecuted, but the Danes were not. When Finnish politician Jussi Halla-aho made offensive statements about Somalis in deliberate and explicit mimicry of another writer's offensive statements about Finns, he was the only one investigated.[172] This policy of criminalizing religious hate speech does not, as policy makers hope, allay social tensions; rather, it simply lurches from a debate about issues to an even more fraught and convoluted debate about what issues can be debated. The judiciary becomes the new battleground for competing religious, social, and political views, and it cripples the freedom to express views honestly and without fear.

Attempts by the state forcibly to regulate the content of speech involving Islam, under either blasphemy bans or, more likely given their rising popularity among Western policy makers, hate-speech laws, will prove futile in societies with growing social pluralism, in which people will inevitably be exposed to views that contradict and criticize their own. As comedian Rowan Atkinson warned, such laws merely produce "a veneer of tolerance concealing a snakepit of unaired and unchallenged views."[173] Even this veneer would be produced only at the expense of the two fundamental freedoms most critical to addressing the challenges confronting Western societies: freedom of expression and freedom of religion, "offensive" as their exercise so often is.

13

Enforcement by Violence and Intimidation

In 2004, Mimount Bousakla, a Belgian senator and the daughter of Moroccan immigrants, was forced into hiding after threats to "ritually slaughter her." She moved to a secret location and was given around-the-clock police protection. A critic of both women's roles in Muslim communities and fundamentalist influences in Belgian mosques, her book Couscous with Belgian Fries *condemned forced marriages. Shortly before the threats, she had harshly criticized an official Belgian Muslim group, the Muslim Executive, for failing to denounce the murder of Theo van Gogh. On November 19, 2004, police arrested a Belgian convert to Islam who confessed to making threats against her.*[1]

In late September 2006, French philosophy teacher Robert Redeker was forced into hiding after publishing an article, "In the Face of Islamist Intimidation, What Must the Free World Do?" The article, written in response to widespread Muslim anger at Pope Benedict XVI's Regensburg address, argued that "[w]hereas Jewish and Christian rites forsake violence and remove its legitimacy, Islam is a religion that, in its very sacred texts, as much as in some of its everyday rites, exalts violence and hatred." Several people responded to Redeker's linking of Islam to violence by threatening to kill him and his family. An Al-Qaeda-linked Web site, Al Hesbah, published his cell phone number and home address, complete with directions for any enterprising assassin. Sheikh Yusuf al-Qaradawi, who enjoys one of the widest audiences of any Islamic preacher in the world, denounced Redeker on Al Jazeera. Egypt and Tunisia banned the Le Figaro *issue containing his article. The French Interior Ministry treated the threats seriously and gave Redeker police protection.*

Redeker noted that, since he was in hiding and couldn't go to work, "the Islamists have succeeded in punishing me on the territory of the republic as if I were guilty of a crime of opinion." The prime minister, Dominique de Villepin, denounced the threats, saying, "Everyone has the right to express his views freely," but added, "of course while respecting others." The mayor of Saint-Orens-de-Gameville, where Redeker worked, the head of his school, the two main French teachers' unions, and human rights groups distanced themselves from him. The education minister expressed an amorphous "solidarity" but stressed that government employees should "show prudence and moderation in all circumstances."[2]

French Muslim leader Dalil Boubakeur criticized the threats. Tariq Ramadan, with his customary equivocation, said that Redeker "is free to write what he likes in Le Figaro, *but he must know what he wanted—he signed a stupidly provocative text." In October, more than twenty French intellectuals called for more government assistance to Redeker since he was having financial difficulty due to having to live in hiding. In 2009, he remained in hiding under the protection of France's domestic intelligence services.[3]*

In April 2008, comedian Ben Elton said that he thought the BBC was "too scared to allow jokes about Islam" and that he was talked out of merely invoking the proverb, "If the mountain won't come to Mohammed, Mohammed must go to the mountain." He added, "The BBC will let vicar gags pass but they would not let imam gags pass. They might pretend that it's, you know, something to do with their moral sensibilities, but it isn't. It's because they're scared." In his view, this was also bad for Muslims: "I'm quite certain that the average Muslim does not want everybody going around thinking, 'We've just got to pretend you don't exist because we're scared that somebody who claims to represent you will threaten to kill us." While the BBC denied the charges, several days later, BBC chief Mark Thompson warned of "a growing nervousness about discussion about Islam and its relationship to the traditions and values of British and Western society as a whole."[4]

Introductory Remarks

In the West, bans on speech perceived as critical of Islam not only threaten legal consequences, but also may be enforced extrajudicially by vigilantes or terrorists. Muslims and non-Muslims alike are subject to intimidation and violence. Those who raise questions about immigration or leave Islam or promote tolerance, critical thought, and human rights within Muslim communities can face very real risks. Both the threat of violence and the fear it engenders in such cases are becoming widespread in the West.

Intimidation and violence in connection with art or films concerning Islam are on the rise. Among the most notorious instances was the November 2004 murder of filmmaker Theo van Gogh, which precipitated a wave of religious violence in the Netherlands as well as a round of soul-searching in Europe. But there are less publicized cases. Too often galleries, media outlets, artists, and performers seem to anticipate Islamist threats and preemptively censor themselves accordingly, often in a manner differing dramatically from their treatment of works that might offend other religious groups. In many cases, censorship takes place without any complaints by Muslims. Indeed, in some almost comical cases, Muslim groups have denied that the censored matter is even offensive to them.

Objects of intimidation and threats of violence range from members of far-right parties to clergymen to philosophers. They include those who made controversial remarks once to those who make a living by criticizing Islam.

Ironically, Britain's left-wing politician George Galloway, a radical opponent of the Iraq war and an advocate of British Islamists, was threatened with death by Islamist extremists for being a "false prophet" and for campaigning in British elections in 2005.[5]

While people of any religious affiliation face danger for purportedly insulting Islam, those born into Muslim families who do so, even in a mild way, are particularly at risk. Those who advocate a more open version of Islam, especially one including greater rights for women, are commonly targeted as blasphemers and may be accused of apostasy, even if they call themselves Muslims. Sometimes Muslim girls and women who don't follow prescribed rules in dress and behavior have been victimized, even by honor killings.[6] Those who actually leave Islam face particular peril. Former Muslims who identify themselves as atheists and agnostics have formed groups in an attempt to combat the violent enforcement of Islamist apostasy prohibitions. Meanwhile, converts from Islam to Christianity or other faiths face problems ranging from social pressure to deadly physical violence.

The Murder of Theo Van Gogh

The brutal murder in 2004 of Dutch filmmaker Theo van Gogh in Amsterdam focused Western attention on the potential consequences of "insulting Islam" in a way unparalleled since the 1989 fatwa against Salman Rushdie. This time, however, the perpetrator was not a foreign government but a member of the Netherlands' own immigrant population.

Van Gogh was a well-known provocateur who offended people of every political and religious stripe and who considered many Muslims immigrants a threat to "atheists, Jews, gays, women and nonbelievers." One of his projects was collaborating with Ayaan Hirsi Ali on *Submission*, a graphic film depicting four women, who wore transparent garments and had Qur'anic verses about women written on their skin, speaking of the suffering inflicted on them by men.[7]

On November 2, 2004, while he was cycling near central Amsterdam, van Gogh was shot several times at close range and then nearly decapitated by a twenty-six-year-old Dutch-Moroccan. The killer, Mohammed Bouyeri, then used the knife to stab a note into van Gogh's chest.[8] One observer reportedly shouted at Bouyeri, "You can't do that!" The killer responded, "Oh, yes I can...now you know what's coming for you." The note was titled "Open Letter to Hirsi Ali," threatening her with death, signed in the name of an Islamic terrorist group, and quoting at length from the Qur'an. Its author claimed that Hirsi Ali "terrorizes Islam" and declared in capital letters, "Ayaan Hirsi Ali, you will smash yourself on Islam!"[9] Bouyeri then started a shootout with the police in hopes of dying a martyr. He also left an article predicting the replacement of the Dutch parliament with a sharia court and stating, "It will not be long before the knights of Allah march into the Hague."

In a later recording, a man who had visited Bouyeri prior to the murder declared: "we slaughtered a lamb in the traditional Islamic fashion. From now on, this will be the punishment for anyone in this land who challenges and insults Allah and his messengers."[10]

Bouyeri was a second-generation immigrant raised in a Moroccan area of Amsterdam. By mid-2003, he had withdrawn from Dutch life at large, fallen under the influence of the radical Syrian preacher Abou Khaled, and become the leader of the "Hofstad network" of Muslim youths.[11] At his public hearing in late January 2005, he came to court holding a Qur'an; he praised Allah and Muhammad and confessed to the murder. He told the court he had been "motivated by the law that commands me to cut off the head of anyone who insults Allah and his prophet." This also, in his interpretation, forbade him from living "in this country, or in any country where free speech is allowed." He told van Gogh's mother, present in the court, "I can't feel for you because I think you're a non-believer." He went on to say, "If I ever get free, I would do it again." He also stated that "the story that I felt insulted as a Moroccan, or because he called me a goat f****r, that is all nonsense. I acted out of faith." In July 2005, he was convicted of van Gogh's murder—as well as the attempted murder of police officers and bystanders—and sentenced to life imprisonment.[12]

The murder shocked a country known for its tolerance. The Dutch prime minister called van Gogh "a champion of the freedom of speech." Amsterdam's mayor, Job Cohen, who had been harshly criticized in van Gogh's final column, declared, "The freedom of speech is a foundation of our society and that foundation was tampered with today ... Theo van Gogh picked fights with many people, myself included, but that is a right in this country." On the night of the murder, 20,000 people turned out to demonstrate against the murder. On November 10, van Gogh's funeral drew thousands more, many carrying pro-free speech banners.[13]

Some Dutch Muslim organizations, such as the Islam and Citizenship Foundation, sent delegations to the gathering to show their opposition to the murder. The European Arab League's Dutch branch, which had denounced *Submission*, condemned the murder and noted, "shots and death threats are not the way to make people think differently." UMMON, an umbrella group of Moroccan mosques, issued a statement in support of free speech and called for imams to include this message in their Friday sermons.[14] However, Zahid Mukhtar, a spokesman of Norway's Islamic Council, claimed that he could "understand" why some Muslims might become angry enough at van Gogh to kill him.[15] When an artist in Rotterdam painted a street mural containing the words "thou shalt not kill" in Dutch, along with the date of van Gogh's murder, a local mosque leader complained to police that the commandment was "racist." The police, on orders of the mayor, sandblasted the mural. A television reporter who stood at the scene in protest was arrested, and police destroyed his film. During November, extremists of all types engaged in violence, and there were twenty attacks on churches, mosques, and Muslim schools.

As for the film *Submission* itself, in January 2005, a planned screening at a film festival in Rotterdam was canceled on the recommendation of the police after the producer received death threats. The producer acknowledged "yielding to terror," explaining, "But I'm not a politician or an antiterrorist police officer; I'm a film producer." In his view, van Gogh's murderer had succeeded in his effort "to frighten the country."[16]

Arts and Media

Among the arts, other targets of threats have included the plays of Voltaire and fifteenth-century Italian frescoes, as well as contemporary European works. Some were by artists of Muslim background. While Sikhs, Hindus, Christians, and others have also occasionally responded violently to controversial art, intimidation has been most widespread regarding perceived insults to Islam.[17]

In June 2001, an Italian Muslim group called for a fresco, *The Last Judgment*, painted by fifteenth-century artist Giovanni de Modena in the San Petronio basilica in Bologna, to be removed or destroyed because it depicted Muhammad in hell. The Union of Italian Muslims, headed by activist Adel Smith, sent letters to Bologna's archbishop and even to the pope demanding its removal, declaring it to be "an even graver offence...than that caused by Salman Rushdie's *The Satanic Verses*." Smith even called for Italian schools in immigrant areas to stop teaching Dante, who, in his *Inferno*, had placed Muhammad in hell. Other Muslims rejected Smith's views. Nabil Baioni of the Islamic Cultural Centre in Bologna commented, "I think this Smith represents only himself."[18] The fresco remains in place but has been subject to violent plots that have been thwarted by police.[19]

In 2005, Britain's Tate Gallery refused to showcase a piece by artist John Latham, titled *God Is Great*, after Islamic scholars suggested that it was offensive because it used a Qur'an, along with the holy books of Judaism and Christianity, each partially embedded in a standing piece of glass. Gallery director Stephen Deuchar stated that, after the July 7 Tube bombings, the gallery worried that the sculpture "might be considered willfully provocative" and would invite some form of attack.[20]

When a French municipal cultural center in Saint-Genis-Pouilly scheduled a reading of Voltaire's play *Fanaticism, or Mahomet the Prophet*, which is an attack on religious intolerance, some French Muslim groups demanded its cancellation. The show took place in December 2005 despite a minor riot in which a car was set on fire. The mayor defended free speech and thought the increasingly frequent controversies were due to the fact that "for a long time we have not confirmed our convictions, so lots of people think they can contest them." The outcome in this case contrasted with another in Geneva in 1993, where a planned production of the same play was canceled following Muslim complaints.[21]

A September 2006 production of Mozart's *Idomeneo* at the Berlin Deutsche Oper was initially canceled because of fear of violence by Muslim extremists.

Director Hans Neuenfels had updated the show's final scene, in which the title character refuses to sacrifice to the gods, to include the severed heads of Muhammad, Jesus, and Buddha, along with that of Poseidon. The revised staging drew audience protests at its December 2003 premiere but was only canceled after German security officials told the Oper's general manager, Kirsten Harms, that there would be "an incalculable security risk to the public and employees" if the production were staged. When the director refused to alter or cut this scene, Harms canceled the show. After government officials and German Muslim representatives criticized this censorship, the opera was performed without disturbance. The production opened December 18 with a police presence, security gates with electronic scanners, and a memo to opera employees on what measures to take in event of bomb threats.[22]

At Berlin's Galerie Nord in February 2008, violence was threatened over an art exhibition that included a poster depicting Islam's most important shrine, the Ka'aba, and bearing the words "stupid stone." The exhibition was temporarily closed until security measures could be put in place.[23] Also in 2008, the Hans Otto Theater in Potsdam planned a stage adaption of Salman Rushdie's *Satanic Verses*. Its director and coauthor Uwe Laufenberg said, "It is time for the Muslim world to say exactly what it finds so provocative about this book," and hoped his production would help shift attention to what was actually in the novel as opposed to a vague belief that it was offensive. While some Muslims expressed regret, the head of the Central Council of Muslims in Germany said that "freedom of opinion and the arts is of a high value and most Muslims are against censorship," but he also noted that "offences against what is sacred in a religion is not something we value." Others were less temperate. A Turkish actor who had planned to take part in the play, Oktay Khan, quit after receiving death threats.[24] In January 2010, the Metropolitan Museum of Art in New York quietly pulled various depictions of Muhammad from its Islamic collection.[25]

The publishing world is also suppressing Islam-related material. As mentioned, in 2009, Yale University Press, in consultation with Yale University, insisted on omitting all illustrations of Muhammad from its "definitive" scholarly book on the 2005–6 Danish cartoon crisis by Jytte Klausen. In addition to any reproduction of the *Jyllands-Posten* page featuring the cartoons, it censored Gustave Doré's nineteenth-century illustration of the Muhammad in hell scene from Dante's *Inferno* and an Ottoman print of the prophet. The university press director, John Donatich, claimed that the requested recommendation from experts (including diplomats, scholars, and counterterrorism officials) to pull the drawings had been "overwhelming and unanimous." A formal press statement highlighted the refusal of mainstream American media outlets to reprint the cartoons during the initial controversy and noted that "republication of the cartoons—not just the original printing of them in Denmark—has repeatedly resulted in violence around the world." It cited UN officials Ibrahim Gambari and Joseph Verner Reed, as well as former U.S. Director of National Intelligence John Negroponte, as warning that inclusion of the cartoons would lead to violence. Gambari stated, "You can count on violence if any illustration of the Prophet is published."

However, Muslim scholar Reza Aslan withdrew a statement of praise he had offered for the book upon learning of Yale's decision, which he deemed "idiotic." Notably, the decision, which author Klausen agreed to only reluctantly, seemed to rest on assumptions directly contradicting the thesis of her book, which argues that the cartoon crisis had its origins in conflicting political interests rather than in a spontaneous outpouring of popular outrage.[26] In an interview with Klausen about this self-censorship, the British watchdog group Index on Censorship also self-censored illustrations of the cartoons, with an explanation that it did so out of fear for the safety of its employees and associates.[27]

In October 2009, the Droste Publishing Company in Germany canceled the publication of a mystery novel about Islamic honor killings. The company said it did not want to anger the Muslim population nor any other religious group in the future. Gabriele Brinkmann, the author of *To Whom Honor Is Due*, refused to remove passages that might be offensive to Muslims.[28] In the same month, the city of Frankfurt canceled a Muhammad look-a-like contest at the Frankfurt Book Fair by the German satirical magazine *Titanic*. Some Muslims had complained and promised that the contest would incite bigger riots than the Danish cartoon.[29]

Several incidents involve works that do not specifically refer to Islam. When Terrence McNally portrayed Jesus Christ and his followers as homosexuals in his play, *Corpus Christi*, he probably anticipated outrage from Christians, of which there was—unsurprisingly—a great deal. But it is unlikely that he foresaw the death fatwa he received in October 1999 from a Muslim group, "The Shari'ah Court of the UK." The court's supporters handed out copies of the fatwa outside the London theater where the play had opened. It was signed by Sheikh Omar Bakri Muhammad, who criticized the Church of England for not seeking to suppress the film, and even stated, "It is blasphemy for them not to take action." Since Muslims consider Jesus a Messenger from God, he asserted that those who insult Allah and the messengers of God "must understand it is a crime." The fatwa declared that McNally "will be arrested and there will be capital punishment." The sheikh further asserted that McNally could escape the death sentence by converting to Islam, whereas, "if he simply repented he would still be killed—but his family would be cared for by the Islamic state."[30]

In March 2006, in Paris, some Muslim youths threatened the owners of a café in their neighborhood with violence if they did not remove cartoons hung on the walls as part of an exhibition "Neither god nor god." The cartoons mocked all religions and did not include any depictions of Muhammad. Nonetheless, some local boys between ten and twelve years old accused the café owners of being racists and tried to smash the pictures with sticks and iron rods. Subsequently, the café received a visit from a slightly older group, who, as one owner said, "warned us that if we didn't take the cartoons down they would call in the Muslim Brothers who would burn the café down. They kept saying: 'This is our home. You cannot act like this here.'" The owners refused to remove the cartoons, which they believed would have been "surrender," but instead covered those that had drawn the youths' ire with sheets of paper bearing the word "censored" so it would still be possible to view them by lifting the paper. They also lodged a complaint with the police.[31]

In October 2006, London's Whitechapel Art Gallery removed erotically themed paintings by German surrealist Hans Bellmer the day before the opening of a new exhibition, reportedly in order "to not shock the population of the Whitechapel neighborhood, which is partly Muslim."[32]

Threats consistently pursue those who do focus on Islam, sometimes even in a sympathetic manner. In December 2000, a theater director in Rotterdam, Gerrit Timmers, planned to stage a play on the life of Aisha, one of Muhammad's wives. His Muslim actors declared that, although they would like to participate, they could not do so due to fear of retaliation by local Islamists: "We are enthusiastic about the play, but fear reigns."[33] In the United States, Random House at the last minute rejected the historical romance novel about Aisha, *Jewel of Medina*, by American writer Sherry Jones. They did so to protect "the safety of the author, employees of Random House, booksellers and anyone else who would be involved in distribution and sale of the novel." The cancellation came after a Middle East Studies professor, consulted by the company, warned Muslims of the possible publication of an offensive novel and also warned Random House of a likely hostile reaction by Muslims. In September 2008, three men were arrested and subsequently sentenced for attempted arson of the home of Martin Rynja, whose British publishing company, Gibson Square, had agreed to carry the book.[34]

There are other examples in the United States of censorship by threat of violence. The comedy cartoon show *South Park* declined to show an image of the Muslim prophet dressed in a bear suit, though it had mocked figures from other religions. In response, Molly Norris, a cartoonist for the *Seattle Weekly*, suggested that to counter such intimidation maybe there should be an "Everybody Draw Mohammed Day!" She withdrew the suggestion and implied that she had been joking; but after she had received many death threats, including some from Al-Qaeda, the FBI advised her that she should go into hiding. She has given up her job, moved, and changed her name. *Seattle Weekly*'s chief editor, Mark Fefer, wrote that her cartoons would no longer be in the paper "because there is no more Molly."[35] On October 3, 2010, about 800 newspapers in the United States refused to run the "Non Sequitur" cartoon drawn for that day run by regular daily cartoonist Wiley Miller, and instead substituted another cartoon by Wiley. The cartoon that they refused to run contained no depiction of Muhammad, but merely a bucolic scene with the caption, "Where's Muhammad?" The *Washington Post* said that it did not run the cartoon because it might upset Muslim readers and seem a "deliberate provocation."[36] Meanwhile, on October 20, 2010, Zachary Chesser, a young convert to Islam, pleaded guilty in Federal Court to supporting Somali terrorists and threatening the creators of *South Park* and was subsequently sentenced to twenty-five years in prison.[37]

Several artists of Muslim background have also faced serious danger in the West. In January 2005, Rachid Ben Ali, a Dutch-Moroccan artist, was forced into hiding after his satirical work denouncing Islamist violence, exhibited by an Amsterdam art museum, drew death threats. His paintings, which depicted suicide bombers and "hate imams," were featured in an exhibition that was opened with a powerful call by Ahmed Aboutaleb, a Muslim politician in the Netherlands, to defend free expression.[38]

Iranian artist Sooreh Hera (a pseudonym) was the target of a fatwa published in Iranian newspapers. She received a number of death threats and could not attend an art festival featuring her own work. Safety concerns arose after she displayed photographs depicting gay Iranian exiles wearing masks and lewdly mimicking Muhammad and his son-in-law, the caliph Ali. In 2008, two invitations for Hera to exhibit were withdrawn for political reasons. An Amsterdam art festival finally agreed to exhibit her work, but with the stipulation that the most controversial pictures be omitted. The sponsoring gallery's director had to obtain police protection due to threats.[39]

These controversies demonstrate that not all Muslims endorse the suppression of productions they view as offensive by fiat or threat. Also, most protests have been peaceful. Nonetheless, intimidation from extremists is quashing artists' appetite for criticizing Islam. In November 2007, British artist Grayson Perry, who had previously not hesitated to target Christianity in his work, stated, "The reason I haven't gone all out attacking Islamism in my art is because I feel real fear that someone will slit my throat." Tim Marlow, exhibitions director at a London art gallery, said Perry had hit upon "something that's there but very few people have explicitly admitted. Institutions, museums and galleries are probably doing most of the censorship." In July 2008, playwright Simon Gray charged that National Theatre director Nicholas Hytner, who had drawn ire from Christians by staging *Jerry Springer: The Opera*, was nonetheless afraid of staging any shows that could be deemed offensive to Muslims. The director of the movie *2012* also admitted that fear prevented him from showing the destruction of Muslim symbols along with St. Peter's Basilica and other religious sites in a scene depicting the end of the world.[40]

Islam and Critical Commentary

Pim Fortuyn

In 2002, Dutch politician Pim Fortuyn was assassinated by a non-Muslim offended by Fortuyn's criticism of Islam. Although frequently described as a right-winger due to his concerns about Muslim immigration, Fortuyn was an openly gay former sociologist who feared that Muslim immigration would undermine the Netherlands' liberal society, in part through crimes against gays and the repression of women. He sought to restrict immigration and called Islam a "backward religion" but vehemently rejected any comparison between himself and figures such as French National Front leader Jean Marie Le Pen. His party, the Lijst Pim Fortuyn, rapidly gained ground in national polls until, on May 6, 2002, Fortuyn was murdered. He was shot repeatedly in a daytime assault by thirty-three-year-old Volkert van der Graaf. During the trial, the killer claimed that he had acted in order "to protect Muslims," whom he claimed Fortuyn used as political "scapegoats."[41]

Ayaan Hirsi Ali

Two prominent Dutch critics of Islam were forced into hiding after van Gogh's slaying: Ayaan Hirsi Ali and Geert Wilders. Both, from different perspectives, are given to sweeping declarations that Islam threatens Western freedoms, and both have been bombarded with threats by radicals who seem determined to prove them right. Hirsi Ali, van Gogh's collaborator on *Submission*, was an immigrant who embraced the liberties of her adopted homeland. The daughter of a Somali opposition leader, she lived in exile with her family in Saudi Arabia, Ethiopia, and then Kenya, for a time falling under the influence of fundamentalists. In 1992, she found asylum in the Netherlands and took menial jobs while learning Dutch. She then became a translator for Dutch social workers working with immigrants, where she encountered abundant reports of domestic abuse. She enrolled at a university to study political science and in 2001 was hired by a Labor Party think tank. After 9/11, she called for an "Islamic Voltaire" and, in 2002, declared herself an atheist. She criticized Dutch multiculturalism and particularly urged the government to protect Muslim women from violence and to stop supporting Muslim organizations that practice gender segregation.

Before long, her father received messages from Somalis in Europe, warning that she would be killed if she continued. Radical Islamist websites also began posting death threats. She responded, "I'm talking from the inside…It's seen as treason. I'm considered an apostate and that's worse than an atheist." After she said on Dutch national television that Islam could in some ways be considered a "backward religion," the threats intensified. In 2002, she was forced to flee temporarily to the United States. In January 2003, Hirsi Ali became a member of the Dutch parliament for the free-market VVD party, where she concentrated on Muslim women's issues, including better enforcement of laws against genital mutilation and "honor killings." She hoped to "confront the European elite's self-image as tolerant while under their noses women are living like slaves." Critics called her an "Enlightenment fundamentalist," and threats against her led Parliament to adopt new security measures.[42]

Shortly after the August 2004 showing of *Submission*, Hirsi Ali began living under around-the-clock protection. She spent six days in secret locations and then, told to leave the country for her own safety, briefly went again to the United

States.[43] In January 2005, authorities uncovered a plot to kill her; nonetheless, she came out of hiding and, with bodyguards, returned to Parliament.[44] That month, two rappers were convicted by a Dutch court for writing a song that spoke of wishing to break her neck. In March, after being kept in hotels and on a naval base for her own protection and with her suggestions for alternative housing repeatedly turned down by officials, she was provided with a safe house.[45]

She continued to raise integration issues, calling for drastic measures such as the closure of Muslim schools.[46] During the peak of the Danish cartoons crisis in February 2006, she gave a lecture in Berlin, "The Right to Offend," charging that many in Europe are afraid to criticize Islam. She decried the cynicism with which "evil governments like Saudi Arabia stage 'grassroots' movements to boycott Danish milk and yoghurt, while they would mercilessly crush a grassroots movement fighting for the right to vote." She also criticized many Islamic teachings on the role of women, the execution of apostates and homosexuals, and punishments for theft and adultery, and she maintained that despite the many peaceful Muslims, it was "a hard-line Islamist movement" within Islam that threatened freedoms.

The Dutch prime minister, Jan Peter Balkenende, said he didn't "have much use" for her comments, and, despite her atheist and feminist stances, she drew heavy criticism from the multiculturalist left and was accused of fueling radicalization in a polarized political atmosphere.[47] In Spring 2006, her neighbors won a court case to evict her for fear of a terrorist attack. In May, she was informed by the immigration minister, Rita Verdonk, of her own party, that her Dutch citizenship was being revoked because she had filed false information on her 1992 asylum application.[48] Although Parliament voted to allow her accelerated naturalization, in September, she left for the American Enterprise Institute in Washington, D.C.[49] Unable to receive protection from the U.S. government as a foreign national, she began living in hiding under privately funded protection.[50]

In February 2008, French philosopher Bernard Henri-Levy told her that her case's connection with freedom of opinion made her a good candidate for citizenship and protection in France. But when she traveled to Paris, Parliament rejected her application. The French Human Rights Minister, Rama Yada, with the backing of President Sarkozy, supported the creation of an EU-based protection fund for victims like Hirsi Ali. However, as of 2011, she continued to live, mainly in isolation, in the United States.[51]

Geert Wilders

Geert Wilders was a controversial—and threatened—figure in the Netherlands even before the international uproar over *Fitna*, discussed in chapter 10. After Wilders called Yasser Arafat a terrorist in October 2003, a man was convicted for writing on an Islamist website that "Wilders should be punished by death for his fascist statements on Islam and the Palestinian cause." In the month following the van Gogh slaying, he received some thirty death threats and was forced into hiding. One online video promised a reward of seventy-two virgins in paradise for his beheading.[52] In 2006, Wilders told an interviewer, "Videos on Islamic websites show my picture and name to the sound of what appears to be knives cutting through flesh while a voiceover says I will be beheaded."[53] However, he declared that if he went silent, "the people who use violence, bullets, and knives to get their way will win."[54]

By 2005, he was moving each night to a different safe house, under the constant protection of bodyguards. He could appear in public only at sessions of Parliament. After living in a cell at the high-security Zeist prison for several months, Wilders finally moved to a permanent safe house in early March 2005. The Dutch government, apparently anticipating a recurring problem, purchased several similar houses to accommodate politicians facing future death threats.[55]

Wilders's proposals themselves raise issues of intolerance. He issued sweeping calls to "stop the Islamization of the Netherlands. That means no more mosques, no more schools, no more imams."[56] He has sought to require imams to preach only in Dutch and to prevent foreign imams from preaching in the Netherlands at all. He has called for the government to pay Muslim immigrants to leave the country. In August 2007, he proposed an all-out ban on the sale, distribution, and use of the Qur'an—at home, in mosques, and for any purpose other than academic research. He charged that Islam's sacred text, which he compared to *Mein Kampf*, "incites hatred and killing" and was to blame for attacks on the founder of an ex-Muslims' group. Claiming to know that the proposal would never make it through the Dutch legislature, Wilders said he only intended it as a warning against using the Qur'an to legitimize violence.[57]

Wilders describes Islam as a "backward religion," "totally incompatible" with democracy, but insists that he makes "a distinction between the religion and the people."[58] He acknowledges the existence of a "majority of moderate Muslims in the Netherlands" who "have nothing to do with terrorism" and maintains that his rage is not aimed at them but at "the growing minority of radical Muslims" who follow a "fascistic" ideology. Toward the latter, he advocates closing known jihadist mosques, revoking the Dutch citizenship of radical imams, and arresting extremists under surveillance by security personnel.[59]

In a setting marked by growing Islamist radicalism and a dearth of more temperate figures willing to address the problem, Wilders has enjoyed political success. He left the liberal VVD party to form the Freedom Party, which won nine seats in the 2006 elections and the second-largest number of seats in the Netherlands' 2009 European parliament elections. In early 2010, he was put on trial by the Dutch government for hate speech against Islam, yet in the June 2010 Dutch elections, the Freedom Party received the third-highest number of votes. He was acquitted of hate speech charges in 2011.

Runar Sogaard

In April 2005, Norwegian Pentecostal preacher Runar Sogaard received death threats and required police protection after the distribution of CDs of one of his sermons, in which he criticized the Islamic prophet. Preaching in March in Stockholm, he made fun of several religions, including Christianity, and called Muhammad "a confused pedophile." Hundreds of Muslims demonstrated outside the church. The leader of Sweden's imam council, in an apparent threat, "demanded that Christian communities repudiate Sogaard's remarks, and promised that Sweden would avoid the ugly scenes experienced in Holland." One Islamist stated to a Swedish paper that "even if I see Runar while he has major police protection I will shoot him to death."[60] An Islamist website of "the Army of Ansar Al-Sunnah in Sweden," which claimed to have established a local terror training camp, vowed to "capture and punish" Sogaard.[61]

Alain Finkielkraut

Far milder comments than Wilders's or Sogaard's have evoked violent responses. During the French urban riots of 2005, French Jewish intellectual Alain Finkielkraut was threatened for stating that the violence had an "ethno-religious character." In a November 18 interview with the Israeli paper *Ha'aretz*, he pointed out that immigrants of religious backgrounds other than Muslim, who faced similar socioeconomic difficulties, were not rioting. He argued that the riots were not a mere response to French racism or simply targeted at "a former colonial power" but were rather "against France, with its Christian or Judeo-Christian tradition."

On November 23, *Le Monde* published an article that cast Finkielkraut as a bigot against Arabs and Muslims. The Movement Against Racism (MRAP) brought racism charges against him, and he received threats of physical harm. The following day, *Le Monde* quoted him saying: "The person portrayed by the [*Le Monde*] article would cause me to feel disdain and even disgust for him." MRAP interpreted this as an apology, and the legal action was dropped. Nonetheless he was "forced to remain cloistered at home." France's then–Interior Minister, Nicolas Sarkozy, stood by Finkielkraut, noting, "If there is so much criticism of him, it might be because he says things that are correct."[62]

Bishop Michael Nazir-Ali

In January 2008, the mere mention of Muslim violence led to threats of yet more violence. The Anglican bishop of Rochester, the Rt. Rev. Michael Nazir-Ali, warned that isolation and extremism in immigrant communities had created "no-go areas" for non-Muslims. He called this intimidation "the other side of the coin to far-Right intimidation" and criticized secularist and multiculturalist policies that had undermined the establishment of the Church of England and called for Britain to turn back to its Christian heritage.[63] Ibrahim Mogra of the Muslim Council of Britain denounced the bishop's comments, which he called "irresponsible for a man of (the bishop's) position."[64]

The son of a Pakistani convert from Islam to Christianity, Nazir-Ali became a bishop in Pakistan but fled that country after receiving death threats. Now in the United Kingdom, also due to death threats, he and his family require police protection: "It was a threat not just to me, but to my family. I took it seriously, so did the police."[65] He has also spoken out on the predicament of Muslim converts to Christianity in the United Kingdom and left his bishopric in 2009 to work full time on defending religious freedom.

Other Examples

Some actual or threatened violence over religious disputes involves a group of Middle Eastern (mainly Egyptian) Islamists who maintain an Arabic website, Barsomyat.com, dedicated to tracking Christian participants in religious arguments with Muslims via PalTalk, an Internet chat service. The site has featured pictures, street addresses, and death threats, all under a banner that showed a sheep's throat being cut.[66]

In March 2009, the Rev. Noble Samuel, a U.K. Christian minister who hosts an Asian gospel TV show, was assaulted in his car by three men who tore his cross off, seized his laptop and Bible, and attempted to smash his head against the steering wheel. Samuel said they threatened to break his legs if he continued broadcasting, which he did nonetheless. Although he emphasized that his show was not "confrontational," Samuel reported having arguments with angry Muslim callers before the attack. The Muslim owner of Samuel's television station condemned the attack on air while Samuel broadcast, and police ruled the attack a case of "faith hate."[67]

Scholars face dangers for doing historical research on Islamic texts. One scholar of ancient Semitic languages in Germany argues that the Qur'an has been mistranslated for centuries and is derived from Christian Aramaic texts misinterpreted by Islamic scholars. Even for such scholarship in obscure journals, for his own protection, he now publishes under the pseudonym Christoph Luxenberg.[68]

Muslim Reformers

Intimidation is a factor within Muslim communities. Some who have merely made a simple remark, and others who have advocated social, political, or theological change have been threatened by extremists. Many of those most threatened are women working in their own communities.

Ahmed Subhy Mansour, Saad Eddin Ibrahim, and Others

On April 10, 2006, a manifesto against Muslim reformers and their families in the West was published online by an Egyptian group, giving them three days to "announce their repentance and disavow their writings...and to repent their support of the countries of unbelief and their rulers." Otherwise, "[W]e will hunt them in every place and every time. They are not far from the swords of the righteous, they are closer to our swords than we to our shoes, they are under our eyes and ears (surveillance) day and night, we are totally aware of their hiding places, residences, schools of their sons, and the times when their wives are alone at home..."[69] Targets included the exiled cleric Ahmed Subhy Mansour of the Quranist group, whose imprisonment in his native Egypt is described in chapter 4; his former colleague, noted Egyptian human rights and democracy activist Saad Eddin Ibrahim; and outspoken Syrian-American ex-Muslim Wafa Sultan, described below. These and many others have continued to speak out, despite a steady stream of anonymous threats. One topic particularly fraught with danger for individuals born into Muslim communities is the position of women. Efforts to defend the human rights of Muslim women are frequently denounced as a form of "insulting Islam," as the following cases demonstrate.

Seyran Ates

In September 2006, Seyran Ates, a Turkish-German lawyer who worked with Muslim women suffering abuse, gave up her Berlin practice after repeated threats. She had been the target of a vilification campaign in a Turkish newspaper in 2005 and has requested, but was denied, police protection. In June 2006, the ex-husband of a client attacked both the client and Ates outside the court. Ates, herself born into a family of Muslim extremists, has criticized ethnic Germans who, in the name of multiculturalism, turn a blind eye to domestic violence and forced marriages. She stated, "We must finally stop allowing human rights violations in Muslim parallel societies to be shrugged off with appeals to German history." Her resignation came after threats left her aware "how dangerous my work as a lawyer is and how little I was and am being protected." The German magazine *Der Spiegel* added, "Those familiar with the Islamic scene doubt whether people fighting for the rights of Muslim women and girls in Germany—lawyers, writers, social workers—receive adequate protection."[70]

Necla Kelek

Another German women's rights activist of Turkish origin, sociologist Necla Kelek, fled her home after being threatened with an axe by her father. She requires police protection to appear publicly.[71] In her book *The Foreign Bride*, she drew attention to the condition of Turkish women and girls imported into Germany for forced marriages to immigrant men and treated "as modern slaves," estimating that 15,000 women annually entered Germany in this manner, and called for a minimum age for foreign brides and harsher punishment for "honor killings."[72] Several Turkish newspapers in Germany denounced her: "They said I was insulting Turkey and Islam." Like Ates, Kelek also criticized German attitudes on women's issues: "Educated Turks, just like many Germans, close their eyes and say that imported brides are a private issue. It isn't. It undermines the values of our own democracy."[73]

Ekin Deligoz

In October 2006, Turkish-born Green Party MP Ekin Deligoz, the first Muslim member of Germany's Parliament, received death threats and had to be placed under police protection after she called, in a newspaper interview, for Muslim women to "take off the head scarf... Show that you have the same civil and human rights as men." The German interior minister, Wolfgang Schauble, defended Deligoz, stressing that "what we as legislators assert with all determination is that this opinion can be expressed, and that one should not need police protection for it."[74] Some Turkish papers responded to Deligoz's statement by vilifying her, even comparing her to the Nazis. Local Muslim leaders, while often criticizing Deligoz's comments, firmly opposed the death threats and affirmed freedom of expression.[75]

Nyamko Sabuni

A similar situation confronted Nyamko Sabuni, who became Sweden's minister of integration and gender equality in October 2006. Born in Burundi to exiled Congolese parents—a Muslim mother and a Christian father (she does not practice either religion)—Sabuni became the first Swedish cabinet minister of African origin. Her appointment was controversial due to her efforts to fight the "honor culture," which she views as the source of abuses such as virginity checks, forced marriages, veiling, female genital mutilation (FGM), and violence against women, particularly within Muslim communities. She has called for compulsory gynecological exams to ensure that teenage girls have not been subjected to FGM and has asserted that girls under the age of fifteen—the age of consent in Sweden—should be prohibited from wearing the veil, arguing, "Nowhere in the Koran does it state that a child should wear a veil; it stops them being children." She has been charged with "Islamophobia" and received strident criticism from Swedish Muslim groups, fifty of which petitioned for her removal soon after she was appointed. Due to death threats, she requires twenty-four-hour security, and her staff has ceased printing her daily activities on her website.[76]

Souad Sbai

Souad Sbai, head of Italy's Association of Moroccan Women, was increasingly threatened after winning a seat in the Italian parliament in 2008. She is not an active Muslim but expresses pride in her heritage, emphasizing, "I've never talked about Islam...I've spoken about Muslims who treat women badly. And this is a crime?" As of April 2009, three men faced trial for making death threats against her and other unknown individuals. Sbai, who supports interfaith dialogue and has criticized the veil and burka, suspects that radical imams "are telling their followers, wrongly, that she insults Islam."[77] In 2009, she brought a court case against "Akrane H.," who, in 2006, penned what she describes as "a death 'fatwa'...for which I had to live in fear for quite some time." In addition to telling Sbai to "begin to pray to God, leave work for men" and that "a woman who does not cover her head must be hanged by the hair," the letter claimed she had "been exposed as a 'massihia' (Christian)," which is, effectively, a charge of apostasy. In a landmark ruling, the court accepted Sbai's argument that such a claim was a de facto death threat.[78]

Kadra Noor

On April 13, 2007, Kadra Noor—a prominent member of a Norwegian-Somali women's organization—was severely beaten in downtown Oslo by a group of Somali men. In a 2000 hidden-camera documentary, she had called attention to Norwegian imams' support for female genital mutilation. She was attacked after telling a Norwegian paper that "the Quran's view of women should be interpreted again" and reported that "while I lay on the pavement they kicked me and screamed that I had trampled on the Koran. Several shouted Allah-o-okbar (God is great) and also recited from the Koran." The Islamic Council of Norway denounced the attack, and two suspects were arrested.[79]

Asra Nomani

In the United States, after promoting a more assertive role for women in Islam, Muslim feminist and former *Wall Street Journal* writer Asra Nomani received death threats, including one from a caller who said he would "slaughter" both her and her parents if she did not "keep [her] mouth shut." She has criticized gender segregation in mosques and helped organize mixed-gender services with female prayer leaders. Critics denounced Nomani as a "troublemaker" and accused her of having CIA and Mossad links. Members of her hometown mosque in Morgantown, West Virginia, have sought to banish her for "disrupting worship and spreading misinformation about Islam." Nonetheless, she has refused to cease her efforts for women or her efforts against Wahhabi-style fundamentalists, who she believes are gaining increasing influence in American mosques with the help of abundant cash flows.[80]

Amina Wadud

Amina Wadud, a Virginia Commonwealth University professor of Islamic studies, led a mixed-gender prayer service in Manhattan. The service was held in an Episcopal church after three mosques declined to host it, and an art gallery offered but changed its mind upon receiving a bomb threat. Wadud was threatened, and the service was denounced widely in the Middle East, including by the Saudi grand mufti, who called it a ploy by "enemies of Islam," and by an official of Al-Azhar University's women's college, who described it as an act of apostasy.[81]

Shabana Rehman

Stand-up comedian and columnist Shabana Rehman has received death threats for addressing questions of women, Islam, and integration through humor. In one routine, Rehman, whose family moved from Karachi to Oslo soon after her birth, comes onstage dressed in a burka, which she quips is not very practical when assembling IKEA furniture but great for scaring children, before shedding it to reveal a red cocktail dress. She criticizes arranged marriages, FGM, and sharia law, as well as Norway's shortcomings in integrating its immigrant population. She mocks Norwegian "halal hippies" who disregard abuses within Islam for the sake of multiculturalism. In 2002, a group of conservative Muslim women symbolically excommunicated her over a protest she had staged against the honor killing of a Kurdish girl. In 2008, several months after she had promised to burn the Qur'an during one of her routines, unknown assailants shot at her sister's Oslo restaurant, though no injuries resulted. Rehman has made such an impression in Norwegian politics that immigration debates are now commonly referred to as the "Shabana debate." In a now-common pattern, critics have charged her with fueling prejudice against immigrants. The Norwegian immigration minister, however, praised her for stimulating conversation about how immigrant culture can be merged with Norwegian culture.[82]

Naser Khader

Those promoting tolerance and democratic values within Islam are also under threat. One is Syrian-born Naser Khader, who in 2001 became the first person of immigrant background to win a seat in the Danish parliament. A consistent foe of Islamic extremism, Khader formulated "Ten Commandments of Democracy," among which he included free expression, nonviolence, and a promise to "separate politics and religion" and "never [to] place religion above the laws of democracy."[83] In September 2005, he refused to attend a meeting on Islamist militancy convened by the Danish prime minister, Anders Fogh Rasmussen, that Khader said would "legitimize radical religious leaders" who were also invited. Soon after his election, Khader required police protection due to death threats from the Nazi far right and Muslim extremists.[84] Amidst the growing cartoon controversy, in 2006, he founded the Democratic Muslims Network to promote the voices of moderate Muslims. Calling himself a "cultural Muslim," he stresses, "Of course you can be a democrat and a practicing Muslim simultaneously.... The goal is not to vote Islam away, but to vote democracy in."

Khader also organized a demonstration of moderate Muslims against Saudi Arabia for its assault on Denmark's freedom of the press. Within a few weeks, his organization had acquired a membership of 1,500 but still remained a minor voice.[85] Khader noted that many members had left the group due to threats, a particular problem for women.[86]

He was threatened with death by Ahmed Akkari, one of the primary cartoon agitators, who said in March 2006 that if he "becomes minister for foreigners, or integration, shouldn't two guys go see him to blow him up, him and his ministry?"[87] After his remarks were captured on hidden camera, Akkari claimed that they were intended as a joke; he was investigated but not charged by Danish police, though the scandal did lead to his removal as spokesman for the Islamic Faith Community.[88]

Ahmed Aboutaleb

Moroccan-born Ahmed Aboutaleb was an Amsterdam alderman who stressed the need for immigrant integration. In 2004, he was denounced by Muslim extremists and Dutch racists alike. In the wake of van Gogh's murder, he received death threats after he told a mosque audience that Muslims must accept common Dutch values, saying, "Anyone who doesn't share these values would be wise to draw their conclusions and leave." Van Gogh's killer, Muhammed Bouyeri, called him a heretic; for his part, Aboutaleb, who has emphasized the complexity of Qur'anic interpretation, said, "it makes me laugh when a kid like Mohammed B. thinks he can derive enough knowledge from the Koran in English and Dutch to think it is his duty to gun a person down."

Aboutaleb was one of the few Muslims present at the Amsterdam demonstration protesting van Gogh's murder. He argued that, despite their possible distaste for van Gogh, others "should have been there to defend the rule of law." He also contended that the Dutch government should have made stronger efforts to initiate a dialogue after van Gogh's killing, emphasizing that "we have to draw a line, not between Muslims and non-Muslims, but between the good people and the bad people."[89] As of early 2005, Aboutaleb had to make his public appearances "always surrounded by people armed to the teeth."[90] In January 2009, he was appointed mayor of Rotterdam and has continued to tell his fellow immigrants, "Stop seeing yourself as victims, and if you don't want to integrate, leave."[91]

Afshin Ellian

Writer and law professor Afshin Ellian was a former member of a far-left Iranian party, who fled to the Netherlands in 1989. He quickly gained degrees in law and philosophy and eventually began contributing to Dutch newspapers. Like Ayaan Hirsi Ali, he has stridently criticized both Islamism and its multiculturalist apologists. He responded to the van Gogh killing in an article titled "Make Jokes about Islam!" and has argued: "Free speech is in danger of being increasingly restricted by invoking 'Islamophobia' and 'racism.' . . . Luther was not a Catholicophobe. He was critical of the church. Voltaire was not a religiophobe. He was simply critical of the intolerant manifestations of religion. Should the Reformation have been warded off on the grounds that Luther 'must not stigmatize all Catholics?'"[92] Like Hirsi Ali, Ellian has been written off as an "Enlightenment fundamentalist" by many of his coreligionists, and he, too, has required constant protection. He believes that "extremists are afraid that if Dutch society becomes a safe haven for an intellectual discussion of political Islam, it will be very dangerous for them."[93]

Canadian Reformers

In Canada, Muslim Canadian Congress (MCC) spokesman Tarek Fatah earned enemies by opposing the use of sharia courts in Canada, advocating for gay rights in Islam, and criticizing a prominent British imam. He was forced to give up his position due to death threats against himself and his family. The leader of the larger and more reactionary Canadian Islamic Congress (CIC), Mohamed Elmasry, wrote in the CIC's journal that Fatah was "well known in Canada for smearing Islam and bashing Muslims." Fatah was attacked in 2003 for allegedly insulting Islam's prophet Muhammad and was called an "apostate" while being assaulted in 2006.[94]

In October 2006, Farzana Hassan Shahid, the MCC's president, said that she and her colleagues were receiving threatening e-mails from Islamist radicals and that she was twice called an apostate for her heterodox positions on sharia and homosexuality, as well as her denunciations of terrorism. She called for Ontario's attorney general, Michael Bryant, to expand hate-crime laws to cover threats made against her and other liberal Muslims, explaining that the law should "include or acknowledge accusations of blasphemy and apostasy into the existing hate laws so the public and legal frame work is sensitized to this issue."[95]

Two other Canadian Muslims, Prof. Salim Mansur, of Indian background, who has spoken against self-censorship in the name of sensitivity, and Raheel Raza, a Pakistani-Canadian, have also both been threatened with death for their views against radical Islam. Both spoke together with Tarek Fatah at an October 2008 conference, condemning gender segregation and criticizing the willingness of some Canadian leftists to abet Islamic extremism.[96]

In April 2007, Pakistani-born journalist Jawaad Faizi was brutally assaulted outside the Canadian home of his editor, Amir Arain of the *Pakistan Post*, over his criticism of the Pakistani Muslim group Minhaj-ul-Quran. His article had questioned whether the group's leader could really have written the prophet Muhammad's name on the moon, as he had claimed. Callers began threatening Faizi and announcing to Arain, "You are not a Muslim, you are supporting Christians." Faizi's assailants told him he must stop writing against Islam, "or he would be attacked again."[97]

In 1972, when she was four years old, Irshad Manji's family fled to Canada to escape Idi Amin's regime in Uganda. Between the ages of nine and fourteen, she studied at a Canadian madrassa and was expelled after challenging her teachers on issues ranging from the prohibition of female prayer leaders to evidence for a Jewish conspiracy against Islam and, finally, for asking why Muhammad ordered his army to destroy a Jewish tribe. She became a highly successful television presenter, taking liberal positions and, as an open lesbian, speaking out on gay issues. Manji chose to call for the reform of Islam rather than abandoning her religion. Her 2004 book, *The Trouble with Islam Today*, denounces human rights abuses committed in the name of Islam, including anti-Semitism, crimes against women, and the continuance of slavery under some Islamic regimes. She argues that scriptural literalism, while a problem in all religions, has become mainstream among Muslims, helping shut down religious debate. In her view, the Qur'an should not be treated as the unquestionable, direct word of God.

In addition to denunciations, she has received enough violent threats to convince her to hire a bodyguard and to bulletproof her home. Nonetheless, Manji avoids bringing a bodyguard to speaking engagements so that she can convince young Muslims, many of whom she believes share her concerns, that it is possible to speak out against extremism. Alongside the threats, she reports messages of gratitude from Muslims, especially young women, saying that she "is saying out loud words they have only whispered." Manji argues: "Muslims in the West are best poised to revive Islam's tradition of independent reasoning...we already enjoy the precious freedom to think, express, challenge and be challenged—all without fear of state reprisal."[98]

Other Reformers

In 2001, Jordanian Islamist Abd al-Munim Abu Zant issued a fatwa calling for the scholar Khalid Duran, a U.S. resident who headed the Ibn Khaldun society, to be killed for apostasy. Duran had not left Islam but was subject to a worldwide smear campaign after the Council on American-Islamic Relations attacked his book, *Children of Abraham: An Introduction to Islam for Jews*. Duran, a strong proponent of interreligious dialogue, had written the book for the American Jewish Committee to "lift [the] cloud" over Jews' perception of Islam as a result of the

Mideast conflict. He wanted to "demonstrate Islam's sublime spirituality" and to "persuade Jews that Islam should not be blamed for its malpractice by certain contemporary Muslims." His car was vandalized, and he had to relocate to a safe house.[99]

During the January 2009 fighting in Gaza, Islamic radicals sent death threats to French imam Hassen Chalghoumi, who was prominently involved in outreach to France's Jewish community. Oil was poured on his car, and he required a bodyguard and police protection; his house had previously been vandalized after he participated in a Holocaust commemoration ceremony and urged Muslims to honor the victims.[100]

In a 2004 *Independent* column, Islamic scholar Akbar Ahmed mourned the suppression of "the gentle voices of Islam" by governments determined to "stay in power at all costs." Part of his article also lamented "vicious personal attacks" on the prophet. In the U.K., however, he was "denounced as an Uncle Tom for being too keen to have dialogue with Jews and Christians and far too impressed by Western civilisation." He spoke at evensong at a Cambridge chapel and gave a lecture for Liberal and Progressive synagogues in the United Kingdom, but "[f]or this I was branded a Zionist agent—and received violent threats both from extremist Muslims appalled at my consorting with the 'enemy' and from racist Britons who told this 'black bastard' to 'go home.'"[101]

Former Muslims

Whether atheists or converts to another religion, some former Muslims live in fear of attacks for apostasy, and those who have spoken out against this oppression often compound their endangerment.[102] In January 2005, Sheikh Omar Bakri Muhammad of the militant Al Muhajiroun group, then living in Britain, declared that in the restored caliphate that he wished to bring about, "Muslims could not convert to Christianity on pain of execution." The Ireland-based European Council for Fatwa and Research—led by the ubiquitous Sheikh al-Qaradawi—sidesteps the question of extrajudicial executions for apostasy by declaring, "Executing whoever reverts from Islam is the responsibility of the state and is to be decided by Islamic governments alone." The council justifies the (properly authorized) killing of "those who declare their action in public and may cause Fitna by bringing down the name of Allah (swt), His prophet (ppbuh) or the Muslims," on the grounds that this is analogous to treason.[103] This problem goes beyond fiery pronouncements by radicals or disingenuous Islamist figures: according to a 2007 report by the think tank Policy Exchange, 36 percent of British Muslims from the ages of sixteen to twenty-four, 37 percent of those between twenty-five and thirty-four, and 31 percent of British Muslims overall agreed "[t]hat Muslim conversion is forbidden and punishable by death."[104]

Ibn Warraq

"Ibn Warraq," a pseudonym historically used by Muslim dissidents, is a Pakistani ex-Muslim living in an undisclosed location in the United States and began writing critiques of Islam in the wake of the 1989 Salman Rushdie affair. To avoid attack, he keeps his identity and whereabouts hidden. Author of many books, including scholarly ones as well as the popular *Why I Am Not a Muslim*, he rarely appears in public. On one exceptional occasion, he did so wearing a disguise, and he has stated that not even his brother knows where he is. He hopes Qur'anic scholarship will help Muslim society grow "less dogmatic, more open," as he believes biblical scholarship has done among Christians.[105]

Mina Ahadi

In 2007, ex-Muslims in three different European countries founded organizations to challenge the repression of apostates, but their leaders have been threatened and have had difficulty finding recruits. In February 2007, Iranian-born human rights activist Mina Ahadi helped establish the Central Council of ex-Muslims in Germany to assist those, particularly women, wishing to leave Islam. The group claimed forty members, many of whom had been active in communist politics in their home countries. Ahadi does not believe in the possibility of modernizing Islam from within but rather hopes to challenge the organizations that claim to represent all Muslims. Shortly after the organization's launch, she received death threats and was placed under police protection. Other members were also "terrorized."[106]

Maryam Namazie

Also in 2007, a group of former Muslims, led by human rights activist and feminist Maryam Namazie, established the Council of ex-Muslims of Britain. The council's mandate was to challenge traditional Islamic punishments for apostasy and, as in Germany, provide non-religious immigrants an "alternative to the likes of the Muslim Council of Britain because we don't think people should be pigeonholed as Muslims or deemed to be represented by regressive organizations like the MCB." Namazie also denounced the British government's "appeasement," which she said had created social division by targeting "specific policies and initiatives" at Muslims. At its launch, twenty-five British ex-Muslims allowed themselves to be named as members. Namazie, who had received death threats, suggested that many people were still wary of joining due to "threats and intimidations."[107]

Ehsan Jami

Ehsan Jami, a local council member for the Dutch Labor Party (PvdA), who moved to the Netherlands from Iran with his family at a young age, was initially attracted to militant Islamic ideology but was later motivated to leave Islam by events, including the van Gogh murder and the Danish cartoon crisis. He suffered three attacks; in one, a group of youths surrounded him at night and held a knife to his throat. After the third assault, in August 2007, when he was struck and pushed to the ground at a shopping center in Voorburg, he was given extra security.[108] Jami launched an ex-Muslims' group on September 11, 2007, calling for ex-Muslims to join in "breaking the taboo that comes with renouncing Islam but also taking a stand for reason, universal rights and values and secularism."[109] He declared, "Sharia schools say that they will kill the ones who leave Islam. In the West people get threatened, thrown out of their family, beaten up ... We want that to change, so that people are free to choose who they want to be and what they want to believe in."[110]

Jami also faced criticism from his own party. The deputy prime minister, Wouter Bos, stated that the group "offends Muslims and their faith." Jami rejected the idea of joining Geert Wilders's Freedom Party since his support of religious freedom placed him at odds with some of Wilders's positions. However, on September 27, he collaborated with Wilders on a joint article, "We Will Never Be Silent," which rejected a government official's calls for them to moderate their rhetoric on Islam. The article urged immediate action against Islamization in the Netherlands, otherwise "we will relive the 1930s. Only that time it was Hitler, this time Mohammed." After its publication, the local Labor party asked Jami to give up his council seat; he remained on the council as an independent. He closed his ex-Muslim committee in April 2008, stating that threats from Muslims were preventing people from joining.[111]

In spring 2008, Jami planned to make an animated film on the life of Muhammad that would have included images of the prophet sexually aroused in the presence of his nine-year-old wife. A Dutch Muslim group announced it would seek a ban on the film, while Jami proclaimed that it would be even more controversial than the 2005 Danish cartoons.[112] However, he dropped the project after a request from the Netherlands' justice minister and a warning that the Dutch government might be unable to protect him.[113] In December 2008, he released a film entitled *Interview with Muhammad*, which contained a mildly confrontational interview with a masked man portraying Islam's Prophet, who seemed in some cases open to a reformist interpretation of his teachings. Various Dutch Muslim groups dismissed the movie as a "tepid piece of fluff," and in February 2009, in protest, the Muslim Spiritual Directorate of Nizhny Novgorod, Russia, called for a boycott of Dutch flowers. Jami continues to face threats and requires constant protection.[114]

Wafa Sultan

Syrian-American psychiatrist Wafa Sultan began to question her faith when, in 1979, Muslim Brotherhood gunmen shouting "God is great" murdered her professor at the University of Aleppo. She maintains that many verses in the Koran say that you must kill those who do not believe in Allah. After emigrating to the United States, she contributed essays critical of extremist Islam to a Muslim reformist website. Sultan gained more attention and, in some quarters, notoriety, after an interview on the Al Jazeera television network in July 2005 in which she linked acts of violence by radical Muslims to "the savage and barbarian instincts aroused by teachings that call for refusing the other, killing him." Her appearance was followed by a barrage of death threats, and Islamist radicals began mentioning her name on their websites.[115]

In a second Al Jazeera appearance on February 21, 2006, Sultan declared that the world was experiencing "not a clash of religions or a clash of civilizations" but "a clash between civilization and backwardness, between the civilized and the primitive, between barbarity and rationality...between those who treat women like beasts and those who treat them like human beings." She also argued, "Only the Muslims defend their beliefs by burning down churches, killing people and destroying embassies." She has subsequently received death threats and, in the summer of 2006, said she and her family were in hiding. She has also expressed concern about the safety of her family in Syria, stating that the secret police questioned two brothers after she appeared on Al Jazeera.[116]

She denounced Islam even more stridently on Al Jazeera in March 2008, and the network apologized for hosting an interview that "offended Islam."[117] This satisfied neither al-Qaradawi, who said that Sultan affronted Islam and blamed Al Jazeera "for allowing such a woman to appear," nor the (American) Muslim Public Affairs Council, which said that Sultan "routinely insults and debases Muslims and everything they hold sacred" and accused Al Jazeera of "spreading Islamophobia."[118]

Converts to Christianity

Converts from Islam to Christianity can face high risks.[119] This can be illustrated by the example of Egyptian actor Omar Sharif, although he did not in fact leave Islam. In October 2005, he simply said, of his role as St. Peter in an Italian TV film, "[p]laying Peter was so important for me that even now I can only speak about it with difficulty." Radicals read his remarks as a sign that he had become a Christian, and an Al-Qaeda-linked website declared, "He is a crusader who is offending Islam and Muslims and receiving applause from the Italian people. I give you this advice, brothers, you must kill him."[120]

Converts do not need to be public figures to become targets. In September 2004, many Muslim-background converts to Christianity participating in a gathering for them in Falls Church, Virginia, stated that they faced death threats for leaving Islam. Registration and entry involved heavy security, and many participants used pseudonyms. Several reported keeping their conversion secret from their own families due to fear of retaliation.

In Austria, a woman of Pakistani background who became a Christian was told by her father that she had two weeks to return to Islam or be killed. When she went to the authorities for help, they were apparently unable to comprehend why anyone would face such risks for the sake of religion and suggested she consider reverting to Islam.[121]

Nissar Hussein, living in a largely Pakistani immigrant area in Bradford, England, converted along with his wife from Islam to Christianity in 1996. Initially ostracized and taunted by their neighbors, the couple became targets of violence in 2001. Groups of young men followed them; a youth drove into Nissar's parked car; an angry group threw rocks at his house, shouted death threats, and gave notice that his house would be burned down unless he returned to Islam. The police allegedly told Nissar to "stop being a crusader and move to another place." Shortly afterward, the empty house next to the couple's was set ablaze, bricks were thrown through their window, and Hussein's wife was held hostage in her home for several hours. Hussein said he had "been utterly failed by the author-ities." Police ignored his complaints, claiming that defending the couple from vio-lence was "not in the public interest." In July 2006, the couple moved to a different neighborhood. Hussein's story is not unique.[122]

A woman called Yasmin, who grew up Muslim in England and converted to Christianity in her thirties, told a *Times* reporter that after her family discovered her conversion, they disowned her. Her husband did the same to her children, a former friend attempted to strangle her, and neighbors forced her from her town: "We had bricks through our windows; I was spat at in the street because they thought I was dishonoring Islam. We had to call the police so many times. I had to go to court to get an injunction against my husband because he was inciting others to attack me." When she moved to a new town, the attacks resumed, but she resolved not to move again. Instead she helped organize a clandestine support group for ex-Muslims. As of February 2005, her group had seventy members.[123]

In December 2007, Bishop Michael Nazir-Ali, who a month later was threat-ened for his comment about "no-go zones," gave a speech warning that Muslim converts to Christianity in the United Kingdom are forced to live in fear. At the same event where he spoke, a thirty-two-year-old woman using the pseudonym "Hannah" recounted how she had fled home at the age of sixteen to escape sexual abuse by her father and an arranged marriage; she eventually had converted to Christianity after being sheltered by a Christian religious education teacher. Death threats against "Hannah" began after she was baptized. Armed with axes, knives, and hammers, a group of forty men, her father and uncle among them, assaulted her home. She said she had to move forty-five times in order to hide from relatives who demanded that she reconvert.

In November 2007, a new round of death threats prompted the police to place "Hannah" on an "at risk" list. Then married to a Church of England employee, she released a memoir titled *The Imam's Daughter*. She said she refused to report her father to the police because of the shame it would bring upon her family, especially her mother, and because she suspected they would either not believe it or simply refuse to help her. According to a 2009 interview with the *Times*, when she had told a schoolteacher that her father was beating her, the school dispatched a social worker from within her community who refused to listen to her allegations and instead informed her father of her accusations, which led to additional abuse. The social worker subsequently told her, "It's not right to betray your community." She describes this as a common problem, when Muslim girls seeking to convert or to deal with abuse encounter British authorities eager to display multicultural sensitivity.[124]

Increased attention to the situation of converts in Europe and around the world came in April 2008, when Italian journalist Magdi Allam, born a Muslim in Egypt, converted from Islam to Christianity in a high-profile baptismal ceremony during an Easter Mass, where he was baptized by Pope Benedict XVI himself. Allam had been a strong critic of Islamic extremism for some time before ultimately deciding that the development of a moderate Islam was impossible. His attacks on radical Islam and support for Israel reportedly earned him a death sentence in 2003 from Hamas. A pro-Israel book he wrote in 2007, which was condemned by the Union of Islamic Communities in Italy, drew so many threats, with some Italian Muslims describing him as a "new Salman Rushdie," that authorities enhanced his security detail.[125]

Allam explained that his conversion followed "a gradual and profound interior meditation," conditioned by the fact that "for five years I have been confined to a life under guard, with permanent surveillance at home and a police escort for my every movement," because of death threats from Islamic extremists in and outside of Italy. The intimidation that he faced as a Muslim reformist helped drive him from Islam. Allam also used the occasion to call for increased protection for Muslim converts to Christianity in Italy, of whom he said thousands "are forced to hide their faith out of fear of being assassinated by Islamic extremists who lurk among us."[126]

The vice president of the Italian Islamic Religious Community expressed concern at the "high-profile" nature of Allam's conversion. Italy's deputy foreign minister for the Middle East, Ugo Intini, publicly attacked Allam's "very harsh criticism" of Islam and called for the Vatican "to distance itself clearly from his statements." Jordanian scholar Aref Ali Nayed of the Royal Islamic Strategic Studies Centre, who had been involved in the "Common Word" initiative to improve Muslim-Christian relations, denounced Allam's baptism as "provocative" and regretted that it came "at a most unfortunate time when sincere Muslims and Catholics are working very hard to mend ruptures between the two communities." A Vatican spokesman later emphasized that the Vatican continued to place great importance on dialogue with Muslims and was not necessarily endorsing Allam's controversial views, but the spokesman also implied that the high-profile baptism may have been carried out in order "to affirm the freedom of religious choice which derives from the dignity of the human person."[127]

Closing

The targets of attacks over alleged insults to Islam are many and varied. Some are avowedly anti-Islam politicians. Others are artists or intellectuals who have intended only to criticize Islamic extremism, or clergymen who speak from their convictions, or even ordinary café owners who found themselves in the wrong neighborhood. Perhaps most targets are of Muslim background. Some are seeking to advance the interests of their coreligionists; others are ex-Muslims, either converts to Christianity or atheists. Some are Muslims with unorthodox views, while others are mainstream Muslims who denounce terrorism and violence. The only thing that they have in common is that they have acted or created or spoken in a way that offends the sensibilities—or frustrates the social and political ambitions—of Muslim fanatics and extremists.

Extrajudicial threats and attacks by vigilantes and terrorists have claimed more victims (including ones brutally murdered), and established a wider pattern of intimidation, silencing, and self-censorship, than have western legal processes. As Ben Elton and others have noted, there is already in place in much of Europe a set of taboos according to which certain things can no longer be said. The legally guaranteed freedom of religion of many European Muslims is restricted by the knowledge that they may be threatened, attacked, or harassed for a word of criticism or a change of faith.

PART IV

MUSLIM CRITICISM OF APOSTASY AND BLASPHEMY LAWS

In this book, we do not analyze the development of notions of apostasy and blasphemy in Islamic or other history, nor do we assess their systematic treatment in Islamic jurisprudence and theology. Our concern is to survey the contemporary use of these notions to justify worldly punishments. Clearly, however, one important step in limiting or stopping their application to repress political and religious freedom is to show that such temporal punishments are not required by Islam. Consequently, we have asked three noted Muslim scholars to address this issue. They all condemn disrespect for others' beliefs, but they argue that Islam does not require temporal punishments for such offenses or purported offenses. Two of these essays are given in part IV, and one, "God Needs No Defense," by the late Kyai Haji Abdurrahman Wahid—the former president of Indonesia, the world's largest Muslim country, and head of Nahdatul Ulama, the world's largest Muslim organization—is the book's foreword.

Wahid outlines the nature of belief itself and argues eloquently that God does not need our defense from human blasphemy or, indeed, anything else. Moreover, those who seek to force their limited understanding on others may themselves be committing blasphemy and certainly coarsen Muslim society. He holds that the origins of blasphemy restrictions lie in the political ramifications of early Islam, when apostasy was tantamount to desertion from the caliph's army. In today's very different situation, temporal punishments for blasphemy and apostasy threaten not only religious minorities but also the right of Muslims to speak freely about their faith; they also hinder faith itself, which always includes growth and seeking for the truth.

In chapter 14, "Renewing Qur'anic Studies in the Contemporary World," the late Professor Abu-Zayd, who was on the receiving end of extremist attacks and at one point was forced to flee his native Egypt, emphasizes that charges of apostasy and blasphemy are "strategically employed to prevent reform of Muslim societies" and "confine the world's Muslim population to a bleak, colorless prison of sociocultural and political conformity." He stresses the enormous social, cultural, and theological diversity in contemporary and historical Islam and outlines the patterns of interpretation used by Muslims. In particular, he argues against an "ahistorical" understanding of Islam and, while carefully never reducing Islam to history, stresses that we need to understand "its historical context...how it emerged and developed within Arabia and other parts of the world." Only then can we understand how Islam should be manifest in our own situation and "liberate the 'deep substance' of the Holy Qur'an's message."

In chapter 15, "Rethinking Classical Muslim Law of Apostasy and the Death Penalty," Abdullah Saeed, some of whose writings have been banned in his native Maldives, emphasizes that current human rights discourse is not merely a Western concern: "It is shared by a large number of Muslims as well." He agrees with Abu-Zayd on the need to understand the political context of early Islam, in particular, the "post-prophetic period against which the classical Islamic law of apostasy was formulated" and which has "played a significant role in the development of this law and associated restrictions on freedom of religion." In that setting of armed conflict among communities, to leave Islam and the Muslims and their allies was to join the opposition; hence, an apostate was "perceived to have automatically joined the non-Muslim side" and "deemed a serious social and political threat to the whole community."

Similarly, the Abbasids curtailed theological debate lest it clash with their state ideology and thus their claim to legitimacy. Hence, "apostasy was more akin to treason," and its punishment was due to its association with treason and rebellion. In contrast to these earlier settings, Muslim communities are not now closed tribes; Muslims move from one area to another, and from country to county, and often live among non-Muslims. Hence, apostasy is no longer akin to treason, is not a violation of state orthodoxy, and should not be subject to laws akin to those against treason.

From these brief essays by skilled scholars, we can see not only that Islam does not require temporal punishments for blasphemy and apostasy but also that such punishments can be understood as opposed to Islamic principles. Countering the use of such accusations and punishments in the Muslim world and the current attempts to spread them to the rest of the world, far from being an attack on Islam, can be seen as a defense of Islam, according to some of its leading scholars.

Renewing Qur'anic Studies in the Contemporary World

NASR HAMID ABU-ZAYD

Introductory Remarks

The events of 9/11 and subsequent terrorist violence have stimulated tremendous interest and concern regarding the sociopolitical and intellectual conditions of the Muslim world and how they impact the West. Yet confusion about the "true" nature of Islam, and the threat we are facing, remains prevalent among Western policy makers, journalists, and the general public. To a substantial extent, this confusion among Western observers arises from the fact that Muslim fundamentalists deliberately and consistently promote a "reading" of Islam whereby every sociopolitical issue must be viewed through a suffocatingly narrow theological lens. As a result, all too many analysts in the West have displayed the unfortunate tendency to conflate the religion of Islam with "Muslims" and "the Muslim world," employing these terms loosely and interchangeably when describing a variety of pathologies that afflict contemporary Muslim societies. This, in turn, has the effect of converting sociopolitical controversies into theological ones, and thereby generating within non-Muslims a profound unease with and mistrust of Islam and its adherents, as well as blindness on how to address the problem of Muslim radicalism.

Promoting the notion of a single unified entity called the *ummah*, the "Community of Believers," Muslim fundamentalists ignore the enormous social, cultural, and theological diversity that exists both within and between the world's various Muslim-majority states. Even within the Arab Middle East, Saudi Arabia's official Wahhabi Islam is highly distinctive and characterized by numerous features completely at odds with the traditional Islam historically practiced by most inhabitants of Mecca, Medina, and the wider Arab and Islamic world. The Wahhabis, like other Muslim fundamentalists, propagate the naive concept of an ideal and ahistorical Islam, which is narrowly defined, restrictive, legalistic, monolithic, compulsory, and supremacist vis-à-vis not only those of other faiths, but even the vast majority of Muslims, who remain traditional in their beliefs. This version of Islam is that of the "sword," as is prominently displayed in the flag of Saudi Arabia. The Islam of mercy, compassion, and profound spiritual devotion, which regards the world's cultural and religious diversity as a divine blessing, is far beyond the reach of the fundamentalists' narrow vision.

Indonesia's former president, Kyai Haji Abdurrahman Wahid, rightly identified this "extreme and perverse ideology in the minds of fanatics"—widely propagated throughout the world, with the aid of Arab petrodollars—as the source of a compelling threat not only to the West but also to Muslims and Islam itself: "This crisis of misunderstanding—of Islam by Muslims themselves—is compounded by the failure of governments, people of other faiths, and the majority of well-intentioned Muslims to resist, isolate and discredit this dangerous ideology. The crisis thus afflicts Muslims and non-Muslims alike, with tragic consequences. Failure to understand the true nature of Islam permits the continued radicalization of Muslims world-wide, while blinding the rest of humanity to a solution which hides in plain sight."[1]

It is imperative that Muslims and non-Muslims alike free themselves from the framework of the fundamentalists' monolithic discourse on Islam. Otherwise, we will either misjudge Islam by conflating it with the dominant discourse of the radicals—just as Dutch parliamentarian Geert Wilders, in his video Fitna, mirrors the ideology of Osama bin Laden—or we will adopt an unrealistic and apologetic stance, decontextualizing Islam from past and present circumstances, so as to convince ourselves that it is "purely a religion of peace," divorced from the violence so often committed in its name.

The first view maintains that Islam is evil, dangerous, and incapable of being reformed. This "anti-Islam discourse" mirrors and echoes the Islamist viewpoint, which is thus taken for granted as representing the one and only "true" Islam. The second approach is equally unrealistic, presenting Islam as a well-defined ethical, spiritual, and purely idealistic ahistorical religious phenomenon. The problem with this approach is that it totally ignores the reality on the ground in the Muslim world, where radicals have often succeeded in donning a mantle of religious authenticity and are rapidly advancing toward their goal of "welding" Islam to their virulent sociopolitical ideology.

Rather than fall into the trap of either demonizing or idealizing Islam and Muslims in general, we must realistically assess conditions in the Muslim world and develop a balanced, mature understanding of Islam itself, consistent with the needs of humanity and life in the modern world.

One highly effective way to accomplish these objectives is to reject the fundamentalists' dogmatic framework and instead locate Islam within its historical context in order to understand how it emerged and developed within Arabia and other parts of the world. In particular, this requires us to approach the Qur'an, Islam's foundational scripture, from an objective historical perspective, examining how it was transmitted, propagated, codified, and ultimately canonized. Through this process, we can begin to determine the "spheres" and limitations of the meanings it provides and thus ascertain its significance within the context of various contemporary societies, free of extremist dogma and the ideology of religious hatred, yet richly imbued with moral and spiritual import.

Such a mature, spiritual, and "contextualized" understanding of the Qur'an will displace the fundamentalists' monolithic and ahistorical worldview. Widely disseminated, it will allow pluralism and tolerance to become the dominant discourse within Muslim societies worldwide. This understanding also represents an appropriate way to respond to criticism of Islam, the Qur'an, and the prophet. Intellectually sound responses that convey the spiritual message of Islam should be employed rather than angry rhetoric, which only encourages violence.

The Sociopolitical and Cultural Contexts

According to Islamic belief, the Qur'an is the speech of God, which conveys the "message" revealed to humans through Muhammad, who was the messenger of God, and human himself. A message represents a communicative link between a speaker and recipient, delivered via a code or linguistic system. Without such a code, messages will not be intelligible to recipients. In the case of the Qur'an, the Arabic language—the human code of the recipient—is the code of communication between the Divine and humans, simply because the Divine code, if any, is unlikely to be comprehended by humans. Besides, the message was not intended for the recipient (Muhammad) alone; rather, it was meant to be transmitted to the recipient's community and beyond. Therefore, it had to be comprehended by the Arabic-speaking community of Mecca and the Arabian Peninsula in general. "We never sent a messenger but with the language of his people, that he might make it clear for them," states the Qur'an (14:4).[2]

Since the speaker, God, cannot be the object of scientific study, it is only possible for scholars to approach the message as encoded in the language of the recipient and his community. To accomplish that objective, scholars need all available information about the first recipient, Muhammad, and his surrounding community. In other words, scholars must begin their analysis of the Qur'anic message by studying its contextual reality and seventh-century Arab culture. "Reality" here refers to the sociopolitical conditions that encompassed those who were addressed by the Qur'an, including its first recipient, and which framed their lives, thoughts, and actions. Culture includes the conceptual framework embodied in a language, in this case, the language in which the Qur'an is expressed.

To analyze the Qur'anic message by studying its sociopolitical and cultural reality is to start with empirical facts. The scholarly analysis of such facts can help us achieve an accurate understanding of the Qur'an, including the realization that the Qur'an is a product of seventh-century Arab culture.

The overarching reality, however, is far more complex than this. While arising within the particular seventh-century culture of Arabia, the Qur'an was taken to heart by its recipients and in turn produced a *new* culture, imbued with profound spiritual as well as sociopolitical and cultural dimensions. The Qur'an's linguistics exhibit a number of unique characteristics that were widely acknowledged and admired by contemporary Arabs, including some of Muhammad's opponents. From this uniqueness emerged the notion of the absolute "inimitability"—*i'jaz*—of the Qur'an.

Although it is necessary to analyse and interpret the Qur'an within the contextual environment in which it originated, the understanding of the Qur'an possessed by the first and subsequent generations of Muslims should by no means be considered absolute or final. The specific linguistic encoding dynamics of the Qur'an allow an endless process of decoding. In this process, we should not simplify or ignore its contextual sociopolitical and cultural meaning; in fact, this "meaning" is vital to indicate the direction of any "new" or contemporary message of the text. This direction facilitates our transition from the text's literal "meaning" to its "significance" in any given sociocultural context, including the present. It also enables the interpreter to correctly and efficiently extract the "historical" and "temporal" elements of the message, which carry no significance in the present context.

In other words, the "deep structure" of the Qur'an must be reconstructed from the surface structure, which was specific to seventh-century Arab culture. Subsequently, this deep structure must give rise to other surface structures, including contemporary ones, suitable to successive generations of Muslim society in various regions of the earth. This entails an interpretive diversity—clearly seen throughout Muslim history, particularly as practiced by Sufis, or Islamic mystics—without which the Message would "harden" and degenerate, and the Qur'an would become, as it is now, subject to political and other forms of self-interested manipulation exercised by so-called guardians of Islam.

The innovative approach to Qur'anic study that I have long proposed in my various writings on the process of modern Qur'anic interpretation entails the use of traditional exegetical methods *and* modern linguistic methodologies, in addition to the analysis of sociohistorical reality and culture.[3] By recognizing the difference between the original contextual "meaning," which is virtually fixed because of its historicity, and the "significance" in a particular sociocultural context, which is changeable, and furthermore, by realizing that the significance must be strongly related and rationally connected to the meaning, we can produce more valid contemporary interpretations. Of course, any interpretations of the Qur'an produced using such a methodology are not exempt from the reality that *every* interpretation is historically and culturally constructed.

Blasphemy and Apostasy Laws Stifle Progress and Hinder Peaceful Coexistence

In early Islam, there emerged a debate between a rational school of theology known as the Mu'tazila that claimed that the Qur'an is "created" not eternal, and other theological schools of thought that held that the Qur'an is the "eternal" verbatim speech of God. In the Mu'tazilites' view, an "uncreated" Qur'an is inconsistent with the concept of pure monotheism, *tawhid*, a pivotal concept in Islam. Sociohistorical analysis demonstrates that these schools did not hold their respective views in a vacuum; rather, they expressed in religious terminologies the different sociopolitical positions of their adherents. Eventually, the notion of an "eternal and uncreated" Qur'an became the dominant accepted dogma in Sunni Islam. Unfortunately, the history of this debate is either unknown or ignored by nearly all contemporary Sunni clerics and scholars. Instead, the doctrine of "eternity" is presented as the Truth, while the doctrine of "creation" is denounced as heresy.

As a result, the notion that religious texts, although Divine and revealed by God, are culturally constructed and historically determined is not only rejected by the Muslim establishment but also actively condemned as "apostasy." There is frequently no clear distinction made among heresy, blasphemy, and apostasy within the Muslim world. Instead, Islamist radicals deliberately conflate these terms in order to attack any discourse that strays from the narrow bounds of their fundamentalist ideology. Having been at the receiving end of such allegations—and driven from my home in Egypt to exile in the Netherlands—I can state with conviction that charges of apostasy and blasphemy are key weapons in the fundamentalists' arsenal, strategically employed to prevent reform of Muslim societies and instead confine the world's Muslim population to a bleak, colorless prison of sociocultural and political conformity. There is little hope of escape from this imprisonment, as long as fundamentalists—and the opportunistic and/or authoritarian regimes that compete with them in a chase to the lowest common denominator of Islam—continue to serve as prison guards and wardens.

Laws penalizing blasphemy and apostasy exist in most Muslim-majority countries throughout the world and act as a severe constraint upon the use of reason to explore and understand the contemporary significance of the Qur'an's profound message. By forcefully silencing critical inquiry, such laws play directly into the hands of Islamic radicals who seek to unify and politicize Muslim societies not only against the West but also against the very concept and principles of modern life, such as freedom, justice, human rights, and the dignity of man, which are themselves inseparable from the right to freedom of conscience and expression. Perhaps the greatest irony is that these core principles—which lie at the heart of any just and humane society—are deeply embedded in the message of the Qur'an itself and yet are ignored by Islam's most fervent, and violent, "defenders."

For although the Qur'an prescribes no earthly punishment for either blasphemy or apostasy, the historical development of Islamic law has widely, though not universally, prescribed the death penalty as punishment for both. A critical historical study of the Qur'an, *hadith*, and *shari'a* would reveal the human origin of these interpretations and hence their complete inappropriateness within a modern context.

This objective historical approach to studying the foundational elements of Islamic law is fiercely resisted by many clerics and mullahs. Yet it is absolutely vital, if we are to liberate the "deep substance" of the Holy Qur'an's message, which proclaims the Prophet Muhammad (and hence, by implication, Islam itself) to be "a blessing for all creation."

Rethinking Classical Muslim Law of Apostasy and the Death Penalty

ABDULLAH SAEED

Some Muslims argue that the right to religious freedom as conceptualized in key international instruments is a product of the West and has no relevance for Muslims.* This argument emanates to a large extent from certain political and religious elites, who have an interest in keeping freedom of belief outside the Muslim domain and do so by relying on ideas, constructs and rulings developed in classical Islamic law. These groups tend to ignore the fact that human rights have growing political backing at the international level, with supporting conventions often enshrined in national legislation, even in Muslim-majority states. This means that the discourse on human rights has developed into a global debate in which Muslims are also participants. Thus religious freedom, as a fundamental human right under international law, has become one of the key rights upon which both Muslims and non-Muslims are increasingly focusing.

Freedom of belief for Muslims—particularly freedom to change religion—is one aspect of the right to religious freedom that is particularly targeted for criticism by many Muslims. They argue that this freedom, as conceptualized in international human rights instruments, is not in line with Islamic norms, values, and laws. According to proponents of this view, Muslims do not have the right to leave Islam and convert to another religion or to no religion at all. Under the classical Islamic law of apostasy, the penalty for leaving Islam is death. In the words of one Muslim religious leader: "The person who knows the truth [Islam] and believes in it, [but] then turns his back on it, does not deserve to live. The punishment for apostasy is prescribed for the protection of the religion and as a deterrent to anyone who is thinking of leaving Islam. There is no doubt that such a serious crime must be met with an equally weighty punishment...."[1]

Nevertheless, classical Muslim apostasy laws, as well as other restrictions on religious freedom in the Muslim world, are increasingly being opposed by Muslims, as well as non-Muslims, at local, national, and international levels. There is growing pressure on Muslims to comply with international standards on human rights from major international bodies such as the United Nations and Amnesty International, as well as from influential powers such as the United States and the European Union.

A careful examination of the debate reveals that current human rights discourse is not just a Western one. It is shared by a large number of Muslims as well. Muslim-majority states, as members of the United Nations, accept in principle the Universal Declaration of Human Rights (UDHR) and many have even ratified major human rights conventions. Constitutions in Muslim states often reflect the principles of the UDHR. Moreover, as a sign of participation in this global discourse, even some more traditionalist Muslims have developed what they consider to be "Muslim" human rights documents. These are generally modeled on the UDHR or similar human rights instruments but use Islamic ideas and terminology.

The political background of the prophetic and post-prophetic period against which the classical Islamic law of apostasy was formulated played a significant role in the development of this law and associated restrictions on freedom of religion. In the political context of the Prophet's time, a person either belonged to the community of believers (Muslims), the unbelievers (non-Muslims) who were at peace with Muslims, or the unbelievers who were at war with Muslims. If one leaves Islam and the Muslims and their allies, there is no option but to join the opposition. An apostate, therefore, was perceived to have automatically joined the non-Muslim side, becoming part of the enemy ranks and using apostasy as a means to attack and inflict maximum harm on the Muslim community. Thus the question of apostasy in early Islamic history was closely associated with the safety and security of the Muslims. Apostates were deemed a serious social and political threat to the whole community.

The punishment for apostasy—based on texts such as the hadith, "If anyone changes his religion, kill him"[2]—came about within this sociopolitical context. The person referred to in the hadith was a *muharib* or someone who was in a state of war against Muslims. Under classical Islamic law anyone who was engaged in war against Muslims could be put to death.[3] Thus one could argue that in early Muslim reasoning, apostasy was more akin to treason, rather than a matter of simply changing one's belief. The death sentence therefore was punishment for committing a serious political crime.

The years following the death of the Prophet Muhammad were also marked by a great deal of social and political tension in the body politic of the Muslim community. This also influenced early conceptions of apostasy and related offences, such as blasphemy and heresy. Problems developed among Muslims that were not simply about political leadership of the community but also about what and who represented religious authority. As the Muslim caliphate expanded and Muslims came into contact with customs, traditions, and practices from outside of Arabia, debates arose as to what was acceptable in Islam, who should be the legitimate political authority, and even who was a Muslim. Some Muslims remained politically neutral in these disputes, while others were eager to take sides. It was in this context that several groups with specific theological or religio-political orientations began to emerge in Arabia, Syria, and Iraq. Such groups included the Kharijis, the Shia, the Qadaris (supporters of free will), and the Jabris (supporters of predestination). Their divisions continued to create tension and conflict within the body politic of the Muslim community.

State involvement in theological matters also began relatively early in Islam, particularly in the Abbasid period (750–1258 CE), which succeeded in wreaking further havoc within the Muslim community. Some rulers played a major role in reducing the scope available for discussion and debate on theological issues when certain views clashed with the state ideology. A good example of this is the Abbasid caliph al-Ma'mun (d. 833). Freedom of belief for Muslims became severely curtailed when those who did not conform to state-adopted theological positions had to flee their towns, remain in hiding, or face torture and persecution, while being branded heretics or blasphemers.

It is important to note the high degree of fluidity and diversity in the understanding of what constitutes apostasy in the course of the development of apostasy laws. This state of affairs has been used by political and religious figures throughout history and up through the present day to control, oppress, persecute, and eliminate opponents. For this reason, the potential for misuse of apostasy laws has always been considerable.

How well the apostasy laws are supported by the Qur'an and the practice of Prophet Muhammad is also debatable. There are significant counterarguments to the view that the punishment of apostasy by death is based on clear Qur'anic or prophetic instructions. Critics argue there is nothing in the Qur'an to justify a temporal punishment, such as death, for apostasy, and little to justify many of the apostasy laws that one finds in classical Islamic legal texts. Many of these laws were developed on the basis of certain isolated (*ahad*) hadith or their interpretations or on the basis of analogy (*qiyas*) and *ijtihad*. For example, the hadith, "Whoever changes his religion, kill him," could be understood to mean converting from any religion to another, and therefore could be taken as a prohibition against converting to any religion. Even if its interpretation was restricted to simply prohibiting conversion from Islam, there are other versions of the hadith that seem to imply a clear connection between the instruction to kill the apostate and rebellion against the Muslim community. In reading such hadith, classical Muslim jurists favored readings and interpretations that supported the death penalty at the expense of those readings that opposed such a penalty. Clear textual proofs that guarantee certainty of knowledge (`*ilm qat*`*i*) were lacking in this debate.

The point is that, because none of the textual proofs provided by Muslim jurists to support the death penalty for apostasy guarantees certainty of knowledge as understood in the principles of Islamic jurisprudence (*usul al-fiqh*), Muslims now have the opportunity to go back and rethink the law. Moreover, if the law is no longer practicable or relevant for the majority of Muslims, there is strong justification for reconsidering it. The argument that such laws have been traditionally backed by consensus (*ijma'*) should not be a deterrent. Numerous other laws in which there previously was a Muslim consensus have been subject to revision; some, as in the cases concerned with slavery and the caliphate, have been dropped altogether.

The nature of today's debate on apostasy and apostasy laws in Muslim states is also important to consider. Malaysia, for example, is a multireligious society in which apostasy laws have been long debated. In various states of Malaysia's federation, apostasy laws, not necessarily with the death penalty, are in place and arguably violate constitutional guarantees of religious freedom by requiring Muslims who want to renounce Islam to repent or endure detention for the purpose of rehabilitation and education.

The apostasy debate in Malaysia is also linked to Malay identity and politics. Both main political parties—the United Malay National Organisation (UMNO) and the opposition and more Islamist Parti Islam Se-Malaysia (PAS)—use the debate to score political points by demonstrating their commitment to Islam. PAS has supported introducing the death penalty to deter Muslims from renouncing Islam, so the more secularist UMNO has been trying to demonstrate its Islamic credentials. As part of this agenda, UMNO has supported the introduction of Islamic banking, insurance, and mortgages and the increase of Islamic programming on television and radio and in other government-controlled media; and it has given more coverage to Islamic festivals than in the past. Several UMNO-governed states within the federation also have introduced or are preparing to introduce legislation making it difficult for Muslims to renounce Islam. Thus support for apostasy laws, along with other features of Islamization, is among the tactics being used to garner political support.

A number of important issues emerge from the Qur'anic treatment of the subject of freedom of religion. It is clear that the Qur'an supports the notion of religious freedom, including religious faith as an individual choice. Religious freedom is presented in the Qur'an in a variety of contexts and ways. Under Muslim rule historically, non-Muslims were allowed to govern their lives under the rules and values of their religious traditions. Muslims were instructed not to abuse or slander adherents to other religions—including idolaters—even though their beliefs, values, and practices were not supported or respected by the Qur'an. The Qur'an also rejected forced conversions, as emphasized in the well-known verse, "There shall be no coercion in matters of faith..."[4] The principle of personal responsibility that is a strong current through the Qur'an also emphasizes that each person is given the capacity to discern right from wrong, and it is a personal decision as to which belief system, if any, to follow. According to the Qur'an, God's plan for humankind is not that everyone should follow the same path.[5] The Prophet's task was primarily to explain the difference between right and wrong. Individuals then had the choice of whether or not to follow God's path. This principle applies equally to Muslims who choose to leave Islam. Every person will be asked about his or her actions on the Day of Judgment and it will be the individual who will ultimately bear the responsibility for that choice in the afterlife.

Despite this, Muslim scholars of the classical period largely limited the scope of freedom available to a Muslim in choosing and adopting a religion or a belief system. They opted instead for a narrow definition of the right to religious freedom, confining it to the freedom given to non-Muslims either to remain under Islamic rule as "protected religious minorities" (*ahl al-dhimma*) or to convert to Islam. Conversion from Islam was banned absolutely. These scholars went against the general ethos of the Qur'an when they argued for state coercion to prevent Muslims from converting to other religions. The view of these early scholars is unsurprising as they functioned at a time when religious freedom and the concept of individual human dignity were not related in the way they are today. In the social and political environment of that earlier time, an individual generally became a "person" through association with a particular religion or tribe; and in the case of Islam, it was the religious tradition rather than the tribe that mattered most. In joining Islam, an individual automatically became part of the community of believers, which also functioned as a political unit, within the caliphate or emirate. Thus there was a conjunction between corporate religious identity rooted in the community and political identity. If someone rejected the community of believers, he or she was automatically excluded from the membership of the political community as well. This meant the complete loss of an individual's basic rights, including the rights to life and to own property, which were conferred upon becoming a Muslim. Since an individual's basic rights were dependent on being part of this community, the whole notion of apostasy and the punishment associated with it in the premodern period made sense.

In contrast, most Muslims today have moved away from this conjunction between religious community and political identity to a sort of separation between the two. Today, a political community in the sense of a nation-state does not have to be based on a religious community, and, in fact, most nation-states in the world are not based on this strict identification. As a rule, an individual can become a citizen of this political unit regardless of religious affiliation. This is true even in the majority of Muslim states, in which modern constitutions often guarantee religious freedom and equality before the law for all. Thus, in general, religious freedom has become a *prima facie* right in the modern period within the functioning of the nation-state. Notions of apostasy, driven by classical Islamic law that depended on the meshing of religious identity and political community, have therefore lost much of their political meaning.

With few exceptions, today's societies are not "closed." People move from one area to another and from country to country in an unprecedented manner. Migration, travel, and dual residence serve the purposes of education, business, recreation, and employment in a world driven by technologically advanced communication networks. Muslims migrate in large numbers to non-Muslim countries and, to a lesser extent, vice versa. Consequently people of diverse religions may live in close proximity or even side by side in the same neighborhood.

This unprecedented interaction and pluralism places substantial pressure on all Islamic scholars to offer new ideas about religious freedom relevant to today's multireligious and multicultural world. The reaffirmation of classical laws, developed for a different time, place, and circumstance, is not particularly practical. In any event, many Muslims have in practice abandoned key aspects of the apostasy laws, particularly punishment by death. It is only in a few Muslim states that the law is still in force. Despite this, the question of apostasy continues to be hotly debated among Muslims. It finds its way into contemporary Islamic legal texts and discourse, with many traditionalists continuing to argue for the implementation of these laws.

On the practical problems posed by apostasy laws, one may argue that these laws have a great potential for abuse. There is a high degree of diversity in Muslim theological, legal, and religio-political positions and thought, and it is difficult to devise a creed that is applicable to and accepted by all Muslims. In addition to premodern divisions, new divisions have emerged among Muslims today, and Muslims from one group still often accuse their opponents of apostasy, heresy, and unbelief. Similarly, in a number of Muslim countries, the government assumes the responsibility of "protecting" local orthodoxies. Those who do not adhere to the government-sanctioned orthodoxy can be branded as deviants, heretics, or apostates. The potential for abuse is all the more real because governments in a number of Muslim countries are either semi-authoritarian or fully authoritarian; thus civil, political, and religious rights remain severely curtailed there. Moreover, religion and religious institutions in these countries are subordinated to the government, which can use its authority to persuade or, if necessary, force religious officials and institutions to question the religious beliefs of political opponents and dissidents. The authoritarian tendencies inherent in these countries also mean that there are very few, if any, institutional safeguards to check abuses, safeguards such as elected representatives of Parliament, independent courts, or a free civic society and media.

For these reasons, it is essential to formulate a concept of religious freedom that is in harmony with our current realities, taking into account both Islamic belief and religious diversity within nation-states. It is premature to believe that nation-states in the Muslim world are going to disappear or that, somehow, a new single Muslim state will emerge with a caliphal system in which one caliph leads the faithful. This idea, modeled on the premodern "caliph," can only be described today as utopian, unrealistic, and impractical. Even a cursory look at the map of the Muslim world—with all its political, theological, economic, and cultural differences—reveals that there are considerable divisions and differences among Muslims that would prevent the realization of such an idea. It is inconceivable that these Muslim states could be politically united under one umbrella, as some Muslims seem to believe, or that all Muslims will one day be residing in a *dar al-islam* (abode of Islam) that accommodates only Muslims as full citizens.

If we are right about world trends, we will see less, not more, compartmentalization of the world into religious blocs. On the contrary, globalization will bring far more linkages and mixes of people from a variety of religious backgrounds into the same space. With the increasing intensity of globalization, interaction, and multiculturalism, many of the classical ideas that Muslims inherited from the past are now impractical and unrealistic. Recognizing these new realities, many Muslim social and political systems have adopted modern ideas associated with religious freedom.

Two important but rarely discussed challenges to laws on apostasy are the increasing religious diversity in the world and the issue of "silent apostasy." Today, nearly all Muslim countries are multireligious societies, and among a nation's Muslim population are people with different legal, theological, or mystical traditions. Even in Saudi Arabia, where all citizens are required by law to be Muslims, there is a significant Shia minority population, in addition to the Sunni majority. Several million Christians, Hindus, and Buddhists also live there as long-term guest workers.

The number of Muslims living as minorities throughout the world is also increasing. Several million Muslims live in the United States and Europe as minorities. There are approximately 50 million Muslims in China and 150 million in India. In those places, apostasy laws have no legal consequences. Muslims are free to convert, apostatize, or simply not follow any religion at all, without any detriment to their basic rights. Today, the classical Islamic law categories of the "abode of Islam" (*dar al-islam*) and "the abode of war" (*dar al-harb*) are not useful to determine where Muslims are located. Given globalization and increasing fluidity and mobility, it is common for people of various faiths to live side by side. In a world of information exchange in which proselytizing is widely practiced, religious conversions will undoubtedly occur and religious boundaries will break down.

Complicating this further is the fact that in all Muslim communities there are both practicing and non-practicing or nominal Muslims. Practicing Muslims themselves vary in their commitment to Islamic rituals, commandments, and prohibitions. Some may be totally committed and devoted to both the fundamentals and non-fundamentals of the religion. Others may adhere only to the fundamentals such as the five daily prayers, fasting, *zakat*, and pilgrimage. Some believers may practice some, or even most, fundamentals but ignore others and be irregular in their practice.

The merely nominal or "cultural" Muslims are those who happen to have been born into a Muslim family and have only minimal affiliation with Islam. Cultural Muslims may carry a Muslim name, live in a Muslim community, and identify with Islam when asked about their religious affiliation. They may also have a superficial, distorted or vague familiarity with what Muslims "do." Cultural Muslims are not usually interested in observing religious practices apart from occasional attendance at *Eid* prayer or participation in community religio-cultural activities. They have little commitment to Islam and do not abide by its command-ments or prohibitions. In all Muslim communities there are large numbers of cultural or nominal Muslims, though there are no reliable studies in this area. Conservative estimates of a quarter of the Muslim population being nominal Muslims would mean that at least 300 million Muslims fall into this category.

Nominal Muslims present a major challenge to the law on apostasy. Under classical Islamic law, such people should be considered apostates. They profess Islam outwardly and perhaps incidentally but have no commitment to it or its practices. A number of classical Muslim scholars held that anyone who did not, for instance, perform the obligatory requirements of the five daily prayers would fall into the category of an apostate. The question then becomes whether they should be put to death as a result. According to Ibn Taymiyya, the Muslim who does not pray the five daily prayers must be ordered to do so; if he refuses, he must be put to death as a *kafir* (unbeliever). He will not be washed before burial, no prayer will be performed for him, and he will not be buried in a Muslim cemetery.[6] Ibn Taymiyya's view is not isolated; as far as fundamental religious obligations are concerned, many *ulama* would concur with him. In fact, many view the first caliph Abu Bakr's engagement in the so-called wars of apostasy as fighting apostates whose crime was the refusal to pay *zakat*, a fundamental obligation of Islam.

If apostasy laws, as understood in classical Islamic law, were rigorously applied, of the 1.2 billion or more Muslims in the world today, it is likely that at least 300 million nominal Muslims would be condemned to death. Those Muslims today who argue for the imposition of the death penalty for apostasy appear to ignore the practical implications of their views, which puts them in an increasingly untenable position. The idea of putting to death hundreds of millions of Muslims is obviously absurd. Perhaps that is why "silent" apostasy is for all practical pur-poses ignored in the current debate.

A primary reason why some Muslims and Muslim regimes feel the need to introduce apostasy laws today is to curtail conversions from Islam. However, Muslims also seek to convert non-Muslims. The fact that Islam is one of the fast-est growing religions in the world is indicative of this. In countries like Malaysia, the number of people converting to Islam is far greater than the number of Muslims who renounce Islam. Therefore, it follows that if Muslim states were to introduce apostasy laws, Muslims are likely to face similar restrictions in non-Muslim-majority states and thus prevent Muslims from converting non-Muslims to Islam. It would be inequitable to suggest that only Muslims should have the right to proselytize. Further, forcing Muslims who do not want to remain Muslim to adhere to Islam would categorize them as hypocrites, according to the Qur'an. People who remain Muslims under the threat of force are unlikely to have anything beneficial to offer to Islam or Muslim communities. Criminalizing apostasy and imposing a death penalty give the impression that Islam is an imposed religion. It may only succeed in offending the overwhelming majority of Muslims in the world who embrace Islam voluntarily. Therefore, a more effective and practical alternative needs to be found to prevent Muslims from renouncing Islam.

It seems that, with the exception of a vocal group of extremists, ultratraditionalists and some political Islamists, the majority of Muslims throughout the Muslim world are moving away from the notion of the need to force Islam on Muslims to the view that Islam is essentially a covenant between the individual and God. This is closer to the Qur'anic idea of noncoercion in religion, which was so strongly emphasized in the Qur'an in a variety of contexts but largely ignored in the formulation of the classical law of apostasy. Unlike the classical period, in which "noncoercion in religion" was considered to have been "abrogated," today the view that is emerging argues that noncoercion was not only *not* abrogated but also remains a fundamental principle of Islam and guarantees religious freedom to all. Nevertheless, many Muslims have remained reluctant to take the logical step of examining apostasy laws and declaring them irrelevant to their life today. Others, although only a few, are arguing for doing away with apostasy laws that adversely affect the individual's basic rights as a person and are pressing for reform in this area.

Given that both the religio-political context in which apostasy laws were first put into effect and the division of the world into categories of the "abode of Islam," "abode of war," and "abode of peace" have lost their meaning and relevance in the modern period, it is important to rethink the punishment for apostasy and apostasy laws. The weak textual basis of the apostasy laws provides a strong religious justification for embarking on the task of reforming these laws and emphasizing religious freedom as a basic human right. This would indeed be a significant contribution to the global discourse on human rights today.

PART V

CONCLUSIONS

‖ 16 ‖

Conclusions

We have surveyed how apostasy and blasphemy rules are applied in many Muslim countries. We have reviewed the impact in the United Nations and in the West of increasing demands that such rules be enforced internationally. And we have presented Islamic scholars who argue that there should be no temporal punishment for such "sins." These three themes are interconnected. Patterns in the Muslim world reveal the destructive effect of such laws and accompanying vigilantism and are a harbinger of the future into which the West is sliding if it should continue to bend to demands to outlaw "defamation of religion." The arguments by the Muslim scholars demonstrate that this is a bitterly contested debate within Islam, in which acquiescence to the demands of repressive regimes and movements undercuts Muslims who argue for and defend—sometimes at the cost of their lives—individual freedoms of religion and expression.

The West is experiencing a diffuse but determined campaign to repress ridicule and critique of or within Islam, in ways analogous to the repression already existing in many Muslim-majority countries. This campaign has made inroads through lawsuits, diplomacy, economic boycotts, and, at times, lethal force and intimidation—all of which are contributing to a broad chilling effect on speech concerning Islam. Few Western leaders and policy makers comprehend the radical nature of the change that is being urged and is in fact already underway. Consequently, there is no concerted or coherent policy response. Instead, the West reacts to the threat of violence largely on an ad hoc basis, through a patchwork of self-censorship and laws restricting speech. Many Western governments embrace hate-speech bans, which serve as proxies for Muslim blasphemy laws.

This book attempts to show that if these demands are successful, the result would be far more sweeping and detrimental to Western society than has been foreseen. At stake are the freedoms of religion and expression that lie at the heart of Western liberal democracies. Furthermore, within Islam itself, compliance with these demands would tip the balance in favor of fundamentalists and extremists, since reformers would be attacked for their views even in the relative safe haven of the West. In his foreword, former Indonesian president Abdurrahman Wahid warned that such efforts "play directly into the hands of fundamentalists, who wish to avoid all criticism of their attempts to narrow the scope of discourse regarding Islam, and to inter 1.3 billion Muslims in a narrow, suffocating chamber of dogmatism."

If Islam, and Islam alone, were to be protected by the state from critique, an illiberal interpretation of Islam would attain a de facto privileged status in the West. Conversely, should Christianity and other religions also benefit from such state protection, fundamental individual freedoms would be essentially negated.

The Muslim World

The background and consequences of this campaign are illustrated by our survey of the customs and norms in many OIC states. It is important to note that governments in Muslim-majority countries, as well as elsewhere, also repress freedom for reasons that have little to do with Islam. Uzbekistan and Turkmenistan restrict any expression, including by peaceful Muslims, which might challenge state authority. Egypt can imprison anyone who "affronts the President of the Republic."[1] Iran imprisons multitudes for religious offenses but also, especially since the protests following the 2009 elections, has imprisoned many others on stated grounds of threatening national security or undermining the regime. It is also important to recognize that the severity of restrictions varies from country to country.

However, despite these caveats, our survey shows that in Muslim-majority countries and areas, restrictions on freedom of religion and expression, based on prohibitions of blasphemy, apostasy, and "insulting Islam," are pervasive, thwart freedom, and cause suffering to millions of people. This survey, extensive though it sometimes is, does not attempt to cover all countries or examples; for reasons of space and to avoid repetition, we limit our review to some twenty Muslim countries, including the worst offenders, and have left out very many cases.[2]

The Muslim World and the West

Despite widespread and growing repression, much of the debate on free speech and freedom of religion in the West and in the UN takes place in isolation from, and often with utter obliviousness toward, the actual application of bans against blasphemy, apostasy, and "insulting religion" throughout much of the Muslim world. However, it is only by examining these practices that we can understand what OIC members and Islamist agitators are pressuring the Western world to adopt.

Some of the pressure takes place through repeated resolutions in the United Nations. It also occurs through such acts as the attacks on Salman Rushdie's translators and international humanitarian workers, threats against Flemming Rose, boycotts of Danish or Norwegian goods, and demands over who should lead

NATO. These actions have been supported variously by Iran, Saudi Arabia, Pakistan, Egypt, Sudan, Turkey, and other Muslim-majority states, sometimes acting together through the OIC. Certainly, the push to outlaw purported criticism of Islam has a grassroots base among some Muslim groups in the West, but it is these governments that have given the movement articulation, respectability, and financial and organizational support.

For example, behind the scenes of the Danish cartoon crisis, the OIC and several of its member states manufactured much of the Muslim outrage, most of which began four months after the cartoons appeared. They stirred Muslim anger and lent legitimacy to the issue, ensuring wide and sustained attention. By the time the crisis subsided, polling showed that an astonishing 99 percent of Jordanians and 98 percent of Egyptians had heard of the Danish cartoons. The media in Jordan and Egypt were tightly controlled by their governments and, according to Reporters without Borders, had press freedom scores of 112 and 143, respectively, with 175 being the worst. Their populations tend to hear about things their governments want them to hear. Iran and Syria were implicated in some of the violence, in an attempt to deflect attention from Iran's nuclear project. Saudi Arabia and Egypt, irate about U.S. foreign policy democratization projects in the region, were instrumental in initiating the boycott and inflaming passions in the street. The OIC voted to condemn the cartoons, issued a démarche against Denmark, and instituted a boycott against private Danish companies.[3]

Not all Muslim-majority governments are responsible for the violence associated with much of the blasphemy ban movement, but several have benefited from that violence and have not hesitated to use it to further their own agendas. At the UN, OIC members have leveraged attacks against Western cartoonists and politicians in order to reinvigorate their long-term diplomatic effort to create a universal blasphemy ban. At the UN Human Rights Council in 2007, Egypt's representative stressed that the Danish cartoon crisis "highlighted the damage that freedom of speech, if left unchecked, may lead to."[4] The expectations of this lobby are thus based partially on what occurs today in their domestic politics and society. The revolutions and political turmoil now sweeping the Arab world appear to be allowing an even greater role for religion in public affairs, so this is not likely to subside.

For these reasons, our survey of practices in many Muslim-majority countries illuminates the type of strictures these states aim to impose on the rest of the world. Taken as a whole, it becomes readily apparent that such strictures constitute one of the major patterns in human rights violations in the world today. Finally, it reveals a key reason why, despite having only minority support, radical views of Islam proliferate: many opponents of radical Islam are silenced by the coercive force of the state or by mobs and vigilantes, often acting with impunity, who justify their violence by claiming to protect Islam from "insult." The practice of punishing blasphemy is an important weapon used by radicals in Islam's ongoing war of ideas.

The Victims of Accusations

Some of the victims are eccentric, like the followers of a Malaysian group who thought that teapots symbolized harmony between people and were therefore sentenced to years in prison, or the Indonesian Sumardi Tappaya, sentenced to six months for heresy after a relative reported that he whistled when he prayed. Others are merely unfortunate, like the multireligious group of Pakistani children who put ointment on an injured donkey; they were accused of insulting Islam and jailed when the ointment smeared into a pattern that a fanatic thought resembled the names of "holy personalities." The donkey was also detained briefly.

However, most victims fall into four basic categories, together comprising millions of people. The first category includes adherents of religious groups that have arisen in the Muslim world in recent centuries. They are accused of thereby maintaining that Muhammad is not the last of the prophets. The two main such groups are the Baha'is and the Ahmadis. These groups differ, in that the latter usually maintains that they are in fact Muslim, while the former do not.

Ahmadis suffer persecution throughout the Muslim world, even in traditionally moderate countries such as Bangladesh and Indonesia. They are viciously persecuted in Pakistan, and the Pakistani constitution even specifically singles them out for persecution: they face up to three years in prison if they call themselves Muslim. On June 9, 2008, the Indonesian government, after persistent pressure from extremist groups, issued a joint ministerial decree ordering the Ahmadiyya community to cease all religious activity in which they described themselves as followers of Islam.

Baha'is also suffer widespread persecution, especially in Iran, their place of origin and home to a large Baha'i community. Since the 1979 Iranian Revolution, hundreds of Baha'is have been killed for their religious beliefs; in 2010, most of the Baha'i leadership was in prison. In 2007, Afghanistan's General Directorate of Fatwas and Accounts, an advisory body to the Supreme Court, pronounced all converts from Islam to Baha'ism to be apostates and declared that all Baha'is are infidels. In Egypt, on March 29, 2009, during a televised discussion of the Baha'i religion, prominent commentator Gamal Abdel Rahem denounced one of the guests, Baha'i Basma Gamal Musa, as an "apostate" who "should be killed!" Baha'is in the village of al-Shuraniya were promptly attacked with rocks and firebombs.

The second category of the persecuted is those who convert, or wish to convert, from Islam to another religion or who simply wish to give up being Muslim. These are regarded as apostates. The persecution of apostates is often extended to anyone thought to be involved in others' apostasy, particularly anyone who talks to Muslims about other religious beliefs. Libya imprisons converts. Iran's Parliament has debated introducing legislation mandating death for apostasy, but even without such legislation, courts have relied on interpretations of sharia, and even quotations from Khomeini, to put to death or otherwise harshly punish apostates. Malaysia has assigned converts, or would-be converts, to reeducation camps. Egypt's security services have tortured converts. Algeria's Minister of Religious Affairs, Ghoulamullah Bouabdellah, has equated Christian evangelism with terrorism. In a 2010 scare over "proselytism," Morocco expelled dozens of expatriate Christians. In 2007, three Turkish Christians in Malatya, including two converts from Islam, were tortured and their throats slit. Saudi Arabia officially instructs that apostates should be killed, and, in 2008, a Saudi member of the *muttawa* burned his daughter to death after she converted. In Afghanistan converts have been killed, and in Somalia, all Somali Christians are being systematically hunted down and killed on the grounds that they are apostates; the Al-Shabab militia openly declares its intention to kill every Christian in the country.

The third category is Muslims of the "wrong" type, such as Shias in predominantly Sunni areas, or Sunnis in Shia areas, and Sufis in many areas.[5] Egypt's government has repressed Shias, and Shia leader Mohamed Ramadan Hussein El-Derini was detained and tortured without charges or trial for fifteen months. One of the detention orders stated that he was "under the influence of Shia ideas and seeks to spread them in his circles." In June 2009, there were reports of as many as 300 arrests of Shias in Egypt. Iran has been arresting Sunni clerics and cracking down on Sufism, with hundreds of arrests. In Saudi Arabia, Shias are commonly viewed as heretics and suffer discrimination and frequent persecution: the situation is even worse for some subgroups, especially Ismailis. In parts of Pakistan, and throughout Iraq, members of Muslim groups are violently attacked, some even as they pray at their mosques and shrines, by Muslims of different sects, with hundreds killed. Turkey discriminates against Alevis, while Morocco is monitoring Shias because of concern that Sunnis are converting.

The fourth category is Muslim reformers and dissidents, including theologians, editors, journalists, authors, democracy activists, and others, especially when they challenge the entrenched power of regimes that claim to be representative of Islam. Those designated as possible heretics or deviants include Bangladeshi feminists, Iranian religious scholars, Egyptian intellectuals, opponents to slavery and corruption in Mauritania, social reformers in Afghanistan, and innumerable others.

In 2002, a group of religious scholars, the Bandung Indonesian Ulemas Forum (FUUI) issued a fatwa saying that reformer Ulil Abshar Abdalla deserved to die after publishing an article in the newspaper *Kompas* titled "Freshening Up Islamic Understanding." Abdalla had already been targeted by the radical Islam Defenders Front. In Afghanistan in 2007, Ghaus Zalmai, formerly an outspoken journalist, who was then spokesman for the attorney general, was arrested for publishing a Dari translation of the Qur'an. Several of Afghanistan's courageous reformist journalists have been charged with blasphemy and imprisoned, especially when they have raised questions abut the status of women. In 2007, Aishath Aniya, formerly the Maldivian Democratic Party's Deputy Secretary-General, was forced to resign and go into hiding after writing an article criticizing the notion that women must wear a veil lest men be tempted. Ali Ahmad Said Asbar is often regarded as the greatest contemporary Arab poet and is more commonly known by his pen names, Adonis or Adunis. In October 2008, after he gave a lecture at Algeria's National Library, arguing that Islamist attempts to impose their religion on society and the state are wrong, Islamists accused him of being an "apostate," and the Minister of Culture denounced his "ideological deterioration" and fired the library's director for inviting him. In Yemen in March 2010, several leading Muslim scholars declared that people pushing for a ban on child brides were apostates.

Vague Charges

One of our main findings is that "blasphemy," "insulting Islam," and even "apostasy," not to mention a myriad of other related offenses, have no clear definitions; what is perceived as an offense varies not only from country to country, but also within countries and regions. Even there, they can be in constant flux. This means that many persons do not know, and cannot know, at any given time and place what is prohibited and what is not. In 2009, Islam Samham, a Jordanian poet and journalist, was sentenced to a year in prison for apostasy for "combining the sacred words of the Qur'an with sexual themes." In usually secular Turkey, one can be punished for insulting the "Turkish nation," which can incorporate a religious dimension because Islam is regarded as an integral part of the Turkish nation.

The possible breadth of what can be banned as blasphemy appears almost limitless. The late Sheikh Abdulaziz bin Baz, while Grand Mufti of Saudi Arabia, declared, "Those who claim that the earth is round and moving around the sun are condemned as apostates and their blood can be shed and their property can be taken in the name of God." He annulled the fatwa in 1985, but for a ten-year period in the late twentieth century, any Copernican in Saudi Arabia was thus declared by the highest religious authority as someone who should be killed and stripped of property. Bin Baz also attempted to provide a comprehensive list of religiously forbidden expressions, including "say[ing] that enforcing the punishments prescribed by Allah, such as amputation of the hand of a thief or stoning of an adulterer, is not suitable for this day and age." He condemned the belief that any system or law that is human in origin can be better than sharia, which would condemn the majority of governments across the Islamic world, most of which have constitutions and incorporate non-sharia laws in their legal and judicial systems. He also listed as banned the belief that "Islam is merely a relationship between Allah and the individual, and that it should not interfere in other aspects of life," a view that would render many Muslims apostate.[6] His fatwas remain in force after his death and are disseminated by the Saudi government around the world. The Saudi government expects such fatwas of its highest religious authorities to be enforced through temporal punishments and, within its borders, seeks to ensure that they are.

Saudi Arabia punishes those whom it deems *mushrikun*, or "polytheists." The term "polytheist" can be used expansively, including against those who celebrate the prophet's birthday, since this can be deemed "an act of imitating Christians." (Christians and Shias are also called "polytheists.") This can also have a multiplier effect whereby "[a]nyone who does not consider the polytheists (*mushrikun*) to be unbelievers, or who has doubts concerning their unbelief, or considers their way to be correct, is himself an unbeliever (*kafir*)." So if you do not celebrate the prophet's birthday, but do not think that those who do so are polytheists, then you too may be a polytheist. Perhaps you might be a polytheist if you disagree with this. Other possible charges in the Kingdom include witchcraft, sorcery, and "harboring destructive thoughts."

Malaysia works on the premise that Muslim Malaysians are very easily confused, and so it outlaws religious speech that could "create confusion among Muslims" or might contain "twisted facts that can undermine the faith of Muslims." Pakistan's blasphemy laws can be violated "by any imputation, innuendo or insinuation, directly or indirectly," which makes knowing when the law is violated extremely difficult. Iran has probably the widest range of crimes, including "friendship with the enemies of God" and "hostility towards friends of God," "fighting against God," "dissension from religious dogma," "spreading lies," and "propagation of spiritual liberalism."

State Repression

Adherents of newer religions, converts, Muslim minorities, and religious, social, and political reformers can be subject to various means of attack as insulters of religion. The dangers they face exist not only in states generally regarded as religiously repressive but also in countries often considered more moderate. Not just Afghanistan, Iran, Pakistan, and Saudi Arabia, but also Egypt and Bangladesh can use the full force of the law, as well as extensive extralegal measures, against them.

Apart from the vagueness of laws relating to blasphemy offenses, the prosecutions in many key Muslim-majority countries also frequently fall far short of international standards of due process and fairness. Proving intent is often not necessary in order to secure criminal convictions, and arguing that what the accused said was in fact true could itself be considered blasphemous. Hence, the accused is deprived of any meaningful defense. In blasphemy cases in Iran, Saudi Arabia, Pakistan, and Sudan, the weight of testimony of a male Muslim is worth more than that of a non-Muslim, and even more again if the non-Muslim is a woman. On this basis, a simple accusation made against a non-Muslim by a Muslim can be enough to secure a conviction. In many places confessions are coerced but are nevertheless routinely allowed as evidence.

Some countries provide little opportunity for a fair hearing and, in others, such as Saudi Arabia, defendants may not even have the right to be present at their own trial. In Iran, the "apostate" Baha'is have no rights whatsoever. In Iran, Pakistan, Afghanistan, Iraq, and other countries, no law is allowed to stand if religious authorities assert that it contradicts the tenets of Islam—as they understand it. Challenging the status of religious offenses is often an offense in its own right, and thus reforming such systems becomes nearly impossible. This produces a circularity such as that which afflicted Afghan editor Ali Mohaqeq Nasab, who was arrested for publishing "un-Islamic" articles after he questioned whether it was right to kill apostates. Criticizing and questioning religious authority is simply forbidden.

Societal Repression

Despite the grave effects of state repression, the greater danger to those accused is from societal forces in attacks that range from calculated assaults by vigilantes and terrorists to sudden attacks by enraged mobs. Pakistan provides striking examples. Although many persons have been persecuted under its blasphemy laws, there have, so far, been no official executions; however, there have been many deaths, and tens of thousands persecuted, through extralegal violence in response to blasphemy accusations. Some of these killings take place while victims are in police custody. As we have described, after an allegation that a Qur'an had been defaced, in March 1997, the town of Shanti Nagar, home to many Christians, was attacked by thousands of Muslims, and, despite the presence of hundreds of police, rioters destroyed 326 houses and fourteen churches. Women and girls were abducted; some were raped, and some forcibly married. On August 1, 2009, about a thousand people, believed to be connected to the Taliban-linked Sipah-e-Sahaba militant group, attacked local Christians in Gojra. Over forty homes were razed, and at least seven Christians were killed, six of whom, including two children, were burned alive.

Yet this extralegal violence does not occur without the cooperation of government authorities. It can in turn be encouraged by state agents, or ignored by them. In 2000, Lahore High Court Judge Nazir Akhtar said publicly that Muslims have a religious obligation immediately to kill anyone accused of blasphemy; they should not wait for legal proceedings. This statement, though later retracted, reveals the degree of prejudice and violence surrounding the issue. Asma Jahangir, who was chair of Pakistan's Human Rights Commission, has said that Pakistan's "pattern" of violence against religious minorities was helped by local politicians who "protect [militants] and keep their names out of police reports."[7]

More particularly, state policies and laws encourage the actions of nonstate actors. Discussing the violent minority within Muslim society, journalist Sabrina Tavernise puts it this way: "an intolerant, aggressive minority terrorizes a more open-minded, peaceful majority, while an opportunistic political class dithers, benefiting from alliances with the aggressors."[8] Brian Grim and Roger Finke's research has shown that "[t]o the extent that governments deny religious freedoms, violent religious persecution and conflict will increase."[9] As the late Shahbaz Bhatti, Pakistan's Minister of Minority Affairs, declared following the Gojra riots against Christians: "The blasphemy law is being used to terrorize minorities in Pakistan."[10] In March 2011, Bhatti himself was murdered for his opposition to the blasphemy law.

Political Manipulation

Since religion and politics overlap everywhere in the world, and especially in the Muslim world, there is no clear line between politically and religiously motivated restrictions. But, very often, apostasy and blasphemy accusations are used in the narrower and more cynical sense of "political," as defined by Ambrose Bierce: "A strife of interests masquerading as a contest of principles. The conduct of public affairs for private advantage."[11] In this style of politics, speech is repressed ostensibly in the defense of religious belief or sentiment, when in fact it is questions of personal advantage, economic gain, and power struggles that are really at issue. In such cases, the elastic nature of apostasy, blasphemy, and insult accusations, combined with lax legal standards and anomic violence, allows them to be put to Machiavellian usage.

In Iran, the government has imprisoned learned clergy who have argued against the regime's purported Islamic justification of its own authority, and its claims for the almost absolute power of the Supreme Leader. Scholar Mohsen Kadivar wrote *The Theories of the State in Shiite Jurisprudence*, a three-volume work containing a comprehensive critique of the official Iranian doctrine of *Velayat-e Faqih*, the rule of the jurist, and concluded that the doctrine was not "a part of Shiite general principles." For this he was sentenced to eighteen months in prison.

After the renewal of protests in Iran in December 2009, Ayatollah Khamenei and government loyalists called for protesters to be arrested and put to death for offending God and the prophet, as well as for insulting Ayatollah Khomeini. As part of this effort, the government charged opposition members with religious crimes, especially *mohareb*, or "making war against God and His Prophet." General Muhammad-Ali Aziz Jaafari has said, "Those who demonstrate against the system are waging war on Allah." In the same period, the regime has been arresting Baha'is for alleged participation in demonstrations as part of its effort to stigmatize the opposition through association with a group deemed heretical. Pro-government demonstrators have carried signs asserting that Mir Hussein Mousavi, the opposition leader, is a Baha'i. On January 5, 2010, a regime-linked paper declared in a headline "The So-Called God-Loving Mousavi's Men Turned Out to be Baha'is and Terrorists."

In Saudi Arabia, reformers Ali al-Domaini, Abdullah al-Hamid, and Matrouk al-Faleh were arrested after they circulated a petition advocating the creation of a constitutional monarchy. Charges against them included "incitement against the Wahhabi school of Islam" and "introducing 'Western terminology'" in their calls for reform. An Interior Ministry spokesman said they had issued "statements which do not serve the unity of the country and the cohesion of society...based on Islamic religion."

Some of the most striking examples are from Sudan, which has used accusations of religious speech and thought crimes to try to quash a wide variety of political opponents. Because of his criticism of the regime, Mohamed Mahmoud Taha—perhaps the country's leading Muslim scholar, as well as the leader of the opposition Republican Brotherhood—was executed in 1985 for apostasy, although there was no such provision in the penal code. In the 1990s, Sudan threatened UN Special Rapporteur Gaspar Biro, a Hungarian lawyer, with allegations of blasphemy because of his reports on human rights in the country. In the most sweeping apostasy fatwa in modern times, in 1992, the Kordofan government declared jihad on the Nuba region, and, in 1993, six government-sponsored Muslim clerics in Kordofan declared: "An insurgent who was previously a Muslim is now an apostate; and a non-Muslim is a non-believer standing as a bulwark against the spread of Islam, and Islam has granted the freedom of killing both of them." This fatwa declared that the Nuba non-Muslims could be wiped out as they were barriers to Islam and that Nuba Muslims were now apostates who not only could be but also should be killed. Hence, half a million people were sentenced to death. Subsequent conditions in the 1990s prompted human right organizations to declare the Nuba mountain region a site of genocide.

Political Closure

Similar political attacks also occur in Muslim countries regarded as more moderate, such as Malaysia. In 2008, legal complaints were lodged against Raja Petra Kamaruddin, a member of the Selangor royal family, editor of the website *Malaysia Today*, and perhaps the country's most prominent political blogger. One of the alleged offenses was that his article, "I Promise to Be a Good, Non-hypocritical Muslim," insulted Islam. He was held without charge in a prison camp for two months.

Malaysia also reveals how religious demagoguery erodes self-critique and moderation. In speaking about the Malaysian government's proposal to criminalize Christians' use of the word "Allah," on the grounds that it gave offense to Muslims, Marina Mahathir, daughter of Malaysia's former long-time prime minister, Mahathir Mohamad, noted that "the furor over religious language will feed on itself.... It's only a few people who are inflamed about it.... But if you keep stoking...sooner or later more and more people will think, 'Oh, maybe we should be upset as well.'"[12] Former finance minister Tengku Razaleigh agreed: "In a complex multiracial society a party and a government whose primary response to a public issue is sunk in the elastic goo of 'sensitivities' rather than founded on principle, drawn from sentiment rather than from the Constitution, is already short of leadership and moral fibre." Razaleigh added, "'Sensitivities' is the favored resort of the gutter politician. With it he raises a mob, fans its resentment and helps it discover a growing list of other sensitivities. This is a road to ruin."[13] Malaysia is also notable in the degree to which the government maintains that it must repress alternative viewpoints because its Muslim population is not capable of dealing with different thoughts and ideas.

When these countries' populations are insulated from alternative viewpoints, they can become ever more pliable, thus perpetuating the system. The 2003 UN Arab Human Development Report, commenting on the fact that more foreign books had been translated by Spain in one recent year than by the entire Arabic-speaking world in the last thousand, noted: "In Arab countries where the political exploitation of religion has intensified, tough punishment for original thinking, especially when it opposes the prevailing powers, intimidates and crushes scholars." Such repression also affects journalists, artists, filmmakers, human rights activists, teachers, dissidents, politicians, religious minorities—all who are perceived as challenging the prevailing order.

Whatever the particular accusations used, the effect is the same: religious minorities are threatened and persecuted, critics of the regime are imprisoned or killed, and debate about the nature of Islam is stifled. As Malaysia's Sisters in Islam stated: "By narrowing the space for open dialogue among citizens and squashing their quest for information and to read, the government's act can be deemed as 'promoting Jahiliah' as it will push us into a more suppressed world where we will blindly follow with no questions asked, lest it disrupts our small worldview...."[14] If Islam cannot be discussed, much of the country's law and politics has been placed beyond discussion and, therefore, beyond reform.

Apart from its internal effects of closing down debate within majority-Muslim countries, restrictions on apostasy, blasphemy, and purported religious insult also shape international affairs by strengthening radical Islam and terrorism. In the contemporary conflict of ideas, the key figures are Muslim defenders of freedom. They already labor under the disadvantages of facing opponents who are well-organized and well-funded, as well as violent and vicious in silencing opposition. Worse, blasphemy restrictions further empower reactionaries to kill, imprison, threaten, and otherwise silence Muslim friends of freedom. Hence, if we do not oppose and resist such restrictions, we abandon the allies of freedom.

The Campaign to Internationalize Blasphemy

While the repression we have described in much of the Muslim-majority world is long-standing, the campaign to internationalize it is recent. It made its first major appearance on February 14, 1989, with Ayatollah Khomeini's fatwa condemning *The Satanic Verses*. This triggered the assassination of the novel's Japanese translator, the stabbing of its Italian translator, the shooting of its Norwegian publisher, the burning to death of thirty-five guests at a Turkish hotel hosting its Turkish publisher, and the lifelong need for security for its author. It also prompted a burning-at-the-stake, albeit a symbolic one, and other forms of censorship. Kenan Malik describes how *Satanic Verses* was destroyed by Muslim protesters in Bradford, England: "The novel was tied to a stake before being set alight in front of the police station. It was an act calculated to shock and offend. It did more than that. The burning book became an icon of the rage of Islam. Sent around the world by a multitude of photographers and TV cameras, the image proclaimed, 'I am a portent of a new kind of conflict and of a new kind of world.'"[15]

Many Sunnis, especially those backed by Saudi oil wealth, joined the bandwagon. Supporters ranging from Islamist Leader Yusuf al-Qaradawi—perhaps the most influential preacher in the Sunni world—to Al-Qaeda, to the members of the OIC have held that, henceforth, those living in non-Muslim jurisdictions, whether Muslim or not, can and should be controlled by amorphous and arbitrarily applied Islamic apostasy and blasphemy rules.[16] On an annual basis for over a decade within the UN, OIC representatives have called for the international criminalization of blasphemy against Islam, either through defamation or hate-speech bans, in order to end what Pakistan's envoy Marghoob Saleem Butt calls the "unrestricted and disrespectful enjoyment of freedom of expression."

This demand is new. In contemporary times, Islamic authorities had not previously insisted that non-Muslim states enforce Islamic rules banning blasphemy and the related sins of apostasy, heresy, and hypocrisy. The practice of forbidding wrong was directed primarily at other Muslims, and certainly not to non-Muslim jurisdictions. Bernard Lewis avers: "[A]t no time, until very recently, did any Muslim authority ever suggest that Shari'a law should be enforced on non-Muslims in non-Muslim countries."[17]

The goal of this program is not to penalize defamation of individual Muslims, which is already banned by traditional Western defamation laws, nor to stop discrimination or violence against Muslims, or others, which are already criminal offenses. Rather, it is to criminalize religious and political criticism of particular versions of Islam. Although the proposed bans are often conflated with personal insults, these are not the core of the complaints. Whether called "defamation," "hate speech," "incitement to hostility," or "Islamophobia," the central issue is criticism against or within Islam. This is clearly evident in the examples that have provoked the most outcry and become emblematic of this movement in the West: the Danish and Swedish cartoons, the Pope's Regensburg speech, the van Gogh film *Submission*, Geert Wilders's *Fitna*, the false *Newsweek* story of Qur'an desecration, and, of course, Rushdie's *Satanic Verses*.[18]

Those targeted range from Theo van Gogh, murdered in Amsterdam for his film *Submission*, to Sister Leonella, a sixty-five-year-old Italian nun in Mogadishu, murdered in "retaliation" for the Regensburg speech, to dozens of blameless Christian villagers in Nigeria, burned and hacked to death by Muslim mobs whipped up to strike out against irreverent cartoons in Denmark. In the six years since Scandinavian newspapers published Muhammed cartoons, plots to kill the cartoonists have been intercepted in Denver, Chicago, Philadelphia, and Waterford, Ireland, while a Somalian would-be axe murderer was apprehended inside the home of one of the caricaturists, Kurt Westergaard. Such violence, combined with more generalized intimidation, as well as threats of legal prosecution, has created a broad chilling effect in the West on public negative expression concerning Islam, including expression by reform-minded Muslims.

Developments in the United Nations

Without Western support, the OIC managed to pass UN resolutions each year for twelve years aimed at criminalizing religious blasphemy, or "defamation of religions," and has now, *with* Western support, passed resolutions urging states to prohibit religious hate speech. In recent years, Western states have responded to OIC demands by offering more aggressively to enforce the International Covenant on Civil and Political Rights' article 20(2), a provision calling for religious and other hate-speech bans that was originally included in the covenant at the insistence of the Soviet bloc and other authoritarian states over vociferous objections from the West.

On October 2, 2009, the United States, seeking to "reach out to Muslim countries," joined with Egypt to introduce a nonbinding resolution urging states to enforce their hate-speech laws, which was adopted by consensus. State Department Legal Adviser Harold Koh praised the resolution as among the Obama administration's most "important successes."[19] Though in the United States, hate-speech crimes have been found unconstitutional, in this resolution, the United States encouraged their enforcement in the rest of the world, which could also lead to efforts to reinterpret the First Amendment at home.[20] Several other prominent American leaders, including a senator and a supreme court justice, also voiced hopes for state-enforced limits on expression involving Qur'an burning when in 2010–11 this became an issue in a small Florida church. To date, such views are in the minority, but they could grow as America's uniquely strong protections of individual freedoms come under increasing pressure.

In its sixteenth session in 2011, the Human Rights Council did not adopt a resolution against defamation of religions—marking the first time the UN's premier human rights body had neglected to do so since 1999. Sensing defeat—brought on by more energetic Western opposition and the recent shock of the assassinations of Pakistan's Minister of Minority Affairs Shahbaz Bhatti and Punjab governor Salman Taseer over their opposition to that country's blasphemy laws—the OIC failed to introduce one. This was a small but essential victory in the

defense of individual rights to freedom of expression and of religion. It demonstrated that concerted pushback from the West on this issue can be effective.
Whether some version of the resolution will be resurrected in subsequent UN
meetings remains to be seen. Meanwhile, the OIC has focused on "hate speech" in
its campaign within the UN for worldwide anti-blasphemy bans.

The West has been unsuccessful in promoting its interpretation of hate speech
that draws a distinction between the protection of the individual followers of a
religion and the protection of the religion itself. The West continues to support
international hate-speech bans undeterred, even while OIC diplomats continue
to use key hate-speech terms, such as "incitement to hostility" and "negative
stereotyping," synonymously with "defamation" and "blasphemy" against Islam.
In fact, one of the OIC's "Subsidiary Organs," of which all member states are
automatically members, is the "International Islamic *Fiqh* [Jurisprudence]
Academy," whose official fatwas stipulate that religious freedom requires forbidding anything that might undercut Islam and call for the judicial punishment of
apostasy.[21]

Unless shelved or defeated, these resolutions, however phrased, are likely to
be interpreted by UN bodies as blasphemy laws and made internationally binding.
Former U.S. Ambassador Jeane Kirkpatrick observed that UN resolutions have a
tendency, like "ground water," to seep into international court opinions whether
binding or not and become customary law.[22] Politicized international bodies will
be authorized to interpret vague hate-speech terms and will be far less scrupu-
lous than Western courts in adhering to fundamental human rights principles.
On this issue, the OIC has already reshaped the focus of the UN Human Rights
Council, and even the General Assembly, as well as the work of several UN Special
Rapporteurs.

If this continues, no longer would the Universal Declaration of Human Rights
be understood as obliging states to ensure respect for rights of the individual to
freedoms of religion and expression. Instead it would be inverted to mandate the
use of state power to coerce individuals to respect specific religions. Western
leaders would be in the dock at UN bodies, while Iran, Saudi Arabia, Egypt,
Pakistan, Sudan, and other states would be legitimized, even lauded, for upholding
international human rights, as they, in the name of fighting religious insult, persecute religious reformers and political dissidents. Conversely, there would be no
international human rights basis for other nations to come to the defense of such
dissidents.

Western Law

Since laws prohibiting blasphemy and heresy against Christianity have become all
but obsolete, it seems far-fetched that the West should now be contemplating a
retreat from its freedoms on behalf of the demands of some members of another

religion. But censorship, book-burnings, and their modern equivalents—blog-purging and the seizure of computer hard drives—are back.

In many Western countries, there are already lawsuits and criminal prosecutions concerning issues involving religion, politics, and society that have customarily been open to debate. Since the mid-1990s, prosecutors in Finland, the Netherlands, and Canada have trawled the websites of anti-immigration advocates looking for evidence that Islam's Prophet may have been mocked or for some other anti-Islamic comment. The Dutch government has taken the added precaution of establishing a standing "Interdepartmental Committee on Cartoons" to monitor irreverent treatment of Islam. In France, Canada, Norway, and Italy, publishers, editors, and authors have been tried for inciting religious hostility and insulting religious sensibilities with their critiques of Islam and Muslim immigration. In Austria, Elisabeth Sabaditsch-Wolff was convicted for her lecture before an anti-immigration political party criticizing Muslim practices she observed abroad. In Germany, a man was convicted for the sacrilegious treatment of the *word* "Koran," not the Islamic sacred text itself. Despite France's "laïcité" system of strict separation of religion and politics, national icon Brigitte Bardot, in her animal-rights advocacy, has been convicted and fined five times under hate-speech laws for denouncing Islamic slaughter practices, as well as for other derogatory statements against Muslim matters.

As in much of the Muslim world, the ambiguity of such laws erodes due process and basic principles of fairness. An Australian lower court found two Christian pastors guilty of "vilifying" Islam in a private religion class and issued a lifelong gag order against their speaking about the Qur'an. Under Norway's hate-speech laws, a handful of political organizations are empowered to bring legal complaints against negative commentary on Islam. A British jury was instructed to ignore whether or not impugned assertions were factually correct. A Helsinki court ruled that an argument made by the defense in a Muslim blasphemy case was inadmissible because "[l]ogic and so-called arguments of reason have no true significance in debating religious questions."

These problems have led to growing legal criticism in Australia, Canada, and the United Kingdom, including by some disillusioned former proponents. Amir Butler, of the Australian Muslim Public Affairs Committee, no longer favors religious hate-speech laws because "at every major Islamic lecture I have attended since [hate speech] litigation began against Catch the Fire Ministries, there have been small groups of evangelical Christians—armed with notepads and pens—jotting down any comment that might be later used as evidence" against the speaker. Vilification laws thus become "a legalistic weapon by which religious groups can silence their ideological opponents, rather than engaging in debate and discussion."[23] Alan Borovoy, an architect of Canada's human rights commissions and general counsel of the Canadian Civil Liberties Association, now laments that, when he labored to create the commissions, "we never imagined that they might ultimately be used against freedom of speech.... No ideology—political, religious or philosophical—can be immune.... A free culture cannot protect people against material that hurts."[24]

Nevertheless, the effort to punish anti-Islamic hate speech is moving forward in both regional and international systems. In 2008, the Council of Europe issued new hate-speech guidelines for the entire region, which specified that, in addition to the offending author or artist, those to be prosecuted will include "those who have directly or indirectly contributed to the circulation of such statement or work of art: a publisher, an editor, a broadcaster, a journalist, an art dealer, an artistic director or a museum manager."

Although so far there have been few convictions, these laws, and the cases they give rise to, chill speech and are a measure of the diminishing value placed by society on freedom and fairness. Western democracies still subscribe to the fundamental importance of freedom of expression. Yet free expression is itself compromised, perhaps fatally, by religious hate- speech bans. To understand why, one has only to look at the Council of Europe's Venice Commission vague and subjective standards, which state that, with respect to religion, "there is no right to offend," that "gratuitously offensive" speech is not protected, and that there is a new "right of [religious freedom of] citizens not to be insulted in their religious feelings."

Censorship, Self-Censorship, and Official Lexicons

Apart from attempted legal prohibitions, governments have sought to regulate language and themes that could possibly touch on Islam.[25] In a 2005 report, England's Chief Inspector of Prisons, Anne Owers, criticized prison staff in Wakefield for wearing tiepins showing St. George's cross, the national flag of England, claiming that they could be "misconstrued" as symbols of the Crusades. Some local Muslims found Ms. Owers's concerns "petty." Indeed, some manifestations of this repressive impulse have been comical, with educators and officials in the United Kingdom continually scrapping pig themes and stories. Sheikh Ibrahim Mogra and other Muslims responded that neither they nor "the vast majority of Muslims" had any objection, and that while Islam forbade Muslims to eat pork, "there is no prohibition about reading stories about pigs"— in fact, such acts by authorities actually worsened the situation of British Muslims: "Every time we get these stories Muslims are seen more and more as misfits."[26]

In 2008, the U.S. Department of Homeland Security and the State Department instructed their employees to avoid the words "salafi," "wahhabist," "caliphate," and "jihadist" as offensive to Muslims when used by non-Muslims. On the advice of unidentified Muslim consultants, the word "liberty" was also dropped in favor of "progress." That year, the U.K. Home Secretary also dropped the term "Islamic terrorism" and instead instituted "anti-Islamic activity." In 2009, the U.S. Homeland Security secretary dropped "Islamic terrorism" in favor of "man-made disasters." The May 2010 U.S. National Security Strategy document, which in previous years had said, "The struggle against militant Islamic radicalism is the great ideological conflict of the early years of the 21st century," dropped any reference to "Islamic extremism."[27]

Leslie Gelb, president emeritus of the Council on Foreign Religions, points out that this creates security challenges: "[T]he failure to nail the problem squarely by name...leads Washington to think of American solutions to terrorism more so than Muslim ones." Senator Joseph Lieberman noted that dropping such words detracts from "important policy questions about how to combat the ideological dimensions of the war that is taking place within Islam." Muslim activist Zuhdi Jasser asks, "If our government officials cannot even employ the terms 'Islamism' or 'Salafism' in their discourse, it remains entirely unclear how they will be able to facilitate this contest of ideas [with Islamist extremists]."[28]

Threat, Violence, and Fear

Even apart from the effects of the law, some who dare to discuss Islam have to change their names or go into hiding. Many come from Muslim backgrounds, such as Ayaan Hirsi Ali, who fled the Netherlands after her coproducer van Gogh was assassinated and a death threat against her was staked with a knife to his corpse. Writer Paul Berman notes:

> When I met Hirsi Ali...she was protected by no less than five bodyguards. Even in the United States she is protected by bodyguards. But this is no longer unusual. [Ian] Buruma himself mentions in *Murder in Amsterdam* that the Dutch Social Democratic politician Ahmed Aboutaleb requires full-time bodyguards. At that same Swedish conference I happened to meet the British writer of immigrant background who has been obliged to adopt the pseudonym Ibn Warraq, out of fear that, in his case because of his Bertrand Russell-influenced philosophical convictions, he might be singled out for assassination. I happened to attend a different conference in Italy a few days earlier and met the very brave Egyptian-Italian journalist Magdi Allam, who writes scathing criticisms of the new totalitarian wave in *Il Corriere della Sera*—and I discovered that Allam, too, was traveling with a full complement of five bodyguards. The Italian journalist Fiamma Nierenstein, because of her well-known sympathies for Israel, was accompanied by her own bodyguards. Caroline Fourest, the author of the most important extended criticism of [Tariq] Ramadan, had to go under police protection for a while. The French philosophy professor Robert Redeker has had to go into hiding.[29]

The West could not have been more unprepared for this new call for censorship on behalf of Islam. Whereas in 1989, Western politicians and intellectuals instinctively sided with Rushdie, by 2007, the announcement that the Queen of England would confer a knighthood on him was met with controversy. Several British Labour and Conservative parliamentarians, journalists, and others publicly denounced the decision. Berman notes this shift: "How times have changed! The Rushdies of today find themselves under criticism, compared unfavorably in the press with the Islamist philosopher who writes prefaces for the collected fatwas of Sheik al-Qaradawi, the theologian of the human bomb.... During the Rushdie affair, courage was saluted. Today it is likened to fascism."[30] Fear is now shaping how we discuss Islam, or whether, apart from platitudes, we dare say anything at all. It has also affected how we view others who, by their expressed ideas, arouse the ire of OIC governments and Islamist extremists. In 2006, Borders and Waldenbooks stores refused, on security grounds, to stock the Council for Secular Humanism's *Free Inquiry* magazine because it reprinted some of the Danish cartoons. Officials at Utrecht University, citing fear of violence from Muslim students, demanded that retiring Professor Pieter W. Van Der Horst omit a passage concerning Islamic anti-Semitism from his valedictory address, even though there had been no threats by Muslim students or anyone else.[31] There have been some notable exceptions to this pattern: for example, in September 2010, the M100 Sanssouci Colloquium, in a ceremony keynoted by German Chancellor Angela Merkel and attended by editors and publishers from Europe's top media companies, awarded its prestigious media prize to Danish cartoonist Kurt Westergaard for his "unbending engagement for freedom of the press and freedom of opinion" and for his courage to defend these democratic values despite threats of death and violence.[32] For the most part, however, in the West's most prominent institutions and associations, there is a growing reluctance to criticize even some of the most extreme manifestations of things done in the name of Islam.

The common Western response of restricting expression about Islam coincides with arguments that such restrictions are necessary to create a social climate that protects minorities from possible discriminatory practices and violence and that religious freedom includes a right to be protected from ridicule, criticism, or dissent; or it springs from an exaggerated sense of multiculturalism. While these rationales are given frequently by policy makers and diplomats, it is actually fear of violence that is the explanation commonly given in the specific incidents. Explicitly citing fear of violence, the British private watchdog group, Index on Censorship, in 2009 declined to show any Danish cartoons when running an interview with author Jytte Klausen on Yale's decision not to publish the cartoons in her book. British political satirist Rory Bremner commented: "When [I'm] writing a sketch about Islam, I'm writing a line and I think, 'If this goes down badly, I'm writing my own death warrant there.'...Where does satire go from there, because we like to be brave but not foolish."[33]

Christopher Hitchens correctly discerns: "a hidden partner in our cultural and academic and publishing and broadcasting world: a shadowy figure that has, uninvited, drawn up a chair to the table. He never speaks. He doesn't have to. But he is very well understood. The late playwright Simon Gray was alluding to him when he said that Nicholas Hytner, the head of London's National Theatre, might put on a play mocking Christianity but never one that questioned Islam."[34] A letter to the *Boston Globe* neatly skewered that paper's claim that it was sensitivity to offense that led to its decision not to publish any Danish cartoons in its coverage of them: "I find all of your editorial cartoons deeply offensive, morally, religiously, philosophically, and spiritually. In fact, I don't like your editorials, either. And the editorializing in your news coverage is annoying as well. In keeping with your cowardly policy not to offend anyone, kindly cease publication at once."[35] The Bart Simpson television cartoon put it more simply. Referring to a death threat causing the creators of the irreverent animation series *South Park* to censor its depiction of Muhammad, the kid Bart, on the Simpsons' website, is seen writing on a blackboard, "South Park—We'd Stand Beside You If We Weren't So Scared."[36]

This fear is not a psychological neurosis or "phobia," but an empirically and rationally grounded, and well-warranted, apprehension about being murdered if one expresses something negative, or something understood as negative, about Islam.

The full extent of Western self-censorship regarding Islam is unknowable, but it is deep, and touches prominent outlets.[37] Yale University Press, Random House, Borders, Waldenbooks, Comedy Central, and even the Index on Censorship have explicitly cited fear of violence as a reason to drop materials that they feared could be seen as impugning Islam. Nelson Carey, President of the American Association of University Professors, said of Yale University Press's decision to censor a book on the Danish cartoons: "We do not negotiate with terrorists. We just accede to their anticipated demands."[38]

Undercutting Muslims

Some Islamic scholars, including those contributing to this book, advocate religious freedom on the basis of Islam itself and reject temporal punishments for apostasy and blasphemy. Abdullah Saeed notes that there is a debate within Islam on whether the Qur'an supports temporal punishment for apostasy and blasphemy. He agrees with Wahid's assessment that such punishment reflects "the early days of Islam, when apostasy generally coincided with desertion from the caliph's army and/or rejection of his authority, and thus constituted treason or rebellion." Saeed argues: "The Prophet's task was primarily to explain the difference between right and wrong. Individuals then had the choice of whether or not to follow God's path. This principle applies equally to Muslims who choose to leave Islam.... [T]he individual ... will ultimately bear the responsibility for that choice in the afterlife." Just as the institution of slavery, which had garnered Muslim and other consensus in the past, has been dropped, punishments for blasphemy and apostasy can also be revised.[39]

But Muslim scholars like these are among those most likely to be persecuted by repressive forces. As we've seen, many moderate Muslim voices are being silenced, especially by apostasy and blasphemy rules, which are key to preserving the tyranny of reactionary forms of Islam. Zeyno Baran explains: "The most important ideological struggle in the world today is within Islam. Moderate and secular Muslims, who embrace the compatibility of Islam and democracy and the individual freedoms we all cherish in the West, are being confronted by Islamists, who are extremist activists that hijack Islam and seek to gain political power and reshape societies."[40] In recent years, political campaigners who call for transparent elections in Iran, democracy activists who demand a constitution in Saudi Arabia, and editors who press to end the criminalization of blasphemy in Afghanistan have all been imprisoned for apostasy or blasphemy. Some, like Pakistan's minister Bhatti and governor Taseer, both strong advocates of blasphemy law reform, have been murdered.

In fact, Muslims at large have much to fear from Islamist extremist violence. Between 2006 and 2008, 98 percent of Al-Qaeda victims were Muslim, and Zawahiri, now Al-Qaeda's commander in chief, has discounted any Muslim concern about this on the basis that, while perhaps some victims were martyrs, most were not real Muslims at all but "apostates."[41] This "takfir" doctrine of declaring dissenting Muslims apostates in order to justify killing them also targets Muslims in the West who advocate open interpretations of Islam.[42] Some of the Muslim women's rights activists described in chapter 13, who have been threatened with "ritual slaughter" and other forms of murder, include Seyran Ates, a German lawyer, Mimount Bousakla, a Belgian senator, and Nyamko Sabuni, a Swedish minister of integration and gender.

Part of the answer to a common post-9/11 refrain—"Where are the moderates?"—is found in the Islamist practice of hurling charges of blasphemy, apostasy, and related accusations that make criticism of all actions and ideas in the name of Islam out of bounds and punishable offenses in this world. And, as Irshad Manji pointedly asks: "In a battle between flaming fundamentalists and mute moderates, who do you think is going to win?"[43]

Apart from the threat of violent attack, such Muslims are undermined by Western blasphemy and hate-speech prosecutions and pressure to self-censor. The Muslim Canadian Congress warned that the Canadian Islamic Congress's complaint against Mark Steyn and *Maclean's* magazine would "serve no purpose other than to reinforce the stereotype that Muslims have little empathy for vigorous debate and democracy." It warned that a Canadian human rights commission's "editorializing" against Steyn and the magazine sent a "very dangerous message to moderate Muslims who reject Sharia and do not take inspiration from overseas Islamic countries or groups." In effect, according to the MCC, the commission had "taken sides in the bitter struggle within Canada's Muslim community where sharia-supporting Islamists are pitted against liberal and secular Muslims." Zeyno Baran, of Turkish Muslim background, comments: "By tolerating intolerance, many in the West make it harder for moderate and reformist Muslims to succeed."[44]

The West undercuts many—especially pro-freedom—forms of Islam by often failing to protect its citizens from radicals, by marginalizing moderates on the basis of radicals' arguments that they are not real Muslims, and by adopting laws restricting speech in compliance with the demand of such radicals. George Weigel observes: "[T]he development of an Islamic 'social doctrine' capable of sustaining tolerance, civility, and pluralism engages the most serious questions of Islamic self-understanding and reminds us that great social and political questions are, more than not, ultimately theological in character."[45] Within Islam, non-Muslims clearly cannot fill this role, but Islamic authorities can, and, where there is individual freedom of religion and expression, many of them do. They need support, not marginalization, in overcoming the reactionary forces who seek to deny them religious and political space and silence their message.

The West at a Crossroads

Although the West remains much freer than the Muslim world, it is experiencing problems stemming from blasphemy restrictions similar to those occurring in the latter—the targeting of a wide range of views, vague and variable laws that are selectively enforced, vigilantism, intimidation and harassment of political opponents, the repression and marginalization of Muslim reformers, and the silencing of political and religious debate. Western actions and reactions concerning insults to religion have generally been uninformed, unfocused, halting, and contradictory, revealing a drift from core principles of freedom in order to silence criticism and dissent in Islamic matters. The UN Arab Development Report noted that cutting off debate that challenges prevailing Islamic strictures has been "inimical to human development." This is because Islam is a complex belief system shaping the views and practices of many of its over one billion followers in culture, politics, economics, science, education, personal and family relations, law and society, as well as what is often called religion. As our survey of Muslim countries demonstrates, under Islamic blasphemy regimes, a large body of ideas is no longer open for debate and inquiry. As Wahid has observed, coercively applied blasphemy laws "narrow the bounds of acceptable discourse...not only about religion, but about vast spheres of life, literature, science and culture in general."

The stakes are high. Most immediately, fundamental freedoms of religion and expression are being eroded. Because of definitional problems, the rule of law and due process rights are also at risk. As the essays of Wahid, Abu-Zayd, and Saeed reveal, accusations of religious insult shape the ideological battle within Islam, between those open to religious and cultural pluralism and those promoting theocratic regimes. This also concerns Western national security interests, since the defeat of extremist interpretations of Islam is tied to whether there is political space for debate, criticism, and interpretation within Islam.

Four major themes have emerged from our survey of the West's legal response to the new demand to enforce respect for Islam.

First, Western hate-speech and public order laws serve as proxies for Muslim blasphemy rules. While blasphemy laws to protect Christianity have been abolished or become all but obsolete, most Western states, with the exception of the United States, respond to complaints of offense concerning Islam with hate-speech laws. Such laws purportedly protect people rather than religions, but, as Council of Europe experts readily acknowledge, the two offenses are "easily blurred." In fact, from Rushdie's novel to the Danish cartoons, it is the perceived defamation of Islam itself, not of persons, which has caused most offense among Muslims and for which many seek state intervention.

Second, religious hate-speech laws are vaguely defined, allowing selective application, which violates the individual's right to freedoms of expression and religion and other basic rights. They often require exceedingly narrow, if not untenable, distinctions between protected social commentary and illegal "gratuitous" insults.[46] The Venice Commission notes that this distinction depends on content-based judgments regarding the statement's worthiness in "furthering progress in human affairs," on whether it is religious or political in substance, on its audience and range of distribution, on whether the speaker is fulfilling a public role, and even on whether the complainant and his religious group "have reacted violently to criticism of their religion."[47] This invites arbitrary enforcement, and governments in Finland, the United Kingdom, the Netherlands, and Austria have not been above selectively prosecuting successful candidates from the political opposition who support immigration restrictions. Furthermore, secular courts find themselves making theological judgments about Qur'anic verses and Islamic practices, for which they are not qualified.

Third, as we have seen, Western courts, including the European Court of Human Rights, sometimes convict and punish those found guilty essentially of sacrilege against Islam. But even those prosecutions that fail, which is probably most of them, have a broad chilling effect. The time and expense of fighting a case on its merits prompts many accused to settle quickly out of court. Ezra Levant, an editor who successfully defended himself against anti-Islamic hate-speech charges in Canada, wrote of the expense and ordeal of being tried: "The process is the punishment."[48] Few authors and fewer outlets are willing to publish negative speech about Islam if there is a potential of prosecution.

Fourth, while some maintain that religious speech controls are made necessary to foster harmony in culturally diverse societies, hate-speech prosecutions have not been proven to reduce hate and instead can exacerbate social tensions. Brian Grim and Roger Finke's surveys indicate that religious restrictions, including those on speech, contribute to internal instability and greater violence.[49] Reviewing the history of European laws against anti-Semitic speech, Elizabeth Powers concludes: "[T]he sad fact is that, despite criminalization of Holocaust denial, Jews in Europe are less secure than at any time since World War II—unlike in the United States, where even Nazis can march down city streets."[50] Clearly factors other than mere expression account for this regional difference.

Rather than alleviate the strains on a religiously pluralistic society, hate-speech laws exacerbate them by stimulating, as in Italy and Australia, a rush by different religious groups to sue and countersue or claim partiality. Some Muslims point to discriminatory pro-Christian blasphemy bans or laws forbidding Holocaust denial. Some Jews and Christians say that, due to fears of reaction and violence, Muslims are, in practice, given greater protection. Such laws also raise Muslim expectations that are then frustrated by the West's general unwillingness to punish defamation of a religion as such. When Britain adopted its hate-speech law, the public prosecutor, anticipating disappointment by British Muslims, felt compelled to explain to them that the law would not "protect them from people being rude or offensive about Islam." Furthermore, as in the Danish cartoons crisis, feelings of offense can be easily manufactured or exacerbated for political ends.

Western efforts to curb negative commentary or defamation of Islam erode liberal democratic tradition, chill speech on a wide array of issues that intersect with Islam, and endanger security, while never being able to satisfy the demands of OIC governments and Islamists.[51]

Recommendations

Western countries need to comprehend and counter the threats posed by demands to stifle negative commentary about and within Islam. This challenge is complicated by policy makers' common lack of knowledge and discomfort in dealing with religious issues generally.

The first recommendation is that diplomats and others take religions seriously enough to learn about them. Former U.S. diplomat and director of the State Department's office of religious freedom, Thomas Farr, writes that "U.S. policy makers and diplomats remain largely ignorant or confused about the effects of religious doctrines, communities, actors, and political theologies" and that "the religion-avoidance syndrome that continues to dominate U.S. policy" has hampered its ability to effectively respond to Islamic extremism.

Second, policy makers must realize that there is a battle within Islam and must discern who are the extremists and their supporters and apologists and who are not. As U.S. Secretary of Defense Robert M. Gates said: "[E]ventual success in the conflict against jihadist extremism will depend less on the results of individual military engagements and more on the overall ideological climate within the world of Islam. Understanding how this climate is likely to evolve over time, and what factors—including U.S. actions—will affect it thus becomes one of the most significant intellectual challenges we face."[52]

Third, the West must reestablish a consensus among its own states on the central importance of individual freedoms of expression and religion to liberal democracy. It must explain that these freedoms are not in conflict but are mutually reinforcing. It must abandon attempts at the international, regional, and national levels to diplomatically and legally finesse proposals to protect religion per se through laws against hate speech. This is a dangerous game that threatens to undermine individual freedoms of both expression and religion.[53]

Fourth, as part of this strategy, we must defend religious freedom, including the right to debate religious views. This is often ignored or even resisted by secular Westerners. Working to expand religious freedom protects religious and ideological pluralism in the Muslim world. This is essential not only to reformist Muslims and Muslim minorities but also to other religious minorities who experience persecution and repression in the same countries that promote blasphemy bans worldwide. Defending the human rights of these victims is an integral part of the contest of ideas. We must insist that religiously offensive speech should be met with more speech and peaceful protest, and not the coercive power of the state, mob intimidation, or vigilante violence.

As Abu-Zayd recounted: "[C]harges of apostasy and blasphemy are key weapons in the fundamentalists' arsenal, strategically employed to prevent reform of Muslim societies and instead confine the world's Muslim population to a bleak, colorless prison of sociocultural and political conformity." The continuing encroachment of blasphemy and apostasy limits in the West will ultimately threaten free speech, free expression, and the free exchange of ideas—whether sacred or secular, ridiculous or respectful. It will permit radical interpretations of one belief system to supersede debate, discussion, and devotion about the nature of faith and religion and the right to reject religious belief altogether. Acquiescence to extremist demands means that voices of dissent will be silenced from Cairo to Copenhagen, from Teheran to Toronto, from Islamabad to Sydney. The suppression of ideas will be felt not only in Muslim-majority states and regions but also in the West and across the world.

As was said by the Pakistani ambassador to the United States, Husain Haqqani, in his eulogy for Shahbaz Bhatti, "Those who would murder a Salman Taseer or a Shahbaz Bhatti deface my religion, my prophet, my Koran and my Allah. Yet there is an overpowering, uncomfortable and unconscionable silence from the great majority of Pakistanis who respect the law, respect the Holy Book, and respect other religions. . . . This silence endangers the future of my nation, and to the extent the silence empowers extremists, it endangers the future of peace and the future of the civilized world.... When a Shahbaz Bhatti is murdered, and we remain silent, we have died with him."[54]

When politics and religion are intertwined, as they necessarily are in debates about blasphemy and insulting Islam, forbidding religious criticism means forbidding political criticism. Conversely, without religious debate there can be no political debate; without religious dissent there can be no political dissent. And without religious freedom, there can be no political freedom.

NOTES

Foreword

1. Descended from a long line of charismatic religious leaders, Kyai Haji Mustofa Bisri heads the Raudlatuth Tholibin Islamic boarding school in Rembang, Central Java. Widely revered as a religious scholar, poet, novelist, painter, and Muslim intellectual, K. H. Mustofa Bisri has strongly influenced the Nahdlatul Ulama's social, educational, and religious development over the past thirty years.
2. Mohammad Asrar Madani, *Verdict of Islamic Law on Blasphemy and Apostasy* (Lahore, Pakistan: Idara-e-Islamiat, 1994).
3. "Everyone has the right to freedom of thought, conscience and religion; this right includes freedom to change his religion or belief, and freedom, either alone or in community with others and in public or private, to manifest his religion or belief in teaching, practice, worship, and observance."
4. Seyyed Hossein Nasr, *Persia: Bridge of Turquoise* (Boston: New York Graphic Society, 1975).
5. Muslims regard *Hadith Qudsi* as the words of God, repeated by Muhammad, and recorded on the condition of an *isnad* (chain of verification by witnesses who heard Muhammad say the hadith).
6. "Everyone has the right to freedom of opinion and expression; this right includes freedom to hold opinions without interference and to seek, receive and impart information and ideas through any media and regardless of frontiers."

Chapter 1

1. The list of purported religious offenses that we cover is very long; a partial list includes "apostasy," "insulting a heavenly religion," "insulting Turkishness," creating "confusion among Muslims," using "twisted facts that can undermine the faith of Muslims," "polytheism," "imitating Christians," "witchcraft," "sorcery," "harboring destructive thoughts," "friendship with the enemies of God," "hostility towards friends of God," "fighting against God," "dissension from religious dogma," "spreading lies, insulting religion and religious authorities," and "propagation of spiritual liberalism." In order to avoid repeating this at each relevant juncture, we will often use "blasphemy" or "insulting Islam" as proxy terms for the whole.
2. Melody Y. Hu, "Chaplain's E-Mail Sparks Controversy," *The Harvard Crimson*, April 14, 2009, http://www.thecrimson.com/article/2009/4/14/chaplains-e-mail-sparks-controversy-span-stylefont-weight.
3. John Innes, "Burger King Recalls 'Sacrilegious' Desserts," *The Scotsman*, September 7, 2005, http://news.scotsman.com/uk.cfm?id=1951292005; "Nike and Islamic Group End Logo Logjam," *CNN.com*, November 21, 1998, http://www.cnn.com/US/9811/21/nike.islamic/;

"Apple's 'Mecca Project' Provokes Muslim Reaction," The Middle East Media Research Institute (MEMRI), Islamist Websites Monitor No. 5, October 11, 2006, http://www.memri.org/report/en/0/0/0/0/0/0/0/1901.htm.

Part II

1. See United States Commission on International Religious Freedom (USCIRF), *The Religion-State Relationship and the Right to Freedom of Religion or Belief: A Comparative Textual Analysis of the Constitutions of Predominantly Muslim Countries*, March 2005, http://www.uscirf.gov/images/stories/pdfComparative_Constitutions/study0305.pdf.
2. See also the discussion of censorship in Lowell H. Schwartz, Todd C. Helmus, Dalia Dassa Kaye, and Nadia Oweidat, *Barriers to the Broad Dissemination of Creative Works in the Arab World* (Santa Monica: Rand Corporation, 2009), http://www.rand.org/pubs/monographs/2009/RAND_MG879.pdf.

Chapter 2

1. "Saudi Gets 8 Years for a Song," SIA News, http://www.Arabianews.org/english/article.cfm?qid=123&sid=2.
2. "Help Save Young Yemeni from Death by Beheading in Saudi Arabia," press release by Saudi Institute, January 27, 2003.
3. Mariam Al Hakeem, "Saudi Man Kills Daughter for Converting to Christianity," *Gulf News*, August 12, 2008, http://www.gulfnews.com/News/Gulf/saudi_arabia/10236558.html.
4. "Saudi Arabia," *International Religious Freedom Report 2009*, U.S. State Department, October 26, 2009, http://www.state.gov/g/drl/rls/irf/2009/127357.htm.
5. Kingdom of Saudi Arabia Ministry of Foreign Affairs, Article 1, "The Basic Law of Governance," http://www.mofa.gov.sa/Detail.asp?InNewsItemID=35297. In October 2007, the Saudi government announced judicial reforms that reformers hope will help reduce clerical power over the judiciary; see "Saudis to Overhaul Legal System," *BBC News*, October 5, 2007, http://news.bbc.co.uk/1/hi/world/middle_east/7029308.stm.
6. Center for Religious Freedom of Hudson Institute with the Institute for Gulf Affairs, *2008 Update: Saudi Arabia's Curriculum of Intolerance*, 45, http://www.hudson.org/files/pdf_upload/saudi_textbooks_final.pdf; U.S. Commission on International Religious Freedom, "Saudi Arabia: USCIRF Confirms Material Inciting Violence, Intolerance Remains in Textbooks Used at Saudi Government's Islamic Saudi Academy," June 11, 2008, http://www.uscirf.gov/index.php?option=com_content&task=view&id=2206.
7. Center for Religious Freedom, *Saudi Publications on Hate Ideology Invade American Mosques* (Washington, D.C.: Freedom House, 2005), 37, 45, http://crf.hudson.org/files/publications/2005%20Saudi%20Report.pdf. "Saudi Cleric Muhammad Al-Munajid Warns: Freedom of Speech Might Lead to Freedom of Belief," MEMRI Clip 1734, March 30, 2008.
8. "Saudi Arabia," *International Religious Freedom Report 2009*.
9. Mariam Al Hakeem, "Saudi Shoura Council Rejects Call for International Pact to Respect All Religions," *Gulf News*, March 19, 2008, http://www.gulfnews.com/news/gulf/saudi_arabia/10198648.html.
10. Aluma Dankowitz, "Saudi Study Offers Critical Analysis of the Kingdom's Religious Curricula," MEMRI Inquiry and Analysis Series 195, November 9, 2004, http://xrdarabia.org/2004/11/18/saudi-report-on-curriculum/.
11. United States Commission on International Religious Freedom, "USCIRF Confirms Violence, Intolerance at Islamic Saudi Academy," June 11, 2008.
12. Hudson Institute/Institute for Gulf Affairs, *2008 Update: Saudi Arabia's Intolerance*, 44, 58.
13. "Saudi Arabia," *International Religious Freedom Report 2009*.
14. See "Affront to Justice: Death Penalty in Saudi Arabia," Amnesty International, October 14, 2008, 8, http://www.amnesty.org/en/library/asset/MDE23/027/2008/en/dc425c41-8bb9-11dd-8e5e-43ea85d15a69/mde230272008en.pdf.

15. "Saudi Arabia," *International Religious Freedom Report 2009.*

16. "Memorandum Submitted by the Kingdom of Saudi Arabia to International Organizations on Human Rights and Their Implementation Within Its Territory," in Hudson Institute/ Institute for Gulf Affairs, *2008 Update: Saudi Arabia's Intolerance*, 64–77.

17. Stephen Schwartz, cited in Daniel Pipes, "Uniting to Exclude Saudi Arabian Airlines," *New York Sun*, August 21, 2007, http://www.danielpipes.org/article/4862.

18. "Christian Prisoner Feared Dead in Saudi Arabia," International Christian Concern, March 7, 2002; "Saudi Arabia: Last Two Christian Prisoners Deported," *Compass Direct News*, April 19, 2002, http://archive.compassdirect.org/en/display.php?page=news&idelement=1219& lang=en&length=short&backpage=archives&critere=&countryname=Saudi%20 Arabia&rowcur=0.

19. "Saudi Christian Convert Arrested and Jailed," *AsiaNews.it*, December 17, 2004, http:// www.asianews.it/index.php?l=en&art=2134.

20. Information provided in e-mail correspondence with a representative of International Christian Concern, April 1, 2008.

21. "Saudi Arabia," *International Religious Freedom Report 2007*, U.S. State Department, September 14, 2007, http://www.state.gov/g/drl/rls/irf/2007/90220.htm.

22. "Saudi Arabia: Authorities Arrest Christian Convert," *Compass Direct News*, January 28, 2009, http://www.compassdirect.org/en/display.php?page=news&lang=en&length=long&i delement=5779&backpage=index&critere=&countryname=&rowcur=225. See also Arabic Network for Human Rights Information, "KSA Arrests Blogger, Blocks His Site. His Life At Risk as He Embraced Christianity," January 14, 2008, http://anhri.net/en/reports/2009/ pr0114.shtml; "Saudi Arabia: Authorities Release Christian Blogger," *Compass Direct News*, April 16, 2009, http://www.compassdirect.org/en/display.php?page=news&lang=en&lengt h=long&idelement=5881; Cairo Institute for Human Rights Studies, *Bastion of Impunity, Mirage of Reform: Human Rights in the Arab Region*, Annual Report 2009, 176, http://www. cihrs.org/Images/ArticleFiles/Original/485.pdf. Hamoud had been arrested twice before.

23. "Saudi Arabia," *International Religious Freedom Report 2007*; Sarah Leah Whitson, "Letter to Saudi King Abdullah bin Abd al-'Aziz Al Sa'ud: Regarding the Religious Persecution of Ahmadis," Human Rights Watch, January 24, 2007, http://www.thepersecution.org/ news/2007/hrwl0124.html; "Saudi Arabia: Stop Religious Persecution of Ahmadis," Human Rights Watch, January 24, 2006, http://www.hrw.org/en/news/2007/01/23/saudi-arabia-stop-religious-persecution-ahmadis.

24. "Saudi Arabia," *International Religious Freedom Report 2007*. For background, see "The Shiite Question in Saudi Arabia," International Crisis Group, Middle East Report N°45–19, September 2005, http://www.crisisgroup.org/en/regions/middle-east-north-africa/iran-gulf/saudi-arabia/045-the-shiite-question-in-saudi-arabia.aspx.

25. "Saudi Arabia," *International Religious Freedom Report 2009.*

26. Hudson Institute/Institute for Gulf Affairs, *2008 Update: Saudi Arabia's Intolerance*, 13.

27. "Saudi Arabia," *International Religious Freedom Report 2007.*

28. Stephen Schwartz, "*Shari'a* in Saudi Arabia, Today and Tomorrow," in *Radical Islam's Rules*, ed. Paul Marshall (Lanham, MD: Rowman & Littlefield, 2005), 30–31.

29. "Saudi Arabia," *International Religious Freedom Report 2007.*

30. Translation of statement provided by Ali al-Ahmed of the Institute for Gulf Affairs; "Saudi Clerics Slam Shias, Hezbollah," *Reuters*, June 1, 2008, http://www.gulf-times.com/site/ topics/printArticle.asp?cu_no=2&item_no=221969&version=1&template_id=37& parent_id=17.

31. Middle East Media Research Institute. "Recent Rise in Sunni-Shi'ite Tension (Part III): Sectarian Strife in Saudi Arabia," *Inquiry & Analysis* 482, December 16, 2008, http://www .memri.org/bin/articles.cgi?Page=archives&Area=ia&ID=IA48208.

32. "Saudi Arabia: An Upsurge in Public Executions," Amnesty International, http://www .amnestyusa.org/document.php?lang=e&id=4FBA416ABC8805C2802569A600603109.

33. "Blasphemer Executed in Saudi Arabia," *Arab News* via Moneyclips, September 4, 1992; "Saudi Arabia, Religious Intolerance: The Arrest, Detention and Torture of Christian

Worshipers and Shi'a Muslims," Amnesty International, 14, 1993, http://www.amnestyusa
.org/document.php?lang=e&id=F9ABD6A906FEFB03802569A600603A2B;
Communication to the Government of Saudi Arabia from UN Special Rapporteur Abdel
Fattah Amor, August 31, 1993, as presented before the UN Commission on Human Rights,
January 20, 1994.

34. See Schwartz, "Shari'a Today and Tomorrow," 29, 35; Additional cases of persecution of
    Shias are available from the Institute of Gulf Affairs, http://www.gulfinstitute.org/artman/
    publish/index.shtml.

35. "Denied Dignity: Systematic Discrimination and Hostility Toward Saudi Shia Citizens,"
    Human Rights Watch, 2009, http://www.hrw.org/en/reports/2009/09/03/denied-dignity-0.

36. Cairo Institute for Human Rights Studies 2009, *Bastion of Impunity, Mirage of Reform*,
    174–75.

37. Kelly McEvers, "Sorcery Charges on the Rise in Saudi Arabia," NPR, December 21, 2009,
    http://www.npr.org/templates/story/story.php?storyId=121715788; "Lawyer Beheading
    Planned in Saudi Sorcery Case," *CNN.com*, April 1, 2010, http://www.cnn.com/2010/
    WORLD/meast/03/31/saudi.arabia.sorcery/index.html.

38. Cairo Institute for Human Rights Studies, *Bastion of Impunity, Mirage of Reform*, 175;
    "Grumbling and Rumbling: Shia Unhappiness Is Rattling Regimes in Saudi Arabia and
    Elsewhere in the Gulf," *The Economist*, February 26, 2009, http://www.economist.com/dis-
    playstory.cfm?story_id=13185773; "Denied Dignity: Systematic Discrimination and
    Hostility toward Saudi Shia Citizens," Human Rights Watch, 2009, 15–23, http://www.hrw
    .org/en/reports/2009/09/03/denied-dignity-0, which also reports (p. 11) that in June
    2009, another Shia was reportedly sentenced to 400 lashes and three months' prison for
    allegedly cursing God. The judge is also reported to have insulted Shias.

39. United States Commission on International Religious Freedom, "Saudi Arabia: USCIRF
    Concerned by Misleading Claims about Release of Religious Prisoners," November 6, 2006.
    For an overview, see "The Ismailis of Najran: Second-class Saudi Citizens," Human Rights
    Watch, September 2008, http://www.hrw.org/reports/2008/saudiarabia0908/.

40. Brian Whitaker, "A Bad Joke," *Guardian*, September 14, 2006, http://www.guardian.co.uk/
    commentisfree/2006/sep/14/abadjoke.

41. "Saudi Religious Prisoner on Strike until Death," Saudi Information Agency, September 8,
    2006, http://www.arabianews.org/english/article.cfm?qid=192&sid=2.

42. "Saudi Arabia: Mentally Ill Prisoner Put in Solitary," Human Rights Watch, February 2,
    2007,   http://www.hrw.org/en/news/2007/02/01/saudi-arabia-mentally-ill-prisoner-
    put-solitary; "Saudi Arabia," *International Religious Freedom Report 2007*. Personal
    correspondence between Ali Al-Ahmed and Msgr. Pietro Parolin, Undersecretary for the
    Holy See's Relations with States, January 15, 2008, confirms that the Vatican raised the
    case with Saudi officials. On the sentence, "Saudi Religious Prisoner on Strike until Death,"
    SIA News, September 8, 2006, says the sentence was changed in 1999; "Saudi Arabia:
    Pardon Ismaili Sentenced to Death," (Letter), Human Rights Watch, October 10, 2006,
    http://hrw.org/english/docs/2006/10/10/saudia14372.htm, implies he still faced a death
    sentence, as does "Saudi Arabia: Stop Trials for Insulting Islam," Human Rights Watch,
    May 13, 2008, http://www.hrw.org/en/news/2008/05/12/saudi-arabia-stop-trials-insult-
    ing-islam; Whitaker, "A Bad Joke," says the King met with Hadi's father and may have
    reduced the sentence.

43. "Saudi Unrest Blamed on 'Sorcerer,'" *BBC News*, April 25, 2000, http://news.bbc.co.uk/2/hi/
    middle_east/725597.stm; Ahmed Al-Haj, "Saudi Security Forces, Ismaili Protestors Clash,
    Many Said Dead," *AP*, April 24, 2000; "Three Foreigners Hurt in Unrest Linked to Ismaili
    Minority: Saudi Minister," *Agence France Presse* (henceforth *AFP*), April 25, 2000; Schwartz,
    "Shari'a Today and Tomorrow," 29–30.

44. Sources agree on their arrest but differ as to their sentences; see "Civil and Political Rights,
    Including Questions Regarding Torture and Detention: Report of Special Rapporteur Nigel
    Rodley," UN Commission on Human Rights, January 25, 2001, http://www.unhchr.ch/
    Huridocda/Huridoca.nsf/0/9d0d08575ef2e1528025687e00516e7a?Opendocument;

Amnesty International document MDE 23/78/00, October 8, 2000, http://www.amnesty.org/en/library/info/MDE23/078/2000/en.

45. "The Ismailis of Najran," Human Rights Watch, September 22, 2008, http://www.hrw.org/en/reports/2008/09/22/ismailis-najran.

46. Report on Saudi Arabia, United States Commission on International Religious Freedom, May 2003.

47. UN Commission on Human Rights, "Report of the Special Rapporteur on the Question of Torture, Theo van Boven, Submitted Pursuant to Commission Resolution 2002/38," E/CN.4/2003/68/Add.1, February 27, 2003, http://www.unhchr.ch/Huridocda/Huridoca.nsf/(Symbol)/E.CN.4.2003.68.Add.1.En?Opendocument; Amnesty International, "Incommunicado Detention/Fear of Torture/Possible Prisoners of Conscience," document 23/002/2002, February 19, 2002, http://www.amnesty.org/en/.../MDE23/002/2002/en/.../mde230022002es.html.

48. World Report 2003–Saudi Arabia, Human Rights Watch, http://www.hrw.org/legacy/wr2k3/mideast6.html; Schwartz, "Shari'a Today and Tomorrow," 29.

49. "Ismaili Leader's Sentence Reduced after International Protest," Saudi Information Agency, May 28, 2002, http://www.arabiaradio.org/english/article.cfm?qid=25&sid=3&printme=1.

50. "Saudi Ismaili 'Arrested over Petition to King,'" AFP, May 15, 2008, http://www.dailystar.com.lb/article.asp?edition_id=10&categ_id=2&article_id=92040; Reuters, "Saudi Shiite Held after Meeting King," *Kuwait Times*, May 19, 2008, http://www.kuwaittimes.net/read_news.php?newsid=MTMzNjMxMTY5NA; Andrew Hammond, "Saudi Shiites Oppose Plan to Settle Sunnis," Reuters, February 18, 2008, http://www.alertnet.org/thenews/newsdesk/L05508688.htm.

51. Center for Islamic Pluralism, http://www.islamicpluralism.org/.

52. Paul Marshall, ed., *Religious Freedom in the World* (Lanham: Rowman & Littlefield, 2008), 348.

53. Adnan R. Khan, "The Push for Religious Reform Is Allowing Sufis to Step into the Pen," March 3, 2005, http://www.sunniforum.com/forum/archive/index.php?t-4762.html; Mahmoud Ahmad, "Makkah Bids Farewell to Maliki," *Arab News*, October 31, 2004.

54. Faiza Saleh Ambah, "In Saudi Arabia, a Resurgence of Sufism," *The Washington Post*, May 2, 2006, http://www.washingtonpost.com/wp-dyn/content/article/2006/05/01/AR2006050101380.html.

55. Schwartz, "Shari'a Today and Tomorrow," 28–29.

56. "Saudi Woman Faces Death for Witchcraft," *Telegraph*, February 15, 2008, http://www.telegraph.co.uk/news/worldnews/1578803/Saudi-woman-faces-death-for-witchcraft.html. Saudi Maher al-Luqman, an entertainer who walks on nails and eats glass and fire, says that the religious police "have stopped us for two years, branding us as sorcerers, and calling for people to fight us and report us." Circus shows have been banned as "contrary to Islam." "The Perils of Eating Fire in Saudi Arabia—Nael Shyoukhi," *Reuters*, July 21, 2010, http://wwrn.org/articles/33894/.

57. Reuters, "Saudi Executes Egyptian for Practicing 'Witchcraft,'" ABC News (Australia), November 2, 2007, http://abc.net.au/news/stories/2007/11/03/2080777.htm?site=news.

58. Amnesty International, "World 2007 Death Penalty statistics, notes and case studies," April 15, 2008, http://www.amnestyusa.org/document.php?id=ENGACT500142008. "Egyptian Faces Death over Saudi Koran Desecration," *Reuters*, April 18, 2007, http://www.signonsandiego.com/news/world/20070418-1015-saudi-crime-koran.html. In March 2009, the Muttawa arrested a "sorcerer" for practicing magic and providing spiritual services to men and women who rejected Islam; "Hai'a Combat with Sorcerers, Magicians," *Saudi Gazette*, March 16, 2009, http://www.saudigazette.com.sa/index.cfm?method=home.regcon&contentID=2009031532193. Other reported arrests for witchcraft between 2006 and 2009 include, in October 2006, Eritrean expatriate Muhammad Burhan. Wafiqat al-Hazza', a Shia woman, was detained for carrying a Shia prayer book at the Jordanian-Saudi border in 2008 and sentenced to six months for witchcraft. In 2009, a Saudi was arrested for smuggling a book discussing witchcraft into the country and an expatriate for using "sorcery" and "charlatanry" to solve others' romantic problems. On March 10, 2010, the General Court in Medina

upheld the death penalty against forty-six-year-old Ali Hussein Subat (also called Shahrzad) for publicly practicing black magic; see Donna Abu-Nasr/*Associated Press*, "Rights Group Rejects Saudi Witchcraft Charges," *ABC News*, November 25, 2009, http://abcnews.go.com/ International/wirestory?id=9171764&page=1; "Denied Dignity: Systematic Discrimination and Hostility Toward Saudi Shia Citizens," Human Rights Watch, 2009, 11, http://www .hrw.org/en/reports/2009/09/03/denied-dignity-0; Dominic Waghorn, "TV Presenter on Death Row for Witchcraft," *Sky News*, November 24, 2009, http://news.sky.com/skynews/ Home/World-News/Saudi-Arabia-Ali-Sibat-Sentenced-To-Death-For-Witchcraft-Over-TV-Predictions/Article/200911415466364); "Saudi Court Upholds Death Sentence against 'Sorcerer,'" *Arabian Business.com*, http://www.arabianbusiness.com/583567-saudi-court-upholds-death-sentence-against-sorcerer.

59. "Saudi Arabia: Stop Trials for 'Insulting' Islam," Human Rights Watch, May 13, 2008, http:// www.hrw.org/en/news/2008/05/12/saudi-arabia-stop-trials-insulting-islam; "Saudi Arabia Court Ratifies Beheading of Turkish Barber," *TurkishPress*, May 1, 2008, http://www.turk-ishpress.com/news.asp?id=228978; Ebtihal Mubarak, "Turkish Barber Detained Over Profane Remarks," *Arab News*, April 17, 2008, http://www.arabnews.com/?page=1&section =0&article=109032.

60. "President Gul May Save Turkish Man Sentenced to Death in Saudi Arabia," *Today's Zaman*, April 14, 2008; "President Gul intervenes to Save Turk in Saudi Arabia," *Turkish Daily News*, April 14, 2008.

61. Ebtihal Mubarak, "Blasphemy Case Moves to Appeals Court," *Arab News*, April 21, 2008, http://www.arabnews.com/?page=1&section=0&article=109150&d=21&m=4&y=2008; "Uskul pleads with Saudi Authorities for Turk Facing Death Penalty," *Today's Zaman*, April 21, 2008; "Saudi Barber Faces Beheading for Cursing," UPI.com, May 30, 2008, http://www .upi.com/Top_News/2008/05/30/Saudi_barber_faces_beheading_for_cursing/UPI-76321212159442/.

62. "Saudi Authorities Set to Release Turkish Man," *Today's Zaman*, May 27, 2008; Ali Khan Ghazanfar, "Barber Facing Death for Slandering Prophet Freed," *Arab News*, June 5, 2008, http://www.arabnews.com/?page=1&section=0&article=110603&d=5&m=6&y=2008.

63. Neil MacFarquhar, "A Few Saudis Defy a Rigid Islam to Debate Their Own Intolerance," *New York Times*, July 12, 2002, http://query.nytimes.com/gst/fullpage.html?res=9506E4D9103 0F931A25754C0A9649C8B63. See also Faiza Saleh Ambah, "An Unprecedented Uproar Over Saudi Religious Police," *The Washington Post*, June 22, 2007, http://www.washington-post.com/wpdyn/content/article/2007/06/21/AR2007062102466.html.

64. Christopher Boucek, "Saudi Arabia's 'Soft' Counterterrorism Strategy: Prevention, Rehabilitation and Aftercare" (Washington, D.C.: Carnegie Endowment for International Peace, 2008), 4, http://www.carnegieendowment.org/files/cp97_boucek_saudi_final.pdf. For other examples, on Turki al-Hamad, see Malu Halasa, "Triumphant Trilogy," *Time.com*, January 9, 2005, http://www.time.com/time/magazine/article/0,9171,1015836,00.html. On Hamza Al-Maziani, a linguistics professor at King Saud University, see Raid Qusti, "Crown Prince Quashes Jail Term of Saudi Writer," *Arab News*, March 22, 2005, http://www. arabnews.com/?page=1&section=0&article=60829&d=22&m=3&y=2005. On Ra'if Badawi, see "Saudi Arabia: Stop Trials for 'Insulting' Islam," Human Rights Watch, May 13, 2008, http://www.hrw.org/en/news/2007/02/08/letter-king-abdullah?print. On Yousef Aba Al-Khail and Abdullah bin Bejad al-Otaibi, see Ian Black, "Intellectuals Condemn Fatwa Against Writers," *The Guardian*, April 3, 2008; Abeer Mishkas, "Of Fatwas and Infidels," *Arab News*, March 27, 2008, http://www.arabnews.com/?page=7&section=0&article=108283&d =27&m=3&y=2008. On further reformers, see "Saudis on Strike: Pressure for Democratic Change in the Middle East Will Continue, with or without U.S. Help," *The Washington Post*, November 7, 2008, A18, http://hub.witness.org/SaudiHungerStrike.

65. "Cleric Issues Fatwa Against Journalists and Writers," Committee to Protect Journalists, September 22, 2008, http://cpj.org/2008/09/cleric-issues-fatwa-against-journalists-and-writer.php; Cairo Institute for Human Rights Studies, *Bastion of Impunity, Mirage of Reform*, 177. In 2008, al-Lihedan was replaced; see Nina Shea, "New Hope for Reform in Saudi

Arabia?" *National Review Online*, "The Corner" blog, February 16, 2009, http://www.nationalreview.com/corner/177439/new-hope-reform-saudi-arabia/nina-shea.

66. "Saudi Cleric Backs Gender Segregation with Fatwa," Reuters, February 23, 2010, http://in.reuters.com/article/worldNews/idININdia-46408620100223. In March 2010, housewife and poet Hissa Hilal, in what was seen, inter alia, as a criticism of al-Barrak, on the "Million's Poet" poetry competition broadcast live every week on Emirati television, blasted clerics who issue evil fatwas. Hilal subsequently received death threats. "Veiled Saudi Poet Rises to Stardom after Bashing Clerics," *AFP*, March 23, 2010, http://www.france24.com/en/20100323-veiled-saudi-poet-rises-stardom-after-bashing-clerics.

67. Center for Religious Freedom, *Saudi Publications on Hate Ideology*, 20, 34.

68. "Saudi Teacher Sentenced to Prison and Flogging for Religious Discussion with Pupils," Network for Education and Academic Rights, November 17, 2005, http://www.nearinternational.org/alert-detail.asp?alertid=408; Ebtihal Mubarak, "Al-Harbi Case Sparks Debate," *Arab News*, November 21, 2005, http://www.arabnews.com/?page=1&section=0&article=73487&d=21&m=11&y=2005; "Saudi Islamic Doctrine Hard to Control," Associated Press, April 19, 2004, http://www.islamdaily.net/EN/Contents.aspx?AID=1005.

69. Ebtihal Mubarak, "Another Teacher Gets Royal Pardon," *Arab News*, December 11, 2005, http://www.arabnews.com/?page=1&section=0&article=74530.

70. Ebtihal Mubarak, "Justice Served in Al-Suhaimi Case," *Arab News*, January 4, 2006, http://www.arabnews.com/?page=1&section=0&article=75762&d=4&m=1&y=2006.

71. Ebtihal Mubarak, "Another Teacher Gets Royal Pardon."

72. From "Due Process and Fair Trial Violations," in *Precarious Justice: Arbitrary Detention and Unfair Trials in the Deficient Criminal Justice System of Saudi Arabia*, Human Rights Watch, March 2008, http://www.hrw.org/en/node/62304/section/13; Information provided to Ali Al-Ahmed by Al-Suhaimi's family and friends. See also examples given in Michael Scott Doran, "The Saudi Paradox," *Foreign Affairs*, January/February 2004, http://www.foreignaffairs.org/20040101faessay83105/michael-scott-doran/the-saudi-paradox.html.

73. According to *AFP*, Al-Domaini, unlike most of the other detainees, had not actually signed this petition; Lydia Georgi, "Three Saudi Reformists Go on Trial after Two Months in Detention: Wife," AFP, May 19, 2004.

74. Claude Salhani, "Politics & Policies: Saudi Jails Reformers," May 16, 2005, http://politicspolicies.wordpress.com/2005/05/16/politics-policies-saudi-jails-reformers/; "Political Reformers Sentenced," Human Rights Watch, http://www.hrw.org/en/news/2005/05/15/saudi-arabia-political-reformers-sentenced.

75. Edgar C. Cadano, "Abdullah Pardons 5 Saudi Reformers," *Saudi Gazette*, August 9, 2005; "Saudi Activists Plan Hunger Strike to Protest Jailing of Reformists," *Washington Post*, November 1, 2008, http://www.washingtonpost.com/wp-dyn/content/article/2008/10/31/AR2008103103410_pf.html.

76. "Saudi Jailed for Discussing the Bible," Reuters, November 14, 2005, http://www.washingtontimes.com/news/2005/nov/14/20051114-015138-3548r/; Ebtihal Mubarak, "Teacher Charged with Mocking Religion Sentenced to Jail," *Arab News*, November 14, 2005, http://www.arabnews.com/?page=1&section=0&article=73171; Network for Education and Academic Rights, "Saudi Teacher Sentenced to Prison and Flogging for Religious Discussion with Pupils," November 17, 2005, http://www.nearinternational.org/alert-detail.asp?alertid=408.

77. "Liberal Journalists Arrested on Apostasy Charges," SIA News, April 7, 2006, http://www.arabianews.org/english/article.cfm?qid=187&sid=2.

78. Ebtihal Mubarak, "Journalist's Car Vandalized," *Arab News*, November 16, 2005, http://www.arabnews.com/?page=1&section=0&article=73279.

79. AFP, "Saudi Frees Journalist Held Over Internet Writings," *Khaleej Times*, April 20, 2006; Ebtihal Mubarak, "Journalist Detained for Internet Remarks," *Arab News*, April 9, 2008, http://www.arabnews.com/?page=1&section=0&article=80462; "Saudi Arabia: Al Qa'ida Critic Arrested for 'Destructive Thoughts,'" Human Rights Watch, April 12, 2006, http://www.hrw.org/en/news/2006/04/11/saudi-arabia-al-qa-ida-critic-arrested-destructive-

thoughts; "Saudi journalist, accused of un-Islamic writings, is freed," Committee to Protect Journalists, April 20, 2006.

80. Neil MacFarquhar, "Saudi Reformers: Seeking Rights, Paying a Price," *New York Times*, June 9, 2005, http://www.nytimes.com/2005/06/09/international/middleeast/09saudi.html; Mahan Abedin, "Saudi Dissent More Than Just Jihadis," Saudi Debate, June 15, 2006, http://www.e-prism.org/images/Saudi_dissent_more_than_just_ihadis_-_15-6-06.pdf; "Jihad and the Saudi petrodollar," *BBC News*, November 15, 2007, http://news.bbc.co.uk/2/hi/middle_east/7093423.stm.

81. Duraid Al Baik, "Journalists Face Possible Blasphemy Charges," *Gulf News*, December 29, 2009, http://gulfnews.com/news/region/egypt/journalists-face-possible-blasphemy-charges-1.559177.

82. Neeral Gangal, "Saudi Blasphemy Case Filed against Writer-paper," *Arabian Business*, March 19, 2010, http://www.arabianbusiness.com/584088-saudi-blasphemy-case-filed-against-writer—paper. Al Arabiya TV was reportedly charged with insulting God, Muhammad, and the Angel Gabriel; however, the Saudi Ministry of Justice says it never received such a case. See Andy Sambige. "Saudi Blasphemy Case Filed against TV Channel-report," *Arabian Business*, October 29, 2009, http://www.arabianbusiness.com/571908-saudis-launch-blasphemy-case-against-tv-channel—report; "Confusion over Al Arabiya Blasphemy Charges," November 1, 2009, http://www.ameinfo.com/214399.html.

83. Middle East Media Research Institute, Special Dispatch #1070: "Saudi Doctorate Encourages the Murder of Arab Intellectuals," January 12, 2006, http://www.memri.org/report/en/0/0/0/0/0/0/1677.htm.

84. Ibid.

85. "The Fatwa Against the Royal Family," *The Economist*, October 11, 2001.

86. Neil MacFarquhar, "For Saudis, Jihad Abroad Is Terror at Home," *New York Times*, April 23, 2004, http://www.mafhoum.com/press7/191P9.htm; Megan K. Stack, "Jihad Hits Home in Saudi Arabia," *Los Angeles Times*, April 25, 2004, http://articles.latimes.com/2004/apr/25/world/fg-saudi25.

Chapter 3

1. "PEN American Center, "Hojjatoleslam Hasan Yousefi Eshkevari," http://www.pen.org/page.php/prmID/422.

2. "Iranian Reformists Condemn Hardline Clerical Court," *CNN.com*, October 19, 2000, http://www.cnn.com/2000/WORLD/meast/10/19/iran.court/.

3. "2005 Report on International Religious Freedom," *International Religious Freedom Report 2005*, U.S. State Department, Bureau of Democracy, Human Rights, and Labor, http://www.state.gov/g/drl/rls/irf/2005/; "Stifling Dissent: The Human Rights Consequences of Inter-Factional Struggle in Iran," Human Rights Watch May 2001, http://www.hrw.org/reports/2001/iran/Iran0501-05.htm; "Iran Court Lifts Death Verdict on Dissident Cleric," *Gulf News*, May 20, 2001, http://gulfnews.com/news/gulf/uae/general/iran-court-lifts-death-verdict-on-dissident-cleric-1.417071; "Mr. Yusefi-Eshkevari Is Tried Behind Closed Doors by Special Court," *Iran Press Service*, October 9, 2000, http://www.iran-press-service.com/articles_2000/oct_2000/eshkevari_trial_91000.htm; "Cleared of Heaviest Charges, Eshkevari Faces Long Term Jail," *Iran Press Service*, October 23, 2000, http://www.iran-press-service.com/articles_2000/oct_2000/eshkevari_reactions_231000.htm; PEN American Center, "Hojjatoleslam Hasan Yousefi Eshkevari."

4. "Convert Couple Arrested, Tortured, Threatened," *Compass Direct News*, June 25, 2008, http://archive.compassdirect.org/en/display.php?page=news&idelement=5448&lang=en&length=short&backpage=archives&critere=&countryname=Iran&rowcur=0; also "New Law in Iran: Death Penalty for 'Online Crimes,'" *Jerusalem Post*, July 8, 2008, http://www.jpost.com/servlet/Satellite?cid=1215330897449&pagename=JPost%2FJPArticle%2FShowFull; "Safe at Last, by Grace of God, but They Still Need Your Prayers," *Open Doors*, July 7, 2009, http://www.opendoors.org.nz/article/67/safe-at-last-by-grace-of-god-but-they-still-need-your-prayers.

5. Mehrangiz Kar, "Shari'a Law in Iran," in *Radical Islam's Rules: The Worldwide Spread of Extreme Sharia Law*, ed. Paul Marshall (Lanham, MD: Rowman and Littlefield, 2005), 46; on religious minorities in Iran, see Eliz Sanasarian, *Religious Minorities in Iran* (Cambridge: Cambridge University Press, 2000); Jamsheed K. Chosky, "Despite Shahs and Mollas: Minority Sociopolitics in Premodern and Modern Iran," *Journal of Asian History* 40, no 2 (2006): 129–84.

6. Ladan Boroumand, "Iran's Resilient Civil Society: The Untold Story of the Fight for Human Rights," *Journal of Democracy* 18, no. 4 (October 1, 2007): 66, http://www.journalofdemocracy.org/articles/gratis/Boroumand-18-4.pdf.

7. Asghar Schirazi, *The Constitution of Iran: Politics and State in the Islamic Republic*, trans. John O'Kane (London: I.B. Tauris, 1997), 35.

8. "Islamic Penal Code of Iran," trans. Mission for Establishment of Human Rights in Iran (MEHR IRAN), http://mehr.org/Islamic_Penal_Code_of_Iran.pdf.

9. Saeed Doroudi, "Apostasy in the Legal System of Iran," *Iran Morning Daily* 8, no. 2032 (January 22, 2002): 6.

10. "Iran—Constitution," http://www.servat.unibe.ch/icl/ir00000_.html. Article 167: "The judge is bound to endeavor to judge each case on the basis of the codified law. In case of the absence of any such law, he has to deliver his judgment on the basis of authoritative Islamic sources and authentic fatawa. He, on the pretext of the silence of or deficiency of law in the matter, or its brevity or contradictory nature, cannot refrain from admitting and examining cases and delivering his judgment."

11. Ayatollah Khomeini's book, *Tahrir ul-Vassileh* (http://www.melliblog.blogfa.com/post-301.aspx), was a central source of the penal codes from the time of the Islamic Revolution, in addition to the new draft bill that would amend the code.

12. "Dhabihullah Mahrami: Prisoner of Conscience," Amnesty International, October 1, 1996, http://web.amnesty.org/library/print/ENGMDE130341996. A "public" or "national" apostate is someone born non-Muslim who first converts into Islam and then leaves the faith. A "natural" apostate is someone born into a Muslim family who converts to a different religion.

13. The Islamic regime uses the absence of a codified law on apostasy to deny that it punishes apostasy. When the UN Special Rapporteur visited Iran in December 1995, government officials assured him that "under the Civil Code, conversion was not a crime and that no one had been punished for converting"; see "Dhabihullah Mahrami: Prisoner of Conscience."

14. For the full text in Persian, see http://www.dadkhahi.net/law/Ghavanin/Ghavanin_Jazaee/layehe_gh_mojazat_eslami.htm. An English translation is available at http://rezaei.typepad.com/hassan_rezaei/2008/02/index.html. On the development of the proposed law on apostasy, which was first introduced under Khatami, see Amir Taheri, *The Persian Night: Iran Under the Khomeinist Revolution* (New York: Encounter, 2009), 343–45.

15. "Draft Iranian Law Threatens Gross Human Rights Violations," *Bahai World News Service*, February 22, 2008, http://news.bahai.org/story/606; "Draft Iranian Penal Code Legislates Death Penalty for Apostasy," http://www.maavanews.ir/NewsPrint/tabid/602/Code/1726/Default.aspx.

16. The word *Melli* in this case means "of parents."

17. *Hadd* in Islamic penal law applies to fixed penalties—not to be changed, reduced, or annulled.

18. "Draft Iranian Law Threatens Rights Violations," *Bahai World News Service*.

19. "Iran Parliament Requires Death for 'Apostates' as Crackdown Continues," *Compass Direct News*, September 30, 2008; "'Apostasy' Bill Appears Likely to Become Law: International Pressure Sought Against Mandatory Death Penalty for 'Apostates,'" *Compass Direct News*, September 23, 2008; "USCIRF Concerned over Apostasy Death Penalty Threat to Christians, Baha'is, Muslim Dissenters; Calls for Release of Prisoners," United States Commission on International Religious Freedom, September 17, 2008.

20. Amnesty International's Comments on the National Report by the Islamic Republic of Iran for the Universal Periodic Review, February 12, 2010, http://www.amnesty.org/en/library/asset/MDE13/021/2010/en.

21. "A Faith Denied: The Persecution of the Baha'is of Iran," Iran Human Rights Documentation Center, 2006, 3, http://www.iranhrdc.org/english/publications/reports/3149-a-faith-denied-the-persecution-of-the-baha-is-of-iran.html; Ervand Abrahamian, *Iran Between Two Revolutions* (Princeton, NJ: Princeton University Press, 1982), 17; Moojan Momen, ed., *The Babi and Baha'i Religions* (Oxford: George Ronald, 1981); Abbas Amanat, *Resurrection and Renewal* (Ithaca, NY: Cornell University Press, 1989).

22. "A Faith Denied," Iran Human Rights Documentation Center, 3; Abrahamian, *Iran Between Two Revolutions*, 17; Momen, *The Babi and Baha'i Religions*, 4; Reza Afshari, *Human Rights in Iran: The Abuse of Cultural Relativism* (Philadelphia: University of Pennsylvania Press, 2001), 16, 120.

23. See "Baha'is Killed Since 1978," (which covers until 1998), Appendix I of "The Baha'i Question: *Cultural* in Iran," Baha'i International Community, http://question.bahai.org/index.php; U.S. Department of State, International Religious Freedom Report 2007," http://www.state.gov/g/drl/rls/irf/2007/90210.htm.]; "The Student Movement in the Islamic Republic of Iran," *Journal of Iranian Research and Analysis* 15, no. 2 (November 1999); Abdolkarim Soroush's official Web site, http://www.drsoroush.com/English/On_DrSoroush/E-CMO-19991100–1.html; "USCIRF Concerned over Apostasy Death Penalty Threat to Christians, Baha'is, Muslim Dissenters; Calls for Release of Prisoners," United States Commission on International Religious Freedom, September 17, 2008; Afshari, *Human Rights in Iran* (n. 22 above), 16, 121.

24. *International Religious Freedom Report 2001*, U.S. State Department, Bureau of Democracy, Human Rights, and Labor, http://www.state.gov/g/drl/rls/irf/2001/; U.S. State Department, *International Religious Freedom Report 2006*, http://www.state.gov/g/drl/rls/irf/2006/71421.htm.

25. See "Confidential Memo from Ministry of Science, Research, and Technology to Expel Bahá'í Students from Universities," *One Country*, October–December 2007, http://www.onecountry.org/e191/e19108as_Iran_Denial_document_story.html; also "Iranian Bahá'ís Face New Attacks—and Also Gain Increased Support," *One Country*, July–September 2008, http://www.onecountry.org/e194idx.html.

26. "Muslim Students Protest Baha'i Expelled from Iranian University," December 1, 2008, http://iran.bahai.us/2008/12/01/muslim-students-protest-baha%E2%80%99i-expelled-from-iranian-university/.

27. *International Religious Freedom Report 2007*.

28. "Iran: Amnesty International Seeking Clarification of Official Letter about Baha'i Minority," Amnesty International, July 24, 2006, http://www.amnesty.ca/resource_centre/news/view.php?load=arcview&article=3620&c=Resource+Centre+News.

29. *International Religious Freedom Report 2007*.

30. "Release Baha'is Detained in Mazandaran," International Campaign for Human Rights in Iran, December 12, 2008, http://www.iranhumanrights.org/2008/12/release-baha%E2%80%99is-detained-in-mazandaran/; "Detention of Bahais Continues," *Iran Human Rights Voice*, November 19, 2008, http://www.ihrv.org/inf/?p=1296.

31. "Six Bahais, Christian Arrested in Iran: Judiciary," *Agence France Presse (AFP)*, January 27, 2009, http://www.google.com/hostednews/afp/article/ALeqM5gx82ftet4H2W9CQ3S1gj8arJnmSA.

32. *International Religious Freedom Report 2007*; "Six Bahá'í Leaders Arrested in Iran; Pattern Matches Deadly Sweeps of Early 1980s," *Bahai World News Service*, May 15, 2008, http://news.bahai.org/story/632.

33. "Iranian Bahá'ís Face New Attacks," 7; also, Freedom House, "Baha'i 'Spying' Case Strikes New Blow Against Religious Freedom in Iran," February 12, 2009, http://newsblaze.com/story/20090213102310zzzz.nb/topstory.html.

34. "A Glimpse of Conditions Faced by Baha'i Prisoners Inside Iran's Evin Prison," *One Country*, July-November 2009, http://www.onecountry.org/e203/e20308as_Roxana_Saberi_Interview.html.

35. "Prison Sentences for Iran's Baha'i Leaders Reportedly Reduced to 10 Years," *Baha'i World News Service*, September 16, 2010, http://news.bahai.org/story/793.

36. "Governments Condemn Iran's Reversal on Jail Terms," *Baha'i World News Service*, April 6, 2011, http://www.news.bahai.org/story/815.

37. "Iran Accuses 7 Jailed Leaders of Bahai Faith of Espionage," *The Washington Post*, February 18, 2009, A9; "Tehran Puts 7 Bahai's on Trial for Spying," AFP, January 9, 2010. Also, U.S. Department of State, "Persecution of Religious Minorities in Iran," February 13, 2009; House Resolution 175, "Condemning the Government of Iran for Its State-sponsored Persecution of Its Bahai Minority and Its Continued Violation of the International Covenants on Human Rights," http://thomas.loc.gov/cgi-bin/bdquery/z?d111:h.res.00175; Iran Visual News Corps, "Iran to Try Seven Baha'is for 'Spying' for Israel," February 11, 2009, http://www.iranvnc.com/floater_article1.aspx?lang=en&t=1&id=7819; Human Rights Without Frontiers, "EU concerned by arrests of Baha'i in Iran," May 21, 2008, http://www.reuters.com/article/idUSL2187451220080521; and U.S. Commission on International Religious Freedom, "Iran: USCIRF Calls for Justice for Baha'i Prisoners," February 13, 2009, http://www.uscirf.gov/index.php?option=com_content&task=view&id=2347&Itemid=1; Senate Resolution 71, "Condemning the Government of Iran for Its State-sponsored Persecution of Its Bahai Minority and Its Continued Violation of the International Covenants on Human Rights," http://iran.bahai.us/wp-content/uploads/2009/03/s-res-71.pdf.

38. "Bahá'í International Community Sends Letter to Iran's Prosecutor General," March 6, 2009, http://iran.bahai.us/2009/03/06/bahai-international-community-sends-letter-to-irans-prosecutor-general/.

39. "Pressure on Iranian Baha'i Community, Which Has Not Been Officially Recognized as a Minority Religious Group by the Islamic Republic, Has Been Steadily Increasing," *Iran Human Rights Voice*, March 5, 2009, http://www.ihrv.org/inf/?p=1957.

40. Open Letter to the Baha'i Community, February 4, 2009, http://www.iranian.com/main/2009/feb/we-are-ashamed.

41. "Iran's Arrest of Baha'is Condemned," Human Rights Without Frontiers, May 19, 2008, http://www.hrwf.net/index.php?option=com_content&view=article&id=124#_Toc207425156.

42. "Baha'i International Community Rejects Allegations That Arrested Baha'is Had Weapons in Their Homes," *Bahai World News Service*, January 9, 2010, http://news.bahai.org/story/747; "Baha'is Arrested in Iran After Protests," Radio Free Europe/Radio Liberty, January 6, 2010, http://www.rferl.org/content/Bahais_Arrested_In_Iran_After_Protests/1922834.html; "Trial of Seven Baha'i Leaders in Iran Looms," *Bahai World News Service*, January 5, 2010, http://news.bahai.org/story/745; "Citizens Speak up for Baha'is in Iran," DNA, January 8, 2010, http://www.dnaindia.com/mumbai/report_citizens-speak-up-for-baha-is-in-iran_1332211.

43. "Next Court Date for Baha'i Leaders Will Be 11 April," *Bahai World News Service*, February 19, 2010, http://news.bahai.org/story/759; "Iranian Crackdown on Baha'is, Opposition Activists, Journalists Continues," *VOA News*, February 14, 2010, http://www1.voanews.com/english/news/middle-east/Iranian-Crackdown-on-Bahais-Opposition-Activists-Journalists-Continues-84347022.html; "Iranian Police Arrest Baha'is Ahead of Protests," Radio Free Europe/Radio Liberty, February 11, 2010, http://www.rferl.org/content/Iranian_Police_Arrest_Bahais_Ahead_Of_Protests/1955669.html; "Iran: End Persecution of Baha'is," Human Rights Watch, February 23, 2010, http://www.hrw.org/en/news/2010/02/23/iran-end-persecution-baha.

44. Headline translated from *Kayhan* by Michael Rubin, in "Religious Freedom Also Taking a Hit in Iran," *National Review Online*, The Corner Blog, January 6, 2010, http://corner.nationalreview.com/post/?q=MWM0NDFhMmYzNWM2NzA0YTQ5YWNjMmJhMGM1MmEyOTA. Firuz Kazemzadeh has provided us with a photograph of a progovernment demonstrator with a placard reading "Baha'i Mousavi should be put to death" (e-mail to the authors, January 2, 2010).

45. "State Injustice: Unfair Trials in the Middle East & North Africa—Appeals Cases," Amnesty International, March 1, 1998, http://web.amnesty.org/library/index/engmde010031998.

46. "Background Information on Recent Event in the Ongoing Persecution of the Baha'is in Iran," *Baha'i Community of the USA*, July 31, 1998, http://www.bahaindex.com/en/news/human-rights/271-mrruhollah-rowhani-executed-in-iran-21-july-1998. Sirus Zabihi-Moghaddam and Hadayat Kashefi-Najafabadi were tried alongside Rowhani. A revolutionary court in Mashad later gave death sentences, lowered in 2000 to seven- and five-year prison terms, respectively. Authorities released Kashefi-Najafabadi in October 2001 and Zabihi-Moghaddam the following June.

47. "The Bahá'í Community of Iran Speaks for Itself," The Bahai Question: Cultural Cleansing in Iran, November 15, 2004, http://question.bahai.org/003_3.php.

48. *International Religious Freedom Report 2006*.

49. *International Religious Freedom Report 2005*.

50. "Iran Nobel Laureate Faces Death Threats," *AFP*, March 16, 2006. In the 2009 presidential election, parliamentarian Mahmoud Ahmadi Bi-Ghash attacked candidate Mehdi Karrubi for supporting "the Bahai sect," *IRNA*, May 27, 2009, http://www.irna.ir/View/FullStory/?NewsId=497035.

51. *International Religious Freedom Report 2007*.

52. *International Religious Freedom Report 1999*, U.S. State Department, Bureau of Democracy, Human Rights, and Labor, excerpt on Iran, Jewish Virtual Library, http://www.jewishvirtuallibrary.org/jsource/anti-semitism/reliran99.html.

53. *International Religious Freedom Report 2001*.

54. Chris Woehr, "Leading Protestant Pastor Executed in Iran, Growing Repression for Iranian Church," *News Network International*, January 11, 1991, 9. SAWAMA, also known as VEVAK, is an acronym for Iran's Ministry of Intelligence and National Security (*Sazman-e Ettela'at va Amniat-e Melli-e Iran*), which replaced the Shah's SAVAK; Barbara Baker, "Iranian Christians in Mashhad Suffering Intense Persecution," *News Network International*, June 30, 1993, 5.

55. "Evangelicals Targeted in Iranian Crackdown," *News Network International*, May 7, 1991, 31; Elisabeth Farrell, "Iranian Pastors Call for Letter Writing Campaign," *News Network International*, January 29, 1993, 23; Barbara Baker, "Iranian Christians in Mashhad Suffering Intense Persecution," *News Network International*, June 30, 1993, 5.

56. "'Apostasy' Bill Appears Likely to Become Law," *Compass Direct News*, September 23, 2008, http://archive.compassdirect.org/en/display.php?page=news&idelement=5599&lang=en&length=short&backpage=archives&critere=&countryname=Iran&rowcur=0; "Hanged for Being a Christian in Iran," *Daily Telegraph*, October 11, 2008, http://www.telegraph.co.uk/news/worldnews/middleeast/iran/3179465/Hanged-for-being-a-Christian-in-Iran.html.

57. "Testimony and Life of Rev. Dibaj in His Own Voice," *Farsi Net*, http://www.farsinet.com/dibaj/; Diana Scimone, "Iranian Church Growing Despite Hardships," *News Network International*, March 27, 1992, 26; "Impassioned Letter from Imprisoned Iranian Pastor Reaches West," *News Network International*, July 21, 1992, 25.

58. "The Written Defense of the Rev. Mehdi Dibaj Delivered to the Sari Court of Justice," *Farsi Net*, December 3, 1993, http://www.farsinet.com/dibaj/; "Evangelicals Targeted in Iranian Crackdown," 31; Scimone, "Iranian Church Growing Despite Hardships," 26; "Impassioned Letter from Imprisoned Iranian Pastor Reaches West," 25.

59. "Iran: Christian Couple Released on Bail," *Compass Direct News*, October 5, 2006, http://archive.compassdirect.org/en/display.php?page=news&idelement=4571&lang=en&length=short&backpage=archives&critere=&countryname=Iran&rowcur=25.

60. Human Rights Watch 1997 Report, http://www.hrw.org/reports/1997/iran/Iran-06.htm.

61. In late 1999, the press revealed that Emami, former Vice Minister of Intelligence, was directly responsible for the "Serial Murders" in the 1980s and 1990s; see *Iran Terror Database*, July 19, 2005, http://www.iranterror.com/content/view/33/52/.

62. Human Rights Watch 1997 Report.

63. Hamid Pourmand, a Naval officer charged with hiding his conversion from his superiors, received a three-year prison term, since, according to Iranian law, only Muslims can be

military officers. "Iran: Authorities Quietly Release Convert Christian Prisoner," *Compass Direct News*, September 12, 2006, http://archive.compassdirect.org/en/display.php?page=ne ws&idelement=4533&lang=en&length=short&backpage=archives&critere=&countryname =Iran&rowcur=25. For other cases, see Ghorban Tourani, "Iran: US Accepts Iranian Christians for Resettlement," *Compass Direct News*, December 6, 2005, http://archive.compassdirect. org/en/display.php?page=news&idelement=4100&lang=en&length=short&backpage=archi ves&critere=&countryname=Iran&rowcur=25; "Iran: Christian Couple Released on Bail," *Compass Direct News*, October 5, 2006, http://archive.compassdirect.org/en/display.php?pag e=news&idelement=4571&lang=en&length=short&backpage=archives&critere=&countryn ame=Iran&rowcur=25. On further cases, including that of Issa Motamedi Mojdehi, see *Compass Direct News*, December 14, 2006, http://archive.compassdirect.org/en/display.php? page=news&idelement=4685&lang=en&length=short&backpage=archives&critere=&count ryname=Iran&rowcur=0; and *Compass Direct News*, December 4, 2006, http://www.compass-direct.org/en/display.php?page=lead&lang=en&length=long&idelement=4515.

64. "Iran: Further Information on Fear of Torture and Ill-treatment/Possible Prisoners of Conscience," Amnesty International, http://www.iranrights.org/english/document-454–973.php; "Iranian Christian Arrested Without Charges," *Compass Direct News*, June 9, 2008, http://archive.com-passdirect.org/en/display.php?page=news&idelement=5421&lang=en&length=short&backpag e=archives&critere=&countryname=Iran&rowcur=0; Farsi Christian News Network, "Court Issues Verdict on 3 Farsi-speaking Christians," March 25, 2009, http://www.fcnn.com//index. php?option=com_content&task=view&id=3006&Itemid=63.

65. BosNewsLife, "Iranian Christians Face Death Penalty in Iran," September 11, 2008, http:// www.rferl.org/content/Two_Iranian_Christians_May_Face_Execution_For_Apostasy /1779217.html; "Iranian Church Leader Released—Son of Hanged Pastor Bailed on Charges of Anti-govt Behavior," Release International, October 23, 2008, http://www.releaseinter-national.org/pages/posts/iranian-church-leader-released—son-of-hanged-pastor-bailed-on-charges-of-anti-govt-activity451.php. For additional cases, see "Tortured Christian Flees," *Compass Direct News*, July 21, 2008, http://archive.compassdirect.org/en/display.ph p?page=news&idelement=5478&lang=en&length=short&backpage=archives&critere=&co untryname=Iran&rowcur=0; "Christian Couple Dies from Police Attack," *Compass Direct News*, August 6, 2008, http://archive.compassdirect.org/en/display.php?page=news&idele ment=5508&lang=en&length=short&backpage=archives&critere=&countryname=Iran&r owcur=0; "Prosecutor Charges Two Christians with Apostasy," *Iran Human Rights Voice*, September 11, 2008, http://www.ihrv.org/inf/?p=884; "Matin Azad and Arash Basirat, Two Christians Charged with Heresy, Are Freed," *Iran Human Rights Voice*, October 4, 2008, http://www.ihrv.org/inf/?p=1060; "Court Finds Way to Acquit Christians of 'Apostasy,'" *Compass Direct News*, October 30, 2008, http://archive.compassdirect.org/en/display.php?p age=news&idelement=5664&lang=en&length=short&backpage=archives&critere=&count ryname=Iran&rowcur=0; "Assyrian Iranian Minister Arrested in Urumieh by Security Agents," Farsi Christian News Network, October 1, 2008, http://www.fcnn.com/index. php?option=com_content&task=view&id=1760&Itemid=63.

66. Human Rights Without Frontiers, "The Calvary of a Female Convert to Christianity," June 9, 2009, in HRWF country report at http://www.hrwf.net/index.php?option=com_ content&view=article&id=105:news-2008-catalogued-by-country&catid=38:freedom-of-religion-and-belief&Itemid=90.

67. "Iran: Three Iranian Christians Arrested from Homes in Tehran," *Compass Direct News*, March 22, 2011, http://archive.compassdirect.org/en/display.php?page=news&idelement=5776&l ang=en&length=short&backpage=archives&critere=&countryname=Iran&rowcur=0; "Wave of Arrests of Christians in Iran," Middle East Concern, January 27, 2009. http://www .givengain.com/cgi-bin/giga.cgi?cmd=cause_dir_news_item&cause_id=1489& news_id=59190&cat_id=434.

68. "Iran: Christian Arrested Without Charges," *Compass Direct News*, June 9, 2008, http:// archive.compassdirect.org/en/display.php?page=news&idelement=5421&lang=en&length =short&backpage=archives&critere=&countryname=Iran&rowcur=0.

69. "Authorities Tighten Grip on Christians As Unrest Roils," *Compass Direct News*, August 11, 2009, http://archive.compassdirect.org/en/display.php?page=news&idelement=6057&lang=en&length=short&backpage=archives&critere=&countryname=Iran&rowcur=0; "Iran Temporarily Releases Christians on Bail," ICC, September 15, 2009/HRWF, September 16, 2009.

70. "Authorities Tighten Grip on Christians as Unrest Roils"; Damaris Kremida, "Iran Releases Two Christian Women from Evin Prison," *Compass Direct News*, November 19, 2009, http://www.compassdirect.org/english/country/iran/11805/; "Iran Detains Christians Without Legal Counsel," *Compass Direct News*, January 28, 2010, http://www.compassdirect.org/english/country/iran/14572; "Iran: Maryam and Marzieh Acquitted," Middle East Concern, May 24, 2010. For additional cases, see "Iranian Authorities Pressure Father of Convert," *Compass Direct News*, May 20, 2009, http://archive.compassdirect.org/en/display.php?page=news&idelement=5932&lang=en&length=short&backpage=archives&critere=&countryname=Iran&rowcur=0.

71. "Iran Detains Christians Without Legal Counsel."

72. "Christian Priest and Wife Arrested in Iran," Radio Free Europe/Radio Liberty, March 4, 2010, http://www.rferl.org/content/Christian_Priest_And_Wife_Arrested_In_Iran/1974682.html; "Torture of Wilson Eisavi, Priest in Assyrian Church," *Iran Human Rights Voice*, March 9, 2010, http://www.ihrv.org/inf/?p=3878; "The Worrying Condition of Rev. 'Wilson Issavi' in Prison," *Farsi Christian News Network*, http://www.fcnn.com/index.php?option=com_content&view=article&id=812:the-worrying-condition-of-rev-qwilson-issaviq-in-prison&catid=127:iranian-christian&Itemid=593. On additional cases, see "Trend Continues Against Churches Previously Protected by Iranian Government," *Assyrian International News Agency*, February 24, 2010, http://www.aina.org/news/20100224011107.htm; Ethan Cole, "Jailed Iranian Pastor Temporarily Freed, in 'Good Spirits,'" *Christian Post*, March 31, 2010, http://www.christianpost.com/article/20100331/jailed-iranian-pastor-temporarily-freed-in-good-spirits.html.

73. "Backgrounder: The Trial of 13 Iranian Jews," Anti-Defamation League, March 2003, http://www.adl.org/backgrounders/Iranian_Jews.asp; "Report on Current Condition for Jews in Iran, Human Rights and Torture," Iranian American Jewish Federation, 2006, 18.

74. In December 2004, the Iranian TV station Sahar 1 began showing a weekly series set in Israel and the West Bank, with the title "For You, Palestine," or "Zahra's Blue Eyes." It portrayed a Jewish eye surgeon who searched for the most attractive Muslim children, paying particular attention to their eyes. Once he found what he was looking for, he deceived the children into having eye surgery and removed their eyes, which were then used as implants for Israeli children. Anti-Semitism has increased significantly since Mahmoud Ahmadinejad's accession to the presidency. He has publicly questioned the existence and scale of the Holocaust. On December 11 and 12, 2006, the government sponsored a conference entitled "Review of the Holocaust: Global Vision" that provided a forum for those who deny the Holocaust. On August 14, 2006, a government-sponsored exhibition of Holocaust cartoons, solicited earlier in the year by the newspaper *Hamshahri* as an international contest, took place in Tehran; see *International Religious Freedom Report 2005* and *2007*.

75. Nazila Fathi, "Wipe Israel 'off the Map' Iranian Says," *The New York Times*, October 27, 2005, http://www.nytimes.com/2005/10/26/world/africa/26iht-iran.html.

76. "One Person's Story: Mr. Habib Elqanian," *Omid: A Memorial in Defense of Human Rights*, http://www.abfiran.org/english/english/person—2861.php.

77. On Iran's Zoroastrians, see Jamsheed K. Chosky, "Despite Shahs and Mollas"; Jamsheed K. Chosky, "Heritage, Faith and Minority Identity: Zoroastrians in the Islamic Republic of Iran," in *Negotiating Identity Amongst the Religious Minorities of Asia*, ed. M. A. Ehrlich (Leiden: E.J. Brill, forthcoming 2011). On Zoroastrians as *kaffers*, see Chosky, "Despite Shāhs and Mollās," 165.

78. Chosky, "Despite Shahs and Mollas," 161.

79. Chosky, "Heritage, Faith and Minority Identity: Zoroastrians in Iran," 5.

80. Chosky, "Despite Shahs and Mollas," 182–83.

81. Khaled Mahmoud, "Iran: Government Bans Sunnis from Praying in State Universities," *Asharq Al-Awsat*, April 28, 2010, http://aawsat.com/english/news.asp?section=1& id=20756.

82. Reza Afshari recounts three government killings of Sunni religious leaders. See Afshari, *Human Rights in Iran: The Abuse of Cultural Relativism* (Philadelphia: University of Pennsylvania Press, 2001), 129, 130.

83. Ladan Boroumand, *Journal of Democracy*, October 2007, http://www.journalofdemocracy.org/articles/gratis/Boroumand-18-4.pdf.

84. Ibid.

85. Nir Boms and Shayan Arya, "On Annan, Robinson, Religion and Hypocrisy," *The Jerusalem Post*, November 10, 2008, http://www.jpost.com/servlet/Satellite?cid=1225910085758&pagename=JPost%2FJPArticle%2FShowFull.

86. Ron Synovitz, "Clashes Highlight 'Demonization' of Sufi Muslims," Radio Free Europe/ Radio Liberty, November 16, 2007, http://www.rferl.org/featuresarticle/2007/11/DEB2FA43–077F-4B8D-9079–97A1EC610C67.html.

87. *International Religious Freedom Report 2006*.

88. The Nematollahi Gonabadi is a Sufi order with traditions similar in several respects to those of Shia.

89. Golnaz Esfandiari, "Local Authorities Try to Evict Sufi Leader," Radio Free Europe/Radio Liberty, October 12, 2006, http://www.rferl.org/featuresarticle/2006/10/81C671EA-C25A-46DB-AB07–328838F1AD99.html; "Security Forces Attack Again Prayer Areas of the Nematollahi Gonabadi Sufis," *Iran Now Network*, November 10, 2006, http://iran-now.net/$202612.

90. "Dozens Injured in Clash Between Sufi Mystics, Iran Paramilitary," *The Jerusalem Post*, November 11, 2007, http://www.jpost.com/IranianThreat/News/Article.aspx?id=81619; Synovitz, "Clashes Highlight 'Demonization' of Sufi Muslims." See also "The New Round of Harrasments (sic) Against Gonabadi Daravish," *Iran Human Rights Voice*, September 17, 2008, http://www.ihrv.org/inf/?p=944#more-944.

91. "Iranian Authorities Destroy Sufi Holy Site in Isfehan," *Payvand News*, February 19, 2009, http://www.payvand.com/news/09/feb/1220.html.

92. Iran Human Rights Voice, "Scuffle with Gonabadi Dervishes in Isfehan Resulted in Forty Arrests," February 22, 2009, http://www.ihrv.org/inf/?p=1904.

93. "A Dervish's Dream for Iran," Radio Free Europe/Radio Liberty, February 22, 2010, http://www.rferl.org/content/A_Dervishs_Dream_For_Iran/1964987.html; Stephen Schwartz, "Iran: Thugs in Clerical Dress' vs. the Sufis," Hudson Institute New York, March 15, 2010, http://www.hudsonny.org/2010/03/iran-thugs-in-clerical-dress-vs-the-sufis.php.

94. Laura Secor, "The Democrat: Iran's Leading Reformist Intellectual Tries to Reconcile Religious Duties and Human Rights," *Boston Globe*, March 14, 2004, http://www.boston.com/news/globe/ideas/articles/2004/03/14/the_democrat/. A good introduction to Akbar Ganji's work is *Reason, Freedom, and Democracy in Islam: Essential Writings of Abdolkarim Soroush* (New York: Oxford University Press, 2002). On Akbar Ganji, see "Iranian Journalist, in Court, Says Security Forces Tortured Him," *New York Times*, November 10, 2000, http://query.nytimes.com/gst/fullpage.html?res=9B00E5DB1438F933A25752C1A9669C8B63&scp=6&sq=akbar+ganji&st=nyt; Shirin Ebadi, *Iran Awakening* (New York: Random House, 2006), 193; Nazila Fathi, "Iranian Writer Released After Serving 6-Year Prison Term," *New York Times*, March 19, 2006, http://www.nytimes.com/2006/03/19/international/middleeast/19iran.html?scp=18&sq=akbar+ganji&st=nyt; "Journalist Tortured to Renounce Writings," Human Rights Watch, November 2, 2005, http://www.hrw.org/english/docs/2005/11/02/iran11958.htm; Country Reports on Human Rights Practices 2005, Bureau of Democracy, Human Rights, and Labor, http://www.state.gov/g/drl/rls/hrrpt/2005/61688.htm; Akbar Ganji, "Money Can't Buy Us Democracy," *New York Times*, August 1, 2006, http://www.nytimes.com/2006/08/01/opinion/01ganji.html?scp=9&sq=akbar+ganji&st=nyt.

95. Official Web site of Abdolkarim Soroush, http://www.drsoroush.com/English/News_Archive/E-NWS-19960531–1.html; "Let the Occasional Chalice Break: Abdolkarim Souroush and Islamic Liberation Theology," *The Iranian*, October 26, 1998, http://www.iranian.com/Opinion/Oct98/Soroush/index.html.

96. "Islam, Catholicism, and the Secular: A Conversation with Jose Casanova and Abdolkarim Soroush," Center for the Study of Islam and Democracy, http://ikhwanweb.com/Article. asp?ID=15280&SectionID=83; official Web site of the Erasmus Prize, http://www.erasmus-prijs.org/eng/index.cfm?paginaID=34&item_ID=12; Scott Macleod, "Abdokarim Souroush, Iran's Democratic Voice," *Time*, April 18, 2005, http://www.time.com/time/subscriber/2005/time100/scientists/100soroush.html; http://www.drsoroush.com/English/News_Archive/E-NWS-20040702-Dr.Soroush_is_Back_in_Tehran.html; Laura Secor, "The Democrat: Iran's Leading Reformist Intellectual."

97. Mohammad Ayatollahi Tabaar, "Who Wrote the Koran?" *New York Times Magazine*, December 5, 2008, http://www.nytimes.com/2008/12/07/magazine/07wwln-essay-t.html.

98. "At Least 40 Followers of Ayatollah Sayed Hossein Kazemeyni Boroujerdi Arrested," Amnesty International report, posted by *Payvand News*, October 3, 2006, http://www.payvand.com/news/06/oct/1016.html.

99. Abdorrahman Boroumand Foundation, http://www.abfiran.org/english/document-298–699.php?searchtext=Ym9yb3VqZXJkaaQ%3D%3D; "News/Imprisoned Cleric's Life in Danger/Ayatollah Boroujerdi in Need of Urgent Medical Care," June 1, 2008. http://mardaninews.de/Deutsch/?p=178.

100. "A Brief Report on the Latest Condition of Ayatullah Borojerdi in Zazd Prison," *Iran Human Rights Voice*, www.ihrv.org/inf/?p=1420.

101. "Unexpected Transfer of Ayatullah Borojerdi to Evin Prison," Iran Human Rights Voice, August 26, 2009.

102. Abdorrahman Boroumand Foundation.

103. Yasuyuki Matsunaga, "Mohsen Kadivar, an Advocate of Postrevivalist Islam in Iran," *British Journal of Middle Eastern Studies*, December 2007, http://www.kadivar.com/Data/Remote/0/Data/Resources/Medias/Kadivar,%20an%20Advocate%20(matsunaga).pdf; Human Rights Watch, *World Report 2001*, Appendix, http://www.hrw.org/legacy/wr2k1/appendix/index.html.

104. Scott Macleod and Nahid Siamdoust, "The Critical Cleric," *Time*, May 5, 2004, http://www.time.com/time/2004/innovators/200405/kadivar.html; Bret Stephens, "Religion of Peace in Iran, a Theological State Is Challenged on Theological Grounds," *Wall Street Journal*, June 23, 2009, http://online.wsj.com/article/SB124571492981739137.html#mod=djemEditorial Page.

105. Mohsen Kadivar, "The Principles of Compatibility of Islam and Modernity," October 7, 2004, http://www.kadivar.com/Index.asp?DocId=831&AC=1&AF=1&ASB=1&AGM=1&AL=1&DT=d tv. See also Mohsen Kadivar, "Freedom of Religion and Belief in Islam," in *The New Voices of Islam: Rethinking Politics and Modernity* (Berkeley: University of California Press, 2006), 119–42.

106. Macleod and Siamdoust, "The Critical Cleric"

107. "This Iranian Form of Theocracy Has Failed," interview with Mohsen Kadivar by Erich Follath and Gabor Steingart, *Spiegel Online*, July 1, 2009, http://www.spiegel.de/international/world/0,1518,633517,00.html.

108. "Reformists in Iran, Despite Pressure, Speak Out More Boldly," *New York Times*, August 4, 2000, http://query.nytimes.com/gst/fullpage.html?res=9B03E5D8173CF937A3575BC0A9669C8B63&scp=5&sq=MOhsen+Kadivar&st=nyt.

109. "Amnesty Highlights the Case of Hashem Aghajari," Iran Mania, November 08, 2002, http://www.iranmania.com/news/ArticleView/Default.asp?NewsCode=12888&NewsKind=CurrentAffairs.

110. Sadeq Saba, "Profile of Abdollah Nouri," *BBC News*, November 27, 1999, http://news.bbc.co.uk/1/hi/world/middle_east/539470.stm; "Abdollah Nouri, Prisoner of Conscience," Amnesty International, June 27, 2002, http://asiapacific.amnesty.org/library/Index/ENGMDE130102002?open&of=ENG-IRN.

111. John Burns, "With Iran's Reforms at Stake, a Moderate Digs In," *New York Times*, October 24, 1999, http://query.nytimes.com/gst/fullpage.html?res=9A0DEEDB1F39F937A15753C1A96F958260; John Burns, "Cleric's Trial Becomes Flash Point of Iran's Political Fate," *New York Times*, October 31, 1999, http://query.nytimes.com/gst/fullpage.html?res=9D01E4DA173BF932A05753C1A96F958260.

112. "Iran Annual Report 2002," Reporters Without Borders, http://www.rsf.org/article. php3?id_article=1438; Said Amir Arjomand, "Civil Society and the Rule of Law in the Constitutional Politics of Iran Under Khatami," *Social Research*, June 22, 2000, at Encyclopedia.com, http://www.encyclopedia.com/doc/1G1-63787333.html.

113. Reporters Without Borders, http://www.rsf.org/article.php3?id_article=28929.

114. Jomhouri Elsami's official Web site, http://www.jomhourieslami.com; Reporters Without Borders, as listed on International Freedom Exchange Network (IFEX), http://www.ifex .org/en/layout/set/print/content/view/full/60511/.

115. Reporters Without Borders, http://www.rsf.org/article.php3?id_article=28929.

116. "Grand Ayatollah Hossein-Ali Montazeri: 'Not Every Conversion is Apostasy,'" (in Persian), *BBC Persian*, http://www.bbc.co.uk/persian/iran/story/2005/02/050202_mj-montzari-renegade.shtml.

117. Robin Wright, "Iran's Opposition Loses a Mentor but Gains a Martyr," *Time*, December 21, 2009, http://www.time.com/time/world/article/0,8599,1949048,00.html; Abbas Milani, "Mourning Montazeri," *The New Republic*, December 21, 2009, http://www.tnr.com/article/ mourning-montazeri; Richard Spencer, "Grand Ayatollah Montazeri Death Sparks Protests," *Telegraph*, December 20, 2009, http://www.telegraph.co.uk/news/worldnews/middleeast/ iran/6851224/Grand-Ayatollah-Montazeri-death-sparks-protests.html.

118. Reporters Without Borders/Network for Education and Academic Rights (NEAR), http://74.125.45.104/search?q=cache:7wDc3CXLXJgJ:www.nearinternational.org/alerts/i ran2420050830en+Mojtaba+Lotfi&hl=en&ct=clnk&cd=1&gl=us&ie=UTF-8.

119. "The Office of Ayatullah Montazeri Condemns Imprisonment of Mojtaba Lotfi, Calling It Illegal and Unfair," *Iran Human Rights Voice*, December 9, 2008, http://www.ihrv.org/ inf/?p=1397.

120. See http://latimesblogs.latimes.com/babylonbeyond/2009/09/iran-grand-ayatollah-calls-government-a-military-regime.html.

121. Wright, "Iran's Opposition Loses a Mentor but Gains a Martyr"; Spencer, "Montazeri Death Sparks Protests"; Milani, "Mourning Montazeri," *The New Republic*, December 21, 2009, http://www.tnr.com/article/mourning-montazeri; *Violent Aftermath: The 2009 Election and Suppression of Dissent in Iran*, Iran Human Rights Documentation Center, 2010, 35–36, http://www.iranhrdc.org/httpdocs/English/pdfs/Reports/Violent%20Aftermath.pdf.

122. Iason Athanasiadis, "Iran Move to Defrock Dissident Ayatollah Opens Rifts in Theocracy," *Christian Science Monitor*, January 6, 2010, http://www.csmonitor.com/World/Middle-East/2010/0106/Iran-move-to-defrock-dissident-ayatollah-opens-rifts-in-theocracy; "Website Says Iran Militia Attack Pro-Reform Cleric's Home," Radio Free Europe/Radio Liberty, December 22, 2009, http://www.rferl.org/content/Website_Says_Iran_Militia_ Attack_Clerics_Home/1911071.html?page=1&x=1#relatedInfoContainer; Mustafa El-Labbad, "The Iranian Triangle," *Al-Ahram*, January 14–20, 2010, http://weekly.ahram.org .eg/2010/981/re10.htm. For the cases of Mojtaba Saminejad, Ehsan Mansouri, Majid Tavakoli, Ahmad Ghassaban, and Hadi Ghabel, see Source: Reporters Without Borders, as listed on International Freedom Exchange (IFEX) Web site, http://www.ifex.org/en/ content/view/full/66707; International Freedom of Expression eXchange, "Blogger Mojtaba Saminejad Gets Two-year Prison Sentence," June 8, 2005, http://www.ifex.org/en/content/ view/full/67227; "Jailed Students Abused to Obtain Forced Confessions," http://www.ifex .org/en/content/view/full/85193/. The government also blocks over five million Web sites deemed to contain immoral or antisocial material: "Iran Blocks Access to over Five Million Websites," *AFP*, November 19, 2008, http://www.breitbart.com/article.php?id=081119173 359.0m09kn48&show_article=1. See also Gozaar: A Forum on Human Rights and Democracy in Iran, http://www.gozaar.org/template1.php?id=782&language=english.

123. Hiedeh Farmani, "Iran's Khamenei Issues Stern Warning to Opposition," *AFP*, December 13, 2009; Anne Barker, "Iran Arrests Hundreds of Dissidents," ABC.net, December 30, 2009, http://www.abc.net.au/news/stories/2009/12/30/2782418.htm.

124. Nazila Fathi, "Protestors Defy Iranian Efforts to Cloak Unrest," *New York Times*, June 17, 2009, http://www.nytimes.com/2009/06/18/world/middleeast/18iran.html?_r=1.

125. Amir Taheri, "Regime on the Brink," *New York Post*, February 13, 2010, http://www.nypost.com/p/news/opinion/opedcolumnists/regime_on_the_brink_xhGnMOyqyk9vQO-l4aWpGfO; "Iran Opposition Leaders Face Execution: Khameini Aide," Reuters, December 29, 2009, http://www.reuters.com/article/idUSLDE5BQ06J20091229.

126. Nazila Fathi, "Iran Accuses Five of Warring Against God," *The New York Times*, January 8, 2010; Edward Yeranian, "Iran Demonstrators Facing Death Sentence," *Voice of America*, January 17, 2010, http://www.voanews.com/english/news/middle-east/Iran-Demonstrators-Facing-Death-Sentence-81930617.html; "Citizens Speak Up for Baha'is in Iran," DNA, January 8, 2010, http://www.dnaindia.com/mumbai/report_citizens-speak-up-for-baha-is-in-iran_1332211; House Resolution 175, "Condemning the Government of Iran for Its State-sponsored Persecution of Its Baha'i Minority and Its Continued Violation of Its International Covenants on Human Rights, 111th Cong., 1st Session (introduced February 13, 2009).

127. The service in question was likely the July 17 Friday prayer, during which Rafsanjani called for an end to arrests and censorship; see *Violent Aftermath: The 2009 Election and Suppression of Dissent in Iran*, Iran Human Rights Documentation Center, 2010, 29, http://www.iranhrdc.org/httpdocs/English/pdfs/Reports/Violent%20Aftermath.pdf.

128. "Twenty Year-Old Student Accused of Moharebeh (Waging War)," *Iran Human Rights Voice*, February 6, 2010, http://www.ihrv.org/inf/?p=3696; "USCIRF Condemns Thirty-One Years of Religious Abuse in Iran," U.S. Commission on International Religious Freedom, February 10, 2010, http://www.uscirf.gov/index2.php?option=com_content&do_pdf=1&id=2973.

129. "One of the Nine Accused of Ashura Protest Sentenced to Death," *Iran Human Rights Voice*, March 4, 2010, http://www.ihrv.org/inf/?p=3846#more-3846.

130. Payman Fatahi, the leader of the hard-to-classify AleYasin society, a self-described "contemplative community," was held in Evin prison for six months and charged with, inter alia, "dissension from religious dogma," "promoting pluralism," and "religious breakdown by attempting to link Islam, Christianity and Judaism." "Report about Crackdown Against AleYasin Community," *Iran Human Rights Voice*, February 2, 2009, http://www.ihrv.org/inf/?p=1763; Elyasin News blog, http://elyasinnews.blogspot.com/.

Chapter 4

1. Sayed Al Qimni, "How Brutal of You My Country," *El Qahera*, January 2, 2007, http://www.hrinfo.net/mena/aodepf/2005/pr0717.shtml; Stephen Ulph, "Al-Qaeda Extends Threats to Journalists and Intellectuals Outside Iraq," *The Jamestown Foundation Terrorism Focus* 2, no. 14 (July 22, 2005): http://www.jamestown.org/programs/gta/single/?tx_ttnews%5Btt_news%5D=530&tx_ttnews%5BbackPid%5D=238&no_cache=1.

2. "Egypt: Security Police Torture Christian Convert Woman," *Compass Direct News*, July 18, 2007, http://archive.compassdirect.org/en/display.php?page=news&idelement=4952&lang=en&length=short&backpage=archives&critere=&countryname=Egypt&rowcur=50; "Egypt: Police Release Christian to Her Violent Family," *Compass Direct News*, July 23, 2007, http://archive.compassdirect.org/en/display.php?page=news&idelement=4956&lang=en&length=short&backpage=archives&critere=&countryname=Egypt&rowcur=50. Five months later, speaking by telephone through a translator, a woman claiming to be al-Sayed said police in Alexandria treated her "not good, but not badly" but contradicted eyewitness testimony, raising questions about whether she was under police pressure; see "Egypt: Mystery Shrouds Release of Woman Convert," *Compass Direct News*, December 10, 2007, http://archive.compassdirect.org/en/display.php?page=news&idelement=5154&lang=en&length=short&backpage=archives&critere=&countryname=Egypt&rowcur=25.

3. "Bahai Homes Attacked after Media Commentary," *Menassat News*, April 3, 2009, http://www.menassat.com/?q=en/news-articles/6305-bahai-homes-attacked-egypt-after-slandering-media-commentary; Egyptian Villagers Torch 'Deviant' Bahai Homes," *Agence France Presse (AFP)*, http://www.alarabiya.net/articles/2009/04/02/69775.html; "Call for Egypt Bahai Attack Probe," *BBC News*, http://news.bbc.co.uk/2/hi/middle_east/7981252.stm.

Two days prior to the *Al-Haqiqa* episode, Abdel Rahimhad wrote in the state-owned newspaper *Al-Gomhuriyah* that Baha'is are "a deviant group which seeks to harm Islam to serve the interests of the enemies of the Muslim religion, in particular world Zionism," "Egyptian Villagers Torch 'Deviant' Bahai Homes," *AFP*.

4. "Constitution of the Arab Republic of Egypt," http://www.egypt.gov.eg/english/laws/Constitution/default.aspx; David J. Warr, "The State of Freedom of Expression in Egypt," November 7, 1997, http://www.cjfe.org/protestlets/1997/egyn07.html.

5. Nadia Abou El-Magd, "When the Professor Can't Teach," *Al-Ahram Weekly*, http://weekly.ahram.org.eg/2000/486/eg6.htm; Mona Eltahawy, "Lives Torn Apart in Battle for the Soul of the Arab World," *The Guardian*, October 20, 1999, http://www.guardian.co.uk/international/story/0,260766,00.html.

6. See Baha'i Faith in Egypt, http://www.bahai-egypt.org.

7. U.S. State Department, "Country Reports on Human Rights Practices 2001: Egypt," http://www.state.gov/g/drl/rls/hrrpt/2001/nea/8248.htm; *International Religious Freedom Report 2007*, http://www.state.gov/g/drl/rls/irf/2007/90209.htm; "Prohibited Identities: State Interference with Religious Freedom," Human Rights Watch, November 11, 2007, http://hrw.org/reports/2007/egypt1107.

8. "Egypt Hearing Highlights ID Card Discrimination for Bahá'ís," *One Country*, July–September 2006, http://www.onecountry.org/e182/e18210as_Cairo_ID_Card_Hearing.htm.

9. HRW/EIPR interview with Diya' Nur al-Din, Cairo, November 13, 2005, in "Prohibited Identities."

10. *International Religious Freedom Report 2007*. For a defense of the Baha'is by a moderate Muslim thinker, see "Egypt: Interview with Gamal El-Banna," Baha'i Faith in Egypt blog, October 25, 2006, http://www.bahai-egypt.org/2006/10/egypt-interview-with-gamal-el-banna.html.

11. *International Religious Freedom Report 2007*; "Prohibited Identities."

12. "Court Decision on Bahai Egyptians Postponed to October 30th," http://www.copticassembly.com/showart.php?main_id=437; "Egypt: Court Rules Against Convert," *Compass Direct News*, January 31, 2008, http://archive.compassdirect.org/en/display.php?page=news&idelement=5209&lang=en&length=short&backpage=archives&critere=&countryname=Egypt&rowcur=25.

13. See Baha'i Web site: http://www.bahai-egypt.org/.

14. Egyptian Initiative for Personal Rights: "Five-year Legal Battle Ends in Favor of Egyptian Bahá'ís," March 16, 2009, http://www.iranpresswatch.org/post/1893.

15. Cairo Institute for Human Rights Studies, *Bastion of Impunity, Mirage of Reform: Human Rights in the Arab Region—Annual Report 2009*, 126, http://www.cihrs.org/Images/ArticleFiles/Original/485.pdf.

16. Photographs of the cards using a dash for "religion" are shown in "First Identification Cards Issued to Egyptian Bahá'ís," *Baha'i World News Service*, August 14, 2009, http://news.bahai.org/story/726.

17. "International Human Rights Report 2009: Egypt," March 11, 2010, U. S. State Department, Bureau of Democracy, Human Rights, and Labor, http://www.state.gov/g/drl/rls/hrrpt/2009/index.htm.

18. Liam Stack, "Egyptians Win the Right to Drop Religion from ID Cards," *The Christian Science Monitor*, April 20, 2009, http://www.csmonitor.com/2009/0420/p06s12-wome.html.

19. Mohamed Abdel Salam, "Egypt's Baha'is Still Having ID Problems," *Bikjamasr*, March 15, 2010, http://bikyamasr.com/wordpress/?p=9906.

20. "The Egyptian Parliament Is Discussing a Bill to Declare All Bahá'ís Criminals," *The Iran Press Watch*, April 29, 2009, http://www.iranpresswatch.org/post/2550.

21. Interviews by Paul Marshall, Cairo, July 2000 and February 5–6, 2001. The massacre at El-Kosheh is described in *Massacre at the Millennium* (Washington: Freedom House, 2001). For an overview of recent attacks on Copts, see *Egyptian Initiative for Personal Rights*, "Two Years of Sectarian Violence: What Happened? Where Do We Begin? An Analytical Study of Jan 2008–Jan 2010," http://eipr.org/sites/default/files/reports/pdf/Sectarian_Violence_inTwoYears_EN.pdf.

22. Mustafa El-Menshawy, "One Step Forward, Two Steps Back," *Al-Ahram Weekly*, October 20–26, 2005, http://weekly.ahram.org.eg/2005/765/eg6.htm; Maamoun Youssef, "Stabbing of Nun Sparks Tension in Alexandria," *Independent Online*, October 20, 2005, http://www.int.iol.co.za/index.php?set_id=1&click_id=85&art_id=qw1129782066324B221; "Three Killed in Egypt Church Riot," *BBC News*, October 22, 2005, http://news.bbc.co.uk/2/hi/middle_east/4366232.stm;2009; Michael Slackman, "Egyptian Police Guard Coptic Church Attacked by Muslims," *New York Times*, October 23, 2005, http://www.nytimes.com/2005/10/23/international/africa/23egypt.html?_r=1.

23. "Authorities Detain Christian Rights Advocates," *Compass Direct News*, August 9, 2007, http://archive.compassdirect.org/en/display.php?page=news&idelement=4982&lang=en&length=short&backpage=archives&critere=&countryname=Egypt&rowcur=25; "More Christian Activists from Rights Group Jailed," *Compass Direct News*, November 12, 2007, http://archive.compassdirect.org/en/display.php?page=news&idelement=5112&lang=en&length=short&backpage=archives&critere=&countryname=Egypt&rowcur=25; "Authorities Free Christian Human Rights Activists," *Compass Direct News*, November 7, 2007, http://archive.compassdirect.org/en/display.php?page=news&idelement=5110&lang=en&length=short&backpage=archives&critere=&countryname=Egypt&rowcur=25.

24. Paul Marshall, interview with Grand Sheik of Al-Azhar, Sheik Tantawi, August 1998. See also Paul Marshall, *Egypt's Endangered Christians* (Washington: Freedom House, 1998), and *Massacre at the Millennium* (Washington: Freedom House, 2000); "Egypt: Copts Appeal Religious Identity Ruling," *Compass Direct News*, June 25, 2007, http://www.compassdirect.org/English/country/Egypt/2007/newsarticle 4921.html.

25. Jubilee Campaign USA, "Egyptian Convert to Christianity Held Captive Since November 2009," July 14, 2010. In July 2007, Ali Gomaa, the grand mufti, made a controversial statement that apostasy only merited punishment in the afterlife. He later clarified that "apostates" could be punished on earth if they were "actively engaged in the subversion of society."

26. As quoted in "Egypt—Religious Freedom Profile," Christian Solidarity Worldwide, January 9, 2009, http://dynamic.csw.org.uk/article.asp?t=report&id=118.

27. *BBC News*, http://news.bbc.co.uk/2/hi/middle_east/7888193.stm 2/26; Article 98(f) specifies penalties of up to five years in prison and a fine of up to LE 1,000.

28. Jubilee Campaign USA, "Egyptian Convert Held Captive."

29. "Egypt: Crack-Down on Converts to Christianity," *Compass Direct News*, November 14, 2003, http://archive.compassdirect.org/en/display.php?page=news&idelement=2417&lang=en&length=short&backpage=archives&critere=&countryname=Egypt&rowcur=75; "Egypt: Convert Ordered Released on Bail," *Compass Direct News*, December 15, 2003, http://archive.compassdirect.org/en/display.php?page=news&idelement=2479&lang=en&length=short&backpage=archives&critere=&countryname=Egypt&rowcur=75.

30. For background, see "Prohibited Identities"; for discriminatory laws concerning marriage, divorce, child custody, and inheritance, see Law no. 25 of 1920; Law no. 52 of 1929; Law no. 77 of 1943. Though it has not caused any hardship so far because no one has successfully converted from Islam, any convert loses his inheritance. This does not apply to converts to Islam.

31. "Egypt," in The United States Commission on International Religious Freedom, *Annual Report 2008*, 224, http://www.uscirf.gov/images/AR2008/egyptar2008_full%20color.pdf.

32. "The International Society for Human Rights nominates Coptic Priest Metaos Wahba as 'Prisoner of the Month of November 2008,'" December 13, 2008, at Voice of the Copts, http://voiceofthecopts.org/en/innocent_behind_bars/the_international_society_for_human_rights_nominates_coptic_prie.html.

33. "Egypt: Convert Locked into Mental Hospital," *Compass Direct News*, May 13, 2005, http://archive.compassdirect.org/en/display.php?page=news&idelement=3816&lang=en&length=short&backpage=archives&critere=&countryname=Egypt&rowcur=75; "Egypt: Convert Released from Mental Hospital," *Compass Direct News*, June 21, 2005, http://archive.compassdirect.org/en/display.php?page=news&idelement=3860&lang=en&length=short&backpage=archives&critere=&countryname=Egypt&rowcur=75.

34. "Egypt: Sheikh Jailed Eight Months Without Charges," *Compass Direct News*, November 23, 2005, http://archive.compassdirect.org/en/display.php?page=news&idelement=4089&lang=en&length=short&backpage=archives&critere=&countryname=Egypt&rowcur=50; "Egypt: Christian Convert from Islam Jailed," http://archive.compassdirect.org/en/display.php?page=news&idelement=4596&lang=en&length=short&backpage=archives&critere=&countryname=Egypt&rowcur=50; "Egypt: Authorities Release Jailed Christian Convert," *Compass Direct News*, May 24, 2007, http://archive.compassdirect.org/en/display.php?page=news&idelement=4883&lang=en&length=short&backpage=archives&critere=&countryname=Egypt&rowcur=50.

35. "Prohibited Identities"; "Police Detain Convert Who Wedded Christian," *Compass Direct News*, November 27, 2007, http://archive.compassdirect.org/en/display.php?page=news&idelement=5126&lang=en&length=short&backpage=archives&critere=&countryname=Egypt&rowcur=25.

36. "Egypt Copt Jailed 45 Years after Father's Conversion," *AFP*, November 22, 2007, http://afp.google.com/article/ALeqM5gWAdeTNMOeMfyPaOwrYpODjNAQJA; "Egypt: Father's Brief Conversion Traps Daughters in Islam," *Compass Direct News*, October 10, 2008, http://archive.compassdirect.org/en/display.php?page=news&idelement=5630&lang=en&length=short&backpage=archives&critere=&countryname=Egypt&rowcur=25; "Bahiya Detained," *Watani International*, http://www.arabwestreport.info/AWR/article_details.php?article_id=19984&aweek=19&ayear=2008&t=s&char=0; "Egypt: Christian in Muslim ID Case Wins Right to Appeal," *Compass Direct News*, December 2, 2008, http://archive.compassdirect.org/en/display.php?page=news&idelement=5708&lang=en&length=short&backpage=archives&critere=&countryname=Egypt&rowcur=0. HRW/EIPR reports that, as of November 2007, there were at least eighty-nine people struggling to have their religion officially recognized after their parents converted them against their will; see "Prohibited Identities."

37. "Egyptian Convert to Christianity Tortured, Raped in Egypt," Assyrian International News Agency, December 20, 2008, http://www.aina.org/news/20081219220247.htm; Voice of the Copts: "Muslim Woman Who Converted to Christianity Arrested at Cairo Airport," http://www.aina.org/news/20081216193035.htm.

38. "Egypt: Judge Tells of Desire to Kill Christian," *Compass Direct News*, January 27, 2009, http://archive.compassdirect.org/en/display.php?page=news&idelement=5778&lang=en&length=short&backpage=archives&critere=&countryname=Egypt&rowcur=0.

39. "Prohibited Identities" says, "Conversion from Islam to Christianity is fraught with legal and social risks.... As a result, the number of persons born Muslim who have converted to Christianity is hard to gauge, but at a minimum it would appear to involve a score or more persons per year, and so cumulatively be in the hundreds if not thousands." Anecdotal evidence from Egypt suggests the number may be much higher. For further background, see the 2008 annual report of the United States Commission on International Religious Freedom, http://www.uscirf.gov/images/AR2008/annual%20report%202008-entire%20document.pdf. See also "Copts Appeal Religious Identity Ruling," *Compass Direct News*, June 25, 2007.

40. *International Religious Freedom Report 2007*; "Egypt Adjourns Muslim Converts' Appeal" *AFP*, September 2, 2007, http://afp.google.com/article/ALeqM5hs761o2Rs9v4unacJxxtyduI-UDA.

41. "Egypt: Converts Win Case but May Face Discrimination," *Compass Direct News*, February 11, 2008, http://archive.compassdirect.org/en/display.php?page=news&idelement=5233&lang=en&length=short&backpage=archives&critere=&countryname=Egypt&rowcur=25.

42. "Penalize 'Re-conversion': Egyptian Fatwa Says," *Al Arabiya*, January 20, 2008, http://www.alarabiya.net/articles/2008/01/20/44471.html; "Egypt: Ex-Muslims Blocked from Declaring Conversion," *Compass Direct News*, March 26, 2008, http://archive.compassdirect.org/en/display.php?page=news&idelement=5309&lang=en&length=short&backpage=archives&critere=&countryname=Egypt&rowcur=25; "Egypt: Citizen Wins Rare Legal Victory to Revert to Christianity," *Compass Direct News*, January 8, 2009, http://archive.compassdirect.org/en/display.php?page=news&idelement=5755&lang=en&length=short&backpage=archives&critere=&countryname=Egypt&rowcur=0.

43. "Egyptian Lawyer Files Suit for Rights of Christian Converts," Assyrian International News Agency, March 16, 2009, http://www.christiantoday.com/article/egyptian.lawyer.files.suit. for.rights.of.christian.converts/22777.htm; Voice of the Copts, "The First Ever Lawsuit Filed by an Egyptian Advocacy," March 12, 2009, http://voiceofthecopts.org/en/breaking_ news/the_first_ever_lawsuit_filed_by_an_egyptian_advocacy.html. On December 20, 2008, an Alexandrian administrative court ruled that Fathi Labib Yousef, who had converted to Islam from Christianity in 1974, and in 2005 sought to revert to Christianity, could have his Christian status shown on his identity card. "Egypt: Citizen Wins Rare Legal Victory to Revert to Christianity," *Compass Direct News*.

44. "Muslim Sues for Right to Convert to Christianity," *Compass Direct News*, August 7, 2007, http://archive.compassdirect.org/en/display.php?page=news&idelement=4978&lang=en& length=short&backpage=archives&critere=&countryname=Egypt&rowcur=25; "Islamists Join Case Against Convert to Christianity," *Compass Direct News*, October 10, 2007, http:// archive.compassdirect.org/en/display.php?page=news&idelement=5069&lang=en&length =short&backpage=archives&critere=&countryname=Egypt&rowcur=25; "In Hiding, Convert Continues Fight for Rights," *Compass Direct News*, November 15, 2007, http:// archive.compassdirect.org/en/display.php?page=news&idelement=5114&lang=en&length =short&backpage=archives&critere=&countryname=Egypt&rowcur=25; "Egypt: Muslim Authorities Call for Beheading of Convert," International Society for Human Rights, August 30, 2007, http://www.ishr.org/index.php?id=697&tx_ttnews%5Btt_news%5D=762&tx_tt news%5BbackPid%5D=296&cHash=c51802de6d; Pierre Loza, "Christian Convert Says He'll Stay the Course, Despite Threats," *Daily Star*, August 9, 2007, http://www.dailystare-gypt.com/article.aspx?ArticleID=8706; "Egypt, Muslim Convert to Christianity Fears for Life," *Middle East Times*, August 14, 2007, http://www.metimes.com/print.php?Story ID=20070814-070417-8160r. Hegazy published a book of poems called *Sherine's Laugh*. In one poem, "Ashraf Pasha," he recalled the abuse he had suffered at the hands of Ashraf Ma'alouf, an SSI officer who reportedly tortured him for converting.

45. "Tempers Flare into Melee at Convert's Hearing," *Compass Direct News*, January 25, 2008, http://archive.compassdirect.org/en/display.php?page=news&idelement=5205&lang= en&length=short&backpage=archives&critere=&countryname=Egypt&rowcur=25; "Egypt: Court Rules Against Convert."

46. "Egypt: Court Rules Against Convert"; "One Egyptian Convert's Never-Ending Struggle," Crosswalk.com, September 15, 2008, http://www.crosswalk.com/news/religiontoday/ 11581771/print/; "Egypt—Religious Freedom Profile."

47. "Another Convert Tries to Change Religious Identification," *Compass Direct News*, August 7, 2008; Magdy Samaan, "Convert to Christianity Takes His Case to Court," *Daily News Egypt*, August 13, 2008, http://www.thedailynewsegypt.com/article.aspx?ArticleID=15722; *BBC News*: "Egyptian Christian's Recognition Struggle," February 13, 2009, http://news.bbc.co.uk/2/hi/ middle_east/7888193.stm; "Egypt: Judge Ejects Lawyer for Christian from Court," *Compass Direct News*, January 13, 2009, http://archive.compassdirect.org/en/display.php?page=news&i delement=5759&lang=en&length=short&backpage=archives&critere=&countryname=Egypt& rowcur=0; "Egypt: Ruling on Bid for Christian ID Expected Soon," *Compass Direct News*, February 10, 2009, http://archive.compassdirect.org/en/display.php?page=news&idelement=5804&lang =en&length=short&backpage=archives&critere=&countryname=Egypt&rowcur=0.

48. "Egypt: Islamic Lawyers Urge Death Sentence for Egyptian Convert," *Compass Direct News*, February 27, 2009, http://archive.compassdirect.org/en/display.php?page=news&ideleme nt=5826&lang=en&length=short&backpage=archives&critere=&countryname=Egypt&ro wcur=0; "Egypt: Citizen Wins Rare Legal Victory" *Compass Direct News* (n. 42 above); "Egypt May Remove Religion from ID Cards," *Al Arabiya*, March 25, 2009, http://www.alarabiya. net/articles/2009/03/25/69227.html.

49. "Egypt Church Issues First Conversion Certificate," *Compass Direct News*, April 14, 2009, http://archive.compassdirect.org/en/display.php?page=news&idelement=5879&lang=en&le ngth=short&backpage=archives&critere=&countryname=Egypt&rowcur=0; "Egypt: Convert's Religious Rights Case Threatens Islamists," *Compass Direct News*, May 12, 2009, http://

archive.compassdirect.org/en/display.php?page=news&idelement=5917&lang=en&length=short&backpage=archives&critere=&countryname=Egypt&rowcur=0.

50. "Egypt: Court Denies Right to Convert to Second Christian," *Compass Direct News*, June 16, 2009, http://archive.compassdirect.org/en/display.php?page=news&idelement=5964&lang=en&length=short&backpage=archives&critere=&countryname=Egypt&rowcur=0.

51. "Muslim Egyptian Girl Who Converted to Christianity Subjected to Acid Attack," *AINA News Service*, April 17, 2010, http://www.aina.org/news/20100416201043.htm.

52. Zyed Krichen, "Censorship and Persecution in the Name of Islam," R,Bli T No. 1072, July 13–19, 2006, excerpted by Assyrian International News Agency, January 9, 2007, http://www.aina.org/news/20070108191217.htm.

53. Warr, "The State of Freedom of Expression in Egypt"; Pakinam Amer, "Censorship of Literary Work Remains Unchallenged in Egypt," February 12, 2007, http://news.monstersandcritics.com/middleeast/features/article_1262896.php/Censorship_of_literary_work_remains_unchallenged_in_Egypt; *International Religious Freedom Report 2005*, U.S. State Department, Bureau of Democracy, Human Rights, and Labor, http://www.state.gov/g/drl/rls/irf/2005/51598.htm; Azza Khattab, "All God's Children," *Egypt Today*, September 2004, http://www.egypttoday.com/article.aspx?ArticleID=2257.

54. Zyed Krichen, "Censorship and Persecution in the Name of Islam." In April 2010, a group of lawyers mounted a *hisba* case to get *One Thousand and One Nights* banned again, to try the government officials who allowed it to be published under Article 178 of the penal code, for publishing something that "offends the public decency"; see Mohamed Abdel Salam, "Egypt Lawyers Call for 1001 Nights to Be Banned," *Bikya Masr*, April 27, 2010, http://bikyamasr.com/?p=12152; Steve Negus, "Brother of Another Color," http://www.mafhoum.com/press2/77S26.htm; "World Press Freedom Review 1998," http://www.freemedia.at/cms/ipi/freedom_detail.html?country=/KW0001/KW0004/KW0091/&year=1998; Committee to Protect Journalists (CPJ), "Ongoing Government Harassment of *Cairo Times* Magazine," June 5, 1998, http://www.ifex.org/fr/content/view/full/6418/.

55. Max Rodenbeck, "Witch Hunt in Egypt," *New York Review of Books*, November 16, 2000.

56. For these and other examples, see "Egyptian Government Censors Books and Writer—Confiscation of Dozens of Publications Reported at Cairo International Book Fair," February 7, 2001, http://canada.ifex.org/es/content/view/full/12641; http://www.thefileroom.org/documents/dyn/DisplayCase.cfm/id/1066; Egyptian Organization for Human Rights (EOHR), "Book Confiscated, EOHR Alarmed by Religious Institutions' Increasing Censorship," November 4, 2003, http://www.ifex.org/eng/content/view/full/54830/; "Behind the Ban," *Al-Ahram Weekly*, No. 767, November 2–9, 2005, http://weekly.ahram.org.eg/2005/767/cu2.htm; "Al-Azhar: The Book 'Modern Clerics and the Industry of Extremism,' Contains Blatant Insults to Islam," *Al-Sharq al-Awsat*, October 19, 2006; *Cairo*, by Ayman al-Qadi and Muhammad Khalil; Jennifer Bryson, "Freedom in Muslim Countries: An Endangered Species," *Public Discourse*, March 27, 2009, http://www.thepublicdiscourse.com/2009/03/75; "Leading Woman Novelist Condemned for 'Insulting Islam,'" *Index on Censorship*, March 2, 2007, http://www.indexonline.org/en/news/articles/2007/1/egypt-leading-woman-novelist-condemned-for-i.shtm. After some strange rulings on Islam, breast-feeding, and drinking urine by senior Al-Azhar figures, Al-Azhar Sheikh Mohamed Sayed Tantawy had to issue a statement that Al-Azhar does not review its own books; see Yasmine Saleh, "Al-Azhar Claims Not to Be in Charge of Reviewing Its Books," *Daily Star Egypt*, June 5, 2007, http://www.dailystaregypt.com/article.aspx?ArticleID=7542.

57. Human Rights Watch 1999 Report, http://www.hrw.org/worldreport99/mideast/egypt.html; Committee on Academic Freedom on the Middle East and North Africa (CAFMENA), letter of May 21, 1998, http://fp.arizona.edu/mesassoc/CAFMEN Aletters.htm.

58. Rasha Saad, "Labyrinths of the Sect," *Al-Ahram Weekly*, No. 817, October 19–25, 2006, http://weekly.ahram.org.eg/2006/817/sc1.htm; *International Religious Freedom Report 2007*.

59. "New Report Documents Arrests and Torture of Shiite Muslims in Egypt," Egyptian Initiative for Personal Rights, August 3, 2004, http://eipr.org/en/report/2004/08/01/570; *International Religious Freedom Report 2005* (n. 53 above).

60. "Mohamed Ramadan Mohamed Hussein El-Derini v. Egypt, Working Group on Arbitrary Detention," U.N. Doc. E/CN.4/2006/7/Add.1 at 25 (2005), http://www1.umn.edu/human-rts/wgad/5-2005.html; *International Religious Freedom Report 2005*; Yasmine Saleh, "Courtroom Dramas: The Lawsuits and Docks of 2007," *Daily News Egypt*, December 30, 2007, http://www.thedailynewsegypt.com/article.aspx?ArticleID=11056. In December 2007, twenty-five members of the *Al-Ahbash* group were arrested for membership in an illegal organization and contempt for religion. *Al-Ahbash* combines Sunni and Shia elements and is Sufi in outlook. In February 2008, they were released without charge. The non-Egyptian members were reportedly deported; see *International Religious Freedom Report 2008*, U.S. State Department, Bureau of Democracy, Human Rights, and Labor, http://www.state.gov/g/drl/rls/irf/2008/108481.htm. From the report: "In 2005 the Maadi misdemeanor court issued a verdict in a blasphemy case involving Ibrahim Ahmad Abu Shusha and 11 of his followers, who had been detained absent an arrest warrant since 2004. The court sentenced Abu Shusha to 3 years' imprisonment for claiming to be divine and denigrating Islam. The court sentenced the 11 other defendants . . . to 1 year of imprisonment. . . . The court also asserted that freedom of belief does not include permission to deny the principles of heavenly religions. An appeals court reaffirmed the Abu Shusha sentences in July 2005." In May 2006, two Azharites—Abdul Sabur al-Kashef and Mohammed Radwan—were tried for blaspheming Islam. Al-Kashef was sentenced to eleven years' imprisonment for claiming to have seen God and Radwan three years for denying the existence of heaven and hell. In mid-January 2007, El-Gamaleya Misdemeanor Court of Appeals reduced Kashef's sentence to 6 years and upheld 3 years for Radwan." See *International Religious Freedom Report 2008*, cited earlier in this note.

61. Cairo Institute for Human Rights Studies, *Bastion of Impunity, Mirage of Reform*.

62. Maurits S. Berger, "Apostasy and Public Policy in Contemporary Egypt: An Evaluation of Recent Cases in Egypt's Highest Courts," *Human Rights Quarterly* 25 (2003): 731; "Book Confiscated, EOHR Alarmed by Religious Institutions' Increasing Censorship."

63. "Human Rights Abuses by Armed Groups," Amnesty International, September 1, 1998, http://web.amnesty.org/library/Index/ENGMDE120221998?open&of=ENG-EGY; Azza Khattab, "All God's Children," *Egypt Today*, September 2004, http://www.egypttoday.com/article.aspx?ArticleID=2257.

64. Ghassan Abdullah, "New Secularism in the Arab World," http://www.ibn-rushd.org/forum/Secularism.htm. There is available on the Web, with no provenance, "Faraj Fodah, *The Hidden Truth*," trans. Ian Hunt of Farag Foda, *Al-hakika al-gha'iba*, Cairo, 1986.

65. See the Web site http://www.thefileroom.org/documents/dyn/DisplayCase.cfm/id/1052; Khattab, "All God's Children."

66. Abdullah, "New Secularism in the Arab World"; "Human Rights Abuses."

67. "Human Rights Abuses"; "Censorship and Persecution in the Name of Islam," Assyrian International News Agency, http://www.aina.org/news/20070108191217.htm; "El Ghazali: A Tender Heart and a Righteous Tongue," Islamonline, http://ww1.islamonline.net/arabic/in_depth/ghazaly/articles/07.shtml.

68. Ahmed Subhy Mansour, *Penalty of Apostasy: A Historical and Fundamental Study* (Cairo: Tiba, 1992; English translation, Toronto: International Publishing and Distributing, 1998), http://www.ahl-alquran.com/English/show_article.php?main_id=523.

69. "Who Is Gamal Al-Banna?" *Egypt Today*, January 2005, http://www.egypttoday.com/article.aspx?ArticleID=3349; Gamal Al-Banna, "The Islamic Renaissance Fellowship: A Position Paper," http://www.islamiccall.org/irfellowship.htm (Islamiccall.org is Al Banna's Web site); Gamal Al-Banna, "An Experiment of Islamic Renovation: The Call for Islamic Revival," http://www.islamiccall.org/Islamic_Revival.htm; "Gamal Al-Banna: A Lifetime of Islamic Call," http://weekly.ahram.org.eg/2009/941/intrvw.htm; *International Religious Freedom Report 2005*.

70. Gamal Al-Banna, "An Experiment of Islamic Renovation"; Gamal Al-Banna, "Our Faith," http://www.islamiccall.org/our_faith.htm; Yasmin Moll, "Gamal Al-Banna," *Egypt Today*, September 2004, http://www.egypttoday.com/article.aspx?ArticleID=2269.

71. Y. Yehoshua, "A Cairo Conference Calling for Reform Raises the Ire of the Egyptian Religious Establishment," October 22, 2004, http://memri.org/bin/articles.cgi?Page=archives&Area=ia&ID=IA19204); "Banna Family Illustrates Complexities of Modern Islam," http://www.utusan.com.my/utusan/content.asp?y=2004&dt=1101&pub=Utusan_Express&sec=Features&pg=fe_05.htm.

72. Yehoshua, "A Cairo Conference Calling for Reform Raises the Ire of the Egyptian Religious Establishment."

73. "Gamal El-Banna Discusses Freedom of Thought and Expression in Islam at the BA," http://www.bibalex.org/english/media/NewsDetails.aspx?NewsID=1607; Gamal Al-Banna, "Our Faith," http://www.islamiccall.org/our_faith.htm; Gamal Al-Banna, "The Islamic Renaissance Fellowship."

74. "You Ask and Gamal Al-Banna Answers about the Truth of Bahá'ís," October 25, 2006, http://translate.google.com/translate?js=y&prev=_t&hl=en&ie=UTF-8&layout=1&eotf=1&u=http%3A%2F%2Fwww.almasry-alyoum.com%2Farticle2.aspx%3FArticleID%3D34264&sl=ar&tl=en.

75. Pierre Loza, "Christian Convert Says He'll Stay the Course, Despite Threats," *Daily News Egypt*, August 9, 2007, http://www.dailystaregypt.com/article.aspx?ArticleID=8706.

76. Moll, "Gamal Al-Banna."

77. Ibid.; Daniel Williams, "Aging Egyptian Says Religion Allows Freedom of Thought and Evolution," *Washington Post Foreign Service*, March 7, 2005; Michael Slackman, "Hints of Pluralism in Egyptian Religious Debates," *New York Times*, August 31, 2009, http://www.nytimes.com/2009/08/31/world/africa/31cairo.html?_r=1.

78. See his Web site, "Nasr Hamid Abu Zayd," http://www.answers.com/topic/nasr-abu-zayd.

79. "From Confiscation to Charges of Apostasy," The Center for Human Rights Legal Aid (CHRLA), September 1996, http://www.wluml.org/node/262; "Writer Dr Nasr Hamed Abu Zeid-Branded an Apostate," IFEX, 1996, http://www.ifex.org/fr/content/view/full/77664/.

80. Mary Anne Weaver, "Revolution by Stealth," *New Yorker*, June 8, 1998, http://www.dhushara.com/book/zulu/islamp/egy.htm; El-Magd, "When the Professor Can't Teach." On May 31, 1995, two weeks before the divorce ruling described below, the Cairo University Council promoted Abu-Zayd to a full professorship.

81. Weaver, "Revolution by Stealth"; "From Confiscation to Charges of Apostasy."

82. Weaver, "Revolution by Stealth." See also Baber Johansen, "Apostasy as Objective and Depersonalised Fact: Two Recent Egyptian Court Judgments," *Social Research* 70, no. 3 (Fall 2003): 687–710.

83. Warr, "The State of Freedom of Expression in Egypt"; Nadia Abou El-Magd, "When the Professor Can't Teach."

84. Warr, "The State of Freedom of Expression in Egypt"; Mona El Tahawy, "Lives Torn Apart in Battle for the Soul of the Arab World," *The Guardian*, October 20, 1999, http://www.guardian.co.uk/international/story/0,,260766,00.html.

85. Weaver, "Revolution by Stealth"; El-Magd, "When the Professor Can't Teach."

86. "Writer Dr Nasr Hamed Abu-Zeid Branded an Apostate"; "From Confiscation to Charges of Apostasy"; "Egypt—Religious Freedom Profile."

87. CHRLA, "From Confiscation to Charges of Apostasy."

88. "Human Rights Abuses by Armed Groups"; Warr, "The State of Freedom of Expression in Egypt."

89. One of the most serious cases was brought against Abu-Zayd's mentor, Hassan Hanafi, professor of philosophy at Cairo University. See Weaver, "Revolution by Stealth."

90. Weaver, "Revolution by Stealth."

91. Amira Howeidy, "Out of Eden," *Al-Ahram Weekly*, January 1999, http://www.library.cornell.edu/colldev/mideast/ahr.htm; "Writer Dr Nasr Hamed Abu-Zeid Branded an Apostate"; Mona Eltahawy, "Meanwhile: Giving Muslims the Tools to Take on Shariah" December 14, 2006, http://www.iht.com/articles/2006/12/14/opinion/edelta.php.

92. "Nasr Hamid Abu Zayd," http://www.answers.com/topic/nasr-abu-zayd; Susan Stephan, "Intellectual Censorship in Islam: A Matter of Life and Death," http://iranscope.ghandchi.

com/Anthology/Islam/intelislam.htm; *International Religious Freedom Report 2005*; Gamal Nkrumah, "To Freely Express Themselves," *Al-Ahram Weekly*, No. 709, September 23–29, 2004, http://weekly.ahram.org.eg/2004/709/eg3.htm; El-Magd, "When the Professor Can't Teach"; Kamal Hasani, "A Great Muslim Hero: Nasr Hamed Abuzayed (1943–2010)," Hudson Institute, July 20, 2010, http://www.hudson-ny.org/1421/muslim-hero-nasr-hamed-abuzayed.

93. On other works by El-Qimni, see p. 136 of his *Thank You . . . Bin Laden!*, unpublished English translation of Arabic *Shukran . . . Bin Laden!* ed. Abdul Munim Fahmi (Cairo: Dar Misr Al Mahroosa, 2004). Thanks to Jennifer Bryson for passing on this translation. Al Qimni contributes to the Arab liberal Web site, http://www.middleeasttransparent.com/, which started by publishing a petition calling for "a treaty banning religious incitement to violence and specifically names 'Sheikhs of Death' (such as Yusuf Al-Qaradawi of Al-Jazeera television), demanding that they be tried before an international court." He also maintains a blog: http://quemny.blogspot.com/.

94. "In Search of What Went Wrong," *Middle East Times*, November 10, 2004, http://www.metimes.com/storyview.php?StoryID=20041110-085834-5258r; Abdullah, "New Secularism in the Arab World."

95. Warr, "The State of Freedom of Expression in Egypt." See also Sayyid Al-Qimni, *Thank You . . . Bin Laden!*

96. Mustafa Suleiman, "Egyptians Protest Award to Controversial Writer," *Al-Arabiya*, July 13, 2009, http://www.alarabiya.net/articles/2009/07/13/78580.html; Michael Slackman, "Hints of Pluralism in Egyptian Religious Debate"; Salam, "Egypt Lawyers Call for 1001 Nights to Be Banned"; Cairo Institute for Human Rights Studies, *Bastion of Impunity, Mirage of Reform*, 125–26.

97. Apart from additional materials cited, biographical materials are taken from "Sheikh Dr. Ahmed Subhy Mansour, Board Member: Summary of Qualifications," http://www.freemuslims.org/about/mansour.php; Ahmed Subhy Mansour, "Outline of Twenty Five Years of Persecution in Egypt," http://ahmed.g3z.com/cv/drahmedcve.htm; and interviews with Paul Marshall and Nina Shea, Washington, D.C., July 2007.

98. Mansour, "Outline of Twenty Five years of persecution in Egypt."

99. The book was originally published under the title *The Quran: Why?* using the pseudonym Abdullah Al Khalifah, but *Al Noor*, a newspaper connected to the Muslim Brotherhood, divulged the author's identity.

100. Ahmed Subhy Mansour, "Freedom of Opinion Between Islam and Muslims," http://www.ahl-alquran.com/English/show_article.php?main_id=2931. His views can be summarized in the principles of the International Quranic Center, which include, inter alia: "1. The Quran is the sole source of Islam and its laws; 2. The Quran is comprehensive, completely sufficient in itself . . .; 4. The Qurannot—the Hadith—was the Prophet Mohamed's only tradition and he was ordered to abide by it alone." The full text is found at http://www.ahl-alquran.com/English/aboutus.php. Mansour maintains a personal Web site at http://www.ahmed.g3z.com/.

101. Ahmed Subhy Mansour, "Penalty of Apostasy: A Historical and Fundamental Study," http://www.ahl-alquran.com/English/show_article.php?main_id=523.

102. Ahmed Subhy Mansour, "Culture of Slaves," http://www.hrinfo.net/en/discussion/2005/h0713.shtml; Ahmed Subhy Mansour, "Outline of Twenty Five Years of Persecution in Egypt"; Ahmed Subhy Mansour, "Penalty of Apostasy: A Historical and Fundamental Study."

103. Fahmi Howaydy, "The Campaign to Dismantle Islam," *Al-Ahram Weekly*, March 29, 2005; Ahmed Subhy Mansour, "Dismantling Fahmi Howaydy," both at http://www.ahl-alquran.com/English/show_article.php?main_id=107.

104. "Alqaeda Online Voice, Alfaluja Website, Calls for Dr. Ahmed Subhy Mansour's Assassination," International Quranic Center, October 1, 2009, http://www.ahl-alquran.com/English/show_news.php?main_id=8321.

105. Ethar Shalaby, "Admin Court to Decide on Quranist's Case on July 31," July 5, 2007, http://free-islam.com/modules.php?name=Forums&file=viewtopic&t=548; Ahmed Subhy Mansour,

"Is It a Conspiracy to Eradicate the Quranists in Egypt?" http://www.ahl-alquran.com/English/show_article.php?main_id=2308; "Arrest of Mr. Amr Tharwat by Egyptian State Security forces. Question to European Parliament by MEP Cappato [ALDE]," June 11, 2006, http://www.npwj.org/2007/06/11/arrest_mr_amr_tharwat_egyptian_state_security_forces_question_european_parliament_mep_cap; Passant Rabie, "EIPR Demands Release of Detained Quranists," July 16, 2007, http://www.dailystaregypt.com/article.aspx?ArticleID=8256; Nadine Qenawi, "Prosecutor Continues Investigation," *El Masry El Youm*, June 4, 2007, http://www.aad-online.org/en/Categories/ArabCategories/Discrimina tionagainstminorities/tabid/97/ctl/Details/mid/482/ItemID/936/Default.aspx; Salonaz Sami, "List lengthens," *Al-Ahram Weekly*, No. 851, 28 June–4 July 2007, http://weekly.ahram.org.eg/2007/851/eg8.htm; "Al-Azhar Elevates Its' Attacks," *Alshark Alawsat*, August 30, 2007, http://www.ahl-alquran.com/English/show_news.php?main_id=460; Ashraf Abdel Maksoud, "Quranists or Ignorants," July 14, 2007, http://translate.google.com/translate?js=y&prev=_t&hl=en&ie=UTF-8&layout=1&eotf=1&u=http%3A%2F%2Fwww.almesryoon.com%2FShowDetailsC.asp%3FNewID%3D35963%26Page%3D7%26Part%3D1&sl=ar&tl=en.

106. International Quranic Center, "International Quranic Center Declares Forced Disappearance Case," December 3, 2008, http://ahl-alquran.com/English/show_news.php?main_id=4216; "Reda Is Finally Released; Tells Interrogation Horrors," January 24, 2009, http://ahl-alquran.com/English/show_news.php?main_id=4740. Also, Ahmed Subhy Mansour, "Egypt Persecutes Muslim Moderates," *International Herald Tribune*, January 23, 2009, http://pewforum.org/news/display.php?NewsID=17405; Cairo Institute for Human Rights Studies, *Bastion of Impunity, Mirage of Reform* (n. 15 above), 125; Sarah Carr, "Quranist Detained at Cairo Airport Released," *Daily News Egypt*, November 29, 2009, http://www.thedailynews-egypt.com/article.aspx?ArticleID=26118.

107. See material at "Writer Haydar Haydar declared an apostate and sentenced to death by Islamists in Egypt for his book 'A Banquet for Seaweed,'" The File Room, http://www.thefileroom.org/documents/dyn/DisplayCase.cfm/id/1065; "Egyptian Government Censors Books and Writer—Confiscation of Dozens of Publications Reported at Cairo International Book Fair"; Country Reports on Human Rights Practices 2001: Egypt," U.S. State Department, Bureau of Democracy, Human Rights, and Labor, http://www.state.gov/g/drl/rls/hrrpt/2001/nea/8248.htm.

108. *International Religious Freedom Report 2006*, U.S. State Department, Bureau of Democracy, Human Rights, and Labor, http://www.state.gov/g/drl/rls/irf/2006/71420.htm.

109. Nadia Abou el Magd, "'Abuse' of Islamic Rule Lands Lawyer in Court," *The National* (UAE), October 9, 2009, http://www.thenational.ae/apps/pbcs.dll/article?AID=/20091009/FOREIGN/710089862/1135; "Egyptians protest award to controversial writer" (n. 96 above). Gobraiel did initiate a *hisba* case in 2004 to ban a film he believed had insulted Christianity, and El-Wahsh even joined his legal team. Coptic representatives have also sought to quash other purportedly offensive works. Nonetheless, such cases are relatively infrequent and unsuccessful compared to those concerning insults against Islam; Amr Hamzawy, "Between Expression and Religion," *Al-Ahram Weekly*, August 6–12, 2009, http://www.carnegieendowment.org/publications/index.cfm?fa=view&id=23508; Sayed Mahmoud, "Double Entry Ledger," *Al-Ahram Weekly*, January 1–6, 2009, http://weekly.ahram.org.eg/2009/928/cu4.htm; Peter Kenyon, "Egyptian Film Stirs Coptic Christian Controversy," *NPR*, April 2, 2009, http://www.npr.org/templates/story/story.php?storyId=102599798; Noha El-Hennawy, "Egypt: Movie Challenges Coptic Restrictions on Divorce," *L.A. Times*, "Babylon & Beyond" blog, February 10, 2009, http://latimesblogs.latimes.com/babylonbeyond/2009/02/egypt-movie-cha.html; Yasmine El-Rashidi, "Cinema Case Unresolved," *Al-Ahram Weekly*, August 12–18, 2004, http://weekly.ahram.org.eg/2004/703/eg7.htm.

110. *Le Monde*, March 8, 1989.

111. See Daniel Pipes, *The Rushdie Affair: The Novel, the Ayatollah, and the West* (New York: Birch Lane Press, 1990), 148. Shortly before his death, he sought permission from Al-Azhar to publish "Children of the Alley" and for Ahmed Kamal Abu El Magd, an Islamist thinker and

Deputy President of the National Council on Human Rights, to write the introduction; see David Hardaker, "Egypt's Nobel Winner Asks Islamists to Approve Book," *The Independent*, January 28, 2006, http://www.independent.co.uk/news/world/middle-east/egypts-nobel-winner-asks-islamists-to-approve-book-524861.html?cmp=ilc-n; Sayed El Bahrawi, "A Question of Ethics," *Al-Ahram Weekly*, No. 781, February 9–15, 2006, http://weekly.ahram.org.eg/2006/781/cu6.htm.

112. On others such as Haydar Haydar, Khalil Abdel Karim, Salah El Din Mohsen, Nawal Al-Sadawi, and Mohammed Futuh, see "Controversy Maker Passes in Silence" *Akhbar Aladab* 48 (April 21, 2002): http://www.akhbarelyom.org.eg/adab/issues/458/0103.html; Warr, "The State of Freedom of Expression in Egypt"; Susan Stephan, "Intellectual Censorship in Islam"; Max Rodenbeck, "Witch Hunt in Egypt"; Jennifer Bryson, "Freedom in Muslim Countries: An Endangered Species"; *International Religious Freedom Report 2007*; "Leading Woman Novelist Condemned for 'Insulting Islam.'" Blogger Abdel Kareem Nabil Suleiman was given a four-year sentence, "[three for] inciting hatred of Islam and one for insulting President Mubarak"; see Robert Mackey, "Egyptian Blogger Remains in Jail," Lede blog, *New York Times*, March 13, 2007, http://thelede.blogs.nytimes.com/2007/03/13/egyptian-blog-ger-remains-in-jail/?scp=1&sq=abdel%20kareem%20nabil%20suleiman&st=cse; "Egypt Court Upholds 4-year Sentence for Blogger," Reuters, December 22, 2009, http://www.reu-ters.com/article/idUSTRE5BL3KB20091222. Kareem was released on November 16, 2010. New reformers are emerging, including Nehro Tantawy and Mohamed El Badry, and, despite the repression of Shias, Ahmed Rassem El Nafees continues his work as a Shia scholar.

113. Magdi Khalil, "On the Eve of September 11, Taking a Stand Between the Advocates of Terrorism and Enlightenment," Ash-Sharq Al-Awsat, September 10, 2005, http://www.defenddemocracy.org/research_topics/research_topics_show.htm?doc_id=297544.

Chapter 5

1. Sister Naseem George and Aftab Alexander Mughal, "Pakistan—Mob Attacks on Christian Villages," Human Rights Solidarity, February 1997, http://www.hrsolidarity.net/mainfile.php/1997vo107no01/237/.

2. Stephen Gill, "Shanti Nagar, Moment to Moment on First Terror Episode Against Christians," *Pakistan Christian Post*, http://www.pakistanchristianpost.com/viewarticles.php?editor ialid=64, no date.

3. See Human Rights Commission of Pakistan, "Fact-finding Report: Filing of Blasphemy Charges Against 5 Ahmadis in Layyah District," February, 1, 2009, under "Mr. Masood Ahmed, representative of the Ahmadiyya community in Layyah," http://www.hrcp-web.org/showfact.asp?id=11.

4. *The Friday Times*, June 15–21, 2001, excerpted in National Commission for Justice and Peace, *A Report on the Religious Minorities in Pakistan* (Lahore: April 2003), 67.

5. Muhammad Ali Jinnah, "Mr. Jinnah's presidential address to the Constituent Assembly of Pakistan (Aug. 11, 1947), http://www.pakistani.org/pakistan/legislation/constituent_address_11aug1947.html. For background, see Maarten G. Barends, "Sharia in Pakistan," in *Radical Islam's Rules: The Worldwide Spread of Extreme Sharia*, ed Paul Marshall (Lanham, MD: Rowman and Littlefield, 2005), 65–85.

6. David Forte, "Apostasy and Blasphemy in Pakistan," *Connecticut Journal of International Law* 10, no. 27 (Fall 1994): 30.

7. Ibid., 32.

8. Rubya Mehdi, *The Islamization of the Law in Pakistan* (Richmond: Curzon Press, 1994).

9. Hamid Ali and Zaka Ali, eds., *The Constitution of the Islamic Republic of Pakistan, 2001*, rev. ed. (Karachi: Ideal Publishers, 2001).

10. Forte, "Apostasy and Blasphemy in Pakistan," 36.

11. Fred Halliday and Hamza Alavi, eds., *State and Ideology in the Middle East and Pakistan* (London: Macmillan, 1988).

12. John L. Esposito and John O. Voll, *Islam and Democracy* (New York: Oxford University Press, 1996).

13. D. P. Collins, "Islamization of Pakistan Law: A Historical Perspective," *Stanford Journal of International Law* 24 (1987): 511–85.

14. Section 295 Pakistan Penal Code in *Criminal major acts Edition March 2002* (Lahore: National Law Book House, 2002). See Barends, "Sharia in Pakistan," 65–85.

15. Ontario Consultants on Religious Tolerance, "Religious Intolerance in Pakistan," July 8, 2003, http://www.religioustolerance.org/rt_pakis.htm; Barends, "Sharia in Pakistan," 65–85.

16. Akbar Ahmad, "Pakistan's Blasphemy Laws: Words Fail Me," *Washington Post*, May 19, 2002, http://www.wright-house.com/religions/islam/pakistan-blasphemy-law.html. Pakistan's guarantees of freedom of religion and speech are constitutionally "subject to any reasonable restrictions imposed by law in the interest of the glory of Islam"; *International Religious Freedom Report 2007*, U.S. State Department, Bureau of Democracy, Human Rights, and Labor, http://www.state.gov/g/drl/rls/irf/2007/90233.htm.

17. Javaid Rehman, "Minority Rights and the Constitutional Dilemmas of Pakistan," in *Netherlands Quarterly of Human Rights* 19, no. 4 (2001): 417–43.

18. Pew Research Center, "Pakistani Public Opinion," August 13, 2009, http://pewglobal.org/reports/display.php?ReportID=265.

19. The Persecution.org (Persecution of the Ahmadiyya Muslim Community), "Apostasy Bill 2006 (Proposed)," http://www.thepersecution.org/50years/apostasybill.html; Qaiser Felix, "New Apostasy Bill to Impose Death on Anyone Who Leaves Islam," *AsiaNews.it*, May 9, 2007, http://www.asianews.it/index.php?l=en&art=9218; *UN Human Rights Council Universal Periodic Review: Pakistan*, submission of The Becket Fund for Religious Liberty, 14 January 2008, see n. 17, http://lib.ohchr.org/HRBodies/UPR/Documents/Session2/PK/BFRL_PAK_UPR_S2_2008_BecketFundforReligiousLiberty_uprsubmission.pdf.

20. "Religious Intolerance in Pakistan."

21. Amnesty International, "Pakistan: Insufficient Protection of Religious Minorities," May 14, 2001, http://www.amnesty.org/en/library/info/ASA33/008/2001/en; Paul Marshall, ed., *Religious Freedom in the World* (Lanham, MD: Rowman & Littlefield, 2008), 321.

22. "Religious Intolerance in Pakistan."

23. Ahmad, "Pakistan's Blasphemy Laws"; U.S. Commission on International Religious Freedom, *Annual Report 2006*, http://www.uscirf.gov/index.php?option=com_content&task=view&id=2191&Itemid=1. Anwar Keneth received a death sentence because (allegedly) "[H]e addressed a letter to a local imam and others stating that Islam was a fake religion. He also claimed in the letter to be Christ." See "Blasphemy Results in Death Sentence," *Associated Press (AP)*, July 18, 2002, http://wwrn.org/articles/11079/.

24. National Commission for Justice and Peace, *A Report on the Religious Minorities in Pakistan*.

25. "Christian Cleared of Blasphemy Charges, Fired from Job, Facing Death Threats," February 22, 2008, http://www.persecution.org/suffering/newssummpopup.php?newscode=7202&PHPSESSID=950237e02e168d2f4ba712d5984333d7; NCJP, *A Report on the Religious Minorities in Pakistan*; Marshall, *Religious Freedom in the World*, 321; Ali Waqar, "60 Accused of 'Blasphemy' in Six Months: NCJP," *The Daily Times* (Islamabad), July 31, 2005, http://www.dailytimes.com.pk/default.asp?page=story_31-7-2005_pg7_22; "More Ahmadis Killed as Government Continues to Ignore Religious Violence," Amnesty International, November 1, 2000, http://asiapacific.amnesty.org/library/Index/ENGASA330132000?open&of=ENG-PAK.

26. Ahmad, "Pakistan's Blasphemy Laws."

27. "Blasphemer Attacked in Pakistan," *BBC News*, August 7, 2009, http://news.bbc.co.uk/2/hi/south_asia/8189209.stm.

28. "Pakistani Government Drafts Bill to Revise Discriminatory Laws," All India Christian Council, July 25, 2007, http://indianchristians.in/news/content/view/137/47/; Amnesty International, "Pakistan: Insufficient Protection of Religious Minorities," May 14, 2001, http://www.amnesty.org/en/library/info/ASA33/008/2001/en.

29. "Pakistan City Tense after 'Blaspheming' Christians Shot," *BBC News*, July 20, 2010, http://www.bbc.co.uk/news/world-south-asia-10696762.

30. "Blasphemy Laws in Pakistan," CSW-US, n.d., http://www.cswusa.com/Countries/Pakistan-blasphemylaws.htm.

31. *Daily Pakistan*, January 30, 2001, excerpted in National Commission for Justice and Peace, *A Report on the Religious Minorities in Pakistan*.

32. Ron Synovitz, "After Facebook, Pakistan Shuts Down YouTube over Blasphemy," Radio Free Europe/Radio Liberty, May 20, 2010, http://www.rferl.org/content/After_Facebook_Pakistan_Shuts_Down_YouTube/2047818.html; "Pakistan to Monitor Google and Yahoo for 'Blasphemy,'" *BBC News*, June 25, 2010, http://news.bbc.co.uk/2/hi/world/south_asia/10418643.stm.

33. "Ahmadisyya Islam," http://www.globalsecurity.org/military/intro/islam-Ahmadis.htm; "Rejected Muslim Sect Keeps Faith: Ahmadis Thriving in Silver Spring Despite Disdain, Fear," *Washington Post*, August 30, 2008, http://www.washingtonpost.com/wp-dyn/content/article/2008/08/29/AR2008082902302.html.

34. Amjad Mahmood Khan, "Persecution of the Ahmadiyya Community in Pakistan: An Analysis Under International Law and International Relations," *Harvard Human Rights Journal* 16 (2003): 217–44, http://www.law.harvard.edu/students/orgs/hrj/iss16/khan.shtml#fn6.

35. "Ahmadisyya Muslim Community," http://www.alislam.org/introduction/index.html.

36. "Ahmadisyya Islam."

37. Barends, "Sharia in Pakistan."

38. USCIRF, *Annual Report 2006*.

39. Testimony of Amjad Mahmood Khan, Esq., before the Tom Lantos Human Rights Commission, House Committee on Foreign Affairs, U.S. House of Representatives, October 8, 2009.

40. Testimony of Mujeeb I. Ijaz before the Tom Lantos Human Rights Commission, House Committee on Foreign Affairs, U.S. Congress, October 8, 2009.

41. Embassy of Pakistan, "Application Form for Passport," http://www.embassyofpakistanusa.org/forms/A%20form%20fillable.pdf.

42. Marshall, *Religious Freedom in the World*, 322. Continuing reports on the persecution of Ahmadis are given at http://www.thepersecution.org/.

43. *International Religious Freedom Report 2002*, U.S. State Department, Bureau of Democracy, Human Rights, and Labor, http://www.state.gov/g/drl/rls/irf/2002/14026.htm; Khan, "Persecution of the Ahmadiyya Community in Pakistan."

44. Marshall, *Religious Freedom in the World*, 321.

45. *International Religious Freedom Report 2008*, U.S. State Department, Bureau of Democracy, Human Rights, and Labor, http://www.state.gov/g/drl/rls/irf/2008.

46. The Persecution.org, "Summary of the Cases," http://thepersecution.org/facts/summary.html. The U.S. State Department records from early 2008: "In January 2008 authorities arrested an Ahmadi in Wazirabad, Punjab, on charges of distributing Ahmadi-related pamphlets. He was granted bail in March 2008 and forced to leave the area after receiving numerous death threats. In January 2008 police charged an Ahmadiyya businessman, *Manzur Ahmed*, with destroying pages that included religious inscriptions.... On March 6, 2008, police arrested 80-year-old Ahmadi Altaf Husain in Kabeerwala for desecrating the Qur'an. According to police, a student saw Husain rip pages out of the Qur'an and throw them on the ground. Members of the Ahmadiyya community stated that Husain was reading the power meter outside his home when the student warned him that he was stepping on a page of the Qur'an.... On June 18, 2008, Mohammad Shafeeq was sentenced to death for blasphemy after he allegedly defiled the Qur'an and used derogatory language to refer to the Prophet Mohammad." See *International Religious Freedom Report 2008*; *International Herald Tribune*, June 18, 2008; "Muslim Man in Pakistan Sentenced to Death for Blasphemy," http://newshopper.sulekha.com/news/muslim-man-in-pakistan-sentenced-to-death-for-blasphemy.htm. For another case, see "Presumed Guilty Five Ahmadis Arrested in Punjab for Blasphemy," *AsiaNews.it*, February 13, 2009, http://www.asianews.it/index.php?l=en&art=14481, and Asian Human Rights Commission, "Four Children and One Man Have Been Arbitrarily Arrested and Charged," January 30, 2009, http://www.ahrchk.net/

statements/mainfile.php/2009statements/1859/. In March 2009, two Ahmadi medical doctors were brutally murdered by unknown assailants. Dr. Shiraz Ahmad Bajwa and his wife, Dr. Noreen Bajwa, pregnant with her first child, were strangled to death in their home and then hung from a fan. There has been no motive attributed to the murders apart from the couple's Ahmadi identity. See "Brutal Murder of Ahmadi Muslim Husband and Wife in Pakistan," Fox Business, March 16, 2009, http://www.reuters.com/article/pressRelease/idUS83347+16-Mar-2009+PRN20090316.

47. "Pakistan: Insufficient Protection of Religious Minorities" (n. 28 above).
48. Ibid.
49. "Pakistan: Two Persons Murdered after an Anchor Person Proposed the Widespread Lynching of Ahmadi Sect Followers," Asian Human Rights Commission, Urgent Appeals Programme, September 10, 2008, http://www.ahrchk.net/ua/mainfile.php/2008/2999/.
50. *Asian Human Rights Commission Statement*, AHRC-STM-062–2009, March 18, 2009, http://www.ahrchk.net/statements/mainfile.php/2009statements/1947/.
51. Jane Perlez and Waqar Gillani, "Sectarian Attacks Hit Two Pakistani Mosques," *New York Times*, May 28, 2010, http://www.nytimes.com/2010/05/29/world/asia/29pstan.html?ref=world; "Pakistan Mosque Attacks in Lahore Kill Scores," *BBC News*, May 28, 2010, http://news.bbc.co.uk/2/hi/south_asia/10181380.stm.
52. M Zulqernain, "Sharif Stuns Pakistan: Calls Ahmedis Brothers," *Indian Express*, June 8, 2010, http://www.indianexpress.com/news/sharif-stuns-pakistan-calls-ahmedis-brother/630800/.
53. "Pakistan: Insufficient Protection of Religious Minorities." See also Javaid Rehman, "Minority Rights and the Constitutional Dilemmas of Pakistan," in *Netherlands Quarterly of Human Rights* 19, no. 4 (2001): 417–43; "Religious Intolerance in Pakistan."
54. On some other cases, see David Pinault, "Loser's Vengeance: Muslim-Christian Relations and Pakistan's Blasphemy Law," *America* 194, no. 13 (April 10, 2006); "Sangla Hill Christian Accused of Blasphemy Released," February 22, 2006, http://www.asianews.it/index.php?art=5456&l=en; International Christian Concern (ICC), "Faces of Persecution in Pakistan," June 6, 2001, http://www.persecution.org/concern/2001/06/p3.html; *Religious Prisoners Congressional Task Force: The Islamic Republic of Pakistan*, http://www.house.gov/pitts/initiatives/humanrights/hr-rp-pak-ayubmasih.htm; Amnesty International, *Annual Report 2002*, http://www.amnesty.org; "Faces of Persecution in Pakistan (continued)," http://www.persecution.org/concern/2001/06/p4.html; "School Owner Muhammad Ibrahim Became Jealous Because the School Run by Pervez Masih Was Attracting More Pupils," Center for Legal Aid Assistance and Settlement, http://www.claas.org.uk/news_detail.aspx?ID=57; Ali Waqar, "84 Year Old Accused of Blasphemy," *The Daily Times*, May 10, 2007. See also http://www.timesonline.co.uk/tol/comment/faith/article1826359.ece.
55. For an overview of the Ayub Masih case, see "Death Sentence Confirmed for Ayub Masih," *Compass Direct News*, August 24, 2001, https://www.strategicnetwork.org/index.php?loc=kb&view=v&id=6899&fto=662&; "Last Appeal for Ayub Masih," *Compass Direct News*, September 21, 2001, http://archive.compassdirect.org/en/display.php?page=news&idelement=264&lang=en&length=short&backpage=archives&critere=&countryname=Pakistan&rowcur=125; "Eleven Christians Currently Jailed on Blasphemy Charges," *Compass Direct News*, July 18, 2002, http://archive.compassdirect.org/en/display.php?page=news&idelement=1503&lang=en&length=short&backpage=archives&critere=&countryname=Pakistan&rowcur=100; "Acquitted Christian Flees to Freedom," *Compass Direct News*, September 13, 2002, http://archive.compassdirect.org/en/display.php?page=news&idelement=1573&lang=en&length=short&backpage=archives&critere=&countryname=Pakistan&rowcur=100.
56. "Religious Intolerance in Pakistan."
57. Christian Solidarity Worldwide, *Briefing: Pakistan, Visit to Pakistan, October 25–November 2, 2004*, 5, http://dynamic.csw.org.uk/article.asp?t=report&id=12&search.
58. "Illiterate Christian Acquitted of Blasphemy," June 16, 2003, http://www.crossroad.to/News/Persecution/alert/compass.htm.

59. Christian Solidarity Worldwide, "Visit to Pakistan," 6.

60. "Illiterate Christian Acquitted of Blasphemy."

61. "Man to Die over Insult," *Daily Herald*, June 2, 2007, 2, http://richarddawkins.net/articleComments,1220,Man-to-die-over-insult,Daily-Herald,page2.

62. Qaiser Felix, "Christian Tortured and Detained on False Charges of Blasphemy," *AsiaNews.it*, July 3, 2009, http://www.asianews.it/news-en/Faisalabad,-a-Christian-tortured-and-detained-on-false-charges-of-blasphemy-15685.html; "Pakistani Christian Sentenced to Life Under Blasphemy Law," *Compass Direct News*, January 22, 2010, http://www.compass-direct.org/english/country/pakistan/14329; Fareed Khan, "Punjab: Christian Couple Touches Qur'an with Dirty Hands, Gets 25 Years in Prison," *AsiaNews.it*, March 3, 2010, http://www.compassdirect.org/english/country/pakistan/14329.

63. "Blasphemer Attacked in Pakistan"; Joshua Partlow, "They Want to Destroy Christians," *The Washington Post*, August 3, 2009, http://www.washingtonpost.com/wp-dyn/content/article/2009/08/02/AR2009080202011.html; "Pakistan Christians Burned to Death in Islamist Attacks," *Compass Direct News*, August 1, 2009, http://blog.christianitytoday.com/ctliveblog/archives/2009/08/pakistan_christ.html; "Gojra Assault Was Planned in Advance: HRCP," Dawn.com, August 7, 2009, http://www.hrcp-web.org/shownews.asp?id=33.

64. "Blasphemer Attacked in Pakistan"; Joshua Partlow, "They Want to Destroy Christians"; "Christians Flee after Muslims Destroy Village," *Union of Catholic Asian News*, July 31, 2009, http://www.ucanews.com/2009/07/31/christians-flee-after-muslims-destroy-village; Sabrina Tavernise, "Hate Engulfs Christians in Pakistan," *The New York Times*, August 3, 2009, http://www.nytimes.com/2009/08/03/world/asia/03pstan.html; Omar Waraich, "Pakistan: Who's Attacking the Christians?" *Time*, August 6, 2009, http://www.time.com/time/world/article/0,8599,1914750,00.html; Zofeen Ebrahim, "Attacks on Christians Spotlight Blasphemy Laws," Inter Press Service, August 25, 2009, http://ipsnews.net/news.asp?idnews=48206; "Reemergence of Violence Against Christians in Pakistan," Report and Analysis by NCJP, August 4, 2009.

65. Tavernise, "Hate Engulfs Christians in Pakistan." For further reports on Gojra and related incidents, see Partlow, "They Want to Destroy Christians"; "Christians Flee after Muslims Destroy Village"; Omar Waraich, "Pakistan: Who's Attacking the Christians?"; Ebrahim, "Attacks on Christians Spotlight Blasphemy Laws"; Salman Masood and Waqar Gillani, "4 Militants Held in Fatal Attack on Christians in Pakistani Town," *New York Times*, September 10, 2009; "5 More Pakistani Christians Killed," *Zenit*, September, 9, 2009, http://www.zenit.org/article-26757?l=english; Fareed Khan, "Punjab, Muslim Extremists Burn Church over Alleged Blasphemy Case," *AsiaNews.it*, September 12, 2009, http://www.asianews.it/index.php?l=en&art=16308; "LHC Grants Bail to Muslims Accused of Gojra Violence: Killers of Robert Danish Will Be Reinstated," *Pakistan Christian Post*, September 18, 2009, http://www.pakistanchristianpost.com/viewnews.php?newsid=1499; "Pakistani Christian Youth Accused of Blasphemy Killed in Sialkot Jail," *Pakistan Christian Post*, September 15, 2009, http://www.pakistanchristianpost.com/viewnews.php?newsid=1496; "Pakistani Church Burned by Muslims," *Zenit*, September, 19, 2009, http://www.zenit.org/article-26875?l=english; "Police Shoot Mourners at Funeral of Christian," *Compass Direct News*, September 17, 2009, http://www.compassdirect.org/english/country/pakistan/9439/; Fareed Khan, "Sialkot: Police Charges Crowd at Funeral for Young Man Killed in Prison for Blasphemy," *AsiaNews.it*, September 16, 2009; Brian Sharma, "Cooperation among Police, Muslim and Christian Leaders Stave Off Religious Brushfires," *Compass Direct News*/HRWF, September 9, 2009; "Archbishop Saldanha Condemns Killing and Carnage in Gojra, Calls for Closure of Christian Institutions for Three Days Mourning in Punjab," Pax Christi press release, August 3, 2009, http://storage.paxchristi.net/2009–0553-en-ap-HR.pdf; "Reemergence of Violence Against Christians in Pakistan" (n. 64 above).

66. Waqar Gillani and Sabrina Tavernise, "Pakistan Rights Groups Seek Answers on Christian's Death," *New York Times*, September 16, 2009, http://www.nytimes.com/2009/09/17/world/asia/17pstan.html. See also ANI, "Pakistan Govt Asked to Review Blasphemy Law," Pakistan News.net, September 2, 2009; "Statement on the Misuse of the Blasphemy Law and the

Security of Religious Minorities in Pakistan," World Council of Churches, September 1, 2009, http://www.oikoumene.org/gr/resources/documents/central-committee/geneva-2009/reports-and-documents/report-on-public-issues/statement-on-the-misuse-of-the-blasphemy-law-and-the-security-of-religious-minorities-in-pakistan.html; see also "Pakistani Christians 'Live in Fear,' Churches Say," Reuters, September 23, 2009.

67. "Muslim Threats to Christians Rise in Pakistan," *The Washington Times*, October 4, 2009, http://www.washingtontimes.com/news/2009/oct/04/muslim-threats-to-christians-on-rise-in-pakistan/?source=newsletter_must-read-stories-today_headlinespage=2; "Pakistan Leader, Pope Talk of Attacks on Christians," *Zenit*, October 1, 2009, http://www.zenit.org/article-27014?l=english; "Zardari Promises Pope to Overcome Discrimination Caused by Religion," *AsiaNews.it*, http://www.asianews.it/index.php?l=en&art=16475&size=A. See also "All Christian Parties Conference to End Blasphemy Law Set to Launch Movement," *Pakistan Christian Post*, October 18, 2009, http://www.pakistanchristianpost.com/headline-newsd.php?hnewsid=1460; Maria Mackay, "Pakistan's Minorities Minister Vows to End Persecution of Christians," *Christian Today*, October 11, 2009, http://www.christiantoday.com/article/pakistans.minorities.minister.vows.to.end.persecution.of.christians/24358.htm; Zeeshan Haider, "Pakistan Intends to Alter Blasphemy Law," Reuters, February 25, 2010, http://www.reuters.com/article/idUSTRE61O1M820100225. According to a Pakistani government official, possible changes included requiring an investigation and a judge's approval before a case could be registered, as well as demanding proof that defendants had intended to commit blasphemy.

68. Ishaq Tanoli, "Life Term for Blasphemy Accused," *Dawn*, February 26, 2010, http://www.dawn.com/wps/wcm/connect/dawn-content-library/dawn/the-newspaper/national/life-term-for-blasphemy-accused-620; Fareed Khan, "Punjab: Christian Couple Touches Qur'an with Dirty Hands"; "Pakistan's 'Blasphemy' Laws Claim Three More Christians," *Compass Direct News*, March 10, 2010.

69. Tanoli, "Life Term for Blasphemy Accused"; Khan, "Punjab: Christian Couple Touches Qur'an with Dirty Hands"; "Pakistan's 'Blasphemy' Laws Claim Three More Christians."

70. " 'Blasphemy Laws' Used to Jail Elderly Christian in Pakistan," *Compass Direct News*, June 29, 2010, http://www.compassdirect.org/english/country/pakistan/22092/. For other cases, see Thomas Kelly, "'Blasphemy Laws' Used to Jail Elderly Christian," *Compass Direct News*, June 26, 2010, http://www.compassdirect.org/english/country/pakistan/22092/; "Lahore: Christians Accused of Blasphemy Flee Extremists and Police," *AsiaNews.it*, July 9, 2010, http://www.asianews.it/news-en/Lahore:-Christians-accused-of-blasphemy-flee-extremists-and-police-18892.html.

71. Rob Crilly and Aoun Sahi, "Christian Woman Sentenced to Death 'for Blasphemy,'" *The Telegraph*, November 9, 2010.

72. *Daily Jang*, July 11, 2001, excerpted in National Commission for Justice and Peace, *A Report on the Religious Minorities in Pakistan*.

73. *International Religious Freedom Report 2008*.

74. Alex Alexiev, "The Taliban of Fact and Washington Fiction," *National Review Online*, May 13, 2009, http://article.nationalreview.com/?q=OGIyNWUwMGVjOWI0MmFmNDIwNTI3YzI1NmFhN2JmMDk.

75. Amnesty International, "Pakistan: Insufficient Protection of Religious Minorities."

76. The following is drawn from *Daily Dawn*, July 10, 2002, excerpted in NCJP, *A Report on the Religious Minorities in Pakistan*, (n. 4 above).

77. *Daily Dawn*, July 7, 2002, excerpted in National Commission for Justice and Peace, *A Report on the Religious Minorities in Pakistan*.

78. Donna E. Arzt, "The Treatment of Religious Dissidents Under Islamic Law," in *Religious Human Rights in Global Perspective: Religious Perspectives*, ed. John Witte, Jr. and Johan D. van der Vyver (The Hague: Martinus Nijhoff, 1996), 430.

79. "Blasphemer Attacked in Pakistan."

80. "Pakistan, Islamists Sign Deal to Enforce Sharia," ABC News, February 16, 2009, http://www.abc.net.au/news/stories/2009/02/16/2493056.htm; Zarar Khan, "Pakistan President

Agrees to Islamic Law in Swat," *AP*, April 13, 2009, http://www.alarabiya.net/articles/2009/04/14/70606.html; "Militants Bomb Ancient Shrine in Pakistan," *The Independent*, March 5, 2009, http://www.independent.co.uk/news/world/asia/militants-bomb-ancient-shrine-in-pakistan-1637955.html; Douglas Feith and Justin Polin, "Radio-Free Swat Valley," *The New York Times*, March 30, 2009, http://www.nytimes.com/2009/03/30/opinion/30feith.html; "Blasphemer Attacked in Pakistan."

81. Nahal Toosi, "Pakistanis Blame US after Shrine Attack Kills 42," *AP*, July 2, 2010, http://news.yahoo.com/s/ap/20100702/ap_on_re_as/as_pakistan; Mubashir Bukhari, "Suicide Bombers Strike Shrine in Lahore, Pakistan, Killing at Least 35," *Washington Post*, July 2, 2010, http://www.washingtonpost.com/wp-dyn/content/article/2010/07/01/AR2010070106081_pf.html.

82. For more information on Shaikh, see Celia Dugger, "Pakistani Sentenced to Death for Blasphemy," *New York Times*, August 20, 2001, http://www.nytimes.com/2001/08/20/international/asia/20DOCT.html; "Dr. Shaikh Sentenced to Death," http://www.rationalistinternational.net/Shaikh/2001.08.26.htm; Ahmad, "Pakistan's Blasphemy Laws"; "Blasphemy Doctor Faces Death," *The Guardian*, August 19, 2001, http://www.guardian.co.uk/international/story/0,3604,539348,00.html. A good overview is given in "Dr Younus Shaikh Free!" International Humanist and Ethical Union, January 23, 2004, http://www.iheu.org/node/85. Dr. Shaikh should not be confused with Younus Shaikh, who, in July, 2007, was sentenced by Karachi's Anti-Terrorism Court to life imprisonment under section 295-B for writing a book that the judge claimed had negated the punishment of *rajam* (stoning to death in the case of adultery). "Blasphemous Writer Gets Life Term," *The News International* (Karachi), July 30, 2007, http://www.thenews.com.pk/daily_detail.asp?id=65594.

83. Dugger, "Pakistani Sentenced to Death for Blasphemy"; see also "Dr. Shaikh Sentenced to Death," http://www.rationalistinternational.net/Shaikh/2001.08.26.htm.

84. Ahmad, "Pakistan's Blasphemy Laws."

85. Dugger, "Pakistani Sentenced to Death for Blasphemy."

86. Ahmad, "Pakistan's Blasphemy Laws."

87. Paul Wiseman, "Words Can Bring Death Sentence in Pakistan," *USA Today*, March 25, 2002, http://www.usatoday.com/news/world/2002/03/26/usat-blasphemy.htm.

88. See "Dr Younus Shaikh Free!"

89. *Daily Dawn*, July 8, 2002, excerpted in National Commission for Justice and Peace, *A Report on the Religious Minorities in Pakistan*.

90. Fasih Ahmed, "The War on Words," *Newsweek*, http://www.newsweek.com/id/167386/output/print; "Death Threat for Editor Najam Sethi over Islamic Cartoon," *Times Online*, July 26, 2008, http://www.timesonline.co.uk/tol/news/world/article4402382.ece.

91. Salman Masood and Carlotta Gall, "Prominent Ally of Pakistan's President Is Assassinated," *New York Times*, January 4, 2011; Zahid Hussain and Tom Wright, "Pakistan Assassin Had Revealed Plans," *Wall Street Journal*, January 5, 2011; "Pope Urges Pakistan to Repeal Blasphemy Law," *BBC*, January 10, 2011, http://www.bbc.co.uk/world-south-asia-12156825

92. Augustine Anthony, "Militants Say Killed Pakistani Minister for Blasphemy," Reuters, March 2, 2011; Nahal Toosi and Chris Brummit, "Militants Kill Sole Christian Minister in Pakistan,: *AP*, March 2, 2011; see "Blasphemer Attacked in Pakistan."

93. Ahmad, "Pakistan's Blasphemy Laws." The BBC suggests that with respect to blasphemy, "Hundreds of people have been lynched since the mid-1980s"; see "Blasphemer Attacked in Pakistan."

94. Sabrina Tavernise, "At Top University, a Fight for Pakistan's Future," *New York Times*, April 20, 2010, http://www.nytimes.com/2010/04/21/world/asia/21university.html.

95. Christian Caryl, "A Eulogy for Pakistan," *Radio Free Europe/Radio Liberty*, March 16, 2011, http://www.rferl.org/content/pakistan_bhatti_washington/2340390.html; Lela Gilbert, "Pakistan and Blasphemy: A Matter of Life and Death," *Jerusalem Post*, April 21, 2011, http://www.jpost.com/Features/InThespotlight/Article.aspx?id=217432; Embassy of the Islamic Republic of Pakistan press release, "Pakistani and US Leaders Urge Tolerance, Harmony in Minister Shahbaz Bhatti Memorial Service at the Embassy," March 10, 2011, http://www.embassyofpakistanusa.org/news474_03102011.php

Chapter 6

1. Kevin Sullivan, "A Body and Spirit Broken by the Taliban," *Washington Post*, January 5, 2002.

2. Alastair Leithead, "Anger over 'Blasphemous' Balls," *BBC News*, August 26, 2007, http://news.bbc.co.uk/2/hi/south_asia/6964564.stm.

3. *Agence France Presse (AFP)*, "Afghan Demands Apology for Football 'Insult,'" *Khaleej Times Online*, September 8, 2007, http://findarticles.com/p/articles/mi_kmafp/is_200709/ai_n19507629/.

4. Amir Shah, "Afghanistan Imposes Death Penalty for Conversion from Islam," *Associated Press (AP)*, January 8, 2001. In June 2001, this provision was amended so that foreigners caught proselytizing would be detained for three to ten days and then deported. See also Barbara G. Baker, "Taliban Refuse International Access to Jailed Christians," *Compass Direct News*, August 24, 2001, http://archive.compassdirect.org/en/display.php?page=news&idelement=563&lang=en&length=short&backpage=archives&critere=&countryname=Afghanistan&rowcur=0.

5. Kathy Gannon, "Workers in Afghanistan Fear Backlash," *AP* via *The Washington Post Online*, August 7, 2001; Amir Shah, "Afghanistan Imposes Death Penalty." *Compass Direct News* referred to the staff as SNI employees, but the *Washington Times* says it was not clear whether Shelter Germany, which directly employed them, was really, as its Web site claimed, a branch of SNI.

6. Baker, "Taliban Refuse International Access to Jailed Christians"; Pamela Constable, "We Are All Good Muslims," *Washington Post*, August 24, 2001, http://imgs.sfgate.com/cgi-bin/article.cgi?f=/c/a/2001/08/24/MN50203.DTL&hw=mohamed&sn=261&sc=036; Barbara G. Baker, "Jailed Christians Left Isolated in Afghanistan," *Compass Direct News*, September 18, 2001, http://www.hrwf.net/religiousfreedom/news/afghanistan2001.html#Kabulcourttoresumechristiantrial; Kathy Gannon, "UN Seeks Afghan Aid Workers Release," *AP* via *Washington Post Online*, August 8, 2001.

7. Barry Bearak, "Afghans Shut Offices of 2 More Christian Relief Groups," *New York Times*, September 1, 2001, http://query.nytimes.com/gst/fullpage.html?res=9D06EED61030F932A3575AC0A9679C8B63; Kathy Gannon, "Expelled Aid Workers Leave Beleaguered Capital," *AP*, September 1, 2001; Roger Boyes and Zahid Hussain, "Aid Groups Ousted in Purge of Christians," *The Times* (London), September 7, 2001; Kathy Gannon, "Afghan Aid Workers of Banned Christian Group Arrested," *AP*, September 9, 2001.

8. Amir Zia, "Foreign Aid Workers' Trial to Reopen Saturday in Kabul," *AP*, September 27, 2001, http://www.boston.com/news/daily/27/aid_worker.htm; Molly Moore, "From Agony to Anxiety, Then Freedom," *Washington Post*, November 16, 2001, http://www.papillonsart-palace.com/from.htm; Christopher Torchia, "Eight Foreign Aid Workers Held in Afghanistan Airlifted to Freedom by U.S. Special Forces Helicopters," *AP*, November 15, 2001.

9. "Five Afghan Christians Martyred," *Compass Direct News*, September 9, 2004, http://archive.compassdirect.org/en/display.php?page=news&idelement=208&lang=en&length=short&backpage=archives&critere=&countryname=Afghanistan&rowcur=0.

10. N. C. Aizenman, "Prominent Afghan Clerics Targeted by Taliban, Authorities Say," *Washington Post*, August 3, 2005, http://www.washingtonpost.com/wp-dyn/content/article/2005/08/02/AR2005080201737_pf.html; "Afghanistan," *Country Reports on Human Rights Practices 2007*, U.S. State Department, Bureau of Democracy, Human Rights, and Labor, March 11, 2008, http://www.state.gov/g/drl/rls/hrrpt/2007/100611.htm.

11. Choe Sang-Hun, "Deal Is Set to Free Korean Hostages," *International Herald Tribune*, August 29, 2007; Fisnik Abrashi, "Taliban Threaten to Kill 18 Abducted South Korean Christians in Afghanistan," *AP*, July 21, 2007, http://www.independent.co.uk/news/world/asia/taliban-threaten-to-kill-18-abducted-isouth-korean-christians-in-afghanistan-458079.html; Lee Jong-Heon, "Analysis: Seoul Striving to Free Hostages," *UPI*, July 23, 2007.

12. "Afghanistan: Constitution Threatens to Institutionalize 'Taliban-lite,'" U.S. Commission on International Religious Freedom press release, November 4, 2003, http://www.uscirf.gov/

index.php?option=com_content&task=view&id=1473. The commission was referring to a draft of the constitution, but the relevant articles remained in the final version. See also Paul Marshall, "Taliban Lite," *National Review Online*, November 7, 2003. Article 2 says: "Followers of other religions are free to exercise their faith and perform their religious rites within the limits of the provisions of the law." However, this protects only "rites," not rights, and almost no religion requires only the practice of rites. Also, the provision "within the limits of the provisions of the law" allows restrictions on even this limited guarantee.

13. Patrick Goodenough, "Trial of Afghan Convert Emphasizes Need for Judicial Reform," Cybercast News Service, March 22, 2006, http://www.studentnewsdaily.com/daily-news-article/trial_of_afghan_convert_emphasizes_need_for_judicial_reform/.

14. Alex Spillius, "Afghans to Carry on Stoning Criminals," *Telegraph* (U.K.), January 24, 2002, http://www.telegraph.co.uk/news/worldnews/asia/afghanistan/1382687/Afghans-to-carry-on-stoning-criminals.html; J. Alexander Their, "The Crescent and the Gavel," *New York Times*, March 26, 2006, http://www.nytimes.com/2006/03/26/opinion/26thier.html.

15. Nina Shea, "Sharia in Kabul?" *National Review*, October 28, 2002, http://www.hudson.org/index.cfm?fuseaction=publication_details&id=4607.

16. Kim Barker, "At the Supreme Court, an Unlikely New Hero," *Chicago Tribune*, January 21, 2007, http://www.chicagotribune.com/news/opinion/chi-0701210351jan21,0,7944559.story.

17. "Afghanistan," *Country Reports on Human Rights Practices 2007*.

18. "Afghanistan Seizes Illegal Images of Prophet," Reuters, March 11, 2003; "Supreme Court Bans Sale of Religious Posters," Radio Free Europe/Radio Liberty via *IPR Strategic Business Information Database*, March 18, 2003.

19. "Afghanistan Seizes Illegal Images of Prophet."

20. Paul Wiseman, "Pop Culture Views with Conservatism in Afghanistan," *USA Today*, June 6, 2008, http://www.usatoday.com/news/world/2008-06-05-afghanmedia_N.htm; "TOLO TV, a Station Fighting Ignorance," Reporters Without Borders, December 7, 2005, http://tolo.tv/index.php?option=com_content&task=view&id=117&Itemid=42; "Afghanistan Pulls Cable Channels," BBC, November 11, 2004, http://news.bbc.co.uk/2/hi/entertainment/4003139.stm; Saad Mohseni, "Pressing for Freedom," *Wall Street Journal*, March 8, 2007; "Afghan Defiance over Indian Soaps," *BBC*, April 15, 2008, http://news.bbc.co.uk/2/hi/south_asia/7348389.stm.

21. "Afghan Preacher Accuses Authorities of Ignoring 'Blasphemous' Iranian Books," Tolo TV via BBC Monitoring International Reports, May 18, 2008.

22. "Afghanistan," *Country Reports on Human Rights Practices 2007*.

23. Ibid. See also USCIRF Annual Report, May 2008, http://www.uscirf.gov/images/AR2008/annual%20report%202008-entire%20document.pdf.

24. Daniel Cooney, "Afghan Christian Could Get Death Sentence," *AP* via *Boston.com*, March 19, 2006, http://www.boston.com/news/world/asia/articles/2006/03/19/afghan_man_prosecuted_for_converting/; Barbara G. Baker, "More Christians Arrested in Wake of Afghan 'Apostasy' Case," *Compass Direct News*, March 22, 2006, http://www.crosswalk.com/1385441/; Maria Sanminiatelli, "Afghan Christian Given Asylum in Italy," *AP*, March 28, 2006.

25. Lloyd de Vries, "Afghan Christian Could Get Death Sentence," *AP* via *CBS News*, March 19, 2006, http://www.cbsnews.com/stories/2006/03/22/world/main1428951.shtml; Kim Barker, "Afghan man faces death for abandoning Islam," *Chicago Tribune*, March 21, 2006.

26. Barker, "Afghan Man Faces Death for Abandoning Islam"; Daniel Cooney, "Afghan Court Drops Christian Convert Case," *AP*, March 26, 2006, http://proteinwisdom.com/?p=6192.

27. Abdul Waheed Wafa, "Preachers in Kabul Urge Execution of Convert to Christianity," *New York Times*, March 25, 2006, http://www.nytimes.com/2006/03/25/international/asia/25convert.html; Pamela Constable, "For Afghans, Allies, a Clash of Values," *Washington Post*, March 23, 2006, http://www.washingtonpost.com/wp-dyn/content/article/2006/03/22/AR2006032201113.html.

28. Sultan M. Munadi, and Christine Hauser, "Afghan Convert to Christianity Is Released, Officials Say," *New York Times*, March 28, 2006, http://www.nytimes.com/2006/03/28/international/asia/28afghan.html.

29. Cooney, "Afghan Court Drops Christian Convert Case"; "Hundreds Protest Report Afghan Convert to Be Freed," *CNN*, March 27, 2006; Amir Shah, "Afghan Convert Released from Prison," *Washington Post*, March 28, 2006; Daniel Williams, "Afghan Convert Arrives in Italy as Protests Mount in Homeland," *Washington Post*, March 30, 2006; "Editorial: Taliban, Pakistan and Modernity," *Daily Times*, March 29, 2006, http://www.dailytimes.com.pk/default.asp?page=2006%5C03%5C29%5Cstory_29-3-2006_pg3_1.

30. Barbara G. Baker, "Whose Law in Afghanistan?" *Christianity Today*, April 6, 2006, http://www.christianitytoday.com/ct/2006/may/5.22.html; Williams, "Afghan Convert Arrives in Italy"; "Afghan Clerics Threaten Trouble over Convert," Reuters, April 2, 2006, http://www.democraticunderground.com/discuss/duboard.php?az=view_all&address=102x2202973.

31. Pamela Constable, "Afghans' Uneasy Peace with Democracy; In Discord over Convert's Trial, Muslims Say They Identify with Islamic Law First," *Washington Post*, April 22, 2006; "Afghan Kidnappers 'Want Convert,'" *BBC News*, October 18, 2006, http://news.bbc.co.uk/2/hi/south_asia/6061236.stm; "Italian's Kidnappers Set Terms for Release: Website," *AFP*, October 17, 2006; "Italian Photographer Freed in Afghanistan after Three Weeks 'in Dark,'" *AFP*, November 3, 2006.

32. Baker, "Whose Law in Afghanistan?"; Baker, "More Christians Arrested in wake of Afghan 'Apostasy' Case."

33. "Christian South Koreans to Be Deported," *Washington Times*, August 4, 2006, http://www.washingtontimes.com/news/2006/aug/03/20060803-095437-1360r/.

34. Matthias Gebauer, "A Community of Faith and Fear," *Spiegel Online*, March 30, 2006, http://www.spiegel.de/international/0,1518,408781,00.html. On other converts, see Mark Morris, "Christian Afghan Fears for Life If Deported," *St. Louis Post-Dispatch*, February 26, 2005; Santosh Digal, "Appeal for Afghan Christians, Sentenced to Death for Their Faith," *AsiaNews.it*, June 15, 2010, http://www.asianews.it/news-en/Appeal-for-Afghan-Christians,-sentenced-to-death-for-their-faith-18680.html#; Mindy Belz, "Kill the Christians: Lawmakers and Protesters in Afghanistan Are Calling for Just That," *World*, June 18, 2010, http://www.worldmag.com/webextra/16862.

35. "Students Protest Against Desecration of Holy Quran," South Asian News Agency, March 4, 2009, http://www.sananews.com.pk/english/2009/03/04/students-protest-against-desecration-of-holy-quran/.

36. Laura King, "Afghans Protest Rumored Desecration of Koran by US Troops," *LATimes.com*, October 26, 2009, http://articles.latimes.com/2009/oct/26/world/fg-afghanistan-koran26; Ben Farmer, "Afghan Police Open Fire after Protesters Burn Effigy of Barack Obama," *Daily Telegraph*, October 25, 2009, http://www.telegraph.co.uk/news/worldnews/asia/afghanistan/6433054/Afghan-police-open-fire-after-protesters-burn-effigy-of-Barack-Obama.html.

37. "Afghan Anger over 'Koran Burning' in Kandahar," *BBC*, January 13, 2010, http://news.bbc.co.uk/2/hi/south_asia/8455788.stm.

38. "Probe Call in Afghan 'Convert' Row," *Aljazeera.net*, May 4, 2009, http://english.aljazeera.net/news/asia/2009/05/20095485025169646.html; "Military Burns Unsolicited Bibles Sent to Afghanistan," *CNN*, May 20, 2009, http://edition.cnn.com/2009/WORLD/asiapcf/05/20/us.military.bibles.burned/index.html?eref=edition.

39. Danna Harman, "Despite Opposition, Afghan Christians Worship in Secret," *The Christian Science Monitor*, February 27, 2009, http://www.csmonitor.com/2009/0227/p04s03-wosc.html.

40. Amir Shah and Heidi Vogt, "Afghan Gov't Destroys Books It Says Insult Sunnis," *AP*, May 27, 2009, http://abcnews.go.com/International/wireStory?id=7689287.

41. Jonathan Steele, "Female Minister 'Is Afghan Rushdie,'" *The Guardian*, June 18, 2002, http://www.guardian.co.uk/world/2002/jun/18/afghanistan.jonathansteele; Kathy Gannon, "Female Afghan Official Fears Threats," *AP*, June 23, 2002.

42. "Afghan Woman Minister Hits Back," *BBC News*, June 18, 2002, http://news.bbc.co.uk/2/hi/south_asia/2051612.stm.

43. Gannon, "Female Afghan Official Fears Threats" (n. 41 above).

44. "Afghan Judiciary Denies Depriving Former Woman Minister from Post," Voice of the Islamic Republic of Iran, Mashhad, translated and supplied by BBC Monitoring, June 24, 2002; "Third Woman in Afghan Government," *BBC News*, June 27, 2002, http://news.bbc. co.uk/2/hi/south_asia/2069560.stm.

45. "Afghanistan: Karzai Fails on Press Freedom," Human Rights Watch news release, June 24, 2003. Mahdavi has started his own blog (http://mhmahdavi.blogspot.com/), where "Holy Fascism" may be read, although the English translation is poor.

46. *Afghanistan—2004 Annual Report*, Reporters Without Borders, http://www.rsf.org/article. php3?id_article=10144.

47. Mir Hussain Mahdavi, "Editor Flees Certain Death in Afghanistan," *The Hamilton Spectator*, May 5, 2007; "Afghan Supreme Court Denies Handing Down Death Sentence in Blasphemy Case," Voice of the Islamic Republic of Iran, Mashhad, via BBC Monitoring International Reports, August 8, 2003; "Jailed Afghan Editor-in-Chief Defends Right to Express Ideas," *Arman-e Melli* via BBC Monitoring, June 20, 2003.

48. "President Karzai Orders Release of Two Journalists," Reporters Without Borders, June 25, 2003, http://www.rsf.org/article.php3?id_article=7288; Amir Shah, "Protestors in Afghan Capital Call for Authorities to Try Journalist Accused of Blasphemy," *AP*, July 3, 2003; *2003 World Press Freedom Review—Afghanistan*, International Press Institute, http://www .freemedia.at/cms/ipi/freedom_detail.html?country=/KW0001/KW0005/KW0109 /&year=2003; Jake Rupert, for CanWest News Service, "Afghan Editor Forced to Flee to Canada," *National Post* (Canada), October 27, 2003. The 2004 State Department religious freedom report says the charges were not dropped; the State Department human rights report says they were; the *National Post* article, written after his arrival in Canada, says Mahdavi was acquitted of insulting Islam under Afghanistan's old press law, but Shinwari was pressing to have him and Sistany tried and convicted under sharia. *Aftab* had its power cut in April 2003, by order of Agriculture Minister Sayeed Hossein Anwari, after it published articles critical of *mujahideen* leaders and Islamist political parties, as well as the article "Secularism as a Third Approach." When approached by the paper's editor for an explanation, Anwari said he could not tolerate "talk against Islam." Mahdavi also faced death threats over articles criticizing Abdul Rabb al-Rasul Sayyaf, leader of the *Ittihad-e-Islami* party and a close Shinwari ally; see "Killing You Is a Very Easy Thing for Us: Human Rights Abuses in Southeast Afghanistan," Human Rights Watch, July 2003, http://www.hrw.org/ reports/2003/afghanistan0703/10.htm#_Toc46287030.

49. Kim Barker, "Editor's Jailing Tests Afghan Democracy," *Chicago Tribune*, November 26, 2005; Wahidullah Amani, "Writer Could Face Death Sentence," Institute for War & Peace Reporting, November 29, 2005, http://www.theasiamediaforum.org/node/380.

50. Amani, "Writer Could Face Death Sentence."

51. Griff Witte, "Post-Taliban Free Speech Blocked by Courts, Clerics," *Washington Post*, December 11, 2005, http://www.washingtonpost.com/wp-dyn/content/article/2005/12/ 10/AR2005121001138.html.

52. Ibid.; Barker, "Editor's Jailing Tests Afghan Democracy"; Daniel Cooney, "U.N. Criticizes Afghan Editor's Jailing," *AP*, October 24, 2005.

53. Witte, "Post-Taliban Free Speech Blocked."

54. "High Court Allows Release of Journalist Ali Mohaqiq Nasab," Reporters Without Borders, December 21, 2005, http://www.rsf.org/article.php3?id_article=16006.

55. Golnaz Esfandiari, "Afghanistan: Imprisoned Journalist Says Freedom of Expression Under Attack," Radio Free Europe/Radio Liberty, December 29, 2005.

56. Khaled Hosseini, "Journalism Is Not a Capital Crime," *Wall Street Journal*, February 1, 2008, http://online.wsj.com/article/SB120182626320733755.html; "Afghanistan: Journalist on Death Row Gives First Interview," Radio Free Europe/Radio Liberty, February 26, 2008; Nora Boustany, "Afghan Reporter's Death Sentence Draws Wide Condemnation," *Washington Post*, January 25, 2008, http://www.washingtonpost.com/wp-dyn/content/article/2008/ 01/24/AR2008012402995.html.

57. "Journalists Under Attack in the North," Institute for War & Peace Reporting, December 11, 2007, http://www.iwpr.net/?p=arr&s=f&o=341348&apc_state=henh; "Afghan journalists seek release of colleague," Reuters, January 12, 2008, http://uk.reuters.com/article/idUKSP33543520080112.

58. Amir Shah, "Afghan Journalist Sentenced to Death for Distributing Paper 'Against Islam,'" *AP*, January 22, 2008, http://www.signonsandiego.com/news/world/20080122-1125-af-ghan-journalist-deathpenalty.html.

59. "Afghan 'Blasphemy' Death Sentence," *BBC News*, January 23, 2008, http://news.bbc.co.uk/2/hi/south_asia/7204341.stm.

60. Kim Sengupta, "Lifeline for Pervez: Afghan Senate Withdraws Demand for Death Sentence," *Independent* (U.K.), February 2, 2008, http://www.independent.co.uk/news/world/asia/lifeline-for-pervez-afghan-senate-withdraws-demand-for-death-sentence-777188.html; Jerome Starkey, "Afghan Government Official Says That Student Will Not Be Executed," *Independent* (U.K.), February 6, 2008, http://www.independent.co.uk/news/world/asia/afghan-government-official-says-that-student-will-not-be-executed-778686.html.

61. "Afghan Journalist Charged with Insulting Islam Appeals Death Sentence," *Fox News*, May 18, 2008, http://www.canadafreepress.com/index.php/site/article/afghan-journalist-charged-with-insulting-islam-appeals-death-sentence/; Jean MacKenzie, "Saving Parwez Kambakhsh," Institute for War & Peace Reporting, June 16, 2008, http://www.iwpr.net/index.php?apc_state=hen&s=o&o=p=arr&s=f&o=345224.

62. "Kambakhsh to Fight On," Institute for War & Peace Reporting, October 23, 2008, http://www.iwpr.net/?p=arr&s=f&o=347301&apc_state=henparr.

63. Kim Sengupta. "Clerics and Hardliners Vent Their Fury at Pervez Release," *The Independent*, September 8, 2009, http://www.independent.co.uk/news/world/asia/clerics-and-hardlin-ers-vent-their-fury-at-pervez-release-1783406.html; "'Blasphemy' Journalist Released from Jail," *The Herald Sun*, September 8, 2009, http://www.heraldsun.com.au/news/break-ing-news/blasphemy-journalist-released-from-jail/story-e6frf7k6-1225770420956.

64. Hafizullah Gardesh, "Koran Translation Provokes Controversy," Institute for War & Peace Reporting, December 6, 2007, http://www.iwpr.net/?p=arr&s=f&o=341229&apc_state=heniarr2007; "Koran translation angers Afghans, publisher arrested," Reuters, November 5, 2007, http://www.reuters.com/article/worldNews/idUSISL15790820071105.

65. Hafizullah Gardesh, "Koran Translation Provokes Controversy," Institute for War & Peace Reporting, December 6, 2007, http://www.iwpr.net/?p=arr&s=f&o=341229&apc_state=heniarr2007.

66. "20 Years' Jail for Errors in Koran Translation," *AFP*, September 13, 2008, http://www.afghanistannewscenter.com/news/2008/september/sep132008.html#14.

67. "Student's Long Blasphemy Term Upheld in Afghanistan," *International Herald Tribune*, March 12, 2009, http://article.wn.com/view/2009/03/12/Students_long_blasphemy_erm_upheld_in_Afghanistan/.

68. "Afghan Editor Arrested for Alleged Blasphemy," *AFP*, January 14, 2009, http://www.google.com/hostednews/afp/article/ALeqM5gzM1w-_aLYhmM2GTgfuG7P8QCB5Q; "Why the Payman Daily Was Closed?" *Kabul Press*, February 7, 2009, http://www.kabulpress.org/my/spip.php?article2964.

69. "*Payman Daily* Staff Arrest by Attorney General's Office," *Media Watch Report*, January 2009, http://www.nai.org.af/IMG/pdf/Media_watch_News_Letter_44_English_Version.pdf.

70. In other incidents, at a *loya jirga*, Abdul Nasim criticized interpretations of Islamic rules that suggested that women are weak-minded and was warned, "you're against *sharia*, you're like Salman Rushdie," and government officials said they could not protect him; see Elizabeth Rubin, "Kabul Dispatch," *The New Republic Online*, July 8, 2002, http://www.afghanistan-newscenter.com/news/2001/november/nov22f2001.html. On the 2004 case of Abdul Latif Pedram, condemned by Shinwari for defending equal rights for women, see "Afghan Supreme Court Calls for Disqualification of Presidential Candidate over Alleged Blasphemy," Radio Free Europe/Radio Liberty, September 2, 2004; Amy Waldman, "Poetic Justice for an Afghan

Gadfly: He's on the Ballot," *New York Times*, October 2, 2004, http://www.nytimes.com/2004/10/02/international/asia/02fprofile.html?fta=y.

Chapter 7

1. "Journalists Escape Prison over Jokes," *New York Times*, January 16, 2007, http://query.nytimes.com/gst/fullpage.html?res=9805EED81030F935A25752C0A9619C8B63; "Editor and Reporter Receive Three-year Suspended Sentences; Newspaper Ordered Closed for Two Months," Reporters Without Borders, January 16, 2007, http://www.rsf.org/Three-year-suspended-sentences-for.html.

2. Barbara G. Baker, "Young Muslims in Turkey Murder Three Christians," *Christianity Today*, April 20, 2007, http://www.christianitytoday.com/ct/2007/aprilweb-only/116-52.0.html, and "Slain Evangelists Were Tortured, Say Doctor," *Hürriyet*, April 21, 2007, http://arama.hurriyet.com.tr/arsivnews.aspx?id=-604288; "Turks in Christian Murder Trial," *BBC News*, November 23, 2007, http://news.bbc.co.uk/2/hi/europe/7108607.stm.

3. "Turkish Court Seeks to Link Murder of Christians to Plan to Destabilize Government," *Compass Direct News*, December 29, 2009, http://www.compassdirect.org/english/country/turkey/13084/.

4. Carolyn Wendell, *The Right to Offend, Shock or Disturb: A Guide to Evolution of Insult Laws in 2007 and 2008* (World Press Freedom Committee, 2009), 127. http://www.ifex.org/international/2009/09/09/insult_laws/.

5. *Official Journal of the Algerian Republic* 12 (March 1, 2006). See analysis by the *Grouping in Defense of Believers of a Faith Other Than Islam in Algeria*, April 20, 2006, http://collectifalgerie.free.fr/english/Comment_gb.htm.

6. "Algeria: Why Authorities Have Begun Clamping Down on Christians," *Compass Direct News*, May 27, 2008, http://archive.compassdirect.org/en/display.php?page=news&idelement=5391&lang=en&length=short&backpage=archives&critere=&countryname=Algeria&rowcur=0.

7. Ibid.

8. "Accuser in Blasphemy Case Linked to Islamists," *Compass Direct News*, July 18, 2008, http://archive.compassdirect.org/en/display.php?page=news&idelement=5477&lang=en&length=short&backpage=archives&critere=&countryname=Algeria&rowcur=0.

9. "Religious Rights Abuses Criticized at UN," *Compass Direct News*, April 16, 2008, http://archive.compassdirect.org/en/display.php?page=news&idelement=5334&lang=en&length=short&backpage=archives&critere=&countryname=Algeria&rowcur=0.

10. "Official Orders Closure of 19 Protestant Congregations," *Compass Direct News*, March 28, 2008, http://archive.compassdirect.org/en/display.php?page=news&idelement=5311&lang=en&length=short&backpage=archives&critere=&countryname=Algeria&rowcur=0.

11. "Algeria: Crackdown on Churches," *Compass Direct News*, March 18, 2008, http://archive.compassdirect.org/en/display.php?page=news&idelement=5290&lang=en&length=short&backpage=archives&critere=&countryname=Algeria&rowcur=0.

12. "Algerian Court Pressures Woman to Renounce Christ," *Compass Direct News*, May 23, 2008, http://www.onenewsnow.com/Persecution/Default.aspx?id=123352.

13. Ibid.; "Une offensive antichrétienne en algérie," *Le Figaro International*, June 27, 2008, http://www.lefigaro.fr/international/2008/05/21/01003-20080521ARTFIG00017-une-offensive-antichretienneen-algerie.php.

14. "L'affaire Habiba Kouider fait polémique," *Radio France Internationale*, May 28, 2008; see also "Algeria," *International Religious Freedom Report 2009*, U.S. State Department, Bureau of Democracy, Human Rights, and Labor, http://www.state.gov/g/drl/rls/irf/2009/127344.htm.

15. "Accuser in Blasphemy Case Linked to Islamists."

16. "Prayer Request: Update on Algerian Christians Attend Appeal Hearing," *Middle East Concern*, November 6, 2008, http://www.givengain.com/cgi-bin/giga.cgi?cmd=cause_dir_news_item&cause_id=1489&news_id=55505&cat_id=434.

17. "Algerian Muslims Block Christmas Service," *Compass Direct News*, December 31, 2009, http://www.compassdirect.org/english/country/13314/13393/.

18. On conversion to Shiism, see Israel Elad-Altman, "The Sunni-Shia Conversion Controversy," in *Current Trends in Islamist Ideology* 5 (2007): 1–10, especially 2–3.

19. "Anouar Ben Malek Stirs Controversy with 'Oh Maria.'" *The Algeria Channel*, September 23, 2006, http://www.algeria.com/forums/literature-film-litt-rature-cin-ma/16835-anouar-ben-malek-stirs-controversy-oh-maria.html.

20. Barry Rubin, "Islamists Are Playing for All of the Marbles," *The Hudson Institute*, February 6, 2009, http://www.hudsonny.org/2009/02/islamists-are-playing-for-all-of-the-marbles.php.

21. "Update on Zena, Iraqi Believer in Jordan," *Middle East Concern*, April 12, 2005.

22. "Jordan," *International Religious Freedom Report 2007*, U.S. State Department, Bureau of Democracy, Human Rights, and Labor, http://www.state.gov/g/drl/rls/irf/2007/90213.htm.

23. "Court Annuls Christian Convert's Marriage," *Compass Direct News*, June 9, 2008, http://archive.compassdirect.org/en/display.php?page=news&idelement=5420&lang=en&length=short&backpage=archives&critere=&countryname=Jordan&rowcur=0. The State Department report mentions other cases but notes that they cannot be verified; see "Jordan," *International Religious Freedom Report 2007*.

24. Wendell, *The Right to Offend, Shock or Disturb*, 137.

25. "Jordan," *International Religious Freedom Report 2007*.

26. "Jordanian Newspaper Editor Slams AFP over Handling of Muhammad Cartoons Story," *Press Gazette*, June 2, 2008, http://www.pressgazette.co.uk/story.asp?storyCode=41294&sectioncode=1.

27. Shafika Mattar, "Jordan Arrests Poet Accused of Insulting Islam," *Associated Press* (henceforth *AP*), October 21, 2009, http://www.theinsider.com/news/1279278_Jordan_arrests_poet_accused_of_insulting_Islam.

28. Suha Malkawi, "Poet Accused of Being Enemy of Islam," *The National*, October 6, 2008, http://www.thenational.ae/apps/pbcs.dll/article?AID=/20081006/FOREIGN/619470860&SearchID=73383472238547; "Jordan Court Decides to Jail Poet for Slandering Islam," *Deutsche Presse-Agentur*, June 22, 2009, http://www.monstersandcritics.com/news/middleeast/news/article_1485020.php/Jordan_court_decides_to_jail_poet_for_slandering_Islam.

29. "Jordan Court to Rule on Cartoon Case," *The National*, May 30, 2008, http://www.thenational.ae/article/20080529/FOREIGN/715595686/1011/SPORT&Profile=1011; "Jordan Charges Dutch Politician with Blasphemy," Reuters, June 1, 2008, http://www.reuters.com/article/worldNews/idUSL015190420080701.

30. "Danish Editors Face Trial in Jordan," *The Copenhagen Post*, June 3, 2008; "Netherlands Concerned on Jordan Arrest Warrant for Wilders," *Europe News*, June 20, 2008, http://www.nisnews.nl/public/210608_3.htm; "Jordan Court Wants Wilders Arrested," *Dutch News*, June 20, 2008, http://www.dutchnews.nl/news/archives/2008/06/wilders_fears_arrest_after_jor.php.

31. Wendell, *The Right to Offend, Shock or Disturb*, 143.

32. Hassan Alaoui, "Morocco Bans French Magazine for Insulting Islam," *AP*, November 2, 2008, http://www.foxnews.com/wires/2008Nov02/0,4670,AFMoroccoIslamMedia,00.html.

33. "Moroccan Christian Serving 15 Years for faith," International Christian Concern, June 17, 2010, http://www.persecution.org/suffering/ICCnews/newsdetail.php?newscode=12565&title=moroccan-christian-serving-15-years-for-faith.

34. "Morocco," *International Religious Freedom Report 2005*, U.S. State Department, Bureau of Democracy, Human Rights, and Labor, http://www.state.gov/g/drl/rls/irf/2005/51606.htm.

35. "Morocco," *International Religious Freedom Report 2005*.

36. "Morocco," *Country Reports on Human Rights Practices 2005*, U.S. State Department, Bureau of Democracy, Human Rights, and Labor, Sec. 2.c., http://www.state.gov/g/drl/rls/hrrpt/2005/.

37. "Moroccan Islamists Use Facebook to Target Christians," *Compass Direct News*, June 17, 2010, http://www.compassdirect.org/english/country/morocco/21797/.

38. Paul Marshall, *Their Blood Cries Out* (Dallas: Word Publishing, 1997), 48.

39. "Morocco Jails German for Trying to Convert Muslims," Reuters, November 29, 2006, http://www.reuters.com/article/idUSL2924248320061129.

40. "Morocco Expels Five Missionaries," *BBC News*, March 30, 2009, http://news.bbc.co.uk/go/pr/fr/-/2/hi/africa/7971491.stm.

41. "Moroccan Officials Raid Bible Study, Arrest Christians," *Compass Direct News*, February 9, 2010, http://www.compassdirect.org/english/country/morocco/15087/.

42. Private reports from Morocco. See also April 27, 2010, letter from Samuel L. Kaplan, the U.S. Ambassador to Morocco, to Leonard Leo, Chair of the U.S. Commission on International Religious Freedom.

43. "Morocco Cuts off Diplomatic Relations with Iran, Accuses It of Spreading Shi'ism in the Country," MEMRI, March 24, 2009, http://www.memri.org/bin/articles.cgi?Page=archives&Area=sd&ID=SP229409.

44. "Morocco," *International Religious Freedom Report 2005*.

45. "Threats for Breaking Morocco Fast," *BBC News*, September, 18, 2009, http://news.bbc.co.uk/2/hi/8262787.stm; Alexandra Sandels, "Morocco: Ramadan 'Protest Picnickers' Face Prosecution," *Los Angeles Times*, September 21, 2009, http://latimesblogs.latimes.com/babylonbeyond/2009/09/morocco-ramadan-protestpicnickers-face-prosecution.html?utm_source=feedburner&utm_medium=feed&utm_campaign=Feed%3A+BabylonBeyond+(Babylon+%26+Beyond+Blog).

46. Paul Marshall, ed., *Religious Freedom in the World* (Lanham, MD: Rowman & Littlefield, 2008), 400–402. For an overview of religious freedom in Turkey, see Otmar Oehring, "Turkey: Religious Freedom Survey, November 2009," *Forum 18 News*, November 27, 2009, http://www.forum18.org/Archive.php?article_id=1379.

47. David Cronin, "Turkey to Be Pushed to Speed Up Reforms," Inter Press Service, September 18, 2008, http://ipsnews.net/news.asp?idnews=43914; Laura Fulton, "A Muted Controversy: Freedom of Speech in Turkey," *Harvard International Review* 30, no. 1 (Spring 2008): http://hir.harvard.edu/index.php?page=article&id=1739&p=2.

48. Güzide Ceyhan, "Turkey: What Causes Intolerance and Violence?" *Forum 18 News*, November 29, 2007, http://www.forum18.org/Archive.php?article_id=1053.

49. Otmar Oehring, "Turkish Nationalism, Ergenekon, and Denial of Religious Freedom," *Forum 18 News*, October 21, 2008, http://www.forum18.org/Archive.php?article_id=1206.

50. Elif Shafak, "The Murder of Hrant Dink," *Wall Street Journal*, January 22, 2007, http://www.pen.org/viewmedia.php/prmMID/1141.

51. Amberin Zaman, "Turkish Journalist Who Spoke Up for Amenians Is Shot Dead in the Street," *The Telegraph*, January 20, 2007, http://www.telegraph.co.uk/news/worldnews/1540051/Turkish-journalist-who-spoke-up-for-Armenians-is-shot-dead-in-the-street.html; Reuters, "High-profile Editor Shot Dead on Istanbul Street," *Gulf Times*, January 20, 2007, http://www.gulf-times.com/site/topics/article.asp?cu_no=2&item_no=128449&version=1&template_id=39&parent_id=21.

52. Susanne Fowler and Sebnem Arsu, "Armenian Editor's Death Leads to Conciliation," *The New York Times*, January 23, 2007, http://www.nytimes.com/2007/01/23/world/europe/23turkey.html?_r=1&scp=1&sq=armenian%20editor%27s%20death%20leads%20to%20conciliation&st=cse; "Teenager 'Confesses to Killing Journalist,'" *Irish Examiner.com*, January 21, 2007, http://www.irishexaminer.com/breakingnews/ireland/cwsneymhsncw/.

53. Christopher Orlet, "Turkish Blood," *American Spectator*, January 22, 2007, http://spectator.org/archives/2007/01/22/turkish-blood.

54. Fowler and Arsu, "Armenian Editor's Death Leads to Conciliation"; "Teenager 'Confesses to Killing Journalist'"; "Key Suspect Followed Till Moment of Dink's Death," *Hurriyet DailyNews.com*, January 23, 2007, http://www.hurriyet.com.tr/english/domestic/10869673.asp?scr=1.

55. Fethiye Çetin and Deniz Tuna, "Two Years On: Lawyers Summarise Dink Trial," *Bianet News*, January 19, 2009, http://www.bianet.org/english/minorities/112015-two-years-on-lawyers-summarise-dink-trial; "Ergenekon Suspect to Give Testimony in Malatya Murder Case," *Today's Zaman*, January 17, 2009, http://www.todayszaman.com/tz-web/detaylar.do?load=detay&link=164331.

56. Ibrahim Usta, "Turkish Author on Trial for Insulting Islam," *Huffington Post*, May 26, 2009, http://www.huffingtonpost.com/2009/05/26/nedim-gursel-turkish-auth_n_207546.html; "Turkish Author Acquitted of Insulting Islam—TV," Reuters, June 25, 2009, http://in.reuters.com/article/worldNews/idINIndia-40605120090625.

57. "Turkey: Converts Charged Under Speech Law," *Compass Direct News*, October 31, 2006, http://archive.compassdirect.org/en/display.php?page=news&idelement=4602&lang=en&length=short&backpage=archives&critere=&countryname=Turkey&rowcur=50; "Turkey: Converts' Trial Shows Tensions Before Pope's Visit," *Compass Direct News*, November 27, 2006, http://archive.compassdirect.org/en/display.php?page=news&idelement=4652&lang=en&length=short&backpage=archives&critere=&countryname=&rowcur=700.

58. Ziya Meral, *No Place to Call Home: Experiences of Apostates from Islam, Failures of the International Community* (Christian Solidarity Worldwide: Surrey, U.K., 2008), 57; "Turkey: Christians' Trial for 'Insulting Turkishness' Stalls Again," *Compass Direct News*, November 12, 2008, http://archive.compassdirect.org/en/display.php?page=news&idelement=5684&lang=en&length=short&backpage=archives&critere=&countryname=Turkey&rowcur=0; "Converts Subjected to Official Harassment," *Compass Direct News*, July 3, 2007, http://archive.compassdirect.org/en/display.php?page=news&idelement=4927&lang=en&length=short&backpage=archives&critere=&countryname=Turkey&rowcur=50; "Turkey: 'Insulting Turkishness' Case Proceeds Under Revised Law," *Compass Direct News*, March 20, 2009, http://archive.compassdirect.org/en/display.php?page=news&idelement=5854&lang=en&length=short&backpage=archives&critere=&countryname=Turkey&rowcur=0.

59. See "Baseless Case Against Turkish Christians Further Prolonged," *Compass Direct News*, February 15, 2010, http://www.compassdirect.org/english/country/turkey/15188/.

60. Güzide Ceyhan, "What Causes Intolerance and Violence?"; Otmar Oehring, "Turkey: Religious Freedom Survey, November 2009"; "Update #7 on Trial of Murderers of Christians in Turkey," *Middle East Concern*, September 16, 2008, http://www.givengain.com/cgi-bin/giga.cgi?cmd=cause_dir_news_item&cause_id=1489&news_id=52735&cat_id=434.

61. Meral, *No Place to Call Home* (n. 58 above), 54.

62. "Turkey's Protestant Churches Complain They Are Being Targeted," *Today's Zaman*, January 19, 2008, http://www.todayszaman.com/tz-web/detaylar.do?load=detay&link=132018. See also "Four Street Evangelists Jailed," *Compass Direct News*, April 27, 2007, http://archive.compassdirect.org/en/display.php?page=news&idelement=4850&lang=en&length=short&backpage=archives&critere=&countryname=Turkey&rowcur=50; "Attackers Firebomb Protestant Church," *Compass Direct News*, November 9, 2006, http://archive.compassdirect.org/en/display.php?page=news&idelement=4620&lang=en&length=short&backpage=archives&critere=&countryname=Turkey&rowcur=50.

63. Oehring, "Turkey: Religious Freedom Survey, November 2009."

64. Marshall, *Religious Freedom in the World*, 402.

65. Ibid.; "Turkey," *International Religious Freedom Report 2008*, U.S. State Department, Bureau of Democracy, Human Rights, and Labor, http://2001-2009.state.gov/g/drl/rls/irf/2008/108476.htm.

66. Benjamin Harvey, "Alevis Push for Tolerance," *AP*, January 10, 2007, http://www.washingtontimes.com/news/2007/jan/09/20070109-111943-2773r/.

67. Marshall, *Religious Freedom in the World*, 402; Martin Van Bruinessen, "Kurds, Turks and the Alevi Revival in Turkey," http://www.uga.edu/islam/alevivanb.html.

68. "European Court Rules on Faith, Names on Turkish ID," *Today's Zaman*, February 2, 2010, http://www.todayszaman.com/tz-web/news-200374-100-european-court-rules-on-faith-names-on-turkish-id.html.

69. *Constitution of the Republic of Yemen, 1994*, Al-Bab, http://www.al-bab.com/yemen/gov/con94.htmFebruary 2, 2010; Marshall, *Religious Freedom in the World*, 432–33.

70. "Yemen: Freedom of Expression in Peril" (London: Article 19 [Global Campaign for Freedom of Expression], 2008), 8, http://www.article19.org/pdfs/publications/yemen-foe-report.pdf.

71. Human Rights Without Frontiers 2008 Yemen report, "Bahai's Imprisoned in Yemen May Face Deportation to Iran," http://www.hrwf.net/index.php?option=com_content&

view=article&id=105:news-2008-catalogued-by-country&catid=38:freedom-of-religion-and-belief&Itemid=90; "Yemen," *International Religious Freedom Report 2008*; "250 Baha'is in Danger," Tagamu News, September 15, 2008, http://www.bahairights.org/2008/09/15/250-bahais-in-danger/.

72. "Official: Yemen Detains 9 People for Converting to Christianity," *AP*, August 19, 2008, http://freecopts.net/english/index.php?option=com_content&task=view&id=948&Itemid=2; "Yemen Court Sentences Somali Convert to Death," *Christianity Today*, July 7, 2000, http://www.christianitytoday.com/ct/2000/julyweb-only/55.0.html; "Freed Somali Christian Arrives in New Zealand," *Christianity Today*, September 1, 2000, http://www.christianitytoday.com/ct/2000/septemberweb-only/36.0.html; "Christians Are Arrested in Yemen for Handing out Bibles," *Christian Telegraph*, July 4, 2008, http://www.christiantele-graph.com/issue2434.html.

73. "Yemeni Novelist under Fire," *Yemen Times*, May 13, 2002, http://www.yementimes.com/02/iss20/front.htm.

74. "Al-Rai Al-Aam Editor Receives Jail Time for Republishing Prophet Mohammed Cartoons," *Yemen Times*, November 26, 2006; "Yemen Editor 'Faces Death Calls,'" *BBC News*, March 8, 2006; "PM Orders Reopening of Three Newspapers Closed for Reprinting Mohammed Cartoons," Reporters Without Borders, May 4, 2006.

75. "Yemen: Ban on Child Brides Is Imperiled," *AP*, March 22, 2010, http://www.nytimes.com/2010/03/23/world/middleeast/23briefs-Yemenbf.html; Ahmad Al-Haj, "Yemen Cleric: Fight Draft Law Banning Child Brides," *AP*, April 27, 2010, http://www.google.com/hosted-news/ap/article/ALeqM5g_F18e6XXJTq8PTcZPXX7joaJ6NgD9F9FUM00.

76. Iraq has gone through many transitions in the last seven years, but, apart from other violence, Al-Qaeda in Iraq (AQI) and its allies have targeted other Muslims with differing views as apostates, including those who participate in elections, since AQI regards democracy itself as apostate. Religious minorities—Christians, by far the largest non-Muslim minority, Mandeans (followers of John the Baptist), Yezidis (an ancient angel-centered religion), Baha'is, and Jews—are also being repeatedly attacked. While only 3 or 4 percent of Iraq's pre-2003 population, they account for 40 percent of its refugees; see Nina Shea, "Obliterating' Iraq's Christians," *Washington Post Online*, May 14, 2010, http://www.hudson.org/index.cfm?fuseaction=publication_details&id=6999.

On threats against Azerbaijan reformist Muslim scholar Nariman Gasimoglu and journalists Samir Huseinov and Rafiq Tagi, see Altay Goyushov, "Islamic Revival in Azerbaijan," *Current Trends in Islamist Ideology* 7 (November 11, 2008): http://www.currenttrends.org/research/detail/islamic-revival-in-azerbaijan. On Gasimoglu, see Felix Corley, "Azerbaijan: Will the State Protect Muslim Scholar from Muslim Death Threats?" *Forum 18 News*, March 30, 2005, http://www.forum18.org/Archive.php?article_id=534. The relevant article by Gasimoglu is "Religious Freedom, the Best Counter to Religious Extremism," *Forum 18 News*, June 10, 2004, http://www.forum18.org/Archive.php?article_id=338. See also "2 Journalists Go on Trial in Azerbaijan for Article Critical of Islam," *AP*, March 20, 2007; "Azerbaijani Journalists Convicted of Inciting Hatred with Article Seen as Criticizing Islam," *AP*, May 4, 2007; Aida Sultanova, "Azerbaijan Prosecutors Investigate Newspaper That Published Criticism of Prophet Muhammad," *AP*, November 14, 2006; "Azerbaijan's President Declares Amnesty Including Some Journalists," *AP*, December 28, 2007.

On Syrian writer, Nabil Fayadh, threatened by Al-Qaeda for a book he had written, see "Death Threats, Al-Qaeda Fatwas Against Syrian Writer," *The Middle East Media Research Institute*, January 18, 2009, http://www.memri.org/bin/latestnews.cgi?ID=Announcement5908. Also, in October 2008, twelve Syrians were convicted of "fomenting sectarian strife" and sentenced to two and a half years in prison after they participated in pro-democracy initiatives.

In Libya, though there is no law forbidding apostasy, the police have harassed, detained, and tortured converts, including some overseas. See "African Christian Imprisoned in Libya," *Middle East Concern*, May 3, 2007; "Ghanaians Demand Justice," *Ghana Today*, February 8, 2008, http://www.ghanatoday.com/index.php?option=news&task=viewarticle&sid=23147;

"Ghana Christian Leaves Libya Jail," *BBC News*, May 1, 2009, http://news.bbc.co.uk/go/pr/fr/-/2/hi/africa/8028980.stm; "Libya Tortures Four Christian Converts from Islam," Assyrian International News Agency via International Christian Concern, March 9, 2009, http://www.persecution.org/suffering/ICCnews/newsdetail.php?newscode=9683&title =libya-tortures-four-christian-converts-from-islam.

Israel has also penalized insults to Islam and Muslims. In 1998, Tatiana Soskin was sentenced to two years in prison after putting up a poster that pictured the Prophet Muhammad as a pig. See "Pig Poster Artist Sentenced to Two Years," *The Washington Post*, January 9, 1998.

77. Saban Kardas, "Religious Freedom Still Tenuous in Turkey," *Eurasia Daily Monitor* 6, no. 38 (February 26, 2009): http://www.jamestown.org/single/?no_cache=1&tx_ttnews%5Btt_news%5D=34559.

Chapter 8

1. "Nigeria: Teacher Accused of Blasphemy Disappears," *Compass Direct News*, March 28, 2006, http://archive.compassdirect.org/en/display.php?page=news&lang=en&length=long&idelement=4277&backpage=archives&critere=&countryname=Nigeria&rowcur=25; "Nigerian Teacher Dies 'over Koran,'" *BBC News*, March 21, 2007, http://news.bbc.co.uk/2/hi/africa/6477177.stm; U. S. State Department, "Nigeria," *International Religious Freedom Report 2008*, http://2001-2009.state.gov/g/drl/rls/irf/2008/108385.htm.

2. "Islamists in Somalia Behead Two Sons of Christian Leader," *Compass Direct News*, July 1, 2009, http://archive.compassdirect.org/en/display.php?page=news&idelement=5986&lang=en&length=short&backpage=archives&critere=&countryname=Somalia&rowcur=0.

3. Alex De Waal, "Averting Genocide in the Nuba Mountains, Sudan," Social Science Research Council, December 22, 2006, http://howgenocidesend.ssrc.org/de_Waal2/. See also Edgar O'Ballance, *Sudan, Civil War and Terrorism: 1956–99* (New York: St. Martin's Press, 2000).

4. On Islam and Christianity in Sub-Saharan Africa, see the Pew Forum's survey, "Tolerance and Tension: Islam and Christianity in Sub-Saharan Africa," April 15, 2010, http://pewforum.org/docs/?DocID=515.

5. These upheavals are usually described as political and/or ethnic, rather than religious, but they often have religious dimensions. As the Roman Catholic archbishop of the Jos Archdiocese asked, "Why were churches and clergy attacked and killed? Why were politicians and political party offices not attacked, if it was a political conflict?" Also, "Nigeria: Six Pastors Killed, Forty Churches Razed in Jos," *Compass Direct News*, December 11, 2008, http://archive.compassdirect.org/en/display.php?page=news&idelement=5725&lang=en&length=short&backpage=archives&critere=&countryname=Nigeria&rowcur=0.

6. See Paul Marshall, *The Talibanization of Nigeria: Sharia Law and Religious Freedom* (Washington: Freedom House, 2002), and "Nigeria: Shari'a in a Fragmented Country," in *Radical Islam's Rules: The Worldwide Spread of Extreme Shari'a Law*, ed. Paul Marshall (Lanham, MD: Rowman and Littlefield, 2005), 113–34.

7. "Nigeria," *International Religious Freedom Report 2008*.

8. Interview with Paul Marshall, May 2001. See also Marshall, *The Talibanization of Nigeria*, and "Nigeria: Shari'a in a Fragmented Country."

9. "Catholic Priest, Member of Parliament Killed in Nigeria," *Newsroom*, May 30, 2000; "Sharia Is Superior to Nigerian Constitution-Sani," an interview with Abdulhaji Ahmed Sani, Governor of Zamfara, with Omolade Adunbi, Abdul Oroh, and Feyi Koya-Adewole, *Church and Society*, January to March 2000. See also Marshall, *The Talibanization of Nigeria*, and "Nigeria: Shari'a in a Fragmented Country."

10. "Nigeria: Two Converts to Christianity Face Death," *Compass Direct News*, May 13, 2002, http://archive.compassdirect.org/en/display.php?page=news&idelement=1243&lang=en&length=short&backpage=archives&critere=&countryname=Nigeria&rowcur=150.

11. "Nigeria: A Teenager Counts the Cost of Embracing Christ," *Compass Direct News*, December 9, 2005, http://archive.compassdirect.org/en/display.php?page=news&lang=en&length=long&idelement=4103&backpage=archives&critere=&countryname=Nigeria&rowcur=50.

12. "Nigeria: Cattleman Severely Tortured for Receiving Christ," *Compass Direct News*, October 31, 2005, http://archive.compassdirect.org/en/display.php?page=news&lang=en&length=long&idelement=4048&backpage=archives&critere=&countryname=Nigeria&rowcur=50.

13. "Nigeria: Teacher Accused of Blasphemy Disappears."

14. "Nigeria: Offhand Comments Spark Latest 'Blasphemy' Rampage," *Compass Direct News*, October 2, 2006, http://archive.compassdirect.org/en/display.php?page=news&lang=en&length=long&idelement=4556&backpage=archives&critere=&countryname=Nigeria&rowcur=25.

15. "Nigeria: Teacher on Trial after Punishing Muslim Student," *Compass Direct News*, October 16, 2006, http://archive.compassdirect.org/en/display.php?page=news&lang=en&length=long&idelement=4594&backpage=archives&critere=&countryname=Nigeria&rowcur=25.

16. "Nigerian Teacher Dies 'Over Koran'"; "Nigeria," *International Religious Freedom Report 2008*.

17. "Nigeria Christian Killed over Blasphemy; Dozens Injured," *BosNewsLife*, February 13, 2008, http://www.bosnewslife.com/3435-3435-nigeria-christians-killed-in-riot-over-blasph; "Nigeria," *International Religious Freedom Report 2008*; "Nigeria: Muslim Rioters Attack Christian in Kano," *Compass Direct News*, April 23, 2008, http://archive.compassdirect.org/en/display.php?page=news&lang=en&length=long&idelement=5344&backpage=archives&critere=&countryname=Nigeria&rowcur=0; "Nigeria: Mob Kills 50-year-old Man for 'Blasphemy,'" *Daily Trust News*, http://allafrica.com/stories/200808110940.html. Ademola Bello, born a Muslim, was once attacked by militants who held a gun to his head and accused him of abandoning Islam because his play *Bondage* criticized sharia; see Ademola Bello, "Al-Qaeda in Nigeria: Grazing in the Sahara," *RealClearWorld*, January 25, 2010, http://www.realclearworld.com/articles/2010/01/25/al_qaeda_in_nigeria_grazing_in_the_sahara_97501.html.

18. "Nigeria's Journalist on the Run," *BBC News*, November 27, 2002, http://news.bbc.co.uk/2/hi/africa/2518977.stm.

19. "Nigerian Government Rejects Fatwa," *BBC News*, November 26, 2002, http://news.bbc.co.uk/2/hi/africa/2514821.stm. There was also widespread violence following the Danish cartoons, which is covered in chapter 10.

20. "Nigerian 'Trained in Afghanistan,'" *BBC News*, September 2, 2009, http://news.bbc.co.uk/2/hi/8233980.stm.

21. "Nigeria: Death Toll Climbs in Attack by Islamic Sect," *Compass Direct News*, August 7, 2009, http://archive.compassdirect.org/en/display.php?page=news&idelement=6056&lang=en&length=short&backpage=archives&critere=&countryname=Nigeria&rowcur=0; Nick Tattersall, "Nigerians Count Cost after Uprising by Islamic Sect," *News Daily*, August 3, 2009, http://www.newsdaily.com/stories/tre5721x5-us-nigeria-sect-scene; "Nigeria's Boko Haram Chief 'Killed,'" *News Africa*, July 31, 2009, http://english.aljazeera.net/news/africa/2009/07/2009730174233896352.html; Senan Murray and Adam Nossiter, "In Nigeria, an Insurgency Leaves a Heavy Toll," *The New York Times*, August 3, 2009, http://www.nytimes.com/2009/08/04/world/africa/04nigeria.html; "Boko Haram Resurrects, Declares Total Jihad," *Vanguard*, August 14, 2009, http://www.vanguardngr.com/2009/08/14/boko-haram-ressurects-declares-total-jihad.

22. Aminu Abubakar, "Nigerian Islamist Sect Threaten to Widen Attacks," *Agence France Presse (AFP)*, March 29, 2010, http://www.google.com/hostednews/afp/article/ALeqM5j1FA1NJrS-ES89YWeX4f--kcQGmA. See also Jon Gambrell, "Internet Video: Muslims Must Rise up in Nigeria," *Associated Press (AP)*, March 16, 2010, http://www.breitbart.com/article.php?id=D9EFSPT80&show_article=1.

23. We have not covered de facto self-governing Somaliland in the north, but there is government-sponsored Islamist religious repression there also. See "Converts from Islam Jailed, Pursued in Somalia's Breakaway Region," *Compass Direct News*, September 16, 2009, http://www.compassdirect.org/english/country/somalia/9383/; "Imprisoned Christian in Somaliland on Hunger Strike," *Compass Direct News*, October 16, 2009, http://www.compassdirect.org/english/country/somalia/10593/.

24. Mohamed Mohamed, "Somali Rage at Grave Desecration," *BBC News*, June 8, 2009, http://news.bbc.co.uk/2/hi/africa/8077725.stm.

25. "Somalia," *International Religious Freedom Report 2008*, U.S. State Department, Bureau of Democracy, Human Rights, and Labor, http://2001-2009.state.gov/g/drl/rls/irf/2008/108391.htm.

26. Sudarsan Raghavan, "In Somalia's War, a New Challenger Is Pushing Back Radical al-Shabab Militia," *Washington Post*, May 28, 2010, http://www.washingtonpost.com/wp-dyn/content/article/2010/05/26/AR2010052605279.html; Jeffrey Gettleman, "For Somalia, Chaos Breeds Religious War," *New York Times*, May 23, 2010, http://www.nytimes.com/2009/05/24/world/africa/24somalia.html?pagewanted=1&_r=1.

27. "Somalia," *International Religious Freedom Report 2008*; "Somalia," *International Religious Freedom Report 2007*, http://www.state.gov/g/drl/rls/irf/2007/90120.htm; "Almost Expunged," *The Economist*, October 22, 2009, http://www.economist.com/world/middlee-ast-africa/displaystory.cfm?story_id=14707279. There are also attacks on Christians in the breakaway region of Somaliland.

28. "Somali Islamists Declare: 'We Will Slaughter Christians'—'Somalis Are 100% Muslim and Will Always Remain So,'" *Militant Islam Monitor*, October 17, 2006, http://www.militan-tislammonitor.org/article/id/2474.

29. "From African Bush to Scotland Yard—the Murder Trail That Led to al-Qaida," *The Guardian*, November 15, 2005, http://www.guardian.co.uk/world/2005/nov/15/rosie-cowan.mainsection.

30. "Italian Nun Killed in Somalia; Islamic Forces Suspected," *Catholic World News*, September 18, 2006, http://www.catholicculture.org/news/features/index.cfm?recnum=46538.

31. "Christian Aid Worker in Somalia Beheaded for Converting from Islam," *Compass Direct News*, October 27, 2008, http://archive.compassdirect.org/en/display.php?page=news&idelement=5661&lang=en&length=short&backpage=archives&critere=&countryname=Somalia&rowcur=0.

32. "Somali Christian Shot and Killed," Voice of the Martyrs Canada, August 6, 2008, http://www.persecution.net/so-2008-08-06.htm.

33. "Somali Christian Shot at Muslim Wedding," *Mission Network News*, October 23, 2008, http://www.mnnonline.org/article/11809.

34. "Somalia: Christian in Kenya Refugee Camp Attacked, Shot," *Compass Direct News*, December 10, 2008, http://archive.compassdirect.org/en/display.php?page=news&lang=en&length=long&idelement=5724&backpage=archives&critere=&countryname=Somalia&rowcur=0.

35. Ibid.

36. Assyrian International News Agency, "Muslims Behead Four Christian Orphanage Workers in Somalia," August 11, 2009, http://www.aina.org/news/20090811144715.htm; "Somali Islamist Hardliners Behead 7 'Spies,'" Reuters, July 10, 2009, http://af.reuters.com/articlePrint?articleId=AFJOE5690BW20090710; "Convert from Islam Shot Dead," *Compass Direct News*, July 20, 2009, http://www.compassdirect.org/english/country/somalia/4496/.

37. "Muslim Militants Slay Long-Time Christian in Somalia," *Compass Direct News*, September 18, 2009, http://www.compassdirect.org/english/country/somalia/9494/.

38. "Islamic Extremists Kill Another Church Leader," *Compass Direct News*, October 1, 2009, http://www.compassdirect.org/english/country/somalia/10010/.

39. "Christian in Somalia Who Refused to Wear Veil Is Killed," *Compass Direct News*, October 27, 2009, http://www.compassdirect.org/english/country/somalia/11061/. For other incidents, see "Convert from Islam Shot Dead"; "Somali Christian Shot Dead Near Kenya Border," *Compass Direct News*, August 22, 2009, http://www.compassdirect.org/english/country/somalia/4893/; "Somali Christian Flees Refugee Camp Under Death Threat," *Compass Direct News*, December 9, 2009, http://www.compassdirect.org/english/country/somalia/12417/.

40. "Islamic Extremists Execute Young Convert," *Compass Direct News*, November 23, 2009, http://www.compassdirect.org/english/country/somalia/11836/.

41. "Islamic Militants Murder Christian Leader," *Compass Direct News*, January 26, 2010, http://www.compassdirect.org/english/country/somalia/14479/.

42. "Al Shabaab Militants Execute Christian Leader," *Compass Direct News*, May 5, 2010, http://www.compassdirect.org/english/country/somalia/18721/.

43. "Islamic Extremists in Somalia Kill Church Leader, Torch Home," *Compass Direct News*, March 24, 2010, http://www.compassdirect.org/english/country/somalia/16692/.

44. For background, see Hamouda Fathelrahman Bello, "Shari'a in Sudan," in Marshall, *Radical Islam's Rules*, 87–112.

45. Bello, "Shari'a in Sudan."

46. Hayder Ibrahim Ali, *The Crisis of Political Islam: The Example of the National Islamic Front in the Sudan* (Cairo: The Centre of Sudanese Studies, 1991); John O. Voll, *Sudan: State and Society in Crisis* (Bloomington: Indiana University Press, 1991), http://books.google.com/books?hl=en &lr=&id=r4ar4LLzIr0C&oi=fnd&pg=PA1&dq=John+O.+Voll+Sudan:+State+and+Society+in +Crisis,+(Bloomington:+Indiana+University+Press,+1991),+Available+at:&ots=RlC7TUCV D0&sig=T1lo3Dpb0vlFFkjac1sZXFVCris#PPA4,M1. On the politics of this period, see J. Millard Burr and Robert O. Collins, *Revolutionary Sudan: Hasan al-Turabi and the Islamist State, 1989–2000* (Leiden: Brill, 2003); Mansour Khalid, *War and Peace in Sudan: A Tale of Two Countries* (London: Kegan Paul International, 2003); Peter Woodward, *Sudan after Nimeiri* (London: Routledge, 1991); "Religion and Human Rights: The Case of Sudan," Proceedings of Conference Convened by the Sudan Human Rights Organization, May 30, 1992.

47. Section 126 of the Sudan penal code of 1992 expressly imposes the death penalty for apostasy, but the death penalty had been used earlier, even when the penal code did not expressly provide for it. See Abdullahi Ahmed An-Na'im, "The Islamic Law of Apostasy and Its Modern Applicability: A Case from the Sudan," *Religion* 16 (1986): 197–223.

48. Gisle Tangenes, "The Islamic Gandhi," *Bit of News*, September 11, 2006, http://www.bits ofnews.com/content/view/3856/42. There is a Web site devoted to Taha's ideas: www .alfikra.org.

49. Mahmoud Mohamed Taha, *The Second Message of Islam* (Syracuse, NY: Syracuse University Press, 1987), 137. For an elaboration of his approach in constitutional, human rights and international law terms, see Abdullahi Ahmed An-Na'im, *Toward an Islamic Reformation: Civil Liberties, Human Rights and International Law* (Syracuse, NY: Syracuse University Press, 1990).

50. George Packer, "The Moderate Martyr," *The New Yorker*, September 11, 2006, http://www .newyorker.com/archive/2006/09/11/060911fa_fact1.

51. USCIRF 2009 Annual Report, 99, http://www.uscirf.gov/images/AR2009/final%20ar 2009%20with%20cover.pdf.

52. "Sudan: Sudanese Convert to Christianity Forced into Hiding," *Compass Direct News*, February 7, 2002, http://archive.compassdirect.org/en/display.php?page=news&idelemen t=1136&lang=en&length=short&backpage=archives&critere=&countryname=Sudan&ro wcur=0; Barbara G. Baker, "Police Launch Manhunt to Find Christian," *Compass Direct News*, March 15, 2002, http://archive.compassdirect.org/en/display.php?page=news&idel ement=1169&lang=en&length=short&backpage=archives&critere=&countryname=Suda n&rowcur=0.

53. "The Application of the Apostasy Law in the World Today," Barnabas Fund, July 3, 2007, http://www.barnabasfund.org/US/News/Articles-research/The-Application-of-the-Apostasy-Law-in-the-World-Today.html?&quicksearch=The+Application+of+the+Apostas.

54. Barbara G. Baker, "Sudanese Police Torture Convert Student," *Compass Direct News*, October 8, 2001, http://www.comeandsee.com/modules.php?name=News&file=article&sid=191.

55. "Converts from Islam Struggle to Survive," *Compass Direct News*, April 14, 2009, http:// archive.compassdirect.org/en/display.php?page=news&lang=en&length=long&idelement= 5878&backpage=archives&critere=&countryname=Sudan&rowcur=0.

56. Rob Crilly and Lucy Bannerman, "Sudan Police Throw Teacher in Jail for Teddy Bear Named Muhammad," *The Times*, 27 November 2007, http://www.timesonline.co.uk/tol/news/ world/africa/article2951262.ece; Jeffrey Gettleman, "Calls in Sudan for Execution of British Teacher," *New York Times*, December 1, 2007, http://www.nytimes.com/2007/12/01/world/ africa/01sudan.html; "Teddy Row Teacher Freed from Jail," *BBC News*, December 3, 2007, http://news.bbc.co.uk/2/hi/uk_news/7124447.stm.

57. "U.N. Aide and Sudan Clash on Islamic Laws," *New York Times*, March 8, 1994, http://query. nytimes.com/gst/fullpage.html?res=9D04EFDA1F3AF93BA35750C0A962958260; *Situation of human rights in the Sudan—Report of the Special Rapporteur, Mr. Gaspar Biro, sub-mitted in accordance with Commission on Human Rights resolution 1993/60*, UN Commission on Human Rights, 50th session, February 1, 1994, E/CN.4/1994/48, 15–16. See also Ken Ringle, "The Next Rushdie?" *Washington Post*, March 26, 1994, and "Human Rights and Islam; Sudan Cites Higher Authority," *The Economist*, March 5, 1994.

58. Ken Ringle, "The Next Rushdie?"; "U.N. Aide and Sudan Clash on Islamic Laws"; Edward Luce, "Sudan Criticizes the Author of a Rights Survey for Blasphemy," *The Guardian*, March 3, 1994.

59. As quoted in *Report of the Secretary-General submitted in accordance with Commission on Human Rights resolution 1995/75*, UN Commission on Human Rights, 52nd session, February 22, 1996, E/CN.4/1996/57, http://www.unhchr.ch/Huridocda/Huridoca.nsf/TestFrame/e2 f2cb75181e115b802566da0040304c?Opendocument.

60. Africa Watch (now incorporated into Human Rights Watch), "Destroying Ethnic Identity: The Secret War Against the Nuba," *News from Africa Watch* 3, no. 15 (December 10, 1991): http://www.swrtc.ca/docs/DESTROYING%20ETHNIC%20IDENTITY%20.PDF; Alex De Waal and Yoanes Ajawin, "Facing Genocide: The Nuba of Sudan" (London: African Rights, 1995), http://www.justiceafrica.org/publishing/online-books/facing-genocide-the-nuba-of-sudan/; Hunud Abia Kadouf, "Marginalization and Resistance: The Plight of the Nuba People," *New Political Science* 23, no. 1 (2001): http://web.ebscohost.com.proxyau.wrlc.org/ehost/pdf?vid=4&hid=3&sid=5ab7726f-b98c-42d2-975d-2d615961328a%40 sessionmgr14.

61. Mohamed Suliman, "The Nuba Mountains of Sudan: Resource Access, Violent Conflict, and Identity," *Sudan Tribune*, September 2, 2003, http://www.sudantribune.com/spip. php?article252.

62. De Waal, "Averting Genocide in the Nuba Mountains, Sudan"; see also O'Ballance, *Sudan, Civil War and Terrorism: 1956–99*.

63. One person who continues this tradition, though now in the United States, is Taha's stu-dent, Abdullahi Ahmed An-Na'im, who teaches at Emory University. His latest work is *Islam and the Secular State: Negotiating the Future of Shari'a* (Cambridge, MA: Harvard University Press, 2008).

64. International Federation of Journalists, "IFJ Condemns Brutal Murder of Sudanese Journalist," September 7, 2006, http://www.sudantribune.com/spip.php?article17482; "Kidnapped Sudan Editor Beheaded," *BBC News*, September 6, 2006, http://news.bbc. co.uk/2/hi/africa/5321368.stm.

65. "Sudan SPLM Official Receives Death Threats over Adultery Bill," *Sudan Tribune*, April 24, 2009, http://www.sudantribune.com/spip.php?article30975.

66. Michael Hoebink, "The Dark Side of Liberal Islam," Radio Netherlands Worldwide, April 26, 2006, http://static.rnw.nl/migratie/www.radionetherlands.nl/currentaffairs/turabi060426-redirected; "Sudan's Turabi Considered Apostate," *Sudan Tribune*, April 24, 2006, http://www.sudantribune.com/article.php3?id_article=15219.

67. Lee Smith, "Sudan's Osama," *Slate*, August 5, 2004, http://www.slate.com/id/2104814; "Profile: Sudan's Islamist leader," *BBC News*, January 15, 2009, http://news.bbc.co.uk/2/hi/africa/3190770.stm; "Sudan Frees Opposition Leader Hassan al-Turabi," *The Times*, March 9, 2009, http://www.timesonline.co.uk/tol/news/world/africa/article5872347.ece.

Chapter 9

1. Mathias Hariyadi, "Clashes in Maluku, 45 Houses and a Church Set on Fire," *AsiaNews.it*, December 10, 2008, http://www.asianews.it/index.php?l=en&art=13974; Elizabeth Kendal, "Maluku, Eastern Indonesia: 'Blasphemy' Triggers Pogrom," World Evangelical Alliance press release, December 12, 2008, http://www.worldevangelicals.org/news/article.htm?id=2274.

2. "Raja Petra Arrested under ISA," *Malaysiakini*, September 12, 2008, http://www1.malaysia-kini.com/news/89544; "Malaysia Detains 'Dissent' Writer," *BBC News*, September 23, 2008, http://news.bbc.co.uk/2/hi/asia-pacific/7630789.stm; "Malaysia Blogger Goes on Trial," *Aljazeera News*, October 6, 2008, http://english.aljazeera.net/news/asia-pacific/2008/10/20081067323419616.html; "Malaysia Blogger's Joy at Release," *BBC News*, November 7, 2008, http://news.bbc.co.uk/2/hi/asia-pacific/7714696.stm; "Religious Department to Act Against any Blogger Who Insults Islam," *New Straits Times*, December 12, 2008.

3. Another religiously repressive state in the area is Brunei. All groups except Shafi'i Islam must register with the government and provide a list of their members, and the government prohibits propagating any view except Shafi'i Islam and has banned many groups (including Silat Lintau, Tariqat Mufarridiyyah, Qadiyania, al-Arqam, Abdul Razak Mohammad, al-Ma'unah, Saihoni Taispan, and the Baha'is). It also prohibits the sale of Bibles. Anyone who "publicly teaches or promotes any deviant beliefs or practices" may be charged under the Islamic Religious Council Act and imprisoned for three months and fined approximately $1,400. In December 2000, three Christians—Malai Taufick, Freddie Chong, and Yunus Murang—were imprisoned for "cult" activities. Amnesty International reports that they were coerced into confessing. As of March 2008, the Internal Security Department had questioned twenty-five Christians for alleged attempts to convert Muslims. See "Institute on Religion and Public Policy: Religious Freedom in Brunei Darussalam," January 19, 2009, http://religionandpolicy.org/cms/index2.php?option=com_content&do_pdf=1&id=2260.

4. Human Rights Watch, *Breach of Faith: Persecution of the Ahmadiyya Community in Bangladesh* 17, no. 6(C) (June 2005). For background on the rise of more radical forms of Islam in Bangladesh, see Maneeza Hossein, *The Road to a Shariah State: Cultural Radicalization in Bangladesh*, Hudson Institute White Paper, November 2006, http://www.hudson.org/files/pdf_upload/Maneeza.pdf, and "Bangladesh," *International Religious Freedom Report 2008*, U.S. State Department, Bureau of Democracy, Human Rights, and Labor, http://2001-2009.state.gov/g/drl/rls/irf/2008/108498.htm.

5. Paul Marshall, ed., *Religious Freedom in the World* (Lanham, MD: Rowman & Littlefield, 2008), 153.

6. "Hasina Wins Bangladesh Landslide," *BBC News*, December 30, 2008, http://news.bbc.co.uk/2/hi/south_asia/7803785.stm; *Thaindian News*, "Bangladesh Islamist Party Pledges Military Training in Seminaries," *Thaindian News*, December 12, 2008, http://www.thaindian.com/newsportal/uncategorized/bangladesh-islamist-party-pledges-military-training-in-seminaries_100130003.html.

7. "Govt to Ensure Minority Rights, CHT Peace Treaty: PM," *The Daily Star*, April 30, 2009, http://www.thedailystar.net/story.php?nid=86226.

8. Marshall, *Religious Freedom in the World*, 153. In 2008, a seventy-year-old woman, Rahima Beoa, was burned to death after a mob reportedly set fire to her house in Cinatuly village in the Rangpur district as punishment for her converting to Christianity; in 2006, many Christian homes in the area were vandalized. See "Elderly Burned Convert Dies in Bangladesh," *BosNewsLife*, February 5, 2008, http://www.bosnewslife.com/3416-3416-news-alert-elderly-burned-convert-dies-in.

9. "Bangladesh Islamist Party Pledges Military Training in Seminaries."

10. "Arrest Warrant Against Cartoonist for 'Blasphemous' Caricature," *Zee News: India Edition*, September 18, 2007, http://www.zeenews.com/news395742.html.

11. The following examples of persecution of Ahmadis are from Human Rights Watch, *Breach of Faith: Persecution of the Ahmadiyya Community in Bangladesh*. For more recent incidents, see: "Attacks on Ahmadiyyas: US Envoy to Report Soon to State Dept," *The Daily Star*, April 24, 2005; "Stop Persecution of the Ahmadiyyas," editorial, *New Age* (Dhaka), October 7, 2006, http://www.newagebd.com/2006/oct/07/edit.html#1; "Ahmadiyya Muslim Community," http://www.alislam.org/introduction/index.html. For background on the Ahmadis, see chapter 5.

12. "Bangladesh: Christian Convert's Life Threatened," *Compass Direct News*, October 16, 2008, http://archive.compassdirect.org/english/country/bangladesh/2008/newsarticle_5634.html.

13. "Bangladesh: Christian Convert's Life Threatened." For a similar case—converts Ishmael Sheikh and his wife Rahima Khatun—see "Bangladesh: Muslims Drive Christian Grandparents from Home," *Compass Direct News*, January 14, 2009, http://archive.compassdirect.org/en/display.php?page=news&idelement=5760&lang=en&length=short&backpage=archives&critere=&countryname=Bangladesh&rowcur=0.

14. "Christian Family Beaten, Cut—and Faces Charges." *Compass Direct News*, December 8, 2008, http://archive.compassdirect.org/en/display.php?page=news&idelement=5722&lang=en&length=short&backpage=archives&critere=&countryname=Bangladesh&rowcur=0.

15. "Christian Convert from Islam and Family Threatened with Death," *AsiaNews.it*, September, 30, 2009, http://www.asianews.it/index.php?l=en&art=16456&size=A. See also the case of Ahsan Ali, "Bangladesh: Christian Convert's Life Threatened."

16. Taslima Nasreen maintains a Web site at http://taslimanasrin.com/.

17. Nupar Banerjee, "Muslim Cleric Targets Feminist Writer," *Associated Press (AP)*, January 16, 2004.

18. Ashling O'Connor, "Feminist Author Rewrites Novel after Death Threats from Muslim Extremists," *The Times*, http://www.timesonline.co.uk/tol/comment/faith/article2978120.ece; Banerjee, "Muslim Cleric Targets Feminist Writer"; "Taslima Nasreen Removes Comment," *BBC News*, http://news.bbc.co.uk/2/hi/south_asia/7120473.stm; "Taslima Nasreen: Controversy's Child," *BBC News*, http://news.bbc.co.uk/2/hi/south_asia/7108880.stm.

19. "Protesters Attack Author Nasreen," *BBC News*, September 8, 2007, http://news.bbc.co.uk/2/hi/south_asia/6938887.stm; Asghar Ali Engineer, "Attack on Taslima: Love of Islam or Love of Power," August 14, 2007, http://indianmuslims.in/attack-on-taslima-love-of-islam-or-love-of-power/; Syed Amin Jafri, "Hyderabad Police Lodge Case Against Taslima Nasreen," *Rediff India Abroad*, August 11, 2007, http://www.rediff.com///news/2007/aug/11taslima.htm.

20. "Taslima Nasreen's Visa Extended," *BBC News*, February 15, 2008, http://news.bbc.co.uk/2/hi/south_asia/7246129.stm; "Another Storm Brews Around Taslima Visa Extension," February 15, 2008, http://www.expressindia.com/latest-news/Another-storm-brews-around-Taslima-visa-extension/273633/; "Banished Within & Without," *Times of India*, February 10, 2008, http://www1.timesofindia.indiatimes.com/articleshow/2770240.cms; see also "Taslima Hopes for Timely Visa Renewal," February 8, 2008, http://www.ndtv.com/convergence/ndtv/story.aspx?id=NEWEN20080040765. On March 1, 2010, two people died in riots in Shimoga and Hassan reacting to an article by Nasreen on Muslim women wearing burkas. See "2 Killed in Shimoga, Hassan Violence," *The Hindu*, March 2, 2010, http://www.thehindu.com/2010/03/02/stories/2010030258380100.htm.

21. "Abiding Shame," February 11, 2008, http://www.outlookindia.com/full.asp?fodname=20080211&fname=taslima&sid=1; Engineer, "Attack on Taslima: Love of Islam or Love of Power."

22. "Journalist Detained," The Committee to Protect Journalists, December 3, 2003. http://cpj.org/2003/12/journalist-detained.php; Bret Stephens, "Darkness in Dhaka," *The Wall Street Journal*, October 10, 2006, http://www.pierretristam.com/Bobst/library/wf-391.htm; "The Risks of Journalism in Bangladesh," *New York Times*, December 14, 2003, http://query.nytimes.com/gst/fullpage.html?res=9E05E6DF123CF937A25751C1A9659C8B63

23. "Man with 'Mosad Links' Held at ZIA," *The Daily Star*, November 30, 2003, http://www.thedailystar.net/2003/11/30/d3113001088.htm.

24. David Harris, "Journalist's Plight Needs Attention," December 8, 2006, http://www.juf.org/news/world.aspx?id=19392.

25. Personal communication with Salauddin Shoaib Choudhury, February 23, 2008.

26. Richard Benkin, "Salah Uddin Shoaib Choudhury Attacked by Goons: Anti-Radical, Pro-Peace Muslim Journalist Savaged in Broad Daylight," *The Canada Free Press*, February 22, 2009, http://canadafreepress.com/index.php/article/8699.

27. "Bangladesh Cartoonist Arrested," September 18, 2007, http://rumiahmed.wordpress.com/2007/09/18/bangladesh-cartoonist-arrested/. The cartoon may be viewed at http://www.islam-watch.org/M.Hussain/Islamic-Rage-Why-Cartoon-in-Bangladesh-Kills-Christians-in-Nigeria.htm. See also Aminesh Roul, "Bangladesh: Cartoon Injustice," October 31, 2007, http://www.speroforum.com/site/article.asp?id=11781.

28. "Bangladesh's Cartoonist Hero," October 1, 2007, http://www.docstrangelove.com/2007/10/01/bangladeshs-cartoonist-hero/.

29. Ain O Shalish Kendra (ASK) press release, January 24, 2008, http://www.askbd.org/main2.php.

30. "Islamists Battle Cats," October 1, 2007, http://www.docstrangelove.com/2007/09/18/islamists-battle-cats/.

31. ASK press release.

32. "Cartoonist Arrested over Harmless Play on Name Mohammed," Reporters Without Borders, http://www.rsf.org/article.php3?id_article=23700.

33. "IPI Protests Jailing of Cartoonist in Bangladesh and Suspension of Publication of Satirical Weekly," September 25, 2007, http://www.freemedia.at/cms/ipi/statements_detail.html?ctxid=CH0055&docid=CMS1190721263476.

34. *The 3rd World View*, http://rezwanul.blogspot.com/.

35. "Cartoonist Jailed," *Agence France Presse* (*AFP*), November 13, 2009, http://www.gulf-times.com/site/topics/article.asp?cu_no=2&item_no=325879&version=1&template_id=44&parent_id=24.

36. William Gomes, "Dhaka, Islamic Leaders Accused of Blasphemy: Protests and More Than 100 Arrests," *AsiaNews.it*, July 1, 2010, http://www.asianews.it/news-en/Dhaka,-Islamic-leaders-accused-of-blasphemy:-protests-and-more-than-100-arrests-18819.html.

37. In the draft of the Jakarta Charter, the first principle was formulated as: "One Lordship with the obligation to carry out the Islamic syari'a for its adherents," but on August 18 the Preparatory Committee for Indonesia's Independence (PPKI) dropped the phrase and affirmed Pancasila in its present form. The phrase "with the obligation to carry out the Islamic syari'a for its adherents" is often known in Indonesia as the "7 words" (in Indonesian, it is seven words) and Islamist groups have often sought to reinstate it.

38. On the advice of Matius Ho, we have put "Lordship" rather than "God" here. In Indonesian, "God" is "Allah," the God of Islam and Christians. But the Pancasila uses "Ketuhanan," a variation of "Tuhan," best translated as "Lord" in English. The prefix "ke-" and the suffix "-an" makes it an abstract idea, reflected best in "Lordship."

39. "Prominent Journalist Tells Court How Indonesia's Religion Law Jailed Him," *Jakarta Glove*, February 10, 2010, http://www.thejakartaglobe.com/home/prominent-journalist-tells-court-how-indonesias-religion-law-jailed-him/357820.

40. For an overview, see the Becket Fund for Religious Liberty, "Indonesian Constitutional Court Hears Challenge to Blasphemy Law," February 9, 2010, and the Becket Fund's Amicus Brief in the case, http://www.becketfund.org/index.php/article/1209.html; "Indonesia," *International Religious Freedom Report 2008*; "Court Chief Promises Fair Ruling," *Jakarta Post*, February 13, 2010, http://www.thejakartapost.com/news/2010/02/13/court-chief-promises-fair-ruling.html; "Constitutional Court Taking Up Indonesia's Thorny Religious Row," *Jakarta Globe*, February 4, 2010, http://www.thejakartaglobe.com/news/constitutional-court-taking-up-indonesias-thorny-religious-row/356799.

41. Chris Blake, "Indonesia Court Upholds Blasphemy Law," *AP*, April 20, 2010, http://www.google.com/hostednews/ap/article/ALeqM5hPQn6EhCh4bg7T1uaEV-Wo5pdnwQD9F6IML01.

42. Sadanand Dhume, "Strict Penalties in Aceh," September 15, 2009, http://www.asiasociety.org/policy-politics/human-rights/strict-penalties-aceh.

43. *Siding and Acting Intolerantly* (*Berpihak dan Bertindak Intoleran*), SETARA Institute for Democracy and Peace (Jakarta), 2008 Annual Report (January 13, 2009), lists 367 violations

of religious freedom in 265 incidents, 103 of which occurred in June 2008, when persecution of Ahmadiyyahss\ escalated.

44. Theresia Sufa, "Thousands besiege Ahmadiyah complex," *Jakarta Post*, July 16, 2005.
45. "Ahmadiyah Prepares Legal Action Against MUI," *Jakarta Post*, July 19, 2005.
46. Rendi A. Witular, "MUI to Formulate Edict Against 'Liberal Thoughts,'" *Jakarta Post*, July 27, 2005.
47. Richard Kraince, "The Challenge to Religious Liberty in Indonesia," The Heritage Foundation, June 1, 2009, http://www.heritage.org/research/reports/2009/06/the-challenge-to-religious-liberty-in-indonesia.
48. "Indonesia," *International Religious Freedom Report 2006*, U.S. State Department, Bureau of Democracy, Human Rights, and Labor, http://www.state.gov/g/drl/rls/irf/2006/71341.htm.
49. Kraince, "The Challenge to Religious Liberty in Indonesia."
50. "English translation of Indonesian Joint Ministerial Decree (SKB) against Ahmadiyah," http://www.thepersecution.org/world/indonesia/docs/skb.html.
51. Kraince, "The Challenge to Religious Liberty in Indonesia."
52. "Govt Calls It a Day for Ahmadiyah," *Jakarta Post*, June 10, 2008.
53. "Jakarta's Slippery Slope," Review and Outlook, *Wall Street Journal*, June 25, 2008; "Indonesian Muslims Urge Ahmadiyya Sect Disbanded," Reuters, August 4, 2008, http://wwrn.org/articles/29134/; "Indonesia," *International Religious Freedom Report 2008* (n. 4 above).
54. Sarah Webb, "Former Indonesian President Urges Religious Tolerance," Reuters, June 25, 2008.
55. "Indonesia: Sunday School Teachers Sentenced to Three Years in Prison," *Compass Direct News*, September 1, 2005, http://archive.compassdirect.org/en/display.php?page=news&lang=en&length=long&idelement=3949&backpage=archives&critere=&countryname=Indonesia&rowcur=50; "Indonesia: High Court Rejects Appeal for School Teachers," *Compass Direct News*, December 21, 2005, http://archive.compassdirect.org/en/display.php?page=news&idelement=4138&lang=en&length=short&backpage=archives&critere=&countryname=Indonesia&rowcur=25; "Indonesia: Court Rejects Legal Intervention for Jailed Teachers," *Compass Direct News*, January 24, 2006, http://archive.compassdirect.org/en/display.php?page=news&idelement=4178&lang=en&length=short&backpage=archives&critere=&countryname=Indonesia&rowcur=25; "Indonesia: Imprisoned Sunday School Teachers Released," *Compass Direct News*, June 8, 2007, http://archive.compassdirect.org/en/display.php?page=news&idelement=4902&lang=en&length=short&backpage=archives&critere=&countryname=Indonesia&rowcur=25.
56. "Indonesia: Christian Lecturer Attacked in West Java," *Compass Direct News*, November 16, 2006, http://archive.compassdirect.org/en/display.php?page=news&lang=en&length=long&idelement=4629&backpage=archives&critere=&countryname=Indonesia&rowcur=25. On September 6, 2007, the Malang District Court sentenced forty-one members of the College Student Services Agency to five years in prison for creating a training video in which, allegedly, trainees placed Qur'ans on the ground. The following August, they were given reprieves as part of Indonesian Day celebrations. See "Indonesia," *International Religious Freedom Report 2009*, U.S. State Department, Bureau of Democracy, Human Rights, and Labor, http://www.state.gov/g/drl/rls/irf/2009/127271.htm.
57. "Indonesia," *International Religious Freedom Report 2008*; "Al-Qiyadah Al-Islamiyah: Mini theocracy in Bogor and Padang," http://www.indonesiamatters.com/1435/theocracy/.
58. "Al-Qiyadah Al-Islamiyah: Mini Theocracy in Bogor and Padang"; "Majelis Ulama: The MUI Rides the Anti-heretic Wave to More Money and Influence," http://www.indonesiamatters.com/1434/ulama/; "Two Former Al-Qiyadah Activists Get 3 Years for Blasphemy," *Jakarta Post*, http://www.thejakartapost.com/news/2008/05/03/two-former-alqiyadah-activists-get-three-years-blasphemy.html; Tad Stahnke, "Obama's Indonesian Opportunity," *Human Rights First*, March 17, 2010.
59. "Indonesia," *International Religious Freedom Report 2006*.
60. "Lia Eden," *Indonesia Matters*, December 31, 2005, http://www.indonesiamatters.com/260/lia-eden-trial.

61. "Indonesian Court Overturns Ruling on Religious Sect, Jails Senior Member," BBC Monitoring Asia Pacific, November 14, 2007; "Indonesia," *International Religious Freedom Report 2008*.

62. Erwida Maulia, "Sect Leader Gets 2.5 Years for Blasphemy," *Jakarta Post*, July 30, 2009, http://www.thejakartapost.com/news/2009/07/30/sect-leader-gets-25-years-blasphemy.html.

63. "Moderate Muslim Threatened with Death Fatwa for Defending Freedom of Religion," *Kompas*, February 9, 2004; Ulil Abshar Abdalla, interview with Paul Marshall, Jakarta, January 2, 2004.

64. Richard Paddock, "Separation of Mosque and State Wanes in Indonesia," *Los Angeles Times*, March 20, 2006.

65. Chris Tryhorn and agencies, "Indonesian Editor Charged with Offending Islam," *MediaGuardian*, July 21, 2006, http://www.guardian.co.uk/media/2006/jul/21/pressand-publishing.race; The Committee to Protect Journalists, "Indonesia Detains Online News Editor over Prophet Drawings," July 20, 2006, http://cpj.org/2006/07/indonesia-detains-online-news-editor-over-prophet.php; "Jakarta Court Dismisses Case Against Santosa," Reporters Without Borders, September 20, 2006, http://www.rsf.org/Jakarta-court-dismisses-case.html.

66. Liz Gooch, "Malaysian Court Ends Ban on Book," *New York Times*, January 26, 2010, http://www.nytimes.com/2010/01/26/world/asia/26malaysia.html?ref=world. See also Perry Smith, "Speak No Evil: Apostasy, Blasphemy and Heresy in Malaysian Syariah Law," *UC Davis Journal of International Law and Policy* 10, no. 2 (Spring 2004): 358–403, http://www.iclrs.org/common/documents/pdf/2393.pdf.

67. Paul Wiseman, "In Malaysia, 'Islamic Civilization' Is Promoted," *USA Today*, November 4, 2004, http://www.usatoday.com/news/world/2004-11-03-malaysia-islam_x.htm.

68. Julia Zappei, "Malaysia: Catholic Paper That Used Allah Can Print," *AP*, January 8, 2009, http://www.foxnews.com/wires/2009Jan08/0,4670,ASMalaysiaCatholicNewspaper,00.html; "Malaysian Government Defeated by History: Christians Have Used the Word "Allah" for Centuries," *AsiaNews.it*, February 25, 2009, http://www.asianews.it/index.php?l=en&art=14574; "Malaysia: Ban Lifted on Malay Section of Catholic Newspaper," *Compass Direct*, January 9, 2009, http://archive.compassdirect.org/en/display.php?page=news&idelement=5757&lang=en&length=short&backpage=archives&critere=&countryname=Malaysia&rowcur=0.

69. "Islamic Councils Against Catholic Magazine of Kuala Lumpur: Forbidden to Use the Word 'Allah,'" *AsiaNews.it*, November 26, 2008, http://www.asianews.it/index.php?l=en&art=13850.

70. "Malaysia Restores 'Allah' Ban for Christians," *AP*, March 2, 2009, http://www.foxnews.com/story/0,2933,503504,00.html. The decision was upheld by the courts in May 2009; see "Malaysia Court Refuses to Let Church Use 'Allah,'" *The Dawn Media Group*, May 28, 2009, http://www.dawn.com/wps/wcm/connect/dawn-content-library/dawn/news/world/14-malaysia-court-refuses-to-let-church-use-allah-zj-06; "Malaysia Court Suspends 'Allah' Ruling," *AFP*, January 6, 2010, http://www.google.com/hostednews/afp/article/ALeqM5jdjxJHhJSxwW0qXtF-tOv447Y4Sw.

71. James Hookway and Celine Fernandez, "'Allah' Ruling May Challenge Malaysia," *Wall Street Journal*, January 2, 2010, http://online.wsj.com/article/SB126239298638513113.html; Hookway and Fernandez, "Malaysia Says It Will Appeal 'Allah' Ruling," *Wall Street Journal*, January 4, 2010, http://online.wsj.com/article/SB126252276477713845.html; "3 Malaysian Churches Attacked in 'Allah' Dispute," AP, January 8, 2010, http://www.christianwebsite.com/forum/showthread.php?p=29185; Rachel Harvey, "Malaysia Church Attacks Continue in Use of 'Allah' Row," *BBC News*, January 11, 2009, http://news.bbc.co.uk/2/hi/asia-pacific/8451630.stm; "Ninth Church Vandalized in Malaysia as Tensions Rise," *New York Times*, January 11, 2010, http://www.nytimes.com/2010/01/12/world/asia/12malaysia.html; "Pig Head Find at Malaysia Mosques," *BBC News*, January 27, 2010, http://news.bbc.co.uk/2/hi/asia-pacific/8482267.stm: "Malaysia Won't Punish Muslims for

Taking Communion," *AP*, March 4, 2010, http://www.siasat.com/english/news/malaysia-wont-punish-muslims-taking-communion.

72. "Non-Muslims Not to Use 35 Islamic terms: Diktat," *Press Trust of India*, January 15, 2010, http://www.zeenews.com/news596153.html. See also Joseph Chinyong Liow, "No God but God: Malaysia's 'Allah' Controversy," *Foreign Affairs*, February 10, 2010, http://www.foreignaffairs.com/articles/65961/joseph-chinyong-liow/no-god-but-god.

73. "Seizure of 15,000 Bibles in Malaysia tuns Christians," *Compass Direct News*, November 7, 2009, http://www.compassdirect.org/english/country/malaysia/11589/; Julia Zappei, "Malaysia Rejects Call to Release 10,000 Bibles," *AP*, November 5, 2009, http://www.boston.com/news/world/asia/articles/2009/11/05/malaysia_rejects_call_to_release_10000_bibles/.

74. "Govt Bans 37 Publications on Islam Containing Twisted Facts," BERNAMA News Agency, June 6, 2007, http://www.bernama.com/bernama/v3/news.php?id=265986.

75. "Govt Bans Two Books Containing Twisted Facts on Islam," BERNAMA News Agency, August 14, 2008, http://www.bernama.com.my/bernama/v5/newsgeneral.php?id=352710; Liz Gooch, "Malaysian Court Ends Ban on Book," *New York Times*, January 26, 2010, http://www.nytimes.com/2010/01/26/world/asia/26malaysia.html?ref=world.

76. See "Mission and Objectives" on Web site http://www.sistersinislam.org.my/index.php?option=com_content&task=view&id=198&Itemid=164. SIS was formed in 1988 and registered as an NGO in 1993 under the name SIS Forum (Malaysia) Berhad. The name Sisters in Islam is retained as an authorship name.

77. Sisters in Islam, "Press Statement: Banning of the Book on 'Muslim Women and the Challenge of Islamic Extremism,'" August 21, 2008, http://www.sistersinislam.org.my/index.php?option=com_content&task=view&id=769&Itemid=1/.

78. Liz Gooch, "Malaysian Court Ends Ban on Book."

79. "Clause Doesn't Cover Muslims," *The Star Online*, February 24, 2009, http://thestar.com.my/news/story.asp?file=/2009/2/24/parliament/3330271&sec=parliament/. For background, see Perry Smith, "Speak No Evil: Apostasy, Blasphemy and Heresy in Malaysian Syariah Law"; Mohamed Azam Mohamed Adil, "Law of Apostasy and Freedom of Religion in Malaysia," *Asian Journal of Comparative Law* 2, no. 1 (2007): 1–36; Thio Li-Ann, "Apostasy and Religious Freedom: Constitutional Issues Arising from the Lina Joy Litigation," *Malayan Law Journal* 2, no. 1 (April 2006). On the earlier treatment of blasphemy and apostasy in Malaysian law, see Mohamed Hashim Kamali, *Freedom of Expression in Islam*, rev. ed. (Cambridge: Islamic Texts Society, 1997), 273–93.

80. "Renouncing Islam a Matter for Syariah Court Only," *New Straits Times*, March 6, 1999.

81. Angela Wu, "Lina Joy," *Wall Street Journal*, September 7, 2006, http://www.becketfund.org/files/c8589.pdf.

82. The card identifies who is a Muslim: information on others' faith is recorded electronically and is not visible to the eye.

83. Ashgar Ali Ali Mohamed, "Lina Joy v Majlis Agama Islam Wilayah & Anor," *Malaysian Law Journal* 2 (2004): 119–44, http://www.becketfund.org/index.php/case/107.html.

84. Doug Bandow, "The Right Not to Be Muslim," *National Review Online*, June 8, 2007, http://article.nationalreview.com/?q=Y2IyZmU2NDljNmEwMjIxNGNmMzI4NzFjZmNiMTQ5YjI.

85. Jonathan Kent, "Malaysia 'Convert' Claims Cruelty," *BBC News*, July 6, 2007, http://news.bbc.co.uk/go/pr/fr/-/2/hi/asia-pacific/6278568.stm.

86. Julia Zappei, "Muslim-Born Woman Seeks Life as Hindu," *ABC News*, July 6, 2007, http://www.bookrags.com/news/muslim-born-woman-seeks-life-as-moc/.

87. "Convert to Know Fate Next Month," *New Straits Times*, July 21, 2007, http://www.malaysianbar.org.my/legal/general_news/convert_to_know_fate_next_month.html?date=2008-03-01/.

88. Sharanjit Singh, "Syariah High Court Declares Convert No Longer a Muslim," *New Straits Times*, May 8, 2008, http://www.malaysianbar.org.my/legal/general_news/landmark_decision_syariah_high_court_declares_convert_no_longer_a_muslim.html.

89. "M'sian Muslims Protest Ruling on Renunciation of Islam," *New Straits Times*, May 16, 2008, http://www.asiaone.com/News/AsiaOne%2BNews/Malaysia/Story/A1Story20080516-65646.html.

90. "Malaysian Court Upholds Muslim Return to Buddhism," *The China Post*, March 17, 2009, http://www.chinapost.com.tw/asia/malaysia/2009/03/17/200426/Malaysian-court.htm/. In the recent case of Lim Yoke Khoon, the Shah Alam Court of Appeal denied her request to reconvert to Christianity on a technicality that Lim is expected to appeal. "Malaysia: Court Denies Woman's Appeal to Leave Islam," *Compass Direct News*, August 15, 2008, http://archive.compassdirect.org/en/display.php?page=news&idelement=5521&lang=en&length=short&backpage=archives&critere=&countryname=Malaysia&rowcur=0. In 2009, Malaysia banned the conversion of children without the consent of both parents; see "Malaysia Tackles Child Conversion," *BBC News*, April 23, 2009, http://news.bbc.co.uk/2/hi/asia-pacific/8014025.stm. There had been a series of cases concerning the religious status of children in cases of conversion; see Sofianni Subki, "Custody Turmoil," *New Straits Times*, September 15, 2003, http://www.hvk.org/articles/0903/203.html; "High Court Declines to Nullify Conversion of Minors to Islam," *New Straits Times*, April 14, 2004, http://www.highbeam.com/doc/1P1-93434957.html. Another grievance for non-Muslims has been that religious authorities can confiscate and bury a body as a Muslim if a sharia judge rules the deceased a Muslim, which requires only the word of one Muslim witness. See "Body-snatching Divides Religions in Malaysia," *The Earth Times*, June 22, 2009, http://www.earthtimes.org/articles/show/274242,body-snatching-divides-religions-in-malaysia-feature.html.

91. "Islamic Authority in Malaysia Bans Moderate Muslim Mosque," *Salem News*, May 1, 2009, http://www.salem-news.com/printview.php?id=10694.

92. Paul Wiseman, "In Malaysia, 'Islamic Civilization' Is Promoted."

93. "59 Sky Kingdom Members Detained," *New Straits Times*, July 21, 2005, http://www.religionnewsblog.com/11755/59-sky-kingdom-members-detained.

94. "Indignant Imams Flatten Teapot Deity's Commune," *AsiaNews.it*, August 2, 2005, http://www.asianews.it/index.php?l=en&art=3837.

95. "Sky Kingdom Member Gets Two Years for Apostasy," *The Star Online*, March 3, 2008, http://thestar.com.my/news/story.asp?file=/2008/3/4/courts/20519214.

96. "Ayah Pin Still Hiding in Thailand," *New Straits Times*, May 3, 2006, http://www.religion-newsblog.com/14499/ayah-pin-still-hiding-in-thailand.

97. "Malaysia Women's Group Sued over 'Islam' in Name," *Jakarta Post*, March 22, 2010, http://www.thejakartapost.com/news/2010/03/22/malaysia-women039s-group-sued-over-039islam039-name.html.

98. "Sharia in Force on Atolls of the Maldives," *AsiaNews.it*, October 20, 2008, http://www.asianews.it/news-en/Sharia-in-force-on-atolls-of-the-Maldives-13522.html. It is unclear if this means that a Maldivian may be stripped of citizenship or if the law applies only to foreigners who wish to gain citizenship; see Odd Larsen, "Maldives: Religious Freedom Survey 2008," *Forum 18 News*, October 15, 2008, http://www.forum18.org/Archive.php?article_id=1203. For more background, see Larsen, "Maldives: What Do Maldivians Understand Freedom of Religion or Belief to Be?" *Forum 18 News*, December 7, 2009, http://www.forum18.org/Archive.php?article_id=1383.

99. Ahmed Naish, "Parliament Takes on Revised Penal Code," *Dhivehi Observer*, October 14, 2009, http://doreview.blogspot.com/2009/10/parliament-takes-on-revised-penal-code.html.

100. Olivia Lang, "'Anni' Heralds New Era in Maldives," *BBC News*, October 29, 2008, http://news.bbc.co.uk/2/hi/south_asia/7697283.stm.

101. "Maldives: Reform in Politics but Not in Religious Liberty," World Evangelical Alliance, December 9, 2008, http://www.worldevangelicals.org/commissions/rlc/rlc_article.htm?id=2264; "No Place for Religious Freedom in the Maldives' Democratic Dispensation," *AsiaNews.it*, February 19, 2009, http://www.asianews.it/index.php?l=en&art=14524&size=A.

102. Maryam Omidi, "Journalists 'Exercise Self-censorship,'" *Minivan News*, June 4, 2009, http://www.mail-archive.com/zestmedia@yahoogroups.com/msg07062.html.

103. "Maldives," *International Religious Freedom Report 1999*, U.S. State Department, Bureau of Democracy, Human Rights, and Labor, http://www.state.gov/www/global/human_rights/irf/irf_rpt/1999/irf_maldives99.html; See, for example, http://www.ctlibrary.com/ct/1998/september7/8ta27d.html, http://www.religioustolerance.org/rt_maldive.htm.

104. J. J. Robinson, "Islamic Foundation Calls for Death Sentence If Apostate Fails to Repent," *Minivan News*, May 30, 2010, http://minivannews.com/politics/islamic-foundation-calls-for-death-sentence-if-apostate-fails-to-repent-7606/print/; "Apostate Publicly Repents and Rejoins Islam, after Counseling," *Minivan News*, June 1, 2010, http://minivannews.com/politics/apostate-publicly-repents-and-rejoins-islam-after-counselling-7704/print/.

105. Hassan Saeed and Abdullah Saeed, *Freedom of Religion, Apostasy and Islam* (Aldershot, U.K.: Ashgate, 2004).

106. South Asia Analysis Group, "On Dr. Hassan Saeed's Book on Freedom of Religion and Apostasy," June 25, 2008, http://www.southasiaanalysis.org/%5Cpapers28%5Cpaper2747.html.

107. "Maldives: Reform in Politics but Not in Religious Liberty," World Evangelical Alliance, December 8, 2008, http://www.ea.org.au/default.aspx?id=4f06b920-cc46-4c2e-a939-7bd24de72c70.

108. Odd Larsen, "Maldives: Almost No Religious Freedom for Migrant Workers," *Forum 18 News*, June 23, 2009, http://www.forum18.org/Archive.php?article_id=1316;

109. Sisters in Islam, "Banning of the Book on 'Muslim Women and the Challenge of Islamic Extremism,'" press statement, August 21, 2008, http://www.sistersinislam.org.my/index.php?option=com_content&task=view&id=769&Itemid=1.

Part III

1. Statement by Ihab Gamaleldin, Egypt, at the 2nd Plenary Meeting of the 6th Session of the UN Human Rights Council, September 13, 2007, UN Human Rights Council archived video, http://www.un.org/webcast/unhrc/archive.asp?go=070913.

2. Resolution 12/16, Freedom of Opinion and Expression, UN Human Rights Council, adopted October 2, 2009.

3. On the tendency of religious repression to increase religious violence, see Brian J. Grim and Roger Finke, "Religious Persecution in Cross-National Context: Clashing Civilizations or Regulated Religious Economies?" *American Sociological Review* 72 (August 2007): 633–58.

Chapter 10

1. Lee Keath, "Friday Brings New Prophet Drawing Protests," *Associated Press* (*AP*), February 10, 2006, http://muzi.com/news/ll/english/10003182.shtml.

2. "Islam-West Divide 'Grows Deeper,'" *BBC News*, February 10, 2006, http://news.bbc.co.uk/2/hi/middle_east/4699716.stm.

3. Sadaqat Jan, "Protestors Rally in Pakistan, Iraq," *AP*, February 21, 2006.

4. "Palestinian Children Demonstrate Against Denmark," *Jerusalem Post*, February 13, 2006.

5. Riaz Khan, "Cleric Announces $1M Bounty on Cartoonist," *AP*, February 17, 2006, http://www.encyclopedia.com/doc/1P1-118608901.html. In Morocco, thousands demonstrated, and lawyers in Tangier claimed the cartoons were part of a campaign beginning with "the profanation of the Qur'an in Guantanamo"; see Oumnia Guedda, "Prophet Caricatures," *Morocco Times*, February 14, 2006. On February 19, tens of thousands demonstrated in Istanbul; see Ali Kotarumalos, "Muslims Assault U.S. Embassy in Indonesia," *AP*, February 19, 2006, http://www.msnbc.msn.com/id/11445755/.

6. In Bhopal, India, about 10,000 held a silent protest, with some banners stating, "Stop all anti-Islamic activities." Thousands demonstrated in Gaza and in the capitals of Pakistan and Bangladesh; see "Islam-West divide 'Grows Deeper.'"

7. Jytte Klausen, *The Cartoons That Shook the World* (New Haven: Yale University Press, 2009), 107.

8. Henryk M. Broder, "How a Film Triggered a Global Panic," *Der Spiegel*, March 20, 2008, http://www.spiegel.de/international/europe/0,1518,542255,00.html; Leander Schaerlackens, "Dutch Film to Slam Islam," *Washington Times*, February 29, 2008, http://

www.washingtontimes.com/news/2008/feb/29/dutch-film-to-slam-islam/; Ian Traynor, "'I Don't Hate Muslims. I Hate Islam,' Says Holland's Rising Political Star," *The Guardian*, February 17, 2008, http://www.guardian.co.uk/world/2008/feb/17/netherlands.islam.

9. "UN Chief Condemns Anti-Islam Film," *BBC News*, March 28, 2008, http://news .bbc.co.uk/2/hi/7319188.stm; "Muslim, UN Outrage over Dutch MP's Anti-Islam Film," *Agence France Presse (AFP)*, March 28, 2008; "Arab, Muslim Leaders Denounce Film by Dutch Filmmaker," *AP*, March 29, 2008, http://www.wsvn.com/news/articles/local/MI81 627/; see also http://www.abc.net.au/news/stories/2008/03/29/2202493.htm?section =justin.

10. "Dutch Chief's Son Killed in Afghanistan for 'Fitna,'" *Al Arabiya*, April 18, 2008, http://www. alarabiya.net/articles/2008/04/18/48527.html.

11. Marcus Eliason, "Khomeini Sanctions Murder of 'Blasphemous Novelist,'" *AP*, February 14, 1989, http://news.google.com/newspapers?nid=860&dat=19890222&id=CjkQAAAAIBAJ &sjid=G48DAAAAIBAJ&pg=5697,5374875; Robert Barr, "'Satanic Verses' Author Scrubs U.S. Trip; Iranians Announce Bounty," *AP*, February 15, 1989, http://news.google.com/new spapers?nid=1928&dat=19890215&id=SQcgAAAAIBAJ&sjid=6GQFAAAAIBAJ&p g=1452,2808617.

12. Daniel Pipes, *The Rushdie Affair* (New Brunswick: Transaction Publishers, 2003), 113–18, notes that the title *The Satanic Verses* caught the attention of many who had not bothered to read the book itself and was frequently misinterpreted, particularly in translation, as meaning that the entire Qur'an was written by the devil.

13. In addition to the book itself (*The Satanic Verses* [New York: Random House, 2008]), this analysis draws on Lawrence Pollard, "Satanic Verses' Polarising Untruths," *BBC News*, February 14, 2009, http://news.bbc.co.uk/2/hi/entertainment/7889974.stm, and Pipes, *The Rushdie Affair*, 53–69.

14. This consists by its own count of fifty-seven Muslim countries (it includes "the State of Palestine" and "Northern Cyprus"), headquartered in Saudi Arabia. See chapter 11.

15. Christopher Walker, "Islamic Leaders Urge Muslim World to Ban 'Blasphemous Rushdie Book,'" *The Times* (London), November 22, 1988.

16. Pipes, *The Rushdie Affair*, 20–24, 134–35; Andrew Morgan, "Muslims Call in for Ban on Rushdie Publishers; Viking-Penguin," *The Times* (London), January 30, 1989; Sheila Rule, "Khomeini Urges Muslims to Kill Author of Novel," *New York Times*, February 15, 1989 http://www.nytimes.com/books/99/04/18/specials/rushdie-khomeini.html.

17. Eliason, "Khomeini Sanctions Murder of 'Blasphemous Novelist'"; Rule, "Khomeini Urges Muslims to Kill Author of Novel"; "French Firm Suspends Publication of 'Satanic Verses,'" *United Press International*, February 15, 1989; "Waldenbooks: We Never Banned 'Satanic Verses,'" *United Press International*, February 24, 1989; "B. Dalton's to Return 'Satanic Verses' to Shelves," *AP*, February 23, 1989, http://www.nytimes.com/1989/02/23/ world/b-dalton-to-resume-its-sales-of-satanic-verses.html?pagewanted=1; Kathleen Maclay, "Bombs Strike Berkeley Bookstores, New York Newspaper," *AP*, February 28, 1989.

18. Eliason, "Khomeini Sanctions Murder of 'Blasphemous Novelist'"; Harvey Morris and Heather Mills, "Rushdie 'Will Not Be Forgiven,'" *The Independent*, February 20, 1989.

19. Rule, "Khomeini Urges Muslims to Kill Author of Novel"; Morris and Mills, "Rushdie 'Will Not Be Forgiven'"; Mona Ziade, "Iran Severs Relations with Britain over Book," *AP*, March 7, 1989, http://news.google.com/newspapers?nid=2002&dat=19890307&id=urkiAAAAIB AJ&sjid=QLUFAAAAIBAJ&pg=4175,1159671; "Islamic Conference denounces Rushdie," *United Press International*, March 16, 1989.

20. "Thousands of Moslems Clash in Protest Against Salman Rushdie," *AP*, May 27, 1989, http:// articles.latimes.com/1989-05-28/news/mn-1613_1_london-protest-rushdie-book-blas- phemy-law-satanic-verses; Angella Johnson, "MPs Call for Verses Ban," *The Guardian*, May 29, 1989.

21. Daniel Pipes, "Salman Rushdie's Delusion, and Ours," *Commentary*, December 1998, http:// www.danielpipes.org/article/301; Karin Davies, "Moslems Picket British Publisher," *United Press International*, January 8, 1990.

22. Karin Davies, "Rushdie: 'I Don't Intend to Be Defeated,'" *United Press International*, April 27, 1990; Alexander Macleod, "Britons Link Novel, Hostage Issue," *Christian Science Monitor*, May 18, 1990.

23. "Rushdie Apologizes for Offending Muslims," *The Globe and Mail*, September 28, 1990; Nicholas de Jongh, "It's Been Hell, Says Contrite Rushdie," *The Guardian*, September 28, 1990; "Threat to Rushdie 'Is Not Changed,'" *The Times*, September 29, 1990.

24. "Iranian Minister: Rushdie Death Decree Irrevocable," *AP*, December 9, 1990, http://news. google.com/newspapers?nid=1893&dat=19901210&id=8MYfAAAAIBAJ&sjid=uNgEAAA AIBAJ&pg=3757,5729637.

25. Angella Johnson, "Rushdie Makes Peace Overtures," *The Guardian*, November 27, 1990; Iqbal Wahhab, "British Muslim Urges Iran to Stay Firm on Rushdie Sentence," *The Independent*, December 4, 1990.

26. Hugo Young, "Commentary: The Muddle of Rushdie's Satanic Prose," *The Guardian*, December 20, 1990.

27. Robert Barr, "Rushdie Embraces Islamic Faith," *Pittsburgh Post-Gazette*, December 25, 1990; "Rushdie Won't Seek Paperback Version," *The News* (Boca Raton), December 25, 1990, http://news.google.com/newspapers?nid=1290&dat=19901225&id=5NkPAAAAIBAJ&sjid =KY0DAAAAIBAJ&pg=6399,5366187.

28. Pipes, *The Rushdie Affair*, 205, suggested that publishers and editors were particularly vulnerable since they were implicated by the ayatollah's edict, yet unlike Rushdie they were not under guard.

29. "Rushdie's Associates Targeted by Islamic Zealots," *AP*, February 13, 1994; "Translator Hurt," *The Independent*, July 4, 1991; "Rushdie, in Rare Public Appearance, Says Hitmen after Him," *AP*, September 15, 1991, http://news.google.com/newspapers?nid=1368&dat= 19910916&id=o20WAAAAIBAJ&sjid=9RIEAAAAIBAJ&pg=5405,3600901.

30. T. R. Reid, "'Satanic Verses' Translator Found Slain," *Washington Post*, July 13, 1991, http:// www.encyclopedia.com/doc/1P2-1074580.html; Kevin Sullivan, "Rushdie Translator Stabbed to Death," *The Guardian*, July 13, 1991; Ashok S. Rai, "Slain 'Verses' Translator Revered, Reviled," *The Nikkei Weekly*, August 3, 1991. Igarashi's murder remained unsolved when the statute of limitations was reached fifteen years later; "Statute of Limitations to Expire on 'Satanic Verses' Murder in Japan," *Japan Economic Newswire*, July 4, 2006.

31. Paris: Editions la Découverte, 1993; English translation, *For Rushdie: Essays by Muslim Writers in Defense of Free Speech* (New York: George Braziller, 1994).

32. Koenraad Elst, postscript to Pipes, *The Rushdie Affair*, 259; "Turkish Paper Publishes 'Satanic Verses,'" *AFP*, May 26, 2003; "Fundamentalists Protest at Satanic Verses," *AFP*, May 28, 1993; "35 Dead, 60 Injured in Hotel Fire Set by Turkish Fundamentalists," *AFP*, July 3, 1993; Hugh Pope, "Turkish Zealots Kill 40 in 'Verses' Attack," *The Independent*, July 3, 1993, http://www.independent.co.uk/news/world/turkish-zealots-kill-40-in-verses-attack-militants-burn-down-hotel-in-riot-over-rushdies-book-1482639.html; "Turkey: Writer Aziz Nesin Denies Engaging in Anti-religious Propaganda," Turkish TV broadcast of July 4, 1993, carried in BBC Summary of World Broadcasts, July 6, 1993; Yalman Onaran, "Burned: An Author Charged with Inciting a Crowd to Kill Him," *Columbia Journalism Review*, November 1994; Rasit Gurdilek, "Fundamentalist Rampage Leaves 35 Dead, 60 Injured," *AP*, July 3, 1993; "Rushdie's Supporters 'Will Also Face Death,'" *The Herald* (Glasgow), July 8, 1993.

33. Doug Mellgren, "Salman Rushdie's Norwegian Publisher Shot," *AP*, April 11, 1993, http:// www.highbeam.com/doc/1P2-969291.html; Mellgren, "Iran Denies Links to Shooting of Rushdie's Publisher," *AP*, October 14, 1993; "Police Hunting Nygaard Gunmen, Iranian Ambassador Called In," *AFP*, October 21, 1993; "Norway Closes Rushdie Inquiry," *Washington Post*, April 22, 1995.

34. "Norway Reopens Satanic Verses Shooting Case," *CBC News*, November 27, 2010, http:// www.cbc.ca/news/arts/books/story/2010/11/27/norway-publisher-rushdie.html.

35. Jamie Wilson and Helen Carter, "Rushdie's Nightmare Years as a Fugitive," *The Guardian*, September 23, 1998; Anne McElvoy, "Banned on the Run," *The Times*, August 26, 1995; Jan

M. Olsen, "Danes Cancel Rushdie Visit, Citing Inadequate Security," *AP*, October 31, 1996; "Tehran Confirms Fatwa Against Rushdie," *AFP*, February 15, 2008; David Pallister, "Rushdie Wins Government Pledge to Combat Fatwa," *The Guardian*, February 17, 1998; "Iran Says It Won't Execute Rushdie," *AP*, March 1, 1998; "Senior Iran Cleric Says Rushdie Death Sentence Is Irrevocable," *AP*, July 24, 1998, http://news.google.com/newspapers?nid=1345&dat=19 910214&id=LMgSAAAAIBAJ&sjid=CfoDAAAAIBAJ&pg=5057,1778807.

36. Pipes, *The Rushdie Affair*, 184–87, describes Iranian state-sponsored assassinations or assassination attempts, particularly against Iranian expatriates in the West, during the 1980s.

37. "French Journalists Win First EU 'For Diversity. Against Discrimination' Award," EU press release IP/05/512, May 2, 2005, http://europa.eu/rapid/pressReleasesAction.do?reference =IP/05/512&format=HTML&aged=0&language=EN&guiLanguage=en.

38. Anthony Shadid and Kevin Sullivan, "Anatomy of the Cartoon Protest Movement," *Washington Post*, February 16, 2006, http://www.washingtonpost.com/wp-dyn/content/ article/2006/02/15/AR2006021502865.html; Paul Marshall, interview with Flemming Rose, Copenhagen, August 6, 2006; Klausen, *Cartoons That Shook the World*, 14–15. Klausen reports that three other cartoonists turned down the assignment, one citing fear and the others unrelated reasons.

39. John Hansen, "The Editor and the 12 Cartoons," interview with Carsten Juste, *Jyllands-Posten*, December 18, 2005, http://jp.dk/udland/article177647.ece.

40. Flemming Rose, "Freedom of Expression: The Face of Muhammad," *Jyllands-Posten*, September 30, 2005, 3, translation available via the Australian Broadcasting Corporation at www.abc.net.au/mediawatch/transcripts/AccompCart.doc.

41. The other images featured were: a Danish schoolboy named Muhammad gesturing to a blackboard that read "*Jyllands-Posten*'s journalists are a bunch of reactionary provocateurs"; Muhammad at the entrance to paradise telling a row of suicide bombers, "stop, stop, we've run out of virgins!"; Muhammad's face with the traditional Islamic crescent around it and the star over his right eye; abstract forms that may have been stylized female figures next to verses that appear to chastise the Prophet for repressing women; Muhammad with a broken halo resembling horns; Muhammad viewing a paper and telling two sword-brandishing men, "Relax...it's just a sketch made by a Dane from southwest Denmark"; Muhammad with eyes obscured by a black bar and sword in hand, standing in front of two frightened-looking women in burkas; Kare Bluitgen, the children's book author in question, with an orange (a symbol for luck), reading "PR-stunt" nestled in a turban on his head and a drawing of a be-turbaned stick figure in his hand; and the image that *Jyllands-Posten* used for the centerpiece in its story, showing a man standing before a lineup of seven figures in turbans, including figures from other religions, Mr. Bluitgen, and a far-right Danish politician, saying "Hm...I don't recognize him."

42. In a 2008 interview, he explained: "the cartoon was...aimed at the terrorists, who use part of Islam as their spiritual ammunition. You could also say that the terrorists have taken the Prophet as their hostage"; interview with Kurt Westergaard by Yassin Musharbash, *Spiegel Online*, August 15, 2008, http://www.spiegel.de/international/europe/0,1518,572330,00.html.

43. Stephen Schwartz, "Muhammad Caricatured," *The Weekly Standard*, February 20, 2006, http://www.weeklystandard.com/Content/Public/Articles/000/000/006/699xftsa.asp; Oleg Grabar, "Seeing Is Believing. The Image of the Prophet in Islam: The Real Story," *The New Republic*, November 4, 2009, http://www.tnr.com/article/books-and-arts/seeing-and-believing.

44. Richard, "In Art Museums, Portraits Illuminate a Religious Taboo," http://www.washing-tonpost.com/wp-dyn/content/article/2006/02/13/AR2006021302407.html; Amir Taheri, "Bonfire of the Pieties," *Wall Street Journal*, February 8, 2006, http://www.opinionjournal .com/editorial/feature.html?id=110007934.

45. "Q&A: Depicting the Prophet Muhammad," *BBC Online*, http://news.bbc.co.uk/2/ hi/4674864.stm; "Q&A," www.sistani.org.

46. Pew Forum, transcript of "Islam and the West: A Conversation with Bernard Lewis," April 27, 2006.

47. "Imam Demands Apology for Mohammed Cartoons," *Copenhagen Post*, October 6, 2005; Lorenzo Vidino, "Creating Outrage," *National Review Online*, February 6, 2006, http://old. nationalreview.com/comment/vidino200602060735.asp; Pernille Ammitzbøll and Lorenzo Vidino, "After the Danish Cartoon Controversy," *Middle East Quarterly*, http://www.mefo-rum.org/1437/after-the-danish-cartoon-controversy.

48. Lorenzo Vidino, "Creating Outrage"; Shadid and Sullivan, "Anatomy of the Cartoon Protest Movement"; Ammitzbøll and Vidino, "After the Danish Cartoon Controversy."

49. Klausen, *Cartoons That Shook the World*, 83.

50. *Copenhagen Post*, "Cartoons Have Muslims Threatening Newspaper," *Jyllands-Posten*, October 12, 2005, http://www.freerepublic.com/focus/f-news/1501392/posts.

51. The ambassadors of Turkey, Saudi Arabia, Iran, Pakistan, Egypt, Indonesia, Algeria, and Bosnia and Herzegovina; a representative of the Libyan Embassy; the *chargé d'affaires* of Morocco; and the Head of the Palestinian General Delegation.

52. Klausen, *Cartoons That Shook the World*, 155–57, discusses the three incidents mentioned aside from the cartoons; pp. 36–37 reproduce the diplomats' letter in full.

53. Reproduced in ibid., 66.

54. "Rent-a-Riot ABCs," *New York Post*, February 9, 2006; Vidino, "Creating Outrage"; Shadid and Sullivan, "Anatomy."

55. "Cartoons of Mohammed Cause Death Threat," *DR Nyheder*, December 2, 2005.

56. Decision on possible criminal proceedings in the case of *Jyllands-Posten*'s article "The Face of Muhammad," The Director of Public Prosecutions (Denmark), File No. RA-2006-41-0151, March 15, 2006, http://www.rigsadvokaten.dk/media/bilag/afgorelse_engelsk.pdf. There were controversies in 1984 and 1992 over a painting on a railway station and a film, respectively, offensive to many Christians, but no legal measures were taken. See *Blasphemy and Film Censorship—Submission to the European Court of Human Rights in Respect of Nigel Wingrove v. the United Kingdom, Article 19 and Interights*, December 1995, 8, http://www .article19.org/pdfs/cases/uk-wingrove-v.-uk.pdf; and "Denmark, Norway, Sweden and Finland," under Caslon's analysis of European blasphemy law and cases, http://www.caslon .com.au/blasphemyprofile9.htm#denmark.

57. "Danes and Muslims," *Wall Street Journal*, January 31, 2006.

58. "Muslim Organization Calls for Boycott of Denmark," *Copenhagen Post*, December 28, 2005; Klausen, *Cartoons That Shook the World*, 63–64.

59. Daniel Howden, "How a Meeting of Leaders in Mecca Set Off the Cartoon Wars Around the World," *The Independent*, February 10, 2006, http://www.independent.co.uk/news/world/middle-east/how-a-meeting-of-leaders-in-mecca-set-off-the-cartoon-wars-around-the-world-466109.html.

60. The Al-Aqsa Martyrs' Brigades claimed responsibility for the incident, which fortunately ended without injury; Donna Abu-Nasr, "Outrage Builds in Mideast over Cartoons," *AP*, January 30, 2006, http://news.google.com/newspapers?nid=1665&dat=20060131&id=MEUaAAAAIBAJ&sjid=RyUEAAAAIBAJ&pg=3424,5641902; Jenny Booth and Reuters, "Kidnapping in Row over Muhammad Cartoons," *The Times*, February 2, 2006, http://www .timesonline.co.uk/tol/news/world/europe/article724944.ece; http://news.google.com/newspapers?nid=1774&dat=20060203&id=45ceAAAAIBAJ&sjid=1oYEAAAAIBAJ&pg=6812,3285523; "Gaza EU Offices Raided by Gunmen," *BBC News*, January 30, 2006, http://news.bbc.co.uk/2/hi/middle_east/4661572.stm; Alan Cowell, "Dane Defends Press Freedom As Muslims Protest Cartoons," *New York Times*, February 1, 2006, http://www .nytimes.com/2006/02/01/international/europe/01danish.html; Nidal al-Mughrabi, "Gazans Burn Danish Flags, Demand Cartoon Apology," Reuters, January 31, 2006.

61. "Gaza EU Offices Raided by Gunmen."

62. "Danes and Muslims."

63. Alan Cowell, "Dane Defends Press Freedom."

64. Shadid and Sullivan, "Anatomy"; Alan Cowell, "More European Papers Print Cartoons of Muhammad, Fueling Dispute with Muslims," *New York Times*, February 2, 2006, http://www.nytimes.com/2006/02/02/international/europe/02danish.html.

65. "Bomb Hoax at France-Soir Follows Similar Threats Against other European Newspapers," Reporters Without Borders, February 7, 2006, http://www.rsf.org/article.php3?id_article=16342.

66. "Envoys Meet As Muslim Anger Grows," *BBC News*, February 3, 2006, http://news.bbc.co.uk/2/hi/europe/4678280.stm.

67. "Behind the Headlines: How the Arab Media Covered the Danish Cartoon Controversy," *Asharq Alawsat*, February 8, 2006, http://www.aawsat.com/english/news.asp?section=5&id=3715; "Clash of Civilization," *Wall Street Journal*, February 11, 2006, http://www.opinionjournal.com/weekend/hottopic/?id=110007956.

68. "Sheikh Al-Qaradawi Responds to Cartoons of Prophet Muhammad," MEMRI Special Dispatch Series 1089, February 9, 2006, http://memri.org/bin/articles.cgi?Page=archives&Area=sd&ID=SP108906.

69. "Cartoons Spark Burning of Embassies," *Washington Post*, February 5, 2006, http://www.washingtonpost.com/wp-dyn/content/article/2006/02/04/AR2006020401208.html; Qassim Abdel-Zahra, "Muslims Again Protest Muhammad Caricatures," *AP*, February 3, 2006, http://www.breitbart.com/article.php?id=D8FHNUPG8&show_article=1; Albert Aji, "Syrians Torch Embassies over Caricatures," *AP*, February 4, 2006, http://www.chinadaily.com.cn/english/doc/2006-02/05/content_517149.htm.

70. "Muslim Cartoon Fury Claims Lives," *BBC News*, February 6, 2006, http://news.bbc.co.uk/2/hi/4684652.stm.

71. "Taleban Say 100 Enlist for Suicide Attacks over Cartoons," *Khaleej Times* (*AFP*), February 9, 2006.

72. Abdullah Shiri, "Saudi Cleric Demands Trial over Drawings," *AP*, February 11, 2006, http://islamdaily.net/EN/Contents.aspx?AID=4063.

73. "Two Die in Pakistan Cartoon Clash," *BBC News*, February 14, 2006, http://news.bbc.co.uk/2/hi/south_asia/4711318.stm.

74. "Fresh Pakistan Cartoon Protests," *BBC News*, February 16, 2006, http://news.bbc.co.uk/2/hi/south_asia/4718958.stm; "40,000 in Karachi Protest Cartoons of Muhammad," *AP*, February 17, 2006, http://www.washingtonpost.com/wpdyn/content/article/2006/02/16/AR2006021602136.html.

75. "Muslim Cartoon Fury Claims Lives"; Lee Keath, "Friday Brings New Prophet Drawing Protests," *AP*, February 10, 2006, http://muzi.com/news/ll/english/10003182.shtml.

76. "Europarliament Condemns Killing of Priest in Turkey," *Zenit*, February 21, 2006, http://www.zenit.org/article-15341?l=english; "CSI Deplores Wave of Islamic Violence against Freedom of Expression," Christian Solidarity International press release, February 8, 2006, http://www.csi-int.org/archives.php?inhId=1139498235&bstFam=2&arc=1&sId=01234280636&sucHL=&sucJahr=; "Benedict XVI Hopes Priest's Murder Stirs Solidarity," *Zenit*, February 6, 2006, http://www.zenit.org/article-15202?l=english.

77. Annia Ciezadlo, "What the Cartoon Jihadists Want," *New Republic*, February 16, 2006.

78. Ali Kotarumalos, "Muslims Assault U.S. Embassy in Indonesia."

79. Peter Lamprecht, "Cartoon Protestors in Pakistan Target Christians," *Compass Direct News*, February 20, 2006.

80. Dean Nelson, "Minister Offers £6m to Behead Cartoonist," *Sunday Times*, February 19, 2006, http://www.timesonline.co.uk/tol/news/world/article732451.ece.

81. "Nigerian Priest: Another Victim of Violence," *Zenit*, February 21, 2006, http://www.zenit.org/article-15339?l=english; Njadvara Musa, "Cartoon Protests Leave 15 Dead in Nigeria," *AP*, February 18, 2006.

82. In Klausen's assessment, by February, Egypt and the OIC had decided to end the conflict and "hand the matter over to the United Nations" but were overtaken by events; see *Cartoons That Shook the World*, 53.

83. "Muslim Cartoon Fury Claims Lives," *BBC News*, February 6, 2006; "Iran President Orders Economic Reprisals for Cartoons," *AFP*, February 5, 2006, http://www.abc.net.au/news/newsitems/200602/s1562601.htm.

84. "Cartoon Crisis is EU Fight," *AFP*, February 22, 2006; "Pakistan Crackdown over Cartoons," *BBC News*, February 17, 2006, http://news.bbc.co.uk/2/hi/south_asia/4722712.stm; the reward was offered for killing the cartoonist (singular) according to the BBC original, and it may be that the bounty offerers, as well as others, were unaware that the cartoons were drawn by twelve different people.

85. Qassim Abdel-Zahra, "Muslims Again Protest Muhammad Caricatures"; Ewen MacAskill, Sandra Laville, and Luke Harding, "Cartoon Controversy Spreads Throughout Muslim World," *The Guardian*, February 4, 2006, http://www.guardian.co.uk/world/2006/feb/04/muhammadcartoons.pressandpublishing; "Musharaff in Cartoon Condemnation," *BBC News*, February 3, 2006, http://news.bbc.co.uk/2/hi/south_asia/4676776.stm.

86. "Two Die in Pakistan Cartoon Clash"; Paivi Munter, Annukka Oksanen, and Roula Khalaf, "Nordic States Fear Spread of Mid East Attacks," *Financial Times*, February 5, 2006.

87. Shiri, "Saudi Cleric Demands Trial over Drawings."

88. "Asia's Moderate Muslims," *Wall Street Journal*, February 8, 2006, http://www.atimes.com/se-asia/CI28Ae01.html.

89. "Islam-West Divide 'Grows Deeper.'"

90. "Dubai Sacks U.S. Prof; Kuwait Echoes 'Calm'; Four Killed," *Arab Times* (Kuwait), February 8, 2006.

91. Qassim Abdel-Zahra, "Muslims again Protest Muhammad Caricatures"; MacAskill, Laville, and Harding, "Cartoon Controversy Spreads Throughout Muslim World"; Sebastian Usher, "Saudi Ppaper 'Shut' in Cartoon Row," *BBC News*, February 20, 2006, http://news.bbc.co.uk/2/hi/4734500.stm; Michael Slackman and Hassan M. Fattah, "Furor over Cartoons Pits Muslim Against Muslim," *New York Times*, February 22, 2006, http://www.nytimes.com/2006/02/22/international/middleeast/22cartoons.html; "Syria: Journalist Charged after Advocating Dialogue," UN Office for the Coordination of Humanitarian Affairs, *Integrated Regional Information Networks*, February 12, 2006, http://www.irinnews.org/report.aspx?reportid=26127.

92. "Declaration of Fatwa by World islamic [sic] Scholars about Danish Cartoons," February 20, 2006, http://www.theamericanmuslim.org/tam.php/features/articles/declaration_of_fatwa_by_world_islamic_scholars_about_danish_cartoons; Klausen, *Cartoons* (n. 7 above), 105.

93. Eli Lake, "A Surprise in a Supermarket in Cairo," *New York Sun*, February 13, 2006.

94. Shiri, "Saudi Cleric Demands Trial over Drawings."

95. European Commission Against Racism and Intolerance, CRI (2006) 18, *Third report on Denmark*, adopted December 16, 2005, released May 16, 2006, http://hudoc.ecri.coe.int/XMLEcri/ENGLISH/Cycle_03/03_CbC_eng/DNK-CbC-III-2006-18-ENG.pdf; "EU Media Code Set to Follow Muslim Cartoons Row," *TheParliament.com*, http://www.eupolitix.com/latestnews/news-article/newsarticle/eu-media-code-set-to-follow-muslim-cartoons-row/; "EU Commissioner Lashes out at Mohammed Drawings," *Copenhagen Post*, December 23, 2005.

96. "Usama bin Laden Criticizes Europe for Anti-Islamic Cartoons, Vows Reaction," *AP*, March 19, 2008; Yassin Musharbash, "Online Magazine Hints at Attacks on Papers That Ran Muhammad Caricatures," *Der Spiegel*, May 5, 2006; "Al-Qaeda Video Calls for Attacks over Mohammed Videos [sic]," *AFP*, May 11, 2006.

97. "Will Kill Mohammed Caricaturists," *Aftenposten*, May 4, 2006.

98. "Mohammed Cartoons 'Sparked Bomb Plot,'" *The Australian*, September 2, 2006.

99. "Cartoons Possible Terror Motive," *Copenhagen Post*, May 10, 2007; "Three Jailed for Planned Copenhagen Astacks," *France 24*, November 23, 2007, http://www.france24.com/france-24Public/en/archives/news/europe/20071123-Denmark-bomb-attack-imprisoned-Muslims-Iraqi-Kurd.php.

100. "A Suspect in the Vollsmose terror Case Said the Cu [sic]," *Copenhagen Post*, October 4, 2007, http://www.cphpost.dk/news/1/4096.html.

101. "Islamic Extremists Threaten Denmark with Poison," *Copenhagen Post*, September 15, 2008.
102. Moumine Ngarmbassa, "Chad Halts 'Holy War' by Muslim Leader, 70 Killed," *Reuters*, July 2, 2008.
103. "Danish Cartoons 'Plotters' Held," *BBC News*, February 12, 2008.
104. "Tunisians Had Planned to Strangle prophet Cartoonist—Report," *Dow Jones Newswires*, June 19, 2009.
105. "Danish court rules on Tunisians held over murder plot," *Deutsche Presse-Agentur (DPA)*, November 19, 2008.
106. "Danish Caricaturist of Muhammad Fame Now Homeless," *Der Spiegel*, February 20, 2008.
107. "Danish Muhammad cartoon reprinted," *BBC News*, February 13, 2008.
108. "European Newspapers Reprint Prophet Mohammed Cartoon," *CNN*, February 13, 2008; Jakob Illeborg, "A Turn for the Worse," *The Guardian*, February 20, 2008, http://www.guardian.co.uk/commentisfree/2008/feb/20/aturnfortheworse, notes that the mood in Europe seems to have changed between the initial controversy and February 2008.
109. Michael Kimmelman, "Outrage at Cartoons Still Tests the Danes," *New York Times*, March 20, 2008; "Danish Muhammad Cartoon Reprinted," *BBC News*, February 13, 2008.
110. Flemming Rose, "Free Speech and Radical Islam," *Wall Street Journal*, February 15, 2008.
111. "Denmark Evacuates Embassies in Algeria, Afghanistan," *AP*, April 23, 2008.
112. "Danish Appeals Court Rejects Lawsuit Against Newspaper That Published Prophet Cartoons," *International Herald Tribune*, June 19, 2008; Souad Mekhennet and Alan Cowell, "Qaeda Group Says It Bombed Embassy," *New York Times*, June 6, 2008, http://www.nytimes.com/2008/06/06/world/asia/06pstan.html?ex=1370404800&en=036b0551a6ac7b3f&ei=5124&partner=permalink&exprod=permalink.
113. "Al Qaeda Repeats Threat to Danes," *New York Times*, September 6, 2008. Investigators also later found that preparations for the attack were "similar to previous attacks by Taliban linked to Al-Qaeda"; see "Pakistani Taliban Targeted Danes after Cartoons: Officials," *AFP*, June 3, 2008.
114. "2 Chicago Men Charged in Terror Plot over Muhammad Cartoons," *Fox News*, October 27, 2009, http://www.foxnews.com/story/0,2933,569780,00.html; James Bone, "'Mickey Mouse' Project Plotted to Kill Muhammad Cartoonist," *Times Online*, October 28, 2009, http://www.timesonline.co.uk/tol/news/world/us_and_americas/article6892968.ece.
115. Matthew Campbell, "Panic Room Saved Artist Kurt Westergaard from Islamist Assassin," *Times* (U.K.), January 3, 2010, http://www.timesonline.co.uk/tol/news/world/article6973966.ece; "Somali Charged over Attack on Danish Cartoonist," *BBC News*, January 2, 2010, http://news.bbc.co.uk/2/hi/europe/8437652.stm.
116. Klausen, *Cartoons That Shook the World*, 107.
117. Ibid., 4.
118. Oleg Grabar, "Seeing Is Believing. The Image of the Prophet in Islam: The Real Story," *The New Republic*, November 4, 2009. Grabar previously had two books published by Yale University Press with such images.
119. Pope Benedict XVI, "Faith, Reason and the University: Memories and Reflections," Lecture of the Holy Father at the University of Regensburg, September 12, 2006, http://www.vatican.va/holy_father/benedict_xvi/speeches/2006/september/documents/hf_ben-xvi_spe_20060912_university-regensburg_en.html. The version currently posted reads "a startling brusqueness, a brusqueness that we find unacceptable," but this passage was not in the original lecture and was added in October 2006. The lecture is discussed in James V. Schall, ed., *The Regensburg Lecture* (South Bend: St. Augustine's Press, 2007).
120. "Pope Criticized over Islam Remarks," *Al Jazeera*, September 15, 2006, http://english.aljazeera.net/archive/2006/09/200849154441682442.html.
121. Benjamin Harvey, "Muslim Anger over Papal Comments Ggrows," *AP*, September 15, 2006; "Report: Rome Tightens Pope's Security after Furor over Islam Remarks," *Ha'aretz*, September 17, 2006; Suzan Fraser, "Turkish Lawmaker compares Pope to Hitler," *AP*, September 16, 2006.
122. "Pope Upset That Muslims Offended," *CNN*, September 16, 2006.

123. "Fresh Criticism of Pope's Remarks," *BBC News*, September 16, 2006.

124. Joelle Bassoul, "Fears of Violent Mideast Backlash to Pope," *AFP*, September 15, 2006; "Pope Upset That Muslims Offended"; Harvey, "Muslim Anger over Papal Comments Grows"; Stephen Brown, "Pope to Give Blessing as Pressure for Apology Grows," Reuters, September 16, 2006; Stephen Brown, "Pope Apology Fails to Stop Backlash," *Herald Sun* (Australia), September 17, 2006; "Rome Tightens Pope's Security after Furor over Islam Remarks"; Fraser, "Turkish Lawmaker Compares Pope to Hitler."

125. "Israeli-US Plot Behind Pope's Remarks: Iran Hardline Press," *AFP*, September 17, 2006; "Cardinal Adds to Islam-violence Debate," Reuters, September 19, 2006.

126. Ian Fisher, "Some Muslim Leaders Want Pope to Apologize," *New York Times*, September 16, 2006. Rana Jawad, "Pakistan Parliament Demands Pope Retract Islam Comments," *AFP*, September 15, 2006; "Pakistan's Parliament Adopts Resolution Condemning Pope's Remarks about Islam," *AP*, September 15, 2006.

127. Stephen Brown, "Pope to Give Blessing as Pressure for Apology Grows."

128. "Pope's Speech Stirs Muslim Anger," *BBC News*, September 14, 2006.

129. "Pope Criticized over Islam Remarks."

130. Fraser, "Turkish Lawmaker Compares Pope to Hitler"; Fisher, "Some Muslim Leaders Want Pope to Apologize."

131. Harvey, "Muslim Anger over Papal Comments Grows"; Anthony Shadid, "Remarks by Pope Prompt Muslim Outrage, Protests," *Washington Post*, September 16, 2006; Bassoul, "Fears of Violent Mideast Backlash to Pope."

132. "Palestinians Open Fire Inside Nablus Church," *AFP*, September 16, 2006; Ali Daraghmeh, "Five Palestinian Area Churches Attacked," *AP*, September 16, 2006; "West Bank Churches Attacked after Pope Remarks," *New York Times*, September 16, 2006.

133. Shadid, "Remarks by Pope Prompt Muslim Outrage, Protests"; "Second Assyrian Christian Killed in Retaliation for Pope's Remarks," *Assyrian International NewsAgency*, September 17, 2006, http://www.aina.org/news/20060917014616.htm.

134. "Egypt's Top Christian Leader Denounces Comments," *The Age* (Australia), September 16, 2006; Nadia Abou El-Magd, "Mideast Christians in Uneasy Position," *AP*, September 17, 2006.

135. "Pope's Statement in Full," *CNN*, September 16, 2006.

136. "Pope Upset That Muslims Offended"; Brown, "Pope Apology Fails to Stop Backlash."

137. "Rome Tightens Pope's Security after Furor over Islam Remarks."

138. "'Jihad' Vowed over Pope's Speech," *SwissInfo*, September 18, 2006; Nadia Abou El-Magd, "Mideast Christians in Uneasy Position," *AP*, September 17, 2006.

139. Mohamed Sheikh Nor, "Italian Nun Slain by Somali Gunmen," *AP*, September 17, 2006; "Religious in Somalia Died Forgiving Her Killers; Sister Loenella Sgorbati to Be Buried in Kenya," *Zenit*, September 18, 2006; "Italian Nun Slain in Somalia," Reuters, September 17, 2006; "Gunmen Shoot Elderly Nun Dead," *The Weekend Australian*, September 16, 2006; "Somali Cleric Calls for Pope's Death," *AFP*, September 17, 2006; "Vatican Denounces Nun's Murder in Somalia," *Zenit*, September 17, 2006; Selcan Hacaoglu, "Muslims Seek Detailed Apology from Pope," *AP*, September 19, 2006; "Benedict XVI Praises Slain Nun," *Zenit*, September 24, 2006.

140. Ian Fisher, "In a Rare Step, Pope Expresses Personal Regret," *New York Times*, September 18, 2006; "Pope's Comments Published in Arabic," *Zenit*, September 19, 2006; *Zenit*, September 28, 2006.

141. "Kashmir City Shuts in Protest over Pope's Remarks," Reuters, September 18, 2006; B. Raman, "LET Issues Fatwa to Kill the Pope," International Terrorism Monitor Paper 133, October 2, 2006; Selcan Hacaoglu, "Lawyer: Pope Gunman Warns Benedict Not to Travel," *AP*, September 18, 2006; "Pope Statement Fails to End Anger," *BBC News*, September 18, 2006.

142. Philip Pullella and Stephen Brown, "Pope Says Anti-Islam Quotes Not His Own Views," Reuters, September 20, 2006; "Pope Expresses 'Deep Respect' for Muslims and Proposes a Positive and Self-Critical Dialogue," *Zenit*, September 20, 2006.

143. Ian Fisher, "In a Rare Step, Pope Expresses Personal Regret," *New York Times*, September 18, 2006. "Cardinal Adds to Islam-violence Debate," Reuters, September 19, 2006. Tracy Ong and Natalie O'Brien, "Pope Row in Past, PM Tells Muslims," *The Australian*, September 20, 2006.

144. "German Bishops Urge Muslims to be Calm," October 4, 2006, ReligionandSpirituality.com, http://www.religionandspirituality.com/view/post/11599361427100/German_bishops_urge_Muslims_to_be_calm/.

145. "German Bishops Urge Muslims to Respect Religious Liberty Describe Criticisms of Papal Address as Unjust," *Zenit*, October 3, 2006.

146. "Pope Stresses Respect for Muslims," *BBC News*, September 25, 2006.

147. Robin Pomery, "Pope Says Christians, Muslims Must Reject Violence," Reuters, September 25, 2009; "Pope Says Dialogue with Islam Vital for Future," *Zenit*, September 25, 2006.

148. "Islamic Foreign Ministers Press Pope to Apologize," Reuters, September 26, 2006; John L. Allen, Jr., "A Challenge, Not a Crusade," *New York Times*, September 19, 2006.

149. "Terror Campaign Targets Chaldean Church in Iraq," *AsiaNews.it*, October 6, 2006, http://www.asianews.it/index.php?l=en&art=7410; Sameer N. Yacoub, "Fourteen Killed in Violence Around Iraq Including Three Baghdad Bombings," *AP*, October 11, 2006; "Relatives of Beheaded Iraqi Priest Say Kidnappers Demanded Apology for Pope," *International Herald Tribune*, October 12, 2006.

150. Maamoun Youssef, "Pan-Arab TV Broadcasts New Bin Laden Tape Calling for Holy War to Liberate Palestine," *AP*, March 20, 2008.

151. John Thavis for Catholic News Service, "Islamic Scholars Write Pope, Take Issue with Remarks in German Speech," *Florida Catholic*, October 18, 2006; "Text: Muslim Scholars' Open Letter to Pope Benedict," *Independent Catholic News*, October 19, 2006, http://www.indcatholicnews.com/news.php?viewStory=6924.

152. Lars Ströman, "The Right to Ridicule a Religion," *Nerikes Allehanda*, English version published August 28, 2007, http://www.na.se/artikel.asp?intId=1209676.

153. James Savage, "Paper Defends Muhammad Dog Cartoon," *The Local* (Sweden), August 28, 2007.

154. Paul Marshall, "A Scandinavian Sequel," *National Review Online*, August 31, 2007; "Iran Protests over Swedish Muhammad Cartoon," *The Local* (Sweden), August 27, 2007.

155. "Ahmedinejad Claims 'Zionists' Behind Swedish Cartoon," *The Local* (Sweden), August 28, 2007.

156. Ministry of Foreign Affairs, Pakistan, "Pakistan Condemns the Publication of Offensive Sketches in Sweden," press release No. 234/2007, August 30, 2007.

157. Peter Hall, "'Jihad Jane' Ccodefendant Pleads Guilty to Terrorism Charge," *Los Angeles Times*, March 10, 2011, http://articles.latimes.com/2011/mar/10/nation/la-na-terror-plea-20110310.

158. Eamon Quinn and John F. Burns, "In Ireland, a Hearing on a Plot to Kill a Swedish Cartoonist," *New York Times*, March 15, 2010, http://www.nytimes.com/2010/03/16/world/europe/16ireland.html; "Arrests in Ireland over Swedish Cartoonist Plot," *New York Times*, March 9, 2010, http://www.nytimes.com/aponline/2010/03/09/world/AP-EU-Swedish-Cartoonist.html; Ian Urbina, "U.S. Woman Charged in Terror Plot Pleads Not Guilty," *New York Times*, March 18, 2010, http://www.nytimes.com/2010/03/19/us/19jane.html; United States Attorney, Eastern District of Pennsylvania, U.S. Department of Justice, "Pennsylvania Woman Indicted in Plot to Recruit Violent Jihadist Fighters and Commit Murder Overseas," March 9, 2010, http://www.justice.gov/usao/pae/News/Pr/2010/mar/larose_release.pdf.

159. "Populist Politician Blasts Koran, Mohammed," *Daily Telegraph* (Australia), February 14, 2007.

160. "Saudi Wants Dutch MP Apology for Islam Offence: Paper," *Reuters*, February 18, 2007.

161. Henryk M. Broder, "How a Film Triggered a Global Panic"; Leander Schaerlackens, "Dutch Film to Slam Islam"; Ian Traynor, "'I Don't Hate Muslims. I Hate Islam,' Says Holland's Rising Political Star."

162. "Dutch Lawmaker Gets Death Threat over Koran Film," *Xinhua*, February 27, 2008; "Al Qaeda Fatwa Against MP Wilders," NIS News Bulletin, February 28, 2008 http://www.freerepublic.com/focus/news/1977320/posts.

163. Stefan Nicola, "Analysis: Anti-Islam Film Scares the Hague," *UPI Energy*, January 22, 2008; Mike Cooper, "Iran Warns Dutch Lawmaker's Anti-Quran Film Would 'Breed Violence,'" *AP*, March 11, 2008; Elettra Neysmith, "Iranians Urge Dutch to Ban Film," *BBC News*, February 16, 2008; "Hundreds of Afghans Protest Danish Prophet Cartoon, Dutch Film Criticizing Quran," *AP*, March 5, 2008; Stephen Graham, "Pakistan Lifts Curbs on YouTube, Says 'Blasphemous' Video Clip Has Been Removed," *AP*, February 27, 2008; Peter Svensson, "Pakistan Attempts to Block Local YouTube Access, Takes out Site for Two-thirds of World," *AP*, February 26, 2008.

164. "A Dutch Antagonist of Islam Waits for His Premiere," *New York Times*, March 22, 2008.

165. "Dutch TV Stations refuse Anti-Muslim Film," *Washington Times*, March 7, 2008; "Dutch Protest Anti-Koran Film," *MSNBC.com*, March 22, 2008; Gregory Crouch, "A Dutch Antagonist of Islam Waits for His Premiere," *New York Times*, March 22, 2008.

166. "Dutch Islam Film Website 'Shut,'" *BBC News*, March 23, 2008, http://news.bbc.co.uk/2/hi/europe/7310439.stm.

167. "Website Withdraws Dutch MP's Anti-Islam Film after Threats," *AFP*, March 29, 2008.

168. "Film Critical of Islam Dropped from Website," *CNN*, March 28, 2008.

169. "Cartoonist to Sue over Islam Film," *BBC News*, March 28, 2008.

170. Michael Steen and Andrew Bounds, "Muslim Reaction to Dutch Film Is Muted," *Financial Times*, March 28, 2008; "Muslim Group Asks for Court Review," *International Herald Tribune*, March 28, 2008; "UN Chief Condemns Anti-Islam Film," *BBC News*, March 28, 2008; Text of UN press release via States News Service, "High Commissioner for Human Rights Condemns Wilders' Film and Calls for Appropriate Legal Responses," March 28, 2008.

171. "Statement by H. E. Professor Ekmeleddin Ihsanoglu, Secretary General of the Organization of the Islamic Conference on the Release of the Blasphemous Documentary Film 'Fitna,'" March 28, 2008, http://www.oic-oci.org/oicnew/topic_detail.asp?t_id=907&x_key.

172. M. Ghazanfar Ali Khan, "Wilders Film Aims to Block Dialogue: WAMY," *Arab News*, March 31, 2008.

173. "Malaysian opposition party calls for Dutch boycott over anti-Islam film," *AP*, March 31, 2008.

174. Niclas Mika for *Reuters*, "Iran, Indonesia Angry over Dutch Koran Film," *National Post* (Canada), March 28, 2008; "Indonesia Criticizes Dutch Film Critical of Islam," *International Herald Tribune*, March 28, 2008; "Indonesia Bans Dutch filmmaker, Warns Against Violent Protest," *AFP*, April 1, 2008; "Indonesian Internet Providers start Blocking Dutch Film: Report," *AFP*, April 5, 2008; "Arab, Muslim Leaders Denounce Film by Dutch Filmmaker," *AP*, March 29, 2008; "UN Chief Condemns Anti-Islam Film," *BBC News*, March 28, 2008; "500 Pak Lawyers Protest Against Anti-Islam Dutch Film," Asian News International, April 15, 2008. Pakistani Christian leaders also protested the film; see "Bishop Condemns Anti-Islam Film and Caricatures," *Daily Times* (Pakistan), April 17, 2008; "Pakistani Islamic Women Protest 'Anti-Islam' Film, Cartoons," *AFP*, April 26, 2008; "Pakistanis Protest Dutch Anti-Koran Film," *AFP*, May 3, 2008.

175. "Muslim, UN Outrage over Dutch MP's Anti-Islam Film," *AFP*, March 28, 2008.

176. Eliane Engeler, "Muslim Countries Slam Dutch Anti-Quran Film at UN," *AP*, April 15, 2008; Human Rights Council—First Universal Periodic Review, Geneva, April 7–18 2008, http://www.un.org/webcast/unhrc/archive.asp?go=080415.

177. Tahir Niaz, "Pakistan Asks EU to Amend Laws on Freedom of Expression," *Daily Times* (Pakistan), June 8, 2008.

178. Asif Shahzad, "Car Bombing Outside Danish Embassy in Pakistan Kills at Least 6," *AP*, June 2, 2008. In the Netherlands itself, on May 29, some Dutch businesses threatened a lawsuit against Wilders for any commercial losses if Muslim countries boycotted Dutch goods in protest against the film; "Dutch Businesses Threaten to Sue over Anti-Islam film," *AFP*, May 29, 2008.

179. Resolution 1510 (2006), Parliamentary Assembly of the Council of Europe (PACE), June 28, 2006, http://assembly.coe.int/main.asp?Link=/documents/adoptedtext/ta06/eres1510.htm.

180. "Arab Columnists: Islam Has Been Harmed More by Muslims Than by the West," MEMRI Special Dispatch No. 1951, June 6, 2008.

Chapter 11

1. "U.N. Aid and Sudan Clash on Islamic Laws," *New York Times*, March 8, 1994, http://www.nytimes.com/1994/03/08/world/un-aide-and-sudan-clash-on-islamic-laws.html?scp=1&sq=U.N.%20Aide%20and%20Sudan%20Clash%20on%20Islamic%20Laws&st=cse. The agreements in question were the Covenant on Civil and Political Rights and the Convention on the Rights of the Child.

2. *Situation of Human Rights in the Sudan—Report of the Special Rapporteur, Mr. Gáspár Bíró, submitted in accordance with Commission on Human Rights Resolution 1993/60*, UN Commission on Human Rights, 50th session, February 1, 1994, E/CN.4/1994/48, pp. 15–16.

3. Letter dated February 18, 1994, from the Permanent Representative of Sudan to the United Nations Office at Geneva addressed to the Assistant Secretary-General for Human Rights, UN Commission on Human Rights, 50th session, March 1, 1994, E/CN.4/1994/122.

4. As quoted in *Report of the Secretary-General submitted in accordance with Commission on Human Rights resolution 1995/75*, UN Commission on Human Rights, 52nd session, February 22, 1996, E/CN.4/1996/57, http://www.unhchr.ch/Huridocda/Huridoca.nsf/TestFrame/e2f2cb75181e115b802566da0040304c?Opendocument.

5. *Report of the Special Rapporteur on freedom of religion or belief, Asma Jahangir, and the Special Rapporteur on contemporary forms of racism, racial discrimination, xenophobia and related intolerance, Doudou Diène, further to Human Rights Council decision 1/107 on incitement to racial and religious hatred and the promotion of tolerance*, UN Human Rights Council, 2nd session, September 20, 2006, A/HRC/2/3, http://daccess-dds-ny.un.org/doc/UNDOC/GEN/G06/139/90/PDF/G0613990.pdf?OpenElement.

6. Membership includes the "State of Palestine." See "Timeline: Organisation of the Islamic Conference," *BBC News*, September 18, 2008, http://news.bbc.co.uk/2/hi/middle_east/country_profiles/1564339.stm. The organization has repeatedly insisted that the international community distinguish between terrorism and what it calls a legitimate fight for self-determination; see, for example, Convention of the Organisation of the Islamic Conference on Combating International Terrorism, http://www.oic-oci.org/english/convenion/terrorism_convention.htm).

7. "Muslim Leaders Want to Curb 'Islamophobia,'" *MSNBC.com*, March 14, 2008, http://www.msnbc.msn.com/id/23639629/; *2nd OIC Observatory Report on Islamophobia (June 2008 to April 2009)*, issued at the 36th Council of Foreign Ministers, Damascus, May 23–25, 2009, http://www.oic-oci.org/uploads/file/Islamphobia/Islamophobia_rep_May_23_25_2009.pdf.

8. Charter of the Organisation of the Islamic Conference, March 14, 2008, http://www.oic-oci.org/is11/english/Charter-en.pdf.

9. *Ten-Year Programme of Action to Meet the Challenges Facing the Muslim Ummah in the 21st Century*, Third Extraordinary Session of the Islamic Summit Conference, Organisation of the Islamic Conference, December 7–8, 2005, http://www.oic-oci.org/ex-summit/english/10-years-plan.htm; "Islamophobia," from OIC journal issue 1, http://www.oic-oci.org/english/article/islamophobia.htm.

10. *Cairo Declaration on Human Rights in Islam*, adopted during the Nineteenth Islamic Conference of Foreign Ministers (Session of Peace, Interdependence and Development), Cairo, Egypt, 31 July to August 5, 1990, http://www.oicun.org/articles/54/1/Cairo-Declaration-on-Human-Rights-in-Islam/1.html. For an analysis of the Declaration, see Anne Elizabeth Mayer, *Islam and Human Rights: Tradition and Politics*, 3rd ed. (Boulder: Westview Press, 1999).

11. *Support by the United Nations system of the efforts of Governments to promote and consolidate new or restored democracies*, Report of the Secretary-General, August 23, 2007, A/62/296, p. 16. For references to Cairo also see, for example, Report of the United Nations High Commissioner for Human Rights, Economic and Social Council, Substantive session of 1999, Geneva, July 29, 1999, E/1999/96, p. 11, and resolution 1998/17 (August 21, 1998)

on the Situation of Women in Afghanistan, which misleadingly pronounced that "the Cairo Declaration on Human Rights in Islam, adopted by the Organization of the Islamic Conference in 1990, guarantees the rights of women in all fields" (in Report of the Sub-Commission on Prevention of Discrimination and Protection of Minorities, E/CN.4/1999/4 (also listed under E/CN.4/Sub.2/1998/45), pp. 49–50. For a complete list search for "Cairo Declaration on Human Rights" in the UN Official Document System, see http://documents.un.org/advance.asp.

12. United Nations Update, *Human Rights Brief* 16, no. 1 (2008): 53–54, http://www.wcl.american.edu/hrbrief/16/1unupdate.pdf?rd=1.

13. "UN Hosts First Meeting Tackling Islam and Human rights," *Agence France Presse (AFP)*, November 9, 1998; "Search for Unity in Cultural Diversity Is Particular Responsibility of the UN, Says UN High Commissioner, Mary Robinson, to Seminar on Islam and Universal Declaration for Human Rights," UN press release, November 9, 1998, http://www.unhchr.ch/huricane/huricane.nsf/(Symbol)/HR.98.85.En?Opendocument.

14. "UN's top human rights official urges action to combat 'Islamophobia,'" UN press release, March 15, 2002, http://www.un.org/apps/news/story.asp?NewsID=3128&Cr=Robinson&Cr1=&Kw1=islam&Kw2=&Kw3.

15. "Islamic Principles Integral Part of Human Rights: UN Rights," *AFP*, March 15, 2002.

16. Summary record of the 20th meeting, 49th session, Sub-Commission on Prevention of Discrimination and Protection of Minorities, UN Commission on Human Rights, held August 19, 1997, released August 22, 1997, E/CN.4/Sub.2/1997/SR.20, p. 7; "Foreign Conspiratorial Schemes Against the Sudan," Resolution 5896, adopted by the Council of the League of Arab States on September 13, 1999, submitted in a letter to the President of the UN Security Council on September 23, 1999, UN document S/1999/997. See also Christian Solidarity International, "Islamic Violence Against Freedom of Expression," letter to UN Secretary-General Kofi Annan, February 8, 2006.

17. *Report by Mr. Maurice Glele-Ahanhanzo, Special Rapporteur on contemporary forms of racism, racial discrimination, xenophobia and related intolerance*, UN Commission on Human Rights, 53rd session, January 16, 1997, E/CN.4/1997/71, p. 14; "UN Rapporteur's 'Offensive' Text Earns Official Rap," *AFP*, April 18, 1997; Summary record of the 68th meeting, 53rd session, UN Commission on Human Rights, April 18, 1997, released September 3, 1997, E/CN.4/SR.68, pp. 4–7; Summary record of the 70th Meeting, 53rd Session, UN Commission on Human Rights, April 28, 1997, E/CN.4/1997/SR.70, p. 7.

18. *Corrigendum to Report by Mr. Maurice Glele-Ahanhanzo, Special Rapportuer on Contemporary Forms of Racism, Racial Intolerance, and Related Discrimination*, UN Commission on Human Rights, July 8, 1997, E/CN.4/1997/71/Corr.1; Summary record of the 11th Meeting, 54th Session, UN Commission on Human Rights, March 25, 1998, E/CN.4/1998/SR.11, p. 10; *Report by Mr. Glele-Ahanhanzo, Special Rapporteur on contemporary forms of racism, racial discrimination, xenophobia and related intolerance*, UN Commission on Human Rights, 55th Session, January 15, 1999, E/CN.4/1999/15, p. 20. See also David Littman, "Islamism Grows Stronger at the United Nations," *Middle East Quarterly* 6, no. 3 (September 1999), http://www.meforum.org/article/477.

19. See for instance A/RES/61/164.

20. Joint written statement submitted by the International Humanist and Ethical Union (IHEU), a nongovernmental organization in special consultative status, the Association for World Education (AWE), and the Association of World Citizens (AWC), nongovernmental organizations on the Roster, UN Human Rights Council, 7th session, submitted February 24, 2008, distributed March 4, 2008, A/HRC/7/NGO/96; "Islamic states seek world freedom curbs: humanists," *Reuters*, March 12, 2008, http://www.reuters.com/article/worldNews/idUSL1277265220080312?feedType=RSS&feedName=worldNews&rpc=22&sp=true.

21. Statement by the International Humanist and Ethical Union at the 21st plenary meeting of the 7th session of the UN Human Rights Council, March 13, 2008, UN Human Rights Council Archived video, http://www.un.org/webcast/unhrc/archive.asp?go=080313; "IHEU

'Ambushed' at Human Rights Council," International Humanist and Ethical Union, March 14, 2008, http://www.iheu.org/node/3115.

22. Joint statement by the Association for World Education and the International Humanist and Ethical Union before the 23rd plenary meeting of the 8th session of the UN Human Rights Council, June 16, 2008, UN Human Rights Council archived video, http://www .un.org/webcast/unhrc/archive.asp?go=080616 (the text of this exchange is found in several different video segments on this page, mostly under the heading "Points of order").

23. Frank Jordans, "Muslim Countries Win Concession Regarding Religious Debates by UN Human Rights Body," *Associated Press (AP)*, June 18, 2008; "U.N.'s Arbour Opposes 'Taboos' in Human Rights Body," Reuters, June 18, 2008, http://www.reuters.com/article/world-News/idUSL1856437520080618.

24. Summary record of the 1st Meeting of the 2nd Session of the UN Human Rights Council, Geneva, September 18, 2006, A/HRC/SR.1, released September 28, 2006.

25. UN Web cast of the 20th Plenary Meeting of the 9th Session of the Human Rights Council, September 23, 2008, http://www.un.org/webcast/unhrc/archive.asp?go=080923.

26. Official record of the 4th plenary meeting of the 54th session of the UN General Assembly, September 20, 1999, A/54/PV.4, p. 34.

27. UN Commission on Human Rights Resolution 1999/82, "Defamation of Religions," adopted April 30, 1999, http://www.unhchr.ch/Huridocda/Huridoca.nsf/(Symbol)/E.CN.4.RES. 1999.82.En?Opendocument.

28. Summary record of the 61st Meeting, 55th session, UN Commission on Human Rights, held April 29, 1999, released October 19, 1999, E/CN.4/1999/SR.61, p. 2.

29. Compare draft resolution "Defamation of Religions," UN Commission on Human Rights, 56th session, April 5, 2000, E/CN.4/2000/L.6, to final resolution 2000/84, April 26, 2000; Pakistani/OIC amendments to the amendments contained in document E/CN.4/2000/L .18 to draft resolution E/CN.4/2000/L.6, UN Commission on Human Rights, 56th session, April 20, 2000, E/CN.4/2000/L.96; see also UNCHR, report on the 56th session, E/CN.4/2000/167 or E/2000/23, pp. 336–38, http://www.unhchr.ch/Huridocda/Huridoca. nsf/(Symbol)/E.CN.4.2000.167+E.2000.23.En?Opendocument.

30. Summary record of the 67th meeting, 56th session, UN Commission on Human Rights, April 26, 2000, released December 1, 2000, E/CN.4/2000/SR.67, pp. 14–15.

31. UNCHR Resolution 2001/4, "Combating Defamation of Religions as a Means to Promote Human Rights, Social Harmony and Religious and Cultural Diversity," adopted April 18, 2001, http://www.unhchr.ch/huridocda/huridoca.nsf/(Symbol)/E.CN.4.RES.2001.4.En?Open document.

32. Audio recording of the 61st meeting of the 57th session of the UN Commission on Human Rights, April 18, 2001, http://www.unhchr.ch/html/menu2/2/57chr/57audio.htm.

33. Guatemala, India, Nigeria, the Republic of Korea, South Africa, and several other African nations abstained. UNCHR, Report on the 57th Session, Supplement No. 3, UN Economic and Social Council, Official Records, 2001, E/2001/23 or E/CN.4/2001/167, p. 372, http:// www.unhchr.ch/Huridocda/Huridoca.nsf/e06a5300f90fa0238025668700518ca4/4788ae 6d51ed9fe8c1256a920035e0ba/$FILE/G0115748.pdf.

34. Summary record of the 39th meeting of the 58th session, UN Commission on Human Rights, April 15, 2002, released April 19, 2002, E/CN.4/2002/SR.39, pp. 6–8.

35. From (in order): *Report by Mr. Doudou Diène, Special Rapporteur on contemporary forms of racism, racial discrimination, xenophobia and related intolerance, submitted pursuant to Commission on Human Rights resolution 2002/9*, UN Commission on Human Rights, 59th session, January 3, 2003, E/CN.4/2003/23; *Situation of Muslim and Arab peoples in various parts of the world—Report by Mr. Doudou Diène, Special Rapporteur on contemporary forms of racism, racial discrimination, xenophobia and related intolerance*, UN Commission on Human Rights, February 23, 2004, E/CN.4/2004/19; *Addendum* to the previous, December 13, 2004, E/ CN.4/2005/18/Add.4.

36. September 2, 2008, A/HRC/9/12.

37. *Situation of Muslim and Arab peoples in various parts of the world* (2004 report); *Situation of Muslim and Arab peoples in various parts of the world – Report by Mr. Doudou Diène, Special Rapporteur on contemporary forms of racism, racial discrimination, xenophobia and related intolerance*, UN Commission on Human Rights, 62nd session, February 13, 2006, E/CN.4/2006/17.

38. January 3, 2003, E/CN.4/2003/23.

39. February 13, 2006, E/CN.4/2006/17, p. 7.

40. February 13, 2006, E/CN.4/2006/17.

41. August 21, 2007, A/HRC/6/6; Statement of Doudou Diène, Special Rapporteur on contemporary forms of racism, racial discrimination, xenophobia and related intolerance (as translated by a UN translator) before the 4th plenary meeting of the 6th session of the UN Human Rights Council, September 14, 2007, UN Human Rights Council archived video, http://www.un.org/webcast/unhrc/archive.asp?go=070914; also see "Islamophobia on Rise, Especially in Europe: UN Envoy," *New York Times*, September 14, 2007. Diène also alleged that Islamophobia was "exceptional" since not only Muslims are attacked but also "the religion itself, Islam, its sacred book, the Koran, and its prophet, Mohammed, which is virtually unparalleled in today's world," February 23, 2004, E/CN.4/2004/19, p. 5.

42. August 21, 2007, A/HRC/6/6; September 2, 2008, A/HRC/9/12; statement before the 4th plenary meeting of the 6th session of the UN Human Rights Council.

43. In a rare instance when he acknowledged that "Islamophobia also stems from the attitude and behavior of some Muslims," he quickly emphasized that this was connected to a "sense of victimization" produced by "the widespread influence of foreign powers over the course of the past century in the Middle East" (August 21, 2007, A/HRC/6/6).

44. December 13, 2004, E/CN.4/2005/18/Add.4.

45. *Report of the Special Rapporteur...Asma Jahangir, and the Special Rapporteur...Doudou Diène*, p. 8.

46. Ibid., 10.

47. Ibid., 12, 15.

48. "Combating Defamation of Religions," UN General Assembly, 60th session, resolution 60/150, adopted December 16, 2005, released January 20, 2006, A/RES/60/150.

49. Official records of the 64th plenary meeting of the 60th session of the UN General Assembly, December 16, 2005, A/60/PV.64, p. 11. Voting patterns were similar to those in the commission: the OIC together with Russia, China, and other allies in Africa, Latin America, and Asia, versus the European Union and other European countries, Australia, Canada, Israel, the United States, and some additional countries, with India and others abstaining.

50. UNCHR Resolution 2005/23, "Combating Defamation of Religions," adopted April 12, 2005, in *Report on the Sixty-First Session, UN Commission on Human Rights, March 14–April 22, 2005, Supplement No. 3*, E/2005/3 or E/CN.4/2005/134, pp. 21–24. The session record for 2005 (E/CN.4/2005/SR.44) is available in French only.

51. "Prophet Cartoons Worry UN Commissioner," *The Copenhagen Post*, December 7, 2005, http://www.freerepublic.com/focus/f-news/1537044/posts; original *Berlingske Tidende* article (Danish), http://www.berlingske.dk/article/20051207/danmark/112070743/.

52. *Ten-Year Programme of Action.*

53. "UN Urged to Ban Attack on Religion," *AlJazeera.net*, January 29, 2006, http://english.aljazeera.net/archive/2006/01/200849154847426825.html, as translated in Middle East Media Research Institute, "Sheikh Al-Qaradhawi Responds to Cartoons of Prophet Muhammad," Special Dispatch Series 1089, February 9, 2006, http://memri.org/bin/latest-news.cgi?ID=SD108906.

54. Summary record of the 48th meeting of the Third Committee, UN General Assembly, 61st session, November 17, 2006, released January 9, 2006, A/C.3/61/SR.48, pp. 3–5.

55. Summary record of the 49th meeting of the Third Committee, 62nd session, UN General Assembly, held November 20, 2007, distributed December 14, 2007, A/C.3/62/SR.49. The U.S. delegate also, troublingly, stated that "[h]is delegation agreed with many of the general tenets in the draft resolution" but felt it focused too much on a single religion.

56. Decision 2006/107, "Incitement to Racial and Religious Hatred and the Promotion of Tolerance," June 30, 2006, in *Report to the General Assembly on the First Session of the Human Rights Council*, UNHRC, July 5, 2006, A/HRC/1/L.10/ADD.1, p. 23.

57. *Report to the General Assembly on the Fourth Session of the Human Rights Council*, UNHRC, released June 12, 2007, A/HRC/4/123, p. 57.

58. References to the UN Charter, the Global Agenda for Dialogue, and the Millennium Declaration were dropped; reference to the World Summit 2005 and to various reports by the special rapporteurs were added; see "Combating Defamation of Religions," UN Human Rights Council, March 30, 2007, A/HRC/RES/4/9.

59. "Intervention at the Fourth Session of the Human Rights Council," Jubilee Campaign, March 28, 2007; "Intervention at the Fourth Regular Session of the Human Rights Council," Becket Fund, March 27, 2007; "Freedom House Condemns Passage of UN Resolution Supporting Limits on Free Speech," Freedom House/IFEX, March 30, 2007.

60. *Combating Defamation of Religions—Report of the Secretary-General*, UN General Assembly, 62nd session, August 29, 2007, A/62/288.

61. Statement by Ihab Gamaleldin, Egypt, at the 2nd Plenary Meeting of the 6th Session of the UN Human Rights Council, September 13, 2007, UN Human Rights Council archived video, http://www.un.org/webcast/unhrc/archive.asp?go=070913.

62. Statement by Marghoob Saleem Butt of Pakistan on behalf of the Organization of the Islamic Conference at the 2nd Plenary Meeting of the 6th Session of the UN Human Rights Council, September 13, 2007, UN Human Rights Council archived video, http://www.un.org/webcast/unhrc/archive.asp?go=070913.

63. Statements by Masood Khan of Pakistan on behalf of the Organisation of the Islamic Conference, Sameh Shoukry for Egypt, and Abdullah Abbas Rashwan for Saudi Arabia, as translated, at the 33rd plenary meeting of the 6th session the UN Human Rights Council, December 14, 2007, UN Human Rights Council Archived video, http://www.un.org/webcast/unhrc/archive.asp?go=071214. On efforts to change the resolution, see Pakistan (on behalf of the Organization of the Islamic Conference): amendments to draft resolution L.15/Rev.1, in document A/HRC/6/L.49, December 13, 2007; compare to draft resolution, "Elimination of All Forms of Intolerance Based on Religion Based on Religion or Belief," UN Human Rights Council, 6th session, agenda item 3, December 11, 2007, A/HRC/6/L.15/Rev.1.

64. *Combating Defamation of Religions*, UN General Assembly, adopted December 19, 2006, released February 21, 2007, A/RES/61/164.

65. The preamble included a new reference to the Declaration on the Elimination of All Forms of Intolerance and of Discrimination Based on Religion or Belief and welcomed "international and regional initiatives to promote cross-cultural and interfaith harmony"; a clause was added to the operative paragraph on "attempts to identify Islam with terrorism," stating that "equating any religion with terrorism should be rejected and combated by all at all levels." See, UN Document A/HRC/9/7, para. 67 (2008) for finding on defamation practices.

66. L. Bennett Graham, "Defamation of Religions: The End of Pluralism?" *Emory International Law Journal* 23, no. 1 (2009): 72.

67. Resolution 7/36, "Mandate of the Special Rapporteur on the Promotion and Protection of the Right to Freedom of Expression," UN Human Rights Council, adopted March 28, 2008, http://ap.ohchr.org/documents/E/HRC/resolutions/A_HRC_RES_7_36.pdf. The vote was thirty-two to none; abstaining were the European block, Canada, Guatemala, Japan, the Philippines, and the Republic of Korea.

68. Resolution 7/36, section 4(d).

69. Eliane Engeler, "US, Europeans Say Islamic Countries Want to Limit Free Speech at the UN," *AP*, April 1, 2008. http://www.jpost.com/International/Article.aspx?id=96792.

70. "Vote on Freedom of Expression Marks the End of Universal Human Rights," International Humanist and Ethical Union (IHEU), March 30, 2008, http://www.iheu.org/vote-on-freedom-of-expression-marks-the-end-of-universal-human-rights.

71. "Release of 2008 International Religious Freedom Report: Remarks by John V. Hanford III, Ambassador at Large for International Religious Freedom," U.S. State Department press

release, September 19, 2008, http://montevideo.usembassy.gov/usaweb/2008/08-446eEN.shtml.

72. "World Newspaper Congress Condemns UN Human Rights Council on Press Freedoms," *AP*, June 3, 2008; full text at United Nations Resolution, World Association of Newspapers, June 3, 2008, http://www.wan-press.org/article17293.html.

73. Office of the United Nations High Commissioner for Human Rights, "Follow-up to the 2008 Expert Seminar on Articles 19 and 20 of the ICCPR with Regard to Freedom of Expression and Incitement to Hatred," http://www2.ohchr.org/english/issues/opinion/articles1920_iccpr/.

74. *Report of the United Nations High Commissioner for Human Rights and Follow-Up to the World Conference on Human Rights—Addendum: Expert seminar on the links between articles 19 and 20 of the International Covenant on Civil and Political Rights . . . (Geneva, 2–3 October 2008)*; UN Human Rights Council, January 16, 2009, A/HRC/10/31/Add.3.

75. This shift has been noted by other observers, e.g., Graham, in "Defamation of Religions: The End of Pluralism?" 82.

76. September 2, 2008, A/HRC/9/12.

77. *2nd OIC Observatory Report on Islamophobia (June 2008–April 2009)*, issued at the 36th Council of Foreign Ministers, Damascus, May 23–25, 2009, http://www.oic-oci.org/uploads/file/Islamphobia/Islamophobia_rep_May_23_25_2009.pdf.

78. Frank LaRue, UN Special Rapporteur on freedom of opinion and expression, Miklos Haraszti, OSCE Representative on Freedom of the Media, Catalina Botero, OAS Special Rapporteur on freedom of expression, and Faith Pansy Tlakula, ACHPR Special Rapporteur on freedom of expression and access to information, "Joint Declaration on Defamation of Religions, and Anti-Terrorism and Anti-Extremism Legislation," December 10, 2008, http://www.osce.org/documents/rfm/2008/12/35705_en.pdf. The statement also attempted to set boundaries for laws restricting speech advocating terrorism and regulating media coverage of terrorism.

79. As noted in Graham, "Defamation of Religions: The End of Pluralism?" 72. See official records of the 70th plenary meeting of the 63rd session of the UN General Assembly, December 18, 2008, A/63/PV.70. The Western block convinced about twenty mainly African and Latin American countries, along with some island states, to end their support; most switched to abstention.

80. Summary record of the 46th meeting (November 24, 2008) of the Third Committee of the UN General Assembly, 63rd session, distributed January 22, 2009, A/C.3/63/SR.46, pp. 5–7. See also Robert Evans, "Don't Link Islam to Terror, Islamic Chief Urges," Reuters, December 19, 2008.

81. See *Racism, Racial Discrimination, Xenophobia and Related Forms of Intolerance, Follow-Up to and Implementation of the Durban Declaration and Programme of Action*, UN Human Rights Council Resolution, March 26, 2009, A/HRC/10/L.2/Rev.1; and Resolution 10/22, *Combating Defamation of Religions*, adopted March 26, 2009, in Draft report of the Human Rights Council on its tenth session, released May 12, 2009, A/HRC/10/L.11, pp. 78–83. Voting was "YES": Bahrain, Bangladesh, Bolivia, Burkina Faso, China, Cuba, Djibouti, Egypt, Indonesia, Jordan, Kyrgyzstan, Nicaragua, Nigeria, Pakistan, Philippines, Qatar, Russian Federation, Saudi Arabia, Senegal, South Africa; "NO": Argentina, Belgium, Chile, France, Hungary, Italy, Mexico, Netherlands, Norway, Republic of Korea, Slovakia, Slovenia, Ukraine, United Kingdom, United States of America, Uruguay, Bosnia and Herzegovina; "ABSTAIN": Brazil, Cameroon, Ghana, India, Japan, Madagascar, Mauritius; "ABSENT": Angola, Gabon. TOTAL: YES: 20, No: 17, Abstentions: 8. This drop in support parallels the General Assembly vote in December 2009, 80 votes for to 61 against, 42 abstaining. This result was the worst ever for the OIC member states and their supporters.

82. Statement by Mr. Zamir Akram of Pakistan for the OIC at the 5th plenary meeting of the 10th session of the UN Human Rights Council, March 26, 2009, http://www.un.org/webcast/unhrc/archive.asp?go=090326.

83. International Covenant on Civil and Political Rights, available via the Office of the UN High Commissioner for Human Rights at http://www2.ohchr.org/english/law/ccpr.htm. Both sections of article 20 were held, without further explanation, to be "fully compatible with the right of freedom of expression as contained in article 19, the exercise of which carries with it special duties and responsibilities," in Office of the High Commissioner for Human Rights, "General Comment No. 11," July 29, 1983, paragraph 2, http://www .unhchr.ch/tbs/doc.nsf/%28Symbol%29/60dcfa23f32d3feac12563ed00491355?Open document.

84. International Convention on the Elimination of All Forms of Racial Discrimination, available via the Office of the UN High Commissioner for Human Rights at http://www2.ohchr. org/english/law/cerd.htm.

85. The first U.S. reservation to the covenant states: "That article 20 does not authorize or require legislation or other action by the United States that would restrict the right of free speech and association protected by the Constitution and laws of the United States." The sixth U.K. reservation declares: "The Government of the United Kingdom interpret Article 20 consistently with the rights conferred by Articles 19 and 21 of the Covenant and having legislated in matters of practical concern in the interests of public order (ordre public) reserve the right not to introduce any further legislations"; Australia's reservation follows the same lines. Belgium declares: "Article 20 as a whole shall be applied taking into account the rights to freedom of thought and religion, freedom of opinion and freedom of assembly and association." Other European states have entered reservations regarding article 20 (1), which concerns propaganda for war, on free expression grounds, but professes no similar concern over 20 (2). See Status of Treaties: International Covenant on Civil and Political Rights, UN Treaty Collection, http://treaties.un.org/Pages/ViewDetails.aspx?src= TREATY &mtdsg_no=IV-4&chapter=4&lang=en; http://www.bayefsky.com/pdf/usa_t2_ccpr.pdf; http:// www1.umn.edu/humanrts/usdocs/civilres.html.

86. Gordon Duguid, "U.S. to Run for Election to the UN Human Rights Council," U.S. State Department press release, March 31, 2009, http://www.state.gov/r/pa/prs/ps/2009/03/ 121049.htm, and Patrick Worsnip, "U.S. Elected to U.N. Rights Council for First Time," *The Washington Post*, May 12, 2009.

87. In *Brandenburg v. Ohio*, the U.S. Supreme Court established the incitement test under which advocacy of use of force or law violation cannot be prohibited except where such "advocacy is directed to inciting or producing imminent lawless action and is likely to incite or produce such action." *Brandenburg v. Ohio*, 395 U.S. 444 (1969).

88. Under federal law, hate crimes are not distinct offenses. They amplify the penalty for traditional crimes in which the perpetrator was motivated by biases considered particularly detrimental to society. See William J. Krouse, *Hate Crime Legislation in the 109th Congress*, Congressional Research Service Report RL 33403 (2009), p. 2. By contrast, European-style hate speech codes can punish hateful utterances standing alone. See, further discussion in chapter on Western law.

89. "Remarks on the Release of the 2009 Annual Report on International Religious Freedom, Remarks of Hillary Rodham Clinton, Secretary of State," Washington, DC, October 26, 2009, http://www.state.gov/secretary/rm/2009a/10/130937.htm.

90. "Briefing on the Release of the 2009 Annual Report on International Religious Freedom, Special Briefing of Michael H. Posner, Assistant Secretary, Bureau of Democracy, Human Rights, and Labor," Washington, DC, October 26, 2009, http://www.state.gov/g/drl/rls/ rm/2009/130948.htm.

91. "International Law as Part of Our Law," 98 *Am. J. Int'l L.* 43, 52–54 (2004) and "The Globalization of Freedom," 26 *Yale L.J.* 305 (2001). In his speech before the American Society of International Law on March 25, 2010, Koh described as an important success: "the adoption by consensus of a freedom of expression resolution, which we co-sponsored with Egypt, that brought warring regional groups together and preserved the resolution as a vehicle to express firm support for freedom of speech and expression. This resolution was a way of implementing some of the themes in President Obama's historic speech in Cairo,

bridging geographic and cultural divides and dealing with global issues of discrimination and intolerance."

92. Durban Review Conference 2009, http://www.un.org/durbanreview2009/index.shtml; "Iran Becomes a Member of the Inner Circle of the Drafting Committee of UN 'Anti-racism' Conference," *Eye on the UN*, July 31, 2008, http://www.eyeontheun.org/durban.asp?p=622; Statement of the Permanent Mission of the Islamic Republic of Iran to the United Nations, No. 330-11/4312, March 14, 2008, http://www.un.org/durbanreview2009/pdf/replies/Iran.pdf; Statement of the representative of Iran before the first plenary meeting of the first substantive session of the Preparatory Committee of the Durban Review Conference, April 21, 2008, UN Human Rights Council archived video, http://www.un.org/webcast/unhrc/archive.asp?go=031.

93. *Note verbale* dated October 8, 2008 from the Permanent Mission of Sri Lanka to the United Nations Office at Geneva addressed to the Office of the United Nations High Commissioner for Human Rights, UN General Assembly, October 10, 2008, A/CONF.211/PC.3/5.

94. See *Note verbale* dated September 13, 2008 from the Permanent Mission of Pakistan to the United Nations Office at Geneva addressed to the Office of the High Commissioner for Human Rights, UN General Assembly, October 3, 2008, A/CONF.211/PC.3/10; Revised version of the technically reviewed text (A/CONF.211/PC/WG.2/CRP.2), January 23, 2009, http://www.un.org/durbanreview2009/pdf/intersession_open_ended19109.pdf; "Durban II – The Human Rights Fraud," *Eye on the UN*, January 28, 2009, http://www.eyeontheun.org/durban.asp?p=718.

95. Hillel Neuer, "The Defamation of Human Rights," *Radio Free Europe/Radio Liberty*, December 22, 2008, http://www.rferl.org/Content/The_Defamation_Of_Human_Rights/1362296.html.

96. Betsy Pisik, "U.S. to Skip Racism Summit," *Washington Times*, February 28, 2009; Robert Wood, "U.S. Posture Toward the Durban Review Conference and Participation in the UN Human Rights Council," State Department press release, February 27, 2009, http://www.state.gov/r/pa/prs/ps/2009/02/119892.htm; "A U.N. Education," *Wall Street Journal*, March 2, 2009, http://online.wsj.com/article/SB123595311981705283.html.

97. Outcome document of the Durban Review Conference, United Nations, http://www.un.org/durbanreview2009/pdf/Durban_Review_outcome_document_En.pdf. "Islamophobia, anti-Semitism, Christianophobia, and anti-Arabism" are discussed in paragraph 12; incitement to hatred in paragraphs 13, 68, 69, 134; freedom of expression is praised in paragraphs 54, 58.

98. Full text of the ICCPR is http://www2.ohchr.org/english/law/ccpr.htm.

99. "Freedom of Expression and Incitement to Racial or Religious Hatred," Joint statement by Mr. Githu Muigai, Special Rapporteur on contemporary forms of racism, racial discrimination, xenophobia and related intolerance, Ms. Asma Jahangir, Special Rapporteur on freedom of religion or belief, and Mr. Frank La Rue, Special Rapporteur on the promotion and protection of the right to freedom of opinion and expression, at an OHCHR side event during the Durban Review Conference, Geneva, April 22, 2009, http://www2.ohchr.org/english/issues/racism/rapporteur/docs/Joint_Statement_SRs.pdf.

100. L. Bennett Graham, "No to an International Blasphemy Law," *The Guardian*, March 25, 2010, http://www.guardian.co.uk/commentisfree/belief/2010/mar/25/blasphemy-law-ad-hoc-committee.

101. Oral statement submitted by the European Centre for Law and Justice (ECLJ), a nongovernmental organization in special consultative status, September 2007, http://www.eclj.org/PDF/070925_ECLJ_Oral_Statement_ENGLISH.pdf.

102. On the difficulties with "defamation of religions" as a legal concept, see also Graham, "Defamation of Religions: The End of Pluralism?" 69–84.

103. *Report of the Special Rapporteur…Asma Jahangir, and the Special Rapporteur…Doudou Diène.*

104. In 2008, the UN High Commissioner for Human Rights found no common understanding among those countries that had laws on the issue and that the laws addressed "somewhat different phenomena," UN Document A/HRC/9/7 (2008), para. 67; see also UN Document A/HRC/9/25 (2008). A 2006 study by the High Commissioner found that incitement norms have a "lack of clarity on key concepts," UN Document A/HRC/2/6 (2006), para. 81.

Chapter 12

1. Mark Steyn, "The Future Belongs to Islam," *Maclean's*, October 20, 2006, http://www. macleans.ca/article.jsp?content=20061023_134898_134898&source.

2. "Islam and Phobias," *The Economist*, January 10, 2008, http://www.economist.com/world/ americas/displaystory.cfm?story_id=10499144.

3. British Columbia Human Rights Tribunal, Elmasry on behalf of Muslim residents of the Province of British Columbia and Habib v. Roger's Publishing and MacQueen (No. 4), 2008 BCHRT 378, p. 37, October 10, 2008, http://www.bchrt.bc.ca/decisions/2008/pdf/oct/378_ Elmasry _and_Habib_v_Rogers_Publishing_and_MacQueen_(No_4)_2008_BCHRT_378.pdf.

4. Interview with Nina Shea, March 19, 2010.

5. Unofficial translation of the Criminal Code of Finland, Ministry of Justice, http://www.finlex .fi/en/laki/kaannokset/1889/en18890039.pdf.

6. Racial and Religious Tolerance Act 2001, No. 47 of 2001, Victorian Consolidated Legislation, http://www.austlii.edu.au/au/legis/vic/consol_act/rarta2001265/.

7. David Palmer and Allan Harman, "Is This Religious Persecution?" *On Line Opinion* (Australia), January 21, 2005, http://www.onlineopinion.com.au/view.asp?article=2956.

8. For analysis on this point see Patrick Parkinson, "Religious Vilification, Anti-Discrimination Laws and Religious Minorities in Australia: The Freedom to Be Different," *University of Sydney Law School Legal Studies Research Paper No. 08/59* (June 2008) (originally in *Australian Law Journal* 81 [2007]: 6–7).

9. Mark Durie, "Catch the Fire and Daniel Scot's (in)credible testimony," February 18, 2005, http://www.onlineopinion.com.au/view.asp?article=3050.

10. Islamic Council of Victoria v. Catch the Fire Ministries Inc (Final) [2004] VCAT 2510 (December 22, 2004), Victoria Civil and Administrative Tribunal, VCAT Reference No. A392/2002, http://www.austlii.edu.au/cgi-bin/sinodisp/au/cases/vic/VCAT/2004/2510.html? query=^catch%20the%20fire, and Judge Higgins, Summary of Reasons for Decision, December 17, 2004, Victoria Civil and Administrative Tribunal, VCAT Reference No. A392/2002, http://www.religionlaw.co.uk/interausaf.pdf.

11. "Muslim Council Agrees to Drop Hate-Speech Suit Against Aussie Pastors after BF Wins Appeal," The Becket Fund, June 26, 2007, http://www.becketfund.org/index.php/ article/676.html.

12. "Anti-Vilification Laws and Their Chilling Effect on Religious Expression," Personal testimony by Pastor Daniel Scot, Geneva—Jubilee meeting, March 28, 2007.

13. The matter of personal libel suits and "libel tourism" is an important subject but distinct from the issues we address in this book. See Testimony of Dr. Rachel Ehrenfeld, Hearing on Libel Tourism, Subcommittee on Commercial and Administrative Law, House Committee on Judiciary, U.S. Congress, February 12, 2009, http://judiciary.house.gov/hearings/pdf/ Ehrenfeld090212.pdf; "Governor Paterson Signs Legislation Protecting New Yorkers Against Infringement of First Amendment Rights by Foreign Libel Judgments," New York State press release, May 1, 2008, http://www.state.ny.us/governor/press/press_0501082. html; Arlen Specter and Joe Lieberman, "Foreign Courts Take Aim at Our Free Speech," *Wall Street Journal*, July 14, 2008; Adam Cohen, "'Libel Tourism': When Free Speech Takes a Holiday," *New York Times*, September 14, 2008, http://www.nytimes.com/2008/09/15/ opinion/15mon4.html?_r=1.

14. In the U.S. there is no federal ban on blasphemy. State-level blasphemy laws are believed to have been invalidated under First Amendment jurisprudence since at least the 1952 Supreme Court case *Burstyn v. Wilson*, in which the court struck down a New York State prohibition on Roberto Rossellini's allegedly sacrilegious film *The Miracle*. The court held that a ban on "sacrilegious" material sets the censor "adrift upon a boundless sea amid a myriad of conflicting currents of religious views, with no charts but those provided by the most vocal and powerful orthodoxies." The justices concluded: "It is not the business of government in our nation to suppress real or imagined attacks upon a particular religious doctrine," U.S. Supreme Court, *Joseph Burstyn, Inc. v. Wilson*, 343 U.S. 495 (1952), http:// laws.findlaw.com/us/343/495.html. See written comments submitted in *Otto-Preminger v.*

Austria, October 14, 1993, http://www.article19.org/pdfs/cases/austria-case-of-otto-prem-inger-v.-austria.pdf. David Nash, *Blasphemy in the Christian World: A History* (New York: Oxford University Press, 2007), 177–78, and ARTICLE 19/INTERIGHTS (see written comments submitted in *Otto-Preminger v. Austria*, October 14, 1993, http://www.article19.org/pdfs/cases/austria-case-of-otto-preminger-v.-austria.pdf) both identify *Burstyn v. Wilson* as the death knell of blasphemy as a crime in the United States despite the fact that statutes against it remained on the books in a number of states in subsequent years. In July 2010, a federal judge struck down Pennsylvania's 1977 statute that forbade the use of certain blasphemous and profane words in companies' names; Shannon P. Duffy, "Filmmaker Can Go with 'Hell' When It Comes to Company Name," Law.Com, July 2, 2010, http://lawyers-law.com/filmmaker-can-go-with-hell-when-it-comes-to-company-name/.

15. Nash, *Blasphemy in the Christian World*, 150–61, 162–66. Heresy could similarly be a capital crime. See Robert Post, "Hate Speech," in *Extreme Speech and Democracy*, ed. Ivan Hare and James Weinstein (Oxford: Oxford University Press, 2009), 131, and Nash, *Blasphemy in the Christian World*, 179. See also Kevin Seamus Hasson, *The Right to Be Wrong: Ending the Culture War over Religion in America* (San Francisco: Encounter Books, 2005), 41; Esther Janssen, "Limits to Expression on Religion in France," Agama & Religiusitas di Eropa, *Journal of European Studies* 5, no. 1 (2009): 22–45, http://www.ivir.nl/publications/janssen/Limits_to_expression_on_religion_in_France.pdf.

16. Defamation Act 2009, July 23, 2009, Irish Statute Book, Office of the Attorney General, http://www.irishstatutebook.ie/2009/en/act/pub/0031/sec0036.html; Carol Coulter, "Crime of Blasphemous Libel Proposed for Defamation Bill," *Irish Times*, April 29, 2009, http://www.irishtimes.com/newspaper/frontpage/2009/0429/1224245599892.html; http://www.irishtimes.com/ newspaper/breaking/2009/0519/breaking53.html. "25 Blasphemous Quotations," *Atheist Ireland*, January 2, 2010, http://www.atheist.ie/2010/01/25-blasphemous-quotations; Karla Adam, "Atheists Challenge Ireland's New Blasphemy Law with Online Postings," *Washington Post*, January 3, 2010, http://www.washingtonpost.com/wp-dyn/content/article/2010/01/02/AR2010010201846.html; "Ireland to Hold Referendum on Blasphemy Law," *The Guardian*, March 15, 2010, http://www.guardian.co.uk/world/2010/mar/15/ireland-referendum-blasphemy-law.

17. Dieter Grimm, "Freedom of Speech in a Globalized World," in *Extreme Speech and Democracy*, 18.

18. In *Rex v. Taylor* (1676); quoted in Russell Sandberg and Norman Doe, "The Strange Death of Blasphemy," *The Modern Law Review* 71, no. 6 (2008): 972; *R v. Ramsay & Foote* and *R v. Bradlaugh* (1883), quoted in Robert Post, "Hate Speech," 127; see also Sandberg and Doe, "Strange Death," 973.

19. Venice Commission 2008, *Analysis of the Domestic Law Concerning Blasphemy, Religious Insult and Inciting Religious Hatred in Albania, Austria, Belgium, Denmark, France, Greece Ireland, Netherlands, Poland, Romania, Turkey, United Kingdom*, Study no. 406/2006, October 10, 2008, 10–11, http://www.venice.coe.int/docs/2008/CDL-AD(2008)026add2-bil.pdf. This document is *Annexe II* to draft report CDL(2008)090 (http://www.venice.coe.int/docs/2008/CDL(2008)090-e.pdf), and will henceforth be cited as *Annexe II*.

20. As of 2008, the law had not been used on behalf of religions other than the Greek Orthodox Church, although it specifically permits such use; see Venice Commission 2008, *Annexe II*, 46–47.

21. Venice Commission 2008, *Annexe II*, 8, 30; ARTICLE 19 and INTERIGHTS, *Blasphemy and Film Censorship—Submission to the European Court of Human Rights in Respect of Nigel Wingrove v. the United Kingdom*, December 1995, p. 6, http://www.article19.org/pdfs/cases/uk-wingrove-v.-uk.pdf; Decision on Possible Criminal Proceedings in the Case of *Jyllands-Posten's* Article "The Face of Muhammad," The Director of Public Prosecutions (Denmark), File No. RA-2006-41-0151, March 15, 2006, http://www.rigsadvokaten.dk/media/bilag/afgorelse_engelsk.pdf.

22. David Rising, "MTV 'Popetown' Ad Draws Complaint," *Associated Press (AP)*, April 25, 2006, http://www.highbeam.com/doc/1P1-122498671.html. In Germany, various cases of anti-Christian blasphemy have been dismissed by the courts. Between 1985 and 1995, two cases

were rejected in Italy; see *Blasphemy and Film Censorship*, 8; "Blasphemy: European Laws and Cases," *Caslon Analytics*, August 2008, http://www.caslon.com.au/blasphemyprofile6. htm#italy. In October 1997, the Catholic Archbishop of Melbourne, Australia, arguing that Andres Serrano's art constituted blasphemous libel, sought an injunction against it but was turned down on a technicality, leaving the validity of the blasphemy law unclear. However, the presiding justice opined that, as a modern pluralist society, "Australia need not bother with blasphemous libel"; see Kate Gilchrist, "God Does Not Live in Victoria," *Art Monthly*, December 1997, http://www.artslaw.com.au/publications/Articles/97Blasphemy.asp; for more on Australian blasphemy cases, see Caslon Analytics, http://www.caslon.com.au/blasphemyprofile5.htm.

23. "Italy Gags 'Porno' Virgin Mary Sites," *BBC News*, July 10, 2002, http://news.bbc.co.uk/2/ hi/europe/2119780.stm; "Website's Pope Pictures Offend Catholics," *Guardian Unlimited*, April 29, 2005, http://www.theage.com.au/news/Breaking/Website-shows-Pope-the-Nazi/2005/05/05/1115092599914.html; Richard Owen, "Comedian Sabina Guzzanti 'Insulted Pope' in 'Poofter Devils' Gag," *The Times*, September 12, 2008, http://www.timesonline.co.uk/tol/news/world/europe/article4732048.ece.

24. Venice Commission 2008, *Annexe II*, 48.

25. Krysia Diver, "Cartoonist Faces Greek Jail for Blasphemy," *The Guardian*, March 23, 2005, http://www.guardian.co.uk/world/2005/mar/23/austria.arts; Miron Varouhakis, "Greek Court Clears Austrian Cartoonist of Blasphemy," *AP*, April 13, 2005, http://www.encyclopedia.com/doc/1P1-107349748.html; "Greek 'Obscene Art' Trial Delayed," *BBC News*, June 3, 2005, http://news.bbc.co.uk/2/hi/europe/4606533.stm; Elinda Labropoulou, "Curator on Trial for 'Obscene' Art," *The Independent*, June 4, 2005, http://www.independent.co.uk/news/world/europe/curator-on-trial-for-obscene-art-492973.html.

26. The Council of Europe, based in Strasbourg, has forty-seven member countries. Founded on May 5, 1949, by ten countries, it seeks to develop throughout Europe common and democratic principles based on the European Convention on Human Rights and other reference texts on the protection of individuals; see http://www.coe.int/aboutCoe/index. asp?page=quisommesnous&l=en.

27. Dirk Voorhoof, "European Court of Human Rights—Case of *Tatlav v. Turkey*," *IRIS* 7, article 2 (2006): 3, http://merlin.obs.coe.int/iris/2006/7/article2.en.html.

28. Convention for the Protection of Human Rights and Fundamental Freedoms, available via Council of Europe at http://conventions.coe.int/Treaty/en/Treaties/Html/005.htm.

29. In 1982, the European Court of Human Rights, which decides which cases will be heard by the Court of Human Rights, rejected an appeal from the publication *Gay News* and its editor Denis Lemon, who had received Britain's first blasphemy conviction in over half a century after publishing a poem that depicted Christ as a homosexual; see *Whitehouse v Lemon* (1979) 2 WLR 281. The European Court similarly found that "the rights of others" justified the suppression of blasphemy in the 1994 case *Otto-Preminger Institut v. Austria*, which upheld Austria's seizure of a film, *Das Liebeskonzil* ("Council in Heaven"), depicting God, Christ, and the Virgin Mary in a mocking and derogatory fashion. In *Wingrove v. UK* (1996), the European Court endorsed the government's decision to uphold the banning of a film on blasphemy grounds; see Application No. 8710/79, X. Ltd. and Y v/United Kingdom, European Commission of Human Rights, May 7, 1982, http://www.menschenrechte.ac.at/ orig/95_2/Wingrove.pdf. In another case concerning a pornographic film, *Visions*, that purportedly depicted the visions of sixteenth-century St. Teresa of Avila, the court again asserted "the right of citizens not to be insulted in their religious feelings."

30. Ian Cram, "The Danish Cartoons, Offensive Expression, and Democratic Legitimacy," in *Extreme Speech and Democracy*, 319; Monica Macovei, "Freedom of Expression: A Guide to the Implementation of Article 10 of the European Convention on Human Rights," Council of Europe Human Rights Handbook No. 2, pp. 54–55, http://www.coe.int/t/dghl/publications/hrhandbooks/index_handbooks_en.asp,; this summary also contains lengthy excerpts from the original court ruling.

31. *Wingrove v. the United Kingdom*—Chamber Judgment, European Court of Human Rights, October 22, 1996, http://www.strasbourgconsortium.org/document.php?DocumentID=370.

32. Ibid.

33. Dirk Voorhoof, "Case of *I.A. v. Turkey*," *IRIS* 10, article 3 (2005): 3, http://merlin.obs.coe.int/iris/2005/10/article3.en.html. A three-judge minority argued that the European Court should "reconsider" its holdings in *Wingrove* and *Otto Preminger* on the grounds that the resulting jurisprudence gave too much support to conformist speech and the *pensée unique*.

34. Nash, *Blasphemy in the Christian World*, 17, 181.

35. "Not Dead, Just Sleeping: Canada's Prohibition on Blasphemous Libel as a Case Study in Obsolete Legislation," *University of British Columbia Law Review* 141 (April 17, 2008): 193, http://papers.ssrn.com/sol3/papers.cfm?abstract_id=1121932.

36. "Bid to Prosecute Rushdie Is Rejected," *New York Times*, April 10, 1990, http://www.nytimes.com/1990/04/10/books/bid-to-prosecute-rushdie-is-rejected.html?pagewanted=1.

37. *Whitehouse v. Lemon* [1979], quoted in Nash, *Blasphemy in the Christian World*, 5.

38. *Regina v. Chief Metropolitan Stipendiary Magistrate*, ex parte Choudhury [1990] 3 W.L.R. 986, Queen's Bench Division, effective April 9, 1990, http://www.religlaw.org/template.php?id=2494.

39. As quoted in *Wingrove v. UK* (European Court of Human Rights, 1996), http://www.strasbourgconsortium.org/document.php?DocumentID=370.

40. Nash, *Blasphemy in the Christian World*, 88–92.

41. The UN Human Rights Committee in November 1996 upheld France's Holocaust denial law on the grounds that it "served the respect of the Jewish community to live free from fear of an atmosphere of anti-Semitism" (Communication No. 550/1993, UN Human Rights Committee, adopted November 8, 1996, CCPR/C/58/D/550/1993, December 16, 1996), http://www1.umn.edu/humanrts/undocs/html/VWS55058.htm. Governments in the past two decades have made active use of such laws. The British Holocaust denier David Irving was fined approximately $6,000 by a German court in 1992, and in 2006, he was sentenced to a three-year jail term in Austria; see Veronika Oleksyn, "Holocaust Denier Gets Three Years in Jail," *AP*, February 20, 2006. See also http://www.vosizneias.com/50997/2010/03/10/budapest-hungary-holocaust-deniers-face-3-years-jail-under-new-law; "Irving Expands on Holocaust Views," *BBC News*, February 28, 2006, http://news.bbc.co.uk/2/hi/europe/4757506.stm. In February 2007, Ernst Zundel was convicted of inciting hatred against Jews and sentenced to five years' imprisonment for activities including his contributions to a Holocaust-denying Web site; see Thomas Seythal, "Holocaust Denier Sentenced to 5 Years," *AP*, February 15, 2007, http://www.encyclopedia.com/doc/1Y1-103301044.html. French laws of this kind were used to charge eminent Princeton historian Bernard Lewis, after a 1993 interview with *Le Monde*, in which Lewis had questioned whether the massacres of Armenians during World War I, which he said did occur, were the result of a deliberate genocidal plan by Ottoman authorities. Although three cases were dismissed, one civil suit resulted in his being condemned and fined for not being "objective," since the European parliament had classified the massacres as genocide; see Gerard Alexander, "Illiberal Europe," *Weekly Standard*, April 10, 2006, http://www.weeklystandard.com/Content/Public/Articles/000/000/012/055sbhvq.asp.

42. Council of Europe, *Recommendation No. R 97(20) of the Committee of Ministers to Member States on "Hate Speech,"* October 30, 1997.

43. Council of Europe, *Additional Protocol to the Convention on Cybercrime, Concerning the Criminalisation of Acts of a Racist and Xenophobic Nature Committed Through Computer Systems*, Strasbourg, January 28, 2003, http://conventions.coe.int/treaty/en/Treaties/Html/189.htm.

44. American Convention on Human Rights, http://www.oas.org/juridico/English/treaties/b-32.html; Joanna Oyediran, "Article 13(5) of the American Convention on Human Rights," in *Striking a Balance: Hate Speech, Freedom of Expression and Non-discrimination*, ed. Sandra Coliver (Colchester, U.K.: University of Essex Human Rights Centre,1992)), 33–34. The U.S. has signed but not ratified this treaty.

45. Ian Black, "EU Agrees New Race Hatred Law," *The Guardian*, April 20, 2007, http://www.guardian.co.uk/eu/story/0,,2061767,00.html; Council of the European Union, "Council Framework Decision on Combating Racism and Xenophobia," 2794th Council meeting, Justice and Home Affairs press release, Luxembourg, 19–20 April 2007, http://www.consilium.europa.eu/ueDocs/cms_Data/docs/pressData/en/jha/93741.pdf.

46. Ingrid Melander, "Britain Limits EU Religious Hatred Ban," Reuters, April 17, 2007; Council of the European Union, *Council Framework Decision 2008/913/JHA of November 28, 2008 on Combating Certain Forms and Expressions of Racism and Xenophobia by Means of Criminal Law*, http://eur-lex.europa.eu/LexUriServ/LexUriServ.do?uri=CELEX:32008F0913:EN:NOT.

47. Council of the European Union, *Framework Decision on Combating Certain Forms of Expression of Racism and Xenophobia*. See also "Framework Decision on Combating Racism and Xenophobia," *Europa*, http://europa.eu/legislation_summaries/justice_freedom_security/combating_discrimination/l33178_en.htm; Council of the European Union, "'A' Item Note," from Permanent Representatives Committee to Council, re: *Proposal for a Council Framework Decision on Combating Certain Forms and Expressions of Racism and Xenophobia by Means of Criminal Law*, November 26, 2008, http://register.consilium.europa.eu/pdf/en/08/st16/st16351-re01.en08.pdf; and Tarlach McGonagle, "Council of the European Union: Framework Decision on Racism Adopted," *IRIS* 2, article 5 (2009): 6, http://merlin.obs.coe.int/iris/2009/2/article5.en.htm.

48. Eric Heinze, "Wild-West Cowboys Versus Cheese-Eating Surrender Monkeys," in *Extreme Speech and Democracy*, 184.

49. Venice Commission 2008, *Annexe II*, 9.

50. Parkinson, "Religious Vilification, Anti-Discrimination Laws and Religious Minorities in Australia," 5.

51. The Venice Commission is charged with upholding Europe's constitutional heritage of democracy, human rights, and the rule of law. Its roster of experts is appointed to four-year terms and acts in their personal capacity. (H. Knox Thames, Chris Seiple, and Amy Rowe, eds., *International Religious Freedom Advocacy*, 70.) See *Report on the Relationship Between Freedom of Expression and Freedom of Religion: The Issue of Regulation and Prosecution of Blasphemy, Religious Insult and Incitement to Religious Hatred, Adopted by the Venice Commission at its 76th Plenary Session (Venice, 17–18 October 2008) on the basis of comments by Mr. Louis-Léon Christians, Mr. Pieter van Dijk, Ms. Finola Flanagan, and Ms. Hanna Suchocka*, Strasbourg, October 23, 2008, http://www.venice.coe.int/docs/2008/CDL-AD(2008)026-e.pdf, henceforth cited as Venice Commission 2008, *Report*. On incitement clauses considered for inclusion in the declaration, see Kevin Boyle, "Religious Intolerance and the Incitement of Hatred," in *Striking a Balance*, 64–65; the resulting distinction between the declaration and the CERD is also emphasized by the UN Special Rapporteur on Freedom of Religion or Belief, who thus cautions against an unthinking application of CERD Article 4 to religious matters; see "Special Rapporteur on Freedom of Religion or Belief—Framework for Communications," Office of the UN High Commissioner for Human Rights, http://www2.ohchr.org/english/issues/religion/IV1.htm. Other states in the OSCE survey had legislation that could easily be interpreted to cover religious groups; for instance, Canada's hate-speech laws cover "any identifiable group," and Germany's refer to "segments of the population."

52. In the United States, the content of speech can be restricted only in narrow circumstances. These include: cases of personal defamation and libel, laws that punish false statements of fact that harm individual persons, not the peaceful criticism of ideas; cases in which, as the Supreme Court ruled in *Brandenburg v. Ohio*, the "advocacy is directed to inciting or producing imminent lawless action and is likely to incite or produce such action" (a much vaguer and attenuated standard was adopted by the UN's International Covenant on Civil and Political Rights, Article 20(2), which obliges states to prohibit by law "[a]ny advocacy of national, racial, or religious hatred that constitutes incitement to discrimination, hostility or violence"); cases of "true" threats, and intimidation, in which "the speaker means to communicate a serious expression of an intent to commit an act of unlawful violence to a particular individual or group of individuals"; cases of "fighting words," which are limited

to face-to-face insults that are likely to arouse an immediate violent response (and even here the Supreme Court has further narrowed the exception by finding statutes criminalizing such words overbroad and vague, or including impermissible content-based restrictions); cases satisfying "strict scrutiny," meaning the restriction is narrowly tailored to serve a compelling government interest, and no less restrictive alternative would be as effective (e.g., grand jury secrecy, or falsely shouting "fire" in a crowded theater); and cases of harassment, as prohibited in most states by statutes covering in various forms: (1) repetitious annoyances; (2) threats specifically conveyed, orally, electronically, or by telephone or mail; or (3) conduct likely to stimulate an immediate violent response. The Supreme Court has never squarely addressed whether harassment, when it takes the form of pure speech, is exempt from First Amendment protection. Boyle, "Overview," in *Striking a Balance*, 4. See also James Weinstein, "An Overview of American Free Speech Doctrine and its Application to Extreme Speech," in *Extreme Speech and Democracy*, 81; in the same volume, Eric Heinze, in "Wild-West Cowboys versus Cheese-Eating Surrender Monkeys" (pp. 182–203), challenges the U.S./European divide as a cultural and practical matter but acknowledges it is a legal reality.

53. *Brandenburg v. Ohio*, 395 U.S. 444 (1969), http://caselaw.lp.findlaw.com/cgi-bin/getcase.pl?court=US&vol=395&invol=444.

54. In the case *National Socialist Party of America v. Village of Skokie*, 432 U.S. 43 (1977), the Supreme Court prevented a state court from banning a neo-Nazi march through a Jewish area on the basis that it unconstitutionally infringed on their First Amendment rights.

55. William J. Krouse, *Hate Crime Legislation in the 109th Congress*, Congressional Research Service Report RL 33403 (2009), 2. A key 1952 Supreme Court precedent is *Joseph Burstyn, Inc. v. Wilson*, 342 U.S. 495, 505 (1952), invalidating a NY statute banning "sacrilegious" films: "It is not the business of government in our nation to suppress real or imagined attacks upon a particular religious doctrine, whether they appear in publications, speeches, or motion pictures." In 1970, a state appellate court overturned a conviction under Maryland's 1860 blasphemy law, finding it violated the First Amendment's religion clauses. (The Supreme Court found it unnecessary to reach the free speech question.) See *Maryland v. West*, 9 Md. App. 270 (1970). Blasphemy laws remain on the books in six states (Massachusetts, Oklahoma, Michigan, South Carolina, Wyoming, and Pennsylvania). Officials expect not to enforce them and could face legal and professional sanctions for bringing obviously untenable cases. Indeed, shortly after the Maryland decision, planned blasphemy prosecutions in neighboring Delaware and Pennsylvania were dropped. See Robert C. Post, "Cultural Heterogeneity and Law: Pornography, Blasphemy, and the First Amendment," 76 Calif. L. Rev note 1 at 316–17, 1988. An exception to the pattern of arcane and unenforced statutes, a 1977 Pennsylvania law, enacted overwhelmingly, banned corporate names containing "words that constitute blasphemy, profane cursing or swearing or that profane the Lord's name" (19 Pa. Code §17.5). In July 2010, a federal judge struck down the statute.

56. Jeffrey Breinholt, in "More Overlooked History: The Muslim Libel Cases," *Counterterrorism Blog*, August 2, 2007, http://counterterrorismblog.org/2007/08/more_overlooked_history_the_mu.php, notes a number of such cases and the likelihood that more remain unknown to the public because the accused opted to settle out of court rather than pay the legal fees for a defense.

57. Paul Marshall and Nina Shea, "Afghan Blowback," *National Review Online*, April 8, 2011, http://www.nationalreview.com/articles/264222/afghan-blowback-paul-marshall; Paul Marshall, "New Koran Campaign Follows Old Patterns, *National Review Online*, April 4, 2011, http://www.nationalreview.com/corner/263779/new-koran-campaign-follows-old-patterns-paul-marshall; Paul Marshall and Nina Shea, "The Source of Their Rage, *National Review* magazine, October 4, 2010; Nina Shea, "A Heckler's Veto Afterall?" *National Review Online*, September 15, 2010, http://www.nationalreview.com/corner/246669/hecklers-veto-after-all-nina-shea; Paul Marshall and Nina Shea, "Burning the Koran," *National Review*

Online, September 7, 2010, http://www.nationalreview.com/articles/245877/burning-koran-nina-shea.

58. Tom Gross, "J'Accuse," *Wall Street Journal*, June 2, 2005; Jon Henley, "Le Monde Editor 'Defamed Jews,'" *The Guardian*, June 4, 2005, http://www.guardian.co.uk/media/2005/jun/04/pressandpublishing.france; Rachel Zabarkes, "Fallaci's Fight," *National Review*, June 26, 2002, http://old.nationalreview.com/comment/comment-zabarkes062602.asp; Lara Marlowe, "'Le Monde' Acquitted of 'Racially' Defaming Israel," *The Irish Times*, July 13, 2006, http://cosmos.ucc.ie/cs1064/jabowen/IPSC/php/art.php?aid=48256; Ben Leach, "Foreign Office Diplomat Arrested over 'Anti-Semitic' Rant," *Telegraph*, February 9, 2009, http://www.telegraph.co.uk/news/newstopics/politics/4564216/Foreign-Office-diplomat-arrested-over-anti-Semitic-rant.html; Shea Peters, "John Galliano Released from Rehab, Fate of Christian Dior Still Unknown," *Examiner*, April 12, 2011, http://www.examiner.com/designer-fashion-in-national/john-galliano-released-from-rehab-fate-of-the-john-galliano-label-still-unknown.

59. See Ian Leigh, "Homophobic Speech, Equality Denial, and Religious Expression," in *Extreme Speech and Democracy*, 379–93.

60. "Sweden—Criminalizing Religious Speech—Ake Green," Becket Fund for Religious Liberty, http://www.becketfund.org/index.php/case/93.html; John Leo, "Canadian Kangaroos," *National Review*, June 20, 2008, http://article.nationalreview.com/361166/canadian-kangaroos/john-leo; Bruce Korol, "Constitutional Rights Must Be Protected," *Calgary Herald*, December 6, 2007, http://www.canada.com/calgaryherald/news/theeditorialpage/story.html?id=02a2999c-f366–47b5–846d-2c0d6e378502; Deborah Tetley, "Alberta Judge Rules in Favor of Author of Anti-gay Letter," *National Post*, December 5, 2009, http://www.nationalpost.com/m/story.html?id=2305614&s=Today%27s%20Newspaper.

61. These cases, many of which began with complaints from the Catholic organization AGRIF (General Alliance Against Racism and for Respect of French and Christian Identity), included complaints concerning posters for the film *The People vs. Larry Flint* (featuring the title character standing as if on a cross) in 1997; Janssen, "Limits to Expression on Religion in France," end page, http://www.ivir.nl/publications/janssen/Limits_to_expression_on_religion_in_France.pdf. On Jehovah's Witnesses, see "Anti-sect Deputy Jean Pierre Brard Sentenced for Hate Speech Against Jehovah's Witnesses," *Human Rights Without Frontiers* (*HRWF*), September 28, 2009, http://hrwf.net/uploads/France%202009.doc; "The Antisect Movements and Money," *Coordination of Associations and Individuals for Freedom of Conscience*, December 16, 2009, http://www.freedomofconscience.eu/the-antisect-movements-and-money/; "The Director of the Weekly Magazine 'Le Point' Sentenced for Defaming Jehovah's Witnesses," *HRWF*, June 7, 2010, http://tech.groups.yahoo.com/group/rael-science-select/message/20364. On a conviction in Russia for perceived anti-Christian art, see "Russians Convicted and Fined over Forbidden Art Show," *BBC News*, July 12, 2010, http://news.bbc.co.uk/2/hi/europe/10595903.stm; Alexander Verkhovsky, "Art Curators' Verdict Not Isolated Instance—This Is a System," *Forum 18*, July 19, 2010, http://www.forum18.org/Archive.php?query=Verkhovsky&religion=all&country=all&results=10.

62. "Four Men Jailed over Cartoon Demo," *BBC News*, July 18, 2007, http://news.bbc.co.uk/2/hi/uk_news/6904622.stm; "Homecoming Soldiers Branded 'Murderers' and 'Terrorists' by Muslim Extremists," *Telegraph* (U.K.), January 5, 2010, http://www.telegraph.co.uk/news/newstopics/onthefrontline/6931203/Homecoming-soldiers-branded-murderers-and-terrorists-by-Muslim-extremists.html; "Hate Crimes and Discrimination Based on Religion or Belief," Human Rights Without Frontiers International, September 1, 2009; Toby Sterling, "Dutch to Prosecute Arabs over Holocaust Cartoon," *AP*, September 2, 2009. Norway's "Act on prohibition of discrimination based on ethnicity, religion, etc. 2005," forbids "statements which have an offensive, frightening, hostile, degrading or humiliating effect, or which are intended to have such an effect." Burden of proof falls on the accused: "If there are circumstances that give reason to believe that a breach of any of the provisions . . . has taken place, such breach shall be assumed to have taken place unless the person responsible for the act, omission or statement produces evidence showing that no such breach has taken place."

Unofficial translation, Norwegian Ministry of Labour, http://www.regjeringen.no/en/dep/aid/doc/lover_regler/reglement/2005/the-anti-discrimination-act.html?id=420606.

63. Nina Shea and Paul Marshall, "We Need to Talk about Islam," *The Wall Street Journal: Europe*, November 8, 2010, http://online.wsj.com/article/SB1000142405274870446270457559048095903 5618.html.

64. In "Postscript" in Daniel Pipes, *The Rushdie Affair*, 2nd ed. (New Brunswick: Transaction Publishers, 2003), 270. A similar case arose in Belgium, where a priest of Turkish extraction was charged with incitement to racial hatred after harshly denouncing Muslims; he was acquitted, and subsequently the law was amended to add religious hate-speech bans. "Hate Crimes and Discrimination Based on Religion or Belief," *HRWF*, September 1, 2009, hrwf .net/.../Religious%20intolerance%20and%20discrimination%202007-2009.doc.

65. Jonathan C. Randal "Brigitte Bardot vs. Muslim Sheep Slaying—Animal-Rights Stand Criticized as Racist in Tone," *Seattle Times*, May 23, 1996, http://community.seattletimes.nwsource.com/archive/?date=19960523&slug=2330801.

66. Nicolas Marmie, "Court Acquits Brigitte Bardot of Racism," *AP*, January 23, 1997.

67. Alex Duval Smith, "Brigitte Bardot Denies Race Hatred Charge," *The Guardian* (U.K.), December 20, 1996, http://news.bbc.co.uk/2/hi/entertainment/3692965.stm; "Bardot Convicted of Inciting Racial Hatred," *AP*, October 9, 1997.

68. "Court again Convicts Bardot of Racism after Anti-Islam Remarks," *Agence France Presse* (*AFP*), January 20, 1998.

69. "Bardot Fined for Racist Remarks," *BBC News*, June 16, 2000, http://news.bbc.co.uk/2/hi/entertainment/793390.stm.

70. "Brigitte Bardot Guilty in Racial Hatred Case," *AP*, June 3, 2008, http://www.msnbc.msn.com/id/24948578/; "Brigitte Bardot on Trial for Muslim Slur," Reuters, April 15, 2008, http://www.reuters.com/article/idUSL1584799120080415.

71. "French Screen Icon Bardot Fined for Anti-Muslim Remarks," *AFP*, June 3, 2008. http://afp.google.com/article/ALeqM5h1N4N6pzrHw9Lunbyjbb4u4yrqxg. In 1990, Archbishop Marcel Lefebvre of the ultratraditionalist Catholic splinter group SSPX received a fine approximately equivalent to $900 for telling non-Muslim listeners that once Europe's Muslim population grew, their wives and children would "be kidnapped and dragged off to a certain kind of places [sic] as they exist in Casablanca"; Koenraad Elst, "The Rushdie Rules," *Middle East Quarterly* 5, no. 2 (June 1998): http://www.meforum.org/395/the-rushdie-rules.

72. "Italian Writer Fallaci Responds to Group's Assessment of Book As 'Islamophobe Attack,'" *AP*, June 11, 2002, http://www.highbeam.com/doc/1P1-53556849.html.

73. "French Court Allows 'Anti-Islamic' Book," *BBC News*, June 21, 2002, http://news.bbc.co.uk/2/hi/europe/2058520.stm.

74. In a 2002 *Le Monde* article; see, e.g., "Swiss Muslim Teacher Fired over Defense of Stoning for Adultery," *AP*, February 5, 2003; "Swiss Muslims File Suit over Fallaci Book," *AFP*, June 20, 2002, http://www.milligazette.com/Archives/01072002/0107200263.htm.

75. Margaret Talbot, "The Agitator; Oriana Fallaci Directs Her Fury Toward Islam," *New Yorker* 82, no. 16 (June 5, 2006): http://www.newyorker.com/archive/2006/06/05/060605fa_fact.

76. Marta Falconi, "Judge Orders Italian Author to Stand Trial on Charges of Public Defamation Against Islam," *AP*, May 25, 2005, http://www.warriorsfortruth.com/oriana-fallaci-muslim-book.html; John Hooper, "Anti-Islamic Italian Author in New Legal Fight," *The Guardian*, July 13, 2005, http://www.guardian.co.uk/world/2005/jul/13/books.italy; Christian Spillman, "Church and Pope Defend Crucifix in Italian Schools," *AFP*, December 11, 2003. His request regarding the crucifixes was upheld by a local judge, but the ruling was later overturned.

77. "Muslim Activist Sues Pope, Cardinal, for Comments about Superiority of Christianity," *AP*, February 28, 2004, http://www.catholicculture.org/news/features/index.cfm?recnum=28012; Maria Sanminiatelli, "From the Fringes, an Italian Muslim Uses Courts to Battle Pope and Others, Defend Islam," *AP*, August 27, 2005.

78. Oriana Fallaci, *The Strength of Reason* (New York: Rizzolo International Publications, Inc., 2006), 263–64.

79. Falconi, "Judge Orders Italian Author to Stand Trial"; Hooper, "Anti-Islamic Italian Author in New Legal Fight"; Barbara McMahon, "Author's Trial for Defaming Islam Begins," *The Guardian*, June 13, 2006, http://www.guardian.co.uk/world/2006/jun/13/books.italy.

80. Francoise Michel, "Death of Oriana Fallaci, War Reporter Turned Scourge of Islam," *AFP*, September 15, 2006.

81. "Adel Smith, 6 Months Sentence for Defaming religion," Agenzia Giornalistica Italia, June 14, 2005; "Italy: Court Rules Against Stiffer Penalties for Catholicism's Slanderers," AdnkronosInternational, April 29, 2005; "Insults Against Catholicism Same As Other Creeds, Court Says," ANSA English Media Service, April, 29, 2005.

82. "Freedom in the World: Country Report—Finland," *Freedom House*, 2009, http://www.freedomhouse.org/template.cfm?page=22&year=2009&country=7608.

83. Decision on possible criminal proceedings in the case of *Jyllands-Posten's* article.

84. Ibid.

85. "Danish Court Rejects Civil Suit," *BBC News*, October 26, 2006, http://news.bbc.co.uk/2/hi/6087506.stm.

86. "Danish Appeals Court Rejects Lawsuit Against Newspaper That Published Prophet Cartoons," *International Herald Tribune*, June 19, 2008, http://www.nytimes.com/2008/06/19/world/europe/19iht-islam.4.13840577.html.

87. *World Report 2009—Denmark*, Reporters Without Borders, May 1, 2009, http://www.unhcr.org/refworld/country,,,,DNK,4562d8b62,49fea994c,0.html.

88. "French Paper Cleared in Muhammad Drawings Case," *AP*, March 22, 2007, http://www.rferl.org/content/article/1075438.html; Janssen, "Limits to expression on religion in France."

89. Philippe Val, "Modern Blasphemy," *Wall Street Journal*, March 21, 2007.

90. "French Paper Cleared"; Val, "Modern Blasphemy."

91. "Editor Defends Prophet Cartoons," *BBC News*, February 7, 2007, http://news.bbc.co.uk/2/hi/6337307.stm; Val, "Modern Blasphemy."

92. "Editor Defends Prophet Cartoons."

93. "French Paper Cleared"; Pascal Mbongo, "Hate Speech, Extreme Speech, and Collective Defamation in French Law," in *Extreme Speech and Democracy*, 232–33; "Danish Newspaper Hails Acquittal in French Cartoons Trial," *AFP*, March 22, 2007, http://neveryetmelted.com/2007/03/22/charlie-hebdo-acquitted/.

94. Janssen, "Limits to Expression on Religion in France."

95. Alberta Human Rights and Citizenship Commission complaint form, http://westernstandard.blogs.com/shotgun/files/soharwardy_complaint.pdf; Syed B. Soharwardy, "Ezra Wrong About Islam," *Calgary Sun* (Alberta), March 20, 2006.

96. Carly Weeks, "Islamic Group Takes Cartoon Case to Tribunal," *Ottawa Citizen*, February 16, 2006, http://www.cbc.ca/arts/story/2008/05/08/herald-cartoon.html.

97. "Alta Human Rights Complaint Filed over Muslim Editorial Cartoons," Canadian *Press NewsWire*, February 15, 2006, http://www.cbc.ca/canada/windsor/story/2010/03/12/mont-gazette-cartoon-niqab-aislin.html; "Alta Crown Suggests No Charges for Publications That Printed Muslim Cartoons," *Canadian Press NewsWire*, February 22, 2006.

98. Jason Fekete, "Publisher Defends Cartoons," *The Calgary Herald*, January 11, 2008, http://www.ctv.ca/servlet/ArticleNews/story/CTVNews/20060213/cartoons_060213/20060213?hub=TopStories; Ezra Levant, "What a Strange Place Canada Is," *Globe and Mail* (online), January 21, 2008, http://www.theglobeandmail.com/news/national/article661959.ece.

99. Ezra Levant, "'Human Rights' vs. Magna Carta," *National Post*, January 15, 2008, http://www.quebecoislibre.org/08/080120-3.htm.

100. Graeme Morton for Canwest News Service, "Muslim Leader Drops Complaint Against Levant," *National Post*, February 13, 2008, http://www.nationalpost.com/news/story.html?id=304005; "Former Publisher to Sue Muslim Leader Who Filed Human Rights

Complaints," *CBC News*, February 13, 2008, http://www.cbc.ca/canada/story/2008/02/13/levant-cartoons.html.

101. Joseph Brean, "Muslim Complaint Rejected Against Danish Cartoons Published in Alberta," *Canwest News Service*, August 6, 2008; Ezra Levant, "How I Beat the Fatwa, and Lost My Freedom," *National Post*, August 6, 2008, http://network.nationalpost.com/np/blogs/fullcomment/archive/2008/08/06/ezra-levant-how-i-beat-the-fatwa-and-lost-my-freedom.aspx.

102. Andrew Higgins, "Why Islam Is Unfunny for a Cartoonist," *Wall Street Journal*, July 12, 2008, http://online.wsj.com/article/SB121581460304047109.html.

103. Andrew Osborn, "Tirade Against Islam Dismays Dutch Muslims," *The Guardian*, January 29, 2003, http://www.guardian.co.uk/world/2003/jan/29/thefarright.islam; Ayaan Hirsi Ali, "Islam's Silent Moderates," *New York Times*, December 7, 2007, http://www.nytimes.com/2007/12/07/opinion/07ali.html.

104. Toby Sterling, "Dutch Politician Can Write Sequel to Controversial Film, Court Rules," *AP*, March 15, 2005. Interview with Hirsi Ali by Nina Shea on November 3, 2010.

105. "Dutch Protest Against Islam Critic's Koran Film," *MSNBC.com*, March 22, 2008, http://www.msnbc.msn.com/id/23757212/; on *Fitna* see above, chap. 10.

106. "Amsterdam Court of Appeals Orders the Criminal Prosecution of the Member of Parliament of the Dutch Second Chamber Geert Wilders," *Rechtspraak.nl*, January 21, 2008, http://www.rechtspraak.nl/Gerechten/Gerechtshoven/Amsterdam/Actualiteiten/Amsterdam+Court+of+Appeal+orders+the+criminal+prosecution+of+the+Member+of+Parliament+of+the+Dutch+S.htm; "Dutch Lawmaker Wilders to Be Prosecuted for Anti-Islam Comments," *Bloomberg*, January 21, 2009, http://www.bloomberg.com/apps/news?pid=20601085&sid=anIUQcBjnZmk&refer=europe.

107. "Anti-Islam Lawmaker Appeals Hate Speech Charges," *International Herald Tribune*, February 3, 2009, http://www.nasdaq.com/aspx/stock-market-news-story.aspx?storyid=200905200911dowjonesdjonline000610; Folkert Jensma, "Has Wilders Broken the Law?" *NRC Handelsblad*, January 19, 2010, http://www.nrc.nl/international/article2462698.ece/Has_Wilders_broken_the_law.

108. Summons of the Accused, District Court Office of the Public Prosecutor, http://www.wilderstontrial.com/images/stories/dagvaarding_ENG.pdf.

109. "Court Limits Wilders' Witness List," *DutchNews.nl*, February 3, 2010, http://www.dutchnews.nl/news/archives/2010/02/court_limits_wilders_witness_l.php.

110. Joan Clements, "Jacqui Smith's Ban on Anti-Muslim Dutch MP Triggers Diplomatic Row with Holland," *Telegraph*, February 11, 2009, http://www.telegraph.co.uk/news/newstopics/politics/4592536/Jacqui-Smiths-ban-on-anti-Muslim-Dutch-MP-triggers-diplomatic-row-with-Holland.html. Baroness Cox and Lord Pearson stated that, while they disagreed with Wilders's proposal to ban the Qur'an, they suspected he would not have been barred from entering the country had he instead proposed banning the Bible.

111. "Banned Dutch MP Held at Heathrow," *BBC News*, February 12, 2009, http://news.bbc.co.uk/2/hi/uk_news/politics/7886491.stm.

112. Beverley Rouse, "Named and Shamed: The 16 Barred from the UK," *The Independent*, May 5, 2009, http://www.independent.co.uk/news/uk/politics/16-banned-from-britain-named-and-shamed-1679127.html; "UK 'Least Wanted' List Published," *BBC News*, May 5, 2009, http://news.bbc.co.uk/2/hi/uk_news/8033060.stm. Similar measures were used in the 1980s and early 1990s against Nation of Islam leader Louis Farrakhan, a German nationalist, and a French Holocaust denier who had planned to speak to a group of neo-Nazis; see Joanna Oyediran, "The United Kingdom's Compliance with Article 4 of the International Convention on the Elimination of All Forms of Racial Discrimination," in *Striking a Balance*, 252–53. They were also used for blasphemy prevention in 1977, when Danish artist Jens Jurgen Thursen was barred from entering the United Kingdom as his plan to shoot the movie *The Sex Life of Christ* was deemed an offense against public morals; see Nash, *Blasphemy in the Christian World*, 205.

113. Alan Travis, "Geert Wilders Wins Appeal Against Ban on Travelling to UK," *The Guardian*, October 13, 2009, http://www.guardian.co.uk/world/2009/oct/13/geert-wilders-wins-appeal-ban-uk; Wilders's legal counsel in his appeal to the tribunal was Arfan Khan, described by the *Guardian* as "a British Muslim barrister."

114. "Leader of British Far-right Party Arrested," *AP*, December 14, 2004, http://www.independent.co.uk/news/uk/politics/bnp-official-arrested-over-claims-he-threatened-to-kill-nick-griffin-1936014.html; Rod Liddle, "Alas, I Must Defend the BNP," *The Sunday Times* (London), February 5, 2006, http://www.timesonline.co.uk/tol/comment/columnists/rod_liddle/article726871.ece.

115. Andrew Norfolk, "BNP Chief Claims Acquittal Is His Victory for Freedom," *The Times*, November 11, 2006, http://www.timesonline.co.uk/tol/news/uk/article633564.ece.

116. "Austrian Politician Threatened after Anti-Islam Comments: Ministry," *AFP*, January 15, 2008, http://www.lexisnexis.com/us/lnacademia/framedo?tokenKey=rsh-20.7447965078 75964.html; "Austria Politician Gets Threats for Anti-Islam rant," *Al Arabiya News*, January 16, 2008, http://www.alarabiya.net/articles/2008/01/16/44271.html; "Austrian Court Rejects Venue Change for Trial of Politician Who Disparaged Prophet Muhammad," *AP*, May 16, 2008, http://austriantimes.at/index.php?id=6017&print=1-newentry; "Austrian Far-right Legislator Convicted of Anti-Muslim Incitement," *Earth Times*, January 22, 2009, http://www.topnews.in/node/113757/list.

117. Christian Wienberg, "Danish Lawmakers Reported to Police for Remarks on Muslim Veils," *Bloomberg*, April 20, 2007, http://blog.taragana.com/politics/2010/01/28/denmark-urges-full-use-of-rules-limiting-muslim-face-veil-says-no-ban-needed-15717/; "Danish MP Who Compared Muslim Veil to Swastika Escapes Charges," *AFP*, September 24, 2007, http://www.alarabiya.net/articles/2007/09/24/39530.html.

118. Simon Bradley, "Anti-racism Body Slams Minaret Posters," *SwissInfo.ch*, October 7, 2009, http://www.swissinfo.ch/eng/Specials/Minaret_Debate/Result_and_reactions/Anti-racism_body_slams_minaret_posters.html?cid=45310; Michael Soukup, "Why the Swiss Are Afraid of Minarets," *Spiegel Online*, October 13, 2009, http://www.spiegel.de/international/europe/0,1518,654963,00.html.

119. "Sweden Democrat Leader Reported for 'Hate Speech,'" *The Local* (Sweden), October 20, 2009, http://www.thelocal.se/22762/20091020; "Politician Calls Islam Threat to Sweden," *United Press International*, October 19, 2009, http://www.upi.com/Top_News/International/2009/10/19/Politician-calls-Islam-threat-to-Sweden/UPI-53791255969898/; http://www.state.gov/g/drl/rls/hrrpt/2009/eur/136060.htm; "Sweden Democrats Lash Out Against Islam," *Sverige Radio*, October 19, 2009, http://www.sr.se/cgi-bin/international/artikel.asp?ProgramID=166&Nyheter=1&artikel=3177393. On a German case, see "German Central Bank Disempowers Board Member over Racist Remarks," *Deutsche Welle*, October 13, 2009, http://www.dw-world.de/dw/article/0,,4787728,00.html.

120. "C4 'Distorted' Mosque Program," *BBC News*, August 8, 2007, http://news.bbc.co.uk/2/hi/uk_news/england/west_midlands/6936681.stm.

121. "Mosque Programme Claims Rejected," *BBC News*, November 19, 2007, http://news.bbc.co.uk/2/hi/uk_news/england/west_midlands/7101728.stm.

122. "Police Apologise over Mosque Show," *BBC News*, May 15, 2008, http://news.bbc.co.uk/2/hi/uk_news/england/west_midlands/7401704.stm.

123. Pierre-Antoine Souchard, "French Author on Trial for Anti-Islam Comments," *AP*, September 17, 2002, http://vigilant.tv/article/2189/upi-french-author-on-trial-for-islam-slurs; Philip Delves Broughton, "Writer Defends Right to Call Islam 'Stupid,'" *Telegraph* (U.K.), September 18, 2002, http://www.telegraph.co.uk/news/worldnews/europe/france/1407582/Writer-defends-right-to-call-Islam-stupid.html; Pierre-Antoine Souchard, "French Court Throws Out Suit Against Writer's Remarks on Islam," *AP*, October 22, 2002; Joseph Coleman, "Trial of French Author Raises Questions about Freedom of Expression," *AP*, October 23, 2002.

124. "German Man Convicted of Disturbing Peace by Printing Name of Quran on Toilet Paper," *AP*, February 23, 2006, http://sheikyermami.com/2008/01/08/german-businessman-who-printed-name-of-quran-on-toilet-paper-will-face-trial/; "Man Who Made 'Koran' Toilet Paper Escapes Jail," *Irish Times*, February 24, 2006.

125. As quoted in "Dutchman Acquitted of Insulting Islam," *NRC Handelsblad*, March 10, 2009, http://www.nrc.nl/international/article2176521.ece/Dutchman_acquitted_of_insulting_Islam.

126. Ms. Sabaditsch-Wolff was interviewed in Vienna by Nina Shea on May 9, 2010, and, through email correspondence, on February 23, 2011.

127. Public Order Act 1986, http://www.opsi.gov.uk/RevisedStatutes/Acts/ukpga/1986/cukpga_19860064_en_2#pt1-l1g6; Crime and Security Act 2001, http://www.opsi.gov.uk/acts/acts2001/ukpga_20010024_en_5#pt5-l1g39. The latter act amended the Crime and Disorder Act 1998, which established categories of "racially aggravated" offenses, to include religion as well.

128. Paul Bracchi, "It May Have Been a Victory for Free Speech, but Why Did Breakfast Insult of Muslim's Faith Case Ever Come to Court?" *Daily Mail*, December 10, 2009, http://www.dailymail.co.uk/news/article-1234680/It-victory-free-speech-did-breakfast-insult-Muslims-faith-case-come-court.html#; Jonathan Wynne-Jones, "Christian Hoteliers Received Violent Threats Over Muslim Guest 'Insult,'" *Telegraph* (U.K.), December 12, 2009, http://www.telegraph.co.uk/news/newstopics/religion/6796508/Christian-hoteliers-received-violent-threats-over-Muslim-guest-insult.html. Also in Liverpool, atheist Harry Taylor left leaflets at the airport mocking Jesus, the pope, and Islam and was given an "Anti-Social Behaviour Order" that forbade him from carrying religiously offensive material in a public place, as well as a six-month sentence, suspended for two years, and was ordered to perform community service and pay costs. "Atheist Given Asbo for Leaflets Mocking Jesus," *Telegraph*, April 23, 2010, http://www.telegraph.co.uk/news/newstopics/religion/7624578/Atheist-given-Asbo-for-leaflets-mocking-Jesus.html.

129. "Inmate Sues to Stop Use of Alpha Course in Jail," news brief, *Charisma*, http://oralroberts.charismamag.com/index.php/component/content/article/232-unorganized/11308-news-briefs.

130. "Catholics Back Muslim Claims Against Evangelical Christians," *Catholic News*, March 22, 2005; Sarah Left, "Australian Ministry Vilified Muslims, Court Rules," *The Guardian*, December 17, 2004, http://www.guardian.co.uk/world/2004/dec/17/australia.religion.

131. Cardinal George Pell, "Religious Vilification," *Our People*, July 3, 2005, http://www.sydney.catholic.org.au/people/archbishop/stc/2005/200573_1095.shtml; see also Andrew West, "Religious Leaders Unite to Fight Vilification Laws," *Sydney Morning Herald*, April 23, 2009, http://www.smh.com.au/national/religious-leaders-unite-to-fight-vilification-laws-20090422-affp.html?page=-1. For Forsyth, see "Pastors Reject Apology Order over Koran Comments," Australian Broadcasting Corporation, June 22, 2005, http://www.abc.net.au/news/newsitems/200506/s1397914.htm.

132. The full text of Butler's article is at http://www.onlineopinion.com.au/view.asp?article=2274.

133. Henri Astier, "Speech Row Rocks Multi-ethnic Canada," *BBC News*, March 24, 2008. http://news.bbc.co.uk/2/hi/7273870.stm.

134. "MCC Shocked at OHRC Decision to Trumpet Islamist Cause," Muslim Canadian Congress, April 9, 2008, http://ezralevant.com/Statement%20on%20OHCR%20Macleans%20complaint.pdf; Randall Palmer, "Muslims Test Press Freedom Limits in Canadian Case," Reuters, January 6, 2008; "Rights Commission Dismisses Complaint Against Maclean's," *CBC News*, June 28, 2008; Brian Hutchinson, "The Court of Last Resort," *National Post*, June 3, 2008; Mohamed Elmasry, Complaint Form, BC Human Rights Tribunal, http://www.steynonline.com/images/macleans%20hr%20bc%20elmasry.pdf; Joseph Brean, "Maclean's Wins Third Round of Hate Fight," *National Post*, October 11, 2008, http://www.nationalpost.com/news/story.html?id=874166.

135. Canadian Human Rights Act, R.S.C. 1985, c. H-6, http://www.canlii.org/en/ca/laws/stat/rsc-1985-c-h-6/latest/rsc-1985-c-h-6.html; Alan Borovoy, "Hearing Complaint Alters Rights Body's Mandate," *The Calgary Herald*, March 16, 2006, http://www.safs.ca/issuescases/aborovoy.html.

136. Response to Stanley Kurtz, "Not Without a Fight," in *The New Criterion* (Summer 2008 supp.): 15.

137. Borovoy, "Hearing Complaint Alters Rights Body's Mandate."

138. Colin Perkel, "Investigators Hijacked Internet Link, Man Alleges," *The Globe and Mail*, April 3, 2008, http://www.theglobeandmail.com/news/national/article677447.ece; Charlie Gillis, "Righteous Crusader or Civil Rights Menace?" *Macleans*, April 9, 2008, http://www.macleans .ca/canada/national/article.jsp?content=20080409_48864_48864&page=1.

139. Athanasios D. Hadjis, *Richard Warman (Complainant) and Canadian Human Rights Commission (Commission) and Marc Lemire (Respondent)*, Canadian Human Rights Tribunal, September 2, 2009, http://chrt-tcdp.gc.ca/aspinc/search/vhtml-eng.asp?doid=981&lg=_e&isruling=0 #1011252.

140. Joseph Brean, "Hate Speech Law Unconstitutional: Rights Tribunal," *National Post*, September 2, 2009, http://www.nationalpost.com/story-printer.html?id=1954734; Karen Kleiss, "Complaints Against Alberta Newspapers Dismissed by Human Rights Commission," *Edmonton Journal*, September 23, 2009, http://www.edmontonjournal.com/news/Complai nts+against+Alberta+newspapers+dismissed+human+rights+commission/2025833/story. html; Deborah Tetley, "Alberta Judge Rules in Favor of Author of Anti-gay Letter," *National Post*, December 5, 2009, http://www.nationalpost.com/m/story.html?id=2305614&s= Today%27s%20Newspaper. On May 26, 2010, Judge Lusting suspended a Canadian Human Rights Tribunal hearing until the status of the section was clarified, see http://chrt-tcdp .gc.ca/aspinc/search/vhtml-eng.asp?doid=1012&lg=_e&isruling=0.

141. Brendan Carlin, "Hatred Bill goes ahead despite Church protests," *Telegraph*, July 12, 2005, http://www.telegraph.co.uk/news/uknews/1493826/Hatred-Bill-goes-ahead-despite-Church-protests.html.

142. "New Effort to Ban Religious Hate," *BBC News*, June 11, 2005, http://news.bbc.co.uk/2/hi/ uk_news/politics/4075442.stm; "Britain's 'Mr. Bean' Attacks Religious Hatred Bill," *New York Times*, December 6, 2004, http://www.telegraph.co.uk/comment/columnists/charles-moore/3613495/Is-it-only-Mr-Bean-who-resists-this-new-religious-intolerance.html; http://www.publications.parliament.uk/pa/ld200506/ldhansrd/vo051011/text/51011-04. htm.

143. "Muslim Poll—November 2004," *The Guardian*/ICM, p. 12, http://image.guardian.co.uk/ sys-files/Guardian/documents/2004/11/30/Muslims-Nov041.pdf.

144. Will Cummins, "We Must Be Allowed to Criticize Islam," *Telegraph* (U.K.), July 12, 2004, http://www.telegraph.co.uk/comment/personal-view/3608288/We-must-be-allowed-to-criticise-Islam.html.

145. Edward Black, "Blackadder's Deadly Serious Attack on 'Religious Hate' Bill," *The Scotsman*, December 7, 2004, http://www3.interscience.wiley.com/journal/118652185/abstract? CRETRY=1&SRETRY=0; David Hencke, "Celebrities Join Fight to Amend Bill on Religious Hatred," *The Guardian*, June 21, 2005, http://www.guardian.co.uk/politics/2005/jun/21/ religion.immigrationpolicy.

146. Sarah Hall and Tania Branigan, "Law to Safeguard Religion Is No Joke, Warns Blackadder," *The Guardian*, December 7, 2004, http://www.guardian.co.uk/media/2004/dec/07/racean-dreligion.broadcasting.

147. "New Effort to Ban Religious Hate."

148. Jon Ungoed-Thomas, "Witches See an Opportunity in New Hate Bill," *The Times*, October 23, 2005. http://www.timesonline.co.uk/tol/news/uk/article581694.ece.

149. "Silence, Blasphemers," *The Economist*, June 25, 2005, http://www.highbeam.com/ doc/1G1-133548709.html; Brendan Carlin, "Hatred Bill Goes ahead Despite Church Protests," *Telegraph*, July 12, 2005, http://www.telegraph.co.uk/news/uknews/1493826/ Hatred-Bill-goes-ahead-despite-Church-protests.html; "Free Speech v. Religion," *The Economist*, December 9, 2004, http://www5.economist.com/research/articlesBySubject/ displaystory.cfm?subjectid=2743324&story_id=E1_PQSSRTG.

150. James Jones, "As a Man of Faith, I Cannot Support the Religious Hatred Bill," *Telegraph* (U.K.), October 24, 2005.

151. "Religious Hatred Law Is No Joke," *Telegraph* (U.K.), December 6, 2004, http://www .guardian.co.uk/media/2004/dec/07/raceandreligion.broadcasting.

152. Maryam Namazie, "Political Islam in the Heart of Secular Europe," address to the International Humanist and Ethical Union Congress, July 6, 2005, http://www.scoop.co.nz/stories/WO0507/S00192.htm.

153. Geoffrey Robertson, "Religion Must Remain Open to Criticism," *The Scotsman*, January 26, 2005.

154. Salman Rushdie, "Democracy Is No Polite Tea Party," *Los Angeles Times*, February 7, 2005, http://articles.latimes.com/2005/feb/07/opinion/oe-rushdie7.

155. House of Commons Debates (Hansard) for June 21, 2005, http://www.publications.parliament.uk/pa/cm200506/cmhansrd/vo050621/debtext/50621-29.htm.

156. Stephen Bates and Julian Glover, "Christian Group May Seek Ban on the Qur'an," *The Guardian*, October 12, 2005, http://www.guardian.co.uk/uk/2005/oct/12/religion.immigrationpolicy.

157. "Muslims Warn Parties on Hate Bill," *Times* (U.K.), February 6, 2005, http://www.timesonline.co.uk/tol/news/uk/article511119.ece.

158. David Charter, "New Laws Will Keep Freedom to Insult Islam," *The Times*, January 26, 2005, http://www.timesonline.co.uk/tol/news/uk/article506510.ece.

159. House of Lords Debates (Hansard), October 11, 2005, http://www.publications.parliament.uk/pa/ld200506/ldhansrd/vo051011/text/51011-04.htm#51011-04_head3, and http://www.publications.parliament.uk/pa/ld200506/ldhansrd/vo051011/text/51011-11.htm.

160. Andrew Sparrow, "Mockery Is Good for the Faithful, Says Carey," *Telegraph* (U.K.), October 21, 2005, http://www.telegraph.co.uk/news/uknews/1501109/Mockery-is-good-for-the-faithful-says-Carey.html.

161. "Government Suffers Chaotic Double Defeat over Bill to Combat Religious Hatred," *The Guardian*, February 1, 2006, http://www.guardian.co.uk/politics/2006/feb/01/religion.immigrationpolicy. See Racial and Religious Hatred Act 2006, Office of Public Sector Information, February 16, 2006, http://www.opsi.gov.uk/acts/acts2006/ukpga_20060001_en_1.

162. "Blasphemy: UK and Eire," Caslon Analytics, http://www.caslon.com.au/blasphemyprofile8.htm; Sandberg and Doe, "Strange Death of Blasphemy," 976–81.

163. In the case, editor Denis Lemon was convicted of blasphemous libel and given a suspended sentence and fined; see Mark Thompson, "Sense Prevailed over Springer 'Blasphemy,'" *Telegraph* (U.K.), June 12, 2007, http://www.telegraph.co.uk/comment/personal-view/3644516/Sense-prevailed-over-Springer-blasphemy.html.

164. Chamber Judgment, *Giniewski v. France*, European Court of Human Rights—Press Release Issued by the Registrar, January 31, 2006, http://www.echr.coe.int/Eng/Press/2006/Jan/ChamberjudgmentGiniewskivFrance310106.htm; Dirk Voorhoof, "European Court of Human Rights—Case of Klein v. Slovakia," *IRIS* 1, article 1 (2007): 2, http://merlin.obs.coe.int/iris/2007/1/article1.en.html.

165. Parliamentary Assembly of the Council of Europe, Resolution 1510 (2006), "Freedom of Expression and Respect for Religious Beliefs," http://assembly.coe.int/Main.asp?link=/Documents/AdoptedText/ta06/ERES1510.htm.

166. Janssen, "Limits to Expression on Religion in France."

167. Venice Commission 2008, *Report*, 16–19.

168. Parliamentary Assembly of the Council of Europe, Recommendation 1805 (2007): "Blasphemy, Religious Insults and Hate Speech Against Persons on Grounds of Their Religion," adopted June 29, 2007, http://assembly.coe.int/Documents/AdoptedText/ta07/EREC1805.htm.

169. Venice Commission 2008, *Report*, 15.

170. "Europe Is Threatened by Bigots—Not by Islam," statement by Terry Davis, Secretary General of the Council of Europe, Press Release—590 (2007), http://www.coe.int/t/dc/av/allreleases_en.asp.

171. Venice Commission 2008, *Report*, 15. The commission reported that Europe's new hate-speech laws could "raise expectations concerning prosecution and conviction that will not be met."

172. Mark Rice-Oxley, "Free Speech in Europe: Mixed Rules," *Christian Science Monitor*, February 8, 2006, http://www.csmonitor.com/2006/0208/p01s01-woeu.html.

173. "Free Speech v. Religion."

Chapter 13

1. Raf Casert, "Belgian Politician Critical of Radical Muslims Moves to Secret Location after Death Threats," *Associated Press* (*AP*), November 17, 2004, http://www.accessmylibrary.com/coms2/summary_0286-14498646_ITM; Sebastian Rotella, "Belgian Killing, Threats Raise Specter of Fundamentalist Violence," *Los Angeles Times*, November 19, 2004, http://articles.latimes.com/2004/nov/19/world/fg-belgium19; Raf Casert, "Arrest Made in Case of Death Threats Against Belgian Politician," *AP*, November 19, 2004, http://articles.latimes.com/2004/nov/19/world/fg-belgium19.

2. Elaine Sciolino, "Teacher in Hiding After Attack on Islam Stirs Threats," *New York Times*, September 30, 2006, http://www.nytimes.com/2006/09/30/world/europe/30france.html; Jenny Percival and agencies, "Teacher Forced into Hiding after Attacking Islam," *The Times*, September 29, 2006, http://www.timesonline.co.uk/tol/news/world/europe/article655333.ece.

3. Charles Bremner, "Philosophers Demand Help for Teacher on Run from Islam threats," *The Times*, October 3, 2006; http://www.timesonline.co.uk/tol/news/world/europe/article658422.ece; "Report: Moroccan Police Arrest Man for Allegedly Threatening tTeacher in France," *International Herald Tribune*, January 9, 2007; http://www.unitedcopts.org/index2.php?option=com_content&do_pdf=1&id=631.

4. Sherna Noah, "BBC 'Too Scared to Allow Jokes about Islam,'" *Independent*, April 2, 2008, http://www.independent.co.uk/arts-entertainment/films/news/bbc-too-scared-to-allow-jokes-about-islam-803807.html; Dan Sabbagh, "BBC Chief Mark Thompson Warns of 'Over-cautious' Islam Coverage," *The Times*, April 10, 2008, http://www.timesonline.co.uk/tol/comment/faith/article3724384.ece. The Ben Elton interview is at http://www.thirdway.org.uk/290.

5. "Galloway Told to Avoid His Home," *BBC News*, April 20, 2005, http://news.bbc.co.uk/1/hi/uk_politics/vote_2005/frontpage/4467147.stm.

6. James Brandon and Salam Hafez, *Crimes of the Community: Honour-Based Violence in the UK* (London: Centre for Social Cohesion, 2008), http://www.londonscb.gov.uk/files/resources/cpp/crimes_of_the_community.pdf.

7. "Theo van Gogh Believed Provocation Was the Ultimate Freedom of Expression," *Agence France Presse* (*AFP*), July 11, 2005; Marlise Simons, "Dutch Filmmaker, an Islam Critic, Is Killed," *New York Times*, November 3, 2004, http://query.nytimes.com/gst/fullpage.html?res=9C06E7D61F3DF930A35752C1A9629C8B63&sec=&spon=&pagewanted=all; Ian Buruma, *Murder in Amsterdam: The Death of Theo van Gogh and the Limits of Tolerance* (London: Penguin, 2006), 87–99.

8. Paul Gallagher and Marcel Michelson, "Dutch Filmmaker, Who Angered Muslims, Shot Dead," Reuters, November 2, 2004, http://www.rense.com/general59/shot.htm.

9. Anthony Deutsch, "Dutch politician threatened in letter left on body of murdered filmmaker," *AP*, November 5, 2004, http://www.freerepublic.com/focus/f-news/1271036/posts; Ronald Rovers, "The Silencing of Theo van Gogh," *Salon*, November 24, 2004, http://dir.salon.com/news/feature/2004/11/24/vangogh/index.html.

10. Toby Sterling, "Alleged Killer of Filmmaker Van Gogh Dreamed of Overthrowing Dutch Government, Prosecutors Say," *AP*, January 26, 2005, http://www.encyclopedia.com/doc/1P1-104744913.html; David Rennie, "Contempt and defiance from Muslim accused of murdering film-maker," *Daily Telegraph*, July 12, 2005.

11. Buruma, *Murder in Amsterdam*, 210–12.

12. Ibid., 189; Glenn Frankel, "From Civic Activist to Alleged Terrorist," *Washington Post*, November 28, 2004, http://www.washingtonpost.com/wp-dyn/articles/A16855-2004Nov27.html; Anthony Browne, "Muslim Radical Confesses to Van Gogh Killing in Court tirade," *The Times*, July 12, 2005, http://www.timesonline.co.uk/tol/news/world/article543212.ece; "Van Gogh Suspect Refuses Defense," *BBC News*, July 11, 2005, http://news.bbc.co.uk/2/hi/europe/4670535.stm; Rennie, "Contempt and Defiance"; Philippe Naughton, "Van Gogh Killer Jailed for Life," *The Times*, July 26,

2005, http://news.bbc.co.uk/2/hi/europe/4716909.stm. In March 2006, nine members of the Hofstad group were convicted of membership in a terrorist organization; some received prison sentences of up to fifteen years and others were deported. See "Up to 15 Years in Prison for Nine Members of Dutch 'Terrorist' Network," *AFP*, March 10, 2006.

13. Anthony Browne, "Film-maker Is Murdered for His Art," *The Times*, November 3, 2004, http://www.timesonline.co.uk/tol/news/world/article502323.ece; Toby Sterling, "Filmmaker Who Criticized Islam Slain," *AP*, November 2, 2005, http://www.encyclopedia.com/doc/1P2-11145726.html; "Some 20,000 Dutch Gather to Pay Homage to Slain Controversial Filmmaker," *AFP*, November 2, 2004, http://www.abc.net.au/news/stories/2004/11/03/1233542.htm.

14. Glenn Frankel, "Controversial Dutch Filmmaker Is Slain," *Washington Post*, November 3, 2004, http://www.encyclopedia.com/doc/1P2-212183.html; "Many Fear Dutch Society Has Lost Its Famed Tolerance after Filmmaker's Murder," *AFP*, November 3, 2004.

15. Jan M. Olsen, "In Denmark, Leading Muslim Cleric Says Slain Dutch Filmmaker's Critique of Islam Unacceptable," *AP*, November 19, 2004; Carin Pettersson, "Norwegian Imam Supports van Gogh Murder," *Nettavisen*, November 19, 2004, http://pub.tv2.no/nettavisen/english/article304803.ece; "Norwegian Politicians March Against Muslim Violence," *AFP*, December 4, 2004.

16. Marlise Simons, "Militant Muslims Act to Suppress Dutch Film and Art Show," *New York Times*, January 31, 2005, http://query.nytimes.com/gst/fullpage.html?res=9801E6D9153BF932A05752C0A9639C8B63&sec=&spon=&pagewanted=all.

17. Michael McDonough, "Hundreds of Protestors Damage Theater in Protest over Sikh Play," *AP*, December 19, 2004; Tania Branigan and Vikram Dodd, "Writer in Hiding As Violence Closes Sikh Play," *The Guardian*, December 21, 2004, http://www.guardian.co.uk/uk/2004/dec/21/religion.arts; Nick Cohen, "Yet Again We Cave into Religious Bigots. And This Time They're Hindus," *The Observer*, May 28, 2006, http://www.guardian.co.uk/commentisfree/2006/may/28/arts.comment; Dan Sabbagh, "'Springer' Row a Threat to Free Speech—BBC Chief," *The Times*, March 8, 2005, http://news.bbc.co.uk/2/hi/uk_news/england/west_midlands/4606085.stm; "Oh Come All Ye Faithful," *The Economist*, January 15, 2005, http://www.economist.com/surveys/displaystory.cfm?story_id=10015239.

18. Richard Owen, "Muslims Say Fresco Must Be Destroyed," *The Times*, June 29, 2001, http://www.hvk.org/articles/0603/86.html.

19. Frank Bruni, "Italy Arrests 5; Fresco Showing Muhammad Is Issue," *New York Times*, August 21, 2002, http://www.nytimes.com/2002/08/21/international/europe/21ITAL.html; *Reuters*, "Italy Frees Fresco Suspects," *New York Times*, August 22, 2002, http://www.nytimes.com/2002/08/22/world/italy-frees-fresco-suspects.html?pagewanted=1; Sabina Castelfranco, "Italy Thwarts Terrorist Attack Days Before Election," *Voice of America News*, April 7, 2006, http://sweetness-light.com/archive/italy-foils-two-terrorist-attacks.

20. John Latham, "At War with the Tate," *Independent*, October 12, 2005, http://www.independent.co.uk/news/people/profiles/john-latham-at-war-with-the-tate-510620.html; Stephen Deuchar, "This Is Not Censorship, It's Safety," *The Guardian*, October 11, 2005, http://www.guardian.co.uk/artanddesign/2005/oct/11/art.terrorism.

21. Andrew Higgins, "Muslims Ask French to Cancel 1741 Play by Voltaire," *AP*, March 6, 2006, http://www.hyscience.com/archives/2006/03/muslims_ask_fre.php.

22. Craig Whitlock, "Fear of Muslim Backlash Cancels Opera," *Washington Post*, September 27, 2006, http://www.washingtonpost.com/wp-dyn/content/article/2006/09/26/AR2006092601352.html; David R. Sands, "Opera Canceled for Fear of Muslim Ire," *Washington Times*, September 27, 2006; Madeline Chambers, "Merkel Warns Against Bowing to Fear of Muslim Violence," *Reuters*, September 27, 2006, http://www.islamfortoday.com/germany01.htm; Craig Whitlock, "In German Opera, Heads Come Off Without Incident," *Washington Post*, December 18, 2006, http://www.washingtonpost.com/wp-dyn/content/article/2006/12/18/AR2006121801255.html; Mark Landler, "At German Conference on Muslim Relations, One Vote is Unanimous: Mozart Must Go On," *New York Times*, September 28, 2006, http://www.nytimes.com/2006/09/28/world/europe/28germany.html.

23. Geir Moulson, "Berlin Gallery Closes Danish Group's Exhibition after Threats over Poster," *AP*, February 29, 2008, http://www.Reuters.com/article/idUSL2860324220080228.

24. Kate Connolly, "Security Stepped Up As German Theater Breaks Taboo by Staging Satanic Verses," *The Guardian*, March 29, 2008, http://www.guardian.co.uk/stage/2008/mar/29/theatre.germany; "German Theater Stages Version of Rushdie's 'The Satanic Verses,'" *AP*, March 31, 2008.

25. Isabel Vincent, "'Jihad' Jitters at Met," *New York Post*, January 10, 2010, http://www.nypost.com/p/news/local/manhattan/jihad_jitters_at_met_76yj3VNUy4hcRAnhOcPCHP.

26. The Jewel of Medina statement by Random House Publishing Group, http://www.random-house.com/rhpg/medinaletter.html; Patricia Cohen, "Yale Press Bans Images of Muhammad in New Book," *New York Times*, August 12, 2009, http://www.nytimes.com/2009/08/13/books/13book.html; statement by Yale University Press, August 14, 2009, http://yalepress.yale.edu/yupbooks/KlausenStatement.asp.

27. For the interview with Klausen, see http://www.thefire.org/article/11418.html; Wendy Kaminer, "Index on Censorship Meets the Enemy Within," *The Atlantic*, December 21, 2010, http://www.theatlantic.com/national/archive/2009/12/index-on-censorship-meets-the-enemy-within/32439/.

28. Sarah Marsh, "German Publisher Cancels Book Seen Insulting Islam," Reuters, October 6, 2009, http://www.reuters.com/article/idUSTRE5952Y120091006.

29. Aaron Eitan Meyer, "Frankfurt Cancels 'Muhammad Look-alike Contest' Out of Fear of Offending Muslims," Legal Project Blog, October 30, 2008, http://www.legal-project.org/blog/2008/10/frankfurt-cancels-muhammad-look-alike.

30. "Fatwa for 'Gay Jesus' Writer," *BBC News*, October 29, 1999, http://news.bbc.co.uk/2/hi/uk/493436.stm. This quotation is of the BBC's paraphrase rather than of Sheik Muhammad's exact words.

31. "Muslim Gang Forces Paris Café to Censor Cartoon Show," *AFP*, March 31, 2006.

32. Ben Sisario, "London Gallery Removes Works," *New York Times*, October 7, 2006, http://query.nytimes.com/gst/fullpage.html?res=9D01E6D91230F934A35753C1A9609C8B63.

33. Giulio Meotti, "In the Casbah of Rotterdam," originally in *il Foglio*, May 14, 2009, trans. Matthew Sherry, http://chiesa.espresso.repubblica.it/articolo/1338480?eng=y.

34. "Men Plotted Against UK Publisher of Mohammad Book," Reuters, April 21, 2009, http://uk.reuters.com/article/idUKTRE53K2SO20090421; Asra Q. Nomani, "You Still Can't Write About Muhammad," *Wall Street Journal*, August 6, 2008, http://online.wsj.com/article/SB121797979078815073.html.

35. "'Draw Mohammad' Cartoonist Goes into Hiding at FBI's Insistence after Assassination Threat," *Fox News*, September 16, 2010.

36. Andrew Alexander, "Where Was the 'Where's Muhammad?' Cartoon?" *Washington Post*, October 10, 2010.

37. Tara Bahrampour, "Out of Suburbia, the Online Extremist," *Washington Post*, November 2, 2010; Nina Mandell, "Zachary Chesser, Man Who Threatened South Park Creators, Sentenced to 25 Years in Prison," *New York Daily News*, February 25, 2011.

38. Marlise Simons, "Militant Muslims Act to Suppress Dutch Film and Art Show," *New York Times*, January 31, 2005, http://query.nytimes.com/gst/fullpage.html?res=9801E6D9153BF932A05752C0A9639C8B63&sec=&spon=&pagewanted=all.

39. Jana Winter, "Iranian Artist Fights to Have Muhammad Art Displayed in Dutch Museums," *Fox News*, May 3, 2008, http://www.foxnews.com/story/0,2933,354075,00.html; Matthew Campbell, "Woman Artist Gets Death Threats over Gay Muslim Photos," *The Sunday Times*, January 6, 2008, http://www.timesonline.co.uk/tol/news/world/europe/article3137510.ece. For a similar case, see also "Swedish Museum Removes Painting after Complaints about Use of Muslim Verses," *AP*, February 3, 2005, http://www.accessmylibrary.com/coms2/summary_0286-18596867_ITM.

40. Ben Hoyle, "Artists Too Frightened to Tackle Radical Islam," *The Times*, November 19, 2007, http://entertainment.timesonline.co.uk/tol/arts_and_entertainment/visual_arts/

article2896431.ece; Tim Walker, "Hytner 'Is Afraid of Offending Muslims,'" *Daily Telegraph*, July 30, 2008, http://www.telegraph.co.uk/news/newstopics/mandrake/2472422/Hytner-is-afraid-of-offending-Muslims.html; Ben Child, "Emmerich Reveals Fear of Fatwa Axed 2012 Scene," *The Guardian*, November 3, 2009, http://www.guardian.co.uk/film/2009/nov/03/roland-emmerich-2012-kaaba.

41. Stephanie Van Den Berg, "Dutch Far-right Leader Fortuyn Shot Dead," *AFP*, May 6, 2002, http://news.bbc.co.uk/2/hi/europe/1971423.stm; Abrose Evans-Pritchard and Joan Clements, "Fortuyn Killed 'to Protect Muslims," *Daily Telegraph* (U.K.), March 28, 2003, http://www.telegraph.co.uk/news/worldnews/europe/netherlands/1425944/Fortuyn-killed-to-protect-Muslims.html.

42. Marlise Simons, "Behind the Veil: A Muslim Woman Speaks Out," *New York Times*, November 9, 2002, http://www.nytimes.com/2002/11/09/world/the-saturday-profile-behind-the-veil-a-muslim-woman-speaks-out.html?pagewanted=1; "I Won't Be Intimidated for Expressing My Views," *Expatica*, September 27, 2004, http://www.expatica.com/nl/main.htm; Christopher Caldwell, "Daughter of the Enlightenment," *New York Times*, March 3, 2005, http://www.nytimes.com/2005/04/03/magazine/03ALI.html; "Moving Stories: Ayaan Hirsi Ali," *BBC News*, December 23, 2003, http://news.bbc.co.uk/2/hi/3322399.stm; "Danger Women," *The Guardian* (U.K.), May 17, 2005, http://www.guardian.co.uk/film/2005/may/17/religion.immigration; Ayaan Hirsi Ali, *Infidel* (New York: Free Press, 2008), 285–86.

43. Ayaan Hirsi Ali, "Grief and Anger over Theo's Murder," *International Herald Tribune*, November 11, 2004, http://www.flameout.org/flameout/vangogh/griefandanger.html; Ronald Rovers, "The Silencing of Theo van Gogh," *Salon*, November 24, 2004; "Another Political Mrrder," *The Economist*, November 6, 2004, http://dir.salon.com/news/feature/2004/11/24/vangogh/index.html.

44. "Threatened Dutch MP out of Hiding," *BBC News*, January 18, 2005, http://news.bbc.co.uk/2/hi/europe/4183697.stm.

45. "Dutch Court Sentences Rappers over Threat lyrics," Reuters, January 27, 2005; Marlise Simons, "Two Dutch Deputies on the Run, from Jihad Death Threats," *New York Times*, March 4, 2005, http://www.nytimes.com/2005/03/04/international/europe/04hague.html; "Threatened MP Wilders Gains Permanent Secured Housing," *Expatica*, April 1, 2005, https://www.osac.gov/News/story.cfm?contentID=26632&print&print.

46. Deborah Scroggings, "The Dutch-Muslim Culture War," *The Nation*, June 9, 2005, http://www.thenation.com/doc/20050627/scroggins; Ayaan Hirsi Ali, "The Right to Offend," *NRC Handelsblad*, February 14, 2006, http://www.nrc.nl/opinie/article1654061.ece/The_Right_to_Offend; Marlise Simons, "Immigration Debate Divides the Dutch," *International Herald Tribune*, May 24, 2006.

47. "PM Has 'No Use' for Hirsi Ali's Cartoon Views," *Expatica*, February 10, 2006, http://www.expatica.com/nl/news/local_news/pm-has-no-use-for-hirsi-alis-cartoon-views-27556.html.

48. John Ward Anderson, "Discredited Somali Quits Dutch Politics," *Washington Post*, May 17, 2006, http://www.washingtonpost.com/wp-dyn/content/article/2006/05/16/AR2006051601872.html; "Dutch Disease," *Wall Street Journal*, May 16, 2006; "Muslim's Loss of Dutch Citizenship Stirs Storm," *New York Times*, May 18, 2006, http://www.nytimes.com/2006/05/18/world/europe/18dutch.html?sq=&st=nyt&scp=301&pagewanted=print; "Intolerant Netherlands," *Washington Post*, May 18, 2006, http://www.washingtonpost.com/wp-dyn/content/article/2006/05/17/AR2006051701903.html.

49. "Dutch Forced to Rethink Decision on Somali-born MP," *The Guardian* (U.K.), May 18, 2006, http://www.guardian.co.uk/world/2006/may/18/mainsection.international1. Also see Hirsi Ali's resignation speech, in "Ayaan Hirsi Ali: 'I Will Continue to Ask Uncomfortable Questions,'" *Middle East Quarterly* (Fall 2006), http://www.meforum.org/1029/ayaan-hirsi-ali-i-will-continue-to-ask; Marlise Simons, "Somali-Born Politician Allowed to Stay a Dutch Citizen," *New York Times*, June 27, 2006, http://www.nytimes.com/2006/06/28/world/europe/28dutch.html?sq=Balkenende&st=nyt&scp=53&pagewanted=all.

50. "Hirsi Ali Says Thanks but No Thanks," *Copenhagen Post*, October 17, 2007, http://larryh. newsvine.com/_news/2007/10/17/1031928-hirsi-ali-says-thanks-but-no-thanks-by-the-copenhagen-post-october-17-2007-1000.

51. "Former Dutch Lawmaker Ayaan Hirsi Ali to Seek Protection in France," *Deutsche Presse-Agentur*, February 10, 2008, http://www.france24.com/en/20080210-ayaan-hirsi-ali-seeks-islaam-dutch-MP-former-french-protection-france; Vanessa Mock, "EU Politicians Make Empty Promises to Hirsi Ali," *Expatica*, February 15, 2008, http://www.expatica.com/nl/lifestyle_leisure/news_focus/EU-politicians-make-empty-promises-to-Hirsi-Al.html? ppager=0.

52. "Man Gets Community Service for Death Threats to Dutch MP," *AFP*, December 3, 2004; Gareth Harding, "Interview: Geert Wilders—the New Fortuyn?" *United Press International*, December 1, 2004; "Dutch Prosecutor Demands Jail Sentence for Death Threat Against Lawmaker," *AFP*, November 19, 2004; "Dutch Shocked by Public Death Wish from Muslim," Reuters, November 24, 2004.

53. Daniel Schwammenthal, "An Ordinary Dutch Life," *Wall Street Journal*, November 18, 2006.

54. Marlise Simons, "2 Dutch Deputies on the Run from Jihad Death Threats," *New York Times*, March 4, 2005 http://www.nytimes.com/2005/03/04/international/europe/04hague.html; Christopher Caldwell, "Holland Daze," *Weekly Standard*, December 27, 2004, http://www .weeklystandard.com/Content/Public/Articles/000/000/005/059darxx.asp.

55. Keith B. Richburg, "In Netherlands, Anti-Islamic Polemic Comes with a Price," *Washington Post*, February 1, 2005, http://www.washingtonpost.com/wp-dyn/articles/A52502-2005Jan31.html; "Threatened MP Wilders Gains Permanent Secured Housing."

56. "Populist Politician Blasts Koran, Mohammed," *Daily Telegraph*, February 14, 2007; Ian Traynor, "'I Don't Hate Muslims. I Hate Islam,' says Holland's Rising Political Star," *The Guardian* (U.K.), February 17, 2008, http://www.guardian.co.uk/world/2008/feb/17/ netherlands.islam.

57. Nicolien den Boer, "'Qur'an Should Be Banned'—Wilders Strikes Again," Radio Netherlands, August 8, 2007, http://static.rnw.nl/migratie/www.radionetherlands.nl/ currentaffairs/ned070808mc-redirected; Michel Hoebink, "Hirsi Ali's Ally Attacked by Fellow Islam Critics," Radio Netherlands, May 4, 2007 http://static.rnw.nl/migratie/www. radionetherlands.nl/currentaffairs/ned070405-redirected; "Dutch Far Right MP Snubs EU, Refuses Seat," *Washington Post*, June 11, 2009, http://tvnz.co.nz/world-news/dutch-far-right-mp-snubs-eu-seat-after-win-2781029, Aaron Gray-Block, "Dutch Anti-Islam Politician Wilders Plans New Film," Reuters, April 16, 2009, http://www.geertwilders.nl/ index.php?option=com_content&task=view&id=1571.

58. Anthony Deutsch, "Popular Dutch Lawmaker Urges Halt to Non-Western Immigrants, Shutting Down Radical Mosques," *AP*, November 19, 2004; Schwammenthal, "An Ordinary Dutch Life"; Harding, "Interview: Geert Wilders—the New Fortuyn?"

59. Anthony Browne, "Death Threats Force Controversial Dutch MP Underground," *The Times* (U.K.), November 20, 2004, http://www.timesonline.co.uk/tol/news/world/article393161 .ece.

60. "Muslims in Sweden Protest Against Preacher Calling Mohammed 'Pedophile,'" *AFP*, April 24, 2005, http://www.aftenposten.no/english/local/article1024117.ece.

61. James Brandon, "Sweden's Rising Muslim Tide," *Christian Science Monitor*, December 6, 2005, http://www.csmonitor.com/2005/1206/p07s02-woeu.html.

62. Lauren Elkin, "Jewish Philosopher at Centre of Riot Debate," *Canadian Jewish News*, December 8, 2005; Hillel Halkin, "Finkielkraut's Plain Talk on Race," *New York Sun*, November 29, 2005, http://www.nysun.com/opinion/finkielkrauts-plain-talk-on-race/23689/; Daniel Ben-Simon, "French Philosopher Alain Finkielkraut Apologizes after Death Threats," *Ha'aretz*, November 27, 2005, http://www.haaretz.com/hasen/pages/ShArt.jhtml? itemNo=650155; Daniel Ben Simon, "France's Sarkozy Backs Beleaguered Finkielkraut over Muslim Riot Comments," *Ha'aretz*, December 7, 2005, http://www.haaretz.com/hasen/ pages/ShArt.jhtml?itemNo=654055.

63. Michael Nazir-Ali, "Extremism Flourished as UK Lost Christianity," *Daily Telegraph* (U.K.), January 5, 2008, http://www.telegraph.co.uk/news/uknews/1574695/Extremism-flourished-as-UK-lost-Christianity.html.

64. "British Bishop Says He Faces Threats after Comments on Islamic Extremism," *AP*, February 2, 2008, http://www.encyclopedia.com/doc/1A1-D8U022503.html; Jonathan Wynne-Jones, "Bishop Warns of No-go Zones for Non-Muslims," *Daily Telegraph* (U.K.), January 5, 2008, http://www.telegraph.co.uk/news/uknews/1574694/Bishop-warns-of-no-go-zones-for-non-Muslims.html.

65. Quoted in Jonathan Wynne-Jones, "Bishop of Rochester Reasserts 'No-go' Claim," *Daily Telegraph*, February 24, 2008, http://www.telegraph.co.uk/news/uknews/1579661/Bishop-of-Rochester-reasserts-no-go-claim.html.

66. Daveed Gartenstein-Ross, "The Freedoms We Fight For," *The Weekly Standard*, blog p. 2, November 28, 2005, http://www.weeklystandard.com/Content/Public/Articles/000/000/006/395unguo.asp.

67. Jonathan Petre, "Minister Beaten after Clashing with Muslims on His TV Show," *Daily Mail*, March 15, 2009, http://www.dailymail.co.uk/news/article-1162039/Minister-beaten-clashing-Muslims-TV-show.html. Attacks also take place outside the West: Father Daniil Sysoyev, a Russian Orthodox priest, was killed in his church on November 19, 2009. He had received fourteen death threats for his attempts to convert Muslims. An Islamic group from the Caucasus claims responsibility for the assassination; see "Islamists Claim Killing of Russian Priest," *AFP*, December 25, 2009, http://www.google.com/hostednews/afp/article/ALeqM5hJOiv_HtszrmgOpKIJWuc5203W3A; "Likely Killer of Priest Daniil Sysoyev Identified," *The Voice of Russia*, January 27, 2010, http://english.ruvr.ru/2010/01/27/3917253.html.

68. Alexander Stille, "Scholars Are Quietly Offering New Theories of the Koran," *New York Times*, March 2, 2002, http://www.nytimes.com/2002/03/02/arts/scholars-are-quietly-offering-new-theories-of-the-koran.html?pagewanted=1.

69. Translation by the Center for Islamic Pluralism in "CIP Urgent Media Bulletin Re Death Threat—April 12, 2006," http://www.islamicpluralism.org/news/2006n/06urgentmediabulletin.htm; Munir al Mawry, "Arab Intellectuals Receive Death Threat," *Asharq Alawsat*, October 4, 2006, http://www.aawsat.com/english/news.asp?section=1&id=4484.

70. Derek Scally, "Muslim Lawyer Shuts Berlin Office," *Irish Times*, September 6, 2006, http://www.irishtimes.com/newspaper/world/2006/0906/1156791421300.html; Peter Schneider, "In Germany, Muslims Grow Apart; Islam in Europe," *International Herald Tribune*, December 3, 2005, http://www.nytimes.com/2005/12/02/world/europe/02iht-islam7.html; "Europe's New Dissidents," *Wall Street Journal*, September 6, 2006, http://online.wsj.com/article/SB113902160067465086.html.

71. "Europe's New Dissidents."

72. Marlise Simons, "Muslim Women Take Charge of Their Faith," *International Herald Tribune*, December 2, 2005, http://www.nytimes.com/2005/12/01/world/europe/01iht-islam6.html.

73. "Necla Kelek, 49, Best-selling Author," *International Herald Tribune*, December 1, 2005, http://www.hewaronline.net/mideast/neclakelek.htm.

74. "Lawmaker Threatened for Head Scarf Comments," *AP*, October 31, 2006, http://www.msnbc.msn.com/id/15501366; see also Douglas Murray and Johan Pieter Verwey, *Victims of Intimidation* (London: Centre for Social Cohesion, 2008), 6–7, http://www.socialcohesion.co.uk/files/1231525439_1.pdf.

75. Stefanie Von Brochowski, "German Lawmaker Gets Death Threats after Urging Muslim Women to take off Head Scarves," *AP*, October 31, 2006, http://legacy.signonsandiego.com/news/world/20061031-1134-germany-headscarves.html; Stefanie Von Brochowski, "German Greens Seek Muslim Support for Lawmaker Threatened over Head Scarf Comments," *AP*, November 1, 2006, http://www.accessmylibrary.com/coms2/summary_0286-23191178_ITM.

76. Sarah Lyall, "Sweden's Lightning Rod in a Storm over Assimilation," *New York Times*, January 13, 2007, http://www.nytimes.com/2007/01/13/world/europe/13profile.html; Helena

Frith Powell, "Sweden's Muslim Minister Turns on Veil," *The Sunday Times*, October 22, 2006, http://www.timesonline.co.uk/tol/news/world/article608929.ece; David Charter, "Young, Black, Swedish—the Minister for Controversy," *The Times*, May 21, 2007, http://www.timesonline.co.uk/tol/news/world/europe/article1816494.ece.

77. Phil Stewart, "Interview—Italy MP Gets Death Threats from Muslim Radicals," Reuters, April 1, 2009, http://dalje.com/en-world/italy-mp-gets-death-threats-from-muslim-radicals/247833.

78. "Italy: MP in Court to Defend Herself Against Death 'Fatwa,'" AdnKronosInternational, June 18, 2009, http://www.adnkronos.com/AKI/English/Religion/?id=3.0.3439029989; Valentina Colombo, "Counter-Jihad by Court: A Historical Victory," http://www.hudsonny.org/2009/07/counter-jihad-by-court-a-historical-victory.php.

79. "Kadra Attacked in Public," *Aftenposten* (Norway), April 13, 2007, http://www.fgmnetwork.org/gonews.php?subaction=showfull&id=1176586438&archive=&start_from=&ucat=1&; "2 Men Arrested in Norway after Attack on Critic of Islam," *AP*, April 16, 2007, http://www.mail-archive.com/osint@yahoogroups.com/msg39607.html.

80. Teresa Wiltz, "The Woman Who Went to the Front of the Mosque," *Washington Post*, June 5, 2005, http://www.washingtonpost.com/wp-dyn/content/article/2005/06/04/AR2005060401646.html.

81. Gary Robertson, "Safety of Muslim VCU Professor Discussed," *Richmond Times-Dispatch*, March 25, 2005; Nadia Abou El-Magd, "N.Y. Prayer Service Irks Mideast Muslims," *AP*, March 18, 2005, http://www.ewoss.com/articles/D88U965G3.aspx.

82. Sarah Coleman, "Shabana Rehman: Making Fun of the Mullahs," *World Press Review* 50, no. 9 (2003): http://www.worldpress.org/Europe/1437.cfm; Craig S. Smith, "Militant Mullah Meets Match in Comic at Norway Nightclub," *New York Times*, April 30, 2004, http://www.nytimes.com/2004/04/30/international/europe/30norw.html?pagewanted=1; Matthew Campbell, "Heard the One about the Rebel Muslim Girl?" February 9, 2003, *Sunday Times*, http://www.timesonline.co.uk/tol/news/world/article869830.ece; Craig S. Smith, "Skien Journal: Where East Meets West Warily, She Makes Them Laugh," *New York Times*, November 14, 2003, http://www.nytimes.com/2003/11/14/world/skien-journal-where-east-meets-west-warily-she-makes-them-laugh.html?pagewanted=1; "Shots Fired at Pakistani-born Comic's Oslo Restaurant," *Daily Times*, August 25, 2005, http://www.dailytimes.com.pk/default.asp?page=story_25-8-2005_pg7_39.

83. "Deputy of Syrian-Palestinian Origin Returned in Danish Poll," *AFP*, November 21, 2001; James Brandon, "Europe's Muslims Divided in Wake of Cartoon Furor," *Christian Science Monitor*, March 6, 2006, http://www.encyclopedia.com/doc/1G1-142850585.html; Lorenzo Vidino, "Finding Partners in Islam," *Boston Globe*, May 9, 2007, http://www.boston.com/news/globe/editorial_opinion/oped/articles/2007/05/09/finding_partners_in_islam/.

84. "Danish PM Hosts Controversial Meeting on Terror and Radical Islam," *AFP*, September 20, 2005; "Moderate Danish Muslims Targets of Attacks and Death Threats," report by *Politiken* via BBC Monitoring Europe, November 22, 2004.

85. Kevin Sullivan, "Turmoil over Cartoons Began Quietly among Danes," *Washington Post*, February 8, 2006, http://pewforum.org/news/display.php?NewsID=6343; Doug Saunders, "A Tale of Two Muslim Danes," *The Globe and Mail* (Canada), February 11, 2006; "Denmark's Democratic Muslims Organization Gains 1,500 Members in First Month," report by *Politiken* via BBC Monitoring Europe, March 7, 2006; "Danish Poll Shows Fall in Support for Democratic Muslims Group over Past Year," text of report by Ritzau Bureau originally titled "Democratic Muslims Losing Support," via BBC Monitoring Europe, January 17, 2007.

86. "Naser Khader and Flemming Rose: Reflections on the Danish Cartoon Controversy," interview by Daniel Pipes, *Middle East Quarterly* 14, no. 4 (Fall 2007): http://www.meforum.org/1758/naser-khader-and-flemming-rose-reflections-on; "Disgruntled Lawmakers Form New Party in Denmark," *AP*, May 7, 2007, http://blog.polilux.dk/#post2; "Liberal Alliance Founder Leaves Party," *The Copenhagen Post*, January 5, 2009, http://www.cphpost.dk/news/politics/90-politics/43917-liberal-alliance-founder-leaves-party.html.

87. Jan M. Olsen, "Denmark PM Discusses Cartoons Crisis with Moderate Muslims," *AP*, February 13, 2006, http://www.accessmylibrary.com/coms2/summary_0286-12698233_ITM; "Report: Spokesman for Danish Imams Appears to Call for Bomb Attack Against Lawmaker," *AP*, March 23, 2006.

88. "Danish Imams Not Charged over Comments in Documentary," report by Danmarks Radio via BBC Monitoring Europe, March 27, 2006; "Danish Islamic Group Removes Spokesman after Apparent Call for Bomb Attack," *AP*, March 25, 2006. For other Danish examples, see "Moderate Muslims Afraid to Speak Out," *Copenhagen Post*, November 16, 2004, http://www.cphpost.dk/get/83602.html; "Moderate Danish Muslims Targets of Attacks and Death Threats."

89. Arthur Max, "Dutch Cabinet Gets Its First Muslims," *AP*, February 21, 2007 http://www.religionnewsblog.com/00017542; Anthony Browne, "The Death of an Easygoing Culture," *The Times*, November 19, 2005, http://www.timesonline.co.uk/tol/news/world/europe/article591787.ece; *Victims of Intimidation*, 2–3; Buruma, *Murder in Amsterdam*, 247–53.

90. Keith B. Richburg, "In Netherlands, Anti-Islamic Polemic Comes with a Price," *Washington Post*, February 2005, http://www.washingtonpost.com/wp-dyn/articles/A52502-2005Jan31.html.

91. Jason Burke, "Holland's First Immigrant Mayor Is Hailed as 'Obama on the Maas,'" *The Guardian*, January 11, 2009, http://www.guardian.co.uk/world/2009/jan/11/netherlands-rotterdam-race-ahmed-aboutaleb.

92. "Stop Capitulating to Threats—a Manifesto," January 21, 2006, http://afshinellian.blogspot.com/2006_01_01_archive.html.

93. Caldwell, "Holland Daze"; Craig Whitlock, "For Public Figures in Netherlands, Terror Becomes a Personal Concern," *Washington Post*, November 11, 2005, http://www.washingtonpost.com/wp-dyn/content/article/2005/11/10/AR2005111002046.html.

94. Sonya Fatah, "Fearing for Safety, Muslim Official Quits," *The Globe and Mail*, August 3, 2006, http://sonyafatah.com/blog/2006/08/03/fearing-for-safety-muslim-official-quits/.

95. Radhika Panjwani, "Muslim Leader Fears Backlash over Liberal Views," *The Mississauga News*, October 13, 2006.

96. Interview with Salim Mansur, May 22, 2010.

97. David B. Harris, "Report from the Northern Front: Montreal Redux," Investigative Project on Terrorism, October 14, 2008, http://www.investigativeproject.org/article/789. Omar El Akkad, "Pakistan-based Muslim Group Behind Attack, Journalist Says," *The Globe and Mail*, April 20, 2007, http://hogtownfront.blogspot.com/2007/04/pakistani-canadian-journalist-may-have.html; "Weekly Journalist on Pakistani Paper Beaten with Cricket Bat," *Reporters Without Borders*, April 23, 2007, http://en.rsf.org/canada-weekly-journalist-on-pakistani-23-04-2007,21880.

98. The book was originally titled *The Trouble with Islam: A Wake Up Call for Honesty and Change* (Toronto: Random House Canada, 2004), but later editions changed this to *The Trouble with Islam Today*, which is the title usually followed in the more than thirty translations; Irshad Manji, "How the West Can Revive Islam," *Time Canada*, September 13, 2004; Irshad Manji, "Outside View: Challenging Islam Is Risky," *United Press International*, November 2, 2004, http://www.irshadmanji.com/news/upi-04-11-02.html; Interview with Irshad Manji by John Glassie, *New York Times*, December 21, 2003, http://www.nytimes.com/2003/12/21/magazine/21QUESTIONS.html?pagewanted=1; DeNeen L. Brown, "'Muslim Refusenik' Incites Furor with Critique of Faith," *Washington Post*, January 19, 2004, http://www.muslim-refusenik.com/news/washingtonpost-040118.html; Irshad Manji, "Salman Rushdie's Knighthood Should Be the Last Thing to Offend Muslims," *The New Republic Online*, June 22, 2007, http://www.irshadmanji.com/news/timesOfLondon_June_26_07.html; Irshad Manji, "Religion Is the Root Cause of Terrorist Threat," *The Australian*, July 5, 2007, http://www.theaustralian.com.au/news/opinion/irshad-manji-religion-is-the-root-cause-of-terrorist-threat/story-e6frg6zo-1111113886840; Clifford Krauss, "An Unlikely Promoter of an Islamic Reformation," *New York Times*, October 4, 2003, http://www.irshadmanji.com/news/nytimes-oct4-03.html.

99. Daniel Pipes, "[Khalid Duran] An American Rushdie?" *Jerusalem Post*, July 4, 2001, http://www.danielpipes.org/384/khalid-duran-an-american-rushdie; Nat Hentoff, "His Blood Could Be Shed," *Washington Times*, July 9, 2001; Khalid Duran, "How CAIR Put My Life in Peril," *The Middle East Quarterly* 9, no. 1 (Winter 2002); Khalid Duran, personal communication, Washington, D.C., February 14, 2009.

100. "Muslim Imam in France Defies Death Threats to Continue Efforts to Reach out to Jewish Neighbors," *International Herald Tribune*, January 22, 2009, http://www.cleveland.com/world/index.ssf/2009/01/muslim_imam_in_france_defies_d.html.

101. Akbar Ahmed, "A Message of Violence and Hatred," *The Independent* (U.K.), July 1, 2004, http://www.independent.co.uk/opinion/commentators/akbar-ahmed-a-message-of-violence-and-hatred-565370.html.

102. See Ibn Warraq, *Leaving Islam; Apostates Speak Out* (New York: Prometheus. 2003).

103. "There Can Be No End to Jihad"—Interview with Sheikh Omar Bakri Muhammad by Anthony McRoy, *Christianity Today*, February 1, 2005, http://www.christianitytoday.com/ct/2005/februaryweb-only/22.0.html; First Collection of Fatwas, trans. Anas Osama Altikriti, European Council for Fatwa and Research, 16–17, www.e-cfr.org/data/cat30072008113814.doc.

104. Munira Mirza, Abi Senthilkumaran, and Zein Ja'far, *Living Apart Together: British Muslims and the Paradox of Multiculturalism* (London: Policy Exchange, 2007), 47, http://www.policyexchange.org.uk/assets/Living_Apart_Together_text.pdf.

105. Ibn Warraq, *Why I Am Not a Muslim* (New York: Prometheus, 2003); "Ibn Warraq: Why I Am Not a Muslim," interview with Stephen Crittenden, on *The Religion Report*, Australian Broadcasting Company (ABC) Radio National, January 23, 2002, http://www.abc.net.au/rn/religionreport/stories/2002/440586.htm; Lee Smith, "Losing His Religion: Apostate Ibn Warraq Campaigns for the Right Not to Be a Muslim," *Boston Globe*, August 17, 2003, http://www.boston.com/news/globe/ideas/articles/2003/08/17/losing_his_religion_boston_globe?mode=PF; Alexander Stille, "Scholars Are Quietly Offering New Theories of the Koran."

106. "'Not Possible to Modernize Islam," *Der Spiegel*, February 27, 2007, http://www.spiegel.de/international/spiegel/0,1518,468828,00.html; "Founder of Ex-Muslim Group Threatened," *United Press International*, February 23, 2007, http://right-mind.us/blogs/blog_0/archive/2007/02/26/50221.aspx.

107. Riazat Butt, "New Ex-Muslim Group Speaks Out," *The Guardian*, June 22, 2007, http://www.guardian.co.uk/uk/2007/jun/22/religion.immigrationpolicy; Jonathan Petre, "New Group for Those Who Renounce Islam," *Daily Telegraph* (U.K.), June 21, 2007, http://www.telegraph.co.uk/news/worldnews/1555263/New-group-for-those-who-renounce-Islam.html; "Europe: New Groups Unite Those Who Renounce Islam," Radio Free Europe, September 11, 2007, http://www.rferl.org/content/article/1078630.html.

108. *Victims of Intimidation*, 8–9; "Extra Security for Ehsan Jami," *Expatica*, August 7, 2007; Toby Sterling, "Muslims Who Renounce Their Faith Band Together in European Countries," *AP*, September 11, 2007, http://www.mail-archive.com/islamkristen@yahoogroups.com/msg108414.html.

109. "Dutch Politician Launches Committee for Ex-Muslims," *AFP*, September 11, 2007, http://static.rnw.nl/migratie/www.radionetherlands.nl/currentaffairs/dut070911mc-redirected.

110. David Charter, "Young Muslims Begin Dangerous Fight for the Right to Abandon Faith," *The Times*, September 11, 2007, http://www.timesonline.co.uk/tol/news/world/europe/article2426314.ece; "Dutch Politician Launches Committee for Ex-Muslims."

111. Johann Hari, "Why Do We Ignore the Plight of Ex-Muslims?" *The Independent* (London), October 25, 2007, http://www.independent.co.uk/opinion/commentators/johann-hari/johann-hari-why-do-we-ignore-the-plight-of-exmuslims-395287.html; "Jami Writes Opinion Piece with Wilders," *Expatica*, September 27, 2007, http://www.expatica.com/nl/news/local_news/jami-writes-opinion-piece-with-wilders-44322_39986.html; "Ex-Muslim Jami Asked to Quit Council Seat," *DutchNews.nl*, October 15, 2007, http://www.dutchnews.nl/news/archives/2007/10/exmuslim_jami_asked_to_quit_co.php; "Councillor shuts down

committee for ex-Muslims," *Expatica*, April 17, 2008, http://www.expatica.com/nl/news/local_news/Councillor-shuts-down-committee-for-ex_Muslims.html.

112. Ab Zagt, "Dutch Concern over New Anti-Muslim Film," *Hollywood Reporter*, March 31, 2008; "Dutch Ex-Muslim Producing the Life of Muhammad," Radio Netherlands, March 27, 2008, http://www.radionetherlands.nl/news/international/5704094/Dutch-exMuslim-producing-IThe-Life-of-MuhammadI.

113. "Dutch Politician Drops Plan for Muhammad Film," Radio Netherlands via BBC Monitoring Europe, March 31, 2008.

114. "Dutch Politician Presents Another Islam Film," Radio Netherlands Worldwide, December 9, 2008, http://www.rnw.nl/node/1304; "Nizhny Novgorod Muftis to Boycott Flowers from Holland," *Interfax*, February 25, 2009, http://www.interfax-religion.com/?act=news&div=5736. A statement by the Dutch government on the Jami film, December 10, 2008, is http://www.government.nl/News/Press_releases_and_news_items/2008/December/Statement_by_the_Dutch_government_on_Jami_film.

115. "Women at War with the Mullahs," *The Times* (U.K.), March 19, 2006, http://www.timesonline.co.uk/tol/news/article742646.ece; Kerry Howley, "Breaking the Silence," *Reader's Digest* (December 2006), http://www.rd.com/your-america-inspiring-people-and-stories/a-woman-speaks-out-against-radical-islam/article31196.html; John M. Broder, "For Muslim Who Says Violence Destroys Islam, Violent Threats," *New York Times*, March 11, 2006, http://www.nytimes.com/2006/03/11/international/middleeast/11sultan.html.

116. "Women at War with the Mullahs"; Kerry Howley, "Breaking the Silence"; John M. Broder, "For Muslim Who Says Violence Destroys Islam, Violent Threats."

117. "Al Jazeera Apology for Guest Remark," *Al Jazeera*, March 5, 2008, http://english.aljazeera.net/news/middleeast/2008/03/200852513839603413.html.

118. "Sheik Yousuf Al-Qaradhawi Accuses Arab-American Psychiatrist Wafa Sultan of Cursing Allah on Al Jazeera TV," MEMRI Clip No. 1718, March 16, 2008, http://www.memritv.org/clip/en/1718.htm; "MPAC Calls on Al Jazeera to Stop Spreading Islamophobia," Muslim Public Affairs Council, March 6, 2008, http://www.mpac.org/article.php?id=617.

119. There is also the phenomenon that some such converts exaggerate their life history in order to impress audiences; see Omar Sacirbey, "Skeptics Challenge Life Stories Offered by High-profile Muslim Converts to Christianity," *Washington Post*, June 26, 2010, http://www.washingtonpost.com/wp-dyn/content/article/2010/06/25/AR2010062504435.html. Nevertheless, this exaggeration should not obscure the very real dangers that many converts face.

120. John Hooper, "St Peter Role Prompts Death Threat," *The Guardian*, October 31, 2005, http://www.guardian.co.uk/world/2005/oct/31/film.alqaida.

121. "Muslim Peril in a New Faith," *Washington Times*, September 6, 2004, http://www.washingtontimes.com/news/2004/sep/06/20040906-124525-1020r/; Gartenstein-Ross, "The Freedoms We Fight For"; Jeffrey Donovan, "Islam's Challenges to 'Universal Human Rights,'" Radio Free Europe/Radio Liberty, December 9, 2008, http://www.rferl.org/content/Islams_Challenges_To_Universal_Human_Rights/1357912.html?spec=2.

122. Anthony Browne, "Muslim Apostates Cast Out and at Risk from Faith and Family," *The Times*, February 5, 2005, http://www.timesonline.co.uk/tol/news/uk/article510589.ece.

123. Browne, "Muslim Apostates Cast Out." See also Ziya Meral, *No Place to Call Home: Experience of Apostates from Islam, Failures of the International Community* (Surrey, U.K.: Christian Solidarity Worldwide, 2008), p. 63.

124. Ruth Gledhill, "British Imam's Daughter under Police Protection after Converting to Christianity," *The Times*, December 5, 2007, http://www.timesonline.co.uk/tol/comment/faith/article3006561.ece; Dominic Lawson, "My Imam Father Came after Me with an Axe," *The Times*, March 15, 2009, http://www.timesonline.co.uk/tol/comment/faith/article5907458.ece.

125. Colby Cosh, "Testing Religious Freedom in the West," *National Post*, March 24, 2008, http://www.nationalpost.com/opinion/columnists/story.html?id=77305e89-def0-4c80-a818-

16d9f571217c&k=6512; Philip Pullella, "Muslim Baptized by Pope Says Life in Danger," *Reuters*, March 23, 2008, http://www.reuters.com/article/idUSL238305320080323; "New 'Salman Rushdie' in Italy? The Case of Magdi Allam," *Al-Bawaba*, July 31, 2007, http://www.albawaba.com/en/countries/Egypt/215622.

126. Magdi Allam's letter to the editor of the *Corriere della Sera*, as quoted in "Magdi Allam Recounts His Path to Conversion," *Zenit*, March, 23, 2008, http://www.zenit.org/rssenglish-22151; "Muslim in Vatican Talks Slams Convert's Baptism," *USA Today*, March 25, 2008, http://www.usatoday.com/news/religion/2008-03-25-vatican-muslim_N.htm; "Terrorism: Italian PM and Christian Convert Targets of Islamist Death Threats," AdnKronosInternational, June 7, 2008, http://www.unitedcopts.org/index.php?option=com_content&task=view&id=2627.

127. Pullella, "Muslim Baptized by Pope Says Life in Danger"; "Scholar denounces Muslim Baptism," *BBC News*, March 26, 2008, http://www.reuters.com/article/idUSL 238305320080323; "Vatican Aide Responds to Muslim Professor," *Zenit*, March 30, 2008, http://www.zenit.org/article-22158?l=english.

Chapter 14

1. Abdurrahman Wahid, "Right Islam vs. Wrong Islam," *Wall Street Journal*, December 30, 2005, http://www.libforall.org/news-WSJ-right-islam-vs.-wrong-islam.html.

2. See my lecture, "The Qur'an: God and Man in Communication" (inaugural lecture for the Cleveringa Chair, Leiden University, Leiden, November 27, 2000), http://www.let.leide-nuniv.nl/forum/01_1/onderzoek/2.htm.

3. I have more recently pursued my work in this area in conjunction with LibForAll Foundation, through its International Institute of Qur'anic Studies (IIQS). The International Institute of Qur'anic Studies has its base of operations in Indonesia, where the late Kyai Haji Abdurrahman Wahid and Dr. Syafi'i Ma'arif—former heads of the world's two largest Muslim organizations, the Nahdlatul Ulama and Muhammadiyah, with a total of seventy million members—have worked closely with the IIQS, serving as its patrons and senior advisors; see http://www.libforall.org/.

Chapter 15

* This chapter is based on the work of the authors Abdullah Saeed and Hassan Saeed, Freedom of Religion, Apostasy and Islam (Aldershot, U.K.: Ashgate, 2004).

1. Sheikh Muhammed Salih Al-Munajjid, "Punishment of the One Who Leaves Islam," Islam QA (Question & Answer), http://islamqa.com/en/ref/696.

2. Muhammad b. Ali b. Muhammad al-Shawkani, *Nayl al-Awtar*, vol. 7 (Beirut: Dar al-Kutub al Ilmiyya, n.d), 191; Al-Qastallani, *Irshad al-Sari li Sharh Sahih al-Bukhari*, 14:396. http://www .archive.org/details/Irshad-Sari-1859.

3. Shawkani, *Nayl al-Awtar*, 7:151–63.

4. Qur'an 2:256.

5. Qur'an 16:9.

6. Ibn Taymiyya, *Majmu` Fatawa Shaykh al-Islam Ahmad b. Taymiyya*, vol. 35 (Mecca: Maktabat al-Nahda al-Haditha, 1404 AH), 105–6.

Chapter 16

1. See article 179 of the Egyptian penal code.

2. The examples mentioned in the conclusions are covered at more length in the relevant chapters, and citations are given there. For further examples, on Mauritania, see Khalid Lum, "An Ex-Islamist Needs US Support," *Wall Street Journal*, February 1, 2010, http://online.wsj

.com/article/SB10001424052748703906204575027462093163750.html?mod=WSJ_
Opinion_LEFTTopOpinion; on Tanzania and Comoros, see "Comoros," *International Religious Freedom Report 2008*, http://2001-2009.state.gov/g/drl/rls/irf/2008/108361
.htm, and "Comoros: Christians Oppressed on Indian Ocean Islands," *Compass Direct News*, December 8, 2008, http://www.christianpersecution.info/news/comoros-christians-oppressed-on-indian-ocean-islands-17355/. We have not covered Iraq since the situation has changed markedly during the writing of this book, but there have been numerous killings on the grounds of heresy, blasphemy, and apostasy. On increasing radicalization in the Muslim world, see Paul Marshall, ed., *Radical Islam's Rules: The Worldwide Spread of Extreme Sharia Law* (Lanham, MD: Rowman and Littlefield, 2005), especially "Introduction: The Rise of Extreme Sharia."

3. Jytte Klausen, *The Cartoons That Shook the World* (New Haven: Yale University Press, 2009).

4. Statement by Ihab Gamaleldin, Egypt, at the 2nd Plenary Meeting of the 6th Session of the UN Human Rights Council, September 13, 2007, http://www.un.org/webcast/unhrc/archive.asp?go=070913.

5. While still accepting them as Muslims, Yusuf Al-Qaradawi, perhaps the best-known Sunni preacher, has been increasingly critical of Shias and has accused them of being heretics, *mubtadiun*, those who introduce unauthorized innovations. Several commentators think that this probably stems from his worries over Iran's political successes; see Jeffrey Fleishman, "Egyptian Sheik's Outburst Against Shiites Roils Iran," *Los Angeles Times*, September 27, 2008, http://articles.latimes.com/2008/sep/28/world/fg-islamic28. See also Israel Elad-Altman, "The Brotherhood and the Shiite Question," in *Current Trends in Islamist Ideology* 9 (2009): 46–63, esp. 54–57; and Israel Elad-Altman, "The Sunni-Shia Conversion Controversy," in *Current Trends in Islamist Ideology* 5 (2007): 1–10, esp. 2–3.

6. Saeed and Saeed note that Ahmad bin Naqib al-Misri (d. 1368) condemned as apostates nearly anyone who undertook scientific inquiry, since his definition of apostasy included the belief "that things in themselves or by their own nature have any causal influence independent of the will of Allah" and also that 'Ali al-Tamimi, a contemporary Islamic teacher raised in the Washington, D.C. area, labels as "apostate" those Muslims who, for instance, believe that Judaism and Christianity are "valid" religions or who "judge by other than the *shari'ah* that Allah sent down to the Prophet Muhammad." Abdullah Saeed and Hassan Saeed, *Freedom of Religion, Apostasy and Islam* (Burlington, VT: Ashgate, 2004), 44–47.

7. Waqar Gillani and Sabrina Tavernise, "Pakistan Rights Groups Seek Answers on Christian's Death," *New York Times*, September 16, 2009, http://www.nytimes.com/2009/09/17/world/asia/17pstan.html.

8. Sabrina Tavernise, "At Top University, a Fight for Pakistan's Future," *New York Times*, April 20, 2010, http://www.nytimes.com/2010/04/21/world/asia/21university.html.

9. Brian J. Grim and Roger Finke, *The Price of Freedom Denied: Religious Persecution and Violence in the 21st Century* (New York: Cambridge University Press, 2010). Grim and Finke describe this as a "core thesis."

10. Sabrina Tavernise, "Hate Engulfs Christians in Pakistan," *New York Times*, August 2, 2009, http://www.nytimes.com/2009/08/03/world/asia/03pstan.html.

11. In his *The Devil's Dictionary* (1911): http://www.alcyone.com/max/lit/devils/.

12. Seth Mydans, "Churches Attacked Amid Furor in Malaysia," *New York Times*, January 10, 2010, http://www.nytimes.com/2010/01/11/world/asia/11malaysia.html.

13. Speech to the ISEAS Regional Forum, January 7, 2010, http://www.iseas.edu.sg/trh7jan10.pdf.

14. "Banning of the Book on 'Muslim Women and the Challenge of Islamic Extremism,'" Sisters in Islam press release, August 21, 2008, http://www.sistersinislam.org.my/index.php?option=com_content&task=view&id=769&Itemid=1.

15. Kenan Malik, "Introduction" in *From Fatwa to Jihad* (London: Atlantic Publishing, 2009), i.

16. Qaradawi also distinguishes between intellectual apostates and others: he calls intellectual apostates "hypocrites" (*munafiqun*) who will go to hell but should not suffer earthly punish-

ment; "Fatwa on Intellectual Apostasy," *IslamOnline*, March 24, 2003, http://www.islamon-
line.net/servlet/Satellite?cid=1119503545098&pagename=IslamOnline-English-
Ask_Scholar%2FFatwaE%2FFatwaE. See also his "Apostasy: Major and Minor," *IslamOnline.
net*, April 13, 2006, http://www.islamonline.net/servlet/Satellite?c=Article_C&cid=11787
24001992&pagename=Zone-English-Living_Shariah%2FLSELayout. See also Fouad Ajami,
The Foreigner's Gift (New York: Free Press, 2006), 74.

17. Michael Cook, *Commanding Right and Forbidding Wrong in Islamic Thought* (New York:
    Cambridge University Press, 2000); Bernard Lewis, *Faith and Power* (New York: Oxford
    University Press, 2010), 188. There is some evidence, however, that blasphemy in Western
    Europe was an issue for Muslim authorities in past centuries. A monologue in Pierre-
    Augustin Caron de Beaumarchais' eighteenth-century *Marriage of Figaro*, Act V, Scene 3: "I
    cobble together a verse comedy about the customs of the harem, assuming that, as a Spanish
    writer, I can say what I like about Mohammed without drawing hostile fire. Next thing,
    some envoy from God knows where turns up and complains that in my play I have offended
    the Ottoman empire, Persia, a large slice of the Indian peninsula, the whole of Egypt, and
    the kingdoms of Barca [Ethiopia], Tripoli, Tunisia, Algeria, and Morocco. And so my play
    sinks without trace, all to placate a bunch of Muslim princes, not one of whom, as far as
    I know, can read but who beat the living daylights out of us and say we are "Christian dogs."
    Since they can't stop a man thinking, they take it out on his hide instead."

18. See "The Dangerous Idea of Protecting Religions from 'Defamation,'" USCIRF Policy Brief,
    October 2009, www.uscirf.gov.

19. Harold Koh, speech to the American Society of International Law, March 25, 2010, http://
    www.state.gov/s/l/releases/remarks/139119.htm. See also Stephanie Farrior, "Molding the
    Matrix: The Historical and Theoretical Foundations of International Law Concerning Hate
    Speech," *Berkeley Journal of International Law* 14, no. 1 (1996): 30.

20. As discussed in chapter 12, the U.S. Supreme Court established an incitement test under
    which advocacy of use of force or law violation cannot be prohibited except where such
    "advocacy is directed to inciting or producing imminent lawless action and is likely to incite
    or produce such action"; *Brandenburg v. Ohio*, 395 U.S. 444 (1969). Under Federal law, hate
    crimes are not distinct offenses: they amplify the penalty for traditional crimes in which the
    perpetrator was motivated by biases considered particularly detrimental to society. By con-
    trast, European-style hate-speech codes punish hateful utterances standing alone. In dis-
    cussing the 2009 U.S.-Egypt resolution, Eugene Volokh suggests how nonbinding UN
    resolutions can enter national law:

    > Advocacy of mere *hostility*—for instance…to radical strains of Islam [or any other
    > religion]—is clearly constitutionally protected here in the U.S.; but the resolution seems to
    > call for its prohibition. If we are constitutionally barred from adhering to it by our domestic
    > Constitution, then we're implicitly criticizing that Constitution, and committing ourselves
    > to do what we can to change it.… [T]he Administration would presumably have to take what
    > steps it can to ensure that supposed 'hate speech' that incites hostility will indeed be pun-
    > ished [by]…filing amicus briefs supporting changes in First Amendment law to allow such
    > punishment, and in principle perhaps the appointment of Justices who would endorse such
    > changes (or even the proposal of express constitutional amendments that would work such
    > changes.…At least it would let other countries fault us for inconsistency when American
    > law fails to punish such speech. And beyond that, I'm worried that the Executive Branch's
    > endorsement of speech-restrictive 'international human rights' norms will affect how the
    > courts interpret the First Amendment, so that over time, 'an international norm against
    > hate speech…[would] supply a basis for prohibiting [hate speech], the First Amendment
    > notwithstanding.' And that worry stems not just from my fevered imagination, but from the
    > views of Prof. Peter Spiro, a noted legal academic who is a *supporter* of this tendency. That's
    > not fearmongering on his part, but hope (hopemongering?) and prediction.

    See "Is the Obama Administration Supporting Calls to Outlaw Supposed Hate Speech?"
    Huffington Post, October 1, 2009, http://www.huffingtonpost.com/eugene-volokh/is-the-
    obama-administrati_b_307132.html. The resolution proved controversial among human

rights advocates, so much so that Secretary of State Hillary Clinton felt compelled to use the release later that month of the State Department's annual religious freedom report to reassert America's commitment to free speech. She stated: "Now, some claim that the best way to protect the freedom of religion is to implement so-called anti-defamation policies that would restrict freedom of expression and the freedom of religion. I strongly disagree.... [W]e are convinced that the best antidote to intolerance is not the defamation of religion's approach of banning and punishing offensive speech, but rather, a combination of robust legal protections against discrimination and hate crimes, proactive government outreach to minority religious groups, and the vigorous defense of both freedom of religion and expression." "Clinton on Release of International Religious Freedom Report 2009," Statement made on October 26, 2009 in http://www.america.gov/st/texttrans-english/2009/October/20091026160243eaifas0.8208277.html&distid=ucs.

21. Other fatwas defend polygamy, husbands preventing their wives from traveling alone, mild beating of spouses, and criminalization of homosexuality; see Paul Marshall, "Ambassador to Islam?" *Weekly Standard* 15, no. 23 (March 1, 2010): http://www.weeklystandard.com/articles/ambassador-islam. Also see talk by Mark Durie at the Hudson Institute, January 19, 2011, http://www.hudson.org/index.cfm?fuseaction=hudson_upcoming_events&id=818.

22. Jeane J. Kirkpatrick, "How the PLO Was Legitimized," *Commentary*, July 1, 1989, www.aei.org/docLib/20030829_KirkpatrickPLO.pdf.

23. For the full text of Butler's article, "Why I've Changed My mind on Victoria's Anti-vilification Laws," see http://www.onlineopinion.com.au/view.asp?article=2274.

24. Alan Borovoy, "Hearing Complaint Alters Rights Body's Mandate," *The Calgary Herald*, March 16, 2006, http://www.safs.ca/issuescases/aborovoy.html.

25. In the future, we may also see greater censorship of the Internet based on a 2009 U.S. change in policy that makes the Internet authority more vulnerable to foreign influence. Jeremy Rabkin and Jeffrey Eisenach, "The U.S. Abandons the Internet," *Wall Street Journal*, October 2, 2009, http://online.wsj.com/article/SB10001424052748704471504574446942665685208.html, raise the concern that "foreign countries will pressure ICANN to impose Internet controls that facilitate their own censorship schemes.... Islamic nations insist that the proper understanding of international human-rights treaties requires suppression of 'Islamophobic' content on the Internet. Will ICANN be better situated to resist such pressures now that it no longer has a formal contract with the U.S. government?"

26. Mark Steyn, "Making a Pig's Ear of Defending Democracy," *Telegraph* (U.K.), October 4, 2005; "Banned, Toy Pigs That Offend Muslims," *Daily Mail*, October 1, 2005; John Brenan, "Toy Pig Ban Climbdown," *Express and Star*, October 19, 2005; "School Bans Pig Stories," *BBC News*, March 4, 2003; Sarah Harris, "'Three Little Pigs CD' Banned from Government-backed Awards for Offending Muslims and Builders," *The Daily Mail*, January 23, 2008. In a variation on the theme, Tayside Police in Scotland apologized after a Muslim member of the police board suggested that a postcard with the force's new number, mailed to local residents, was offensive because it featured a puppy—dogs are unclean in Islam. Other Muslim groups said the picture would not be generally offensive to Muslims; see Martyn McLaughlin, "Apology on the Cards as Police Pup Picture Sparks Warning over Offence to Muslims," *The Scotsman*, July 2, 2008, http://thescotsman.scotsman.com/scotland/Apology-on-the-cards-as.4243889.jp.

27. Associated Press (AP), "Obama Bans Islam, Jihad from US Security sStrategy," *Boston Herald*, April 7, 2010, http://www.bostonherald.com/news/us_politics/view/20100407obama_bans_islam_jihad_from_us_security_strategy/.

28. Leslie Gelb, "Only Muslims Can Stop Muslim Terror," *Daily Beast*, January 7, 2010, http://www.thedailybeast.com/blogs-and-stories/2010-01-07/only-muslims-can-stop-muslim-terror/; Joseph I. Lieberman, "Who's the Enemy in the War on Terror?" *Wall Street Journal*, June 15, 2010; Zuhdi Jasser, "Americanism versus Islamism," in *The Other Muslims: Moderate and Secular*, ed. Zeyno Baran (New York: Palgrave Macmillan, 2010), 187. This may also have been a factor in the murder of American soldiers. The fellow soldiers

of Ft. Hood gunman, Major Nidal Hasan, said that, despite his anti-American rhetoric and open, and illegal, proselytizing, fear of appearing discriminatory against a Muslim kept officers from filing complaints; see Stephen F. Hayes, "Malign Neglect," *The Weekly Standard*, November 30, 2009, http://www.weeklystandard.com/Content/Public/Articles/000/000/017/250ieqfn.asp.

29. Paul Berman, "Who's Afraid of Tariq Ramadan?" *The New Republic*, May 29, 2007, http://www.tnr.com/article/who%E2%80%99s-afraid-tariq-ramadan. See also Berman's *The Flight of the Intellectuals* (Brooklyn, NY: Melville House Publishing, 2010).

30. Berman, "Who's Afraid of Tariq Ramadan?"

31. *AP*, "Two Chains Reject Magazine with Muhammad Cartoons," *Washington Post*, March 30, 2006, http://www.washingtonpost.com/wp-dyn/content/article/2006/03/29/AR2006032902219.html; Pieter W. Van Der Horst, "Tying Down Academic Freedom," *Wall Street Journal*, June 30, 2006.

32. "German Group, Merkel to Honor Controversial Danish Cartoonist," *Radio Free Europe/ Radio Liberty*, September 8, 2010, http://www.rferl.org/content/Danish_Muhammad_Cartoonist_To_Receive_German_Media_Freedom_Prize_/2151531.html.

33. Nick Collins, "Rory Bremner 'Afraid' to Joke about Islam," *Telegraph*, June 21, 2010, http://www.telegraph.co.uk/news/newstopics/religion/7828813/Rory-Bremner-afraid-to-joke-about-Islam.html.

34. Christopher Hitchens, "Assassins of the Mind," *Vanity Fair*, February 2009, http://www.vanityfair.com/politics/features/2009/02/hitchens200902?printable=true&current Page=1.

35. Letter from Bob Flavell of Duxbury, MA, *Boston Globe*, February 8, 2006.

36. Nina Shea, "Self-Censoring *South Park*," *National Review Online*, April 27, 2010, http://article.nationalreview.com/432601/self-censoring-isouth-parki/nina-shea.

37. English companies have restricted the showing of the English flag lest its cross offend Muslims; see Modi Kreitman, "England Afraid to Fly Its Own Flag," *Ynetnews*, June 4, 2006, http://www.ynetnews.com/articles/0,7340,L-3258613,00.html. Italian football team Inter Milan ran into problems for using a red cross on their jerseys, even though it is the symbol of the city of Milan. Similar kerfuffles affected Eintracht Frankfurt and FC Barcelona; see "Uproar over Crossed Football Shirts," *Al Jazeera*, December 15, 2007, http://english.aljazeera.net/sport/2007/12/2008526103049396918.html; Reuters, "German Soccer Team Shies Away from Cross on Jersey," *FaithWorld* blog, March 22, 2008, http://blogs.reuters.com/faithworld/2008/03/22/german-soccer-team-shies-away-from-cross-on-jersey; Xavier G. Luque, "Los países islámicos retocan el escudo del Barça para no herir sensibilidades," *La Vanguardia*, December 15, 2007, http://www.lavanguardia.es/premium/publica/publica?COMPID=53418724457&ID_PAGINA=22088&ID_FORMATO=9&turbourl=false.

38. "Yale Alums Protest Cutting Muslim Toons," *CBS News*, September 8, 2009, http://www.cbsnews.com/stories/2009/09/08/national/main5293364.shtml.

39. Apart from sources referenced elsewhere in this book, for distinctions between and among apostasy, blasphemy, heresy, and disbelief and on the difference between Muslim and non-Muslim in this respect, and on the question of repentance, see also Mohamed Hashim Kamali, *Freedom of Expression in Islam*, rev. ed. (Cambridge: Islamic Texts Society, 1997), 212–58. For short overviews of apostasy in Islam, see Ruud Peters and G. J. J. de Vries, "Apostasy in Islam," *Die Welt des Islams* 17 (1976–77): 1–25, http://home.medewerker.uva.nl/r.peters/bestanden/apostasy%20in%20islam.pdf; Yohanan Friedmann, *Tolerance and Coercion in Islam: Interfaith Relations in the Muslim Tradition* (Cambridge, MA: Cambridge University Press, 2003), esp. 121–59. For debates on apostasy, see Islam Abdul-Aziz, "Apostasy: Scholars Differ on the Penalty" (a report on Proceedings of the 19th Session of the International Islamic Fiqh Academy), May 6, 2009, http://www.islamonline.net/serv-let/Satellite?c=Article_C&cid=1239888697368&pagename=Zone-English-Living_Shariah%2FLSELayout; Abdullah bin Hamid Ali, "Preserving the Freedom for Faith: Reevaluating the Politics of Compulsion," *Lamppost Productions*, July 2009, http://www.lamppostproductions.com/files/articles/PRESERVING%20THE%20FREEDOM%20

FOR%20FAITH.pdf; Jamal Badawi, "Is Apostasy a Capital Crime in Islam?" April 26, 2006, http://www.islamonline.net/servlet/Satellite?c=Article_C&pagename=Zone-English-Living_Shariah/LSELayout&cid=1178724000686; Abdullahi Ahmed An-Na'im, "*The Future of Sharia: Negotiating Islam in the context of the Secular State*," section 2.3b, n.d., http://sharia.law.emory.edu/en/freedom_religion. See also Mohamed Talbi, "Religious Liberty: A Muslim Perspective," in *The New Voices of Islam: A Reader*, ed. Mehran Kamrava (Berkeley: University of California Press, 2006), 105–18; Mohsen Kadivar, "Freedom of Religion and Belief in Islam," in Kamrava, op. cit., 119–42. Others arguing against civil penalties for apostasy include Ahmad Subhy Mansour, *Penalty of Apostasy: A Historical and Fundamental Study* (Toronto: International Publishing, 1998); see also "*The Punishment for Apostasy and Reform in Islamic Fiqh*," 92–116, of Sayyid Al-Qimni, *Thank You...Bin Laden!*, unpublished English translation of Arabic *Shukran...Bin Laden!* ed. Abdul Munim Fahmi (Cairo: Dar Misr Al Mahroosa, 2004). Our thanks to Jennifer Bryson for passing on this translation. Mohammad Omar Farooq, "On Apostasy and Islam: 100+ Notable Islamic Voices affirming the Freedom of Faith," April 2, 2007, http://apostasyandislam.blogspot.com/, gives a listing of and quotations from a wide range of Muslim scholars and organizations opposing civil penalties for apostasy. See also Abdulaziz Abdulhussein Sachedina, *The Islamic Roots of Democratic Pluralism* (New York: Oxford University Press, 2001); *Islam and the Challenge of Human Rights* (New York: Oxford University Press, 2009), esp. 180–87. Olivier Roy notes that in recent years, even fundamentalists have stressed excluding apostates from the community rather than killing them; see his *Secularism Confronts Islam* (New York: Columbia University Press, 2007), 81.

40. Baran, *The Other Muslims*, 1.

41. Scott Helfstein, Nassir Abdullah, and Muhammad al-Obaidi, "Deadly Vanguards: A Study of al-Qa'ida's Violence Against Muslims," Combating Terrorism Center at West Point, Occasional Paper Series, December 2009. Osama bin Laden has opined: "Aiding America, or the Allawi government [in Iraq] which is apostate [*Murtada*], or the Karzai government [in Afghanistan], or the Mahmoud Abbas government [in the Palestinian Authority] which is apostate, or the other apostate governments in their war against the Muslims, is the greatest apostasy of all, and amounts to abandonment of the Muslim community...." He continued: "Anyone who participates in these elections...has committed apostasy against Allah"; see "To the Muslims in Iraq in Particular and the [Islamic] Nation in General," letter from Osama bin Laden, released December 27, 2004 by the Al-Sahab Institute for Media Productions, Memri Special Dispatch No. 837, December 30, 2004, http://www.memri.org/bin/articles.cgi?Area=sd&ID=SP83704&Page=archives. Thomas Hegghammer argues that Al-Qaeda largely avoided *takfiri* language before about 2003 but that now it is much more common; see his "The Ideological Hybridization of Jihadi Groups," *Current Trends in Islamist Ideology* 9 (2009): 26–45. Meanwhile, Zawahiri denounced U.S. Ambassador to Iraq Zalmay Khalilzad as "the Afghan apostate," *Al Jazeera*, June 23, 2006; see also "Dr. Ayman al Zawahiri: Elegizing the Ummah's Martyr and Commander of the Martyrdom-seekers," in Laura Mansfield, ed., *Al Qaeda 2006 Yearbook* (Old Tappan, NJ: TLG Publications, 2007), 190–93. The late Abu Musab al-Zarqawi, for a time the head of Al-Qaeda in Iraq, condemned Shias as "the insurmountable obstacle, the lurking snake, the crafty and malicious scorpion, the spying enemy, and the penetrating venom." He maintained that Shiism is "patent polytheism" and "other forms of infidelity and manifestations of atheism"; see "Text from Abu Mus'ab al-Zarqawi Letter" February 12, 2004, Coalition Provisional Authority, http://www.globalsecurity.org/wmd/library/news/iraq/2004/02/040212-al-zarqawi.htm.

42. This growing practice of mutual *takfir* has led to broad-based efforts to condemn the practice. Leading Muslim authorities have jointly forbidden the accusation that any adherent to any one of the eight schools of Islamic jurisprudence is apostate, see http://www.amman-message.com/; Mahmoud Al Abed, "Clerics Forbid Takfir," *Jordan Times*, July 7, 2005, http://www.jordanembassyus.org/07072005001.htm. Also, the Federación Española de Entidades Religiosas Islámicas, the main body representing Spain's million Muslims, condemned Osama bin Laden by name for what it termed Al-Qaeda's attempt to invent legal justifications

from Qur'anic and hadith sources in order to defend terrorism, and that by so doing they [Al-Qaeda] had "made themselves apostates"; see Stephen Ulph, "A Fatwa and Defiance at the Madrid Conference," *Terrorism Focus* 2, no. 6 (March 16, 2005): http://www.jamestown. org/programs/gta/single/?tx_ttnews%5Btt_news%5D=27709&tx_ttnews%5Bback Pid%5D=238&no_cache=1. See also "Religious Scholars Endorse Edicts," King Abdullah Web site, July 6, 2005, http://www.kingabdullah.jo/news/details.php?kn_serial=3409& menu_id=&lang_hmka1=1.

43. John Glassie, "Questions for Irshad Manji: In Good Faith," *New York Times*, December 21, 2003, http://www.nytimes.com/2003/12/21/magazine/21QUESTIONS.html?scp=1&sq= Interview%20with%20Irshad%20Manji&st=cse; DeNeen L. Brown, "'Muslim Refusenik' Incites Furor with Critique of Faith," *Washington Post*, January 19, 2004, http://www.wash-ingtonpost.com/ac2/wp-dyn/A28039-2004Jan18?language=printer; Irshad Manji, "Salman Rushdie's Knighthood Should Be the Last Thing to Offend Muslims," *The New Republic Online*, June 22, 2007, http://www.tnr.com/article/clerical-error.

44. Baran, *The Other Muslims*, 2, 189.

45. George Weigel, *The Cube and the Cathedral* (New York: Basic Books, 2005), 141.

46. In contrast, the United States has "hate-crimes" legislation but not hate-speech bans or blasphemy crimes, due to the free speech protections in the First Amendment of the U.S. Constitution. Incitement to violence is a crime in the United States only when the expression is directed to inciting violence that is likely and imminent.

47. "Report on the Relationship Between Freedom of Expression and Freedom of Religion: The Issue of Regulation and Prosecution of Blasphemy, Religious Insult and Incitement to Religious Hatred," adopted by the Venice Commission at its 76th Plenary Session (Venice, 17–18 October 2008), 11, http://www2.ohchr.org/english/issues/religion/IV1.htm.

48. Ezra Levant, "Rev. Stephen Boissoin's Conviction Overturned," blog entry, http://ezrale-vant.com/cgi-bin/mt/mt-search.cgi?IncludeBlogs=1&search=HRC.

49. Grim and Finke, *The Price of Freedom Denied: Religious Persecution and Violence in the 21st Century*.

50. Elizabeth Powers, "Liberty for All Free Speech is the American Way," *The Weekly Standard*, April 19, 2010. C. Edwin Baker finds that hate-speech regulation has no real effect on curbing "hate"; see Ivan Hare and James Weinstein, eds., *Extreme Speech and Democracy* (New York: Oxford University Press, 2010).

51. In his June 4, 2009 Cairo speech, President Obama pledged to "fight against negative stereotypes of Islam wherever they appear." Lamin Sanneh rightly asks "why Catholic and other religious groups cannot be given the same degree of enforcement of their religious rights"; see "President Obama and America's New Beginning with Islam: A Response" (unpublished paper, Yale University, June 4, 2009), available through Professor Sanneh.

52. Robert M. Gates, speech, April 14, 2008, http://www.defense.gov/speeches/speech. aspx?speechid=1228. As Farr observes, "There is no systematic approach to what ought to be a central task of U.S. national security strategy, namely, understanding the religious wellsprings of Islamist extremism and its origins in places such as Saudi Arabia. There is too little thought given to supporting religious actors capable of altering the climate of opinion that nurtures the terrorists, their extremist religious views, and the export of those views." See Thomas Farr, *World of Faith and Freedom* (New York: Oxford University Press, 2008), 218. However, traditional Muslims, precisely because they have not pursued a religiously based political agenda, lack a national infrastructure, and their organizations are virtually invisible to state and national governments. Western governments tend to rely heavily in their Muslim outreach on individuals and institutions that are prominent simply because they have Saudi and Gulf support, often espousing views starkly at odds with fundamental freedoms of speech and religion; see Hedieh Mirahmadi, "Navigating Islam in America," in Baran, *The Other Muslims*, 29; Nina Shea and James Woolsey, "What About Muslim Moderates?" *Wall Street Journal*, July 10, 2007.

53. ICCPR Article 20(2), calling for states to ban "incitement to religious hostility," is commonly cited as the legal authority for mandating laws against religious hate speech, but it was proposed by the Soviet bloc, Saudi Arabia, and some other authoritarian states; no Western European state voted for it. See Stephanie Farrior, *Molding the Matrix: The Historical and Theoretical Foundations of International Law Concerning Hate Speech, Berkeley Journal of International Law* 14, no. 1 (1996): n. 231. Eleanor Roosevelt, representing the United States, warned that it was a provision "likely to be exploited by totalitarian States for the purpose of rendering the other articles null and void." Upon signing the ICCPR, the United States provided as follows: (1) the U.S. understands that Article 20 "does not authorize or require legislation or other action by the United States that would restrict the right of free speech and association protected by the Constitution and laws of the United States"; (2) "For the United States, article 5, paragraph 2, which provides that fundamental human rights existing in any State Party may not be diminished on the pretext that the Covenant recognizes them to a lesser extent, has particular relevance to article 19, paragraph 3 which would permit certain restrictions on the freedom of expression.." The U.K. delegate echoed this concern: "Unscrupulous governments like nothing better than a moral justification for their actions."

54. Christian Caryl, "A Eulogy for Pakistan," *Radio Free Europe/Radio Liberty*, March 16, 2011, http://www.rferl.org/content/pakistan_bhatti_washington/2340390.html; Lela Gilbert, "Pakistan and Blasphemy: A Matter of Life and Death," *Jerusalem Post*, April 21, 2011, http://www.jpost.com/Features/InThespotlight/Article.aspx?id=217432; "Pakistani and US Leaders Urge Tolerance, Harmony in Minister Shahbaz Bhatti Memorial Service at the Embassy," Embassy of the Islamic Republic of Pakistan press release, March 10, 2011, http://www.embassyofpakistanusa.org/news474_03102011.php

INDEX